The Nicknames of Major League Baseball

2021

By

Joseph Ross
with
Richard M. Renneboog

Rosstrum Publishing
Nashua, NH

Also available from Rosstrum Publishing

Non-Fiction

Fast Track for Caregivers

366 Tips for a Successful Job Search

Listen to the Cry of the Child

The Dave Maynard Spin (also in Large Print)

The Happy Heart Cookbook

Journey of a Beam

States Have Powers

Teacher Within the Coach (can be a textbook)

Fiction

Timberline

Dark Horizon

Death in Cedar Canyon

Missing

Pursuit

Tapping In to Murder

Lawless in Brazil

Dr. Lawless I Presume

Emotions in Motion (poetry)

Wind Castle (Large Print)

An Unwelcome Arrangement

Advance Praise for
The Nicknames of Major League Baseball

For times when the SABR-brain gets numbed by statistical data analysis, here's a sweet diversion. A tip of the cap to Joe Ross and Richard M. Renneboog for putting this together.

David Daniel, co-author, "Murder at the Baseball Hall of Fame,"
Creator of the prize-winning Alex Rasmussen mystery series.

~~~

I have been a baseball fan ever since I started listening on a short-wave radio night after night as "Diamond Jim" Gentile blasted 46 homers with 141 RBIs and batted .302 for the Baltimore Orioles in 1961. In 1973, my 40-year career as a beat writer covering the Red Sox coincided with the first MLB game in history featuring designated hitters Ron "Boomer" Bloomberg of the New York Yankees and Boston's Orlando "Cha-Cha" Cepeda. How did they get those nicknames? How did any ballplayer get his nickname? Many might be obvious and some I might take a guess, but I didn't know for certain until I read Joe Ross's and Richard M. Renneboog's painstakingly researched, encyclopedic, and intriguing book of baseball nicknames.

Why was John Martin, already nicknamed "Pepper," also called "The Wild Horse of the Osage?" Why were the Hall of Fame Waner brothers, Paul and Lloyd, nicknamed "Big Poison" and "Little Poison?" How did Jim "Toy Cannon" Wynn and Dennis "Oil Can" Boyd get their nicknames?

These and a thousand more questions are answered here, and you will be surprised to learn many of the obvious nicknames were not as obvious as you thought. If you were under the impression, as was I, that the most colorful nicknames disappeared with the players of the distant past, and that modern players are too corporate and colorless for nicknames, think again.

Baseball may change slowly, but some things never change.

Chaz Scoggins, Author of:
"Game of My Life: Memorable Stories of Boston Red Sox Baseball,"
"Tales from the Impossible Dream Red Sox,"
"Bricks and Bats: Professional Baseball in Lowell, Massachusetts"
(with Rico Petrocelli),
Official Scorer, Boston Red Sox and three All-Star games.

~~~

I have been an avid follower of the game since the age of seven, the year the Red Sox played the "Big Red Machine" in the 1975 World Series. What a way to begin my lifelong pursuit of baseball! I will forever be thankful for my Dad letting me stay up to watch those pivotal games. If he hadn't, I never would have seen Carlton "Pudge" Fisk willing his home run inside the foul pole in Game 6!

Nicknames have long been synonymous with the game of baseball. From "Three Finger" Brown to the Splendid Splinter and Hammerin' Hank, to more recently Big Papi and The Wild Horse, followers of America's national pastime have been treated to some of the most colorful descriptions of our greatest heroes. In "The Nicknames of Major League Baseball," Joe Ross and Richard Renneboog take readers on a fascinating journey through some of the stranger monikers that have attached themselves to some of baseball's greatest heroes.

Chris Carpenter, co-author, "Murder at the Baseball Hall of Fame,"
Journalist, The Christian Broadcasting Network.

Also by Joseph Ross

Fast Track for Caregivers (with Esther Ross)

Also by Richard M. Renneboog

(Fiction)

Flayer
Tallest
Gridlock - A Daekel Adventure
Billier's Book
Twist
Faiths
Five Short Stories
Tales fro the Falactic Campground
To Marry an Elf
To Marry an Elf, Part Two
To Marry an Elf, Part Three

(Non-fiction)

Chemical Balance
It's a Gas! An Introduction to the Gas Laws
Sugar World

The Nicknames of Major League Baseball
2021

The Nicknames of Major League Baseball 2021 © 2021 Joseph Ross and Richard M. Renneboog. All rights reserved.

No portion of this book may be reproduced mechanically, electronically, or by any other means now in existence or invented in the future, including photocopying, except for brief passages used as part of a review, without the written permission of the publisher or author.

Rosstrum Publishing books are available at discount when purchased in bulk for premiums or promotions as well as for fundraising or educational use. Based on quantities, special editions can be created to specification. For details,
contact the publisher.

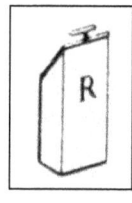

Rosstrum Publishing
A division of The Border Company, LLC
8 Strawberry Bank Rd.
Suite 20
Nashua, NH 03062-2763
Rosstrumpublishing@gmail.com
www.rosstrumpublishing.com

Library of Congress Cataloging-in-Publication Data

Authors: Ross, Joseph and Renneboog, Richard M.
Title: The Nicknames of Major League Baseball, 2021/ Joseph Ross and Richard M. Renneboog—
1st Rosstrum paperback ed.
1. Baseball. 2. Nicknames. 3. Sports. 4. Ross, Joseph.
5. Renneboog, Richard M. 6. Title 7. Major Leagues

Library of Congress Control Number 2021933311
Manufactured in the United States of America
1 3 5 7 9 10 8 6 4 2

Cover field © Jordan Rowland, unsplash.com
Running player ©Nathan Shively, unsplash.com

ISBN 978-1-62570-057-5
ISBN 978-1-62570-058-2 (ebook)

This book is dedicated to the millions of baseball fans, players, and officials who have made the game of baseball our National Pastime.

Introduction

This book was designed as a reference tool. The authors have included as many nicknames as we could possibly find. When possible, the origins of those nicknames are included. Many players had more nicknames than years of major league experience, some even more than Major League games played. Some of the names were gained at birth for a variety of reasons. Others were acquired during their playing careers. Some make sense. Some make no sense.

In addition to serving as a general reference, the book will also provide enjoyable reading and a guidebook for some baseball-related word games. Try making a menu for dinner using only baseball nicknames from Major League players. That is fairly easy because there are so many choices, from breakfast cereal to after-dinner cookies or nuts.

Here is a word game for baseball fans. If we say "BABE," what is the first name that comes to mind? Most fans will say "Ruth." But there are at least 30 other Babes listed in this book who played in the Major Leagues.

"Babe" is not the most common nickname. That unimaginative moniker belongs to "Lefty." The authors found nearly 200 instances where a player, pitchers for the most part, were called "Lefty." Following that were more than 170 players who were big: Big Stan, Big Bill, Big whatever or whomever. Some were called big because they were, at least in size, sometimes in stature. Others were called big because they were extremely short for the major leagues.

Another category was based on hair color: 145 were Red; only 35 were Whitey. The 13 players referred to as Baldy or Bald [anything] were probably under-representing that particular group.

There were at least 83 players referred to as "Doc" and another 10 as "Dr." or "Doctor." Some of these actually were doctors, either before, during, or after their baseball careers.

Other more popular nicknames included, in no particular order, Buck, Bud, Cy, and Rube. Twenty-one players were referred to as the "Franchise." "Kid" may sometimes have referred to a player whose coach or manager could not pronounce or remember his name.

Some players were referred to by a location. For instance, Casey Stengel got his nickname because he was from Kansas City, which became KC, which in turn became Casey. Nearly 100 players had a nickname including a reference to a location, either a city, state, or region.

Many players used their middle names. We tried to ignore these. More than 50 players chose to be known simply by their initials, either first and last or first and middle, occasionally all three.

Species of bird were considerably under-represented. We found Warbler, Vulture, Sparrow, Robin, and just plain Bird.

For those interested in food, there are 43 mentions of various foods from Buttermilk to Yams. That does not include animals that provide food, such as chicken, various varieties of seafood, and beef. That list has names from Ant to Weasel. There are birds, real and imagined, along with some non-existent creatures like Unicorn, Werewolf, Dragon, or Ghost.

Many players have adopted names of people. Some were given these names at birth. Why their parents did not give those players their nicknames as actual names is something we will probably never know. Others received them in honor or memory of a favorite player, someone to strive to emulate. Most interesting in that category is Mickey Mantle. He was named after Mickey Cochrane. Mantle was said to be very happy that his parents did not know that Cochrane was really named Gordon. Mantle hated the thought of being named Gordan Mantle.

Some players were called Pat, Bill, Marty, or almost anything else. Some had female names, like Mary or Liz. Others were named after cartoon characters.

For readers who crave their childhood memories of cops and robbers, or cowboys and Indians, good news awaits: there is only one Outlaw and three Killers. They have only eight Bullets and five Shotguns. They would undoubtedly lose to the 18 Sheriffs, one member of the Police, and two Officers. The good guys report to 14 Captains, 35 Chiefs, 6 Colonels, 3 Generals, 4 Majors, and The Lone Ranger.

Mention the King of Swing: baseball fans again think of Babe Ruth. Many older folks think of Benny Goodman. Benny did not play baseball, but that's all right. Ruth didn't play the clarinet. Many of the older readers may have liked Ike, but that is not referring to the 17 Major League baseball players with that nickname.

We hope you enjoy this book as much as we enjoyed preparing it. We relied on information available from hundreds of sources and hundreds of writers. We remain eternally grateful for their efforts.

All errors are ours.

The authors

A Note About Certain Nicknames

A number of nicknames are very common. Every player, primarily pitchers, who bats and throws left-handed is going to be nicknamed "Lefty" at some point. Every player with red hair or a reddish complexion is eventually going to get stuck with the nickname "Red" or "'Reddy". The nickname of "Whitey" generally refers to light or white hair. We leave off those explanations. In less politically correct times, almost every player who came to the big leagues from a country or foreign background, often uneducated, was nicknamed something akin to "'Rube'" or "Dutch" by his "more worldly" colleagues. Similarly, a lot of players who bore a dark complexion were called "Nig" or "Niggy," the origin of the term requiring no further explanation.

Many players have a familiar name that is just a shortened version of one of their given names or a name with a 'y' or 'ie' added, while some prefer to be known just by their initials or a middle name instead of an actual nickname. The former can't be considered actual nicknames by any standards and are often not included in this list. It is debatable whether the latter should be properly considered nicknames, but they are included here for the unique manner in which they identify the individual. Also not necessarily included in this list are interchangeable names such as 'Jack' for 'John' and 'Hal' for 'Harold', etc.

Some players are given nicknames by their peers that recall another player who was highly regarded, because they seem to have a certain respected quality that characterized that other player. The context in which such a nickname is given is important, since the two players will have also played the same positions. A pitcher might be nicknamed "Cy" or "Rube" in this way, in reference to Cy Young or Rube Waddell; a power hitter might be tagged with 'Babe', for Babe Ruth, and so on.

In many cases, it isn't at all clear why the player got his unique nickname – "Wagon Tongue" and "Dorf", for example – and in other cases it is all too obvious – "Three-Fingered" and "One-Armed" being the prime examples of that situation. Who first gave a nickname may also be a mystery that may be lost in time, unless someone who actually knows first-hand can fill in the blanks and provide that information for baseball historians.

NOTES:

For this book, we have accepted the definition of a "Major League" and of team names from Baseball-Reference.com, even when the MLB website may disagree, especially for those teams which played in the early days of the sport. For that reason, we also do not include the Negro Leagues, although some great players played in that venue and, based on recent MLB action, will surely be included in the next edition of this book.

We have used parentheses to indicate middle names, even if only an initial or two middle names: (James, Billy John). For first and middle names that do not match the listed name, brackets: [John David]. For pronunciation, we use braces: {MAR-tell}. Some pronunciations are not listed exactly as editors may like but are listed as the authors deem easiest for broadcasters.

Some names may not appear as they do on Baseball-Reference.com. That has more to do with the quirks of putting together this tome than for any other reason. Please do not attempt to insert any importance to that ocurrence.

In the index, many nicknames have names attached (for instance, Uncle Tom, Miltie, etc.; or Happy Jack, Bill, etc.). These may be referenced only by the adjective (Honest, Home Run, Rowdy) but are listed completely by player.

The Players

Aardsma David (Allan)
    The DA
    Giants, Cubs, White Sox, Red Sox, Mariners, Yankees, Mets, Braves, 2004-2015

Aaron, Henry (Louis)
    Hammer;
    Hammerin' Hank
        From teammates for his power.
    Bad Henry
        Given by opposing pitchers.
    Pork Chops
        First nickname (minor leagues), given because "it was the only thing I knew to order off the menu."
    Braves, Brewers, 1954-1976

Abad, Fausto (Andres)
    Andy
    Athletics, Red Sox, Reds, 2001-2006

Abbaticchio, Ed [Edward James]
    Batty
        A shortened version of his name and not because of his mental actions.
    Beaneaters, Pirates, Doves, Phillies, 1897-1910

Abbott, Dan [Leander Franklin]
    Big Dan
        Inspired by his size (5'11", 190 lbs.).
    Maumees, 1890

Aber, Al [Albert Julius]
    Lefty
    Indians, Tigers, Athletics, 1950-1957

Abernathy, Talmadge (Lafayette)
    Ted
        An easier nickname than *Tal*.
    Athletics, 1942-1944

Aberson, Clifford (Alexander)
    Kif
    Cubs, 1947-1949

Ables, Harry (Terrell)
    Hans
    Browns, Naps, Highlanders, 1905-1911

Abrams, Cal [Calvin Ross]
    Abie
    Dodgers, Reds, Pirates, 1949-1954

Abreu, Bobby [Bob Kelly] {ah-BRAY-oo}
    El Come Dulce: La Leche
    Astros, Phillies, Yankees, Angels, Dodgers, Mets, 1996-2014

Abreu, José (Dariel) {ah-BRAY-oo}
    Oso: Yogi: Mal Tiempo
    White Sox, 2014-

Abstein, William (Henry)
    Big Bill
        Six foot, 185, he was big for the time.
    Pirates, Browns, 1906-1910

Aceves, Alfredo {a-SEV-ess}
    Ace
    Yankees, Red Sox, 2008-

Acosta, José
    Acostica
        In Spanish, meaning *Little Acosta*.
    Senators, White Sox, 1920-1922

Acuña, Ron Jr. (Jose) [ah COON ya]
    The Beast
        From teammates for his rookie performance.
    Braves, 2018-

Adair, Jerry [Kenneth Jerry]
    Towhead: Casper the Friendly Ghost
    Iceman
        College football nickname.
    Mr. Clutch
        From broadcaster Ken Coleman.
    Orioles, White Sox, Red Sox, Royals, 1958-1970

Adair, Jimmy [James Aubrey]
    Choppy
    Cubs, 1931

Adams, Charles (Benjamin)
    Babe
        The story of his nickname was given as: 1. A woman asking for an autograph said he had a nice round face like a baby's; or 2. A female fan yelled at him, "Oh, you babe."
    Cardinals, Pirates, 1906-1926

Adams, Dan Le [Daniel Leslie]
    Rube
    Packers, 1914-1915

Adams, Dan Lu [Daniel Lucius]
    Doc

Adams, Earl

Graduated from Harvard and had a general medical practice in New York.
Knickerbockers, 1853-1859

Adams, Earl (John)
Sparky
Cubs, Pirates, Cardinals, Reds, 1922-1934

Adams, Joe [Joseph Edward]
Wagon Tongue
His bat feels too heavy in the late part of the season, like the tongue of a wagon wheel stuck in the mud.
Cardinals, 1902

Adams, Karl (Tutwiler)
Rebel
Born in Georgia (rebel territory).
Reds, Cubs, 1914-1915

Adams, Lane (Weston)
LA Swiftness
Royals, Braves, 2014-2018

Adams, Matt [Matthew James]
Big City
Cardinals, Braves, Nationals, 2012-

Adduci, Jim (Charles)
Deuce
Rangers, Tigers, Cubs, 2013-2019

Addy, Bob [Robert Edward]
The Magnet
Forest Citys, Whites, Red Stockings, Dark Blues, White Stockings, Reds, 1871-1874

Adkins, Grady (Emmett)
Butcher Boy
White Sox, 1928-1929

Adleman, Tim [Timothy Max] {add-ull-man}
The Microwave
Reds, 2016-2017

Adrianza, Ehire (Enrique) {AY-ray ad-dree-AHN-zuh}
Guarenero
Giants, Twins, 2013-

Agganis, Harry
The Golden Greek
Greek heritage.
Red Sox, 1954-1955

Agnew, Sam [Samuel Lester]
Slam
Browns, Red Sox, Senators, 1913-1919

Aguilar, Jesus (Alexander) {AH-gee-lar}
Dino
Indians, Brewers, Rays, Marlins, 2014-

Ainsmith, Ed [Edward Wilbur]
Dorf
Senators, Tigers, Cardinals, Robins, Giants, 1910-1924

Aker, Jack [Jackie Delane]
Chief
A strong reliever.
Athletics, Pilots, Yankees, Cubs, Braves, Mets, 1964-1974

Akers, William (G)
Bump
Tigers, Braves, 1929-1932

Alberto, Hanser (Joel)
Radio
Rangers, Orioles, 2015-

Alberts, Francis (Burt)
Butch
Preceded his baseball career.
Blue Jays, 1978

Alberts, Frederick (Joseph)
Cy
Cardinals, 1910

Albosta, Edward (John)
Rube
Dodgers, Pirates, 1941, 1946

Alcock, John (Forbes)
Scotty
Played way before the Star Trek era, when Scotty became a household name.
White Sox, 1914

Alexander, David (Dale)
Moose
6'3", 210 lbs.
Tigers, Red Sox, 1929-1933

Alexander, Grover (Cleveland)
Pete
He called himself *Pete*, so his teammates did also.
Old Pete
Old Pete played until he was well into his 40s.
Alexander the Great
Leadership skills were likened to those of the ancient Greek ruler.
Phillies, Cubs, Cardinals, 1911-1930

Alexander, William (Henry)

Nin
    Predates baseball career.
Cowboys, Browns, 1884
Alfaro, Jorge (Mario) {HOAR-hay al-FAR-oh}
    The Legend: El Oso
Phillies, Marlins, 2016-
Alfonseca, Antonio {al-fahn-SAKE-ah}
    El Pulpo
        Spanish for 'The Octopus.'
    The Octopus
        Ability to snag everything within arm's reach.
Marlins, Cubs, Braves, Rangers, Phillies, 1997-2007
Alfonzo, Edgardo (Antonio)
    Fonzie
        Fonzie Fonzarelli of TV sitcom fame was the epitome of cool.
Mets, Giants, Angels, Blue Jays, 1995-2006
Allen, Artemus (Ward)
    Nick
    Roarin' Nick
        He had a penchant for arguing with umpires.
Buffeds, Blues, Cubs, Reds, 1914-1920
Allen, Cody (Edward)
    Pollo
Indians, Angels, 2012-
Allen, Cyrus (Alban)
    Jack
Stars, Blues, 1879
Allen, Fletcher (Manson)
    Sled
Browns, 1910
Allen, Frank (Erwin)
    Ham
Mansfields, 1872
Allen, Harold (Andrew)
    Hank
Senators, Brewers, White Sox, 1966-1973
Allen, Horace (Tanner)
    Pug
Robins, 1919
Allen, Jesse (Hall)
    Pete
Spiders, 1893
Allen, Myron (Smith)
    Zeke
Blues, Cowboys, Gothams, Beaneaters, 1883-1888
Allen, Richard (Anthony)
    Wampum Walloper
        Extreme strength, ability to hit the long ball, was born in Wampum, PA.
    Crash Helmet
        He wore his batting helmet on the field.
    Crash
Phillies, Cardinals, Dodgers, White Sox, Athletics, 1963-1977
Allen, Robert (Earl)
    Thin Man
        At 6'1", only 165.
Phillies, 1937
Allred, Dale (LeBeau)
    Beau
Indians, 1989-1991
Almeida, Rafael (D)
    Mike
Reds, 1911-1913
Almonte, Abraham
    El Varon
Mariners, Padres, Indians, Royals, Diamondbacks, 2013-
Almora, Albert [Reinaldo Albert]
    Tico
Cubs, 2016-
Alomá, Luis
    Witto
White Sox, 1950-1953
Alomar, Santos Jr. {AL-oh-mar}
    Sandy
        A common nickname for Santos.
Padres, Indians, White Sox, Rockies, Rangers, Dodgers, Mets, 1988-2007
Alomar, Santos Sr. {AL-oh-mar}
    Sandy
        A common contraction of his first name.
    Iron Pony
        Played in 648 consecutive games.
Braves, Mets, White Sox, Angels, Yankees, Rangers, 1964-1978
Alonso, Pete [Peter Morgan]
    Polar Bear

Mets, 2019-

Alonso, Yonder
Mr. 305
Reds, Padres, Athletics, Mariners, Indians, White Sox, Rockies, 2010-

Alou, Felipe (Rojas)
El Panqué de Haina
> Translates to *Sweet bread from Haina*. He was born in Bajos de Haina, San Cristobal, Dominican Republic.

Giants, Braves, Athletics, Yankees, Expos, Brewers, 1958-1974

Alou, Jesús {HAY-Zeus}
Jay
> Given by sportswriters to avoid headlines like, "Jesus Saves Giants," before they determined the pronunciation.

Giants, Astros, Athletics, Mets, 1963-1979

Alpermann, Charles (Augustus)
Whitey
Superbas, 1906-1909

Alston, Walter (Emmons)
Smokey
> Given in high school because of his fastball.

The Quiet Man
> Generally calm, quiet demeanor.

Cardinals, 1936

Alten, Ernie [Ernest Matthias]
Lefty
Tigers, 1920

Altherr, Aaron (Samuel) {all-TAIR}
The Fresh Prince of Altherr
Rhineland Rocket
Phillies, Giants, Mets, 2014-2019

Altizer, David (Tilden)
Filipino
> Born in Pearl, Illinois. He served in the Philippines during the Spanish-American war.

Daredevil
> Given to him in later stories.

Senators, Naps, White Sox, Reds, 1906-1911

Altman, George (Lee)
Big George

He was 6'4", 200 lbs.
Cubs, Cardinals, Mets, 1959-1967

Alvarado, José (Antonio)
El Pocho
Rays, 2017-

Alvarado, Luis (Cesar)
Pimba
> 'Pimba' is generally suggestive of sexual pleasures and bad behavior.

Mijita
> Spanish term of endearment meaning *my dear child*.

Red Sox, White Sox, Cardinals, Indians, Mets, Tigers, 1968-1977

Alvarez, Henderson (Javier III)
The Entertainer
Blue Jays, Marlins, Phillies, 2011-

Álvarez, Pedro (Manuel)
El Toro
Pirates, Orioles, 2010-2018

Alvord, William (Crawford)
Uncle Bill
> Usually given to an older player, but he was only 21 when he made the majors.

Cowboys, Maumees, Spiders, Statesmen, 1885-1893

Amarista, Alexi (Jose) {ah-mah-REE-sta}
Little Ninja
> Versatility and strength, despite his small (5'5", 150 lbs.) body size.

Mighty Mouse
> Small, but powerful.

Angels, Padres, 2011 -

Ambres, Raymond (Payne) {AM-briss}
Chip
Royals, Mets, Padres, 2005-2008

Ames, Leon (Kessling)
Red
Giants, Reds, Cardinals, Phillies, 1903-19

Amole, Morris (F) {ah-*MOE-lee*}
Doc
> From boyhood. Not educational.

Orioles, Senators, 1897-1898

Amorós, Edmundo {AM-or-ohs}
Sandy
> Resemblance to boxing champion Sandy Saddler.

Dodgers, Tigers, 1952-1960

Andersen, Larry (Eugene)
LA
Mr. Jello
Indians, Mariners, Phillies, Astros, Red Sox, Padres, 1975-1994
Anderson, Arnold (Revola)
Red
Senators, 1937-1941
Anderson, Brian (James)
Antic
Angels, Indians, Diamondbacks, Royals, 1993-2005
Anderson, Chase [Robert Chase]
Texas
Diamondbacks, Brewers, Blue Jays, 2014-
Anderson, Edward (John)
Goat
Pirates, 1907
Anderson, George (Lee)
Sparky
    Given by a broadcaster for his feisty play in the Texas League in 1955.
Captain Hook
    Penchant for yanking his starting pitcher at the first sign of weakness.
Phillies, 1959
Anderson, Harry (Walter)
Harry the Horse
    6'3", 205 lbs.
Phillies, Reds, 1957-1961
Anderson, John (Joseph)
Honest John
    Rarely protested calls by umpires.
Long John
    Because he was 6'2" tall.
Big John
    Lest anyone forget how tall he was.
Terrible Swede
    He was born in Norway.
Swedish Apollo
    For his Scandinavian roots.
Grooms, Bridegrooms, Senators, Superbas, Brewers, Browns, Yankees, Senators, White Sox, 1894-1908
Anderson, Karl (Adam)
Bud
Indians, 1982-1983
Anderson, Tim [Timothy Devon]
B. Moss
White Sox, 2016-
Anderson, Tyler (John)
Ricky F
Rockies, Giants, 2016-
Anderson, Walter (Carl)
Lefty
Athletics, 1917, 1919
Anderson, William (Edward)
Lefty
Braves, 1925
Andres, Ernest (Henry)
Junie
    He was Ernest Jr.
Red Sox, 1946
Andrews, Ivy (Paul)
Poison
    Named after poison ivy because his pitching ability was noxious poison to opposing batters.
Yankees, Red Sox, Browns, Indians, 1931-1938
Andrews, Stanley (Joseph)
Polo
Bees, Dodgers, Phillies, 1939-1945
Andrus, Elvis (Augusto) {an-DROOS}
Comando
Rangers, 2009-
Ankenman, Frederick (Norman)
Pat
Cardinals, Dodgers, 1936-1944
Anson, Adrian (Constantine)
Capt
    From teammates; he was the captain of the Chicago White Stockings.
Uncle
    He was the oldest member of the team.
The Marshalltown Infant
Pop
    Obvious - he played for 27 years.
Cap
    From baseball writers and historians after his retirement.
Forest Citys, Athletics, White Stockings, Colts, 1871-1897
Aparicio, Luis (Ernesto) {ap-pa-REESE-ee-oh}
El Grande de Venezuela
    Spanish for "the big guy from

Venezuela."
    Obviously, he was born in Venezuela.
Little Louis
    His father was also Luis.
Luisito
    Spanish for "Little Louie."
White Sox, Orioles, Red Sox, 1956-1973

Appier, Kevin [Robert Kevin] {APE-ee-er}
Ape
Royals, Athletics, Mets, Angels, 1989-2004

Applegate, Frederick (Romaine)
Snitz
Athletics, 1904

Appleton, Edward (Samuel)
Whitey
Robins, 1915-1916

Appleton, Peter (William)
Jake
Jabby
    A short version of his birth name, Jablonowski.
Polish Wizard
    Polish extraction.
Reds, Indians, Red Sox, Yankees, Senators, White Sox, Browns, 1927-1945

Appling, Lucius (Benjamin)
Luke: Luscious Luke
Ol' Aches and Pains
    Given by teammates because of the constant complaining of a hypochondriac.
White Sox, 1930-1950

Aragón, Ángel (father)
Pete
Yankees, 1914-1917

Aragón, Angel (son)
Jack
Giants, 1941

Archdeacon, Maurice (John)
Flash: Comet
    Both nicknames came from his minor league days when he set a speed record of 13.4 seconds to circle the bases. It was a pre-game exhibition.
White Sox, 1923-1925

Archer, Chris [Christopher Alan]
Flaco Fuerte
Rays, Pirates, 2012-

Archer, Frederick (Marvin)
Lefty
Athletics, 1936-1937

Arcia, Orlando (Jesus) {ARR-see-ya}
El Nino
Brewers, 2016-

Ardizoia, Rinaldo (Joseph)
Rugger
Yankees, 1947

Ardner, Joseph (A)
Old Hoss
    No relation to Dan Blocker (Hoss Cartwright of Bonanza).
Blues, Spiders, 1884, 1890

Arenado, Nolan (James)
Sandblaster
Rockies, 2013-

Arencibia, Jonathan (Paul) {ar-en-SEE-bee-ah}
J.P.
Blue Jays, Rangers, 2010 -

Arft, Hank [Henry Irven]
Bow Wow
    His name sounds like Little Orphan Anñe's dog, Sandy, in the radio show. Bill Veeck sent a teletype message offering to sell Arft's contract. The machine jammed and printed, "ARFARFARFARFARFARFARF." Hank Greenberg replied that Veeck should "keep that dog in St. Louis." It may have had something to do with getting the nickname to stick.
Browns, 1948-1952

Arlett, Russell (Loris) {ar-LET}
Buzz
    Cut through opposing batters like a buzz saw.
Phillies, 1931

Armstrong, Noble (George)
Dodo
Athletics, 1946

Arnold, Willis (S)
Billy
Mansfields, 1872

Arnovich, Morris

Snooker
Proficient at the British style of billiards.
Son of Israel
As a Jewish player, he kept kosher for his entire career.
Phillies, Reds, Giants, 1936-1946

Arntzen, Orie (Edgar)
Old Folks
Major league debut at the age of 33.
Athletics, 1943

Arrieta, Jake [Jacob Joseph] {air-ee-etta}
Snake
Orioles, Cubs, Phillies, 2010-

Arroyo, Bronson (Anthony)
Saturn Nuts
From a Red Sox booster club because he was viewed as a young kid pitching in high pressure situations but not letting anything get to him.
Smokey: Tacks: Dirty: BroYo: Free Love
Pirates, Red Sox, Reds, Diamondbacks
2000-2017

Arundel, John (Thomas)
Tug
Athletics, Blue Stockings, Hoosiers, Nationals, 1882-1888

Asbell, James (Marion)
Big Train
Cubs, 1938

Asbjornson, Robert (Anthony)
Casper
He changed his name to "Asby," after his career was under way.
Red Sox, Reds, 1928-1932

Ashburn, Richie [Don Richard]
Put-Put
A name given him by either Ted Williams or Stan Musial because "he ran so fast you would think he had twin motors in his pants."
Tilden Flash
He was born in Tilden, Nebraska.
Whitey
Phillies, Cubs, Mets, 1948-1962

Asher, Alec (Edward)
The Big Cat
Phillies, Orioles, Brewers, 2015-2018

Ashford, Thomas (Steven)
Tucker
Padres, Rangers, Yankees, Mets, Royals, 1976-1984

Ashley, Billy (Manual)
Light-Tower Power
A strong hitter with enough power to put the ball over the light towers.
Dodgers, Red Sox, 1992-1998

Astudillo, Willians (Jose)
{ah-stew-DEE-yo}
Tortuga
Twins, 2018-

Atherton, Charles (Morgan Herbert)
Prexy
His father was the president of Penn State University.
Senators, 1899

Atkins, Francis (Montgomery)
Tommy
Athletics, 1909-1910

Atkinson, Hubert (Burley)
Lefty
Senators, 1927

Atwell, Maurice (Dailey)
Toby
Cubs, Pirates, Braves, 1952-1956

Atz, Jacob (Henry)
John
John is a nickname because some people mistakenly thought he changed his name. He didn't.
Senators, White Sox, 1902-1909

Aubrey, Harry (Herbert)
Chub
Beaneaters, 1903

Auerbach, Frederick (Steven)
Rick
A not very common shortening of his first name.
Brewers, Dodgers, Reds, Mariners, 1971-1981

Auker, Elden (LeRoy) {OCK-er}
Submarine
A submarine style pitcher.
Big Six
A college nickname. He played in the Big Six conference.

Mule Ears
   From and used by manager Mickey Cochrane.
Tigers, Red Sox, Browns, 1933-1942
Aulds, Leycester (Doyle)
Tex
   Grew up in Corpus Cristi, Texas.
Red Sox, 1947
Austin, James (Philip)
Pepper
The Pepper Kid
   Given by manager George Stallings because he liked Austin's hustle.
Yankees, Browns, 1909-1929
Autry, Martin (Gordon)
Chick
Yankees, Indians, White Sox, 1924-1930
Autry, William (Askew)
Chick
Reds, Doves, 1907, 1909
Averill, Howard (Earl) {A-ver-ill}
Rock
   He had a powerful build and bulging forearms.
The Earl of Snohomish
   Born in Snohomish, Washington.
Indians, Tigers, Braves, 1929-1941
Avila, Alex [Alexander Thomas]
Titanium Catcher
Tigers, White Sox, Cubs, Diamondbacks, Twins, 2009-
Avrea, James (Epherium)
Jay
Reds, 1959
Axford, John (Berton)
The Ax Man
   Either a pun based on his last name or a name given him for his ability to give batters "the axe."
Brewers, Cardinals, Indians, 2009-
Ayala, Benigno {eye-ALL-ah}
Felix
   Félix was his mother's maiden name.
Mets, Cardinals, Orioles, Indians, 1974-1985
Aybar, Erick (Johan) {EYE-bar}
Admiral
Angels, Braves, Tigers, Padres, 2006-
Ayers, Yancy (Wyatt)
Doc
   Went to medical school, although he quit to concentrate on baseball.
Senators, Tigers, 1913-1921
Aylward, Richard (John)
Dandy
Indians, 1953
Azcue, José (Joaquin)
The Immortal Azcue
   Known for his strong throwing arm.
Reds, Athletics, Indians, Red Sox, Angels, Brewers, 1960-1972
Babe, Loren (Rolland)
Bee Bee
Yankees, Angels, 1952-1953
Babitt, Mack (Neal)
Shooty
Athletics, 1981
Backman, Walter (Wayne)
Cabbage Patch
Mets, Twins, Pirates, Phillies, Mariners, 1980-1993
Baczewski, Fred [Frederic John] {BAA-jess-key}
Lefty
Cubs, Reds, 1953-1955
Bader, Lore (Verne)
King
Iron Man
Two Pairs
   He loved playing cards.
   Given by the *Sporting News*, based on his minor league career.
Giants, Red Sox, 1912-1918
Badgro, Morris (Hiram)
Red
Browns, 1929-1930
Baerga, Carlos (Obed) {By-AIR-ga}
One if...
   Chris Berman-ism; One if by land, two if by sea, three if by air-ga, because of his ability to hit triples.
Indians, Mets, Padres, Red Sox, Diamondbacks, 1990-2004
Báez, Javier [Ednel Javier]
El Mago

Cubs, 2014-
Báez, Pedro (Alberys)
    The Human Rain Delay: La Mula
    Dodgers, 2014-
Bagby, James Sr. (Charles Jacob)
    Sarge
        From teammates, based on a character in a Broadway play at the time.
    Reds, Indians, Pirates, 1912-1923
Bagwell, Jeff [Jeffrey Robert]
    Brown Paper
        A Chris Berman-ism, introducing his name as "Jeff Brown Paper Bagwell.
    BagPipes
    Astros, 1991-2005
Bagwell, William (Mallory)
    Big Bill
        His 6'1", 175 lb. stature.
    Braves, Athletics, 1923, 1925
Bahnsen, Stanley (Raymond)
    Bahnsen Burner
        Based on the chem lab instrument.
    Stanley Struggle
        Was able to keep runners stranded.
    Bonce
    Yankees, White Sox, Athletics, Expos, Angels, 1966-1982
Bailey, Abraham (Lincoln)
    Sweetbread
    Cubs, Robins, 1919-1921
Bailey, David (Dewitt)
    Homer
        Terrible name for a pitcher but he was actually named for his grandfather.
    Reds, Royals, Athletics, Twins, 2007-
Bailey, Frederick (Middleton)
    Penny
    Braves, 1916-1918
Bailey, Harry (Lewis)
    Bill
        The popular song of the era was, "Won't you come home, Bill Bailey?"
    Yankees, 1911
Bailey, Linwood (Clifton)
    King
        Ace of his minor league team.
    Reds, 1895
Baker, Charles
    Bock: Smiling Bock
    Blues, Athletics, 1901
Baker, Jesse
    Tiny
    Senators, 1919
Baker, John (Franklin)
    Home Run
        Teammates gave him this name because of two home runs. They were hit in championship games, where they counted most. He consistently led the league in home runs ... with 12 in his best season.
    Athletics, Yankees, 1908-1924
Baker, Johnnie (B)
    Dusty
    Braves, Dodgers, Giants, Athletics, 1968-1986
Baker, Kirtley
    Whitey
    Alleghenys, Orioles, Senators, 1890-1899
Baker, Thomas (Calvin)
    Rattlesnake
    Dodgers, Giants, 1935-1938
Bakley, Edward (Enoch)
    Jersey
    Athletics, Keystones, Quicksteps, Cowboys, Blues, Spiders, Infants, Statesmen, Orioles, 1883-1891
Balas, Mitchell (Francis)
    Mike
    Bees, 1938
Balboni, Stephen (Charles)
    Bye-Bye
        He said that to the ball when he hit a home run. Pitchers said it to him when he struck out.
    Bones
        A malapropism for Balboni.
    Ug
        From high school
    Yankees, Royals, Mariners, Rangers, 1981-1993
Baldelli, Rocco (Dan)
    The Woonsocket Rocket
        He was fast and from Woonsocket, RI.
    Devil Rays, Rays, Red Sox, 2003-2010

Baldwin, Charles (B)
Lady
Because of his "quiet ways" and his refusal to swear or come into contact with liquor or tobacco.
Brewers, Wolverines, Bridegrooms, Bisons, 1884-1890

Baldwin, Clarence (Geoghan)
Kid
A nickname given in the 19th century to scrappy, feisty little athletes.
Cowboys, Browns, Unions, Red Stockings, Reds, Athletics, 1884-1890

Baldwin, Henry (Clay)
Ted
Phillies, 1927

Baldwin, Howard (Edward)
Harry
Giants, 1924-1925

Baldwin, Mark [Marcus Elmore]
Fido
White Stockings, Solons, White Sox, Pirates, Giants, 1887-1893

Baldwin, Robert (Harvey)
Billy
Tigers, Mets, 1975-1976

Bamberger, Harold (Earl)
Dutch
Giants, 1948

Bancker, John (V)
Studs
Elm Citys, 1875

Bancroft, David (James)
Beauty
Given by other players for his habit of calling good pitches he missed as "a beauty."
Phillies, Giants, Braves, Robins, 1915-1930

Bando, Sal [Salvatore Leonard]
Captain Sal
Athletics, Brewers, 1966-1981

Bandy, Jett (Adam)
Sinker-Slider
Angels, Brewers, 2015-2018

Banks, Ernie [Ernest]
Mr. Cub
Spent his entire career with one club.
Mr. Sunshine
This speaks to his disposition.
Cubs, 1953-1971

Bannon, James (Henry)
Foxy Grandpa
Strange, since he was in his 20s as a player. Thomas Bannon was his OLDER brother.
Browns, Beaneaters, 1893-1896

Bannon, Thomas (Edward)
Ward Six: Uncle Tom
Giants, 1895-1896

Barbare, Walter (Lawrence) {BAW-bar}
Dinty
Naps, Indians, Red Sox, Pirates, Braves, 1914-1922

Barbary, Donald (Odell)
Red
Senators, 1943

Barbeau, William (Joseph)
Jap
Naps, Pirates, Cardinals, 1905-1910

Barclay, George (Oliver)
Deerfoot
He was fleet of foot.
The Rose
He had an eye for the ladies and was concerned with his looks.
Cardinals, Beaneaters, 1902-1905

Barfoot, Clyde (Raymond)
Foots
Cardinals, Tigers, 1922-1926

Barger, Eros (Bolivar)
Cy
Highlanders, Superbas, Dodgers, Rebels, 1906-1915

Barker, Len [Leonard Harold]
Large Lenny
Rangers, Indians, Braves, Brewers, 1976-1987

Barker, Raymond (Herrell)
Buddy
Orioles, Indians, Yankees, 1960-1967

Barmes, Bruce (Raymond)
Squaky
Senators, 1953

Barna, Herbert (Paul)
Babe

Athletics, Giants, Red Sox, 1937-1943
Barnes, Austin (Scott)
Sam
Dodgers, 2015-
Barnes, Charles (Roscoe)
Ross
Red Stockings, White Stockings, Reds, 1871-1881
Barnes, Emile (Deering)
Red
Senators, White Sox, 1927-1930
Barnes, Everett (Duane)
Eppie
Pirates, 1923-1924
Barnes, Frank (Samuel)
Lefty
Tigers, Yankees, 1929-1930
Barnes, Jacob (Andrew)
Caveman
Brewers, Royals, Angels, 2016-
Barnes, Jesse (Lawrence)
Nubby
 A variant of 'doorknob,' a nickname given him because he had the smallest hat size in the majors.
Braves, Giants, Robins, 1915-1927
Barnes, John (Francis)
Honey
Yankees, 1926
Barnes, Junie (Shoaf)
Lefty
Reds, 1934
Barnes, Matt [Matthew David]
Barnicles
Red Sox, 2014-
Barnes, Robert (Avery)
Lefty
White Sox, 1924
Barnes, Virgil (Jennings)
Zeke
 From childhood.
Giants, Braves, 1919-1928
Barnes, William (Henry)
Skeeter
Crash Davis
 Based on a fictional character in the movie, Bull Durham, who spent most of his career in the minors.

Reds, Expos, Cardinals, Tigers, 1983-94
Barnhart, Clyde (Lee)
Pooch
Pirates, 1920-1928
Barnie, William (Harrison)
Bald Billy
Dark Blues, Westerns, Mutuals, Orioles, 1874-1886
Barr, Hyder (Edward)
Scotty
 Obviously predated Star Trek.
Athletics, 1908-1909
Barraclough, Kyle (david) {bear-claw}
Bear
Marlins, Nationals, Giants, 2015-
Barragan, Facundo (Anthony)
Cuno
Cubs, 1961-1963
Barrett, Aaron (James)
Bear
Nationals, 2014-
Barrett, Charles (Henry)
Red
Reds, Braves, Cardinals, 1937-1949
Barrett, Frank [Francis Joseph]
Red
Cardinals, Red Sox, Braves, Pirates, 1939-1950
Barrett, John (Joseph)
Jack
Pirates, Braves, 1942-1946
Barrett, Robert (Schley)
Jumbo
Cubs, Robins, Red Sox, 1923-1929
Barrett, Tracy (Souter)
Dick
 A reference to comic strip detective, Dick Tracy.
Kewpie Dick
 He was cute as a Kewpie doll.
Athletics, Braves, Cubs, Phillies, 1933-45
Barrett, William (Joseph)
Whispering Bill
 He was very soft spoken.
Athletics, White Sox, Red Sox, Senators, 1921-1930
Barron, David (Irenus)
Red

No relation to Snoopy's nemesis from the Peanuts cartoons, which didn't start until 1950.
Braves, 1929

Barrows, Roland
Cuke
White Sox, 1909-1912

Barry, Edward
Jumbo
> Tall (6'3") for the day.
Americans, 1905-1907

Barry, Hardin
Finn
Athletics, 1912

Barry, John C
Shad
Senators, Beaneaters, Phillies, Cubs, Reds, Cardinals, Giants, 1900-1908

Barry, John J (Joseph)
Black Jack
Athletics, Red Sox, 1908-1919

Bartell, Richard (William)
Rowdy Richard
> He had an aggressive style of play and a fiery attitude.
Shortwave
> He was an aggressive shortstop.
Pirates, Phillies, Giants, Cubs, Tigers, 1927-1946

Barthold, John (Francis)
Hans
Athletics, 1904

Basgall, Romanus
Monty
Pirates, 1948-1951

Basinski, Edwin (Frank)
Bazooka
Fiddler
> Trained for 16 years as a violinist and played for the Baltimore Symphony.
Dodgers, Pirates, 1944-1947

Baskette, James (Blaine)
Big Jim
> He was 6'2", 185 lbs.
Naps, 1911-1913

Bass, William (Capers)
Doc
> There is no indication of any medical training.
Braves, 1918

Batch, Emil
Heinie
Ace
Superbas, 1904-1907

Batchelder, Joe [Joseph Edward]
Win
Braves, 1923-1925

Bates, Creed (Napoleon)
Frank
Spiders, Prefectos, 1898-1899

Bates, Hubert (Edgar)
Bud
Phillies, 1939

Batista, Leocadio (Francisco) {bah-TEESE-ta}
Tony
Athletics, Diamondbacks, Blue Jays, Orioles, Expos, Twins, Nationals, 1996-2007

Batista, Rafael
El Gallo
> The translation is "The Rooster."
> Perhaps an early riser.
Astros, 1973, 1975

Bauer, Trevor (Andrew)
Bauer Outage
> Rhymes with Power
Diamondbacks, Indians, Reds, 2012-

Baumann, Charles (John)
Paddy
Tigers, Yankees, 1911-1017

Baumann, Frank (Matt) {BOW-man}
Beau
Red Sox, White Sox, Cubs, 1955-1965

Bautista, Jose (Antonio) {bah-TEE-stah}
Joey Bats
> First used by Pittsburgh media. The name comes from a YouTube character he played in "The Hitman," a MLB Fan Cave commercial.
Orioles, Devil Rays, Royals, Pirates, Blue Jays, Phillies, 2004-2018.

Baxes, Dimitrios (Speros)
Jim

Dodgers, Indians, 1959
Baxter, John (Morris)
Moose
He was 6'2", 200 lbs.
Cardinals, 1907
Bay, Harry (Elbert)
Deerfoot
He was a high school track and field star and an American League stolen base leader.
Reds, Bronchos, Naps, 1901-1908
Bayer, Christopher (Andy)
Burley
Colonels, 1899
Baylor, Don (Edward)
Groove
In his rookie season with Baltimore, he told a reporter that he would break into the starting lineup as soon as he got "in the groove."
Sneak Thief
A name bestowed by Billy North of the Athletics when Baylor stole four bases in one game as part of a streak of 25 straight steals.
Orioles, Athletics, Yankees, Red Sox, Twins, 1970-1988
Bayne, William (Lear)
Beverly
Referenced in several encyclopedias but never used by his family.
Browns, Indians, Red Sox, 1919-1930
Beam, Theodore (Lester)
T.J.
Yankees, Pirates, 2006, 2008
Beamon, Clifford
Trey
Generally given to the son of a Jr.
Pirates, Padres, Tigers, 1996-1998
Bean, Beveric (Benton)
Belve
Belve is short for Belveric, which is given as his name on some sites, but his name has no 'L.'
Bill

An easier name to use than Belve or Beveric.
Indians, Senators, 1930-1935
Beatty, Desmond (Aloysius)
Desperate
Giants, 1914
Beaumont, Clarence (Howeth)
Ginger
Nicknamed for his thick red hair.
Pirates, Doves, Cubs, 1899-1910
Beazley, Johnny [John Andrew]
Nig
A nickname given him by his grandfather at about 3 months old.
Yankee Killer
For his World Series mastery in 1942.
Cardinals, Braves, 1941-1949
Becannon James (Melvin)
Buck
Metropolitans, Giants 1884-1887
Beck, Chris [Christopher Michael]
Bubba
White Sox, Mets, 2015-2018
Beck, Clyde (Eugene)
Jersey
Cubs, Reds, 1926-1931
Beck, Ervin (F)
Dutch
Superbas, Blues, Reds, Tigers, 1899-1902
Beck, Rodney (Roy)
Shooter
Giants, Cubs, Red Sox, Padres, 1991-2004
Beck, Walter (William)
Boom-Boom
In 1934, he allowed many line drives which made that sound when hitting the outfield wall.
Browns, Dodgers, Phillies, Tigers, Reds, Pirates, 1924-1945
Beckendorf, Henry (Ward)
Heinie
Tigers, Senators, 1909-1910

Becker, Charles (Schlagel)
Buck
Senators, 1911-1912

Becker, Heinz (Reinhard)
Dutch
> He was born in Germany.

Bunions
> He suffered from severe bunions and foot deformities.

Cubs, Indians, 1943-1947

Beckham, Tim [Timothy Lamar]
Swaggy T
Rays, Orioles, Mariners, 2013-2019

Beckley, Jake [Jacob Peter]
Eagle Eye
> A nickname given him for his batting skill.

Alleghenys, Burghers, Pirates, Giants, Reds, Cardinals, 1888-1907

Bedrosian, Cam [Cameron Rock] {beh-DROW-zee-uhn}
Bedrock
> Son of Steve, also Bedrock.

Angels, 2014-

Bedrosian, Steve [Stephen Wayne] {beh-DROW-zee-uhn}
Bedrock
> Solid relief pitcher.

Braves, Phillies, Giants, Twins, 1981-1995

Beecher, Roy [Leroy]
Colonel
Giants, 1907-1908

Beeler, Joseph (Samuel)
Jodie
Reds, 1944

Beggs, Joseph (Stanley)
Fireman
> Of his 238 games played, most were in relief.

Yankees, Reds, Giants, 1938-1948

Begley, James (Lawrence)
Imp
> Usually implies a short player, but he wasn't.

Reds, 1924

Behan, Charles (Frederick)
Petie
Phillies, 1921-1923

Bejma, Aloysius (Frank) {BAY-ma}
Ollie
> It has been said that he may have looked a bit like Oliver Hardy, the Ollie of the Laurel and Hardy comedy duo.

Browns, White Sox, 1934-1939

Belanger, Mark (Henry) {buh-LAN-jer}
The Blade
> He gained the nickname because of his stature: 6'1" but only 170 lbs.

Orioles, Dodgers, 1965-1982

Belinsky, Robert
Bo
> Nicknamed for the middleweight boxer Bobo Olson in tribute to his street brawling.

Angels, Phillies, Astros, Pirates, Reds, 1962-1970

Bell, Chad [Chadwick Micah]
Wick
Tigers, 2017-2018

Bell, David G (Gus)
Buddy
> Shares a first name with his more famous baseball father.

Indians, Rangers, Reds, Astros, 1972-1989

Bell, David R (Russell)
Gus
> Gus is David Jr. His parents nicknamed him Gus because of their admiration for catcher Gus Mancuso.

Pirates, Reds, Mets, Braves, 1950-1964

Bell, Fernando (Jerome Lee)
Danny
Pirates, 1939-1940

Bell, George A (Antonio)
Liberty
Taco

Chris Berman-ism who always used it between his first and last names.
Blue Jays, Cubs, White Sox, 1981-1993

Bell, George G (Glenn)
Farmer
Born in Greenwood, NY, then a farming community.
Superbas, Dodgers, 1907-1911

Bell, Heath (Justin)
Heater
He is a power pitcher.
Mets, Padres, Marlins, Diamondbacks, Rays 2004-2014

Bell, Herman (S)
Hi
Cardinals, Giants, 1924-1934

Bell, Josh [Joshua Evan]
J.B.
Pirates, 2016-

Bell, Juan
Tito
Orioles, Phillies, Brewers, Expos, Red Sox, 1989-1995

Bell, Ralph (Albert)
Lefty
White Sox, 1912

Bell, Roy (Chester)
Beau
Beau is French for *Belle*, which means *beautiful*.
Browns, Tigers, Indians, 1935-1941

Bell, Wilbur (Gary)
Ding Dong
A Hostess pastry which used an ad featuring a ringing bell.
Indians, Red Sox, Pilots, White Sox, 1958-1969

Bell, William (Samuel)
Ding Dong
A Hostess pastry which used an ad featuring a ringing bell.
Pirates, 1952, 1955

Bella, John
Zeke
He took his nickname as a tribute to Giants' first baseman, Zeke Bonura, his favorite player.
Yankees, Athletics, 1957, 1959

Belle, Albert (Jojuan)
Joey
A short version of his middle name.
Mr. Freeze
Indians, White Sox, Orioles, 1989-2000

Belliard, Rafael (Leonidas)
Pac-Man
Pirates, Braves, 1982-1998

Bellinger, Cody (James)
Cody Love
Dodgers, 2017-

Bellman, Jack (Hutchins)
Happy Jack
Browns, 1889

Belt, Brandon (Kyle) {BRAN-din}
Baby Giraffe
Given by broadcaster Duane Kuiper. Belt's long loping strides were reminiscent of a baby giraffe trying to run.
Giants, 2011-

Beltré, Adrián
El Koja
Dodgers, Mariners, Rangers, 1998-2018

Bench, Johnny (Lee)
The Little General
Reflects his strategic ability in calling for pitches.
Reds, 1967-1983

Bender, Charles (Albert)
Chief
Born on the Chippewa Reservation; often called *Chief* by manager Connie Mack.
Athletics, Terrapins, Phillies, White Sox, 1903-1925

Benes, Andy (Charles) {BEN-ess}
Rain Man
Most often refers to the movie of

that name which tells the story of
an abrasive, selfish Yuppie.
Padres, Mariners, Cardinals,
Diamondbacks, 1989-2002
Benes, Joe [Joseph Anthony]
Bananas
Based on his last name.
Cardinals, 1931
Benge, Ray [Raymond Adelphia] {benj}
Cal: Silent Cal
Indians, Phillies, Dodgers, Bees, Reds,
1925-1938
Bennett, Francis (Allen)
Chip
Red Sox, 1927-1928
Bennett, James (Fred)
Red
Browns, Pirates, 1928, 1931
Bennett, Joseph (Harley)
Bugs
Browns, White Sox, 1918, 1921
Bennett, Justin (Titus)
Pug
Cardinals, 1906-1907
Benson, Allen (Wilbert)
Bullet Ben
Senators, 1934
Bentley, Clytus (George)
Cy
Mansfields, 1872
Benton, Alfred (Lee)
Butch
Mets, Cubs, Indians, 1978-1985
Benton, John (Cleave)
Rube
His pitching style was similar to
that of Rube Waddell.
Reds, Giants, 1910-1925
Benton, Stan [Stanley W]
Rabbit
Phillies, 1922
Benz, Joseph (Louis)
Blitzen: Butcher Boy
White Sox, 1911-1919
Benzinger, Todd (Eric)
Mercedes

Red Sox, Reds, Royals, Dodgers,
Giants, 1987-1995
Berenguer, Juan (Bautista)
Señor Smoke: El Gasolino
Both of these nicknames were
given him by fans because of his
mid-90s fastball.
Pancho Villa
Bestowed by teammates because
of his looks.
Mets, Royals, Blue Jays, Tigers,
Giants, Twins, Braves, 1978-1992
Berger, Charles (Carl)
Heinie
Naps, 1907-1910
Berger, Joe [Joseph August]
Fats
An undeserved nickname. He was
only 170 lbs.
White Sox, 1913-1914
Berger, John (Henry)
Tun
A tun is a wine cask measure. He
was over 200 lbs.
Alleghenys, Pirates, Senators,
1890-1892
Berger, Louis (William)
Boze
Indians, White Sox, Red Sox,
1932-1939
Berghammer, Marty [Martin Andrew]
Pepper
White Sox, Reds, Rebels, 1911-1915
Bergman, Alfred (Henry)
Dutch
Big Dutch
Sets him apart from his younger
brother, Little Dutch.
Indians, 1916
Berkman, Lance [William Lance]
Fat Elvis
Even he doesn't know how he got
that nickname.
Big Puma
Self-given when asked in an
interview what nickname he

would choose, because "pumas are sleek, fast, powerful and secretive."
Astros, Yankees, Cardinals, Rangers, 1999-2013

Bernadina, Roger [Rogearvin Argelo] {burn-a-DEAN-ah}
The Shark
Nationals, Phillies, Reds, Dodgers, 2008-2014

Bernard, Joseph (Carl)
J.C.
Cardinals, 1909

Bernhard, Bill [William Henry]
Strawberry Bill
Phillies, Athletics, Broncos, Naps, 1899-1907

Berra, Dale (Anthony)
Boo Boo
  Son of Yogi
Pirates, Yankees, Astros, 1977-1987

Berra, Lawrence (Peter)
Yogi
  Acquired as a teen when a friend, Bobby Hofman, said he looked like a Hindu yogi when sitting with arms and legs crossed, as they had seen in a movie.
Yankees, Mets, 1946-1965

Berríos, José (Orlando)
The Machine: La Maquina: Orlandito
Twins, 2016-

Berroa, Gerónimo (Emiliano Letta)
Chief
Braves, Reds, Marlins, Athletics, Orioles, Indians, Tigers, Blue Jays, Dodgers, 1989-2000

Berry Claude (Elzy)
Admiral
White Sox, Athletics, Rebels, 1904-15

Berry, Joe Jr. [Joseph Howard]
Nig
  Usually given to one with a dark complexion
Giants, 1921-1922

Berry, Joe Sr. [Joseph Howard]
Hodge
Phillies, 1902

Berry, Jonas (Arthur)
Jittery Joe
Cubs, Athletics, Indians, 1942-1946

Bertaina, Frank (Louis)
Toys in the Attic
Orioles, Senators, Cardinals, 1964-70

Bertoia, Pierino (Peter) {brr-TOY-ah}
Reno
  The last part of his first name.
Tigers, Senators, Twins, Athletics, 1953-1962

Bertrand, Roman (Mathias)
Lefty
Phillies, 1936

Bessent, Fred (Donald) {BESS-ent}
The Weasel
  Given by his teammates.
Dodgers, 1955-1958

Betances, Dellin {buh-TAN-sis}
D Dawg
Yankees, Mets, 2011-

Bethea, Bill [William Lamar]
Spot
Twins, 1964

Bettis, Chad (Robert)
Betty
Rockies, 2013-2019

Betts, Harry [Harold Matthew]
Chubby
  He was 5'10", 200 lbs.
Ginger
Cardinals, Reds, 1903, 1913

Betts, Mookie [Markus, Lynn]
Mookie Batts
Red Sox, Dodgers, 2014-

Betts, Walter (McKinley)
Huck
Phillies, Braves, 1920-1935

Bevens, Floyd (Clifford)
Bill
Yankees, 1944-1947

Biancalana, Roland (Americo)
Buddy
  In high school, he was known as

Buddy Alphabet.
Royals, Astros, 1982-1987
Bibens-Dirkx, Austin (M)
{BIBB-ins DIRKS}
El Rubio
Rangers, 2017-2018
Bicknell, Charles (Stephen)
Bud
Phillies, 1948-1949
Biddle, Lee (Francis)
Rocky
White Sox, Expos, 2000-2004
Biecher, Ed [Edward]
Scrap Iron
A scrappy style of play.
Browns, Spiders, 1897-1898
Bigbee, Carson (Lee)
Skeeter
He stole 182 bases in his major league career.
Pirates, 1916-1926
Bigbee, Lyle (Rudolph)
Al
Babe
A high school nickname.
Athletics, Pirates, 1920-1921
Bigelow, Elliot (Allardice)
Babe
Given in the minor leagues because of his long home runs.
Gilly
Widely used in the minor leagues
Red Sox, 1929
Bildilli, Emil
Hillbilly
"Hillbilly Bildilly" was fun to say.
Browns, 1937-1941
Billings, John (Augustus)
Josh
Naps, Indians, Browns 1913-1923
Billingsley, Brett (Aaron)
Brent
Marlins, 1999
Binks, George (Alvin)
Bingo
Senators, Athletics, Browns, 1944-1948
Bird, Frank (Zephrin)
Dodo
The Dodo Bird is an extinct species.
Browns, 1892
Bird, Greg [Gregory Paul]
Bird Dog
Yankees, 2015-
Bird, James (Edward)
Red
Senators, 1921
Birkofer, Ralph (Joseph)
Lefty
Pirates, Dodgers, 1933-1937
Birmingham, Joseph (Leo)
Dode
Naps, 1906-1914
Birrer, Werner (Joseph)
Babe
Earned on one day when he hit two 3-run homers.
Tigers, Orioles, Dodgers, 1955-1958
Biscan, Frank (Stephen)
Porky
He was 5'11" and weighed 190 lbs.
Browns, 1942-1948
Bischoff, John (George)
Smiley
Either a sunny disposition or unusually dour.
White Sox, Red Sox, 1925-1926
Bishop, Max (Frederick)
Tilly
Bestowed because he held his arms stiff at his sides when he ran.
Camera Eye
Based on his ability to know the strike zone.
Athletics, Red Sox, 1924-1935
Bishop, William (Henry)
Lefty
Athletics, 1921
Bittmann, Henry (Peter)
Red
Cowboys, 1889

Blach, Ty (Tyson Michael)
> The Preacher
> Giants, Orioles, 2016-2019

Black, Bill [John William]
> Jigger
> White Sox, 1924

Black, Harry (Ralston)
> Buddy
> Mariners, Royals, Indians, Blue Jays, Giants, 1981-1995

Black, Joe [Joseph]
> The Workhorse
>> In the 1952 World Series, he pitched three games in seven days.
>
> Dodgers, Redlegs, Senators, 1952-1957

Black, William (Carroll)
> Bud
> Tigers, 1952-1956

Blackburn, Foster (Edwin)
> Charlie
> Packers, White Sox, 1915, 1921

Blackburn, George (W)
> Smiling George
> Orioles, 1897

Blackburn, James (Ray)
> Bones
> Reds, 1948, 1951

Blackburne, Russell (Aubrey)
> Lena
>> A minor league fan compared him to a female player of the day.
>
> Slats
> White Sox, Reds, Braves, Phillies, 1910-1929

Blackmon, Charlie [Charles Cobb]
> Chuck Nazty
> Rockies, 2011-

Blackwell, Ewell
> The Whip
>> Based on his sidearm, snap delivery.
>
> Reds, Yankees, Athletics, 1942-1955

Blair, Clarence (Vick)
> Footsie
> Cubs, 1929-1931

Blair, Louis (Nathan)
> Buddy
> Athletics, 1942

Blair, Paul (L.D.)
> Motormouth
>> A talkative nature.
>
> Orioles, Yankees, Reds, 1964-1980

Blair, Walter (Allen)
> Heavy
>> Confusing, since he was only 185 at 6 ft.
>
> Highlanders, Buffeds, Blues, 1907-1915

Blaisdell, Howard (Carleton)
> Dick
> Unions, 1884

Blake, John (Frederick)
> Sheriff
> Pirates, Cubs, Phillies, Browns, Cardinals, 1920-1937

Blanco, Andrés (Eloy) {BLAHN-koh}
> Whitey
> Royals, Cubs, Rangers, Phillies, 2004-2017

Blanco, Gil [Gilbert Henry]
> Bambi
> Yankees, Athletics, 1965-1966

Blanco, Grégor (Miguel)
> {GREH-goer BLAHN-koh}
> White Shark
> Braves, Royals, Giants, Diamondbacks, 2008-2018

Blanco, Henry (Ramon) {BLAHN-koh}
> Hank White
>> "Hank" is short for "Henry." "White" is the English translation of "Blanco."
>
> Dodgers, Brewers, Braves, Twins, Cubs, Padres, Mets, Diamondbacks, Blue Jays, Mariners, 1997-2013

Blanding, Frederick (James)
> Fritz
> Naps, 1910-1914

Blank, Frank (Ignatz)
> Coonie
> Cardinals, 1909

Blankenship, Homer
Si
White Sox, Pirates, 1922-1928
Blankenship, Lance (Robert)
You Sunk My
Chris Bermanism, a reminder of the game.
Athletics, 1988-1993
Blanks, Larvell
Sugar Bear
By minor league teammates. He had an aggressive batting style.
Braves, Indians, Rangers, 1972-1980
Blanton, Darrell (Elijah)
Cy
Pirates, Phillies, 1934-1942
Blasingame, Don (Lee)
Blazer
A hustler both in the field and on the bases.
Cardinals, Giants, Reds, Senators, Athletics, 1955-1966
Blattner, Robert (Garnett)
Buddy
Cardinals, Giants, Phillies, 1942-1949
Blefary, Curt [Curtis Leroy] {BLEFF-ah-ree}
Clank
Bestowed by Frank Robinson because of his below-average fielding ability.
Cuckoo
His tirades got in the way of his career.
Cadillac Curt
A minor league nickname given because of his home run trot.
Orioles, Astros, Yankees, Athletics, Padres, 1965-1972
Blessitt, Isaiah
Ike
Tigers, 1972
Blethen, Clarence (Waldo)
Climax
Named after his favorite brand of chewing tobacco.
Red Sox, Robins, 1923, 1929
Blevins, Jerry (Richard)
Gordo
Athletics, Nationals, Mets, Braves, 2007-
Block, James (John)
Bruno
Senators, White Sox, Chi-Feds, 1907-1914
Block, Seymour
Cy
Cubs, 1942-1946
Blomberg, Ron [Ronald Mark] {BLOOM-berg}
Boomer
Yankees, White Sox, 1969-1978
Bloomfield, Clyde (Stalcup)
Bud
His father was also named Clyde.
Cardinals, Twins, 1963-1964
Bloomquist, Willie [William Paul]
Spork
Mariners, Royals, Reds, Diamondbacks, 2002-2015
Bluege, Otto (Adam) {BLUE-gee}
Squeaky
Reds, 1932-1933
Bluhm, Harvey (Fred)
Red
Red Sox, 1918
Blyleven, Bert [Rik Aalbert] {BLY-lev-en}
The Dutchman
Born in the Netherlands.
The Minnesota Gopher
He gave up 430 gopher balls (home runs.
Frying Dutchman
As a prank, he lit a fire to teammates' shoelaces.
Be Home
Chris Berman-ism "Bert Be Home by Eleven."
Twins, Rangers, Pirates, Indians, Angels, 1970-1992
Bodie, Frank (Stephen)
Ping

From the sound made when his 52 oz. bat hit the "dead" ball.
The Wonderful Wop
His given name was Francesco Pezzolo.
White Sox, Athletics, Yankees, 1911-1921

Boeckel, Norman (Doxie)
Tony
Pirates, Braves, 1917-1923

Boever, Joseph (Martin) {BAY-ver}
Boever the Saver
A rhyme: He was a closer.
Cardinals, Braves, Phillies, Astros, Athletics, Tigers, Pirates, 1985-1996

Bogart, John (Renzie)
Big John
6'2", 195 lbs.
Tigers, 1920

Boggs, Ray [Raymond Joseph]
Lefty
Braves, 1928

Boggs, Wade (Anthony)
Chicken Man
He ate chicken before every game.
Red Sox, Yankees, Devil Rays, 1982-1999

Bohen, Leo (Ignatius)
Pat
Athletics, Pirates, 1913-1914

Bold, Charles (Dickens)
Dutch
He was born in Sweden.
Browns, 1914

Bolden, William (Horace)
Big Bill
He was 6'4" tall, 200 lbs.
Cardinals, 1919

Boley, John (Peter)
Joe
Silent Joe
Because of his quiet personality.
Athletics, Indians, 1927-1932

Bolger, James (Cyril)
Dutch
Reds, Redlegs Cubs, Indians, Phillies, 1950-1959

Bolton, Cecil (Glenford)
Glenn
Shorthand for his middle name.
Indians, 1928

Bonds, Barry (Lamar)
U.S.
Chris Berman-ism.
Pirates, Giants, 1986-2007

Boney, Henry (Tate)
Haney
Giants, 1927

Bongiovanni, Anthony (Thomas)
Nino
Reds, 1938-1939

Bonham, Ernest (Edward)
Tiny
Ironic: 6'2" and over 200 lbs.
Yankees, Pirates, 1940-1949

Bonilla, Bobby [Roberto Martin Antonio] {bo-KNEE-ya}
Bobby-Bo
White Sox, Pirates, Mets, Orioles, Marlins, Dodgers, Braves, Cardinals, 1986-2001

Bonnell, Barry [Robert Barry]
Preacher
Braves, Blue Jays, Mariners, 1977-1986

Bonness, William (John)
Lefty
Indians, 1944

Bono, Adlai (Wendell)
Gus
Senators, 1920

Bonura, Henry (John)
Zeke
His nickname was from Knute Rockne at Notre Dame, who saw him and said, "What a physique."
White Sox, Senators, Giants, Cubs, 1934-1940

Booker, Richard (Lee)
Buddy
Indians, White Sox, 1966, 1968

Boone, James (Albert)

Dan
: From the western adventurer.
Athletics, Tigers, Indians, 1919-1923
Boone, Luke [Lute Joseph]
Danny
: A reference to Daniel Boone.
Yankees, Pirates, 1913-1918
Boone, Raymond (Otis)
Ike
Indians, Tigers, White Sox, Athletics, Braves, Red Sox, 1948-1960
Booles, Seabron (Jesse)
Red
Naps, 1909
Booth, Amos (Smith)
Darling
Reds, Orioles, Eclipse, 1876-1882
Borchers, George (Bernard)
Chief
White Stockings, Colonels, 1888, 1895
Bordagaray, Stanley (George) {bor-duh-gah-RAY}
Frenchy
: His mother gave him his nickname because of his French background.
White Sox, Dodgers, Cardinals, Reds, Yankees, 1934-1945
Boris, Paul (Stanley)
Lone Ranger
Twins, 1982
Borkowski, Bob [Robert Vilarian]
Bush
: Early neighbors could not pronounce his last name.
Cubs, Reds, Dodgers, 1950-1955
Borland, Tom [Thomas Bruce]
Spike
Red Sox, 1960-1961
Borom, Edward (Jones)
Red
Tigers, 1944-1945
Borton, William (Baker)
Babe
White Sox, Yankees, Terriers, Browns, 1912-1916
Boscan, Jean (Carlos)
J.C.
Braves, Cubs, 2010-2013
Boshers, Jeffrey (Alan) {bo-SHEERS}
Buddy
Angels, Twins, Blue Jays, 2013-
Boss, Harley [Elmer Harley]
Lefty
: Left handed but not a pitcher.
Senators, Indians, 1928-1933
Bostock, Lyman (Wesley)
Abdul Jibber-Jabber
: He was always talking.
Red Bone
: Childhood nickname: a scrawny kid, turned red in the sun.
Twins, Angels, 1975-1978
Bottomly, Jim [James Leroy]
Sunny Jim
: Swagger, rakish cap angle and constant smile.
Cardinals, Reds, Browns, 1922-1937
Boucher, Al [Alexander Francis]
Bo
: Short for his last name.
Terriers, 1914
Boudreau, Lou [Louis] {BOO-dro}
Old Shufflefoot: Handsome Lou
Boordee
: Connie Mack mispronunciation.
The Good Kid
Indians, Red Sox, 1938-1952
Bour, Justin (James) {BORE}
Papito: Bourtobello Crushroom
Marlins, Phillies, Angels, 2014-2019
Bourjos, Peter (Christopher) {BORE-jus}
Needler: Gorgeous: Fleet Pete
Angels, Cardinals, Phillies, Rays, Braves, 2010-2019
Bouton, Jim [James Alan] {BOUT-un}
Bulldog
: A reflection of his tenacity.
Yankees, Pilots, Astros, Braves, 1962-1978
Bowa, Larry [Lawrence Robert]

Gnat: Bo: Pee Wee
Phillies, Cubs, Mets, 1970-1985
Bowen, Emmons (Joseph)
Chick
Only 5'7".
Giants, 1919
Bowen, Sutherland (McCoy)
Cy
Giants, 1896
Bowerman, Frank (Eugene)
Mike
Orioles, Pirates, Giants, Doves, 1895-1909
Bowers, Stewart (Cole)
Doc
His father was a doctor.
Red Sox, 1935-1936
Bowler, Grant (Tierney)
Moose
6', 190 lbs.
White Sox, 1931-1932
Bowles, Emmett (Jerome)
Chief
White Sox, 1922
Bowlin, Weldon [Lois Weldon]
Hoss
Athletics, 1967
Bowman, Alvah (Edson)
Abe
Naps, Indians, 1914-1915
Bowman, Elmer [Elmari Wilhelm]
Big Bow
6'1", 196 lbs.
Senators, 1920
Bowser, James (Harvey)
Red
White Sox, 1910
Boyd, Dennis (Ray)
Oil Can
In his area of Mississippi, Oil was a slang term for beer. He claimed that an ice-cold beverage went down so smooth it was like drinking oil.
Red Sox, Expos, Rangers, 1982-1991
Boyd, Robert (Richard)

The Rope
A line drive hitter.
White Sox, Orioles, Athletics, Braves, 1951-1961
Boyer, Blaine (Thomas)
Grande Rojo
Braves, Cardinals, Diamondbacks, Padres, Twins, Brewers, Red Sox, Royals, 2005-2018
Boyer, Clete [Cletis Leroy]
The Glove
Great ability to catch the ball.
Athletics, Yankees, Braves, 1955-1971
Boyer, Cloyd (Victor)
Junior
His father was NOT Cloyd Sr.
Cardinals, Athletics, 1949-1955
Boyland, Dorian (Scott)
Doe
One syllable version of his first name.
Pirates, 1978-1981
Boyle, Henry (J)
Handsome Henry
Maroons, Hoosiers, 1884-1889
Boyle, John (Anthony)
Honest Jack
Also spent time as an umpire.
Red Stockings, Browns, Pirates, Browns, Giants, Phillies, 1886-1898
Boyle, Ralph (Francis)
Buzz
Braves, Dodgers, 1929-1935
Boyles, Harry
Stretch
6'5", 185 lbs.
White Sox, 1938-1939
Brack, Gilbert (Herman)
Gibby
Dodgers, Phillies, 1937-1939
Bradford, Charles (William)
Buddy
White Sox, Indians, Reds, Cardinals, 1966-1976
Bradley, Archie (N)

Hollywood
Diamondbacks, Reds, 2015-
Bradley, George H.
Foghorn
Red Stockings, 1876
Bradley, George W (Washington)
Grin
Brown Stockings, White Stockings, Trojans, Grays, Blues, Athletics, Outlaw Reds, 1875-1884
Bradley, Hugh (Frederick)
Corns
Red Sox, Rebels, Tip-Tops, Pepper, 1910-1915
Bradley, Jackie
JBJ
    He is a Junior
Red Sox, 2013-
Bradshaw, Dallas (Carl)
Windy
Athletics, 1917
Brady, Bill [William Aloysius]
King
Braves, 1912
Brady, James W (Ward)
King
Phillies, Pirates, Red Sox, Braves, 1905-1912
Brady, Jim [James Joseph]
Diamond Jim
    Named after the more famous Diamond Jim Brady and also because baseball is played on a diamond.
Tigers, 1956
Brady, Michael (Peter)
Spike
White Stockings, 1875
Bragan, Bobby [Robert Randall]
Nig
Mr. Baseball
    Given to him locally for his more than 60-year association with the game.
Phillies, Dodgers, 1940-1948
Brainard, Asa [Asahel]

Count
Ace
    The top pitcher on the staff.
Olympics, Mansfields, Canaries, 1871-1874
Branca, Ralph (Theodore Joseph)
Honker
    Given by teammates for his large nose.
Hawk
    Based on his oversized nose.
Dodgers, Tigers, Yankees, 1944-1956
Brancato, Al [Albert] {BRON-cad-oh}
Bronk
Athletics, 1939-1945
Branch, Norm [Norman Downs]
Red
Yankees, 1941-1942
Brandom, Chester (Milton)
Chick
Pirates, Pepper, 1908-1915
Brandon, Darrell (G)
Bucky
    In the minors, he bought a glove from an Indian youth with buck teeth. The glove had Bucky written on it.
Red Sox, Pilots, Twins, Phillies, 1966-1973
Brandt, Ed [Edward Arthur]
Big Ed
    6'1", 190 lbs.
Braves, Dodgers, Pirates, 1928-1938
Branom, Edgar (Dudley)
Dud
    Sounds bad but came from his middle name.
Athletics, 1927
Bransfield, William (Edward)
Kid
Kitty
    Given by a reporter who mis-heard his "Kid" nickname.
Beaneaters, Pirates, Phillies, Cubs 1898-1911
Brantley, Michael (Charles)

Dr. Smooth
Indians, Astros, 2009-
Branyan, Russell (Oles)
Russell the Muscle
    He hit long distance home runs.
Indians, Reds, Brewers, Devil Rays, Padres, Phillies, Cardinals, Mariners, Diamondbacks, Angels, 1998-2011
Brashear, Norman (Cobb)
Kitty
Colonels, 1899
Bratcher, Joe [Joseph Warwick]
Goobers
Cardinals, 1924
Bratschi, Fred [Frederick Oscar]
Fritz
    A common nickname for Frederick.
White Sox, Red Sox, 1921-1927
Braun, Ryan (Joseph)
The Hebrew Hammer
    A recognized slugger who is also Jewish.
Ocho
Brewers, 2007-
Bray, Clarence (Wilbur)
Buster
Braves, 1941
Brazle, Al [Alpha Eugene]
Cotton
    White-blond hair.
Cardinals, 1943-1954
Brecheen, Harry (David) {bru-KEEN}
Harry the Cat
    For his ability to field bunts.
Cardinals, Browns, 1940-1953
Brenegan, Olaf (Selmar)
Sam
    From his middle name.
Pirates, 1914
Brennan, Tom [Thomas Martin]
Gray Flamingo
Indians, White Sox, Dodgers, 1981-1985
Brenner, Bert [Delbert Henry]
Dutch

Naps, 1912
Brenton, Lynn (Davis)
Buck: Herb
Naps, Indians, Reds, 1913-1921
Bresnahan, Roger (Philip)
The Duke of Tralee
    He often claimed he was from Tralee, Ireland, where his parents were from. Actually, he was born in Toledo.
Senators, Orphans, Orioles, Giants, Cardinals, Cubs, 1897-1915
Bressler, Raymond (Bloom)
Rube
Athletics, Reds, Robins, Phillies, Cardinals, 1914-1932
Breton, John (Frederick)
Jim
White Sox, 1913-1915
Brett, George (Howard)
Mullet
    From Royals manager for missing practice.
Lou
    By himself: he crossed out Mullet on a card he then autographed.
Royals, 1973-1993
Brett, Herbert (James)
Duke
Cubs, 1924-1925
Brett, Ken [Kenneth Alven]
Kemer {KEM-mer}
    Derived from his brother Jim's baby attempt to pronounce his name.
Red Sox, Brewers, Phillies, Pirates, Yankees, White Sox, Angels, Twins, Dodgers, Royals, 1967-1981
Breuer, Marv [Marvin Howard]
Baby Face
Yankees, 1939-1943
Brewer, Jack (Herndon)
Buddy
Giants, 1944-1946
Bridges, Everett (Lamar)
Rocky

As a kid, he got into many scrapes.
Dodgers, Reds, Redlegs, Senators, Tigers, Indians, Cardinals, Angels, 1951-1961

Bridges, Marshall
Fox
Sheriff
Sheriff and Marshall are both officers of the law.
Cardinals, Reds Yankees, Senators, 1959-1965

Brief, Anthony (Vincent)
Bunny
Browns, White Sox, Pirates, 1912-1917

Briggs, Herbert (Theodore)
Buttons
Colts, Orphans, Cubs, 1896-1905

Briley, Greg [Gregory]
Peewee
He was 5'9", 175 lbs.
Mariners, Marlins, 1988-1993

Brinker, Bill [William Hutchinson]
Dode
Phillies, 1912

Brinson, Lewis (Lamont)
Brin Diesel
Brewers, Marlins, 2017-

Briody, Frank [Charles Frank]
Alderman
A reference to his leadership qualities, although, after his playing career, he served only as a ward committeeman.
Fatty
He was only 5'8", but 190 lbs.
Trojans, Blues, Outlaw Reds, Maroons, Cowboys, Wolverines, 1880-1888

Brissie, Leland (Victor)
Lou
He was actually Leland Jr.
Athletics, Indians, 1947-1953

Broadway, Mike [Michael Allen]
Bone Crusher
Giants, 2015-2016

Brock, Lou [Louis Clark]
The Franchise: The Rocket
Cubs, Cardinals, 1961-1979

Brockett, Lewis (Albert)
King
HIghlanders, 1907-1911

Brodie, Walter (Scott)
Steve
Names for a contemporary daredevil for Brodie's all-out manner of playing.
Beaneaters, Browns, Orioles, Pirates, Giants, 1890-1902

Bronkie, Herman (Charles)
Dutch
Naps, Cubs, Cardinals, Browns, 1910-1922

Brookens, Edward (Dwain)
Ike
Tigers, 1975

Brookens, Tom [Thomas Dale]
Pennsylvania Poker
Given by Broadcaster Ernie Harwell, who combined Tom's hitting prowess, birthplace, and some musical history.
Tigers, Yankees, Indians, 1979-1990

Brooks, Jonathan
Mandy
Cubs, 1925-1926

Brosius, Scott (David) {BRO-shus}
Supercalifragilisticexpialadosius
A Chris Berman-ism because it rhymes with his last name.
Athletics, Yankees, 1991-2001

Broskie, Sig [Sigmund Theodore]
Chops
Bees, 1940

Brouthers, Dennis (Joseph) {BROO-thers}
Dan
Big Dan
As a youth, he was big for his age.
Trojans, Bisons, Wolverines, Beaneaters, Reds, Grooms, Orioles, Colonels, Phillies, 1879-1904

Brovia, Joe [Joseph John]

Ox
: As in "strong as an ..." because of his 6'3" frame.

Joltin' Joe: Big Joe

Davenport Destroyer
: He was born and lived in Davenport, CA.

Jolter
: The previous four relate mainly to an outstanding minor league career.

Italian Paisano
: His parents were Italian immigrants.

Redlegs, 1955

Brower, Frank (Willard)
Turkeyfoot
Senators, Indians, 1920-1924

Brown, Alton (Leo)
Deacon
Senators, 1951

Brown, Carroll (William)
Boardwalk
Athletics, Yankees, 1911-1915

Brown, Charles E (Edward)
Yank
Buster
: A probable reference to Buster Brown Shoe company.

Cardinals, Phillies, Doves, Rustlers, Braves. 1905-1913

Brown, Charles R (Roy)
Curly
: Usually a comment about hairdos. We didn't see a photo without a cap.

Lefty
Browns, Reds, 1911-1915

Brown, Dermal (Bram)
Dee
Royals, Athletics, 1998-2007

Brown, Domonic (Larun) {DA-muh-nick}
Downtown
Total Package
: Given by then teammate Ryan Howard after watching Brown in batting practice.

Phillies, 2010-2015

Brown, Eddie [Edward William]
Glass Arm Eddie
Giants, Robins, Braves, 1920-1928

Brown, Elmer (Young)
Shook
Browns, Superbas, Robins, 1911-1915

Brown, Hal [Hector Harold]
Skinny
: Nicknamed by his parents because he was a chubby baby.

White Sox, Red Sox, Orioles, Yankees, Colt 45s, 1951-1964

Brown, Jim [James Donaldson]
Mouse
Don
: From his middle name.

Cardinals, Athletics, 1915-1916

Brown, Jerald (Ray)
Jake
Giants, 1975

Brown, John J
Ad
Bridegrooms, 1897

Brown, John L (Lindsay)
Red
Dodgers, 1937

Brown, Lew [Lewis J]
Blower: Hoss: Horse
Red Stockings, Grays, White Stockings, Wolverines, Beaneaters, Eclipse, Reds, 1876-1884

Brown, Lloyd (Andrew)
Gimpy
: From a leg injury.

El Grandote Burro
: Minor league. Translation-*The big burro*.

Robins, Senators, Browns, Red Sox, Indians, Phillies, 1925-1940

Brown, Mordecai (Peter Centennial) {MOR-deh-chai (like clearing your throat)}
Three Finger
: He lost a finger as a child in a farm

Brown, Ollie

machinery accident.
Miner
   He was a coal miner.
Cardinals, Cubs, Reds, Terriers, Tip Tops, Whales, 1903-1916

Brown, Ollie (Lee)
Downtown
   Many home runs in class A Fresno; the fences faced the downtown.
Giants, Padres, Athletics, Brewers, Astros, Phillies, 1965-1977

Brown, Paul (Percival)
Ray
Cubs, 1909

Brown, Richard (P)
Stub
   Perhaps since he was Richard Jr.
Orioles, Reds, 1893-1897

Brown, Robert (William)
Doc
   Received his MD degree from Tulane University.
The Golden Boy
Yankees, 1946-1954

Brown, Thomas (Michael)
Buckshot
   He scattered his throws all over the first base side of the diamond like buckshot.
Dodgers, Phillies, Cubs, 1944-1953

Brown, Walter (George)
Jumbo: Walter the Whale
Big Brownie: Jolly Falstaffian Flinger
Big Bertha
   He was 6'4", 295 lbs.
Athletic Oliver Hardy
Cubs, Indians, Yankees, Reds, Giants, 1925-1941

Brown, William J (James)
Gates
   His mother nicknamed him but never told him why.
Governor
Gator
   Always supported teammates.
Tigers, 1963-1975

Brown, William M
Big Bill
California
   Born in California.
Giants, Phillies, Orioles, Colonels, Browns, 1887-1894

Browne, Earl (James)
Snitz
   Snitz refers to sliced apples among Pennsylvanians of German ancestry. We don't know if that's a connection.
Phillies, 1935-1938

Browne, Jerry [Jerome Austin]
The Governor
   After the California Governor.
The Guv'nor
Rangers, Indians, Athletics, Marlins, 1986-1995

Browne, Prentice (Almont) {BROWN-ee}
Pidge
Colt 45s, 1962

Browning, Frank
Dutch
Tigers, 1910

Browning, Louis (Rogers)
Pete
Gladiator
   Constant battles with the media.
Louisville Slugger
   He was the first to have his bats custom made.
Eclipse, Colonels, Infants, Pirates, Reds, Browns, Grooms, 1882-1894

Bruett, Joseph (Timothy)
J.T.
Twins, 1992-1993

Brunet, George (Stuart) {Broo-NET}
Lefty: Red
Athletics, Braves, Colt 45s, Orioles, Angels, Pilots, Senators, Pirates, Cardinals, 1956-1971

Bryant, Don [Donald Ray]
Bear
Cubs, Astros, 1966-1970

Bryant, Kris [Kristopher Lee]
  Sparkles: Silk
  Cubs, 2015-
Brynan, Charles (Ruley)
  Tod
  White Stockings, Beaneaters,
  1888, 1891
Buckeye, Garland (Maires)
  Gob
  Senators, Indians, Giants, 1918-1928
Buckles, Jesse (Robert)
  Jim
  Yankees, 1916
Buckner, Bill [William Joseph]
  Billy Buck
  Dodgers, Cubs, Red Sox, Angels,
  Royals, 1969-1990
Buelow, Fred [Frederick William Alexander]
  Fritz
    German nickname for Frederick.
  Perfectos, Cardinals, Tigers, Naps,
  Browns, 1899-1907
Buhner, Jay (Campbell) {BYOU-ner}
  Bone
  Yankees, Mariners, 1987-2001
Buker, Henry (Leslie)
  Happy
  Wolverines, 1884
Bullard, George (Donald)
  Curly
  Tigers, 1954
Bullas, Sim [Simeon Edward]
  Bullets
    Gained because of his ability to
    catch pitchers with strong arms.
  Blue Stockings, 1884
Bulling, Terry (Charles)
  Bud
  Twins, Mariners, 1977-1983
Bullock, Malton (Joseph)
  Red
  Athletics, 1936
Bumbry, Al [Alonza Benjamin]
  The Bee
  Orioles, Padres, 1972-1985

Burdock, Jack [John Joseph]
  Black Jack: Birdie
  Atlantics, Mutuals, Dark Blues,
  Hartfords, Red Stockings, Beaneaters,
  Bridegrooms, Grooms, 1872-1891
Burgess, Forrest (Harrill)
  Smoky
    He inherited his nickname from
    his father. He lived on Tobacco
    Road in North Carolina.
  Cubs, Phillies, Redlegs, Pirates, White
  Sox, 1949-1967
Burgess, Tom [Thomas Roland]
  Tim
  Cardinals, Angels, 1954, 1962
Burk, Charles (Sanford)
  Sandy
    Normal nickname for his middle
    name.
  Superbas, Dodgers, Cardinals, Rebels,
  1910-1915
Burkart, Elmer (Robert)
  Swede
  Phillies, 1936-1939
Burke, Bob [Robert James]
  Lefty
  Senators, Phillies, 1927-1937
Burke, Jimmy [James Timothy]
  Sunset Jimmy
  Spiders, Perfectos, Brewers, White
  Sox, Pirates, Cardinals, 1898-1905
Burke, Les [Leslie Kingston]
  Buck
  Tigers, 1923-1926
Burkett, Jesse (Cail) {BURR-ket}
  Crab
    He was crabby, arguing with
    players, umpires and fans.
  Giants, Spiders, Perfectos, Cardinals,
  Browns, Americans, 1890-1905
Burleson, Rick [Richard Paul]
  Rooster
    Given by Don Zimmer, when
    Burleson was fielding Zimmer
    ground balls without a hat and his
    hair stood up "like a rooster."

Red Sox, Angels, Orioles, 1974-1987

Burnett, Allan (James)
A. J.
Marlins, Blue Jays, Yankees, Pirates, Phillies, 1999-2015

Burns, Charles (Brittingham)
C.B.
Orioles, 1902

Burns, George (Henry)
Tioga George
Tioga Kid
> He lived in Tioga, PA. The names separated him from another George Burns.

Tigers, Athletics, Indians, Red Sox, Yankees, 1914-1929

Burns, Jack [John Irving]
Slug
Browns, Tigers, 1930-1936

Burns, James (Joseph)
Farmer
> Strange, because he was a glass worker, not a farmer.

Slab
> Based on his looks at 5'7", 168 lbs.

The Ashtabula Midget
Cardinals, 1901

Burns, Thomas (P)
Oyster
> He sold shellfish in the off-season.

Quicksteps, Orioles, Bridegrooms, Grooms, Giants, 1884-1895

Burns, William (Thomas)
Sleepy Bill
> Could fall asleep anywhere, any time.

Senators, White Sox, Reds, Phillies, Tigers, 1908-1912

Burrell, Frank (Andrew)
Buster
Giants, Grooms, Bridegrooms, 1891-1897

Burrell, Patrick (Brian) {BURL}
Pat the Bat
> He hit at least 20 home runs for 8 straight seasons.

Phillies, Rays, Giants, 2000-2011

Burright, Larry (Allen)
Possum
Dodgers, Mets, 1962-1964

Burrus, Maurice (Lennon)
Dick
> Never used in the minors or non-baseball references.

Athletics, Braves, 1919-1928

Burton, Ellis (Narrington)
Bones
> At 5'11" and only 160 lbs, he was all skin and...

Cardinals, Indians, Cubs, 1958-1965

Busby, Paul (Miller)
Red
Phillies, 1941, 1943

Busenitz, Alan (Paul) {BOOZE-nits}
Boozy
Twins, 2017-2018

Bush, Guy (Terrell)
The Mississippi Mudcat
> Given by sportswriters for his down-home Mississippi demeanor.

Cubs, Pirates, Bees, Cardinals, Reds, 1923-1945

Bush, Leslie (Ambrose)
Bullet Joe
> Bestowed by Eddie Collins because of his hard fastball. The Missoula club president called him Joe after a local bronco buster.

Athletics, Red Sox, Yankees, Browns, Senators, Pirates, Giants, 1912-1928

Bush, Matt [Matthew Brian]
Matty Ice
Rangers, 2016-

Bush, Owen (Joseph)
Donie {DOE- knee}
> A telegraph error of his name.

Tigers, Senators, 1908-1923

Bushong, Albert (John)
Doc
> A practicing dentist.

Atlantics, Athletics, Ruby Legs, Blues,

Browns, Bridegrooms, 1875-1890
Buskey, Joe [Joseph Henry]
Jazzbow
    He was never involved in the music industry.
Phillies, 1926
Buss, Nick [Nicholas Gregory]
Chili
Dodgers, Angels, 2013, 2016
Butera, Drew [Andrew Edward]
{byoo-TAIR-uh}
The Don: Vito
Twins, Dodgers, Angels, Royals, Rockies, 2010-
Butka, Ed [Edward Luke]
Babe
Senators, 1943-1944
Butler, Billy (Ray)
Country Breakfast
Royals, Athletics, Yankees, 2007-2016
Butler, Brett (Morgan)
Bugsy
Braves, Indians, Giants, Dodgers, Mets, 1981-1997
Butler, Cecil (Dean)
Slewfoot
Braves, 1962, 1964
Butler, Frank B
Stuffy: Goldbrick
Giants, 1895
Butler, Frank E (Edward)
Kid
    At 23, he looked like he was 15.
Reds, 1884
Butler, John (Stephen)
Trolley Line
Robins, Cubs, Cardinals, 1926-1929
Butler, Willis (Everett)
Kid
    He looked like one.
Browns, 1907
Buxton, Byron (Keiron)
Buck
Twins, 2015-
Buxton, Ralph (Stanley)
Buck
The Cheater
    Given in the minors when he was found to use pine tar.
Athletics, Yankees, 1938, 1949
Byerly, Eldred (William)
Bud
    From his youth.
Cardinals, Reds, Senators, Red Sox, Giants, 1943-1960
Byrd, Sammy [Samuel Dewey]
Babe Ruth's Legs
    Used as a pinch runner near the end of Ruth's career.
Alabama Flash
    His outfield speed.
Yankees, Reds, 1929-1936
Byrne, Tommy [Thomas Joseph]
The Wild Man
    A reference to his control problems.
Yankees, Browns, White Sox, Senators, 1943-1957
Byrnes, Eric (James)
The Human Crash Test Dummy
Pigpen
Athletics, Rockies, Orioles, Diamondbacks, Mariners, 2000-2010
Byrnes, Milt [Milton John]
Skippy
    From a popular comic strip character.
Browns, 1943-1945
Caballero, Ralph (Joseph)
Putsy
    From boyhood.
Putz
    Used by announcers until they discovered it was insulting to Jewish fans.
Phillies, 1944-1952
Cabell, Enos (Milton) {ca-BELL}
Big E
    He was certainly big at 6'4".
Orioles, Astros, Giants, Tigers, Dodgers, 1972-1986

Cabrera, Al [Alfredo A]
El Pajaro
Spanish for 'bird.' He was born in the Canary Islands.
Cabbage
Play on his last name.
Cardinals, 1913

Cabrera, Asdrúbal (Jose) {as-DROO-bull}
Cabbie: Chiquitin
Indians, Nationals, Rays, Mets, Phillies, Rangers, 2007-

Cabrera, Melky {MEL-key Ka-BRAIR-uh}
The Melk Man
A play on his first name.
Leche
Spanish for 'milk.'
Yankees, Braves, Royals, Giants, Blue Jays, 2005-2019

Cabrera, Orlando (Luis) {ka-brair-RAH}
O.C.: O-Dog
Expos, Red Sox, Angels, White Sox, Athletics, Twins, Reds, Indians, Giants, 1997-2011

Cady, Forrest (Leroy)
Hollick
From youth.
Hick
Shortened version, by minor league teammates.
Red Sox, Phillies, 1912-1919

Caffie, Joe [Joseph Clifford]
Rabbit
Known for his speed.
Indians, 1956-1957

Cahill, John (Patrick Parnell)
Patsy
Buckeyes, Maroons, Hoosiers, 1884-1887

Cain, Lorenzo (Lamar)
CrunchWrap
Brewers, Royals, 2010-

Cain, Matt [Matthew Thomas]
The Horse
Big Daddy
Given by his high school coach.
Big Sugar
Likes sweets, perhaps.
Giants, 2005-2017

Cain, Merritt (Patrick)
Sugar
Automatic nickname.
Athletics, Browns, White Sox, 1932-1938

Cain, Robert (Max)
Sugar
White Sox, Tigers, Browns, 1949-53

Caithammer, George (Thodore)
Sidee
White Sox, 1934

Caldwell, Earl (Welton)
Teach
Teacher/principal before baseball.
Phillies, Browns, White Sox, Red Sox, 1928-1948

Caldwell, Ralph (Grant)
Lefty
Phillies, 1904-1905

Caldwell, Ray [Raymond Benjamin]
Rube
Grantland Rice said he could be another Rube Waddell.
Sum
Slim
Elongated face, 6'2", 190 lbs.
Yankees, Red Sox, Indians, 1910-1921

Calero, Enrique (Nomar) {kuh-LEHR-oh}
Kiko {KEE-ko}
Cardinals, Athletics, Marlins, 2003-2009

Calhoun, Bill [William Davitte]
Mary
Braves, 1913

Calhoun, Jack [John Charles]
Red
Cardinals, 1902

Calhoun, Kole (Alan)
Red Baron
Angels, Diamondbacks, 2012-

Calhoun, Willie (Shawn Lamont)
June
Rangers, 2017-

Callahan, Jim [James Timothy]
Red
Giants, 1902
Callahan, Jimmy [James Joseph]
Nixey
  A childhood nickname, mostly abandoned.
Phillies, Colts, Orphans, White Sox, 1894-1913
Callahan, Ray [Raymond James]
Pat
Reds, 1915
Camargo, Johan (Valentin) {YO-hahn}
J.C.
Braves, 2017-
Cameron, Jack [John Stanley]
Happy Jack
Beaneaters, 1906
Camnitz, Howie [Samuel Howard]
Red
Rosebud
  Also based on his red hair.
Pirates, Phillies, Rebels, 1904-1915
Camp, Howie [Howard Lee]
Red
Yankees, 1917
Camp, Winfield (Scott)
Kid
Pirates, Colts, 1892, 1894
Campau, Charles (Columbus) {com-po}
Count
  Resembled an Italian nobleman.
Wolverines, Browns, Senators, 1888-1894
Campbell, Archie [Archibald Stewart]
Iron Man
Yankees, Senators, Reds, 1928-1930
Campbell, Bill [William Richard]
Soup
  Brand reference.
Twins, Red Sox, Cubs, Phillies, Cardinals, Tigers, Expos, 1973-1987
Campbell, Clarence
Soup
  Brand reference.
Indians, 1940-1941

Campbell, Dave [David Wilson]
Soup
  Brand reference.
Tigers, Padres, Cardinals, Astros, 1967-1974
Campbell, Eric (Singleton)
Soup
  Brand reference.
Mets, 2014-2016
Campfield, William (Holton)
Sal
Giants, 1896
Canavan, Hugh (Edward)
Hugo
Braves, 1918
Candelaria, John (Robert)
Candy Man
Pirates, Angels, Mets, Yankees, Expos, Twins, Blue Jays, Dodgers, 1975-1993
Candelario, Jeimer
{JAY-mer can-duh-LAR-ee-oh}
Baby Ruth: Candy
Cubs, Tigers, 2016-
Candiotti, Tom [Thomas Caesar]
Cotton
Brewers, Indians, Blue Jays, Dodgers, Athletics, 1983-1999
Cannell, Wirt (Virgin)
Rip
Beaneaters, 1904-1905
Cannon, Joe [Joseph Jerome]
J.J.
Astros, Blue Jays, 1977-1980
Canseco, José
The Chemist: Master Blaster
Parkway José
  A minor league nickname, for his long home runs.
Bash Brother
  Given to Canseco and Mark McGwire for their combined stats.
Athletics, Rangers, Red Sox, Blue Jays, Devil Rays, Yankees, White Sox, 1985-2001
Cantillon, Joe [Joseph D]

Pongo Joe
Senators, 1907-1909
Cantrell, Guy (Dewey)
Gunner
Robins, Athletics, Tigers, 1925-1930
Capra, Lee (William)
Buzz
Mets, Braves, 1971-1977
Cardenal, José (Rosario Domec)
{car-duh-NAHL}
Junior
Giants, Angels, Indians, Cardinals, Brewers, Cubs, Phillies, Mets, Royals, 1963-1980
Cárdenas, Leo [Leonardo Lazaro]
Chico
Mr. Automatic
    Based on his defensive prowess.
Reds, Twins, Angels, Indians, Rangers, 1960-1975
Cardoni, Armand (Joseph)
Ben: Big Ben
Braves, 1943-1945
Carey, George (C)
Scoops
Scoop 'em Up
    From minor league press.
Orioles, Colonels, Senators, 1895-1903
Carey, Max (George)
Scoops
    Based on his ability to catch fly balls.
Pirates, Robins, 1910-1929
Carey, Tom [Thomas Francis Aloysius]
Scoops
The Hoboken Harp
    A derogatory reference. Born in Hoboken.
Browns, Red Sox, 1935-1946
Carleton, James (Otto)
Tex
    From Comanche, Texas.
Cardinals, Cubs, Dodgers, 1932-1940
Carlisle, Walter
Rosy
Red Sox, 1908
Carlson, Leon (Alton)
Swede
Senators, 1920
Carlstrom, Albin (Oscar)
Swede
Red Sox, 1911
Carlton, Steven (Norman)
Lefty
Silent Steve
    He hated talking to the press.
Cardinals, Phillies, Giants, White Sox, Indians, Twins, 1965-1988
Carlyle, Earl (L)
Buddy
Padres, Dodgers, Braves, Yankees, Mets, 1999-2015
Carlyle, Roy (Edward)
Dizzy
Senators, Red Sox, Yankees, 1925-1926
Carmel, Leon (James)
Duke
    Acquired in high school.
Cardinals, Mets, Yankees, 1959-1965
Carnett, Eddie [Edwin Elliott]
Lefty
Braves, White Sox, Indians, 1941-1945
Carney, Jack [John Joseph]
Handsome Jack
Nationals, Bisons, Infants, Kelly's Killers, Brewers, 1889-1891
Carney, Pat [Patrick Joseph]
Doc
Beaneaters, 1901-1904
Carpenter, Charles (Sydney)
Bubba
    Born in Texas but went to high school and college in Arkansas.
Rockies, 2000
Carpenter, Warren (William)
Hick: Old Hickory: Old Hick
Stars, Reds, Ruby Legs, Red Stockings, Browns, 1879-1892
Carrasco, Carlos (Luis) {kuh-RAZZ-koh}

Cookie
Indians, 2009-
Carrasco, Daniel (Jose)
D.J.
Royals, White Sox, Pirates, Diamondbacks, Mets, 2003-2012
Carrasquel, Alfonso
Chico
White Sox, Indians, Athletics, Orioles, 1950-1959
Carreon, Mark (Steven)
My Wayward Son
> From Chris Berman, who refers to Kansas's popular rock anthem, "Carry On My Wayward Son."

Mets, Tigers, Giants, Indians, 1987-1996
Carrick, Bill [William Martin]
Doughnut Bill
Giants, Senators, 1898-1902
Carrigan, Bill [William Francis]
Rough
Americans, Red Sox, 1906-1916
Carroll, Clay (Palmer)
Hawk
Braves, Reds, White Sox, Cardinals, Pirates, 1964-1978
Carroll, Dick [Richard Thomas]
Shadow
Highlanders, 1909
Carroll, Dorsey (Lee)
Dixie
> Born in Padukah, Kentucky.

Braves, 1919
Carroll, John (E)
Scrappy
> Due to his "pugnacious disposition."

Whitecaps, Bisons, Blues, 1884-1887
Carroll, Owen (Thomas)
Ownie
Tigers, Yankees, Reds, Dodgers, 1925-1934
Carroll, Ralph (Arthur)
Doc
> A dentist who graduated from Tufts University.

Red
Athletics, 1916
Carsey, Wilfred
Kid
> He was a kid. He began his baseball career at 15.

Statesmen, Phillies, Browns, Spiders, Senators, Superbas, 1891-1901
Carson, Al [Albert James]
Soldier
> Served in the Army from 1901-07.

Cubs, 1910
Carson, Walter (Lloyd)
Kit
> A reference to the western hero.

Indians, 1934-1935
Carter, Arnold (Lee)
Hook: Lefty
Reds, 1944-1945
Carter, Chris [William Christopher]
Animal
Red Sox, Mets, 2008-2010
Carter, Conrad (Powell)
Nick
Athletics, 1908
Carter, Gary (Edmund)
The Kid
> Given by teammates in his first spring training.

Expos, Mets, Giants, Dodgers, 1974-1992
Carter, Otis (Leonard)
Blackie
> He was not black.

Giants, 1925-1926
Carter, Paul (Warren)
Nick
Naps, Indians, Cubs, 1914-1920
Carter, Solomon (Mobley)
Buck
Athletics, 1931
Cartwright, Ed [Edward Charles]
Jumbo
> He was 5'10, 220 lbs.

Browns, Senators, 1890-1897

Carty, Rico [Ricardo Adolfo Jacobo]
    Beeg Boy
        6'3, 200 lbs.
    Braves, Rangers, Cubs, Athletics, Indians, Blue Jays, 1963-1979

Caruthers, Bob [Robert Lee]
    Parisian Bob
        Nickname was the result of him negotiating a contract from Paris. He was born in Tennessee.
    Browns, Bridegrooms, Grooms, Colts, Reds, 1884-1893

Cary, Scott (Russell)
    Red
    Senators, 1947

Casale, Gennaro (Joseph)
    Jerry
        Based on pronunciation of his first name.
    Red Sox, Angels, Tigers, 1958-1962

Cascarella, Joe [Joseph Thomas]
    Crooning Joe
        He sang tenor on the radio and in night clubs.
    Athletics, Red Sox, Senators, Reds, 1934-1938

Casey, Hugh (Thomas)
    Fireman
    Cubs, Dodgers, Pirates, Yankees, 1935-1949

Casey, James (Patrick)
    Doc
        A dentist who helped teammates with their teeth.
    Senators, Superbas, Tigers, Cubs, 1898-1907

Casey, Sean (Thomas)
    The Mayor
        Named for his friendliness to opposing runners and his public charity work.
    Indians, Reds, Pirates, Tigers, Red Sox, 1997-2008

Cash, Dave [David]
    Action Dog
    Pirates, Expos, Padres, 1969-1980

Cash, Norm [Norman Dalton]
    Stormin' Norman
        Bestowed by broadcaster Ernie Harwell because of Cash's temper.
    White Sox, Tigers, 1958-1974

Casilla, Santiago {cah-SEE-ya}
    Willi
    Athletics, Giants, 2004-2018

Cassel, Joseph (Buren)
    Jack
    Padres, Astros, 2007-2008

Cassini, Jack (Dempsey)
    Gabby
        He was a Fuller Brush salesman.
    Scat
        A stolen base champion in the minors.
    Pirates, 1949

Caster, George (Jasper)
    Ug
    Athletics, Browns, Tigers, 1934-1946

Castillo, Luis (Miguel)
    La Piedra
    Reds, 2017-

Castillo, Welington (Andres)
{cas-TEE-yo}
    Beef
    Cubs, Mariners, Diamondbacks, Orioles, White Sox, 2010-

Castleman, Clydell
    Slick
    Giants, 1934-1939

Castner, Paul (Henry)
    Lefty
    White Sox, 1923

Castro, Lou [Luis Miguel]
    Jud
        A shortened version of "Judge," given after a banquet speech.
    Athletics, 1902

Castro, Miguel (Angel)
    Come Hombre: Ni
    Blue Jays, Orioles, Mets, 2015-

Castro, Ramón (Abraham)
    Bigote
        Means "mustache."

Marlins, Mets, White Sox, 1999-2011
Castro, Starlin (DeJesus)
    All-Starlin
    Cubs, Yankees, Marlins, Nationals, 2010-
Cathey, Hardin (Abner)
    Li'l Abner
        His middle name. 6'4, 190 lbs. from Tenn. Built like the comic strip character.
    Senators, 1942
Caton, James (Howard)
    Howdy
        His middle name is Howard.
    Buster
    Pirates, 1917-1920
Caudill, Bill [William Holland]
    Inspector
    Cubs, Mariners, Athletics, Blue Jays, 1979-1987
Caulfield, John (Joseph)
    Jake
    Athletics, 1946
Causey, Cecil (Algerton)
    Red: The Florida Flamingo
    Giants, Braves, Phillies, 1918-1922
Cavarretta, Phil [Philip Joseph]
    Philliabuck
    Cubs, White Sox, 1934-1955
Caveney, James (Christopher)
    Ike
    Reds, 1922-1925
Cavet, Tillar (H)
    Pug
    Tigers, 1911-1915
Ceccarelli, Art [Arthur Edward]
{chick-a-RELL-ee}
    Chic
    Athletics, Orioles, Cubs, 1955-1960
Center, Marvin (Earl)
    Pete
    Indians, 1942-1946
Cepeda, Orlando (Manuel)
{suh-PAY-duh}
    Baby Bull
        His father was known as The Bull.
    Cha Cha
    Giants, Cardinals, Braves, Athletics, Red Sox, Royals, 1958-1974
Céspedes, Yoenis
{YO-en-ease CESS-peh-dez}
    La Potencia: El Talento
    Athletics, Red Sox, Tigers, Mets, 2012-
Cey, Ron [Ronald Charles] {SAY}
    Penguin
        Named by Tommy Lasorda because of an awkward, stiff-legged running style.
    Dodgers, Cubs, Athletics, 1971-1987
Chacin, Jhoulys (Jose)
{yo-LEASE sha-SEEN}
    Makina
    Rockies, Diamondbacks, Braves, Angels, Padres, Brewers, Red Sox, 2009-
Chafin, Andrew (Gregory) {CHAY-fin}
    The Sheriff
    Diamondbacks, Cubs, 2014-
Chakales, Bob [Robert Edward]
{SHACK-ulls}
    The Golden Greek
        His heritage.
    Indians, Orioles, White Sox, Senators, Red Sox, 1951-1957
Chalmers, George (W)
    Dut
    Phillies, 1910-1916
Chamberlain, Elton (P)
    Ice Box
        Calm to the point of ice water in his veins.
    Colonels, Browns, Solons, Athletics, Reds, Spiders, 1886-1896
Chamberlain, Justin (Louis)
    Joba {JA-ba}
        A young cousin's mispronunciation.
    Yankees, Tigers, 2007-
Chambers, Cliff [Clifford Day]
    Lefty
    Cubs, Pirates, Cardinals, 1948-1953

Chambers, Richard (Jerome)
Rome
From his middle name.
Beaneaters, 1900
Chance, Frank (Leroy)
Husk
Based on his husky physical stature
Peerless Leader (of the Cubs)
From a Chicago baseball writer.
Orphans, Cubs, Yankees, 1898-1914
Chandler, Spurgeon (Ferdinand)
Spud
A shorter and preferred version of his first name.
Yankees, 1937-1947
Channell, Les [Lester Clark]
Goat: Gint
Highlanders, Yankees, 1910, 1914
Chaplin James (Bailey)
Tiny
He was anything but: 6'1", 195 lbs.
Giants, Bees, 1928-1936
Chapman, Aroldis [Albertin Aroldis] {ah-ROLL-dis}
The Cuban Missile
The Missile
A fast runner from Cuba.
Reds, Yankees, Cubs, 2010-
Chapman, Glenn (Justice)
Pete
Dodgers, 1934
Chapman, Jack [John Curtis]
Death to Flying Things
He chased down fly balls.
Atlantics, Brown Stockings, Grays, 1874-1876
Chapman, Matt (James)
Pegasus
Athletics, 2017-
Chappell, LaVerne (Ashford)
Larry
White Sox, Indians, Braves, 1913-17
Chappelle, Bill [William Hogan]
Big Bill
He was 6'2", 206 lbs.
Doves, Reds, Tip-Tops, 1908-1914
Charboneau, Joe [Joseph]
Super Joe: Joltin' Joe: Bazooka Joe
Indians, 1980-1982
Charles, Ed [Edwin Douglas]
Ez
Gum
Inherited from his father.
The Poet
Wrote poetry and appeared on television about racism and baseball while in the minors.
The Glider
A graceful runner.
Athletics, Mets, 1962-1969
Charles, Raymond
Chappy
Cardinals, Reds, 1908-1910
Charlton, Norm [Norman Wood]
The Sheriff
Named for his determined stride to the mound.
Reds, Mariners, Phillies, Orioles, Braves, Devil Rays, 1988-2001
Chartak, Mike [Michael George]
Shotgun
Yankees, Senators, Browns, 1940-44
Charton, Frank (Lane)
Pete
Red Sox, 1964
Chase, Hal [Harold Homer]
Prince Hal
Based on charm, grace, and apparent sincerity.
Highlanders, Yankees, White Sox, Buffeds, Blues, Reds, Giants, 1905-1919
Chase, Ken [Kendall Fay]
Lefty
Senators, Red Sox, Giants, 1936-1943
Chatham, Charles (Lorenzo)
Buster
Little Giant
He was only 5'7".
Braves, 1930-1931
Chavez, Jesse (David)

Flaco
  Pirates, Braves, Royals, Athletics, Blue Jays, Dodgers, Angels, Rangers, Cubs, 2008-
Chavis, Michael (Scott)
  Ice Horse
  Red Sox, 2019-
Cheeves, Virgil (Earl)
  Chief
  Cubs, Indians, Giants, 1920-1927
Chelini, Italo (Vincent)
  Chilly
    A takeoff of his name.
  Lefty
  White Sox, 1935-1937
Chesbro, Jack [John Dwight]
  Happy Jack
    Positive personality while working in a mental institution.
  Pirates, Highlanders, Red Sox, 1899-1909
Childress, Rodney (Osborne)
  Rocky
  Phillies, Astros, 1985-1988
Childs, Clarence (Lemuel)
  Cupid
    As a youngster, he resembled the fictional character.
  Fats
    A newspaper nickname based on his 5'8" 192 lb. frame.
  Fatty
    Another newspaper nickname.
  Paca
    Newspaper nickname; a short, fat rodent.
  The Dumpling
    Newspaper nickname.
  Quakers, Stars, Spiders, Perfectos, Orphans, 1888-1901
Chiles, Pearce (Nuget)
  What's the Use
    His taunt at opposing batters who popped up to him.
  Phillies, 1899-1900
Chipman, Bob [Robert Howard]

  Mr. Chips
  Dodgers, Cubs, Braves, 1941-1952
Chirinos, Robinson (David)
  {chee-REE-nose}
  Pelo Buche
  Rays, Rangers, Astros, Mets, 2011-
Chisenhall, Lonnie (David)
  Lonnie Baseball
  Indians, 2011-2018
Choo, Shin-Soo
  Tokki 1
  Mariners, Indians, Reds, Rangers, 2005-
Chouneau, William
  Chief
  White Sox, 1910
Christenbury, Lloyd (Reid)
  Low
  Braves, 1919-1922
Christensen, Walter (Neils)
  Cuckoo
    He would do somersaults in the outfield... before making a catch.
  Seacap
  Reds, 1926-1927
Christman, Marquette (Joseph)
  Mark
  Tigers, Browns, Senators, 1938-1949
Christopher, Russ [Russell Ormand]
  Daddy Long Legs
  Athletics, Indians, 1942-1948
Church, Emory (Nicholas)
  Bubba
  Phillies, Reds, Cubs, 1950-1955
Churn, Clarence (Nottingham)
  Chuck
  Pirates, Indians, Dodgers, 1957-1959
Ciaffone, Larry [Lawrence Thomas]
  Symphony Larry
  Cardinals, 1951
Cianfrocco, Angelo (Dominic)
  Archi
  Expos, Padres, 1992-1998
Cicero, Joe [Joseph John]
  Dody
    Acquired while playing sandlot

baseball.
Red Sox, Athletics, 1929-1945
Cicotte, Al [Alva Warren] {SEE-cot}
Bozo
Yankees, Senators, Tigers, Indians,
Cardinals, Colt 45s, 1957-1962
Cicotte, Eddie [Edgar Victor] {SEE-cot}
Knuckles
Known as the founder of the knuckleball.
Tigers, Red Sox, White Sox, 1905-1920
Cihocki, Ed [Edward Joseph]
Cy
A shortening of his last name.
Athletics, 1932-1933
Cishek, Steve [Steven R] {SEE-sheck}
Speedpass
Marlins, Cardinals, Mariners, Rays, Cubs, White Sox, 2010-
Clabaugh, John (William)
Moose
Robins, 1926
Clack, Bobby [Robert Suter]
Gentlemanly Bob
Atlantics, Reds, 1874-1876
Clancy, John (William)
Bud
White Sox, Dodgers, Phillies, 1924-34
Clanton, Uke [Eucal]
Cat
Indians, 1922
Clapp, Richard (Keith)
Stubby
He was 5'8", 175 lbs.
Cardinals, 2001
Clark, Bryan (Donald)
Gas Can
Mariners, Blue Jays, Indians, White Sox, 1981-1990
Clark, Fred [Alfred Robert]
Dad
Orphans, 1902
Clark, Harry
Pep
White Sox, 1903

Clark, Harvey (Daniel)
Ginger
Bronchos, 1902
Clark, Jack (Anthony)
Jack the Ripper
A power hitter.
Giants, Cardinals, Yankees, Padres, Red Sox, 1975-1992
Clark, John (Carroll)
Cap
Phillies, 1938
Clark, Owen (F)
Spider
Nationals, Bisons, 1889-1890
Clark, Roy (Elliott)
Pepper
Giants, 1902
Clark, Tony [Anthony Christopher]
Tony the Tiger
Think Wheaties.
Tigers, Red Sox, Mets, Yankees, Diamondbacks, Padres, 1995-2009
Clark, Will [William Nuschler]
The Franchise; Will the Thrill
Giants, Rangers, Orioles, Cardinals, 1986-2000
Clark, William W (Watson)
Watty; Lefty
Indians, Robins, Dodgers, Giants, 1924-1937
Clark, Willie [William Otis]
Wee Willie
One of the smallest players in the game at 5'4".
Giants, Pirates, 1895-1899
Clarke, Alan (Thomas)
Lefty
Reds, 1921
Clarke, Fred (Clifford)
Cap
Colonels, Pirates, 1894-1915
Clarke, Horace (Meredith)
Hoss
Yankees, Padres, 1965-1974
Clarke, Jay (Justin)
Nig

Naps, Tigers, Browns, Phillies,
Pirates, 1905-1920
Clarke, Josh [Joshua Baldwin]
Pepper
Colonels, Cardinals, Naps, Rustlers,
1898-1911
Clarke, Richard (Grey)
Noisy
White Sox, 1944
Clarke, Vibert (Ernesto)
Webbo
Senators, 1955
Clarke, William H
Dad
> He looked older than he was.

White Stockings, Solons, Giants,
Colonels, 1888-1898
Clarke, William J (Jones)
Boileryard
> Named because of his voice.

Orioles, Beaneaters, Senators, Giants,
1893-1905
Clarkson, Arthur (Hamilton)
Dad
Giants, Beaneaters, Browns, Orioles,
1891-1896
Clarkson, James (Buster)
Buzz: Bus
Braves, 1952
Clarkson, John (Gibson)
Sensitive John
> He had a very sensitive character.

Ruby Legs, White Stockings,
Beaneaters, Spiders, 1882-1894
Clarkson, William (Henry)
Blackie
Giants, Braves, 1927-1929
Clary, Ellis
Cat
Senators, Browns, 1942-1945
Claset, Gowell (Sylvester)
Lefty
Athletics, 1933
Claudio, Álex [Alexander]
Chomo
Rangers, Brewers, 2014-

Clausen, Frederick (William)
Fritz
Colonels, Colts, 1892-1896
Clauss, Al [Albert Stanley]
Lefty
Tigers, 1913
Clay, Dain (Elmer)
Sniffy: Ding-a-ling
Reds, 1943-1946
Clay, Frederick (C)
Bill
Phillies, 1902
Cleary, Joe [Joseph Christopher]
Fire
Senators, 1945
Clemens, Clem [Clement Lambert]
Count
Chi-Feds, Whales, Cubs, 1914-1916
Clemens, Roger [William Roger]
The Rocket
K-Man
> Based on super strike-out capability.

The Texas Con Man: The Franchise
Red Sox, Blue Jays, Yankees, Astros,
1984-2007
Clemente, Roberto
Arriba: The Great One
Pirates, 1955-1972
Clemons, Verne (James)
Stinger: Tubby
Browns, Cardinals, 1916-1924
Clevenger, Truman (Eugene)
Tex
> Johnny Pesky saw a resemblance to Tex Hughson.

Red Sox, Senators, Angels, Yankees,
1954-1962
Clevinger, Mike [Michael Anthony]
Sunshine
Indians, Padres, 2016-
Clift, Harlond (Benton)
Darkie
> Given by a teammate who thought his first name was Harlem.

Browns, Senators, 1934-1945

Clifton, Herman (Earl)
Flea
Invented when minor league manager, Del Baker, on being pestered by Clifton, said, "You're worse than a sand flea."
Tigers, 1934-1937

Cline, John (P)
Monk
Orioles, Eclipse, Colonels, Cowboys, 1882-1891

Clinton, Jim [James Lawrence]
Big Jim
6'2", 195 lbs.
Eckfords, Resolutes, Atlantics, Grays, Ruby Legs, Orioles, Red Stockings, 1872-1886

Clippard, Tyler (Lee)
The Yankee Clippard
A pun based on Joe DiMaggio, the Yankee Clipper.
Yankees, Nationals, Athletics, Mets, Diamondbacks, White Sox, Astros, Blue Jays, Indians, Twins, 2007-

Closser, Jeffrey (Darrin) {CLAUS-sir}
J.D.
His initials. He legally changed his first name to JD.
Rockies, 2004-2006

Clough, Ed [Edgar George]
Big Ed: Spec
Cardinals, 1924-1926

Clymer, Bill [William Johnston]
Derby Day Bill
Athletics, 1891

Clymer, Otis (Edgar)
Grumpy
Pirates, Senators, Cubs, Braves, 1905-1913

Coachman, Bobby (Dean)
Pete
Angels, 1990

Coates, Jim [James Alton]
Mummy
Came from his funereal visage on the mound.
Yankees, Senators, Reds, Angels, 1956-1967

Cobb, Ty [Tyrus Raymond]
The Georgia Peach
Born and raised in Georgia.
Tigers, Athletics, 1905-1928

Cochran, Al [Alvah Jackson]
Goat
Reds, 1915

Cochrane, Gordon (Stanley)
Mickey
He was just another "Irish Mick."
Black Mike
He had a difficult time coping with stress.
Kid
A nickname that predated his major league career.
Athletics, Tigers, 1925-1937

Coffman, George (David)
Slick
Tigers, Browns, 1937-1940

Cohen, Alta (Albert)
Schoolboy
Robins, Dodgers, Phillies, 1931-1933

Colavito, Rocco (Domenico) {co-la-VEE-toe}
Rocky
Helped distinguish him from his father, Rocco.
Indians, Tigers, Athletics, White Sox, Dodgers, Yankees, 1955-1968

Cole, Gerrit (Alan) {GAIR-it}
Cole Train
Pirates, Astros, Yankees, 2013-

Cole, Leonard (Leslie)
King
Cubs, Pirates, Yankees, 1909-1915

Coleman, Clarence
Choo-Choo
Given by childhood friends because he was fast.
Phillies, Mets, 1961-1966

Coleman, Michael (Donnell)
Prime Time
Red Sox, Yankees, 1997-2001

Coleman, Pierce (Devon)
Percy
Browns, Reds, 1897-1898
Coleman, Vince [Vincent Maurice]
Vincent Van Go
> Based on his base-stealing ability (led the league 6 years in a row).

Cardinals, Mets, Royals Mariners, Reds, Tigers, 1985-1997
Coleman, Walter (Gary)
Rip
Yankees, Athletics, Orioles, 1955-1960
Colgan, William (H)
Ed: Little Willie: Shorty
Alleghenys, 1884
Collard, Earl (Clinton)
Hap
Indians, Phillies, 1927-1930
Collins, Charles (Augustine)
Chub
Bisons, Hoosiers, Wolverines, 1884-1885
Collins, Eddie [Edward Trowbridge]
Cocky
> One of the smartest players ... and knew it.

Athletics, White Sox, 1906-1930
Collins, Harry (Warren)
Rip
> Named because of his penchant for Ripa Whiskey.

Yankees, Red Sox, Tigers, Browns, 1920-1931
Collins, James (Anthony)
Ripper
Cardinals, Cubs, Pirates, 1931-1941
Collins, John E (Edgar)
Zip
Pirates, Braves, Athletics, 1914-1921
Collins, John F (Francis)
Shano
> Given to him by White Sox teammates. Gaelic equivalent to Sean, which is, of course, not his name.

White Sox, Red Sox, 1910-1925
Collins, Kevin (Michael)
Casey
> His initials form the word.

Mets, Expos, Tigers, 1965-1971
Collins, Orth (Stein)
Buck
Highlanders, Senators, 1904, 1909
Collins, Philip (Eugene)
Fidgety Phil
Cubs, Phillies, Cardinals, 1923-1935
Collins, Tim [Timothy Michael]
Tiny
> Stood only 5'7" tall and weighed only 165.

Royals, Nationals, Cubs, 2011-
Collmenter, Josh [Joshua Michael]
Tomahawk
Diamondbacks, Braves, 2011-2017
Colomé, Alex [Alexander Manuel]
[COAL-uh-may}
The Horse
Rays, Mariners, White Sox, 2013-
Colon, Bartolo
Big Bart: Big Sexy
Indians, Expos, White Sox, Angels, Red Sox, Yankees, Athletics, Mets, Braves, Twins, Rangers, 1997-2018
Combs, Earle (Bryan) {KOOMZ}
The Mail Carrier
> Based on his speed getting from base to base in the minors.

The Waiter
> Staying on a base waiting for the big hitters in the majors.

The Kentucky Colonel
> Good manners and quiet dignity.

Yankees, 1924-1935
Combs, Merrill (Russell)
Merl
Red Sox, Senators, Indians, 1947-1952
Comellas, Jorge
Pancho
Cubs, 1945
Comiskey, Charles (Albert)

Command, Jim

Commy
   Shortening of his name, not his politics.
The Old Roman
   Based on his aggressive and imperious manner.
Brown Stockings, Browns, Pirates, Reds, 1882-1984
Command, Jim [James Dalton]
Igor
Gor
   Short version of Igor.
Phillies, 1954-1955
Compton, Anna (Sebastian)
Pete: Bash
Browns, Terriers, Braves, Pirates, Giants, 1911-1918
Compton, Harry (Leroy)
Jack
Reds, 1911
Conde, Ramón (Luis)
Wito
White Sox, 1962
Conforto, Michael (Thomas)
Scooter
Mets, 2015-
Congalton, William (Millar)
Bunk
   A childhood nickname, even after death.
Orphans, Naps, Americans, 1902-07
Conger, Hyun (Choi)
Hank
Angels, Astros, Rays, 2010-2016
Conigliaro, Tony [Anthony Richard]
Tony C
Red Sox, Angels, 1964-1975
Conine, Jeffrey (Guy) {CO-nine}
Nine
   The back end of his last name.
The Barbarian
   A Chris Berman nickname from a reference to Conan the Barbarian movie.
Mr. Marlin
Royals, Marlins, Orioles Phillies, Reds, Mets, 1990-2007
Conkwright, Allen (Howard)
Red
Tigers, 1920
Conlan, John (Bertrand)
Jocko
White Sox, 1934-1935
Conley, James (Patrick Michael)
Snipe
   The name stuck when teammates took the rookie on a snipe hunt as part of an initiation.
Terrapins, Reds, 1914-1918
Conlon, Arthur (Joseph)
Jocko
Braves, 1923
Connally, George (Walter)
Sarge
   Earned during his service in World War I.
White Sox, Indians, 1921-1934
Connally, John (M)
Red
Maroons, 1886
Connatser, Broadus (Milburn)
Bruce
Indians, 1931-1932
Connelly, William (Wirt)
Wild Bill
   He allowed 7.23 walks per nine innings.
Athletics, White Sox Tigers, Giants, 1945-1953
Connolly, Joe [Joseph Henry]
Coaster Joe
Giants, Indians, Red Sox, 1921-1924
Connolly, Mervin (Thomas)
Mike: Bud
Red Sox, 1925
Connolly, Tom [Thomas Francis]
Blackie: Ham
Senators, 1915
Connor, Edward
Ned
Haymakers, 1871
Connor, Roger

Dear Old Roger
A fan-given characterization.
Trojans, Gothams, Giants, Phillies, Browns, 1880-1897

Connors, Kevin (Joseph Aloysius)
Chuck
Gained in college by saying, "Chuck it to me."
The Rifleman
His post-baseball career as TVs Lucas McCain.
Dodgers, Cubs, 1949, 1951

Conover, Theodore
Huck
Red Stockings, 1889

Conroy, Bernard (Patrick)
Ben
Athletics, 1890

Conroy, William E (Edward)
Wid
An abbreviation for Widow, his sandlot nickname based on the amount of time he spent playing ball.
Brewers, Pirates, Highlanders, Senators, 1901-1911

Conroy, William F (Frederick)
Pep
Senators, 1923

Constable, Jim [Jimmy Lee]
Sheriff
A Sheriff is a constable.
Giants, Indians, Senators, Braves, 1956-1963

Contreras, Arnaldo (Juan)
Nardi
White Sox, 1980

Contreras, William (Jesus)
Killer
Braves, 2020-

Conway, Richard (Daniel)
Rip
Braves, 1918

Conwell, Ed [Edward James]
Irish
Cardinals, 1911

Cook, Luther (Almus)
Doc
Yankees, 1913-1916

Cooke, Allen (Lindsey)
Dusty
Based on his slides into second.
Yankees, Red Sox, Reds, 1930-1938

Cooley, Duff (Gordon)
Sir Richard
Based on his aristocratic manner.
Dick
A nickname for his nickname.
Browns, Phillies, Pirates, Beaneaters, Tigers, 1893-1905

Coombs, Jack [John Wesley]
Colby Jack
Named after his alma mater, Colby College.
Athletics, Robins, Tigers, 1906-1920

Coombs, Raymond (Franklin)
Bobby
Athletics, Giants, 1933, 1943

Cooney, Bill [William Ambrose]
Cush
Doves, 1909-1910

Cooney, Jimmy [James Edward]
Scoops
His oversized hands scooped up ground balls.
Red Sox, Giants, Cardinals, Cubs, Phillies, Braves, 1917-1928

Cooper, Guy (Evans)
Rebel
Youthful escapades.
Yankees, Red Sox, 1914-1915

Coppinger, John (Thomas)
Rocky
Orioles, Brewers, 1996-2001

Corcoran, Art (Andrew)
Bunny
Athletics, 1915

Corcoran, Michael (Joseph)
Mickey
Reds, 1910

Corcoran, Tommy [Thomas William]
Corky

Tommy the Cork
    Based on his last name.
Burghers, Athletics, Grooms,
Bridegrooms, Reds, Giants,
1890-1907
Cordero, Chad (Patrick)
The Chief
    Given to a strong relief pitcher.
Expos, Nationals, Mariners,
2003-2010
Corey, Ed [Edward Norman]
Ike
    Typical Jewish name. He was born Abe Cohen.
White Sox, 1918
Corhan, Roy (George)
Irish
White Sox, Cardinals, 1911, 1916
Corkhill, John (Stewart)
Pop
Red Stockings, Bridegrooms,
Athletics, Reds, Pirates, 1883-1892
Cornejo, Mardie [Nieves Mardie]
The Chief
Mets, 1978
Corrales, Pat [Patrick] {core-AL-iss}
Ike
    Named after *Ozark Ike*, brawny, plodding comic book character.
Phillies, Cardinals, Reds, Padres,
1964-1973
Correa, Carlos (Javier)
The Captain: Showrrea
Astros, 2015-
Correia, Ronald (Douglas)
Rod
Angels, 1993-1995
Corriden, John Sr. (Michael)
Red
Browns, Tigers, Cubs, 1910-1915
Corridon, Frank [Francis Joseph]
Fiddler
    A violinist in the off-season.
Cubs, Phillies, Cardinals, 1904-1910
Cortazzo, John (Francis)
Jess: Shine

White Sox, 1923
Corwin, Elmer (Nathan)
Al
Giants, 1951-1955
Costello, Dan [Daniel Francis]
Dashing Dan
Yankees, Pirates, 1913-1916
Cotter, Harvey (Louis)
Hooks
Cubs, 1922, 1924
Coughlin, Bill [William Paul]
Scranton Bill
    His birthplace.
Senators, Tigers, 1899-1908
Coughlin, William E (Edward)
Roscoe
Colts, Giants, 1890-1891
Coulombe, Danny [Daniel Paul]
{KOO-loam}
Frenchie
Dodgers, Athletics, Twins, 2014-
Coulter, Thomas (Lee)
Chip
Cardinals, 1969
Coumbe, Fred [Frederick Nicholas]
Fritz
    Given to most people of the era named Frederick.
Red Sox, Naps, Indians, Reds,
1914-1921
Counsell, Craig (John)
Chicken
Rockies, Marlins, Dodgers,
Diamondbacks, Brewers 1995-2011
Courtney, Clint [Clinton Dawson]
Scrap Iron
    An aggressive temperament.
The Toy Bulldog
    Had the toughness of a bulldog.
Yankees, Browns Orioles, White Sox,
Senators, Athletics, 1951-1961
Cousineau, Edward (Thomas)
Dee
Braves, 1923-1925
Coveleski, Harry (Frank)
{ko-va-LESS-key}

The Giant Killer
    Given for his successful pitching
    against the New York Giants in the
    1908 pennant race.
Phillies, Reds, Tigers, 1907-1918
Coveleski, Stanley (Anthony)
{ko-va-LESS-key}
    The Greased Pole
        His deceptive pitching style
        likened getting a hit being as hard
        as climbing a greased pole.
    Athletics, Indians, Senators, Yankees,
    1912-1928
Covington, Chet [Chester Rogers]
    Chesty: Lefty
    Chester the Great
        A showoff for the fans.
    Tex
        He was not born, lived in, nor died
        in Texas and never played for a
        Texas based team.
    Phillies, 1944
Covington, Clarence (Calvert)
    Sam
    Browns, Braves, 1913-1918
Covington, William (Wilkes)
    Tex
    Tigers, 1911-1912
Cowens, Alfred (Edward)
    A.C.
    Royals, Angels, Tigers, Mariners,
    1974-1986
Cox, Elmer (Joseph)
    Dick
    Robins, 1925-1926
Cox, Frank [Francis Bernard]
    Runt
        He stood 5'6" tall.
    Wolverines, 1884
Cox, Plateau (Preston Rex)
    Red
    Tigers, 1920
Coyne, Martin (Albert)
    Toots
    Athletics, 1914
Cozart, Zack [Zachary Warren]

Coach
Reds, Angels, 2011-
Craft, Harry (Francis)
    Wildfire
        His argument over a home run led
        to netting around the foul pole to
        help umpires.
    Reds, 1937-1942
Craft, Maurice (Montague)
    Molly
    Senators, 1916-1919
Craghead, Howard (Oliver)
    Judge: Professor
        Both from his scholarly manner.
    Indians, 1931, 1933
Craig, Allen (Thomas)
    The Wrench
    Cardinals, Red Sox, 2010-2015
Craig, George (McCarty)
    Lefty
    Athletics, 1907
Cramer, Roger (Maxwell)
    Doc
        Earned because of a friendship
        with Dr. Hilliard in NJ.
    Flit
        The name of an insecticide, given
        by a sportswriter for his ability to
        judge fly balls. "death to flies."
    Athletics, Red Sox, Senators, Tigers,
    1929-1948
Crandall, James (Otis)
    Doc
        The physician of pitching
        emergencies.
    Giants, Terriers, Browns, Braves,
    1908-1918
Crane, Ed [Edward Nicholas]
    Cannonball
        That's what his pitches seemed
        like.
    Big Ed: Big Ned: Hercules
        These three referred to his 5'10",
        200+ stature.
    Reds, Nationals, Giants, Kelly's
    Killers, Giants, Grooms, 1884-1893

Crane, Sam [Samuel Byrem]
    Lucky: Red
    Leaping Sam
        Had an ability to jump and catch line drives.
    Athletics, Senators, Reds, Robins, 1914-1922

Cravath, Clifford (Carlton)
{Cruh-VATH}
    Gavvy
        A contraction of *gaviota*, Spanish for *seagull*, after he supposedly killed one with a line drive.
    Cactus
        Reflecting his western background.
    Red Sox, White Sox, Senators, Phillies, 1908-1920

Crawford, Carl (Demonte)
    The Perfect Storm
    Devil Rays, Rays, Red Sox, Dodgers, 2002-2016

Crawford, Charles (Lowrie)
    Larry
    Phillies, 1937

Crawford, Clifford (Rankin)
    Pat
    Giants, Reds, Cardinals, 1929-1934

Crawford, Glenn (Martin)
    Shorty
        5'9", 165; Doesn't seem quite right.
    Cardinals, Phillies, 1945-1946

Crawford, Jim [James Frederick]
    Catfish
        A takeoff of Craw Daddy.
    Craw Daddy
        Given by teammates based on his last name.
    Astros, Tigers, 1973-1978

Crawford, Sam [Samuel Earl]
    Wahoo Sam
        He came from Wahoo, Nebraska and insisted that name be used on his Hall of Fame plaque.
    Reds, Tigers, 1899-1917

Creeden, Cornelius (Stephen)
    Connie
    Braves, 1943

Creeden, Pat [Patrick Francis]
    Paddy
    Whoops
        Self-reported nickname. Based on his fielding?
    Brockton Flash
        College football nickname.
    Red Sox, 1931

Creel, Jack (Dalton)
    Tex
        Born, died, buried in Texas.
    Cardinals, 1945

Cregan, Pete [Peter James]
    Peekskill Pete
        Born in Kingston, NY, about an hour from Peekskill.
    Giants, Reds, 1899, 1903

Cremins, Bob [Robert Anthony]
    Lefty
    Crooked Arm
        Given by teammates because he was a lefty.
    Red Sox, 1927

Crespi, Frank (Angelo Joseph)
    Creepy
        He chased grounders full speed, from a crouch: creepy.
        Also creepy looks; dark eyebrows, dark deep-set eyes.
    Cardinals, 1938-1942

Cress, Walker (James)
    Foots
    Reds, 1948-1949

Crisp, Covelli (Loyce)
    Coco
        Given by his sister and brother for his resemblance to the cereal box character. He legally changed his name in 2013.
    Indians, Red Sox, Royals, Athletics, 2002-2016

Crist, Ches [Chester Arthur]
    Squak

Phillies, 1906
Cristall, Bill [William Arthur]
Lefty
Blues, 1901
Cromer, David (Thomas)
D.T.
Reds, 2000-2001
Cromer, Roy (Bunyan)
Tripp
   He is Roy III
Cardinals, Dodgers, Astros, 1993-2003
Crompton, Herb [Herbert Bryan]
Workhorse
   A minor league nickname.
Senators, Yankees, 1937, 1945
Cronin, Bill [William Patrick]
Crungy
Braves, 1928-1931
Crosby, Richard (Stephen)
Bubba
   At his birth, his older, by 18 months, sister could not say, "Brother."
Dodgers, Yankees, 2003-2006
Crosetti, Frank (Peter Joseph)
Crow
   The team's high pitched "holler guy."
Yankees, 1932-1948
Cross, Frank (Atwell)
Mickey
Blues, 1901
Cross, George (Lewis)
Lem
Reds, 1893-1894
Cross, Lafayette (Napoleon)
Lave
Colonels, Athletics, Phillies, Browns, Spiders, Perfectos, Cardinals, Superbas, Senators, 1887-1907
Crouch, Bill [William Henry]
Skip
Browns, 1910
Crouch, Jack (Albert)
Roxy
Browns, Reds, 1930-1933
Croucher, Frank (Donald)
Dingle
Tigers, Senators, 1939-1942
Crouse, Clyde (Ellsworth)
Buck
White Sox, 1923-1930
Crowder, Alvin (Floyd)
General
   Adopted from General Enoch Crowder, designer of the WW1 draft lottery.
Senators, Browns, Tigers, 1926-1936
Crowe, George (Daniel)
Big George
   6'2", 210 lbs.
Braves, Redlegs, Cardinals, 1952-1961
Crowell, Minot (Joy)
Cap
Athletics, 1915-1916
Crumling, Gene [Eugene Leon]
Lefty
   A catcher who batted and threw righty. As a kid, he threw left-handed. The kids called him "Lefty."
Cardinals, 1945
Cruz, Hector (Louis)
Heity
Cardinals, Cubs, Giants, Reds, 1973-1982
Cruz, José
Cheo
Cardinals, Astros, Yankees, 1970-1988
Cruz, Luis (Alfonso)
   Luis Serge in SR-06
Pirates, Brewers, Dodgers, Yankees, 2008-2013
Cruz, Nelson (Ramon)
Boomstick
Brewers, Rangers, Orioles, Mariners, Twins, 2005-
Cuccinello, Tony [Anthony Francis]
{coo-chi-NELL-oh}

Cooch: Chick
Reds, Dodgers, Bees, Giants, Braves, White Sox, 1930-1945
Cuccurullo, Arthur (Joseph)
Cookie
Pirates, 1943-1945
Cuellar, Jesus (Patracis) {KWAY-are}
Charlie
White Sox, 1950
Cuellar, Miguel (Angel) {KWAY-are}
Mike
Redlegs, Cardinals, Astros, Orioles, Angels, 1959-1977
Cueto, Johnny
Johnny Beisbol: Cinco
Reds, Royals, Giants, 2008-
Cueto, Manuel
Potato
> A mislisting for Patato.
Patato
> A Cuban-bestowed nickname, meaning "short."
El Hombre Diablo (The Devil Man)
> Given by fans because he was always lively and making funny faces.
Terriers, Reds, 1914-1919
Cullop, Nick [Henry Nicholas]
Tomato Face
> His face turned bright red whenever he got angry.
Yankees, Senators, Indians, Robins, Reds, 1926-1931
Cummings, William (Arthur)
Candy
> A Civil War-era superlative meaning the best.
Mutuals, Canaries, Whites, Dark Blues, Reds, 1872-1877
Cunningham, Elmer (Ellsworth)
Bert
Grays, Orioles, Athletics, Bisons, Colonels, Orphans, 1887-1901
Cunningham, Mody
Mike
Athletics, 1906

Cunningham, Thomas (David)
Todd: Rich Homie
Braves, Angels, 2013-2016
Cuppy, George (Joseph)
Nig: The Cuban Warrior
The Cuban Hero
> Based on complexion. He was from Indiana.
The Famous Slow Pitcher
> He took a long time between pitches.
Spiders, Perfectos, Beaneaters, Americans, 1892-1901
Curley, Walter (James)
Doc
> Went to UMass, Holy Cross, and UVa.
Orphans, 1899
Curran, Simon (Francis)
Sammy
Beaneaters, 1902
Curry, George (James)
Soldier Boy
> He was in the armed forces.
Browns, 1911
Curtis, Gene [Eugene Holmes]
Eude
Pirates, 1903
Curtis, Vern [Vernon Eugene]
Turk
Senators, 1943-1946
Curtiss, Ervin (Duane)
Jim
Reds, Statesmen, 1891
Cuthbert, Edgar (Edward)
Ned
Athletics, Whites, White Stockings, Reds, Brown Stockings, Browns, Monumentals, 1871-1884
Cutshaw, George (William)
Clancy
Dodgers, Superbas, Robins, Pirates, Tigers, 1912-1923
Cuyler, Hazen (Shirley)
{KAI-ler, rhymes with GUY}
Cuy {pronounced KAI}

Kiki {Kai-Kai}
  1. From the call about who should catch a ball.
  2. From his stutter in giving his last name.
  Pirates, Cubs, Reds, Dodgers, 1921-1938
D'Amico, Jeff [Jeffrey Charles] {duh-MEEK-oh}
  Big Daddy
  Brewers, Mets, Pirates, Indians, 1996-2004
d'Arnaud, Travis (E) {dar-NO}
  Lil D
  Mets, Dodgers, Rays, Braves, 2013-
Dagres, Angelo (George)
  Junior
  Orioles, 1955
Dahlen, Bill [William Frederick] {rhymes with ALLEN}
  Bad Bill
    He had a ferocious temperament.
  Colts, Orphans, Superbas, Giants, Doves, Dodgers, 1891-1911
Dahlgren, Ellsworth (Tenney)
  Babe
  Red Sox, Yankees, Braves, Cubs, Browns Dodgers, Phillies, Pirates, 1935-1946
Dahlke, Jerry [Jerome Alexander]
  Joe
  White Sox, 1956
Daily Cornelius (F)
  Con
  Grays, Beaneaters, Hoosiers, Ward's Wonders, Grooms, Colts, 1885-1896
Daily, Hugh (Ignatius)
  One Arm
    That's what he had.
  Bisons, Blues, Chicago/Pittsburgh, Nationals, Maroons, 1882-1887
Daley, Leavitt (Leo)
  Bud
    His mother wanted a child like her cousin, Buddy Walker.
  Indians, Athletics, Yankees, 1955-64

Daley, Tom [Thomas Francis]
  Pete
  Reds, Athletics, Yankees, 1908-1915
Dallessandro, Dom
  Dim Dom
  Dim Dom Dal
    Named by newspapers as Diminutive Dom. He was 5'5".
  Red Sox, Cubs, 1937-1947
Dalrymple, Clay [Clayton Errol]
  Dimples
    He had one in the middle of his chin.
  Phillies, Orioles, 1960-1971
Dalton, Tolbert (Percy)
  Jack
  Demon Jack
    Hit .319 in 1914, his best year.
  Superbas, Robins, Blues, Tigers, 1910-1916
Daly, George (Josephs)
  Pecks
  Giants, 1909
Daly, Tom [Thomas Peter]
  Tido
  Keystones, White Stockings, Nationals, Bridegrooms, Grooms, Superbas, White Sox, Reds, 1884-1903
Dammann, Bill [William Henry]
  Wee Willie
    5'7", 155 lbs.
  Reds, 1897-1899
Damon, Johnny (David)
  Caveman
  Royals, Athletics, Red Sox, Yankees, Tigers, Rays, Indians, 1995-2012
Danforth, Dave [David Charles]
  Dauntless Dave
    Given by teammate Eddie Collins because of the many controversies he encountered.
  Athletics, White Sox, Browns, 1911-1925
Daniels, Bernard (Elmer)
  Bert

Highlanders, Yankees, Reds, 1910-1914
Daniels, Frederick (Clinton)
Tony
Phillies, 1945
Daniels, Harold (Jack)
Sour Mash Jack
: Obvious choice. His middle name is Jack.
Braves, 1952
Daniels, Pete [Peter J]
Smiling Pete
Alleghenys, Browns, 1890, 1898
Danner, Henry (Frederick)
Buck
Athletics, 1915
Danning, Harry
Harry the Horse
: Named for a Damon Runyon Broadway character.
Giants, 1933-1942
Danning, Isaac
Ike
Browns, 1928
Dantonio, John (James)
Fats
: Given by a childhood friend.
Dodgers, 1944-1945
Danzig, Harold (Paul)
Babe
: Family nickname from his size and a reference to Babe of Paul Bunyan fame.
Red Sox, 1909
Darby, George (William)
Deacon
Reds, 1893
Daringer, Cliff [Clifford Clarence]
Shanty
Packers, 1914
Dark, Alvin (Ralph)
Blackie
The Swamp Fox
: From flooding first base to slow Maury Wills' stealing.
Braves, Giants, Cardinals, Cubs, Phillies, 1946-1960
Darling, Conrad
Dell
: May have something to do with a song of the time with the phrase, "Dell, Darling."
Bisons, White Stockings, Pirates, Browns, 1883-1891
Darragh, James (S)
Jack
Colonels, 1891
Darwin, Danny [Daniel Wayne]
Donham Bullet
: He was born in Donham, Texas.
Dr. Death
: Named by Nolan Ryan because he was tough and supposedly won lots of fights.
Rangers, Brewers, Astros, Red Sox, Blue Jays, Pirates, White Sox, Giants, 1978-1998
Dashner, Lee (Claire)
Lefty
Naps, 1913
Datz, Jeff [Jeffrey William]
Polar Bear
Tigers, 1989
Daub, Dan [Daniel William]
Mickey
Reds, Grooms, Bridegrooms, 1892-1897
Daubach, Brian (Michael) {DAW-back}
Belleville Basher
: Hometown-Belleville, IL, and was a consistent hitter.
Marlins, Red Sox, White Sox, Mets, 1998-2005
Daubert, Harry (J)
Jake
Pirates, 1915
Daugherty, Harold (Ray)
Doc
: Not a doctor, but it could be related to his last name.
Tigers, 1951
Daughters, Bob [Robert Francis]

Red
Red Sox, 1937
Daulton, Darren (Arthur)
Dutch
Phillies, Marlins, 1983-1997
Dauss, George (August)
Hooks
Named for his curve ball.
Tigers, 1912-1926
Davenport, Claude (Edwin)
Big Dave
His brother was Dave.
Shorty
He stood 6'6".
Giants, 1920
Davidson, Homer (Hurd)
Divvy
Naps, 1908
Davidson, Thomas (Eugene)
Ted
First, middle, last name initials.
Reds, Braves, 1965-1968
Davies, Lloyd (Garrison)
Chick
Athletics, Giants, 1914-1926
Davies, Zack [Zachary Ryan]
Bat Boy
Brewers, Padres, 2015-
Davis, Alfonzo (DeFord)
Lefty
Left-handed, but not a pitcher.
Superbas, Pirates, Highlanders, Reds, 1901-1907
Davis, Bill [Arthur Willard]
Jolly Green Giant
6'6", 215 lbs.
Indians, Padres, 1965-1969
Davis, Charles (Theodore)
Chili
A family-given haircut at age 12 looked like a chili bowl on his head.
Giants, Angels, Twins, Royals, Yankees, 1981-1999

Davis, Chris [Christopher Lyn]
Crush
Based on his ability to crush the ball.
Rangers, Orioles, 2008-
Davis, Curt [Curtis Benton]
Coonskin
He was born in Missouri.
Phillies, Cubs, Cardinals, Dodgers, 1934-1946
Davis, Eric (Keith)
Eric the Red
Best part of his career was with Cincinnati.
The Franchise
First to have 30 HR and 50 SB in the same year.
Rifleman
Reds, Dodgers, Tigers, Orioles, Cardinals, Giants, 1984-2001
Davis, Frank (Talmadge)
Dixie
Born in North Carolina.
Reds, White Sox, Phillies, Browns, 1912-1926
Davis, George E (Earl)
Storm
He was a cyclone like Jim Palmer. OR based on a book his mother read while pregnant.
Orioles, Padres, Athletics, Royals, Tigers, 1982-1994
Davis, George W (Willis)
Kiddo
Yankees, Phillies, Giants, Cardinals, Reds, 1926-1938
Davis, Harry A (Albert)
Stinky
He resembled a comic book character with that name.
Tigers, Browns, 1932-1937
Davis, Harry H
Added his own middle initial to separate from others with the same name.
Jasper

Given by schoolmates at Girard
College.
Giants, Pirates, Colonels, Senators,
Athletics, Naps, 1895-1917
Davis, Ira [James Ira]
Slats: Scratch: Mosquito
Giants, 1899
Davis, Isaac B (Benjamin)
Ike
Mets, Pirates, Athletics, Yankees,
2010-2016
Davis, Isaac M (Marion)
Ike
Senators, White Sox, 1919-1925
Davis, James (Joseph)
Jumbo
5'11", 195 lbs., not particularly
jumbo.
Cowboys, Orioles, Browns,
Gladiators, Statesmen, 1884-1891
Davis, J. D. [Jonathan Gregory]
Sun Bear: Bubbles
Astros, Mets, 2017-
Davis, Jerry (C)
J.J.
Strange, since his initials are J.C.
Pirates, Nationals, 2002-2005
Davis, John Henry (Albert)
Daisy
Browns, Beaneaters, 1884-1885
Davis, John Humphrey
Red
Giants, 1941
Davis, John W (Wilbur)
Bud: Country
Athletics, 1915
Davis, Khris [Khristoppher Adrian]
Khrush
Brewers, Athletics, 2013-
Davis, Lawrence (Columbus)
Crash
Collided with a teammate at 14.
Athletics, 1940-1942
Davis, Mark (Christopher)
Ben
Big Ben

Related to his stature: 6'4".
Padres, Mariners, White Sox,
1998-2004
Davis, Otis (Allen)
Scat
6', but only 160 lbs.: he was fast.
Dodgers, 1946
Davis, Virgil (Lawrence)
Spud
Cardinals, Phillies, Reds, Pirates,
1928-1945
Davis, Wallace (McArthur)
Butch
Royals, Pirates, Orioles, Dodgers,
Rangers, 1983-1994
Davis, Willie [William Henry]
3-Dog
His uniform number was 3.
Dodgers, Expos, Rangers, Cardinals,
Padres, Angels, 1960-1979
Davis, Woody [Woodrow Wilson]
Babe
Tigers, 1938
Dawkins, Travis (Sentell)
Gookie
Reds, Royals, 1999-2003
Dawson, Andre (Nolan)
The Hawk
Given by an uncle for his Hawk
eye at the plate.
Expos, Cubs, Red Sox, Marlins,
1976-1996
Dawson, Ralph (Fenton)
Joe
Indians, Pirates, 1924-1929
Day, Charles (Frederick)
Boots
Cardinals, Cubs, Expos, 1969-1974
Day, Henry (Clyde)
Pea Ridge
He grew up in Pea Ridge, Missouri.
Cardinals, Reds, Robins, 1924-1931
De La Cruz, Eulogio {ay-oo-low-HEE oh}
Frankie
Tigers, Marlins, Padres, Brewers,
2007-2011

De La Rosa, Jorge (Alberto)
{HOR-hay day-la-ROW-suh}
   George
   Brewers, Royals, Rockies,
   Diamondbacks, Cubs, 2004-2018

Deal, Ellis (Ferguson)
   Cot
      Cotton-top hair color.
   Red Sox, Cardinals, 1947-1954

Deal, John (Wesley)
   Snake
   Reds, 1906

Dean, Alfred (Lovell)
   Chubby
      Not particularly: 5'11", 181 lbs.
   Athletics, Indians, 1936-1943

Dean, Charles (Wilson)
   Dory
   Reds, 1876

Dean, Jay (Hanna)
   Dizzy
      An army moniker for his quirky view of the world.
   The Great Man
   Cardinals, Cubs, Browns, 1930-1947

Dean, Paul (Dee)
   Daffy
      A press creation.
   Cardinals, Giants, Browns, 1934-43

DeArmond, Charlie (Hommer)
   Hummer
   Reds, 1903

Deasley, Thomas (H)
   Pat
   Red Stockings, Browns, Giants, Nationals, 1881-1888

DeBerry, John (Herman)
   Hank
   Indians, Robins, 1916-1930

Decker, Cody (Marshall)
   Antihero
   Padres, 2015

Decker, George A
   Gentleman George
   Colts, Browns, Colonels, Senators, 1892-1899

Decker, George H (Henry)
   Joe
   Cubs, Twins, Mariners, 1969-1979

Dedeaux, Raoul (Martial) {DAY-doe}
   Rod
   Dodgers, 1935

Dee, Maurice (Leo)
   Shorty
      He was only 5'6".
   Browns, 1915

Deegan, William (Joseph)
   Dummy
      He was a deaf-mute.
   Giants, 1901

DeFate, Clyde (Herbert)
   Tony
   Cardinals, Tigers, 1917

deGrom, Jacob (Anthony)
   deGrominator: deGoat
   Mets, 2014-

Dehlman, Herman (J)
   Dutch
   Atlantics, Brown Stockings, 1872-77

Deininger, Otto (Charles)
   Pep
   Americans, Phillies, 1902-1909

Delahanty, Ed [Edward James)
   Big Ed
      He was 6'1", but a power hitter.
   King of Swat
      A dominant slugger.
   Quakers, Infants, Phillies, Senators, 1888-1903

Delahanty, Frank (George)
   Pudgie
      5'9", 160 lbs., hardly pudgie.
   Highlanders, Naps, Buffeds, Rebels, 1905-1915

Delaney, Arthur (Dewey)
   Swede
   Cardinals, Braves, 1924-1929

Delgado, Luis (Felipe)
   Puchy
   Mariners, 1977

Delgado, Randall (Enrique)
   Pupi

Braves, Diamondbacks, 2011-2018
Delhi, Lee (William)
Flame
Bestowed by a sportswriter for his blazing fastball and his red hair.
Turk: Red: Demon
Three high school nicknames.
White Sox, 1912
Dell, William (George)
Wheezer
Cardinals, Robins, 1912-1917
DeMaestri, Joe [Joseph Paul]
Oats: Froggy
White Sox, Browns, Athletics, Yankees, 1951-1961
DeMars, William (Lester)
Kid
Athletics, Browns, 1948-1951
DeMerit, John (Stephen)
Thumper
Braves, Mets, 1957-1962
Dempsey, Cornelius (Francis)
Con
Pirates, 1951
Dennehey, Thomas (Francis)
Tod
Phillies, 1923
Denning, Otto (George)
Dutch
Indians, 1942-1943
Dent, Russell (Earl)
Bucky
Bucky F***ing Dent
Given by Red Sox fans after he hit a pennant winning homer in a 1978 playoff game.
White Sox, Yankees, Rangers, Royals, 1973-1984
Dente, Sam [Samuel Joseph]
Blackie
Red Sox, Browns, Senators, White Sox, Indians, 1947-1955
Denzer, Roger
Peaceful Valley
He resembled one of the stars in the play by that name.

Colts, Giants, 1897, 1901
Derby, George (Henry)
Jonah
Wolverines, Bisons, 1881-1883
Derrick, Claud (Lester)
Deek
Athletics, Yankees, Reds, Cubs, 1910-1914
Derringer, Samuel (Paul)
Duke: Dude
Both based on his sartorial splendor.
Oom Paul
Dutch for Uncle Paul Also based on his 6'3½", 205 lb. (admitted. Could be more).
Control King
Gave up fewer than two walks per 9-innings.
Cardinals, Reds, Cubs, 1931-1945
Derrington, Jim [Charles James]
Blackie
White Sox, 1956-1957
Des Jardien, Paul (Raymond)
Shorty
College nickname: Ironic since he was 6'4", 200 lbs.
Indians, 1916
Desautels, Gene [Eugene Abraham] {deh-ZUH-tell}
Red
Tigers, Red Sox, Indians, Athletics, 1930-1946
DeSclafani, Anthony (James) {DEE-scla-faw-knee}
Disco
Marlins, Reds, 2014-
DeShaies, James (Joseph) {de-SHAYS}
J.D.
Two Silhouettes On
A Chris Berman nickname, a pun of the Herman's Hermits song, "Two Silhouettes on the Shades."
Yankees, Astros, Padres, Twins, Giants, Phillies, 1984-1995
DeShields, Delino D (Diaab)

Snacks: Poppa
Rangers, Indians, 2015-
DeShields, Delino L (Lamont)
Bop
Expos, Dodgers, Cardinals, Orioles, Cubs, 1990-2002
Desmond, Ian (Morgan)
Charron
Nationals, Rangers, Rockies, 2009-
Dessau, Frank (Rolland)
Rube
Doves, Superbas, 1907, 1910
Detweiler, Robert (Sterling)
{DEBT-why-ler}
Ducky
Braves, 1942, 1946
Detwiler, Ross (Emery) {DEBT-why-ler}
National Det
> A pun combining his team and his name.

Nationals, Rangers, Braves, Indians, Athletics, Mariners, White Sox, 2007-
Devenski, Chris [Christopher Michael]
Devo the Dragon: The Dragon
Astros, 2016-
Devers, Rafael (Calcano)
Carita: Raffy Big Stick
Red Sox, 2017-
Devine, William (Patrick)
Mickey
> The name he used as a boxer, before baseball.

Skull
> So named by a Boston Globe sportswriter.

Phillies, Red Sox, Giants, 1918-1925
Dewald, Charles (H)
Carl
> A childhood name, his father's middle name.

Infants, 1890
Diaz, Baudilio (Jose)
Bo
Red Sox, Indians, Phillies, Reds, 1977-1989
Diaz, Carlos (Antonio)

Bimbo
Braves, Mets, Dodgers, 1982-1986
Díaz, Dayan (Enrique)
Jumbito
Reds, Astros, 2016-2017
Díaz, Edgar
Kiki
Brewers, 1986, 1990
Díaz, Edwin (Orlando)
Sugar
Mariners, Mets, 2016-
Díaz, Jose (Rafael)
Jumbo
Reds, Rays, 2014-
Díaz, Victor (Israel)
Baby Manny: Big Vic
Mets, Rangers, 2004-2007
Dibble, Rob [Robert Keith]
Nasty Boy
> He was a brawler with a quick temper.

Officer
Reds, White Sox, Brewers, 1988-1995
Dickerson, Alex [Alexander Ross]
Grandpa
Padres, Giants, 2015-
Dickerson, Lewis (Pessano)
Buttercup
> Mentioned once, from an opera *HMS Pinafore* character.

Reds, Trojans, Ruby Legs, Alleghenys, Maroons, Orioles, Eclipse, Bisons, 1878-1885
Dickey, Bill [William Malcolm]
Man Nobody Knows
> Played in the shadow of Ruth, Gehrig and DiMaggio.

Yankees, 1928-1946
Dickey, George (Willard)
Skeets
Red Sox, White Sox, 1935-1947
Dickey, Robert (Allen)
R.A.
Rangers, Mariners, Twins, Mets, Blue Jays, Braves, 2001-2017
Dickshot, Johnny [John Oscar]

Ugly
> Self named. He thought himself the ugliest man in baseball.

Pirates, Giants, White Sox, 1936-45

Dickson, Brandon (Lee)
Cotton
> From Alabama, the Cotton State.

Cardinals, 2011-2012

Dickson, Walt [Walter Raleigh]
Hickory

Giants, Braves, Rebels, 1910-1915

Didier, Bob [Robert Daniel] {DEE-dee-eh}
Diddy Bal
Bob Ball

Braves, Tigers, Red Sox, 1969-1974

Dietrich, Bill [William John]
Bullfrog
> From either his hopping gait or his big glasses.

Athletics, Senators, White Sox, 1933-1948

Dietz, Dick [Richard Allen]
Mule

Giants, Dodgers, Braves, 1966-1973

Dietz, Lloyd (Arthur)
Dutch

Pirates, Phillies, 1940-1943

Difani, Clarence (Joseph)
Jay

Senators, 1948-1949

Difo, Wilmer (Francisco) {DEE-foe}
El Lindo

Nationals, 2015-

Dillard, Robert (Lee)
Pat

Cardinals, 1900

Dillhoefer, William (Martin)
Pickles
> A play on dill pickles.

Cubs, Phillies, Cardinals, 1917-1921

Dillinger, Harley (Hugh)
Hoke: Lefty

Naps, 1914

Dillinger, Robert (Bernard)
Duke

Browns, Athletics, Pirates, White Sox, 1946-1951

Dillon, Frank (Edward)
Pop
> His hair turned gray in his 20s.

Cap
> From the Pacific Coast League.

Pirates, Tigers, Orioles, Superbas, 1899-1904

Dillon, Patrick (Henry)
Packy

Red Stockings, 1875

DiMaggio, Dom [Dominic Paul]
The Little Professor
> Slight build and glasses made him look like it.

Red Sox, 1940-1953

DiMaggio, Joe [Joseph Paul]
Joe D
Joltin Joe
> For his hitting ability

The Yankee Clipper
> The unequalled team leader

Yankees, 1936-1951

Dinneen, Bill [William Henry]
Big Bill
> 6'1", 190 lbs.

Senators, Beaneaters, Americans, Browns, 1898-1909

Distel, George (Adam)
Dutch

Cardinals, 1918

Dixon, John (Craig)
Sonny

Senators, Athletics, Yankees, 1953-1956

Doak, Bill [William Leopold]
Spittin' Bill
> A grandfathered spitball pitcher.

Lumbago Bill
> Back problems made it tough to get to first quickly.

Reds, Cardinals, Robins, 1912-1929

Dobb, John (Kenneth)
Lefty

White Sox, 1924

Dobens, Ray [Raymond Joseph]

Lefty
Red Sox, 1929
Dobson, Joe [Joseph Gordon]
Burrhead
Curly
    Both as a reference to his wavy hair.
Indians, Red Sox, White Sox, 1939-1954
Dockins, George (Woodrow)
Lefty
Cardinals, Dodgers, 1945, 1947
Doe, Fred [Alfred George]
Count
Bisons, Burghers, 1890
Doherty, John (Michael)
Pup
Angels, 1974-1975
Dolan, Albert (James)
Cozy
Reds, Highlanders, Phillies, Pirates, Cardinals, Giants, 1909-1922
Dolan, Patrick (Henry)
Cozy
Beaneaters, Orphans, Superbas, White Sox, Reds, 1895-1906
Doll, Art [Arthur James]
Moose
    6'1", 190 lbs.
Bees, 1935, 1938
Donahue, Charles (Michael)
She
Cardinals, Phillies, 1904
Donahue, Francis (L)
Red
Giants, Browns, Phillies, Naps, Tigers, 1893-1906
Donahue, John A (Augustine)
Jiggs
Pirates, Brewers, Browns, White Sox, Senators, 1900-1909
Donahue, John F (Frederick)
Jiggs
    Given by newspapers as thoughtless referral to John A.
Red Sox, 1923

Donahue, Tim [Timothy Cornelius]
Bridget
    His mother's name.
Reds, Colts, Orphans, Senators, 1891-1902
Donald, Atley [Richard Atley]
Swampy
Yankees, 1938-1945
Donalds, Ed [Edward Alexander]
Erston: Skipper
Reds, 1912
Donaldson, Josh [Joshua Adam]
Bringer of Rain
Athletics, Blue Jays, Indians, Braves, Twins, 2010-
Dondero, Len [Leonard Peter]
Mike
Browns, 1929
Donlin, Mike [Michael Joseph]
Turkey Mike
    Named by teammates, he had a red neck and odd walk.
Perfectos, Cardinals, Orioles, reds, Giants, Rustlers, Pirates, 1899-1914
Donnelly, Ed [Edward]
Big Ed
    6'1", 205 lbs.
Ned
Rustlers, Braves, 1911-1912
Donovan, Bill [William Edward]
Wild Bill
    Erratic control and explosive temper.
Smiling Bill
    Genial and engaging, according to sportswriters.
Senators, Superbas, Tigers, Yankees, 1898-1918
Dooin, Charles (Sebastian)
Red
Phillies, Reds, Giants, 1902-1916
Doolin, Mickey [Michael Joseph]
Doc
    A dentist.
Phillies, Terrapins, Whales, Cubs, Giants, Robins, 1905-1918

Dooms, Harry [Henry E]
  Jack
    Colonels, 1892
Doran, Tom [Thomas J]
  Long Tom
    5'11", but only 152 lbs.
    Americans, Tigers, 1904-1906
Dorish, Harry
  Fritz
    Listed his ancestry as Russian.
  Schoolboy Fritz
    An early minor-league nickname.
    Red Sox, Browns, White Sox, Orioles, 1947-1956
Dorman, Charles D (Dwight)
  Red: Curlie
    Indians, 1928
Dorman, Charlie [Charles William]
  Slats
    White Sox, 1923
Dorsett, Cal [Calvin Leavelle]
  Preacher
    Indians, 1940-1947
Doscher, John (Henry)
  Herm
    Atlantics, Nationals, Trojans, White Stockings, Blues, 1872-1882
Dotterer, Henry (John)
  Dutch
    Redlegs, Reds, Senators, 1957-1961
Doty, Elmer (L)
  Babe
    Maumees, 1890
Dougherty, Tom [Thomas James]
  Sugar Boy
    White Sox, 1904
Douglas, Charles (William)
  Whammy
    He used to wham the ball over the net...in ping pong.
    Pirates, 1957
Douglas, Phil [Phillip Brooks]
  Shufflin' Phil
    White Sox, Reds, Robins, Cubs, Giants, 1912-1922
Douglass, William (Bingham)
  Klondike
    Browns, Phillies, 1896-1904
Dowd, Raymond (Bernard)
  Snooks
    Tigers, Athletics, Robins, 1919, 1926
Dowd, Tommy [Thomas Jefferson]
  Buttermilk Tommy
    Reds, Statesmen, Senators, Browns, Phillies, Spiders, Americans, 1981-1901
Downey, Alexander (Cummings)
  Red
    Superbas, 1909
Downing, Brian (Jay)
  The Incredible Hulk
    A dedicated weightlifter, but not big: 5'10", 170 lbs.
    White Sox, Angels, Rangers, 1973-1992
Downs, Jerome (Willis)
  Red
    Tigers, Dodgers, Cubs, 1907-1912
Downs, Scott (Jeremy)
  Snakeface
    Cubs, Expos, Blue Jays, Angels, Braves, White Sox, Royals, 2000-14
Doyle, Cornelius (J)
  Conny
    Quakers, Alleghenys, 1883-1884
Doyle, Howard (James)
  Danny
    Red Sox, 1943
Doyle, Jack [John Joseph]
  Dirty Jack
    Given for his aggressive base-running and the belief that the base path belongs to the runner, not the fielder.
    Solons, Spiders, Giants, Orioles, Senators, Orphans, Superbas, Phillies, Highlanders, 1889-1905
Doyle, Judd (Bruce)
  Slow Joe
    Took a long time between pitches.
    Highlanders, Reds, 1906-1910
Doyle, Larry [Lawrence Joseph]

Laughing Larry
Giants, Cubs, 1907-1920
Dozier, William H (Henry)
D.J.
Mets, 1992
Dozier, William J (Joseph)
Buzz
Senators, 1947, 1949
Drabowsky, Myron (Walter)
Moe
Cubs, Braves, Reds, Athletics, Orioles, Royals, Cardinals, White Sox, 1956-1972
Drake, Logan (Gaffney)
L.G.
Indians, 1922-1924
Drake, Oliver (Gardner)
Bucko
Orioles, Brewers, Indians, Angels, Blue Jays, Twins, Rays, 2015-
Dreisewerd, Clem [Clemens Johann] {DRIZE- werd}
Steamboat
Red Sox, Browns, Giants, 1944-1948
Drescher, Bill [William Clayton]
Dutch
Yankees, 1944-1946
Drew, David (Jonathan)
J.D.
Cardinals, Graves, Dodgers, Red Sox, 1998-2011
Drew, Stephen (Oris)
Dirt
Diamondbacks, Athletics, Red Sox, Yankees, Nationals, 2006-2017
Driessen, Dan [Daniel]
Cobra
    Quick, uncoiling batting style.
Reds, Expos, Giants, Astros, Cardinals, 1973-1987
Driscoll, John F
Denny
    The real name of another Driscoll who played around that time.
Bisons, Alleghenys, Eclipse, 1880-84
Driscoll, John L (Leo)

Paddy
Cubs, 1917
Dropo, Walt [Walter]
Moose
    1: 6'5", 220 lbs. 2. From Moosup, Connecticut
Red Sox, Tigers, White Sox, Redlegs, Orioles, 1949-1961
Drott, Dick [Richard Fred]
Hummer
Cubs, Colt .45s, 1957-1963
Druhot, Carl (A)
Collie
Reds, Cardinals, 1906-1907
Drysdale, Don [Donald Scott]
Big D
    6'6" tall.
Airedale
Dodgers, 1956-1969
Dubiel, Walt [Walter John]
Monk
Yankees, Phillies, Cubs, 1944-1952
Dubuc, Jean (Joseph Octave) {duh-BUKE}
Chauncey
Reds, Tigers, Red Sox, Giants, 1908-1919
Duda, Lucas (Christopher)
The Big Lebowski: The Dude
Mets, Rays, Royals, Braves, 2010-19
Duensing, Brian (Matthew) {DONE-sing}
Deuce
Twins, Orioles, Cubs, 2009-2018
Duff, Cecil (Elba)
Larry
White Sox, 1922
Duffee, Charlie [Charles Edward]
Home Run
Browns, Solons, Senators, Reds, 1889-1893
Duffey, Tyler (Blinn)
The Doof
Twins, 2015-
Duffy, Danny [Daniel Richard]
Bear
Royals, 2011-
Duffy, Hugh

Sir Hugh
White Stockings, Pirates, Reds, Beaneaters, Brewers, Phillies, 1888-1906

Duffy, Matt [Matthew Michael]
Duffman
Giants, Rays, 2014-2019

Dugan, Joe [Joseph Anthony]
Jumping Joe
> Given by a sportswriter for his penchant for leaving the team when things got tough.

Athletics, Red Sox, Yankees, Braves, Tigers, 1917-1931

Dugey, Oscar (Joseph)
Kid
> A Texas newspaper nickname, given in the minors.

Jake
> Childhood nickname because his father was also Oscar.

Braves, Phillies, 1913-1920

Duggan, Jim [James Elmer]
Mer
Browns, 1911

Duggleby, Bill [William James]
Frosty Bill
> Reluctant to make friends among his teammates.

Phillies, Athletics, Pirates, 1898-1907

Duke, Martin (F)
Duck
> His birth name.

Statesmen, 1891

Duliba, Bob [Robert John]
Ach
> A play on the German phrase, *ach du lieber*. Given by a minor league manager.

Cardinals, Angels, Red Sox, Athletics, 1959-1967

Dumont, George (Henry)
Monte: Pea Soup
Senators, Red Sox, 1915-1919

Duncan, Louis (Baird)
Pat
> Reflected his Irish heritage.

Pirates, Reds, 1915-1924

Dundon, Ed [Edward Joseph]
Dummy
> Deaf mute

Buckeyes, 1883-1884

Dunham, Henry (Houston)
Wiley
Cardinals, 1902

Dunlap, Fred [Frederick C]
Sure Shot
> Based on strength and accuracy throwing to first.

King of Second Basemen
Blues, Maroons, Wolverines, Alleghenys, Giants, Statesmen, 1880-1891

Dunlap, Grant (Lester)
Snap
Cardinals, 1953

Dunn, Adam (Troy)
Big Donkey
> Teammate given. He was not known for base-path speed.

Reds, Diamondbacks, Nationals, White Sox, Athletics 2001-2014

Durbin, Joseph (Adam)
Real Deal
> High school coach bestowed.

J.D.
Twins, Diamondbacks, Phillies, 2004, 2007

Durham, Ed [Edward Fant]
Bull
> Standard nickname for anyone named Durham.

Red Sox, White Sox, 1929-1933

Durham, Joe [Joseph Vann]
Pop
Orioles, Cardinals, 1954-1959

Durham, Leon
Bull
> Obvious choice.

Cardinals, Cubs, Reds, 1980-1989

Durnbaugh, Bobby [Robert Eugene]
Scroggy

Redlegs, 1957
Durocher, Leo (Ernest) {du-ROW- sher}
Lippy
An often arguer.
The Lip
One of the most ejected managers/coaches in history.
Peerless Leader
As manager of the Cardinals.
All-American Out
Given by Babe Ruth, based on his low batting average.
Yankees, Reds, Cardinals, Dodgers, 1925-1945
Durrett, Elmer (Cable)
Red
Dodgers, 1944-1945
Duryea, James (Newton)
Jesse: Cyclone Jim
Red Stockings, Reds, Browns, Senators, 1889-1893
Dusak, Erv [Ervin Frank]
Four Sack
From a poem written by a minor league fan.
Cardinals, Pirates, 1941-1952
Dwyer, Jim [James Edward]
Pig Pen
Cardinals, Expos, Mets, Giants, Red Sox, Orioles, Twins, 1973-1990
Dwyer, Joe [Joseph Michael]
Double
Reds, 1937
Dwyer, John (E)
Jumbo
Blues, 1882
Dyer, Don (Robert)
Duffy
Named at birth because, when he was born, the family was listening to *Duffy's Tavern*, a radio program.
Mets, Pirates, Expos, Tigers, 1968-1981
Dygert, Jimmy [James Henry]
Sunny Jim
Athletics, 1905-1910

Dykstra, Lenny [Leonard Kyle]
The Franchise: Dude
Nails
Hard-nosed personality.
Dr. Dirt
Given by sportscasters for being down and dirty, brash, and outspoken.
Mets, Phillies, 1985-1996
Dyson, Jarrod (Martel)
Zoombiya
Royals, Mariners, Diamondbacks, Pirates, White Sox, 2010-
Dyson, Sam [Samuel Isaac]
Rojo
Blue Jays, Marlins, Rangers, Giants, Twins, 2012-2019
Eagan, Bill [William]
Bad Bill
Based on his rowdy behavior.
Browns, Colts, Pirates, 1891-1898
Eagan, Charles (Eugene)
Truck
5'11", 190 lbs., build like a truck.
Pirates, Blues, 1901
Earl, Howard (J)
Slim Jim
6'2" but only 180 lbs.
Colts, Brewers, 1890-1991
Earle, Billy [William Moffat]
The Little Globetrotter
Named by the St. Paul Globe as one of [Cap] Anson's Globe Trotters.
Red Stockings, Browns, Pirates, Colonels, Grooms, 1889-1894
Earnshaw, George (Livingston)
Moose
6'4", 210 lbs.
Athletics, White Sox, Dodgers, Cardinals, 1928-1936
Easler, Mike [Michael Anthony]
Hit Man: Line Drive: Easy
Astros, Angels, Pirates, Red Sox, Yankees, Phillies, 1973-1987
Eason, Mal [Malcolm Wayne]
Kid

Orphans, Beaneaters, Tigers, Superbas, 1900-1906
Easterwood, Roy (Charles)
Shag
Cubs, 1944
Easton, John (David)
Goose
Phillies, 1955, 1959
Eaton, Adam (Cory)
Spanky: Mouse
Diamondbacks, White Sox, Nationals, 2012-
Eaton, Zeb [Zebulon Vance]
Red
Tigers, 1944-1945
Eaves, Vallie (Ennis)
Chief
>He was one-quarter Cherokee.

Tom
Athletics, White Sox, Cubs, 1935-1942
Ebright, Hi [Hiram C]
Buck
Nationals, 1889
Eccles, Harry (Josiah)
Bugs
Athletics, 1915
Eckert, Al [Albert George]
Obbie
Reds, Cardinals, 1930-1935
Eckert, Charlie [Charles William]
Buzz
Athletics, 1919-1922
Eckhardt, Oscar (George)
Ox
Braves, Dodgers, 1932, 1936
Eckstein, David (Mark)
X Factor: Just Enough
Angels, Cardinals, Blue Jays, Diamondbacks, Padres, 2001-2010
Edelen, Ed [Edward Joseph]
Doc
>He was a practicing physician.

Senators, 1932
Edge, Claude (Lee)
Butch
Blue Jays, 1979
Edmonds, Jim [James Patrick] {ED-muns}
Jimmy Baseball
Angels, Cardinals, Padres, Cubs, Brewers, Reds, 1993-2010
Edmondson, George (Henderson)
Big Ed
>6'1", 179 lbs.

Indians, 1922-1924
Edmonston, Sam [Samuel Sherwood]
Big Sam
Senators, 1907
Edwards, Bruce [Charles Bruce]
Bull
Dodgers, Cubs, Senators, Redlegs, 1946-1956
Edwards, Carl Jr (Fleming)
The String Bean Slinger: Carl's Jr
Cubs, Padres, Mariners, 2015-
Edwards, Howard (Rodney)
Doc
>He served as a Navy medic.

Indians, Athletics, Yankees, Phillies, 1962-1970
Edwards, James (Corbette)
Little Joe
Indians, White Sox, Reds, 1922-1928
Eells, Harry (Archibald)
Slippery
>Eels are the epitome of slippery.

Naps, 1906
Egan, Aloysius (Jerome)
Wishy
>Short form. From his first name. {al-oh-WISH-us}

Tigers, Cardinals, 1902-1906
Egan, Arthur (Augustus)
Ben
>Had a better-known childhood friend named Ben.

Athletics, Naps, Indians, 1908-1915
Egan, Jack [John Joseph]
Silver Fox: Rip
Senators, 1894
Egan, Jim [James K]
Troy Terrier

Played his one major league season for the Troy club.
Trojans, 1882

Eggert, Elmer (Albert)
Mose
Origin unknown, but pre-dated his baseball years.
Moose
A misspelling of Mose.
Red Sox, 1927

Ehmke, Howard (John) {EM-key}
Bob
Called Bob at childhood. Not his first or middle name.
Blues, Tigers, Red Sox, Athletics, 1915-1930

Ehret, Philip (Sydney)
Red
Red hair and a redness in his face from a ruddy complexion.
Cowboys, Colonels, Pirates, Browns, Reds, 1888-1898

Ehrhardt, Welton (Claude)
Rube
Robins, Reds, 1924-1929

Eichhorn, Mark (Anthony)
Dr. Funk
Popeye
He could imitate the cartoon character.
Blue Jays, Braves, Angels, Orioles, 1982-1996

Elberfeld, Norman (Arthur)
Kid
Childhood nickname.
The Tabasco Kid
Named for his temper and peppery style by sportswriter Sam Crane.
Phillies, Reds, Tigers, Highlanders, Senators, Robins, 1898-1914

Eldred, Brad [Bradley Ross]
Big Country: King Kong
Pirates, Rockies, Tigers, 2005-2012

Elko, Pete [Peter]
Piccolo Pete
Cubs, 1943-1944

Ellam, Roy
Slippery
Pun from the Slippery Elm tree, mispronouncing his last name as El Lum.
Whitey
Reds, Pirates, 1909, 1918

Eller, Horace (Owen)
Hod
Reds, 1917-1921

Ellerbe, Frank [Francis Rogers]
Governor
Senators, Browns, Indians, 1919-24

Elliott, Allen (Clifford)
Ace
First, middle and last names.
Cubs, 1923-1924

Elliott, Bob [Robert Irving]
Mr. Team
So named because he was so integral to the Braves.
Pirates, Braves, Giants, Browns, White Sox, 1939-1953

Elliott, Claude (Judson)
Chaucer: Old Pardee
Reds, Giants, 1904-1905

Elliott, Glenn [Herbert Glenn]
Lefty
Silent Glenn
Not very outgoing until he got to know you.
Braves, 1947-1949

Elliott, Harold (Bell)
Rowdy
Doves, Cubs, Robins, 1910-1920

Ellis, Andrew (James)
A.J.
Dodgers, Phillies, Marlins, Padres, 2008-2018

Ellis, George (William)
Rube
Cardinals, 1909-1912

Ellison, Bert (Herbert)
Babe
Tigers, 1916-1920

Ellsbury, Jacoby (McCabe)
  Tacoby Bellsbury
    Sort of rhymes with "Taco Bell."
  Chief
  Red Sox, Yankees, 2007-2017
Elsh, Eugene (Raybold)
  Roy
  White Sox, 1923-1925
Elston, Don [Donald Ray]
  Every Day
  Cubs, Dodgers, 1953-1964
Ely, William (Frederick)
  Bones
  Bisons, Colonels, Stars, Grooms, Browns, Pirates, Athletics, Senators, 1884-1902
Embree, Charles (Willard)
  Red
  Indians, Yankees, Browns, 1941-1949
Embry, Charles (Akin)
  Slim
    6'2" but only 184 lbs.
  White Sox, 1923
Emerson, Chester (Arthur)
  Chuck
  Athletics, 1911-1912
Emery, Herrick (Smith)
  Spoke
  Phillies, 1924
Emmerich, William (Peter)
  Slim
    At 6'1", 170 lbs., he had fine features, even looked slim.
  Giants, 1945-1946
Emslie, Bob [Robert Daniel]
  Blind Bob
    Given by John McGraw during his umpiring career.
  Wig
    He wore a hairpiece because of premature baldness.
  Orioles, Athletics, 1883-1885
Encarnacion, Edwin [Elpidio]
{en-car-nah-see-OWN}
  Double-E: EE
    Sports announcers found it easier than his name.
  Reds, Blue Jays, Indians, Mariners, Yankees, White Sox, 2005-
Engle, Charlie (August)
  Cholly
  Athletics, Pirates, 1925-1930
Engle, Clyde [Arthur Clyde]
  Hack
    He resembled pro wrestler Georg Hackenschmidt.
  Highlanders, Red Sox, Buffeds, Blues, Indians, 1909-1916
Ennis, Russ [Russell Edward]
  Hack
  Senators, 1926
Ens, Anton
  Mutz
  White Sox, 1912
Enzenroth, Clarence (Herman)
  Jack
  Browns, Packers, 1914-1915
Enzmann, Johnny [John]
  Gentleman John
  Robins, Indians, Phillies, 1914-1920
Epperly, Al [Alpert Paul]
  Tub: Pard
  Cubs, Dodgers, 1938, 1950
Epps, Aubrey (Lee)
  Yo-Yo
    Proficient with the toy.
  Pirates, 1935
Epstein, Mike [Michael Peter] {EP-stine}
  SuperJew
    Given by rival manager Rocky Bridges for his 1965 efforts in the California League.
  Orioles, Senators, Athletics, Rangers, Angels, 1966-1974
Erautt, Joe [Joseph Michael]
  Stubby
  White Sox, 1950-1951
Erickson, Hank [Henry Nels]
  Popeye
    After the cartoon character.
  Reds, 1935
Erickson, Paul (Walford)

Li'l Abner
: 6'2", 200 lbs., at the height of the comic strip.
: Cubs, Phillies, Giants, 1941-1948

Ermer, Cal [Calvin Coolidge]
Pres
: Senators, 1947

Errickson, Dick [Richard Merriwell]
Lief
: Bees, Braves, Cubs, 1938-1942

Erskine, Carl (Daniel)
Oisk
: Short for Oiskin, a Brooklyn mispronunciation.
: Dodgers, 1948-1959

Erwin, Ross (Emil)
Tex
: Born in Texas.
: Tigers, Superbas, Dodgers, Robins, Reds, 1907-1914

Escarrega, Ernesto
Chico
: White Sox, 1982

Escobar, Eduardo (Jose)
El De La Pica
: White Sox, Twins, Diamondbacks, 2011-

Esper, Charles (H)
Duke
: Athletics, Alleghenys, Phillies, Pirates, Senators, Orioles, Browns, 1890-1898

Espineli, Eugene (MacAlalag)
Geno
: Giants, 2008

Espinosa, Arnulfo (Acevedo)
Niño
: Spanish for *Little Boy*. He stood 6'1", 192 lbs.
: Mets, Phillies, Blue Jays, 1974-1981

Essick, Bill [William Earl]
Vinegar Bill
: Gained from the large German immigrant population of Cincinnati. *Essig* in German means Vinegar.
: Reds, 1906-1907

Esterbrook, Thomas (John)
Dude
: Colorful, flamboyant and eccentric.
: Bisons, Blues, Metropolitans, Giants, Hoosiers, Colonels, Grooms, 1880-1891

Estrada, Frank [Francisco]
PaquÃn
: Mets, 1971

Etchison, Clarence (Hampton)
Buck
: Braves, 1943-1944

Etheridge, Bobby (Lamar)
Luke
: Giants, 1967, 1969

Ethier, Andre (Everett)
Daddy
: Dodgers, 2006-2017

Eubank, John (Franklin)
Honest John
: Tigers, 1905-1907

Eubanks, Eul (Melvin)
Poss
: Cubs, 1922

Eunick, Ferd [Fernandes Bowen]
Dutch
: Indians, 1917

Eusebio, Tony [Raul Antonio Bare]
{you-SAY-be-oh}
The Astro Clipper
: Astros, 1991-2001

Evans, Charles (Franklin)
Chick
: Doves, 1909-1910

Evans, Darrell (Wayne)
Howdy-Doody
: He resembled the famous puppet.
UFO
: He spoke often about seeing UFOs.
: Braves, Giants, Tigers, 1969-1989

Evans, Dwight (Michael)
Dewey
: Red Sox, Orioles, 1972-1991

Evans, Joe [Joseph Patton]

Doc
Indians, Senators, Browns, 1915-25
Evans, Louis (Richard)
Steve
Giants, Cardinals, Tip-Tops, Terrapins, 1908-1915
Evans, Russell (Edison)
Red
White Sox, Dodgers, 1936, 1939
Evans, Uriah (L P)
Jake: Bloody Jake
Trojans, Ruby Legs, Blues, Orioles, 1879-1885
Everett, Carl (Edward)
C-Rex
Jurassic Carl
> Named by Boston Columnist Dan Shaughnessy when Carl denied the existence of dinosaurs.
Marlins, Mets, Astros, Red Sox, Rangers, White Sox, Expos, Mariners, 1993-2006
Everitt, Bill [William Lee]
Wild Bill
Colts, Orphans, Senators, 1895-1901
Evers, Johnny [John Joseph] {EE-verz}
Crab
> His temperament.
Human Crab
> Because of his unorthodox manner of sliding over to ground balls.
Trojan
> From Troy, his birth town and the name of his first team.
Orphans, Cubs, Braves, Phillies, White Sox, 1902-1929
Evers, Walt [Walter Arthur] {EE-verz}
Hoot
> Named for Hoot Gibson, a cowboy he emulated as a kid.
Tigers, Red Sox, Giants, Orioles, Indians, 1941-1956
Ewing, George (Lemuel)
Bob
> Adopted in childhood instead of using George.
Long Bob
6'1", 170 lbs.
Reds, Phillies, Cardinals, 1902-1912
Ewing, John
Long John
6'1", 168 lbs.
Browns, Outlaw Reds, Nationals, Colonels, Giants, 1883-1891
Ewing, William
Buck
> A nickname bestowed in his youth.
Trojans, Giants, Spiders, Reds, 1880-1897
Ewoldt, Art [Arthur Lee]
Sheriff
Athletics, 1919
Faber, Urban (Clarence)
Red
White Sox, 1914-1933
Fabrique, Albert (LaVerne)
Bunny
Robins, 1916-1917
Fagan, Bill [William A]
Clinkers
Metropolitans, Cowboys, 1887-1888
Fahey, Howard (Simpson)
Cap: Kid
Athletics, 1912
Fahrer, Clarence (Willie)
Pete
Reds, 1914
Fain, Ferris (Roy)
Burrhead: Cocky
Athletics, White Sox, Tigers, Indians, 1947-1955
Fairbank, Jim [James Lee]
Smokey
Athletics, 1903-1904
Faircloth, James (Lamar)
Rags
> The opposite of Fair-cloth.
Phillies, 1919
Falk, Bibb (August)
Jockey

Based on the merciless way he rode
opponents.
White Sox, Indians, 1920-1931
Falk, Chet [Chester Emanuel]
Spot
Browns, 1925-1927
Falkenberg, Frederick (Peter)
Cy
Speculation: He reminded
someone of Cy Young.
Pirates, Senators, Naps, Hoosiers,
Pepper, Tip-Tops, Athletics,
1903-1917
Fallenstein, Ed [Edward Joseph]
Ace
Phillies, Braves, 1931, 1933
Fallon, George (Decatur)
Flash
Dodgers, Cardinals, 1937-1945
Fannin, Cliff [Clifford Bryson]
Mule
Browns, 1945-1952
Fanok, Harry (Michael)
The Flame Thrower
One of the hardest throwing
pitchers of all time.
Cardinals, 1963-1964
Fanovich, Frank (Joseph)
Lefty
Reds, Athletics, 1949, 1953
Farmer, Floyd (Haskell)
Jack
Pirates, Indians, 1916, 1918
Farrell, Charles (Andrew)
Duke
Named by a concessionaire as the
Duke of Marlborough.
White Stockings, Pirates, Reds,
Senators, Giants, Superbas,
Americans, 1888-1905
Farrell, Edward (Stephen)
Doc
A dentist.
Giants, Braves, Cardinals, Cubs,
Yankees, Red Sox, 1925-1935
Farrell, Jack A [John A]
Moose
Stars, Grays, Quakers, Nationals,
Orioles, 1879-1889
Farrell, Jack [John]
Hartford Jack
His home town. There are 3 major
league Jack Farrells.
Dark Blues, 1874
Farrell, Richard (Joseph)
Big Turk
Based on size; 6'4", 215 lbs.
Turk
Shortened form of Big Turk.
Phillies, Dodgers, Cold 45s, Astros,
1956-1969
Faszholz, Jack [John Edward]
Preacher
An ordained pastor.
Cardinals, 1953
Faulkner, Jim [James Leroy]
Lefty
Giants, Robins, 1927-1930
Fausett, Robert (Shaw) {FAW-set}
Buck: Leaky
Reds, 1944
Faust, Charlie [Charles Victor]
Victory
Sparked the Giants to wins as the
mascot.
Giants, 1911
Fauver, Clay [Clayton King]
Cayt: Pop
Colonels, 1899
Federoff, Al [Alfred]
Whitey
Tigers, 1951-1952
Federowicz, Tim [Timothy Joseph]
{fehd-er-oh-vich}
Fedex
Dodgers, Cubs, Giants, Astros, Reds,
Rangers, 2011-2019
Fehring, William (Paul)
Dutch
Named in high school as the
Flying Dutchman when he ran a
kickoff back for a touchdown.

White Sox, 1934
Feinberg, Eddie [Edward Isidore]
: Itzzy
: Phillies, 1938-1939

Felder, Mike [Michael Otis]
: Tiny
: 5'8", 160 lbs.
: Brewers, Giants, Mariners, Astros, 1985-1994

Felderman, Marv [Marvn Wilfred]
: Coonie
: Cubs, 1942

Feliciano, Pedro (Juan)
: Perpetual Pedro
: : Named by a broadcaster because of his large number of appearances.
: Mets, 2002-2013

Feliz, Michael
: Fuego
: Astros, Pirates, 2015-

Feliz, Pedro (Julio)
: Happy Pete
: Giants, Phillies, Astros, Cardinals, 2000-2010

Feller, Bob [Robert William Andrew]
: Rapid Robert
: : His fastball was once clocked at 107 MPH.
: Bullet Bob
: : Same fastball reason.
: The Heater from Van Meter
: : A good fastball and his hometown.
: Indians, 1936-1956

Felsch, Oscar (Emil)
: Happy
: : Easygoing nature and winning smile.
: White Sox, 1915-1920

Fenner, Horace (Alfred)
: Hod
: White Sox, 1921

Ferens, Stan [Stanley]
: Lefty
: Browns, 1942, 1946

Ferguson, Bob [Robert Vavasour]
: Death to Flying Things
: : Based on his defensive prowess.
: Mutuals, Atlantics, Dark Blues, Hartfords, White Stockings, Trojans, Quakers, Alleghenys, 1871-1884

Fernandez, Froilan
: Nanny
: : Short nickname for his last name.
: Braves, Pirates, 1942-1950

Fernández, Humberto
: Chico
: Dodgers, Phillies, Tigers, Mets, 1956-1963

Fernández, José (D)
: Niño
: Marlins, 2013-2016

Fernández, Lorenzo (Marto)
: Chico
: Orioles, 1968

Fernandez, Sid [Charles Sidney]
: El Sid
: : A take-off of El Cid, from the movie, and his Spanish name.
: Dodgers, Mets, Orioles, Phillies, Astros, 1983-1997

Fernández, Tony [Octavio Antonio]
: Flipper
: : Nickname given by teammates for his use of his glove to flip the ball to first base.
: El Cabeza
: : Means "the head," given as a youngster from his oversized noggin.
: El Fantasma
: The Gadget Man
: : Given by teammates because he always had a new gadget.
: Blue Jays, Padres, Mets, Reds, Yankees, Indians, Brewers, 1983-2001

Ferrara, Al [Alfred John]
: The Bull
: : Named by sportswriter for his build and reckless abandon in the field.
: Dodgers, Padres, Reds, 1963-1971

Ferris, Albert (Samuel)
Hobe
Americans, Browns, 1901-1909
Ferriss, Dave [David Meadow]
Boo
    An infant inability to pronounce
    "Brother."
Red Sox, 1945-1950
Ferry, Alfred (Joseph)
Cy
Tigers, Naps, 1904-1905
Ferson, Alex [Alexander]
Colonel
Nationals, Bisons, Orioles, 1889-1892
Fewster, Wilson [Lloyd]
Chick
Yankees, Red Sox, Indians, Robins, 1917-1927
Fick, Charles (Joseph)
C.J.
Cardinals, Astros, 2012
Fidrych, Mark (Steven)
The Bird
    Considered bird-brained for talking to the ball and manicuring the mound on hands and knees. Resembled Big Bird of Sesame Street fame.
Tigers, 1976-1980
Fieber, Clarence (Thomas)
Lefty
White Sox, 1932
Fielder, Cecil (Grant) {SESS-ill}
Big Daddy
    Fan given: big smile, peaceful temperament, massive physical stature.
Wild Bear
    Japan nickname: Wild implies power; bear for his bulk.
Blue Jays, Tigers, Yankees, Angels, Indians, 1985-1998
Fielder, Prince (Semien)
Uncle Phil
Brewers, tigers, Rangers, 2005-2016
Fields, Josh [Joshua Dean]
Okie
    Born in Oklahoma.
White Sox, Royals, 2006-2010
Fien, Casey (Michael) {FEEN}
Fien Machine
Tigers, Twins, Dodgers, Mariners, Phillies, 2009-2017
Fiene, Lou [Louis Henry]
Big Finn
White Sox, 1906-1909
Fiers, Mike [Michael Bruce]
Kai
Brewers, Astros, Tigers, Athletics, 2011-
Figgins, Desmond (DeChone {SHAWN})
Chone
Angels, Mariners, Dodgers, 2002-14
Figueroa, Luis (R)
Wicho
Pirates, Blue Jays, Giants, 2001-2007
Filipowicz, Steve [Stephen Charles]
Flip
    Easier than using his entire last name.
Giants, Reds, 1944-1948
Finn, Neal [Cornelius Francis]
Mickey
    Based on the drink called a Mickey Finn.
Robins, Dodgers, Phillies, 1930-1933
Finneran, Joseph (Ignatius)
Happy: Smokey Joe
Phillies, Tip-Tops, Tigers, Yankees, 1912-1918
Fischer, Charles (William)
Carl
    Given to differentiate him from his father, Charles H.
The Medina Mauler
    Given by fans. He came from Medina, NY.
Senators, Browns, Tigers, White Sox, Indians, 1930-1937
Fischer, Hank [Henry William]
Bulldog
    Earned for his aggressive

demeanor... in basketball.
Braves, Reds, Red Sox, 1962-1967
Fisher, Charles (Edward)
Carlos
Reds, 2009-2011
Fisher, Chauncey (Burr)
Peach
Whoa Bill
Spiders, Reds, Bridegrooms, Giants
Cardinals, 1893-1901
Fisher, Frederick (Brown)
Fritz
Tigers, 1964
Fisher, George (Aloys)
Showboat
Gained in 1930 when the show, "Showboat" was a hit.
Senators, Cardinals, Browns, 1923-1932
Fisher, Isaac (Newton)
Ike
Phillies, 1898
Fisher, Jack [John Howard]
Fat Jack
6'2", 215 lbs.
Orioles, Giants, Mets, White Sox, Reds, 1959-1969
Fisher, John (Gustave)
Red
Browns, 1910
Fisher, Ray (Lyle)
Pick
Short for pickerel, given in college (we have no idea why).
Highlanders, Yankees, Reds, 1910-1920
Fisher, Tom C [Thomasd Chalmers]
Red
Beaneaters, 1904
Fisher, Tom G [Thomas Gene]
Big Fish
Orioles, 1967
Fisher, William (Charles)
Cherokee
Forest Cities, Canaries, Athletics, Dark Blues, Whites, Reds, Grays, 1871-1978
Fisk, Carlton (Ernest)
Pudge
Chubby as a youngster.
Red Sox, White Sox, 1969-1993
Fiske, Max [Maximilian Patrick]
Ski
A short version of his last name.
Chi-Feds, 1914
Fisler, Wes [Weston Dickson]
Icicle
Athletics, 1871-1876
Fister, Doug [Douglas Wildes]
Dougie Fresh
Mariners, Tigers, Nationals Astros, Red Sox, Rangers, 2009-2018
Fitzgerald, Howard (chumney)
Lefty
Although he was a lefty, he was not a pitcher.
Cubs, Red Sox, 1922-1926
Fitzgerald, Justin (Howard)
Mike
Yankees, Phillies, 1911, 1918
Fitzsimmons Freddie [Fred Landis]
Fat Freddie
5'11", a stocky 185 lbs.
Giants, Dodgers, 1925-1943
Flagstead, Ira (James)
Pete
Tigers, Red Sox, Senators, Pirates, 1917-1930
Flaherty, John [Timothy] {FLAY-er-tee}
Flash
Red Sox, Tigers, Padres, Devil Rays, Yankees, 1992-2005
Flaherty, Ryan (Edward)
Flash
Orioles, Braves, Indians, 2012-2019
Flair, Al [Albert Dell]
Broadway
Red Sox, 1941
Flanagan, Ed [Edward F]
Sleepy
Athletics, Colonels, 1887, 1889
Flanagan, James (Paul)

Steamer
: Related to his speed and his size, like a locomotive.
: Pirates, 1905

Flaskamper, Ray [Raymond Harold] {FLASH-cam-per}
Flash
: White Sox, 1927

Fleming, Les [Leslie Harvey]
Mae
: Tigers, Indians, Pirates, 1939-1949

Fleming, Leslie (Fletcherd)
Bill
: Red Sox, Cubs, 1940-1946

Fleming, Tom [Thomas Vincent]
Sleuth
: Giants, Phillies, 1899-1904

Flener, Gregory (Alan)
Huck
: Blue Jays, 1993-1997

Flick, Lew [Lewis Miller]
Noisy
: Athletics, 1943-1944

Flint, Frank (Sylvester)
Silver
: Red Stockings, Blues, White Stockings, 1875-1889

Flohr, Mort [Moritz Herman]
Dutch
: Athletics, 1934

Florence, Paul (Robert)
Pep
: Giants, 1926

Flores, Wilmer (Alejandro)
Ca Tire
: Mets, Diamondbacks, Giants, 2013-

Flowers, D'Arcy (Raymond)
Jake
: Cardinals, Robins, Dodgers, Reds, 1923-1934

Floyd, Leslie (Roe)
Bubba
: Tigers, 1944

Flynn, Cornelius (Francis Xavier)
Carney
: Reds, Giants, Senators, 1894, 1896

Flynn, George (Albert)
Dibby
: Colts, 1896

Flynn, John (A)
Jocko
: White Stockings, 1886-1887

Flynn, William
Clipper
: Haymakers, Olympics, 1871-1872

Fodge, Gene (Arlan)
Suds
Pops
: Given primarily by his grandchildren.
: Cubs, 1958

Fogg, Josh [Joshua Smith]
Dragon Slayer
: White Sox, Pirates, Rockies, Reds, 2001-2009

Foley, Charles (Joseph)
Curry
Old Authority
: Player given for his memory of all things baseball.
: Red Stockings, Bisons, 1879-1883

Forbes, Patrick (Joseph)
P.J.
: Orioles, Phillies, 1998, 2001

Force, Davy [David W]
Wee Davy: Tom Thumb
: 5'4", 130 lbs.
: Olympics, Haymakers, Canaries, White Stockings, Athletics, Mutuals, Brown Stockings, Bisons, Nationals, 1871-1886

Ford, Darnell (Glenn)
Dan
Disco Dan
: Danced on the base path and was passed by another runner.
: Twins, Angels, Orioles, 1975-1985

Ford, Edward (Charles)
Slick
: Given for hidden means of doctoring the ball.
Whitey

Chairman of the Board
: Had a calm, cool demeanor in tough situations.
: Yankees, 1950-1967

Ford, Horace (Hills)
: Hod
: Braves, Phillies, Robins, Reds, Cardinals, 1919-1933

Foreman, August (G)
: Happy
: White Sox, Red Sox, 1924, 1926

Foreman, Frank [Francis Isaiah]
: Monkey
:: On-field antics included a simian impersonation.
: Chicago/Pittsburgh, Cowboys, Orioles, Reds, Statesmen, Senators, Giants, Americans, 1884-1902

Foreman, John (Davis)
: Brownie
: Pirates, Reds, 1895-1896

Fornieles, Jose (Miguel) {for-NEE-lis}
: Mike
:: Translation for Miguel
: Senators, White Sox, Orioles, Red Sox, Twins, 1952-1963

Forsythe, Logan [John Logan]
: Logie Bear
: Padres, Rays, Dodgers, Twins, Rangers, Marlins, 2011-

Foss, George (Dueward)
: Deeby
: Senators, 1921

Fossas, Tony [Emilio Antonio]
: The Mechanic
: Rangers, Brewers, Red Sox, Cardinals, Mariners, Cubs, Yankees, 1988-1999

Fosse, Ray [Raymond Earl] {FOSS-ee}
: Marion Mule
:: He is from Marion, Illinois.
:: Big and strong, stubborn as a mule.
: Indians, Athletes, Mariners, Brewers, 1967-1979

Fossum, Casey (Paul)
: The Blade
: Red Sox, Diamondbacks, Devil Rays, Tigers, Mets, 2001-2009

Foster, Clarence (Francis)
: Pop
: Giants, Senators, White Sox, 1898-1901

Foster, Ed [Edward Lee]
: Slim
: Naps, 1908

Foster, Eddie [Edward Cunningham]
: Kid
:: At 5'6", 145 lbs, the name was given by *Sporting Life*.
: The Evangelist
:: Given by newspapers as the understudy to Billy Sunday.
: Highlanders, Senators, Red Sox, Browns, 1910-1923

Foster, George
: Rube
:: A farmer from Oklahoma.
: Red Sox, 1913-1917

Foster, George A (Arthur)
: Yahtzee
: Giants, Reds, Mets, White Sox, 1969-1986

Foster, Oscar (E)
: Reddy
: Giants, 1896

Fothergill, Bob [Robert Roy]
: Fats
: Fatty
:: Officially 230 lbs., but on a diet, went down to 256.
: Tigers, White Sox, Red Sox, 1922-33

Fournier, Henry [Julius Henry]
: Frenchy
: Reds, 1894

Foutz, Dave [David Luther]
: Scissors
:: Based on a tall, but thin build.
: Browns, Bridegrooms, Grooms, 1884-1896

Fowler, Dexter [William Dexter]
: Daddy Long Legs
:: 6'5". 195 lbs.

Rockies, Astros, Cubs, Cardinals, 2008-

Fowler, Jesse (Peter)
Pete
Cardinals, 1924

Fowler, Joseph (Chester)
Boob: Gink: Chet
Reds, Red Sox, 1923-1926

Fox, Charlie [Charles Francis]
Irish
Giants, 1942

Fox, Ervin
Pete
Based on a minor league nickname: Rabbit (Peter...)
Tigers, Red Sox, 1933-1945

Fox, Nellie [Jacob Nelson]
Mighty Mite: Little Nel
Athletics, White Sox, Colt 45s Astros, 1947-1965

Foxx, Jimmie [James Emory]
Double X
Based on the two Xs in his last name.
The Beast
Given by the press.
Athletics, Red Sox, Cubs, Phillies, 1925-1945

France, Ossie [Osman Beverly]
O.B.
Colts, 1890

Franco, Maikel (Antonio)
Compa F
Phillies, Royals, 2014-

Francoeur, Jeff [Jeffrey Braden]
{Fran-COOR}
Frenchy
Braves, Mets, Rangers, Royals, Giants, Padres, Phillies, Marlins, 2005-2016

Francona, John (Patsy)
Tito
Means "The little one." Given by his father.
Orioles, White Sox, Tigers, Indians, Cardinals, Phillies, Braves, Athletics, Brewers, 1956-1970

Francona, Terry (Jon)
Tito
Nickname inherited from his father, John.
Expos, Cubs, Reds, Indians, Brewers, 1981-1990

Franklin, John (William)
Jay
Padres, 1971

Franklin, Murray (Asher)
Moe
Typical nickname for a Jewish person named Murray.
Tigers, 1941-1942

Fraser, Charles (Carrolton)
Chick
Colonels, Spiders, Phillies, Athletics, Beaneaters, Reds, Cubs, 1896-1909

Frazier, Clint (Jackson)
Bubba: Red Thunder
Yankees, 2017-

Frazier, Todd (Brian)
The ToddFather
Reds, White Sox, Yankees, Mets, Rangers, 2011-

Freeman, Alexander (Vernon)
Buck
Cubs, 1921-1922

Freeman, Harvey (Bayard)
Buck
Athletics, 1921

Freeman, Hersh [Hershell Baskin]
Buster
Red Sox, Redlegs, Cubs, 1952-1958

Freeman, Jerry [Frank Ellsworth]
Buck
Senators, 1908-1909

Freeman, John (Frank)
Buck
Statesmen, Senators, Beaneaters, Americans, 1891-1907

Freeman, Marvin
Starvin' Marvin
6'6", but only 180 lbs.
Phillies, Braves, Rockies, White Sox,

Freeman, Raphael

1986-1996
Freeman, Raphael
Choo
Rockies, 2004-2006
Freeman, Sam [Samuel Douglas]
Freezy
Cardinals, Rangers, Brewers, Braves, Angels, Nationals, 2012-
Freese, David (Richard)
DaveHuman
Cardinals, Angels, Pirates, Dodgers, 2009-2019
Freese, Gene [Eugene Lewis]
Augie
Pirates, Cardinals, Phillies, White Sox, Reds, Astros, 1955-1966
Freese, George (Walter)
Bud
Tigers, Pirates, Cubs, 1953-1961
Freeze, Carl (Alexander)
Jake
White Sox, 1925
Fregosi, Jim [James Louis]
Skip
Angels, Mets, Rangers, Pirates, 1961-1978
Freigau, Howard (Earl)
Ty
Cardinals, Cubs, Robins, Braves, 1922-1928
French, Frank (Alexander)
Pat
Athletics, 1917
French, Walt [Walter Edward]
Piggy: Fitz
Athletics, 1923-1929

Freund, Lawrence (Joseph)
Frank
Colonels, 1896
Frey, Linus (Reinhard) {FRY}
Lonny
  A childhood nickname.
Junior
  He was not a junior and did not like the nickname.
Dodgers, Cubs, Reds, Yankees, Giants, 1933-1948
Frías, Jesus (Maria)
Pepe
Expos, Braves, Rangers, Dodgers, 1973-1981
Friday, Grier (William)
Skipper
Senators, 1923
Fridley, Jim [James Riley]
Big Jim
6'2", 205 lbs.
Indians, Orioles, Reds, 1952-1958
Fried, Arthur (Edwin)
Cy
Tigers, 1920
Friedrich, Christian (Louis Patrick)
Bird
Rockies, Padres, 2012-2016
Friend, Bob [Robert Bartmess]
Warrior
  Gained playing high school football and baseball.
Pirates, Yankees, Mets, 1951-1966
Friend, Owen (Lacey)
Red
Browns, Tigers, Indians, Red Sox, Cubs, 1949-1956
Frieri, Ernesto {free AIR ee}
Big Ern
Padres, Angels, Pirates, Rays, Rangers, 2009-2017
Frierson, Robert (Lawrence)
Buck
Indians, 1941
Frisbee, Charlie [Charles Augustus]
Bunt
Beaneaters, Giants, 1899-1900
Frisch, Frankie [Frank Francis]
The Fordham Flash
  Came from Fordham (Prep and University). A track star.
Giants, Cardinals, 1919-1937
Frisella, Danny [Daniel Vincent]
Bear

Mets, Braves, Padres, Cardinals,
Brewers, 1967-1976
Fritz, Harry (Koch)
Dutchman
Athletics, Chi-Feds, Whales,
1913-1915
Fry, Johnson
Jay
Indians, 1923
Fuentes, Brian (Christopher)
{foo-WHEN-taze}
T-Rex
6'4", 250 lbs.
Mariners, Rockies, Angels, Twins,
Athletics, Cardinals, 2001-2012
Fuentes, Rey [Reymond Louis]
Coqui
Padres, Royals, Diamondbacks,
2013-2017
Fuentes, Rigiberto
Tito: Parakeet
Giants, Padres, Tigers, Athletics,
1965-1978
Fuhrman, Alfred (George)
Ollie
Athletics, 1922
Fulghum, James (Lavoisier)
Dot
From childhood. He liked the
book, *Dot and Her Kittens*.
Athletics, 1921
Fuller, Charles (F)
Nig
Superbas, 1902
Fuller, Frank (Edward)
Rabbit
Tigers, Red Sox, 1915-1923
Fuller, Henry (W)
Harry
Browns, 1891
Fuller, William (Benjamin)
Shorty
5'6".
Nationals, Browns, Giants, 1888-96
Fullis, Charles (Philip)
Chick

Giants, Phillies, Cardinals, 1928-1936
Fulmer, Carson (Springer)
Filthy Fulmer
White Sox, Tigers, Orioles, 2016-
Fulmer, Charles (John)
Chick
Normal nickname for Charles.
Forest Citys, Mutuals, Whites, Grays,
Bisons, Red Stockings, Browns,
1871-1884
Fulmer, Michael (Joseph)
Fulm Piece
Tigers, 2016-
Funk, Elias (Calvin)
Liz
Yankees, Tigers, White Sox,
1929-1933
Furillo, Carl (Anthony)
Skoonj
Given by teammates because of
fondness for scungilli (the edible
part of an aquatic snail).
The Reading Rifle
Based on his throwing arm and his
hometown.
The Arm
Based on his throwing prowess.
Dodgers, 1946-1960
Furmaniak, Jason (Joseph)
{fur-MAN-ee-ak}
J.J.
Pirates, Athletics, 2005, 2007
Fussell, Fred [Frederick Morris]
Moonlight Ace
Cubs, Pirates, 1922-1929
Gabler, Frank (Harold)
The Great Gabbo
A play on his name. Also, Greta
Garbo was in her prime.
Giants, Bees, White Sox, 1935-1938
Gabler, William (Louis)
Gabe
Cubs, 1958
Gables, Kenneth (Harlin)
Coral
Pirates, 1945-1947

Gaddy, John (Wilson)
  Sheriff
  Dodgers, 1938
Gaetti, Gary (Joseph) {guy-ETT-ee}
  The Rat: G-Man: Zorn
  Twins, Angels, Royals, Cardinals,
  Cubs, Red Sox, 1981-2000
Gagnon, Harold (Dennis)
  Chick
  Tigers, Senators, 1922, 1924
Gainer, Del [Dellas Clinton]
  Sheriff
    He was a deputy U.S. marshal in
    Wheeling, WV.
  Tigers, Red Sox, Cardinals, 1909-22
Gainer, Johnathan (Keith)
  Jay
  Rockies, 1993
Gainey, Telmanch
  Ty
  Astros, 1985-1987
Gaines, Willard (Roland)
  Nemo
    Graduated from the Naval
    Academy.
  Senators, 1921
Galarraga, Andrés (Jose)
  {Gahl-la-RAH-ga}
  Big Cat: The Cat
    Names from teammates for his
    graceful, catlike moves.
  Expos, Cardinals, Rockies, Braves,
  Rangers, Giants, Angels, 1985-2004
Gallagher, Alan (Mitchell Edward
George Patrick Henry)
  Filthy McNasty: Pigpen: Dirty Al
    College nicknames acquired when
    he refused to change during a
    hitting streak.
  Giants, Angels, 1970-1973
Gallagher, Charles (William)
  Shorty
  Blues, 1901
Gallagher, Ed [Edward Michael]
  Lefty
  Red Sox, 1932

Gallagher, John (Laurence)
  Jackie
  Indians, 1923
Gallagher, Joseph (Emmett)
  Muscles
    6'2", 210 lbs.
  Yankees, Browns, Dodgers,
  1939-1940
Gallagher, Lawrence (Kirby)
  Gil
  Braves, 1922
Gallen, Zac [Zachary Peter]
  Milkman
  Marlins, Diamondbacks, 2019-
Gallego, Mike [Michael Anthony]
  {gah-YAY-go}
  Lego
  Athletics, Yankees, Cardinals,
  1985-1997
Gallia, Melvin (Allys)
  Bert
  Senators, Browns, Phillies,
  1912-1920
Galloway, Clarence (Edward)
  Chick
  Athletics, Tigers, 1919-1928
Galloway, Jim [James Cato]
  Bad News
  Cardinals, 1912
Galvin, James (Francis)
  Gentle Jeems
    Named for his gentle personality.
  The Little Steam Engine
    From teammates based on "The
    Little Engine that Could." He was
    small but powerful.
  Pud
    His favorite dessert was pudding
    OR he made pudding of opposing
    batters OR he had 11 children OR
    a pudgy body.
  Brown Stockings, Bisons, Alleghenys,
  Burghers, Pirates, Browns, 1875-92
Galvis, Freddy (Jose)
  Toco
  Phillies, Padres, Blue Jays, Reds, 2012-

Gammons, John (Ashley)
Daff
Acquired in college, but no one knows the significance.
Beaneaters, 1901

Gandil, Arnold
Chick
White Sox, Senators, Indians, White Sox, 1910-1919

Gandy, Bob [Robert Brinkley]
String
6'3", 180 lbs
Phillies, 1916

Gannon, James (Edward)
Gussie
Pirates, 1895

Gantenbein, Joe [Joseph Steven]
Sep
Athletics, 1939-1940

Gantner, Jim [James Elmer]
Gumby
Brewers, 1976-1992

Ganzel, Foster (Pirie)
Babe
Senators, 1927-1928

Garcés, Richard (Aron) {gar-SEZ}
El Guapo
Spanish for *the Handsome one*.
Twins, Cubs, Marlins, Red Sox, 1990-2002

García, Adolis [José Adolis]
El Bombi
Cardinals, Rangers, 2018-

García, Adonis
La Maravilla
Braves, 2015-

Garcia, Alfonso (Rafael)
Kiko
From his grandmother; common Hispanic nickname.
Orioles, Astros, Phillies, 1976-1985

García, Avisaíl (Antonio) {ah-vee-cy-EEL}
Mini Miggy
Tigers, White Sox, Rays, Brewers, 2012-

García, Dámaso (Domingo)
Damo
Yankees, Blue Jays, Braves, Expos, 1978-1989

García, Edward (Miguel)
Mike
English for his middle name.
Big Bear
Had short black hair and walked a bit like a bear.
Indians, White Sox, Senators, 1948-1961

García, Freddy (Antonio)
The Chief: The Rock
Big Game
Earned while a member of the White Sox.
Mariners, White Sox, Phillies, Tigers, Yankees, Orioles, Braves, 1999-2013

García, Leury
El Molleto
Rangers, White Sox, 2013-

García, Vinicio (Otilio)
Chico
Orioles, 1954

Garciaparra, Nomar [Anthony Nomar] {GAR-SEE-AH-par-uh}
Nomah
Name with a Boston accent.
Mr. Nice Guy
Chris Bermanism, from Alice Cooper's, "No More Mr...."
Red Sox, Cubs, Dodgers, Athletics, 1996-2009

Gardner, Billy [William Frederick]
Whitey
Shotgun
Had a potent throwing arm.
Slick
Either his speed at turning a double play or his pool shots.
Giants, Orioles, Senators, Twins, Yankees, Red Sox, 1954-1963

Gardner, Franklin (Washington)
Gid
Trojans, Blues, Orioles,

Chicago/Pittsburgh,
Monumentals, Orioles, Hoosiers,
Nationals, Quakers, 1879-1888
Gardner, Richard (Frank)
Rob
> Short for Robin, a baby nickname used by his mother.

Mets, Cubs, Indians, Yankees, Athletics, Brewers, 1965-1973
Garms, Debs (C)
Tex
Browns, Bees, Pirates, Cardinals, 1932-1945
Garneau, Dustin (Thomas)
Drago
Rockies, Athletics, White Sox, Angels, Astros, 2015-
Garner, Phil [Philip Mason]
Scrap Iron
> Tough, gritty, sometimes a brawler.

Athletics, Pirates, Astros, Dodgers, Giants, 1973-1988
Garr, Ralph (Allen)
Gator
The Road Runner
> He was quick running the bases.

Braves, White Sox, Angels, 1968-80
Garrett, Amir (Jamal)
A.G.
Reds, 2017-
Garrett, Clarence (Raymond)
Laz
Indians, 1915
Garrett, Henry (Adrian)
Pat
> Might be referencing Billy the Kid folklore.

Smokey
> Walt Hriniak thought he looked like Smokey Joe Wood.

Braves, Cubs, Athletics, Angels, 1966-1976
Garrison, Robert (Ford)
Rocky: Snapper
Red Sox, Athletics, 1943-1946

Garrity, Francis (Joseph)
Hank
White Sox, 1931
Garver, Mitch [Mitchell Lyn]
Garv Sauce
Twins, 2017-
Garvin, Virgil (Lee)
Ned
The Navasota Tarantula
> His hometown was Navasota, Texas.

Phillies, Orphans, Brewers, White Sox, Superbas, Highlanders, 1896-1904
Garza, Matt [Matthew Scott]
The Count
Twins, Rays, Cubs, Rangers, Brewers, 2006-2017
Gassaway, Charlie [Charles Cason]
Sheriff
Cubs, Athletics, Indians, 1944-1946
Gaston, Clarence (Edwin)
{SEE-toe GAS-tone}
Cito
> Given by a childhood friend, who thought there was a resemblance to a Mexican Wrestler with a stage name of Cito.

Braves, Padres, Pirates, 1967-1978
Gattis, Evan [James Evan] {GATT-iss}
El Oso Blanco
> Spanish for "The White Bear."

The Bull
The White Bear
> Bear-like strength displayed in winter ball in Venezuela.

Braves, Astros, 2013-2018
Gautreau, Walter (Paul)
Doc
> In high school. An alternative to Punk at photo time.

Punk
> He was 5'2", 129 lbs.

Athletics, Braves, 1925-1928
Gautreaux, Sidney (Allen)
Pudge

5'8", 190 lbs.
Dodgers, 1936-1937
Gazella, Mike [Michael]
Gazook
Yankees, 1923-1928
Gaw, George (Joseph)
Chippy
Cubs, 1920
Gearhart, Lloyd (William)
Gary
Giants, 1947
Gearin, Dennis (John)
Dinty: Little Nemo: Kewpie
Dinny: Angel: Denny: Dainty
Gill of the Shamrock: Hermit
Little Forkhander: Nemo
Little Irishman: Midget
Midget Southpaw
Mighty Mite: Sawed Off Red Head
Smallest pitcher in captivity
Wee Dinny
Wee Sprig of the Shamrock
All related to size: 5'4", 150 lbs. All from the minors.
Giants, Braves, 1923-1924
Geary, Bob [Robert Norton]
Speed
Athletics, Reds, 1918-1921
Geary, Eugene (Francis Joseph)
Huck
Pirates, 1942-1943
Gebrian, Pete [Peter]
Gabe
White Sox, 1947
Gedney, Alfred (W)
Count
Haymakers, Eckfords, Mutuals, Athletics, 1872-1875
Gee, Johnny [John Alexander]
Whiz
Pirates, Giants, 1939-1946
Geggus, Charlie [Charles Frederick]
Buck
Nationals, 1884
Gehrig, Lou [Henry Louis]
Larruping Lou
Based on a barnstorming team in the off-season.
Columbia
His alma mater.
Biscuit Pants
His thighs and butt (biscuits) looked large in pinstripes.
The Iron Horse
Did not sit out in 2,130 games over 15 seasons.
Buster
Yankees, 1923-1939
Gehringer, Charlie [Charles Leonard]
The Mechanical Man
Attributed to Lefty Grove because of his consistency.
Tigers, 1924-1942
Gehrman, Paul (Arthur)
Dutch
Lefty
Unusual: he was a right-handed pitcher.
Reds, 1937
Geier, Phil [Philip Louis]
Little Phil
5'7", 145 lbs.
Phillies, Reds, Athletics, Brewers, Beaneaters, 1896-1904
Genins, Frank [C Frank]
Frenchy
Browns, Reds, Pirates, Blues, 1892-1901
Gennett, Ryan (Joseph) {jen-ETT}
Scooter
Named as a 5-year-old, as a fan of a Muppets character.
Brewers, Reds, Giants, 2013-2019
Gentile, Jim [James Edward] {jen-TEEL}
Diamond Jim
Campanella considered him a diamond in the rough.
Dodgers, Orioles, Athletics, Astros, Indians, 1957-1966
Gentry, Craig (Alan)
Kitten Face
Rangers, Athletics, Angels, Orioles,

2009-2018
George, Charles (Peter)
Greek
Indians, Dodgers, Cubs, Athletics, 1935-1945
George, Thomas (Edward)
Not to be confused with George Thomas
Lefty
Browns, Naps, Reds, Braves, 1911-18
Gerber, Wally
Spooks
He had a skeleton-like frame.
Pirates, Browns, Red Sox, 1914-1929
Gerhardt, Allen (Russell)
Rusty
Padres, 1974
Gerhardt, Joe [John Joseph]
Move Up Joe
Given for his habit of shouting it at baserunners.
Blue Legs, Canaries, Mutuals, Grays, Reds, Wolverines, Eclipse, Giants, Metropolitans, Gladiators, Browns, Colonels, 1873-1891
Gerheauser, Al [Albert]
Lefty
Phillies, Pirates, Browns, 1943-1948
Gerken, George (Herbert)
Pickles
Gherkins are sweet pickles.
Indians, 1927-1928
Gerkin, Steve [Stephen Paul]
Splinter
6'1" but only 162 lbs.
Athletics, 1945
Gerner, Ed [Edwin Frederick]
Lefty
Reds, 1919
Geronimo, Cesar (Francisco)
The Chief
Astros, Reds, Royals, 1969-1983
Gerut, Joseph (Diego) {GARE-et}
Jody
Indians, Cubs, Pirates, Padres, Brewers, 2003-2010

Gervais, Lucien (Edward)
Lefty
Braves, 1913
Gessler, Henry (Homer)
Doc
Medical degree from Baltimore Medical College
Lefty: Brownie Schultz
He played under that alias before the majors.
Tigers, Superbas, Cubs, Red Sox, Senators, 1903-1911
Gettel, Al [Allen Jones]
Two Gun
Appeared in several television and movie westerns.
Yankees, Indians, White Sox, Senators, Giants, Cardinals, 1945-1955
Getz, Gus [Gustave]
Gee-Gee
His initials were G.G.
Doves, Robins, Reds, Indians, Pirates, 1909-1918
Getzien, Charles (H)
Pretzels
Either German heritage or ability to throw double curve.
Wolverines, Hoosiers, Beaneaters, Spiders, Browns, 1884-1892
Geyer, Jacob (Bowman)
Rube
Cardinals, 1910-1913
Geygan, James (Edward)
Chappie
A Prep school nickname.
Red Sox, 1924-1926
Giambi, Jason (Gilbert) {gee-AHM-bee}
Giambino
6'3", 250 lbs.; rhymes with Bambino.
Athletics, Yankees, Rockies, Indians, 1995-2014
Giard, Joe [Joseph Oscar]
Peco

Browns, Yankees, 1925-1927
Gibbs, Jerry (Dean)
Jake
Dead-Eye
　Based on a strong hit record.
Yankees, 1962-1971
Gibson, Bob [Robert]
Hoot
　Given in reference to cowboy actor, Hoot Gibson.
Cardinals, 1959-1975
Gibson, George (C)
Moon
　He played on a sandlot team named the "Mooneys."
Gibby: Hack
Pirates, Giants, 1905-1918
Gibson, Leighton (P)
Whitey
Athletics, 1888
Gil, Gerónimo {hair-ON-i-mo HEEL}
The Chief
Orioles, Rockies, 2001-2007
Gilbert, Alfred (Gideon)
Bill
Orioles, 1892
Gilbert, Drew (Edward)
Buddy
Reds, 1959
Gilbert, Harold (Joseph)
Tookie
Giants, 1950, 1953
Gilbert, Jack [John Robert]
Jackrabbit
Senators, Giants, Pirates, 1898-1904
Gile, Don [Donald Loren]
Bear
　6'6", 220 lbs.
Red Sox, 1959-1962
Giles, Ken [Kenneth Robert]
100 Miles Giles
Phillies, Astros, Blue Jays, 2014-
Gilhooley, Frank (Patrick)
Flash
　Speedy on the bases.
Cardinals, Yankees, Red Sox, 1911-1919
Gilkey, Bernard [Otis Bernard]
Innocent Until Proven
　Chris Berman pun on his last name.
Cardinals, Mets, Diamondbacks, Red Sox, Braves, 1990-2001
Gill, Harold (Edward)
Haddie
Reds, 1923
Gill, Johnny [John Wesley]
Patcheye
Indians, Senators, Cubs, 1927-1636
Gill, Warren (Darst)
Doc
Pirates, 1908
Gillespie, Bob [Robert William]
Bunch
Tigers, White Sox, Red Sox, 1944-1950
Gillespie, John (Patrick)
Silent John
Reds, 1922
Gilliam, Jim [James William]
Junior
　Bestowed by a Negro League manager.
Junebug
　Teammate bestowed.
Sweet Lips
　Tightly pursed lips when swinging at a pitch.
Devil
　He played pool and always asked, "Who's going to pay the Devil?"
Dodgers, 1953-1966
Gilliford, Paul (Gant)
Gorilla
　5'11", 210 lbs., built like a gorilla.
Orioles, 1967
Gilligan, Andrew (Bernard)
Barney: Mouse
Blues, Grays, Nationals, Wolverines, 1879-1888
Gilmore, Frank [Franklin T]
Shadow

Nationals, 1886-1888
Gilmore, Len [Leonard Preston]
  Meow
  Pirates, 1944
Gilson, Hal [Harold]
  Lefty
  Cardinals, Astros, 1968
Ginsberg, Myron (Nathan)
  Joe
  Little Joe
    Nicknamed Little Joe after his father, Joe.
  Tigers, Indians, Athletics, Orioles, White Sox, Red Sox, Mets, 1948-1962
Giordano, Tommy [Thomas Arthur]
  T-Bone
  Athletics, 1953
Giuliani, Angelo (John)
  Tony
    Assigned by Rogers Hornsby in his early days.
  Julio
    Given by some of the press.
  Browns, Senators, Dodgers, 1936-1943
Gladden, Dan [Clinton Daniel]
  Dazzle: The Dazzle Man: Wrench
  Giants, Twins, Tigers, 1983-1993
Glade, Fred [Frederick Monroe]
  Lucky
  Orphans, Browns, Highlanders, 1902-1908
Gladmon, James (Henry)
  Buck
  Quakers, Nationals, 1883-1886
Glaiser, John (Burke)
  Bert
  Tigers, 1920
Glasscock, Jack [John Wesley]
  Pebbly Jack
    Picked up and tossed stones in the infield.
  Blues, Outlaw Reds, Marooms, Hoosers, Giants, Browns, Pirates, Colonels, Senators, 1879-1895
Glaviano, Tommy [Thoomas Giatano]
  Rabbit
  Cardinals, Phillies, 1949-1953
Glazner, Charles (Franklin)
  Whitey
  Pirates, Phillies, 1920-1924
Gleason, William (J)
  Kid
    Only 5'7", under 160 lbs.
  Quakers, Phillies, Browns, Orioles, Giants, Tigers, White Sox, 1888-1912
Gleeson, Jim [James Joseph]
  Gee-Gee
  Indians, Cubs, Reds, 1936-1942
Gleich, Frank (Elmer)
  Inch
  Yankees, 1919-1920
Glenn, Burdette
  Bob
  Cardinals, 1920
Glenn, Ed [Edward C]
  Mouse
  Virginians, Alleghenys, Cowboys, Beaneaters, 1884-1888
Glenn, Harry (Melville)
  Husky
  Cardinals, 1915
Glenn, Joe [Joseph Charles]
  Gabby
  Yankees, Browns, Red Sox, 1932-1940
Glynn, Ed [Edward Paul]
  The Flushing Flash
  Tigers, Mets, Indians, Expos, 1975-1985
Goar, Joshua (Mercer)
  Jot
  Pirates, Reds, 1896-1898
Godley, Zack [Zachary Thomas]
  Bull
  Diamondbacks, Blue Jays, Red Sox, 2015-
Godwin, John (Henry)
  Bunny
    Reported by his daughter.
  Honest John
  Americans, 1905-1906

Goeddel, Erik (Van Norman) {guh-DEHL}
Goopy
Mets, Mariners, Dodgers, 2014-2018
Goins, Ryan (Matthew)
Go Go
Blue Jays, Royals, White Sox, 2013-
Goldschmidt, Paul (Edward)
America's First Baseman
Diamondbacks, Cardinals, 2011-
Goldsmith, Warren (M)
Wally
Kekiongas, Olympics, Westerns, 1871-1875
Goldstein, Leslie (Elmer)
Lon
    Resembled famous actor, Lon Chaney.
Reds, 1943, 1946
Goletz, Stan [Stanley]
Stash
    Common for a Stanley of Polish ancestry.
White Sox, 1941
Gomes, Jonny [Jonathan Johnson]
Ironsides
Hacksaw
    Given by Boston players for his playing style.
Devil Rays, Rays, Reds, Nationals, Athletics, Red Sox, Braves, Royals, 2003-2015
Gomes, Yan
Obi Yan: The Yanimal
Blue Jays, Indians, Nationals, 2012-
Gómez, Carlos (Argelis)
Go-Go: Cargo: El Titere
Mets, Twins, Brewers, Astros, Rangers, Rays, 2007-2019
Gómez, José (Luis)
Chile
    Born and died in Mexico, not Chile.
Phillies, Senators, 1935-1942
Gomez, Vernon (Louis)
Lefty
Goofy
    Given when he "invented" a revolving goldfish bowl ... for retired goldfish.
Gay Caballero
    Based on the Disney cartoon of that name. Goofy was not in it.
El Goofy
    A fun-loving goofy character (license plate - GOOF).
The Singular Señor: The Lanky Castilian: The Hibernian-Hildago
The Castilian Celt
    Based on his heritage.
Yankees, Senators, 1930-1943
Gonzales, Joe (Madrid)
Smokey
    Given as a reference to Smokey Joe Wood.
Goofy Joe
    A college nickname.
Red Sox, 1937
Gonzales, Wenceslao
Vince
    An abbreviation of the closest English pronunciation.
Senators, 1955
González, Adrián (Sabin)
El Titan
Rangers, Padres, Red Sox, Dodgers, Mets, 2004-2018
González, Álex [Alexander]
{gon-SAH-less}
Sea Bass
    Given while playing in Florida.
Marlins, Red Sox, Reds, Blue Jays, Braves, Brewers, Tigers, 1998-2014
González, Alexander
Chi Chi
Rangers, Rockies, 2015-
González, Angel (Manuel)
Andy
White Sox, Indians, Marlins, 2007-2009
González, Carlos (Eduardo)
Cargo
Athletics, Rockies, Indians, Cubs,

González, Erik
  2008-2019
González, Erik
  El Mago
  Indians, Pirates, 2016-
González, Eusebio (Miguel)
  Papo
    Widely known nickname... in Cuba.
  Red Sox, 1918
González, Giovany (Aramis)
  {gun-ZAH-lezz}
    Gio {JEE-oh}: Double G
  Athletics, Nationals, 2008-
González, Juan (Alberto)
  Igor
    From childhood, from Igor the Magnificent, a wrestler.
  Juan Gone
    Rhyming nickname, takeoff of his name.
  Rangers, Tigers, Indians, Royals, 1989-2005
Gonzalez, Luis (Emilio) {lou-EESE}
  Gonzo
    Either from his last name or from the Muppet.
  Astros, Cubs, Tigers, Diamondbacks, Dodgers, Marlins, 1990-2008
González, Miguel (Angel)
  El Jaliscience
  Orioles, White Sox, Rangers, 2012-2018
Good, Ralph (Nelson)
  Holy
  Doves, 1910
Good, Wilbur (David)
  Lefty
  Highlanders, Naps, Doves, Rustlers, Cubs, Phillies, White Sox, 1905-1918
Goodell, John (Henry William)
  Lefty
  White Sox, 1928
Gooden, Dwight (Eugene)
  Doc: The Franchise
  K-Man: Dr. K
    All based on his strikeout ability.
  Mets, Yankees, Indians, Devil Rays, Astros, 1984-2000
Goodman, Ival (Richard)
  Ol' Mate
  Reds, Cubs, 1935-1944
Goodwin, Claire (Vernon)
  Pep
  Packers, 1914-1915
Goolsby, Ray [Raymond Daniel]
  Ox
  Senators, 1946
Gordon, Joe [Joseph Lowell]
  Flash
    From the Sci-fi character.
  Yankees, Indians, 1938-1950
Gordon, Tom [Thomas]
  Flash
    From the Sci-fi character.
  Royals, Red Sox, Cubs, Astros, White Sox, Yankees, Phillies, Diamondbacks, 1988-2009
Gore, George (F)
  Piano Legs
  White Stockings, Giants, Browns, 1879-1892
Gorman, Howie [Howard Paul]
  Lefty
  Phillies, 1937-1938
Gorman, John (F)
  Stooping Jack
  Browns, Cowboys, Alleghenys, 1883-1884
Gorman, Tom D [Thomas David]
  Big Tom
    6'2", 200 lbs.
  Giants, 1939
Gorman, Tom P [Thomas Patrick]
  Gorfax
  Expos, Mets, Phillies, Padres, 1981-1987
Goslin, Leon (Allen)
  Goose
    A young goose is a gosling.
    Flapped his arms like a goose when chasing balls in the outfield.
  Senators, Browns, Tigers, 1921-1938

Gossage, Rich [Richard Michael]
　Goose
　　A reporter noted that his neck stuck out looking for a sign.
　White Sox, Pirates, Yankees, Padres, Cubs, Giants, Rangers, Athletics, Mariners, 1972-1994

Gosselin, Phil [Philip David]
　Goose: Barrels
　Braves, Diamondbacks, Pirates, Rangers, Reds, Phillies, 2013-

Gossett, John (Star)
　Dick
　Yankees, 1913-1914

Gould, Al [Albert Frank]
　Pudgy
　　Only 5'6", but 160 lbs.
　Indians, 1916-1917

Gozzo, Mauro (Paul)
　Goose
　Blue Jays, Indians, Twins, Mets, 1989-1994

Grabarkewitz, Billy (Cordell)
　Gabby
　　Big on jokes. Once said, "I was so tired last night, I fell asleep in mid sentence."
　Dodgers, Angels, Phillies, Cubs, Athletics, 1969-1975

Grabowski, John (Patrick)
　Nig
　White Sox, Yankees, Tigers, 1924-31

Grace, Mark (Eugene)
　Amazing
　　Probably more from the hymn than his career.
　Little Hurt
　Cubs, Diamondbacks, 1988-2003

Graff, Louis (George)
　Chappie
　Stars, 1890

Graham, Archibald (Wright)
　Moonlight
　　All zeros in his two-inning career. Known only for his character in the movie, *Field of Dreams*.
　Doc
　　A medical doctor.
　Giants, 1905

Graham, Arthur (William)
　Skinny
　　5'7", 162 lbs., not really skinny.
　Young Skinny
　　His father, Arthur Sr., was the original Skinny Graham.
　Red Sox, 1934-1935

Graham, Bert
　B.G.
　Browns, 1910

Graham, Dawson (Francis)
　Tiny
　　6'2", 185 lbs. If he's Tiny, we'd hate to see Large.
　Reds, 1914

Graham, George (Frederick)
　Peaches
　Broncos, Cubs, Doves, Rustlers, Phillies, 1902-1912

Graham, Kyle
　Skinny
　　6'2", only 172 lbs.
　Braves, Tigers, 1924-1929

Grandal, Yasmani
　YRG Jr
　Padres, Dodgers, Brewers, White Sox, 2012-

Granderson, Curtis
　Grandy Man
　　Rhymes with Candy Man.
　Tigers, Yankees, Mets, Dodgers, Blue Jays, Brewers, 2004-2019

Grant, Eddie [Edward Leslie]
　Harvard Eddie
　　Went to Harvard University and Harvard Law School.
　Naps, Phillies, Reds, Giants, 1905-1915

Grant, Jim [James Timothy]
　Mudcat
　　Given in the minor leagues.
　Indians, Twins, Dodgers, Expos, Cardinals, Athletics, Pirates,

Grant, Mark

1958-1971
Grant, Mark (Andrew)
Mud
Giants, Padres, Braves, Mariners, Astros, Rockies, 1984-1993
Grantham, George (Farley)
Boots
Cubs, Pirates, Reds, Giants, 1922-34
Grasso, Newton (Michael)
Mickey
    Given for a resemblance to Mickey Cochrane.
Giants, Senators, Indians, 1946-1955
Grate, Don
Buckeye
    Born and went to school in Ohio.
Phillies, 1945-1946
Graveman, Kendall (Chase)
Digger
Blue Jays, Athletics, Mariners, 2014-
Graves, Danny [Daniel Peter]
Baby-Faced Assassin
Indians, Reds, Mets, 1996-2006
Graves, Sid [Samuel Sidney]
Whitey
Braves, 1927
Gray, George (Edward)
Chummy
Pirates, 1899
Gray, Jim [James W]
Reddy
Alleghenys, Burghers, Pirates, 1884-1893
Gray, Sam [Samuel David]
Sad Sam
Athletics, Browns, 1924-1933
Gray, William (Denton)
Dolly
    From a song: Darling Nellie or Goodbye Dollie Gray.
Senators, 1909-1911
Greason, Bill [William Henry]
Booster
Cardinals, 1954
Grebeck, Craig (Allen)
Little Hurt
White Sox, Marlins, Angels, Blue Jays, Red Sox, 1990-2001
Green, Edward
Danny
Orphans, White Sox, 1898-1905
Green, Elijah (Jerry)
Pumpsie
    His mother's pet name for him.
Red Sox, Mets, 1959-1963
Green, Harvey (George)
Buck
Dodgers, 1935
Greenberg, Hank [Henry Benjamin]
Hammerin' Hank: The Big Moose
King Kong: Lanky: Greenie
Tigers, Pirates, 1930-1947
Greene, Nelson (George)
Lefty
Dodgers, 1924-1925
Greene, Tommy [Ira Thomas]
Jethro: Tee the Greene
Braves, Phillies, Astros, 1989-1997
Greenwell, Mike [Michael Lewis]
Gator
    Wrestled alligators in Florida.
New Green Monster
    A power hitter for Boston, home of the Green Monster left-field wall.
Red Sox, 1985-1996
Greer, Thurman (Clyde)
The Red Baron: Rusty
Rangers, 1994-2002
Gregerson, Luke [Lucas John]
Duke
Padres, Athletics, Astros, Cardinals, 2009-2019
Gregg, Dave [David Charles]
Highpockets
Naps, 1913
Gregg, Hal [Harold Dana]
Skeets
Dodgers, Pirates, Giants, 1943-1952
Gregorius, Mariekson (Julius)
Didi: Sir Didi
Reds, Diamondbacks, Yankees,

Phillies, 2012-
Gregory, Paul (Edwin)
Pop
White Sox, 1932-1933
Gremminger, Ed [Lorenzo Edward]
Battleship
Spiders, Beaneaters, Tigers,
1895-1904
Gremp, Lewis (Edward)
Buddy
Bees, Braves, 1940-1942
Grey, Romer (Carl)
Reddy
    Flaming red hair.
Pirates, 1903
Griesenbeck, Carlos (Phillipe)
Tim
Cardinals, 1920
Griffey, Ken Jr. [George Kenneth]
The Franchise : Rifleman
The Kid: Junior
The Natural
    A natural swing.
Mariners, Reds, White Sox,
1989-2010
Griffin, Arthur (Joseph)
A.J.
Athletics, Rangers, 2012-2017
Griffin, Doug [Douglas Lee]
Dude
Skeleton
    Luis Tiant said he was thin and lightweight.
Angels, Red Sox, 1970-1977
Griffin, Francis (Arthur)
Pug
Athletics, Giants, 1917, 1920
Griffin, James (Linton)
Hank: Pepper
Cubs, Rustlers, Braves, 1911-1912
Griffin, Tobias (Charles)
Sandy
Gothams, Broncos, Statesmen, Browns, 1884-1893
Griffith, Bert [Bartholonew Joseph]
Buck

Robins, Senators, 1922-1924
Griffith, Clark (Calvin)
Old Fox
    Based on cunning and guile.
Browns, Reds, Colts, Orphans, White Sox, Highlanders, Senators,
1891-1914
Grimes, Burleigh (Arland)
Ol' Stubblebeard
    Unshaven appearances.
Pirates, Robins, Giants, Braves, Cardinals, Cubs, Yankees, 1916-1934
Grimes, Austin (Roy)
Bummer
Giants, 1920
Grimes, Oscar (Ray)
Bummer
Red Sox, Cubs, Phillies, 1920-1926
Grimm, Charlie [Charles John]
Jolly Cholly
    Had fun playing and managing baseball.
Athletics, Cardinals, Pirates, Cubs,
1916-1936
Grimshaw, Myron (Frederick)
Moose
    Awkward looking.
Americans, 1905-1907
Grimsley, Ross Jr. (Albert)
Animal
    Teammate given for lack of hygiene. Also, habit of mooning passersby from the team bus.
Scuz: Crazy Eyes
Reds, Orioles, Expos, Indians,
1971-1982
Griner, Donald (Dexter)
Dan: Rusty
Cardinals, Robins, 1912-1918
Groh, Henry (Knight)
Heinie
Giants, Reds, Pirates, 1912-1927
Groh, Lewis (Carl)
Silver
Athletics, 1919
Groom, Bob [Robert]

The Toothpick Twirler: Sir Robert
Senators, Terriers, Browns, Indians,
1909-1918
Groom, Wedsel (Gary)
Buddy
Tigers, Marlins, Athletics, Orioles,
Yankees, Diamondbacks, 1992-2005
Groskloss, Howard (Hoffman)
Howdy
Pirates, 1930-1932
Gross, Ewell
Turkey
Red Sox, 1925
Groth, Ernie [Ernest John]
Dango
Cubs, 1904
Grove, Robert (Moses)
Lefty: Old Mose
Groves
> The usual reference by Connie Mack.
Athletics, Red Sox, 1925-1941
Grover, Charlie [Charles Byrd]
Bugs
Tigers, 1913
Grubbs, Tom [Thomas Dillard]
Judge
Giants, 1920
Grube, Frank [Franklin Thomas]
Hans
> From teammates for his Pennsylvania Dutch heritage.
White Sox, Browns, 1931-1941.
Gruber, Kelly (Wayne)
Xanthos
> Greek: "blond male"; refers to his long blonde hair.
Goob
> Given by Toronto teammates
Chin
> Given by teammates for his oversized, protruding chin.
Blue Jays, Angels, 1984-1993
Grunwald, Al [Alfred Henry]
Stretch
Pirates, Athletics, 1955, 1959

Gsellman, Robert (John) {guh-SELL-man}
G-Man
Mets, 2016-
Guardado, Eddie [Edward Adrain] {gwar-DAH-doe}
Everyday Eddie
> From his durable arm with the Twins
Twins, Mariners, Reds, Rangers, 1993-2009
Guerra, Fermin {GARE-ah}
Mike: Cuba's Mighty Mite
Senators, Athletics, Red Sox, 1937-51
Guerra, Junior (J)
Cabezon
White Sox, Brewers, Diamondbacks, 2015-
Guerrero, Vlad [Vladimir]
Vlad the Impaler
> From a Romanian Prince Vlad, for how he treated his defeated enemies.
Expos, Angels, Rangers, Orioles, 1996-2011
Guese, Theodore
Whitey
Reds, 1901
Guidry, Ron [Ronald Ames] {GID-ree}
Gator
Louisiana Lightning
> From Lafayette, Louisiana.
Yankees, 1975-1988
Guinn, Drannon (Eugene)
Skip
Braves, Astros, 1968-1971
Guise, Witt (Orison)
Lefty
Old Lefthander
> By a reporter in the minors.
Reds, 1940
Gumbert, Harry (Edwards)
Gunboat
Giants, Cardinals, Reds, Pirates, 1935-1950
Gunkel, Woodward (William)

Red
Indians, 1916
Gurriel, Yuli [Yulieski] {goo-ree-ELL}
La Piña
Astros, 2016-
Gust, Ernie [Ernest Herman Frank]
Red
Browns, 1911
Guth, Charles (Henry)
Bucky
Twins, 1972
Gutiérrez, César (Dario)
Cocoa
Giants, Tigers, 1967-1971
Gutierrez, Franklin (Rafael)
Death to Flying Things
    Given by sportscaster Dave
    Niehaus after a diving catch.
Indians, Mariners, Dodgers,
2005-2017
Gutiérrez, Joaquin (Fernando)
Jackie
Red Sox, Orioles, Phillies, 1983-1988
Gutiérrez, Juan (Carlos)
J.C.
Astros, Diamondbacks, Royals
Angels, Giants, 2007-2014
Guyer, Brandon (Eric)
B.G.
Rays, Indians, 2011-2018
Guzmán, Ronald (Enmanuel)
{gooz-MAHN}
Condor
Rangers, 2018-
Guzmán, Dionini (Ramon)
Johnny
    Closest English pronunciation of
    his Spanish name.
Athletics, 1991-1992
Gwosdz, Doug (Wayne) {GOO-sh}
Eyechart
    The back of his jersey looked like
    an eye chart.
Padres, 1981-1984
Gwynn, Tony Sr. [Anthony Keith]
Captain Video
    Used video before it was popular
    to study his swing.
Mr. Padre
    Beloved by the city; played his
    entire career with 1 team.
Padres, 1982-2001
Haas, Bruno
Boon
Athletics, 1915
Haas, Bryan (Edmund)
Moose
    Given at birth by his father.
Brewers, Athletics, 1976-1987
Haas, George (William)
Mule
    Minor league writer said his bat
    had the kick of a mule.
Pirates, Athletics, White Sox,
1925-1938
Habenicht, Bob [Robert Julius]
Hobby
Cardinals, Browns, 1951, 1953
Hach, Irv [Irvin William]
Major
Colonels, 1897
Hack, Stan [Stanley Camfield]
Smiling Stan
    Good nature, handsome looks.
Cubs, 1932-1947
Hackett, Jim [James Joseph]
Sunny Jim
    Amiable personality.
Cardinals, 1902-1903
Hackett, Mortimer (Martin)
Mert
Beaneaters, Cowboys, Hoosiers,
1883-1887
Haddix, Harvey
Kitten
    A minor league manager called
    him a second Harry "the Cat"
    Brecheen.
Cardinals, Phillies, Redlegs, Pirates,
Orioles, 1952-1965
Haddock, George (Silas)
Gentleman George

Scornful: he had a gentlemanly approach to the game.
Nationals, Bisons, Reds, Grooms, Phillies, Senators, 1888-1894
Hadley, Irving (Darius)
Bump
    Had a resemblance to comic-strip character, Bumpus.
Bumps
    Given by a teammate when he had the mumps.
Senators, White Sox, Browns, Yankees, Giants, Athletics, 1926-41
Haefner, Milton (Arnold)
Mickey
Senators, White Sox, Braves, 1943-50
Hafey, Charles (James)
Chick
Cardinals, Reds, 1924-1937
Hafey, Daniel (Albert)
Bud
White Sox, Pirates, Reds, Phillies, 1935-1939
Hafey, Tom [Thomas Francis]
Heave-O: The Arm
Giants, Browns, 1939, 1944
Hafner, Travis (Lee)
Project
    Given by Cleveland scouts while getting him to play for them.
Donkey
    From the way he looked when he ran the bases.
Pronk
    Combination of his other two nicknames.
Rangers, Indians, Yankees, 2002-13
Hageman, Kurt (Moritz)
Casey
Red Sox, Cardinals, Cubs, 1911-1914
Hagerman, Zerah (Zequiel)
Rip
Chelito
    A Cuban nickname from a female admirer.
ZZ: ZeeZee: Rip Zip
    All from sportswriters.
Cubs, Naps, Indians, 1909-1916
Hahn, Frank (George)
Noodles
    Acquired as a youngster, possibly from bringing his father noodle soup for lunch every day.
Reds, Highlanders, 1899-1906
Haines, Henry (Luther)
Hinkey
Yankees, 1923
Haines, Jesse (Joseph)
Pop: Ol' Pop
    Both because he was old compared to his teammates.
Reds, Cardinals, 1918-1937
Haislip, Jim [James Clifton]
Slim
    6'1" but only 186 lbs.
Phillies, 1913
Hale, Arvel (Odell)
Bad News
    Given by minor league writers after 5 homers in 5 days.
Sammy: Bing
Chief
    He was partially Choctaw Indian.
Indians, Red Sox, Giants, 1931-1941
Hale, George (Wagner)
Ducky
Browns, 1914-1918
Hale, Ray (Luther)
Dad
    Strange; played in his 20s.
Beaneaters, Orioles, 1902
Hale, Walter (William)
Chip
Twins, Dodgers, 1989-1997
Haley, Raymond (Timothy)
Pat
Red Sox, Athletics, 1915-1917
Hall, Archibald (W)
Al
Trojans, Blues, 1879-1880
Hall, Bill [William Bernard]
Beanie

Superbas, 1913
Hall, Charley [Charles Louis]
Sea Lion
> Given by Boston fans for his hoarse coaching voice.

Reds, Red Sox, Cardinals, Tigers, 1906-1918
Hall, Charlie [Charles Walter]
Doc
Metropolitans, 1887
Hall, Herb [Herbert Silas]
Iron Duke
Tigers, 1918
Hall, Tom (Edward)
The Blade
Twins, Reds, Mets, Royals, 1968-77
Halladay, Roy [Harry Leroy]
{HAL-ah-day}
Doc
> Pitch control reminded others of Doc Holliday. Coined by Tom Cheek, Toronto play-by-play announcer.

Blue Jays, Phillies, 1998-2013
Hallahan, Bill [William Anthony]
Wild Bill
> A leader in walks and wild pitches.

Moon
> From catcher Earl Smith: round face, close-cropped hair, pronounced ears.

Pug: Lefty
Sweet William
> From sportswriters when he pitched well.

Cardinals, Reds, Phillies, 1925-1938
Halligan, William (E)
Jocko
Bisons, Reds, Orioles, 1890-1892
Hallstrom, Charlie [Charles Emil]
Swedish Wonder
> From Jönköping, Sweden.

Grays, 1885
Hamann, Elmer (Joseph)
Doc

Indians, 1922
Hamby, Jim [James Sanford]
Cracker
Giants, 1926-1927
Hamels, Cole [Colbert Michael]
Hollywood
> From a teammate because he was "so good on the big stage."

Phillies, Rangers, Cubs, 2006-
Hamilton, Billy R
B-Ham
Bone
Reds, Royals, Braves, Mets, Cubs, 2013-
Hamilton, Billy [William Robert]
Sliding Billy
> Self named for complaining when his 914 stolen bases was not recognized as being greater than Ty Cobb. He slid head-first.

Cowboys, Phillies, Beaneters, 1888-1901
Hamilton, Josh [Joshua Holt]
The Great Hambino
Athletics, 1952-1953
Hamlin, Lewis (Dennison)
Luke
Hot Potato
> Had a habit of juggling the ball while pitching.

Tigers, Dodgers, Pirates, Athletics, 1933-1944
Hammel, Jason (Aaron)
Hammer
Devil Rays, Rays, Rockies, Orioles, Cubs, Athletics, Royals, 2006-2018
Hammond, Walter (Charles)
Jack: Wobby
Indians, Pirates, 1915, 1922
Hamner, Ralph (Conant)
Bruz
White Sox, Cubs, 1946-1949
Hampton, Isaac (Bernard)
Ike
Mets, Angels, 1974-1979
Hancken, Morris (Medlock)

Buddy
: Athletics, 1940
Hand, Brad [Bradley Richard]
: Brotato
: Marlins, Padres, Indians, 2011-
Handiboe, Aloysius (James)
: Mike: Coalyard Mike
: Highlanders, 1911
Handiboe, Jim [James Edward]
: Nick
: Alleghenys, 1886
Handley, Lee (Elmer)
: Jeep
: Reds, Pirates, Phillies, 1936-1947
Hands, Bill [William Alfred]
: Froggy
: Style reminiscent of Don Larsen, who had the nickname.
: Giants, Cubs, Twins, Rangers, 1965-1975
Haney, Fred (Girard)
: Pudge
: 5'6" but 170 lbs. Given by teammates.
: Tigers, Red Sox, Cubs, Cardinals, 1922-1929
Hanlon, Bill [William Joseph]
: Big Bill
: 6', 175 lbs.
: Cubs, 1903
Hanlon, Ed [Edwad Hugh]
: Foxy Ned
: Invented new strategies: hit and run, squeeze play, sacrifice bunt, double steal, and Baltimore chop.
: Blues, Wolverines, Alleghenys, Burghers, Pirates, Orioles, 1880-1892
Hannah, James (Harrison)
: Truck
: Perhaps because he was built like one.
: Harry
: Given to avoid confusion with his father, James J.
: Yankees, 1918-1920
Hannahan, Jack [John Joseph]
: Supermanahan
: Tigers, Athletics, Mariners, Indians, Reds, 2006-2014
Hansen, Andy [Andrew Viggo]
: Swede
: Despite his Danish ancestry.
: Giants, Phillies, 1944-1953
Hansen, Roy E (Emil Frederick)
: Snipe
: Was sent on a snipe hunt during his first spring training.
: Phillies, Browns, 1930-1935
Hansen, Roy I (Inglof)
: Ing
: Senators, 1918
Hanson, Alen (Rery)
: El Chamaquito
: Pirates, White Sox, Giants, Blue Jays, 2016-2019
Hanson, Earl (Sylvester)
: Ollie
: Cubs, 1921
Happ, James (Anthony)
: J.A.
: Initials, pronounced as 'Jay.'
: Happer
: Phillies, Astros, Mariners, Blue Jays, Pirates, Yankees, 2007-
Happenny, John (Clifford)
: Cliff
: White Sox, 1923
Harbridge, Bill [William Albert]
: Yaller Bill
: Dark Blues, Hartfords, White Stockings, Trojans, Quakers, Outlaw Reds, 1875-1884
Harder, Mel [Melvin Leroy]
: Chief
: For his leadership ability.
: Wimpy
: from teammates because of a fondness for hamburgers.
: Indians, 1928-1947
Hardgrove, William (Henry)
: Pat
: White Sox, 1918

Hardin, William (Edgar)
Bud
Cubs, 1952
Harding, Charlie [Charles Harold]
Slim
6'2", 172 lbs.
Tigers, 1913
Hardy, Alex [David Alexander]
Dooney
Orphans, Cubs, 1902-1903
Hardy, Francis (Joseph)
Red
Giants, 1951
Hardy, James (Jerry)
J.J.
Brewers, Twins, Orioles, 2005-2017
Hargrave, Eugene (Franklin)
Bubbles
One theory: an effervescent way of suggesting and guiding.
Cubs, Reds, Yankees, 1913-1930
Hargrave, William (McKinley)
Pinky
Senators, Browns, Tigers, Braves, 1923-1933
Hargrove, Mike [Dudley Michael]
The Human Rain Delay
Constantly left the batter's box to make adjustments.
Rangers, Padres, Indians, 1974-1985
Harkins, John (Joseph)
Pa
Blues, Grays, Orioles, 1884-1888
Harkness, Frederick (Harvey)
Spec
Very round face. Spec is German for bacon or bacon fat.
Naps, 1910-1911
Harkness, Thomas (William)
Tim
Dodgers, Mets, 1961-1964
Harley, Henry (Risk)
Dick
Beaneaters, 1905
Harmon, Bob [Robert Green]
Hickory Bob
Cardinals, Pirates, 1909-1908
Harper, Bill [William Homer]
Blue Sleeve
Browns, 1911
Harper, Bryce (Aron Max)
Bam-Bam: Mondo: Big Kid
Nationals, Phillies, 2012-
Harper, Charles (William)
Jack
Self-adopted as a youngster.
Spiders, Cardinals, Browns, Reds, Cubs, 1899-1906
Harrah, Colbert (Dale) {HAIR-ah}
Toby
Senators, Rangers, Indians, Yankees, 1969-1986
Harrell, Oscar (Martin)
Slim
6'3" but only 180 lbs.
Athletics, 1912
Harrell, Ray [Raymond James]
Cowboy
Born in Texas.
Cardinals, Cubs, Phillies, Pirates, Giants, 1935-1945
Harrelson, Derrel (McKinley)
Bud
Given by his brother who couldn't pronounce Derrel. Called him Brother, which morphed into Bud.
Mighty Mouse
Twiggy
Light weight and short stature.
Mini-Hawk
He started at the tail end of Hawk Harrelson's career.
Mets, Phillies, Rangers, 1965-1980
Harrelson, Ken [Kenneth Smith]
Henrietta Hawk
Hawk
From Dick Howser for the shape of his nose. Looked like a cartoon character popular at the time.
Athletics, Senators, Red Sox, Indians, 1963-1971

Harrington, Charles (Michael)
Mickey
Phillies, 1963

Harris, Alonzo
Candy
Astros, 1967

Harris, Charles
Bubba
From Alabama.
Athletics, Indians, 1948-1951

Harris, Dave [David Stanley]
Sheriff
Was once a deputy chasing mule thieves.
Braves, White Sox, Senators, 1925-34

Harris, Herb [Herbert Benjamin]
Hub
Lefty
Phillies, 1936

Harris, Hernando (Petrocelli)
Pep
Angels, 1996-1998

Harris, Joe [Joseph]
Moon
Used during World War I.
Yankees, Indians, Red Sox, Senators, Pirates, Robins, 1914-1928

Harris, Maurice (Charles)
Mickey
Childhood nickname used by his father.
Red Sox, Senators, Indians, 1940-52

Harris, Stanley (Raymond)
Bucky
A friend said he bucked like a bronco playing basketball.
Senators, Tigers, 1919-1931

Harris, Walter (Francis)
Buddy
Astros, 1970-1971

Harrison, Josh [Joshua Isaiah]
J Hay
Pirates, Tigers, Nationals, 2011-

Harriss, William (Jennings Bryan)
Slim
6'6" but only 180 lbs.
Athletics, Red Sox, 1920-1928

Harrist, Earl
Irish
Reds, White Sox, Senators, Browns, Tigers, 1945-1953

Hart, James (Henry)
Hub
Gained in college because he was central to most plays.
White Sox, 1905-1907

Hart, Robert (Lee)
Billy
Browns, 1890

Hart, Tom [Thomas Henry]
Bushy
Statesmen, 1891

Hartenstein, Chuck [Charles Oscar]
Twiggy
Slight frame reminiscent of Twiggy, the model.
Cubs, Pirates, Cardinals, Red Sox, Blue Jays, 1965-1977

Harter, Frank [Franklin Pierce]
Chief
Reds, Hoosiers, 1912-1914

Harting, Edward
Jumbo
5'9", 213 lbs.
Browns, 1886

Hartley, Grover (Allen)
Slick
Based on his range and quickness at shortstop.
Giants, Terriers, Browns, Red Sox, Indians, 1911-1934

Hartley, Walter (Scott)
Chick
Giants, 1902

Hartman, Frederick (Orrin)
Dutch
Pirates, Browns, Giants, White Sox, Cardinals, 1894-1902

Hartman, J C
Cool
Colt 45s, 1962-1963

Hartnett, Charles (Leo)

Gabby
    Newsman reference to "that gabby kid" at his first training camp.
Old Tomato Face
    In photos, his face reminds one...
Dowdy
    Local nickname as a child.
Cubs, Giants, 1922-1941

Hartnett, Pat [Patrick J]
Happy
Browns, 1890

Hartsel, Tully (Frederick)
Topsy
    Sportswriter coined, "You're as light as Topsy of Uncle Tom's Cabin is black."
Colonels, Reds, Orphans, Athletics, 1898-1911

Hartsfield, Roy (Thomas)
Spec
    Optical technician in the navy.
Braves, 1950-1952

Hartung, Clint [Clinton Clarence]
Floppy
The Hondo Hurricane
    From Hondo, Texas.
Giants, 1947-1952

Harvel, Luther (Raymond)
Red
Indians, 1928

Harvey, Ervin (King)
Zaza
Orphans, White Sox, Blues, Broncos, 1900-1902

Harvey, Matt [Matthew Edward]
Real Deal
    Given by Dwight Gooden after seeing him pitch.
The Dark Knight of Gotham
    A magazine cover compared him to Batman.
Mets, Reds, Angels, Royals, 2012-

Hasbrook, Robert (Lyndon)
Ziggy
White Sox, 1916-1917

Haseley, Adam (Donald)
Rev
Phillies, 2019-

Haslin, Michael (Joseph)
Mickey
Phillies, Bees, Giants, 1933-1938

Hassemaer, Bill [William Louis]
Roaring Bill
Senators, Colonels, 1894-1896

Hassett, John (Aloysius)
Buddy
The Bronx Thrush
    Had a great tenor voice.
Dodgers, Bees, Braves, Yankees, 1936-1942

Hatcher, Michael (Vaughn)
Mickey
Dodgers, Twins, 1979-1990

Hatfield, Gil [Gilbert]
Colonel
Bisons, Giants, Reds, Statesmen, Grooms, Colonels, 1885-1895

Haughey, Chris [Christopher Francis]
Bud
Dodgers, 1943

Hauser, Arnold (George)
Peewee
    Only 5'6", 145 lbs.
Stub
    He was short for a ball player.
Cardinals, Whales, 1910-1915

Hauser, Joe [Joseph John]
Unser Choe
    German, meaning "our Joe."
    From minor leagues.
Athletics, Indians, 1922-1929

Hawke, Bill [William Victor]
Dick
Browns, Orioles, 1892-1894

Hawker, Art [Arthur J]
Sunday
Ward's Wonders, 1890

Hawks, Nelson (Louis)
Chicken
    Based on the Chicken Hawk.
Yankees, Phillies, 1921, 1925

Hawley, Emerson (Pink)
 Pink
 Browns, Pirates, Reds, Giants, Brewers, 1892-1901
Haworth, Homer (Harold)
 Howie: Cully
 Indians, 1915
Hayden, Eugene (Franklin)
 Lefty
 Redlegs, 1958
Hayes, Frankie [Franklin Witman]
 Blimp
  Had nothing to do with size: 6', 185 lbs.
 Athletics, Browns, Indians, White Sox, Red Sox, 1933-1947
Hayes, Jim [James Millard]
 Whitey
 Senators, 1935
Hayes, Minter (Carney)
 Jackie
 Senators, White Sox, 1927-1940
Hayes, Von (Francis)
 Five-For-One
  Went to Phillies in a five for one deal. He was the one.
 Indians, Phillies, Angels, 1981-1992
Hayworth, Myron (Claude)
 Red
 Browns, 1944-1945
Hazle, Bob [Robert Sidney]
 Hurricane
  Named after Hurricane Hazel which had just hit.
 Redlegs, Braves, Tigers, 1955-1958
Hazleton, Willard (Carpenter)
 Doc
 Cardinals, 1902
Healy, John (J)
 Long John
  He was tall and slim.
 Egyptian
  From teammates. Hometown— Cairo (Illinois, not Egypt)
 Maroons, Hoosiers, Nationals, White Stockings, Maumees, Orioles, Colonels, 1885-1892
Heard, Johosie
 Jay
 Orioles, 1954
Hearn, Elmer (Lafayette)
 Bunny
 Braves, 1926-1929
Hearn, Jim [James Tolbert]
 Jumbo Jim
 Cardinals, Giants, Phillies, 1947-1959
Heath, Minor (Wilson)
 Mickey
 Reds, 1931-1932
Heaverlo, Dave [David Wallace]
 {HAVE-er-low}
 Kojak
 Giants, Athletics, Mariners, 1975-81
Hebert, Wally [Wallace Andrew]
 {AY-bare}
 Preacher
  Possibly from wearing a preacher's hat in first grade.
 Mississippi Mudcat
  Self described, but dropped because there was another with that nickname.
 Browns, Pirates, 1931-1943
Hebner, Richie [Richard Joseph]
 The Gravedigger
  His job at a cemetery run by his father.
 Digger
  Shortened form.
 Hacker: Hack
  For his exuberance at the plate.
 Pirates, Phillies, Mets, Tigers, Cubs, 1968-1985
Hechavarría, Adeiny
 {a-DAY-knee etch-eh-var-EE-ah}
 La Pantera
 Blue Jays, Marlins, Rays, Pirates, Yankees, Mets, Braves, 2012-
Hedlund, Mike [Michael Dvid]
 Red
 Indians, Royals, 1965-1972
Heffner, Don [Donald Henry]

Jeep
Yankees, Browns, Athletics, Tigers, 1934-1944
Hegan, Jim [James Edward]
Shanty
Indians, Tigers, Phillies, Giants, Cubs, 1941-1960
Hehl, Herman (Charles)
Jake
Robins, 1918
Heidrick, Emmet [Robert Emmet]
Snags
    Exceptional range in center field.
Kid
    Minor league name as a teen.
Spiders, Perfectos, Cardinals, Browns, 1898-1908
Heifer, Frank [Franklin]
Heck
Red Stockings, 1875
Heileman, John (George)
Chink
Reds, 1901
Heilmann, Harry (Edwin)
{HILE-man}
Slug: Harry the Horse
Tigers, Reds, 1914-1932
Heimach, Fred [Frederick Amos]
Lefty: Fritz
Athletics, Red Sox, Yankees, Robins, Dodgers, 1920-1933
Heine, William (Henry)
Bud
Giants, 1921
Heise, Clarence (Edward)
Lefty
Cardinals, 1934
Heismann, Christian (Ernst)
Crese
Reds, Orioles, 1901-1902
Heitmuller, William (Frederick)
Heinie
    Popular nickname for German ancestry.
Athletics, 1909-1910
Held, Mel [Melvin Nicholas]

Country
Orioles, 1956
Helfrich, Emory (Wilbur)
Ty
Tip-Tops, 1915
Hellickson, Jeremy (Robert)
Hellboy
Rays, Diamondbacks, Phillies, Orioles, Nationals, 2010-2019
Helton, Todd (Lynn)
The Todfather
    A pun on the Godfather franchise.
Highway To
    A Chris Berman-ism: Refers to Highway to Hell(ton) by the rock band, AC/DC.
Rockies, 1997-2013
Heltzel, William (Wade)
Heinie
Braves, Phillies, 1943-1944
Hembree, Heath [Richard Heath]
Heater
Giants, Red Sox, Phillies, 2013-
Hemming, George (Earl)
Old Wax Figger
Infants, Ward's Wonders, Grooms, Reds, Colonels, Orioles, 1890-1897
Hemp, William (H)
Ducky
Colonels, Alleghenys, Stars, 1887-1890
Hemphill, Charlie [Charles Judson]
Eagle Eye
Perfectos, Spiders, Americans, Bronchos, Browns, Highlanders, 1899-1911
Hemsley, Ralston (Burdett)
Rollie: Rollicking Rollie
Pirates, Cubs, Reds, Browns, Indians, Yankees, Phillies, 1928-1947
Henderson, Bernie
Barnyard
Indians, 1921
Henderson, Dave [David Lee]
Hendu

Shortened from his last name.
Mariners, Red Sox, Giants, Athletics, Royals, 1981-1994

Henderson, Rickey (Nelson Henley)
The Franchise
The Man of Steal
Based on his records for stolen bases and his speed, like Superman.
Athletics, Yankees, Blue Jays, Padres, Angels, Mets, Mariners, Red Sox, Dodgers, 1979-2003

Henderson, Steve [Steven Curtis]
Stevie Wonder
Mets, Cubs, Mariners, Athletics, Astros, 1977-1988

Hendrick, George (Andrew)
Silent George
Uneasy when talking to media.
Athletics, Indians, Padres, Cardinals, Pirates, Angels, 1971-1988

Hendrick, Harvey
Gink
Yankees, Indians, Robins, Reds, Cardinals, Cubs, Phillies, 1923-1934

Hendricks, Ed [Edward]
Big Ed
6'3", 200 lbs.
Giants, 1910

Hendricks, Kyle (Christian)
The Professor
Cubs, 2014-

Hendriks, Liam (Johnson)
Slydah
Twins, Blue Jays, Royals, Athletics, 2011-

Hengel, Emery (J)
Moxie
Chicago/Pittsburgh, White Caps, Bisons, 1884-1885

Henke, Tom [Thomas Anthony]
{HEN-key}
The Terminator
From teammate John Cerutti after seeing the movie. A reliever who struck out more than 1 batter per inning.
Rangers, Blue Jays, Cardinals, 1982-1995

Henline, Walter (John)
Butch
Giants, Phillies, Robins, White Sox, 1921-1931

Hennessey, George
Three Star
Browns, Phillies, Cubs, 1937-1945

Henning, Ernest (Herman)
Pete
Packers, 1914-1915

Henrich, Frank (Wilde)
Fritz
Phillies, 1924

Henrich, Tommy [Thomas David]
The Clutch
From teammates: Could make key hits in the clutch.
Old Reliable
Delivered key hits for the 1947 Yankees.
Yankees, 1937-1950

Henriksen, Olaf
Swede
From Denmark, not Sweden.
The Little General
Given by friends and teammates when younger.
The Owl
From childhood friends.
Kid
From childhood friends.
Little Henriksen
One of nine kids in the family.
Red Sox, 1911-1917

Henry, Earl (Clifford)
Hook
Indians, 1944-1945

Henry, Floyd (Bluford)
Butch
Astros, Rockies, Expos, Red Sox, Mariners, 1992-1999

Henry, Frank (John)
Dutch

Browns, Robins, Giants, White Sox, 1921-1930
Henry, Frederick (Marshall)
Snake
Braves, 1922-1923
Henry, John (Park)
Bull
Senators, Braves, 1910-1918
Hensiek, Phil [Philip Frank]
Sid
Senators, 1935
Herbert, Ernie [Earn Albert]
Tex
Reds, Terriers, 1913-1915
Heredia, Guillermo
{gee-YAIR-moe her-ED-dee-uh}
El Conde
Mariners, Rays, Pirates, Mets, 2016-
Herman, Floyd (Caves)
Babe
From a minor league fan. He reminded her of a prize fighter named Babe Herman.
Robins, Reds, Cubs, Pirates, Tigers, Dodgers, 1926-1945
Hernández, Adrián (R)
The Little Duke
Had a similar pitching style to Orlando Hernández.
El Duquecito
Spanish for The Little Duke.
Yankees, Brewers, 2001-2004
Hernández, César (Augusto)
Cesita
Phillies, Indians, 2013-
Hernández, Enrique (J)
Kiké {KEE-kay}
Astros, Marlins, Dodgers, 2014-
Hernández, Félix (Abraham Graham)
King Felix
Coined by sports bloggers from Single-A for potential.
Mariners, 2005-2019
Hernández, Jacinto
Jackie
Anglicized version of his first name.
Angels, Twins, Royals, Pirates, 1965-1973
Hernandez, Keith
Mex
Origin mis-characterized because of his name.
Cardinals, Mets, Indians, 1974-1990
Hernández, Orlando (P)
El Duque
The same nickname as his father; means The Duke.
Yankees, White Sox, Dia-mondbacks, Mets, 1998-2007
Hernández, Roberto
Known as Fausto Carmona from 2006-2011
Indians, Rays, Phillies, Dodgers, Astros, Braves, 2006-2016
Hernández, Salvador (Jose)
Chico
Cubs, 1942-1943
Hernandez, Xavier [Francis Xavier]
X-Man
Blue Jays, Astros, Yankees, Reds, Rangers, 1989-1998
Herndon, Harry (Francis)
Junior
Padres, 2001
Herrell, Walt (William)
Reds
Senators, 1911
Herrera, José (Concepcion)
Loco
Astros, Expos, 1967-1970
Herrera, Juan (Francisco)
Pancho
Usually a nickname for Francisco Panchón. His nickname in Cuba.
Ponchón
Behind his back, referring to his many strikeouts.
Phillies, 1958-1961
Herrera, Odúbel [David Odúbel]
{oh-DOO-bull air-RARE-uh}

113

El Torito
: Means Little Bull. Given by father because he was short and strong.
Phillies, 2015-

Herrera, Procopio
Bobby: Tito
Browns, 1951

Herrera, Ramón
Mike
Paito
: A Cuban nickname.
Red Sox, 1925-1926

Herriage, William (Troy)
Dutch
Athletics, 1956

Herring, Art (Arthur L)
Red: Sandy
Tigers, Dodgers, White Sox, Pirates, 1929-1947

Herring, Bill [William Francis]
Smoke: Smokey: Smoked Herring
Tip-Tops, 1915

Herring, Silas (Clarke)
Lefty
Senators, 1899, 1904

Herrmann, Chris [Christopher Ryan]
Herm the Worm
Twins, Diamondbacks, Mariners, Athletics, 2012-2019

Herrmann, Marty [Martin John]
Lefty
Robins, 1918

Hershberger, Willard (McKee)
Bill
Little Slug
: He hit .345 in 1939.
Reds, 1938-1940

Hershiser, Orel (Leonard)
Bulldog
: Named by Tommy Lasorda for fierce competitive spirit.
Dodgers, Indians, Giants, Mets, 1983-2000

Herzog, Charles (Lincoln)
Buck
Choke 'em Charley
: From his motto, "When you get 'em down, choke 'em."
Giants, Doves, Rustlers, Reds, Braves, Cubs, 1908-1920

Herzog, Dorrel (Norman Elvert)
The White Rat
Whitey
: Sportswriter named for light blonde hair.
Whiteyball
: A style of play instituted as a manager.
Senators, Athletics, Orioles, Tigers, 1956-1963

Heusser, Ed [Edward Burlton]
The Wild Elk of the Wasatch
Cardinals, Phillies, Athletics, Reds, 1935-1948

Heyward, Jason (Alias)
The J-Hey Kid
Braves, Cardinals, Cubs, 2010-

Hickey, Jim [James Robert]
Sid
Braves, 1942, 1944

Hickman, Charlie [Charles Taylor]
Cheerful Charlie
: Fan favorite with no personal enemies.
Piano Legs
: 5'9", 215 lbs., thick legs.
Cheerful Hick
: A measure of fan appreciation.
Beaneaters, Giants, Americans, Bronchos, Naps, Tigers, Senators, White Sox, 1897-1908

Hickman, Jim [James Lucius]
Gentleman Jim
Mets, Dodgers, Cubs, Cardinals, 1962-1974

Hicks, Aaron (Michael)
A-A-Ron
Twins, Yankees, 2013-

Hicks, Clarence (Walter)
Buddy
Tigers, 1956

Higgins, Eddie [Thomas Edward]
Doc
> Never went to college.

Irish
> Born and died in Illinois.

Cardinals, 1909-1910

Higgins, Michael (Franklin)
Pinky
> From his rosy complexion as an infant.

Athletics, Red Sox, Tigers, 1930-1946

High, Andy [Andrew Aird]
Handy Andy
> A clutch performer for the Cardinals.

Knee
> From his short height, 5'6."

Robins, Braves, Cardinals, Reds, Phillies, 1922-1934

High, Ed [Edward Thomas]
Lefty
Tigers, 1901

High, Hugh (Jenkin)
Bunny
Tigers, Yankees, 1913-1918

Hilcher, Walter (Frank)
Whitey
Reds, 1931-1936

Hildebrand, Palmer (Marion)
Pete
Cardinals, 1913

Hill, Bill [William Cicero]
Still Bill
Colonels, Reds, Spiders, Orioles, Superbas, 1896-1899

Hill, Carmen (Proctor)
Specs
> Because he wore glasses.

Bunker
Pirates, Giants, Cardinals, 1915-1930

Hill, Clifford (Joseph)
Red
Athletics, 1917

Hill, Glenallen
Spiderman
> An arachnophobe, he injured himself when he "sleep-crawled" to get away from spiders during a dream.

Blue Jays, Indians, Cubs, Giants, Mariners, Yankees, 1989-2001

Hill, Hunter (Benjamin)
Texas Hill
> Born and died in Austin, TX.

Browns, Senators, 1903-1905

Hill, Marc (Kevin)
Booter
Cardinals, Giants, Mariners, White Sox, 1973-1986

Hill, Rich [Richard Joseph]
Brice
Cubs, Orioles, Red Sox, Indians, Angels, Yankees, Athletics, Dodgers, Twins, 2005-

Hiller, Frank (Walter)
Dutch
> His parents were German immigrants.

Yankees, Cubs, Reds, Giants, 1946-1953

Hiller, Harvey (Max)
Hob: Hobby
Red Sox, 1920-1921

Hilley, Ed [Edward Garfield]
Whitey
Athletics, 1903

Hillis, Malcolm (David)
Mack
Yankees, Pirates, 1924, 1928

Hillman, Darius (Dutton)
Dave
Cubs, Red Sox, Reds, Mets, 1955-1962

Hilly, William (Edward)
Pat
Phillies, 1914

Hinch, Andrew (Jay)
A.J.
Athletics, Royals, Tigers, Phillies, 1998-2004

Hines, Henry (Fred)
Hunky

Grooms, 1895
Hinrichs, Paul (Edwin)
Herky
Red Sox, 1951
Hinrichs, William (Louis)
Dutch
Senators, 1910
Hinton, John (Robert)
Red
Beaneaters, 1901
Hitt, Roy (Wesley)
Rhino
    He had a "roly-poly" girth.
Reds, 1907
Hittle, Lloyd (Eldon)
Red
Senators, 1949-1950
Hoak, Don [Donald Albert]
Tiger
    Broadcaster named for his ferociousness on the field.
El Divino Loco
    Means "the divine Madman," for his hard-headedness.
Dodgers, Cubs, Redlegs, Pirates, Phillies, 1954-1964
Hobbs, Bill [William Lee]
Smokey
Reds, 1913, 1916
Hoblitzell, Dick [Richard Carleton]
Doc
    Was in the Army Dental Corps.
Reds, Red Sox, 1908-1918
Hobson, Clell (Lavern)
Butch
Red Sox, Angels, Yankees, 1975-1982
Hockett, Oris (Leon)
Brown
Dodgers, Indians, White Sox, 1938-1945
Hockette, George (Edward)
Lefty
Red Sox, 1934-1935
Hodge, Clarence (Clemet)
Shovel: Mutt
White Sox, 1920-1922

Hodge, Harold (Morris)
Gomer
    Named for his resemblance to Jim Nabors (Gomer Pyle).
Indians, 1971
Hodkey, Aloysius (Joseph)
Eli
Phillies, 1946
Hoeft, Billy [William Frederick]
Nul
Tigers, Red Sox, Orioles, Giants, Braves, Cubs, 1952-1966
Hoelskoetter, Art [Arthur William]
Holley
    Short form of his last name.
Hoss
Cardinals, 1905-1908
Hoerst, Frank (Joseph)
Lefty
Phillies, 1940-1947
Hoes, Jerome (O'Bryan)
L.J.
Orioles, Astros, 2012-2015
Hoff, Chester (Cornelius)
Red
Highlanders, Yankees, Browns, 1911-1915
Hoffer, Bill [William Leopold]
Chick: Wizard
Orioles, Pirates, Blues, 1895-1901
Hoffman, Clarence (Casper)
Dutch: C.C.
White Sox, 1929
Hoffman, Edward (Adolph)
Tex
    Born in San Antonio, Texas.
Indians, 1915
Hoffman, Frank (Jacob)
The Texas Wonder
    From Houston, Texas, but born in Mississippi.
Cowboys, 1888
Hoffman, Harry (Camp)
Izzy
Senators, Doves, 1904, 1907
Hoffman, John (Edward)

Pork Chop
Astros, 1964-1965
Hoffman, William (A)
Sonny: Hickey
Blues, 1879
Hofman, Arthur (Frederick)
Circus Solly
> From either his circus catches or a comic strip character.

Pirates, Cubs, Tip-Tops, Blues, Yankees, 1903-1916
Hofmann, Fred
Bootnose
> An apt description. Look at his picture.

Yankees, Red Sox, 1919-1928
Hogan, James (Francis)
Shanty
Braves, Giants, Senators, 1925-1937
Hogg, Bert [Wilbert George]
Sonny
Dodgers, 1934
Hogg, William (Johnston)
Buffalo Bill
> Born in Michigan, died in Louisiana.

Highlanders, 1905-1908.
Hogsett, Elon (Chester)
Chief
> A belief that he was part indian; "looked" like an indian.

Tigers, Browns, Senators, 1929-1944
Holbrook, James (Marbury)
Sammy
Senators, 1935
Holden, Joe [Joseph Francis]
Socks
Phillies, 1934-1936
Holdsworth, Jim [James]
Long Jim
Forest Citys, Eckfords, Mutuals, Whites, Hartfords, Trojans, Hoosiers, 1872-1884
Holke, Walter (Henry)
Union Man
Giants, Braves, Phillies, Reds, 1914-1925
Hollahan, Bill [William James]
Happy
Senators, 1920
Holland, Al [Alfred Willis]
Mr. T
Pirates, Giants, Phillies, Angels, Yankees, 1977-1987
Holland, Bill [William David]
Dutch
Senators, 1939
Holland, Derek (Lane)
Dutch Oven
> Dutch last name; Dutch Oven brings the heat.

Rangers, White Sox, Giants, Cubs, Pirates, 2009-
Holland, Howard (Arthur)
Mul
Reds, Giants, Cardinals, 1926-1929
Holland, Robert (Clyde)
Dutch
Braves, Indians, 1932-1934
Holliday, James (Wear)
Bug
> At 151 lbs, he looked as small as a bug in the outfield.

Red Stockings, Reds, 1889-1898
Holliday, Matt [Matthew Thomas]
Big Daddy
> 6'4", 250 lbs.

Rockies, Athletics, Cardinals, Yankees, 2004-2018
Hollingsworth, Al [Albert Wayne]
Boots
> Gained because he made an error... at first base.

Reds, Phillies, Dodgers, Senators, Browns, White Sox, 1935-1946
Hollingsworth, John (Burnette)
Bonnie
Pirates, Senators, Robins, Braves, 1922-1928
Hollins, Dave [David Michael]
Head: Headley
Phillies, Red Sox, Twins, Mariners,

Angels, Blue Jays, 1990-2002
Hollison, John (Henry)
Swede
Colts, 1892
Hollmig, Stan [Stanley Ernest]
Hondo
Phillies, 1949-1951
Holloman, Alva (Lee)
Bobo
> A minor league owner reminded him of Bobo Newsome.

Junior
> His father was Alva, Sr.

Big Indian Chief
> A minor league nickname.

Browns, 1953
Holm, Roscoe (Albert)
Wattie
Cardinals, 1924-1932
Holmberg, David (A)
DH
Diamondbacks, Reds, White Sox, 2013-2017
Holmes, Elwood (Marter)
Chick
Athletics, 1918
Holmes, Howard (Elbert)
Ducky
Cardinals, 1906
Holmes, James (William)
Ducky
Colonels, Giants, Browns, Orioles, Tigers, Senators, White Sox, 1895-1905
Holmes, Tommy [Thomas Francis]
Kelly
> A childhood nickname, given by his friends.

Braves, Dodgers, 1942-1952
Holt, Brock (Wyatt)
Brock Star
Pirates, Red Sox, Brewers, Nationals, 2012-
Holt, James (Emmett Madison)
Red
Athletics, 1925

Holtgrave, Vern [Lavern George]
Woody
Tigers, 1965
Honeycutt, Frederick (Wayne)
Rick
Mariners, Rangers, Dodgers, Athletics, Yankees, Cardinals, 1977-1997
Hood, Albie (Larrison)
Abie
> Possible misspelling.

Braves, 1925
Hook, James (Wesley)
Jay
Professor
> From Casey Stengel. Jay attended Northwestern in the offseason.

Redlegs, Reds, Mets, 1957-1964
Hooker, William (Edward)
Buck
Reds, 1902-1903
Hooton, Burt (Carlton)
Happy
> Named by Tommy Lasorda because he rarely smiled.

Cubs, Dodgers, Rangers, 1971-1985
Hoover, James (Allen)
J.J.
Reds, Diamondbacks, 2012-2018
Hoover, William (James)
Buster
Keystones, Quakers, Orioles, Reds, 1884-1892
Hopkins, John (Winton)
Buck
Sis
> There was a female comedienne by that name.

Cardinals, 1907
Hopkins, Meredith (Hilliard)
Marty
Phillies, White Sox, 1934-1935
Hopkins, Mike [Michael Joseph]
Skinner
Sis
> There was a female comedienne

by that name.
Pirates, 1902
Hopp, Johnny [John Leonard]
Cotney
  Blonde, cotton-top hair.
Hippity
  As in hippity hop.
Cardinals, Braves, Pirates, Dodgers, Yankees, Tigers, 1939-1952
Hopper, Bill [William Booth]
Bird Dog
Cardinals, Senators, 1913-1915
Hopper, Clarence (Franklin)
Lefty
Bridegrooms, 1898
Horan, Joseph (Patrick)
Shags
Yankees, 1924
Horlen, Joe [Joel Edward]
Hard Luck
White Sox, Athletics, 1961-1972
Horne, Berlyn (Dale)
Trader
  nicknamed in reference to explorer, Trader Horne.
Sonny
Cubs, 1929
Horner, William (Frank)
Jack
Orioles, 1894
Hornsby, Rogers
The Rajah
  After Rudolph Valentino in *The Sheik*.
The Rajah of Swat
  Similar to Babe Ruth's Sultan of Swat before it was shortened.
Cardinals, Giants, Braves, Cubs, Browns, 1915-1937
Hornung, Joe [Michael Joseph]
Ubbo Ubbo
  He would shout that when he made a hit or a good play.
Bisons, Red Stockings, Beaneaters, Orioles, Giants, 1879-1890
Horton, Elmer (Edward)

Herky Jerky
Pirates, Bridegrooms, 1896, 1898
Horton, Willie [William Wattison]
Willie the Wonder
The Ancient Mariner
Tigers, Rangers, Indians, Athletics, Blue Jays, Mariners, 1963-1980
Hoskins, Rhys (Dean)
Big Hosk: Big Fella: Rhys Lightning
Phillies, 2017-
Hosmer, Eric (John)
Papo
Royals, Padres, 2011-
Host, Gene [Eugene Earl]
Twinkles: Slick
Tigers, Athletics, 1956-1957
Hotaling, Pete [Peter James]
Monkey
  Reference to his catcher's mask, unusual for the time.
Reds, Blues, Ruby Legs, Red Stockings, Grays, 1879-1888
Houck, Byron (Simon)
Duke
Athletics, Tip-Tops, Browns, 1912-1918
Houck, Sargent (Perry)
Sadie
Red Stockings, Grays, Wolverines, Athletics, Orioles, Nationals, Metropolitans, 1879-1887
Houk, Ralph (George)
Major
  He finished in WWII as a major.
Yankees, 1947-1954
Houlton, Dennis (Sean)
D.J.
Dodgers, 2005, 2007
House, Frank [Henry Franklin]
Pig
  As a baby, he was "big as a house." Couldn't say "Big."
Tigers, Athletics, Reds, 1950-1961
House, James (Rodger)
J.R.
Pirates, Astros, Orioles, 2003-2008

119

House, Willard (Edwin)
  Fred
  Tigers, 1913
Houtz, Fred (Fritz)
  Lefty
  Reds, 1899
Hovley, Steve [Stephen Eugene]
  Tennis Ball Head
  Pilots, Brewers, Athletics, Royals, 1969-1973
Howard, Dave [David Austin]
  Del
  Senators, Tip-Tops, 1912, 1915
Howard, Frank (Oliver)
  Hondo
    Named after John Wayne for his size: 6'7", 255 lbs.
  The Capital Punisher
    Punished AL pitching with his batting ability.
  The Washington Monument
  Dodgers, Senators, Ranger, Tigers, 1958-1973
Howard, George (Elmer)
  Del
  Pitates, Beaneaters, Doves, Cubs, 1905-1909
Howard, Paul (Joseph)
  Del
  Red Sox, 1909
Howard, Ryan (James)
  Big Piece
    6'4", 240 lbs.
  Phillies, 2004-2016
Howe, John
  Shorty
  Giants, 1890, 1893
Howe, Les [Lester Curtis]
  Lucky: Luck
  Red Sox, 1923-1924
Howell, Homer (Elliott)
  Dixie
  Pirates, Reds, Dodgers, 1947-1956
Howell, James (Phillip)
  J.P.
  Royals, Devil Rays, Rays, Dodgers, Blue Jays, 2005-2017
Howell, Millard
  Dixie
    Southern black background.
  Indians, Reds, White Sox, 1940-1958
Howell, Murray (Donald)
  Red: Porky
  Indians, 1941
Howell, Roland (Boatner)
  Billiken
  Cardinals, 1912
Howerton, Bill [William Ray]
  Hopalong
  Cardinals, Pirates, Giants, 1949-1952
Howley, Dan [Daniel Philip]
  Howling Dan: Dapper Dan
  Phillies, 1913
Hoy, William (Ellsworth)
  Dummy
    He was deaf and mute from childhood meningitis.
  Nationals, Bisons, Browns, Senators, Reds, Colonels, White Sox, 1888-1902
Hoyle, Roland (Edison)
  Tex
    He walked like cowboys in western movies.
  Athletics, 1952
Hoyt, Waite (Charles)
  Schoolboy
  The Schoolboy Wonder
    At 18, he was extremely young.
  The Merry Mortician
    When not playing, he worked as a funeral director and in vaudeville.
  Giants, Red Sox, Yankees, Tigers, Athletics, Dodgers, Pirates, 1918-38
Hrabosky, Al [Alan Thomas]
  {ru-BOSS-key}
  Hungo
  Mad Hungarian
    From his unusual last name and colorful character.
  Cardinals, Royals, Braves, 1970-1982

Hrbek, Kent (Allen) {HER-beck}
  Herbie
  Twins, 1981-1994
Hubbard, Trenidad (Aviel)
  Trent
  Rockies, Giants, Indians, Dodgers, Braves, Orioles, Royals, Padres, Cubs, 1994-2003
Hubbell, Carl (Owen)
  King Carl: Old Long Pants
  The Meal Ticket
  Giants, 1928-1943
Huber, Clarence (Bill)Gilly
  Tigers, Phillies, 1920-1926
Hudler, Rex (Allen)
  The Wonder Dog
    From Rex the Wonder Dog after a TV cartoon of the era.
  Bug-Eater
    On a bet, he ate a June bug that landed on his cap.
  Yankees, Orioles, Expos, Cardinals, Angels, Phillies, 1984-1998
Hudlin, Willis [George Willis]
  Ace
  Indians, Senators, Browns, Giants, 1926-1944
Hudson, Hal (Campbell)
  Bud: Lefty
  Browns, White Sox 1952-1953
Hudson, Johnny [John Wilson]
  Mr. Chips
  Little Mr. Chips
    Hit well when the chips were down.
  Bryanite
  Bryan Boy (and variations)
    Lived and died in Bryan, Texas.
  Dodgers, Cubs, Giants, 1936-1945
Hudson, Orlando (Thill)
  O-Dog
    A hip-hop nickname. Hip-hop artists called everyone Dog.
  Blue Jays, Diamondbacks, Dodgers, Twins, Padres, White Sox, 2002-2012

Huff, Aubrey (Lewis)
  Huff Daddy
    Hip hop nickname based on Puff Daddy (Shawn Coombs).
  Devil Rays, Astros, Orioles, Tigers, Giants, 2000-2012
Huggins, Miller (James)
  Rabbit: Little Hug: Hug
  The Mighty Mite
    Only 5'2", 125 lbs.
  Reds, Cardinals, 1904-1916
Hughes, Jared [William Jared]
  Bull
  Pirates, Brewers, Reds, Phillies, Mets, 2011-
Hughes, Jim [James Michael]
  Bluegill
  Twins, 1974-1977
Hughes, Michael (F)
  Mickey
  Bridegrooms, Athletics 1888-1890.
Hughes, Phil [Philip Joseph]
  Peej
  Yankees, Twins, Padres, 2007-2018
Hughes, Roy (John)
  Jeep: Sage
  Indians, Browns, Phillies, Cubs, 1935-1946
Hughes, Tom J [Thomas James]
  Long Tom
  Orphans, Orioles, Americans, Highlanders, Senators, 1900-1913
Hughes, Tom L [Thomas L.]
  Salida Tom
    Raised in Salida, Colorado.
  Highlanders, Braves, 1906-1918
Hughes, Vern [Vernon Alexander]
  Lefty
  Terrapins, 1914
Hughey, Jim [James Ulysses]
  Coldwater Jim
    Began his career in Coldwater, Michigan.
  Smiling Jim
    Smiled sarcastically before striking out a batter.

Brewers, Colts, Pirates, Browns, Spiders, Cardinals, 1891-1900
Huhn, Emil (Hugo) {HOON}
Hap
Hunnie
Given by fans and teammates.
Pepper, Reds, 1915-1917
Hulett, Timothy (Craig)
Tug
Mariners, Royals, 2008-2009
Hulvey, James (Hensel)
Hank
Athletics, 1923
Hummel, John (Edwin)
Silent John
He decided to never complain.
Rowdy John
Named by a teammate when he complained on a pitch.
Honest John
He was always trying to win.
Colonel Pinch
Able to hit in a pinch.
Superbas, Dodgers, Robins, Yankees, 1905-1918
Hundley, Randy [Cecil Randolph]
Rebel
Giants, Cubs, Twins, Padres, 1964-77
Hungling, Bernie [Bernard Herman]
Bud
Robins, Browns, 1922-1930
Hunnefield, Bill [William Fenton]
Wild Bill
White Sox, Indians, Braves, Giants, 1926-1931
Hunt, Ben [Benjamin Franklin]
High Pockets
6'5" tall.
Two-story Twirler: Beanpole
Two nicknames attributed to the Deseret Evening News.
Stringer
Another reference to his height.
Red Sox, Cardinals, 1910, 1913
Hunt, Joel [Oliver Joel]
Jodie
Cardinals, 1931-1932
Hunter, Frederick (Creighton)
Newt
Pirates, 1911
Hunter, Harold (James)
Buddy
Red Sox, 1971-1975
Hunter, Jim [James Augustus]
Catfish
Made up by Charlie Finley for no good reason.
Athletics, Yankees, 1965-1979
Hunter, Tommy [Raymond Thomas]
Tommy Two Towel
Rangers, Orioles, Cubs, Indians, Rays, Phillies, 2008-
Hunter, Torii (Kedar) {TORE-ee}
Spiderman
Twins, Angels, Tigers, 1997-2015
Huntzinger, Walt [Walter Henry]
Shakes
Giants, Cardinals, Cubs, 1923-1926
Hurd, Tom [Thomas Carr]
Whitey
Red Sox, 1954-1956
Hurley, William (H)
Dick
Olympics, 1872
Huskey, Robert (Leon)
Butch
Mets, Mariners, Red Sox, Twins, Rockies, 1993-2000
Husta, Carl (Lawrence)
Sox
Athletics, 1925
Husting, Bert [Berthold Juneau]
Pete
Acquired in childhood, he preferred it to Bert.
Pirates, Brewers, Americans, Athletics, 1900-1902
Hutcheson, Joe [Joseph Johnson]
Poodles: Slug
Dodgers, 1933
Hutchison, Bill [William Forrest]

Wild Bill
Cowboys, White Stockings, Colts,
Browns,
1884-1897
Hynes, Joshua (Colt)
Colt
Padres, Blue Jays, 2013, 2015
Iannetta, Chris [christopher, Domenic]
{eye-uh-NET-uh}
Sponge: Destructobeam
Rockies, Angels, Mariners,
Diamondbacks,
2006-
Iglesias, José (Antonio)
{e-GLAY-see-us}
Candelita
Red Sox, Tigers, Reds, Orioles
2011-
Incaviglia, Pete [Peter Joseph]
Load
Rangers, Tigers, Astros, Phillies,
Orioles, Yankees,
1986-1998
Infante, Gregory (Alexander)
{in-FON-tay}
El Meteorico
White Sox, 2010-
Iott, Frederick (Bidds)
Happy: Happy Jack: Biddo
Naps, 1903
Irelan, Hal [Harold]
Grump
Phillies, 1914
Irvin, Cole (R)
Swirvin Irvin
Phillies, 2019-
Irvin, Monte [Monford Merrill]
Mr. Murder
Giants, Cubs, 1949-1956
Irwin, Arthur (Albert)
Doc: Sandy: Foxy
Ruby Legs, Grays, Quakers,
Nationals, Reds, Phillies,
1880-1894
Irwin, Bill [William Franklin]

Phil
Red Stockings, 1886
Isbell, Frank [William Frank]
Bald Eagle
Orphans, White Sox, 1898-1909
Ishikawa, Travis (Takashi)
{EE-she-kaw-wuh}
Smoky
Giants, Brewers, Orioles, Yankees,
Pirates, 2006-2015
Izturis, Maicer {my-sair iss-TUR-iss}
Mighty Mouse
Expos, Angels, Blue Jays, 2004-2014
Jablonski, Ray [Raymond Leo]
Jabbo: Jolting Jabbo
Cardinals, Reds, Giants, Athletics,
1953-1960
Jackson, Austin (Jarriel)
Ajax
Tigers, Mariners, Cubs, White Sox,
Indians, Giants, Mets, 2010-2018
Jackson, Charlie [Charles Herbert]
Lefty
White Sox, Pirates, 1615, 1917
Jackson, Danny (Lynn)
D.J.: Jason
Royals, Reds, Cubs, Pirates, Phillies,
Cardinals, Padres, 1983-1997
Jackson, Edwin
E Jax
Dodgers, Rays, Tigers,
Diamondbacks, White Sox, Cardinals,
Nationals, Cubs, Braves, Marlins,
Orioles, Athletics, Blue Jays,
2003-
Jackson, George (Christopher)
Hickory
Rustlers, Braves, 1911-1913
Jackson, Grant (Dwight)
Buck
From the minors; he walked bow
legged, ready to draw a gun, as he
walked to the mound.
Phillies, Orioles, Yankees, Pirates,
Expos, Royals, Pirates, 1965-1982
Jackson, Joe [Joseph Walker]

Played one game in stocking feet.
His shoes were not broken in.
Athletics, Naps, Indians, White Sox,
1908-1920
Jackson, Luke (Ray)
Fireman
Rangers, Braves, 2015-
Jackson, Randy [Ransom Joseph]
Handsom Ransom
Cubs, Dodgers, Indians, 1950-1959
Jackson, Reggie [Reginald Martinez]
Mr. October
Black Babe Ruth
> After a 3-homer game in the World Series.

Athletics, Orioles, Yankees, Athletics, 1967-1987
Jackson, Ron [Ronnie Damien]
Papa Jack: Papa Up
Angels, Twins, Tigers, Orioles, 1975-1984
Jackson, Travis (Calvin)
Stonewall
Stoney
> Stopped balls from going through the infield, much as the General held troops at bay.

Giants, 1922-1936
Jackson, Vincent (Edward)
Bo: Bo Knows
Royals, White Sox, Angels, 1986-94
Jacobs, Forrest (Vandergrift)
Spook
Athletics, Pirates, 1954-1956
Jacobson, William (Chester)
Baby Doll
> In the minors, they played You Beautiful Doll. He hit a homer on the first pitch. A fan said he must be that doll.

Tigers, Browns, Red Sox, Indians, Athletics, 1915-1927
Jaeger, Joe [Joseph Peter]
Zip
Cubs, 1920
Jamerson, Charles (Dewey)

Lefty
The Young Collegian
> Already 24 but a (rare) college graduate.

Red Sox, 1924
James, Art [Arthur]
Spider
Tigers, 1975
James, Bert [Berton Hulon]
Jesse
Cardinals, 1909
James, Bill H [William Henry]
Big Bill
Naps, Browns, Tigers, Red Sox, White Sox, 1911-1919
James, Bill L [William Lawrence]
Seattle Bill
> Played in Seattle; to avoid confusion with Bill H.

Braves, 1913-1919
James, Jeff [Jeffrey Lynn]
Jesse
Phillies, 1968-1969
James, William (L)
Lefty
Naps, 1912-1914
Jamieson, Charlie [Charles Devine]
Cuckoo
> Had a trick shot at pool.

Kid Twirler
> As a newlywed in the silk industry.

Senators, Athletics, Indians, 1915-1932
Jankowski, Travis (Paul)
Fred
Padres, Reds, 2015-
Jansen, Kenley (Geronimo)
Kenleyfornia: Ma'montro
Dodgers, 2010-
Janvrin, Hal [Harold Chandler]
Childe Harold
Red Sox, Senators, Cardinals, Dodgers, 1911-1922
Jaso, John (Edward)
Easy J

Rays, Mariners, Athletics, Pirates,
2008-2017
Javery, Al [Alva William]
Beartracks
Bees, Braves, 1940-1946
Javier, Julián [Manuel Julian]
{hoo-lee-ON HA-vee-air}
The Phantom
> Smooth around second base.

Cardinals, Reds, 1960-1972
Jay, Jon [Jonathan Henry]
The Federalist: 305J
Cardinals, Padres, Cubs, Royals,
Diamondbacks, White Sox, 2010-
Jelincich, Frank (Anthony)
Jelly
Cubs, 1941
Jenkins, Fergie [Ferguson Arthur]
Fly
Phillies, Cubs, Rangers, Red Sox,
1965-1983
Jenkins, Tom [Thomas Griffith]
Tut
Red Sox, Athletics, Browns,
1925-1932
Jennings, Dan [Daniel Lee]
D.J.
Marlins, White Sox, Rays, Brewers,
Nationals, 2012-2019
Jensen, Jackie [Jack Eugene]
Golden Boy
Yankees, Senators, Red Sox, 1950-61
Jeter, Derek (Sanderson)
Mr. November
> A fan held up a homemade sign.

The Captain: Captain Clutch: DJ
Dr. Hardball
> From the David Letterman show.

Yankees, 1995-2014
Jethroe, Sam [Samuel]
Jet
Braves, Pirates, 1950-1954
Jiménez, Eloy (Arturo)
Big Baby
White Sox, 2019-
Jiménez, Ubaldo
U: Big U
Rockies, Indians, Orioles, 2006-2017
Johns, Augie [Augustus Francis]
Lefty
Tigers, 1926-1927
Johnson, Art [Arthur Henry]
Lefty
Bees, Braves, 1940-1942
Johnson, Bart [Clair Barth]
Toys in the Attic
White Sox, 1969-1977
Johnson, Billy [William Russell]
Bull
Yankees, Cardinals, 1943-1953
Johnson, Bob [Robert Lee]
Indian Bob
> Born on an Indian reservation.

Athletics, Senators, Red Sox, 1933-45
Johnson, Charlie [Charles Cleveland]
Home Run
Phillies, 1908
Johnson, Chet [Chester Lillis]
Chesty Chet
Browns, 1946
Johnson, Cliff [Clifford]
Heathcliff
Astros, Yankees, Indians, Cubs,
Athletics, Blue Jays, Rangers,
1972-1986
Johnson, Daniel
Jet
Indians, 2020-
Johnson, Don [Donald Spore]
Pep
Cubs, 1943-1948
Johnson, Earl (Douglas)
Lefty
Smiling Swedish Southpaw
> At least he was a southpaw.

Blond Southpaw Hurler
> From the Associated Press.

Red Sox, Tigers, 1940-1951
Johnson, Elmer (Ellsworth)
Hickory
Giants, 1914
Johnson, Fred [Frederick Edward]

Deacon: Cactus
Giants, Browns, 1922-1939

Johnson, George (Howard)
Chief: Murphy: Big Murph
Reds, Packers, 1913-1915

Johnson, Howard (Michael)
HoJo
Tigers, Mets, Rockies, Cubs, 1982-1995

Johnson, Johnny [John Clifford]
Swede
Yankees, White Sox, 1944-1945

Johnson, Ken [Kenneth Wandersee]
Hook
Cardinals, Phillies, Tigers, 1947-1952

Johnson, Lance [Kenneth Lance]
One Dog
Cardinals, White Sox, Mets, Cubs, Yankees, 1987-2000

Johnson, Lloyd (William)
Eppa
Pirates, 1934

Johnson, Lou [Louis Brown]
Sweet Lou: Slick
Cubs, Angels, Braves, Dodgers, Indians, 1960-1969

Johnson, Randy [Randall David]
Bug Unit
From an outfield collision during batting practice.
Expos, Mariners, Astros, Diamondbacks, Yankees, Giants, 1988-2009

Johnson, Rankin [Adam Rankin]
Tex
Red Sox, Chi-Feds, Whales, Terrapins, Cardinals, 1914-1918

Johnson, Richard (Allan)
Footer: Treads
Cubs, 1958

Johnson, Roy
Hardrock
Athletics, 1918

Johnson, Walter (Perry)
Barney
After race car driver, Barney Oldfield.
The Big Train
Blazing fastball.
Weiser Wonder
Minor league nickname.
Senators, 1907-1927

Johnson, William (F)
Lefty: Sleepy Bill
Keystones, Hoosiers, Orioles, 1884-1892

Joiner, Roy (Merrill)
Pop
Cubs, Giants, 1934-1940

Jok, Stan [Stanley Edward]
Tucker
Phillies, White Sox, 1954-1955

Jolley, Smead (Powell)
Guinea: Smudge: Happy
Arkansas Assassin
From a Sporting News comparison to Babe Ruth.
White Sox, Red Sox, 1930-1933

Jolly, Dave [David]
Gabby
Opposite of his quiet, calm demeanor.
Braves, 1953-1957

Jones, Adam (LaMarque)
Pappo: A.J.
Mariners, Orioles, Diamondbacks, 2006-2019

Jones, Albert (Edward)
Cowboy: Bronco
Spiders, Perfectos, Cardinals, 1898-1901

Jones, Andruw (Rudolf)
The Curaçao Kid
Braves, Dodgers, Rangers, White Sox, Yankees, 1996-2012

Jones, Bill [William Dennis]
Midget
Rustlers, Braves, 1911-1912

Jones, Bob [Robert Walter]
Ducky
Tigers, 1917-1925

Jones, Charley [Charles Wesley]

Baby
Westerns, Dark Blues, Reds, White Stockings, Red Stockings, Metropolitans, Cowboys, 1875-1888

Jones, Charlie [Charles Claude]
Casey
Americans, White Sox, Senators, Browns, 1901-1908

Jones, Dale (Eldon)
Nubs
Phillies, 1941

Jones, Daniel (Albion)
Jumping Jack: Jack
Wolverines, Athletics, 1883

Jones, Davy [David Jefferson]
Kangaroo
Brewers, Browns, Orphans, Cubs, Tigers, White Sox, Rebels, 1901-1918

Jones, Earl (Leslie)
Lefty
Browns, 1945

Jones, Elijah (Albert)
Bumpus
Tigers, 1907, 1909

Jones, Garrett (Thomas)
G.I. Jones
Twins, Pirates, Marlins, Yankees, 2007-2015

Jones, Henry (Monroe)
Baldy
Wolverines, 1884

Jones, Howie [Howard]
Cotton
Cardinals, 1921

Jones, Jim [James Tilford]
Sheriff
Colonels, Giants, 1897-1902

Jones, John (William)
Skins
Athletics, 1923, 1932

Jones, Johnny [John Paul]
Admiral
Giants, Braves, 1919-1920

Jones, Ken [Kenneth Frederick]
Broadway
Tigers, Braves, 1924, 1930

Jones, Mack (Fletcher)
Mack The Knife
Braves, Reds, Expos, 1961-1971

Jones, Oscar (Lafayette)
Flip Flap
Superbas, 1903-1905

Jones, Ri [Uriah Louis]
Angel Sleeves
Eclipse, Outlaw Reds, 1883-1884

Jones, Sam [Samuel]
Toothpick Sam
    Always had one in his mouth.
Sad Sam: Red
    Early nickname.
Indians, Cubs, Cardinals, Giants, Tigers, Orioles, 1951-1964

Jones, Sam P [Samuel Pond]
Sad Sam
    Looked sad from the press box.
Naps, Indians, Red Sox, Yankees, Browns, Senators, White Sox, 1914-1935

Jones, Sheldon (Leslie)
Available
    Willing to accept any mound assignment. Derived from the Al Capp Li'l Abner comic strip.
Giants, Braves, Cubs, 1946-1953

Jones, Sherman (Jarvis)
Roadblock
Giants, Reds, Mets, 1960-1962

Jones, Willie (Edward)
Puddin' Head
    Had a very slow drawl.
Phillies, Indians, Reds, 1947-1961

Jordan, Charlie [Charles T]
Kid
Phillies, 1896

Jordan, Jimmy [James William]
Lord
Dodgers, 1933-1936

Jordan, Mike [Michael Henry]
Mitty
Alleghenys, 1890

Jordan, Paul (Scott)
Ricky: Cool Papa

Phillies, Mariners, 1988-1996
Jordan, Raymond (Willis)
Rip: Lanky
White Sox, Senators, 1912, 1919
Joseph, Caleb (Martin)
Cabob
Orioles, Diamondbacks, Blue Jays, 2014-
Joseph, Tommy [Thomas Richard]
ToJo: The Scorpion
Phillies, 2016-2017
Joyce, Bill [William Michael]
Scrappy Bill
Ward's Wonders, Reds, Grooms, Senators, Giants, 1890-1898
Joyner, Wally [Wallace Keith]
Wally World
> Life-long misadventures mirror the star of the movie.

Angels, Royals, Padres, Braves, 1986-2001
Judge, Aaron (James)
All Rise
Yankees, 2016-
Judy, Lyle (Leroy)
Punch
Cardinals, 1935
Juelich, John (Samuel)
Red: Jackie
Pirates, 1939
Jungels, Ken [Kenneth Peter]
Curly
Indians, Pirates, 1937-1942
Justis, Walt [Walter Newton]
Smoke
Tigers, 1905
Kaat, Jim [James Lee] {COTT}
Kitty: Little Jimmy
Senators, Twins, White Sox, Phillies, Yankees, Cardinals, 1959-1983
Kafora, Jake [Frank Jacob]
Tomatoes
Pirates, 1913-1914
Kahdot, Isaac (Leonard)
Ike: Chief
> Has native American heritage.

Indians, 1922
Kahler, George (Runnells)
Krum
Naps, 1910-1914
Kahn, Owen (Earle)
Jack
Braves, 1930
Kaiser, Al [Alfred Edward]
Deerfoot
Cubs, Rustlers, Braves, Hoosiers, 1911-1914
Kaiser, Bob [Robert Thomas]
Chisel
Indians, 1971
Kaiser, Don [Clyde Donald]
Tiger
Cubs, 1955-1957
Kalbfus, Charlie [Charles Henry]
Skinny
> 5'11" but only 145 lbs.

Nationals, 1884
Kalfass, Bill [William Philip]
Lefty
Athletics, 1937
Kalin, Frank (Bruno)
Fats
Pirates, White Sox, 1940, 1943
Kaline, Al [Albert William] {KAY-line}
Mr. Tiger
> His association with the club lasted more than 50 years.

Baltimore Greyhound
> Earned when he scored from first on a double play.

Tigers, 1953-1974
Kamp, Alphonse (Francis)
Ike
Braves, 1924-1925
Kane, Frank [Francis Thomas]
Sugar
Tip-Tops, Yankees, 1915, 1919
Kane, Harry
Klondike
Browns, Tigers, Phillies, 1902-1906
Kane, Jim [James Joseph]
Shamus

Pirates, 1908
Kane, Tom [Thomas Joseph]
Sugar
    From Sugar-cane.
Bees, 1938
Kanehl, Rod [Roderick Edwin]
{Kah-NEEL}
Hot Rod
    Known for his all-out play and agressiveness.
Mets, 1962-1964
Kantlehner, Erv [Erving Leslie]
Peanuts
Pirates, Phillies, 1914-1916
Kapler, Gabe [Gabriel Stefan]
Welcome Back
    Chris Berman-ism: Gabe Kaplan played Gabe Kotter in the TV show, "Welcome Back, Kotter."
Kap
The Body
    Named by a Boston Globe columnist. An avid weightlifter.
Hebrew Hammer
    Long ball hitter who was Jewish.
Tigers, Rangers, Rockies, Red Sox, Brewers, Rays, 1998-2010
Kappel, Henry
Heinie
    Based on German ancestry.
Red Stockings, Solons, 1887-1889
Kardow, Paul (Otto)
Tex
    Born and died in Texas.
Man Mountain
    High school nickname for his size.
Punjab
    A newspaper nickname.
Indians, 1936
Karger, Ed [Edwin]
Loose
    He was described as "fast and loose."
Pirates, Cardinals, Reds, Red Sox, 1906-1911
Karkovice, Ron [Ronald Joseph]
Officer
    Named by Ken Harrelson because he resembled the stereotypical police officer and had skill at solving clubhouse crimes.
White Sox, 1986-1997
Karlon, Bill [William John]
Hank
The Palmer Kid
    Born in Palmer, Mass.
Yankees, 1930
Karpel, Herbert
Lefty
Yankees, 1946
Karr, Benn [Benjamin Joyce]
Baldy
    A pre-baseball nickname.
Red Sox, Indians, 1920-1927
Karst, John (Gottlieb)
Big Jack
    5'11", 175 lbs.
King
Robins, 1915
Katoll, Jack [John]
Big Jack
    5'11", 195 lbs.
Orphans, White Sox, Orioles, 1898-1902
Kavanagh, Charlie [Charles Hugh]
Silk
White Sox, 1914
Kawasaki, Munenori
Satsurō
    Gained in Japan.
Noodle
Buffalo Chicken
    Self-applied when referred to as Noodle.
Mariners, Blue Jays, Cubs, 2012-2016
Kay, Walter (Brocton)
Bill: King Bill

Kazmir, Scott

Senators, 1907
Kazmir, Scott (Edward)
{KAZ-mere}
    Kazmanian Devil: Pizza Man
    Devil Rays, rays, Angels, Indians,
    Athletics, Astros, Dodgers,
    2004-2016
Kearns, Edward (Joseph)
    Teddy
    Athletics, Cubs, 1920-1925
Kearns, Tom [Thomas J]
    Dasher
    Bisons, Wolverines, 1880-84
Kearse, Eddie [Edward Paul]
    Truck
    Yankees, 1942
Keating, Walter (Francis)
    Chick
    Cubs, Phillies, 1913-1926
Keck, Frank (Joseph)
    Cactus
    Reds, 1922-1923
Keefe, Tim [Timothy John]
    Sir Timothy
        Named in the poem, "Casey at the
        Bat." Had a gentlemanly
        behavior.
    Smiling Tim
    Trojans, Metropolitans, Giants,
    Phillies, 1880-1893
Keegan, Bob [Robert Charles]
    Smiley
    White Sox, 1953-1958
Keeler, Willie [William Henry]
    Wee Willie
        From teammates and spectators:
        5'4", 140 lbs.
    Hit 'Em Where They Ain't
        It was what he told reporters.
    Giants, Grooms, Orioles, Superbas,
    Highlanders, 1892-1910
Keeley, Burt [Burton Elwood]
    Speed
    Senators,
    1908-1909
Keen, Bill [William Brown]
    Buster: Hammerhead
    Pirates, 1911
Keenan, Jimmie [James William]
    Sparkplug
    Phillies, 1920-1921
Keener, Harry [Joshua Harry]
    Beans
    Phillies, 1896
Keifer, Sherman (Carl)
    Katsy
    Hoosiers, 1914
Keister, Bill [William Hoffman]
    Wagon Tongue
    Orioles, Beaneaters, Cardinals,
    Senators, Phillies, 1896-1903
Kelb, George (Francis)
    Pugger: Lefty
    Spiders, 1898
Keliher, Maurice (Michael)
    Mickey
    Pirates, 1911-1912
Kell, Everett (Lee)
    Skeeter
    Athletics, 1952
Kelleher, Albert (Aloysius)
    Duke
    Giants, 1916
Keller, Charlie [Charles Ernest]
    King Kong
        Gained in college for his
        muscular physique.
    Yankees, Tigers, 1939-1952
Kellett, Donald (Stafford)
    Red
    Red Sox, 1934
Kelly, Shawn (Andrew)
    Bak-Pak
    Mariners, Yankees, Padres, Nationals,
    Athletics, Rangers, 2009-2019
Kelliher, Frank [Francis Mortiford]
    Yucca
    Senators, 1919
Kelly, Albert (Michael)
    Red
    White Sox, 1910
Kelly, Bill [William Henry]

Big Bill
Athletics, Phillies, 1920, 1928
Kelly, George (Lange)
High Pockets
    Tall (6'4") with long legs; hence high pockets.
Giants, Pirates, Reds, Cubs, Dodgers, 1915-1932
Kelly, Herb [Herbert Barrett]
Moke
Pirates, 1914-1915
Kelly, Joe [Joseph William]
J.K.
Cardinals, Red Sox, Dodgers, 2012-
Kelly, John F (Francis)
Honest John: Father
Blues, Orioles, Quakers, Out-law Reds, Nationals 1879-84
Kelly, John O.
Kick
    Given by teammates. He was an umpire baiter.
Honest John
    Earned respect for umpiring ability.
Diamond John
    A commanding presence.
Smiling John
    From the press for his sarcasm as a manager.
Stars, Trojans, 1879
Kelly, Michael (Joseph)
King
    From the press for his salary. He dressed the part.
The $10,000 Beauty
    Mammoth salary for the time.
The Only Kelly
    Reflective of his fame and adulation.
Reds, White Stockings, Beaneaters, Kelly's Killers, Giants, 1878-1893
Kelly, R.B. (his given "name")
Speed
Senators, 1909
Kelly, Tom [Jay Thomas]
T.K.
Twins, 1975
Kelly, Ty [Tyler Patrick]
T.K.
Mets, Phillies, 2016-2018
Keltner, Ken [Kenneth Frederick]
Butch
The Culprit
    Given by Joe Dimaggio after he stopped Joe's streak.
Benny Beltner
    Given by his roommate after he sparked a clutch team win.
Indians, Red Sox, 1937-1950
Kelty, John (James)
Chief
Alleghenys, 1890
Kemmerer, Russ [Russell Paul]
Rusty: Dutch: Kimmersak
Red Sox, Senators, White Sox, Astros, 1954-1963
Kemner, Herman (John)
Dutch
Reds, 1929
Kemp, Matt [Matthew Ryan]
The Bison
    Given by Don Sutton, TV announcer, who said he looked like a buffalo. Color man changed it to Bison.
Dodgers, Padres, Braves, Reds, Rockies, 2006-
Kenna, Ed [Edward Benninghaus]
The Pitching Poet
    Had 2 anthologies of his poetry published.
The Poet Pitcher
    A variation of the Pitching Poet.
Athletics, 1902
Kenna, Eddie [Edward Aloysius]
Scrap Iron
Senators, 1928
Kennedy, Bill [William Aulton]
Lefty
Indians, Browns, White Sox, Red Sox, Redlegs, 1948-1957

Kennedy, Ian (Patrick)
    I.P.K.
    Yankees, Diamondbacks, Padres, Royals 2007-

Kennedy, John (Edward)
    SuperSub
    Senators, Dodgers, Yankees, Pilots, Brewers, Red Sox, 1962-1974

Kennedy, Michael (Joseph)
    Doc
    Blues, Bisons, 1879-1883

Kennedy, Sherman (Montgomery)
    Snapper
    Orphans, 1902

Kennedy, William (Park)
    Brickyard
        Worked in a brickyard in the off-season.
    Roaring Bill
        For his foghorn voice, and loud ragging of others.
    Perk
        Given by *Sporting Life*.
    Grooms, Bridegrooms, Superbas, Giants, Pirates, 1892-1903

Kent, Jeff [Jeffrey Franklin]
    Clark
        Chris Berman-ism between names: think Superman.
    Blue Jays, Mets, Indians, Giants, Astros, Dodgers, 1992-2008

Kenworthy, William (Jennings)
    Duke: Iron Duke
    Senators, Packers, Browns, 1912-1917

Kepler, Max [Maximilian]
    Rozycki
    Twins, 2015-

Keriazakos, Constantine (Nicholas)
    Gus
    White Sox, Senators, Athletics, 1950-1955

Kerlin, Orie (Milton)
    Cy
    Rebels, 1915

Kerr, John (Jonas)
    Doc
    Rebels, Terrapins, 1914-1915

Kerr, John (Joseph)
    Buddy
    Giants, Braves, 1943-1951

Kershaw, Clayton (Edward)
    The Claw: Kid K: The Minotaur
    Dodgers, 2008-

Kessler, Henry
    Lucky
    Atlantics, Reds, 1873-1877

Kibbie, Horace (Kent)
    Hod
    Braves, 1925

Kibble, Jack [John Westly]
    Happy: Happy Jack
    Naps, 1912

Kiefer, Joe [Joseph William]
    Harlem Joe
        He never lived in Harlem.
    Smoke
    White Sox, Red Sox, 1920-1926

Kiely, Leo (Patrick)
    Kiki : Le-Ki
    Blackie
        Given by a priest.
    Black Cat
        Had a habit of bringing a toy black cat to the bullpen.
    Red Sox, Athletics, 1951-1960

Kiermaier, Kevin (James)
    Outlaw
    Rays, 2013-

Kilhullen, Joseph (Isadore)
    Pat
    Pirates, 1914

Killebrew, Harmon (Clayton)
    Killer
        A combinatin of his name and tape-measure homers.
    Senators, Twins, Royals, 1954-1975

Killefer, Bill [William]
    Reindeer Bill
        Based on his running speed.
    Browns, Phillies, Cubs, 1909-1921

Killefer, Wade

Red: Lollypop: Radiant Red
Red Dog
King of Nuts
    Had a walnut farm while managing.
Hermosa Hermit
    Lived in Hermosa Beach, CA.
Doc
    Had an education in osteopathy. Treated teammates.
Tigers, Senators, Reds, Giants, 1907-1916

Killen, Frank (Bissell)
Lefty
Brewers, Senators, Pirates, Beaneaters, Orphans, 1891-1900

Killian, Ed [Edwin Henry]
Twilight Ed
    Pitched extra inning games into darkness.
Naps, Tigers, 1903-1910

Kilroy, Matt [Matthew Aloysius]
Matches
Boy Wonder
    An amateur nickname as a 14-year-old.
The Phenomenal Kid
    A professional level nickname.
Orioles, Reds, Kelly's Killers, Senators, Colonels, Orphans, 1886-1898

Kim, Hyun Soo {hee-yuhn sue kim}
Hitting Machine: Iron Man
Orioles, Phillies, 2016-2017

Kim, Kwang Hyun {kwang}
KK
Cardinals, 2020-

Kimball, Newell (Whitney)
Newt
Cubs, Dodgers, Cardinals, Phillies, 1937-1943

Kimberlin, Harry (Lydle)
Murphy: Mule Trader
Browns, 1936-1939

Kimbrel, Craig (Michael)
Dirty Craig
Braves, Padres, Red Sox, Cubs, 2010-

Kime, Hal [Harold Lee]
Lefty
Cardinals, 1920

Kimsey, Clyde (Elias)
Chad
Browns, White Sox, Tigers, 1929-36

Kindall, Jerry [Gerald Donald]
Slim
    6'2" but only 175 lbs.
Cubs, Indians, Twins, 1956-1965

Kinder, Ellis (Raymond)
Old Folks
    He pitched into his 40s and was a rookie at 31.
Browns, Red Sox, Cardinals, White Sox, 1946-1957

Kiner-Falefa, Isiah
{KYE-nuhr fuh-LEH-fuh}
Hawaiian Hustle
Rangers, 2018-

King, Charles F (Frederick)
Silver
    Combination of his hair color and a translation of his surname.
Cowboys, Browns, Pirates, Giants, Reds, Senators, 1886-1897

King, Charles G (Gilbert)
Chick
Tigers, Cubs, Cardinals, 1954-1959

King, Lynn (Paul)
Dig
Cardinals, 1935-1939

King, Ray [Raymond Keith]
Burger
Cubs, Brewers, Braves, Cardinals, Rockies, Nationals, 1999-2008

Kingery, Scott (M)
Scotty Jetpacks
Phillies, 2018-

Kingman, Dave [David Arthur]
Kong: King Kong: Sky King
Giants, Mets, Padres, Angels, Yankees, Cubs, Mets, Athletics, 1971-86

Kinsella, Bob [Robert Francis]
Red
Giants, 1919-1920

Kinsella, Ed [Edward William]
Rube
Pirates, Browns, 1905, 1910

Kinsler, Ian (Michael)
Bootsie
Rangers, Tigers, Angels, Red Sox, Padres, 2006-

Kinzy, Harry (Hersel)
Slim
 6'4", but only 185 lbs.
White Sox, 1934

Kipnis, Jason (Michael)
Dirtbag
 Consistently gets his uniform dirty during a game.
Indians, Cubs, 2011-

Kippert, Ed [Edward August]
Kickapoo
Reds, 1914

Kirke, Judson (Fabian)
Jay
Tigers, Rustlers, Braves, Naps, Indians, Giants, 1910-1918

Kirkpatrick, Ed [Edgar Leon]
Spanky
Angels, Royals, Pirates, Rangers, Brewers, 1962-1977

Kirsch, Harry (Louis)
Casey
Naps, 1910

Kisinger, Charles (Samuel)
Rube
Tigers, 1902-1903

Kissinger, Bill [William Francis]
Shang: Shaney
Orioles, Browns, 1895-1897

Kivlehan, Patrick (Anthony)
Believe
Padres, Reds, Diamondbacks, 2016-2018

Klaerner, Hugo (Emil)
Dutch
White Sox, 1934

Klawitter, Al [Albert Herman]
Dutch
 From Pennsylvania Dutch country.
Giants, Tigers, 1909-1913

Klee, Ollie (Chester)
Babe
Reds, 1925

Klein, Chuck [Charles Herbert]
The Hoosier Hammer
 From Indiana and a power hitter.
Phillies, Cubs, Pirates, 1928-1944

Kleinke, Norbert (George)
Nub
Cardinals, 1935, 1937

Kleinow, John (Peter)
Red
Highlanders, Red Sox, Phillies, 1904-1911

Klepfer, Ed [Edward Lloyd]
Big Ed
Highlanders, Yankees, White Sox, Indians, 1911-1919

Klieman, Ed [Edward Frederick]
Specs: Babe
Indians, Senators, White Sox, Athletics, 1943-1950

Kline, Bob [Robert George]
Junior
 By teammates; he made the majors at 21.
Red Sox, Athletics, Senators, 1930-34

Kling, Johnny [John]
Noisy
 Maintained a constant chatter.
Orphans, Cubs, Rustlers, Braves, Reds, 1900-1913

Klobedanz, Fred [Frederick Augustus]
Duke
Beaneaters, 1896-1902

Klopp, Stan [Stanley Harold]
Betz
Braves, 1944

Kloza, John (Clarence)
Nap
Browns, 1931-1932

Kluber, Corey (Scott)
Klubot: Hans
Indians, Rangers, 2011-

Kluszewski, Ted [Theodore Bernard]
{kluh-ZOO-ski}
    Big Klu
    Reds, Redlegs, Pirates, White Sox,
    Angels, 1947-1961

Klutts, Gene (Ellis)
    Mickey
    Yankees, Athletics, Blue Jays,
    1976-1983

Knabe, Franz (Otto)
    Dutch
        Pennsylvania native.
    Pirates, Phillies, Terrapins, Cubs,
    1905-1916

Knapp, Andrew (Michael)
    California Kid: Knapp Time
    Phillies, 2017-

Knaupp, Henry (Antone)
    Cotton
        He was described as blond or
        towheaded.
    Naps, 1910-1911

Knebel, Corey (Andrew) {kuh-NAY-bull}
    Bird Dog
    Tigers, Brewers, 2014-

Knetzer, Elmer (Ellsworth)
    Baron: Pretzel
    Superbas, Dodgers, Rebels, Braves,
    Reds, 1909-1917

Knight, Elmer (Russell)
    Jack
    Cardinals, Phillies, Braves, 1922-27

Knight, Joe [Jonah William]
    Quiet Joe
    Quakers, Reds, 1884, 1890

Knight, John (Wesley)
    Schoolboy
        Signed straight from high school.
    Athletics, Americans, Highlanders,
    Senators, Yankees, 1905-1913

Knoblauch, Chuck [Edward Charles]
{NOB-lock}
    Skippy
    Fundamentally Sound
        From ESPN personalities, from
        his deteriorating fielding.
    Twins, Yankees, Royals, 1991-2002

Knode, Bob [Robert Troxell]
    Ray
    Indians, 1923-1926

Knode, Kenneth (Thomson)
    Mike
    Cardinals, 1920

Knoll, Charles (Elmer)
    Punch
    Senators, 1905

Knolls, Oscar (Edward)
    Hub
    Superbas, 1906

Knothe, Wilfred (Edgar)
    Fritz
    Braves, Phillies, 1932-1933

Knouff, Ed [Edward Augustine]
    Fred
    Athletics, Orioles, Browns, Blues,
    1885-1889

Knowles, Jimmy [James]
    Darby
    Alleghenys, Atlantics, Nationals,
    Metropolitans, Broncos, Giants,
    1884-1892

Knowlson, Tom [Thomas Herbert]
    Doc
    Athletics, 1915

Knox, Andy [Andrew Jackson]
    Dasher
    Athletics, 1890

Knox, Cliff [Clifford Hiram]
    Bud
    Hard
        Gained in the minor leagues.
    Pirates, 1924

Knudson, Guido (Joel)
{GEE-doe ka-NUDE-son}
    Geets: G-Man
    Tigers, 2015

Koehler, Tom [Thomas R]
    TK: Big Salad
    Marlins, Blue Jays, 2012-2017

Koehler, Bernard (James)
    Ben
    Browns, 1905-1906

Koehler, Horace (Levering)
   Pip
   Giants, 1925
Koestner, Elmer (Joseph)
   Bob
   Naps, Cubs, Reds, 1910, 1914
Kohlman, Joe [Joseph James]
   Blackie
   Senators, 1937-1938
Kolloway, Don [Dnald Martin]
   Butch: Cab
   White Sox, Tigers, Athletics, 1940-53
Kolp, Ray [Raymond Carl]
   Jockey
      A bench jockey, needling opponents regularly.
   Jack
      A youth-baseball nickname.
   Browns, Reds, 1921-1934
Kommers, Fred [Frederick Raymond]
   Bugs
   Pirates, Terriers, Terrapins, 1913-14
Konetchy, Ed [Edward Joseph]
   Big Ed: Edward the Mighty
   The Candy Kid
      Worked in a candy factory.
   The LaCrosse Lulu
      Born in LaCrosse.
   The Big Bohemian
      His parents were Bohemian immigrants.
   Cardinals, Pirates, Rebels, Braves, Robins, Phillies, 1907-1921
Konikowski, Alex [Alexander James]
   Whitey
   Giants, 1948-1954
Kopacz, George (Felix)
   Sonny
   Braves, Pirates, 1966, 1970
Kopf, William (Lorenz)
   Larry
   Naps, Athletics, Reds, Braves, 1913-1923
Kopp, Merlin (Henry)
   Manny
   Senators, Athletics, 1915-1919

Korchek, Steve [Stephen Joseph]
   Hoss
   Senators, 1954-1959
Kores, Art [Arthur Emil]
   Dutch
   Terriers, 1915
Korince, George (Eugene)
   Moose
   Tigers, 1966-1967
Korwan, Jim [James]
   Long Jim
   Grooms, Colts, 1894, 1897
Koshorek, Clem [Clement John]
   Scooter
   Pirates, 1952-1953
Koski, Bill [William John]
   T-Bone
   Pirates, 1951
Koster, Fred [Frederick Charles]
   Fritz
   Phillies, 1931
Koufax, Sandy [Sanford] {KOE-fax}
   Koo
      From sportswriters mispronouncing his name.
   The Left Arm of God
   Dodgers, 1955-1966
Koy, Ernie [Ernest Anyz]
   Chief
   Dodgers, Cardinals, Reds, Phillies, 1938-1942
Kracher, Joe [Joseph Peter]
   Jug
   Phillies, 1939
Kraft, Clarence (Otto)
   Big Boy
   Braves, 1914
Kraly, Steve (Charles)
   Lefty
   Yankees, 1953
Kranepool, Ed [Edward Emil]
   The Krane
   Mets, 1962-1979
Krapp, Gene [Eugene Hamlet]
   Rubber Arm
      Based on his durability.

Rubber
: A newspaper writer's abbreviation of Rubber Arm.
Naps, Buffeds, Blues, 1911-1915

Kraus, Jack [John William]
Tex
Texas Jack
: Born and died in Texas.
Phillies, Giants, 1943-1946

Kravitz, Danny [Daniel]
Dusty: Beak
Pirates, Athletics, 1956-1960

Kreitner, Albert (Joseph)
Mickey
Cubs, 1943-1944

Kreitz, Ralph (Wesley)
Red
White Sox, 1911

Kremer, Remy (Peter) {KRAY-mer}
Ray: Wiz
Bush Wiz
: Bush league reference.
The Frenchman
: Sportswriter reference.
Pirates, 1924-1933

Kress, Ralph
Red
Browns, White Sox, Senators, Tigers, Giants, 1927-1946

Kretlow, Lou [Louis Henry]
Lena
Tigers, Browns, White Sox, Orioles, Athletics, 1946-1956

Krieger, Kurt (Ferdinand)
Dutch
Cardinals, 1949, 1951

Krist, Howie [Howard Wilbur]
Spud
: Boyish good looks, his big smile.
Cardinals, 1937-1946

Kroh, Floyd (Myron)
Rube
Americans, Cubs, Braves, 1906-1912

Krol, Ian (A)
King Krol
Nationals, Tigers, Braves, Angels, 2013-2018

Krsnich, Rocco (Peter)
Rocky
White Sox, 1949-1953

Krueger, Arthur (William)
Otto
Oom Paul
: Refers to Paul Kruger, a president of Transvaal, called Oom Paul, Afrikaans for Uncle Paul.
Spiders, Cardinals, Pirates, Phillies, 1899-1905

Krug, Everett (Ben) {KROOG}
Chris
Cubs, Padres, 1965-1969

Kruk, John (Marvin)
The Krukker: Jake: One-Nut Kruk
Padres, Phillies, White Sox, 1986-95

Krukow, Mike [Michael Edward] {CREW-koh}
The Polish Prince
Cubs, Phillies, Giants, 1976-1989

Kuczek, Stanislaw (Leo)
Steve
Braves, 1949

Kuczynski, Bernard (Carl)
Bert
Athletics, 1943

Kuhl, Chad (Michael) {COOL}
Sasquatch
Pirates, 2016-

Kuhn, Walt [Charles Walter]
Red
White Sox, 1912-1914

Kuiper, Duane (Eugene) {KYE-per}
Smoothie
Indians, Giants, 1974-1985

Kunz, Earl (Dewey)
Pinches
Pirates, 1923

Kurowski, George (John)
Whitey
: Had white hair as a child.
Cardinals, 1941-1949

Kurtz, Hal [Harold James]
Bud

Indians, 1968
Kusick, Craig (Robert)
Mongo
Twins, Blue Jays, 1973-1979
Kustus, Joe [Joseph Julius]
Jul: Kul
Superbas, 1909
Kutyna, Marion (John)
Marty
Athletics, Senators, 1959-1962
Kuzava, Bob [Robert Leroy]
Sarge
The White Rat
   Had a flat-top style of blonde hair.
Indians, White Sox, Senators, Yankees, Orioles Phillies, Pirates, Cardinals, 1946-1957
La Stella, Tommy [Thomas F]
3 A.M.
Braves, Cubs, Angels, Athletics, 2014-
Laboy, José (Alberto)
Coco
   From his mother, but he never knew why.
Expos, 1969-1973
LaChance, George (Joseph)
Candy
   From teammates: he chewed peppermint candy instead of tobacco.
Grooms, Bridegrooms, Orioles, Blues, Americans, 1893-1905
LaCock, Ralph (Pierre)
Pete
   English short name for his middle name.
Cubs, Royals, 1972-1980
Ladd, Pete [Peter Linwood]
Bigfoot: Sasquatch
Astros, Brewers, Mariners, 1979-86
Ladd, Arthur (Clifford)
Hi
Pirates, Beaneaters, 1898
Lade, Doyle (Marion)
Porky

Cubs, 1946-1950
Lafferty, Frank (Bernard)
Flip
Athletics, Grays, 1876-1877
Lafitte, Ed [Edward Francis]
Doc
   A practicing dentist.
Tigers, Tip-Tops, Blues, 1909-1915
LaForest, Byron (Joseph)
Ty
Red Sox, 1945
LaForest, Pierre (Luc)
Pete
   English translation of Pierre.
Devil Rays, Padres, Phillies, 2003-07
Laird, Gerald (Lee)
G-Money
Rangers, Tigers, Cardinals, Braves, Diamondbacks, 2003-2015
Lajoie, Nap [Napoleon] {LAJ-way}
Larry
   From a teammate who had trouble pronouncing Lajoie.
Poli
   A less-common abbreviation of Napoleon.
Sandy
   From early teammates to mask his presence from his mother.
The Slugging Cabby
   His "regular" job was driving for a livery stable.
The Frenchman
   Family background is French-Canadian.
Phillies, Athletics, Bronchos, Naps, 1896-1916
Lake, Eddie [Edward Erving]
Sparky
Cardinals, Red Sox, Tigers, 1939-50
Lakeman, Al [Albert Wesley]
Moose
   Named by minor league manager Jocko Munch, for his hulking stature.
Reds, Phillies, Braves, Tigers, 1942-54

Lamabe, Jack [John Alexander]
{la-MABE}
   Tomato Face: Tomatoes
   Pirates, Red Sox, Astros, White Sox,
   Mets, Cardinals, Cubs, 1962-1968

LaManna, Frank
   Hank
   Bees, Braves, 1940-1942

Lamanske, Frank (James)
   Lefty
   Dodgers, 1935

Lamar, Bill [William Harmong]
   Good Time Bill
   Yankees, Red Sox, Robins, Athletics,
   1917-1927

Lamer, Pierre
   Pete
      English translation of Pierre.
   Orphans, Reds, 1902, 1907

Lamet, Dinelson {dee-NEL-sun lu-MET}
   El Flaco
   Padres, 2017-

Lamlein, Fred [Frederick Arthur]
   Dutch
   White Sox, Cardinals, 1212, 1915

Land, William (Gilbert)
   Doc
      His given name was Doc Burrell
      Land.
   Senators, 1929

Landenberger, Ken [Kenneth Henry]
   Red
   White Sox, 1952

Landis, Samuel (H)
   Doc
   Athletics, Orioles, 1882

Landrum, Terry (Lee)
   Tito
   Cardinals, Orioles, Dodgers, 1980-88

Lane, George (M)
   Chappy
   Alleghenys, Blue Stockings,
   1882, 1984

Lane, Hunter [James Hunter]
   Dodo
   Braves, 1924

Lanford, Lewis (Grover)
   Sam
   Senators, 1907

Lang, Robert (David)
   Chip
   Expos, 1975-1976

Lange, Bill [William Alexander]
   Little Eva
      Sometimes walked with an
      affected strut.
   Colts, Orphans, 1893-1899

Lange, Erwin (Henry)
   Erv
   Chi-Feds, 1914

Lange, Frank (Herman Carl)
   Seagan
      Short version of Seaganbuck.
   Seaganbuck
      Unknown meaning; given by his
      father's co-workers.
   Bill
   White Sox, 1910-1913

Langford, Elton
   Sam
   Red Sox, Indians, 1926-1928

Lanier, Lorenzo
   Rimp
   Pirates, 1971

Lanning, Johnny [John Young]
   Tobacco Chewin' Johnny
   Bees, Pirates, Braves, 1936-1947

Lanning, Lester (Alfred)
   Red
   Athletics, 1916

Lansing, Gene [Eugene Hewitt]
   Jigger
   Braves, 1922

LaPalme, Paul (Edmore)
   Lefty
   Pirates, Cardinals, Redlegs, White
   Sox, 1951-1957

Lapihuska, Andy [Andrew]
   Apples
   Phillies, 1942-1943

LaPointe, Raoul (Robert)
   Ralph

Chick
: Childhood nickname.
: Phillies, Cardinals, 1947-1948

LaPorte, Frank (Breyfogle)
Pot
: Highlanders, Red Sox, Browns, Senators, Hoosiers, Pepper, 1905-15

Larkin, Frank (S)
Terry
: Mutuals, Hartfords of Brooklyn, White Stockings Trojans, Virginians, 1876-1884

Larkin, Henry (E)
Ted
: Athletics, Infants, Senators, 1884-93

Larmore, Bob [Robert McKahan]
Red
: Cardinals, 1918

LaRoche, Adam [David Adam]
The Rock
: Braves, Pirates, Red Sox, Diamondbacks, Nationals, White Sox, 2004-2015

LaRocque, Simeon (Henry Jean)
Sam
: Wolverines, Alleghenys, Pirates, Colonels, 1888-1891

LaRoss, Harry (Raymond)
Spike
: Reds, 1914

Larsen, Don (James)
Gooney Bird
: From teammates: protruding ears, pear-shaped body, dangling arms.
: Browns, Orioles, Yankees, Athletics, White Sox, Giants, Colt 45s, Astros, Cubs, 1953-1967

Larsen, Erling (Adell)
Swede
: Bees, 1936

LaRue, Jason [Michael Jason]
Rusty
: Reds, Royals, Cardinals, 1999-2010

Lary, Frank (Strong)
Mule

Taters
: Given after he wrote *Taters* on a train dining car order.
The Yankee Killer
: Won more than ²/₃ of his decisions against the Yankees.
: Tigers, Mets, Braves, White Sox, 1954-1965

Lary, Lyn [Lynford Hobart]
Broadway
: Loved the theater in New York.
: Yankees, Red Sox, Senators, Browns, Indians, Dodgers, Cardinals, 1929-40

Lasorda, Tommy [Thomas Charles]
Gerbil
: Given by Bill "Spaceman" Lee, who said he looked like one.
: Dodgers, Athletics, 1954-1956

Latham, Arlie [Walter Arlington]
The Dude
: A rich dresser.
The Freshest Man on Earth
: Self-description, based on a song of the day.
The Hustler from Hustletown
: From his athletic play.
: Bisons, Browns, Pirates, Reds, Senators, Giants, 1880-1909

Latham, George (Warren)
Jumbo
: 5'8", 250 lbs. (eventually).
Juice
: A reference to his energy while playing and coaching.
: Red Stockings, Elm Citys, Grays, Athletics, Eclipse, 1875-1884

Lathers, Charles (Ten Eyck)
Chick
: Tigers, 1910-1911

Latimer, Clifford (Wesley)
Tacks
: Given by a teammate in the minors.
: Giants, Colonels, Pirates, Orioles, Superbas, 1898-1902

Lattimore, Bill [William Hershel]

Slothful Bill
Naps, 1908
Laureano, Ramón
Razor: Laser
Athletics, 2018-
Lavagetto, Harry (Arthur) {lav-a-JET-oh}
Cookie
> Short version of Cookie's Boy

Cookie's Boy
> Signed by and named for the then owner of the Oakland Oaks.

Pirates, Dodgers, 1934-1947
LaValliere, Mike [Michael Eugene] {la-VALL-yer}
Spanky
Phillies, Cardinals, Pirates, White Sox, 1984-1995
Lavan, John (Leonard)
Doc
> Navy surgeon, practicing doctor, Director of Research for the National Foundation of Infantile Paralysis.

Browns, Athletics, Senators, Cardinals, 1913-1924
Lavelle, Gary (Robert)
Pudge
> Given by teammates for size: 6'1", 200 lbs.

Giants, Blue Jays, Athletics, 1974-87
Law, Vance (Aaron)
Long Arm of the Law
Pirates, White Sox, Expos, Cubs, Athletics, 1980-1991
Law, Vern [Vernon Sanders]
Deacon
> He was a church deacon by the age of 12.

Preacher
> Ordained a priest at the age of 17.

Pirates, 1950-1967
Lawing, Garland (Frederick)
Knobby: Butch
Reds, Giants, 1946
Lawrence, Brooks (Ulysses)
Bull
> Given by Cardinals manager, Eddie Stanky.

Cardinals, Redlegs, Reds, 1954-1960
Lawry, Otis (Carroll)
Rabbit
Athletics, 1916-1917
Lawson, Alfred (Voyle)
Roxie
Indians, Tigers, Browns, 1930-1940
Layne, Hillis [Ivoria Hillis]
Tony
> His friends called him Tony.

Mandrake
> From Seattle writers for his post-career work with kids.

Larruper Lane
> A newspaper reference while working with area kids.

The Chattanooga Choo Choo
> Gained when he played there in the minors.

Senators, 1941-1945
Lazzeri, Tony [Anthony Michael]
Poosh 'Em Up Tony
> An incorrect translation of an Italian phrase meaning "hit it out." Often shouted by Italian fans.

Yankees, Cubs, Dodgers, Giants, 1926-1939
Lear, Charles (Bernard)
King
> Think Shakespeare.

Reds, 1914-1915
Lear, Fred [Frederick Francis]
King
> Think Shakespeare.

Athletics, Cubs, Giants, 1915-1920
Leard, Bill [William Wallace]
Wild Bill
Robins, 1917
Leary, John (J)
Jack
Red Stockings, Wolverines, Alleghenys, Orioles, Eclipse, Mountain City, Chicago/Pittsburgh, 1880-1884

Leathers, Hal [Harold Langford]
Chuck
Cubs, 1920

Leathersich, Jack [John Victor]
Leather Rocket
Mets, Cubs, Pirates, 2015-2017

LeBlanc, Wade (Matthew)
Frenchy
Padres, Marlins, Astros, Angels, Yankees, Mariners, Pirates, Orioles, 2008-

LeBourveau, DeWitt (Wiley)
{luh BORE vo}
Bevo
A takeoff on his last name.
Phillies, Athletics, 1919-1929

LeClair, George (Lewis)
Frenchy
French-Canadian background.
Rebels, Blues, Terrapins, 1914-1915

Leclerc, José (Ramon)
Pico
Rangers, 2016-

Ledbetter, Ralph (Overton)
Razor
Tigers, 1915

Lee Bill C [William Crutcher]
Big Bill
Cubs, Phillies, Braves, 1934-1947

Lee, Bill F [William Francis]
Spaceman
Outrageous behavior, irreverent personality.
Red Sox, Expos, 1969-1982

Lee, Bob [Robert Dean]
Moose: Big Bob
Horse
6'3", 225 lbs.
Angels, Dodgers, Reds, 1964-68

Lee, Carlos
El Caballo
Spanish for 'the horse' and given by Hawk Harrelson when he said that Lee was 'an RBI horse.'
White Sox, Brewers, Rangers, Astros, Marlins, 1999-2012

Lee, Chen (-Chang)
C.C.
Indians, 2013-2015

Lee, Dae-ho
Big Boy: Pig Tiger
Mariners, 2019

Lee, David (Emmer)
Diesel
From teammates. He drove the team bus when the driver was ill, went to a gas station and yelled, "I need some diesel."
Rockies, Padres, Indians, 1999-2004

Lee Derrek (Leon)
D-Lee
Padres, Marlins, Cubs, Braves, Orioles, Pirates, 1997-2011

Lee, Ernest (Holford)
Dud
Browns, Red Sox, 1920-1926

Lee, Hal [Harold Burnham]
Sheriff
Robins, Phillies, Braves, Bees, 1930-1936

Lee, Manuel (Lora)
Manny
Blue Jays, Rangers, Cardinals, 1985-1995

Lee, Thornton (Starr)
Lefty
Indians, White Sox, Giants, 1933-48

Lee, Wyatt (Arnold)
Watty
A misspelling of his first name.
Senators, Pirates, 1901-1904

Leever, Sam
Deacon
The Goshen Schoolmaster
A teacher who was born in Goshen, Ohio.
Pirates, 1898-1910

LeFebvre, Bill
Lefty
Red Sox, Senators, 1938-1944

Legett, Lou [Louis Alfred]
Doc

A dentist before and after major
league baseball.
Dutch
   Childhood nickname.
Braves, Red Sox, 1929-1935
Lehner, Paul (Eugene)
Peanuts
   Small stature, 5'9", 160 lbs.
Gulliver
   He traveled; went AWOL from
   the Army several times.
Browns, Athletics, White Sox,
Indians, Red Sox, 1946-1952
Lehr, Charles (Larry) {LEER}
Justin
Athletics, Brewers, Reds, 2004-2009
Lehr, Clarence (Emanuel)
King
   Shakespearean reference.
Phillies, 1911
Lehr, Norm [Norman Carl Michael]
King
   Shakespearean reference.
Indians, 1926
Leibold, Harry (Loran) {LYE-bold}
Nemo
   Named for comic strip character,
   "Little Nemo."
Half-Pint
Naps, Indians, White Sox, Red Sox,
Senators, 1913-1925
Leifield, Albert (Peter)
Lefty
Pirates, Cubs, Browns, 1905-1920
Leiter, Al [Alois Terry] {LIE-turr}
Cigarette
   A Chris Berman-ism, as in "Al
   Cigarette Lighter."
Yankees, Blue Jays, Marlins, Mets,
1987-2005
Leith, Bill [William]
Shady Bill
Senators, 1899
Leitner, George A (Aloysius)
Doc
   A member of the American
College of Surgeons.
Hoosiers, 1887
Leitner, George M (Michael)
Dummy
   Typical nickname for a deaf
   person.
Athletics, Giants, Bronchos, White
Sox, 1901-1902
LeJohn, Don [Donald Everett]
Ducky
Dodgers, 1965
LeMahieu, DJ [David John]
Machine
Cubs, Rockies, Yankees, 2011-
Lemon, Chet [Chester Earl]
The Jet
   For his great speed in the field.
White Sox, Tigers, 1975-1990
Lenhardt, Don [Donald Eugene]
Footsie
   Always had trouble finding shoes
   that fit.
Browns, White Sox, Red Sox, Tigers,
Orioles, 1950-1954
Lennon, Bob [Robert Albert]
Archie
   His accent reminds of a character
   on *Duffy's Tavern*.
Giants, Cubs, 1954-1957
Lennox, Ed [James Edgar]
Eggie
Athletics, Superbas, Cubs, Rebels,
1906-1915
León, Sandy (David)
Noah
Nationals, Red Sox, Indians, 2012-
Leonard, Elmer (Ellsworth)
Tiny
   6'3", 210". Not exactly tiny.
Athletics, 1911
Leonard, Emil (John)
Dutch
   Nicknamed after another Dutch
   Leonard, who also was not Dutch.
Dodgers, Senators, Phillies, Cubs,
1933-1953

Leonard, Hubert (Benjamin)
    Dutch
        From childhood because he "looked like a Dutchman."
    Red Sox, Tigers, 1913-1925

Leonard, Jeffrey
    Penitentiary Face
        Somber, lead-lidded stare, thick mustache.
    HacMan
        From teammates because he swung at first pitch rather than taking.
    One Flap Down
        Based on his home run trot, with one hand hanging down.
    Dodgers, Astros, Giants, Brewers, Mariners, 1977-1990

LePine, Louis (Joseph)
    Pete
    Tigers, 1902

Leppert, Don E (Eugene)
    Tiger
    Orioles, 1955

Lerchen, Bertram (Roe)
    Dutch
        Ancestors from Germany.
    Red Sox, 1910

Lerian, Walt [Walter Irvin]
    Peck
        Threw out base stealers from a crouch, brushing the dirt to look like a "chicken pecking corn."
    Phillies, 1928-1929

LeRoy, Louis (Paul)
    Chief
        Was a native American.
    Highlanders, Red Sox, 1905-1910

Leskanic, Curt [Curtis John]
{les-CAN-ick}
    Let's Panic
        Rhyming...
    Rockies, Brewers, Royals, Red Sox, 1993-2004

Lesley, Brad [Bradley Jay]
    The Animal
        By Johnny Bench because of his good-natured screaming and stomping.
    Reds, Brewers, 1982-1985

Leslie, Sam [Samuel Andrew]
    Sambo
    Giants, Dodgers, 1929-1938

Leverenz, Walt [Walter Fred]
    Tiny
    Browns, 1913-1915

Leverett, Gorham (Vance)
    Dixie
    White Sox, Braves, 1922-1929

Leverette, Horace (Wilbur)
    Hod
    Browns, 1920

Levsen, Emil (Henry)
    Dutch
    Indians, 1923-1928

Lewis, Allan (Sydney)
    The Panamanian Express
        Charles O. Finley made him a "designated runner."
    Athletics, 1967-1973

Lewis, Bill {William Henry]
    Buddy
    Cardinals, Braves, Bees, 1933-1936

Lewis, Colby (Preston)
    Cobra
    Rangers, Tigers, Athletics, 2002-2016

Lewis, Edward (Morgan)
    Ted
    Parson
        Was an ordained minister.
    The Pitching Professor
        Was president of UNH and UMass (then Mass Agricultural College) after teaching at Columbia Univ.
    Beaneaters, Americans, 1896-1901

Lewis, George (Edward)
    Duffy
        From his mother's maiden name.
    Red Sox, Yankees, Senators, 1910-21

Lewis, John (Kelly)
    Buddy
        Nickname from childhood.

J.K.
    A teenage nickname.
Senators, 1935-1949
Leyritz, Jim [James Joseph]
    The King
Yankees, Angels, Rangers, Red Sox, Padres, Dodgers, 1990-2000
Lidge, Brad [Bradley Thomas] {LIJ}
    Lights Out
Astros, Phillies, Nationals, 2002-2012
Lieber, Charles (Edwin)
    Dutch
Athletics, 1935-1936
Liebhardt, Glenn (Ignatius)
    Sandy
Athletics, Browns, 1930-1938
Lillie, Jim [James J]
    Grasshopper
Bisons, Cowboys, 1883-1886
Lima, José (Desiderio Rodriguez) {LEE-ma}
    Lima Time
        His rally cry from an exuberant character.
    Mambo
        From a band he formed: "Banda Mambo."
Tigers, Astros, Royals, Dodgers, Mets, 1994-2006
Lincecum, Tim [Timothy LeRoy] {LIN-si-come}
    The Freak
        From his ability to throw powerful pitches.
    The Franchise: The Freaky Franchise
    Big Time Timmy Jim
Giants, Angelsm 2007-2016
Lind, Adam (Alan)
    Donnie
Blue Jays, Brewers, Mariners, Nationals, 2006-2017
Lind, Carl [Henry Carl]
    Hooks
Indians, 1927-1930
Lind, José {LEEND}
    Chico
Pirates, Royals, Angels, 1987-1995
Lindgren, Jacob (Stephen)
    The Strikeout Factory
Yankees, 2015-
Lindor, Francisco (Miguel)
    Mr. Smile
Indians, 2015-
Lindsay, Chris [Christian Haller]
    Pinky: The Crab
Tigers, 1905-1906
Link, Fred [Frederick Theodore]
    Laddie
Naps, Browns, 1910
Linke, Ed [Edward Karl]
    Babe
Senators, Browns, 1933-1938
Linton, Claud (Clarence)
    Bob
Pirates, 1929
Lipon, Johnny [John Joseph] {LIP-on}
    Skids
Tigers, Red Sox, Browns, Redlegs, 1942-1954
Lipscomb, Gerard
    Nig
Browns, 1937
Lisenbee, Horace (Milton)
    Hod: Lizzy
Senators, Red Sox, Athletics, Reds, 1927-1945
Lister, Morris (Elmer)
    Pete
Naps, 1907
Littell, Mark (Alan)
    Country
Royals, Cardinals, 1973-1982
Little, Bryan [Richard Bryan]
    Twig
Expos, White Sox, Yankees, 1982-86
Little, William (Arthur)
    Jack
Highlanders, 1912
Lively, Ben [Edward Bennett]
    Bee-bo
Phillies, Royals, 2017-2019
Lively, Everett (Adrian)

Buddy: Red
Reds, 1947-1949
Lively, Henry (Everett)
Jack
Tigers, 1911
Loan, William (Joseph)
Mike
Phillies, 1912
Loaisiga, Jonathan (Stanley)
{low-EYE-sig-ah}
Jonny Lasagna
Yankees, 2018-
Lobert, John (Bernard)
Hans
German version of Johannes, his given name.
Honus
Hans Number Two
Given by Honus Wagner, who shared his first name and was Hans Number One.
Pirates, Cubs, Reds, Phillies, Giants, 1903-1917
Locke, Lawrence (Donald)
Bobby
His nickname as far back as he could remember.
Indians, Cardinals, Phillies, Reds, Angels, 1959-1968
Lockman, Carroll (Walter)
Whitey
Light blonde hair in the majors.
Pickle
Early nickname in honor of a neighborhood policeman.
Giants, Cardinals, Orioles, Reds, 1945-1960
Lockwood, Claude (Edward)
Skip
Nickname given at the age of two.
Athletics, Pilots, Brewers, Angels, Mets, Red Sox, 1965-1980
Logan, Bob [Robert Dean]
Lefty
Dodgers, Tigers, Cubs, Reds, Braves, 1935-1945

Logan, Exavier (Prente)
Nook
Tigers, Nationals, 2004-2007
Logan, Johnny [John]
Yatch
Yatcha
Childhood nickname derived from "Yah-shoo," a combination of Russian and Croatian meaning, "be quiet."
Braves, Pirates, 1951-1963
Lohman, George (Frederick)
Pete
Statesmen, 1891
Lohrke, Jack (Wayne)
Lucky
Avoided death in war and accidents at least 6 times.
Giants, Phillies, 1947-1953
Lombardi, Ernie [Ernesto Natali]
Bocci
From his Italian heritage.
Schnozz
From his big nose.
Lumbago: Cyrano of the Iron Mask
Robins, Reds, Braves, Giants, 1931-47
Long, Herman (C)
Germany: Flying Dutchman
Cowboys, Beaneaters, Highlanders, Tigers, Phillies, 1889-1904
Long, Lester
Lep
Athletics, 1911
Long, Nelson
Red
Beaneaters, 1902
Long, Tom [Thomas Francis]
Little Hawk
Robins, 1924
Loos, Ivan
Pete
Athletics, 1901
Lopat, Eddie [Edmund Walter]
Junkman: The Cute Little Lefthander
Steady Eddie
From broadcaster Mel Allen.

White Sox, Yankees, Orioles, 1944-55
Lopata, Stan [Stanley Edward]
Stash: Big Stash: Lop
Phillies, Braves, 1948-1960
López, Aurelio (Alejandro)
Señor Smoke
   Latino relief pitcher who threw hard and pitched well.
El Lanzallama
   "Flamethrower:" Nickname in Mexico.
El Buitre de Tecamachalco
   Mexican: "The Vulture of Tecamachalco."
Royals, Cardinals, Tigers, Astros, 1974-1987
López, Héctor (Headley)
The Panama Clipper
What a Pair of Hands
Athletics, Yankees, 1955-1966
Lopez, Raymond (Michael)
Mickey
   From his Middle name.
Mariners, 2004
Lord, Bris [Bristol Robotham]
The Human Eyeball
Athletics, Naps, Braves, 1905-1913
Lorenzen, Adolph (Andreas)
Lefty
Tigers, 1913
Lorenzen, Michael (Clifton)
Cowboy: Zen Master
Reds, 2015-
Lotz, Joe [Joseph Peter]
Smokey
Smokey Joe
   Based on his fast ball.
Iron Man Pitcher
   Based on his fortitude and consistency.
Cardinals, 1916
Louden, William (P)
Baldy
Highlanders, Tigers, Buffeds, Blues, Reds, 1907-1916
Love, Edward (Haughton)
Slim
   6'7 $^1/_2$" but only 195 lbs.
The Human Giraffe
   Tallest player in Major League history until 1982.
The Altitudinous Twirler
   Used by *Sporting Life*.
The Human Office Building
   Used by the *Atlanta Constitution*.
The Eiffel Tower
Senators, Yankees, Tigers, 1913-1920
Lovett, Merritt [Merritt Marwood]
Mem
White Sox, 1933
Loviglio, John (Paul)
Jay
Phillies, White Sox, Cubs, 1980-1983
Lowdermilk, Grover (Cleveland)
Slim
   6'4", 190 lbs.
Cardinals, Cubs, Browns, Tigers, Indians, White Sox, 1909-1920
Lowe, Bobby [Robert Lincoln]
Link
Beaneaters, Orphans, Cubs, Pirates, Tigers, 1890-1907
Lowe, George (Wesley)
Doc
Reds, 1920
Lown, Omar {rhymes with Town} (Joseph)
Turk
   He had a fondness for turkey.
Cubs, Redlegs, White Sox, 1951-1962
Lowrey, Harry (Lee)
Peanuts
   His grandfather said he was "no bigger than a peanut." Or: An actress promised him some peanuts for good behavior.
Cubs, Reds, Cardinals, Phillies, 1942-1955
Luby, Hugh (Max)
Hal
Athletics, Giants, 1936, 1944
Luby, John (Perkins)
Pat

Given in reference books, but no proof it was ever used.
Colts, Colonels, 1890-1895

Lucas, Charles (Fred)
Red
The Nashville Narcissus
Coined by a reporter for the Cincinnati Tribune.
Giants, Braves, Reds, Pirates, 1923-38

Lucas, Fred [Frederick Warrington]
Fritz
Phillies, 1935

Lucas, Johnny [John Charles]
Buster
Lucky Lucas
Boston Herald used this when announcing his signing.
Red Sox, 1931-1932

Lucchesi, Joey [Joseph George] {loo-KAY-see}
Fuego
Padres, 2018-

Lucey, Joe [Joseph Earl]
Scootch
Gained in childhood. No one knows why.
Yankees, Red Sox, 1920, 1925

Lucid, Cornelius (Cecil)
Con
Colonels, Grooms, Phillies, Browns, 1893-1897

Ludolph, Willie [William Francis]
Wee Willie
Not so wee: 6'1", 170 lbs.
Tigers, 1924

Lugo, Seth [Jacob Seth]
Quarterrican
Mets, 2016-

Luhrsen, William (Ferdinand)
Wild Bill
Pirates, 1913

Lukon, Eddie [Edward Paul]
Mongoose
Reds, 1941-1947

Lumley, Harry (Garfield)
Judge
Superbas, 1904-1910

Luna, Guillermo
Memo
Cardinals, 1954

Lunsford, James (Lewis)
Trey
Giants, 2002-2003

Lupien, Ulysses (John)
Tony
The result of an Italian night promotion in Scranton.
Cookie
A semipro nickname in Chelmsford, Mass.
Red Sox, Phillies, White Sox, 1940-48

Luque, Dolf [Adolpho Domingo de Guzman] {LOO-kay}
The Pride of Havana: Papá Montero
Braves, Reds, Robins, Giants, 1914-35

Lutenberg, Charles (William)
Luke
Colonels, 1894

Lutz, Louis (William)
Red
Reds, 1922

Lutzke, Walter (John)
Rube
Smoky Rube
Based on his pitching prowess in the minors.
Indians, 1923-1927

Luzardo, Jesús (G)
Lizard King
Athletics, 2019-

Luzinski, Greg [Gregory Michael]
The Bull
Thick chest and productive bat.
Phillies, White Sox, 1970-1984

Lyle, Albert (Walter)
Sparky: The Count
Red Sox, Yankees, Rangers, Phillies, White Sox, 1967-1982

Lynch, Jerry [Gerald Thomas]
The Hat
Pirates, Redlegs, Reds, 1954-1966

Lynch, Matthew (Daniel)

Dummy
Cubs, 1948
Lynch, Walt (Walter Edward)
Jabber
Red Sox, 1922
Lynn, Byrd
Birdie
White Sox, 1916-1920
Lynn, Japhet (Monroe)
Red
Tigers, Giants, Cubs, 1939-1944
Lyons, Ed [Edward Hoyte]
Mouse
Senators, 1947
Lyons, George (Tony)
Smooth
Cardinals, Browns, 1920, 1924
Lyons, Steve [Stephen John]
Psycho
   His eccentricities included hangman in the dirt with opponents.
Moon Man
   Pulled his pants down to empty the dirt after a slide.
Red Sox, White Sox, Braves, Expos, 1985-1993
Lyons, Ted [Theodore Amar]
Sunday Teddy
   Started only on Sundays for much of his career.
White Sox, 1923-1946
Lyons, Thomas (Arthur)
Toby
Stars, 1890
Lytle, Edward (Benson)
Dad
Pop
   He was 28 when in the majors.
Colts, Alleghenys, 1890
Maas, Duane (Frederick)
Duke
Tigers, Athletics, Yankees, 1955-61
MacDougal, Robert (Meiklejohn)
Mike
Mack the Ninth
   Primarily a short reliever: 407 games, 394 innings.
Royals, White Sox, Nationals, Cardinals, Dodgers, 2001-2012
MacFayden, Danny [Daniel Knowles]
Deacon Danny
   A dour demeanor, from Dan Daniel.
Dismal Danny
   Another name from columnist Dan Daniel.
Somerville Scot
   Went to Somerville high school.
Red Sox, Yankees, Reds, Bees, Pirates, Senators, Braves, 1926-1943
Machado, Dixon (Javier)
Skippy: Mowly
Tigers, 2015-2018
Machado, Manny [Manuel Arturo]
Hakuna Machado: Baby Face Assassin
El Ministro de Defensa: Mr. Miami
Orioles, Dodgers, Padres, 2012-
Machemer, Dave [David Ritchie]
Mach One
Angels, Tigers, 1978-1979
Machi, Jean (Manuel) {gene ma-CHEE}
Baquiro
Giants, Red Sox, Mariners, 2012-17
Macias, Andres (Apolonio)
Drew
   Short for Andrew, English translation of Andres.
Padres, 2007-2009
Mack, Connie [Cornelius Alexander]
The Tall Tactician
The Grand Old Man of Baseball
   Managerial nicknames.
Slats
   From his friends at an early age.
Mr. Baseball
   From his Hall of Fame plaque.
Nationals, Bisons, Pirates, 1886-1896
Mack, Frank (George)
Stubby
White Sox, 1922-1925
Mack, Joseph

Reddy
Colonels, Orioles, 1885-1890
MacPhee, Walter (Scott)
Waddy
Giants, 1922
Macullar, Jimmy [James F]
Little Mac
> Only 5'6", 155 lbs.

Stars, Red Stockings, Orioles, 1879-1886
Madden, Frank [Francis A]
Red
Rebels, 1914
Madden, Len [Leonard Joseph]
Lefty
Cubs, 1912
Madden, Michael (Joseph)
Kid
> Made his pro debut at 19: frail and childlike appearing.

Beaneaters, Reds, Orioles, 1887-1891
Madden, Thomas (Francis)
Bunny
Red Sox, Phillies, 1909-1911
Maddox, Garry (Lee)
Secretary of Defense
> Given by a columninst for his play in center field.

Giants, Phillies, 1972-1986
Maddux, Greg [Gregory Alan]
Mad Dog: The Professor
Cubs, Braves, Dodgers, Padres, 1986-2008
Madigan, William (J)
Tony: Tice
Nationals, 1886
Madlock, Bill
Mad Dog
> He had a temper.

Rangers, Cubs, Giants, Pirates, Dodgers, Tigers, 1973-1987
Madson, Ryan (Michael)
Mad Dog: Blest
Phillies, Royals, Athletics, Nationals, Dodgers, 2003-2018
Maeda, Kenta {NAH-eh-da}
MaeKen
Dodgers, Twins, 2016-
Maglie, Sal [Salvatore Anthony]
Mother Maglie
> From his "mother-hen" approach to coaching.

The Barber
> He shaved hitters close with high inside pitches.

Giants, Indians, Dodgers, Yankees, Cardinals, 1945-1958
Magner, Edmund (Burke)
Stubby
> He was only 5'3."

Highlanders, 1911
Magnifico, Damien (Jack)
Wild Thing
Brewers, Angels, 2016-2017
Magoon, George (Henry)
Topsy
> From his spinning top-like movements in the infield.

Bridegrooms, Orioles, Orphans, Reds, White Sox, 1898-1903
Mahaffey, Roy [Lee Roy]
Popeye
Workhorse
> From his willingness to pitch.

Speed
> From teammates for his fastballs.

Pirates, Athletics, Browns, 1926-1936
Mahon, Al [Alfred Gwynn]
Lefty
Athletics, 1930
Mahoney, George (W)
Mike
Big Mike
> 6'4", 220 lbs.

Beaneaters, Browns, 1897-1898
Mahoney, Jim [James Thomas]
Moe
Red Sox, Senators, Indians, Astros, 1959-1965
Mahtook, Mikie [Michael Anthony]
Night Hawk
Rays, Tigers, 2015-

Mailho, Emil (Pierre)
Lefty
Fast Mail
> From minor league stolen base records.

Athletics, 1936

Mails, John (Walter)
The Great: Duster
Robins, Indians, Cardinals, 1915-26

Main, Forrest (Harry)
Woody
Pirates, 1948-1953

Main, Miles (Grant)
Alex
Tigers, Packers, Phillies, 1914-1918

Mains, Willard (Eben)
Grasshopper
White Stockings, Kelly's Killers, Brewers, Beaneaters, 1888-1896

Maisel, Frederick (Charles) {MY-zell}
Fritz:Flash
> From his speed on the basepaths.

Catonsville Flash
> Born in Catonsville, Maryland.

Yankees, Browns, 1913-1918

Majeski, Hank [Henry]
Heeney
> Childhood nickname.

Bees, Braves, Yankees, Athletics, White Sox, Indians, Orioles, 1939-55

Malarkey, John (S)
Liz
King Mull
> Based on his alliance with a minor league team captain.

Senators, Orphans, Beaneaters, 1894-1903

Maldonado, Candido
Candy
Candyman
> A Chris Berman nickname

The 4th out
Dodgers, Giants, Indians, Brewers, Blue Jays, Cubs, Rangers, 1981-1995

Maldonado, Martin (Benjamin) {mar-TEEN}
Cascajo
Brewers, Angels, Astros, Royals, Cubs, 2011-

Mallonee, Ben [Howard Bennett]
Lefty
Athletics, 1921

Mallory, Jim [James Baugh]
Sunny Jim
Senators, Cardinals, Giants, 1940, 45

Malloy, Alex [Archibald Alexander]
Lick
Browns, 1910

Malloy, Herm [John Herman]
Tug
Tigers, 1907-1908

Malmberg, Harry (William)
Swede
Tigers, 1955

Malone, Perce (Leigh)
Pat
> Self-named as a youngster. Perce sounded too "sissy."

Blubber
> From writers for his whale-like physical stature.

Cubs, Yankees, 1928-1937

Maloy, Paul (Augustus)
Biff
Red Sox, 1913

Manaea, Sean (Anthony) {muh-NYE-uh}
Baby Giraffe: Da Kid
Athletics, 2016-

Mancini, Trey [Joseph Anthony]
Boomer
Orioles, 2016-

Mancuso, Gus [August Rodney]
Blackie
Cardinals, Giants, Cubs, Dodgers, Phillies, 1928-1945

Mangum, Leo (Allan)
Blackie
> Dark hair and complexion.

Banjo Blackie
> Played banjo, guitar and ukelele.

White Sox, Giants, Braves, 1924-35

Manion, Clyde (Jennings)
Pete
Tigers, Browns, Reds, 1920-1934
Manlove, Charlie [Charles Henry Weeks]
Chick
Mountain City, Gothams, 1884
Mann, Garth [Ben Garth]
Red
Cubs, 1944
Mann, Les [Leslie]
Major
Braves, Whales, Cubs, Cardinals,
Reds, Giants, 1913-1928
Manning, Ernie [Ernest Devon]
Ed
Browns, 1914
Manning, Rick [Richard Eugene]
Archie
Indians, Brewers, 1975-1987
Manning, Walter (Sanderson)
Rube: Puss
Highlanders, 1907-1910
Mansell, John
Doc
Athletics, 1882
Mansell, Thomas (Edward)
Brick
Trojans, Stars, Wolverines, Browns,
Red Stockings, Buckeyes, 1879-1884
Mantei, Matt [Matthew Bruce] {MAN-tie}
The Ice Man
Marlins, Diamondbacks, Red Sox,
1995-2005
Mantle, Mickey (Charles)
The Oklahoma Kid
   He was from Oklahoma.
The Commerce Comet
   He was fast and from Commerce, Oklahoma.
The Mick: Muscles
Yankees, 1951-1968
Manuel, Mark (Garfield)
Moxie
Senators, White Sox, 1905, 1908
Manush, Henry (Emmett) {ma-NOOSH}
Heinie
   Tigers, Browns, Senators, Red Sox, Dodgers, Pirates, 1923-1939
Manwaring, Kirt (Dean)
What is That
   A Chris Berman-ism. "Kirt What is that Man waring."
Giants, Astros, Rockies, 1987-1999
Mapel, Rolla (Hamilton)
Lefty
Browns, 1919
Mapes, Cliff [Clifford Franklin]
Tiger
Yankees, Browns, Tigers, 1948-1952
Maranville, Walter (James Vincent)
Rabbit
   A 7-year-old said he hopped and bounded around like one.
Stumpy
   Childhood nickname.
Bunny
   Childhood nickname.
Braves, Pirates, Cubs, Robins,
Cardinals, 1912-1935
Marberry, Fred [Frederick]
Firpo
   A big man who resembled boxer Luis Firpo.
Senators, Tigers, Giants, 1923-1936
Marchildon, Phil [Philip Joseph]
{MAR-shill-done}
Babe
Athletics, Red Sox, 1940-1950
Marcum, Johnny [John Alfred]
Footsie
   The biggest feet in baseball.
Athletics, Red Sox, Browns, White Sox, 1933-1939
Margot, Manuel {mar-GO}
Yoandry
Padres, Rays, 2016-
Marichal, Juan (Antonio)
{MARE-ih-shall}
Manito: The Dominican Dandy
The Dominican Comet: Laughing Boy
   Given by Gus Triandos because of a constant smile and laugh at the

opposition.
Giants, Red Sox, Dodgers, 1960-1975
Marion, Donald (George)
Dan: Rube
Tip-Tops, 1914-1915
Marion, John (Wyeth)
Red
Senators, 1935, 1943
Marion, Marty [Martin Whiteford]
Slats
The skinny member of "Abbie an' Slats," comic strip of the day.
The Octopus
Long legs and arms.
Mr. Shortstop
Cardinals, Browns, 1940-1953
Marisnick, Jake [Jacob Shawn]
{muh-RIZ-nick}
Big Fudge
Marlins, Astros, Mets, 2013-
Markakis, Nick [Nicholas, William]
{mar-KAY-kiss}
TTT
Orioles, Braves, 2006-
Markland, Gene [Cleneth Eugene]
Mousey
Athletics, 1950
Marolewski, Fred (Daniel)
Fritz
Cardinals, 1953
Marquard, Richard (William)
{MAR-qward}
Rube
Given by reporter. He resembled Rube Waddell.
The $11,000 Peach
Named by the Giants for their huge bid to get Marquard.
The $11,000 Lemon
Failed to live up to the hype of his (then) large contract.
The $11,000 Beauty
He did live up to the hype.
Giants, Robins, Reds, Braves, 1908-25
Marquardt, Albert (Ludwig)
Ollie

Red Sox, 1931
Márquez, Luis (Ángel)
Canena
Given by his mother, a name he was known by.
El fogón Boricua
Gained in the Amateur World Series in Venezuela.
Braves, Cubs, Pirates, 1951, 1954
Marquis, Roger (Julian)
Noonie
Orioles, 1955
Marr, Charles (W)
Lefty
Red Stockings, Solons, Reds, Kelly's Killers, 1886-1891
Marrero, Chris [Christopher]
Nene
Nationals, Giants, 2011-2017
Marrow, Charles (Kennon)
Buck
Tigers, Dodgers, 1932-1938
Marshall, Charles (Anthony)
Chip: Chick
Cardinals, 1941
Marshall, Clarence (Westly)
Cuddles
Clancy
Gained in his later years.
Yankees, Browns, 1946-1950
Marshall, Eddie [Edward Harbert]
Doc
Giants, 1929-1932
Marshall, Joe [Joseph Hanley]
Home Run Joe
Home Run Marshall
A minor league acquisition.
Pirates, Cardinals, 1903, 1906
Marshall, Milo (May)
Max
Reds, 1942-1944
Marshall, Roy (DeVerne)
Rube
Cy
Phillies, Blues, 1912-1915
Marshall, William (Riddle)

153

Doc
> Practiced medicine for 45 years.

Phillies, Giants, Beaneaters, Cardinals, Cubs, Superbas, 1904-1909

Martell, Marty [Leon Alphonsus]
Doc
Phillies, Doves, 1909-1910

Martes, Francis (Euclides)
Chanchi
Astros, 2017-

Martin, Alfred (Manuel)
Billy
> Based on an infant nickname, Belli, given by his maternal grandmother.

Billy the Kid
> A media nickname.

Yankees, Athletics, Tigers, Indians, Reds, Braves, Twins, 1950-1961

Martin, Boris (Michael)
Baby
> The youngest in the family.

Babe
> He got too old to be called baby.

Hungarian Hot Shot
> Family was from Yugoslavia. A reporter got it wrong.

Browns, Red Sox, 1944-1953

Martin, Elwood (Good)
Speed
Browns, Cubs, 1917-1922

Martin, Harold (Winthrop)
Doc
> He was actually a doctor.

Athletics, 1908-1912

Martin, John (Dale)
J.D.
Nationals, 2009-2010

Martin, Johnny [John Leonard Robinson]
Pepper
> A minor league owner reacted to his chatter and base running.

The Wild Horse of the Osage
> A daring, aggressive base runner.

Cardinals, 1928-1944

Martin, Joe [William Joseph]
Smokey Joe
Giants, White Sox, 1936, 1938

Martin, Joseph C. (Clifton)
J.C.
> First and middle names, to avoid confusion. Both grandparents were named Joseph.

White Sox, Mets, Cubs, 1959-1972

Martin, Joseph S. (Samuel)
Silent Joe
Senators, Browns, 1903

Martin, Morrie [Morris Webster]
Lefty
Dodgers, Athletics, White Sox, Orioles, Cardinals, Indians, Cubs, 1949-1959

Martin, Russell (Nathan Coltrane0)
Muscle
Dodgers, Yankees, Pirates, Blue Jays, 2006-2019

Martina, John (Joseph)
Oyster Joe
> In the minors in 1921, he was traded for two barrels of oysters.

Senators, 1924

Martínez, Carlos A (Alberto Escobar)
Cafe
White Sox, Indians, Angels, 1988-95

Martínez, Carlos E (Ernesto)
Tsunami
> Same as his Twitter handle.

Little Pedro
> For similarities to Pedro Martinez.

Baby Pedro
> Also comparing him to Pedro Martinez.

Cardinals, 2013-

Martínez, Dennis [José Dennis]
El Presidente
> Given by a teammate in 1976.

El Chirizo
> By Nicaraguans based on his shock of hair.

Orioles, Expos, Indians, Mariners,

Braves, 1976-1998
Martinez, Edgar
   Gar
      Short for his first name.
   Papi: El Papa
   Mariners, 1987-2004
Martinez, Felix (Anthony)
   Tippy
   Yankees, Oriles, Twins, 1974-1988
Martinez, John (Albert)
   Buck
   Royals, Brewers, Blue Jays, 1969-86
Martínez, José (Alberto)
   Cafecito: Cafe
   Cardinals, Rays, Cubs, 2016-
Martinez, Julio (Daniel)
   J.D.
   Flaco
   Astros, Tigers, Diamondbacks, Red Sox, 2011-
Martínez, Michael (Gabriel)
   Pelucita
   Mini-Mart
      At 5'9", 180 lbs., hardly mini.
   Phillies, Indians, Red Sox, Rays, 2011-2017
Martínez, Pedro (Jaime)
   Pedro el Grande: Petey
   Dodgers, Expos, Red Sox, Mets, Phillies, 1992-2009
Martinez, Reyenaldo (Ignacio)
   Chito
   Orioles, 1991-1993
Martínez, Rogelio (Bautista)
   Limonar
      The name of the first team he played for in Cuba.
   Senators, 1950
Martinez, Tino [Constantino]
   Bamtino
      From a home run in the World Series.
   Mariners, Yankees, Cardinals, Devil Rays, 1990-2005
Martinez, Victor (Jesus)
   Papicho
   Indians, Red Sox, Tigers, 2002-2018
Martini, Guido (Joe)
   Wedo: Southern
   Athletics, 1935
Mason, Hank [Henry]
   Pistol
   Phillies, 1958, 1960
Massa, Gordon (Richard)
   Moose
      6'3", 210 lbs.
   Duke
   Cubs, 1957-1958
Massey, Bill [William Henry]
   Big Bill
      5'11", 168 lbs., not particularly big.
   Reds, 1894
Massey, Roy (Hardee)
   Red
   Braves, 1918
Massey, William (Herbert)
   Mike: Virgil Van Mijk
   Braves, 1917
Masterson, Justin (Daniel)
   Bat Masterson
      From the TV character.
   Big Masty: Nasty Masty
   Red Sox, Indians, Browns, 2008-2015
Masterson, Paul (Nicholas)
   Lefty
   Phillies, 1940-1942
Mathews, Eddie [Edwin Lee]
   Santa Barbara Bomber: Cap'n Eddie
   Brookfield Bomber: Eddie Mattress
   Braves, Astros, Tigers, 1952-1968
Mathews, Timothy (Jay)
   T.J.
   Cardinals, Athletics, Astros, 1995-2002
Mathewson, Christy [Christopher]
   Gun Boots
      From his football drop-kicking ability.
   The Christian Gentleman
      Refused to pitch on Sundays.
   The Gentleman's Hurler

Husk
: From childhood playmates.
Big Six
: From a baseball writer: He was one of the "big six of pitchers." He was compared to a New York fire company, quickest to get to a fire.
: Giants, Reds, 1900-1916

Mathias, Carl (Lynwood)
Stubby
: Indians, Senators, 1960-1961

Mathis, Jeff [Jeffrey Stephen]
Six
: Angels, Blue Jays, Marlins, Diamondbacks, Rangers, 2005-

Matsui, Hideki {mat-SOO-ee}
Godzilla
: A terror from Japan.
The Japanese Moe Howard
: Yankees, Angels Athletics, Rays, 2003-2012

Matsuzaka, Daisuke
{DICE-kay matt-soo-ZAH-kah}
Dice-K
: The correct Japanese pronunciation of his first name.
The Monster of the Heisei Era
: Nickname in Japan.
: Red Sox, Mets, 2007-2014

Matteson, Clifford (Virgil)
C.V.
: Maroons, 1884

Matthews, Gary Jr. (Nathaniel)
Little Sarge
: Son of Gary Sr.
Sarge Junior
: Son of Sarge Sr.
: Padres, Cubs, Pirates, Mets, Orioles, Rangers, Angels, 1999-2010

Matthews, Gary Sr. (Nathaniel)
Sarge
: Giants, Braves, Phillies, Cubs, Mariners, 1972-1987

Matthews, Joe [John Joseph]
Lefty
: Braves, 1922

Mattick, Wally [Walter Joseph]
Chink
: Bestowed by a newspaper.
Chick
: White Sox, Cardinals, 1912-1918

Mattingly, Don [Donald Arthur]
The Franchise: Donnie Baseball
The Hit Man: Cap
: Yankees, 1982-1995

Mattox, Cloy (Mitchell)
Monk
: Athletics, 1929

Matz, Steven (Jakob)
Rend
: Mets, 2015-

Mauch, Gene (William) {MOCK}
Skip
: Originally, Skippy or Skipper from American Legion days.
: Dodgers, Pirates, Cubs, Braves, Cardinals, Red Sox, 1944-1957

Mauck, Alfred (Maris)
Hal
: Colts, 1893

Maul, Al [Albert Joseph]
Smiling Al
: Keystones, Quakers, Alleghenys, Burghers, Pirates, Senators, Orioles, Superbas, Giants, 1884-1901

Mauldin, Marshall (Reese)
Mark
: White Sox, 1934

Maurer, Brandon (Eugene)
Mauer Power
: Mariners, Padres, Royals, 2013-2018

Mauriello, Ralph
Tami
: Dodgers, 1958

Maxwell, Bruce (Tyrone)
Baby Prince
: Athletics, 2016-

Maxwell, Charlie [Charles Richard]
Smokey
Paw Paw
: After marriage, he lived in that

town.
Sunday Punch: Sunday Charlie
The Sabbath Smasher
> Propensity for hitting homers on Sundays.

Home Run Charlie
> Earned in the minors at Roanoke.

The People's Choice
> From a Detroit sportswriter, for his hustle and hitting.

Red Sox, Orioles, Tigers, White Sox, 1950-1964

May, Frank (Spruiell)
Jakie
The Wee Carolinian
> 5'8", but slight frame.

Cardinals, Reds, Cubs, 1917-1932

May, Lee (Andrew)
Big Bopper
> Listed at 6'3", 195 lbs.

Big Bopper of Birmingham
> Named by teammate. He was from Birmingham.

Reds, Astros, Orioles, Royals, 1965-1982

May, Merrill (Glend)
Pinky
> Gained in college, perpetuated by sportswriters.

Phillies, 1939-1943

May, Rudy [Rudolph]
E.T.
Angels, Yankees, Orioles, Expos, 1965-1983

May, William (Herbert)
Buckshot
Pirates, 1924

Maybin, Cameron (Keith)
Slim: Killa Cam
Hammerin' Cameron
> From Yankees radio announcer.

Tigers, Marlins, Padres, Braves, Angels, Astros, Mariners, Yankees, Cubs, 2007-

Mayes, Adair (Bushyhead)
Paddy

Phillies, 1911

Maynard, James (Walter)
Buster
Giants, 1940-1946

Maynard, Leroy (Evans)
Chick
Red Sox, 1922

Mayo, Eddie [Edward Joseph]
Hotshot
Steady Eddie
> His reliable presence on and off the field.

Giants, Bees, Athletics, Tigers, 1936-1948

Mays, Carl (William)
Sub
> For his submarine pitching motion.

Red Sox, Yankees, Reds, Giants, 1915-1929

Mays, Willie (Howard)
Wonderful Willie
> For the caliber of his playing ability.

Say Hey Kid
> "Hey" was his first response to anything.

Buck
> Used by the Black Barons at the start of his career.

Popeye
> From Trenton teammates, large forearms *ala* Popeye.

Cap
> Used by Giants players when he was captain.

Giants, Mets, 1951-1973

Mazara, Nomar (Shamir)
The Big Chill
Rangers, White Sox, 2016-

Mazzera, Mel [Melvin Leonard]
Mike
Browns, Phillies, 1935-1940

McAdams, George (Decalve)
Jack
Cardinals, 1911

McAleer, Jimmy [James Robert]
  Loafer
  Spiders, Infants, Blues, Browns, 1889-1907
McAllister, Lewis (William)
  Sport
  Texas Jack
    Occassional nickname in the press.
  Spiders, Tigers, Orioles, 1896-1903
McAllister, Zach [Zachary Taylor]
  EZ Mac: Mac the Knife: Z-Mac
  Indians, Tigers, 2011-2018
McArthur, Oland (Alexander)
  Dixie
  Pirates, 1914
McAtee, Michael (James)
  Bub: Butch
  White Stockings, Haymakers, 1871-1872
McAuley, James (Earl)
  Ike
  Pirates, Cardinals, Cubs, 1914-1925
McAvoy, James (Eugene)
  Wickey
  Athletics, 1913-1919
McBee, Pryor (Edward)
  Lefty
  White Sox, 1926
McBride, Arnold (Ray)
  Little Bake
    His father was also Bake.
  Bake
    The same nickname as his father.
  Shake 'n Bake
    From fans in Philadelphia.
  The Callaway Kid
    His home county.
  Cardinals, Phillies, Indians, 1973-83
McCabe, James (Arthur)
  Swat
  Reds, 1909-1910
McCabe, Ralph (Herbert)
  Mack
  Indians, 1946
McCaffrey, Charles (P)
  Sparrow
    One of the lightest players ever.
  Solons, 1889
McCall, Brian (Allen)
  Bam
  White Sox, 1962-1963
McCall, John (William)
  Windy
    From Ted Williams, because he liked to talk.
  Red Sox, Pirates, Giants, 1948-1957
McCall, Robert (Leonard)
  Dutch
  Cubs, 1948
McCandless, Scott (Cook)
  Jack
  Terrapins, 1914-1915
McCann, Brian (Michael)
  Heap
    From teammates for how he unpacked on road trips.
  Fun Police
  Braves, Yankees, Astros, 2005-2019
McCann, Gene [Harry Eugene]
  Mike
  Superbas, 1901-1902
McCann, James (Thomas)
  McCannon
  Tigers, White Sox, 2014-
McChesney, Harry (Vincent)
  Pud
  Cubs, 1904
McClanahan, Robert (Hugh)
  Pete
  Pirates, 1931
McClellan, Hervey (McDowell)
  Little Mac
    5'9" but only 143 lbs.
  White Sox, 1919-1924
McCloskey, Jim [James Ellwood]
  Irish
  Bees, 1936
McClure, Hal [Harold Murray]
  Mac
  Red Stockings, 1882
McColl, Alex [Alexander Boyd]

Red
Senators, 1933-1934
McConnell, George (Neely)
Slats
Highlanders, Yankees, Cubs, Whales, 1909-1916
McCormack, Mike [Michael Joseph]
Kid: Dude
Superbas, 1904
McCormick, Frank (Andrew)
Buck
Named after Frank Buck, big-game hunter/movie director.
Wildcat
Given as part of a Cincinnati infield.
Reds, Phillies, Braves, 1934-1948
McCormick, Harry (Elwood)
Moose
A high school nickname for his size, big for the day.
Giants, Pirates, Phillies, 1904-1913
McCormick, Myron (Winthrop)
Mike
Reds, Braves, Dodgers, Giants, White Sox, Senators, 1940-1951
McCormick, Patrick (Henry)
Harry
Stars, Ruby Legs, Red Stockings, 1879-1883
McCormick, William (Joseph)
Barry
Youth nickname, Irish for fair-haired.
Colonels, Colts, Orphans, Browns, Senators, 1895-1904
McCovey, Willie (Lee)
Willie Mac: Mac: Big Mac
Stretch
From his ability to stretch for off-target throws at first.
Giants, Padres, Athletics, 1959-1980
McCrabb, Les [Lester William]
Buster
Refers to actor, Buster Crabbe.
Athletics, 1939-1950

McCredie, Walter (Henry)
Judge
Went to law school...before dropping out.
Loyal
Childhood nickname.
Superbas, 1903
McCreery, Esley (Porterfield)
Ed: Big Ed
Tigers, 1914
McCullers, Lance Jr (Graye)
Snap Dragon 1
Astros, 2015-
McCullers, Lance Sr (Graye)
Baby Goose
Padres, Yankees, Tigers, Rangers, 1985-1992
McCullough, Pinson (Lamar)
Phil
From his college, referring to his initials.
Senators, 1942
McCurdy, Harry (Henry)
Hank: Uncle Larry
Cardinals, White Sox, Phillies, Reds, 1922-1934
McCutchen, Andrew (Stefan)
Cutch
Pirates, Giants, Yankees, Phillies, 2009-
McDermott, Frank (Aloyious)
Red
Tigers, 1912
McDermott, Maury [Maurice Joseph]
Mickey
Red Sox, Senators, Yankees, Athletics, Tigers, Cardinals, 1948-1961
McDermott, Thomas (Nathaniel)
Sandy
Orioles, 1885
McDonald, Charles (C)
Tex
Born and died in Texas.
Crab
He sulked and got huffy when he dropped a fly ball.

Reds, Braves, Rebels, Buffeds, Blues, 1912-1915

McDonald, Daniel
Jack
Atlantics, Eckfords, 1872

McDonald, Jim [Jimmie Le Roy]
Hot Rod
A hot rod driver by avocation.
Red Sox, Browns, Yankees, Orioles, White Sox, 1950-1958

McDonnell, Jim [James William]
Mack
Indians, 1943-1945

McDougal, James (H)
Dewey
Browns, 1895-1896

McDougal, John (Auchanbolt)
Sandy
Grooms, Cardinals, 1895, 1905

McDowell, Jack (Burns)
Black Jack
From color commentator Ken Harrelson.
White Sox, Yankees, Indians, Angels, 1987-1999

McDowell, Sam [Samuel Edward Thomas]
Sudden Sam
Based on his fastball, coined by a baseball beat writer.
Indians, Giants, Yankees, Pirates, 1961-1975

McElveen, Pryor (Mynatt)
Humpty
Superbas, Dodgers, 1909-1911

McEwing, Joe [Joseph Earl]
Super Joe
Little Unit
A reference to success against Randy Johnson (Big Unit).
Cardinals, Mets, Royals, Astros, 1998-2006

McFadden, Bernard (Joseph)
Barney
Reds, Phillies, 1901-1902

McFarland, Charles (Amos)
Chappie
Cardinals, Pirates, Superbas, 1902-06

McFarland, Timothy (John)
T.J.: Mac
Orioles, Diamondbacks, Athletics, 2013-

McGaffigan, Mark (Andrew)
Patsy
Phillies, 1917-1918

McGann, Dan [Dennis Lawrence]
Cap
Beaneaters, Orioles, Superbas, Senators, Cardinals, Orioles, Giants, Doves, 1896-1908

McGann, Dennis (Lawrence)
Dan: Cap
Beaneaters, Orioles, Superbas, Senators, Cardinals, Orioles, Giants, Doves, 1896-1908

McGarr, James B.
Chippy
Chicago/Pittsburgh, Athletics, Browns, Cowboys, Orioles, Beaneaters, Spiders, 1884-1896

McGarr, Jim [James Vincent]
Reds
Tigers, 1912

McGee, Bill [William Henry]
Fiddler Bill
Cardinals, Giants, 1935-1942

McGee, Willie (Dean)
E.T.
Cardinals, Athletics, Giants, Red Sox, 1982-1999

McGehee, Casey (Michael) {muh-GHEE}
Hits McGehee
Cubs, Brewers, Pirates, Yankees, Marlins, Giants, Tigers, 2008-2016

McGhee, Bill [William Mac]
Fibber
Named after the lead in *Fibber McGhee and Molly*.
Athletics, 1944-1945

McGeehan, Cornelius (Bernard)
Connie
Athletics, 1903

McGill, Bill [William Jacob]

Parson
Browns, 1907
McGill, Willie [William Vaness]
Wee Willie
Kid
    Made his major league debut at the age of 16.
Infants, Kelly's Killers, Browns, Reds, Colts, Phillies, 1890-1896
McGillicuddy, Cornelius
Connie Mack: The Tall Tactician
The Grand Old Man of Baseball
The Grand Old Gentleman: Mack
Mr. Baseball
    From his Hall of Fame plaque.
Slats
    An early nickname from childhood friends.
Nationals, Bisons, Pirates, 1886-1896
McGilvray, Bill [William Alexander]
Big Bill
Bald Eagle of Colorado
    Given by a spring training observer in 1908.
Reds, 1908
McGinnis, George (Washington)
Jumbo
    A 200-pounder during the off season.
Mac
    From a *Sporting Life* correspondent.
Brown Stockings, Browns, Orioles, Red Stockings, 1882-1887
McGinnity, Joe [Joseph Jerome]
Iron Man
    Offseason work in an iron foundry.
Orioles, Superbas, Giants, 1899-1908
McGlothin, Ezra (Malachi)
Pat
Dodgers, 1949-1950
McGlothin, Jim [James Milton]
Red
Angels, Reds, White Sox, 1965-1973
McGlynn, Ulysses (Simpson Grant)

Stoney
Iron Man
    From his durability as a semi-pro and in minor and major leagues.
Cardinals, 1906-1908
McGowan, Dustin (Michael)
D-Mac
Blue Jays, Phillies, Marlins, 2005-17
McGowan, Frank (Bernard)
Beauty
Athletics, Browns, Bees, 1922-1937
McGowan, Tullis (Earl)
Mickey
Giants, 1948
McGraner, Howard
Muck
Reds, 1912
McGraw, Frank (Edwin)
Tug: Tugger: The Barber
Mets, Phillies, 1965-1984
McGraw, John (Joseph)
The Batboy
    Small stature-only 5.7".
Little Napoleon
    His management style, on a raised seat in the dugout.
Mugsy
Orioles, Cardinals, Giants, 1891-1907
McGrew, Walter (Howard)
Slim
    6'7", 235 lbs.
Senators, 1922-1924
McGriff, Fred [Frederick Stanley]
Crime Dog
    From Chris Berman based on the public service character, McGruff the Crime Dog.
Blue Jays, Padres, Braves, Devil Rays, Cubs, Dodgers 1986-2004
McGuire, James (Thomas)
Deacon
    Experienced religion at a revival meeting.
Deacon Jim
    A gentlemanly, fair-play approach to the game.

Blue Stockings, Wolverines, Quakers,
Blues, Broncos, Statesmen, Senators,
Superbas, Tigers, Highlanders,
Americans, Naps, 1884-1912

McGuire, Tom [Thomas Patrick]
Elmer
Chi-Feds, White Sox, 1914, 1919

McGunnigle, Bill [William Henry]
Gunner
> Strong throwing arm.

Bisons, Ruby Legs, Blues, 1879-1882

McGwire, Mark (David)
Big Mac: McZilla
Eve of Destruction
> Chris Berman-ism, used between names, referring to a '60s protest song by Barry McGuire.

Athletics, Cardinals, 1986-2001

McHale, Bob [Robert Emmet]
Rabbit
Senators, 1898

McHale, Jim [James Bernard]
J.B.
Red Sox, 1908

McHenry, Austin (Bush)
Mac
Cardinals, 1918-1922

McIlveen, Henry (Cooke)
Irish
> Born in Belfast, Ireland.

Pirates, Highlanders, 1906-1909

McIlwain, Stover (William
Smokey
> A hard thrower.

White Sox, 1957-1958

McInnis, Jack [John Phalen]
Stuffy
> Boyhood nickname for shouting "That's the stuff."

Athletics, Red Sox, Indians, Braves, Pirates, Phillies, 1909-1927

McIntire, John (Reid)
Harry: Handsome Harry
Superbas, Cubs, Reds, 1905-1913

McJames, James (McCutchen)
Doc

> He was a medical doctor.

Senators, Orioles, Superbas, 1895-1901

McKain, Archie (Richard)
Happy
Red Sox, Tigers, Browns, 1937-1943

McKay, Reeve (Stewart)
Rip
Browns, 1915

McKean, Ed [Edwin John]
Mack
Blues, Spiders, Perfectos, 1887-1899

McKechnie, Bill [William Boyd]
Deacon
> Sang baritone in church choir.

Pirates, Braves, Yankees, Hoosiers, Pepper, Giants, Reds, 1907-1920

McKee, Raymond (Ellis)
Red
Tigers, 1913-1916

McKeithan, Emmett (James)
Tim
Athletics, 1932-1934

McKenna, James (William)
Kit
Bridegrooms, Orioles, 1898-1899

McKenry, Frank (Gordon)
Limb: Big Pete
Reds, 1915-1916

McKenry, Michael (Charles)
The Fort
Fort McKenry
> References to Fort McHenry from the War of 1812.

Rockies, Pirates, Cardinals, 2010-16

McKenzie, Triston (Andrew)
Dr. Sticks
Indians, 2020-

McLarry, Howard (Zell)
Polly
White Sox, Cubs, 1912, 1915

McLaughlin, Bernard
Barney
Cowboys, Quakers, Stars, 1884-1890

McLaughlin, James (Anson)
Kid: Sunshine

Reds, 1914
McLaughlin, Justin (Theodore)
>Jud
>Red Sox, 1931-1933

McLaughlin, Michael (Duane)
>Bo
>Grim Bimbledon
>>An alias after being hit and almost killed by a line drive.
>
>Astros, Braves, Athletics, 1976-1982

McLean, Al [Albert Eldon]
>Elrod
>Senators, 1935

McLean, John (Bannerman)
>Larry
>>From a resemblance to Nap "Larry" Lajoie.
>
>Americans, Cubs, Cardinals, Reds, Giants, 1901-1915

McLeland, Wayne (Gaffney)
>Nubbin
>Tigers, 1951-1952

McLish, Cal [Calvin Coolidge Julius Caesar Tuskahoma]
>Buster
>>Given by teammates.
>
>Bus
>>Short for Buster.
>
>Dodgers, Pirates, Cubs, Indians, Reds, White Sox, Phillies, 1944-1964

McMahon, Henry (John)
>Doc
>>Had a degree in dentistry.
>
>Red Sox 1908

McMahon, John (Joseph)
>Sadie
>>A baseball only nickname.
>
>Athletics, Orioles, Bridegrooms, 1889-1897

McMakin, John (Weaver)
>Spartanburg John
>>Born in Spartanburg, SC.
>
>Superbas, 1902

McMillan, Geeorge (A)
>Reddy
>Giants, 1890

McMillan, Norm [Norman Alexis]
>Bub
>Yankees, Red Sox, Browns, Cubs, 1922-1929

McMillan, Tommy [Thomas Law]
>Rebel
>Superbas, Reds, Highlanders, 1908-1912

McMullin, John (F)
>Lefty
>Haymakers, Mutuals, Athletics, Whites, 1871-1875

McNabb, Carl (Mack)
>Skinny
>Tigers, 1945

McNabb, Edgar (J)
>Texas: Pete
>Orioles, 1893

McNair, Eric [Donald Eric]
>Boob
>>From the title of Boob McNutt, a comic strip.
>
>Rabbit
>Athletics, Red Sox, White Sox, Tigers, 1929-1942

McNally, Mike [Michael Joseph]
>Minooka Mike
>>Born in Minooka, PA.
>
>Ghost
>>Very slender build.
>
>Red Sox, Yankees, Senators, 1915-25

McNamara, John (Raymond)
>Dinny
>Braves, 1927-1928

McNeal, Jeff
>Squirrel
>>Gained in college.
>
>Mets, 2018-

McNeal, John (Harley)
>Harry
>Blues, 1901

McNealy, Robert (Lee)
>Rusty
>Athletics, 1983

McPhee, John (Alexander)
>Bid

Red Stockings, Reds, 1882-1899
McQuery, William (Thomas)
Mox: Big Mox
Outlaw Reds, Wolverines, Cowboys, Stars, Statesmen, 1884-1891
McQuillan, Alvin (Hugh)
Handsome Hugh
Braves, Giants, 1918-1927
McQuillen, Glenn (Richard)
Red
Browns, 1938-1947
McReynolds, Kevin [Walter Kevin]
Big Mac
Padres, Mets, Royals, 1983-1994
McSorley, John (Bernard)
Trick
Red Stockings, Blue Stockings, Maroons, Browns, 1875-1886
McTigue, Bill [William Patrick]
Rebel
Rustlers, Braves, Tigers, 1911-1916
McWeeny, Doug [Douglas Lawrence]
Buzz
White Sox, Robins, Reds, 1921-1930
Meadows, Henry (Lee)
Specs
> First modern major leaguer to wear glasses.

Cardinals, Phillies, Pirates, 1915-29
Meadows, Mike [Michael Ray]
Louie
Astros, Phillies, 1986-1990
Meara, Charlie [Charles Edward]
Goggy
Yankees, 1914
Medeiros, Ray (Antone)
Pep
Reds, 1945
Medich, George (Francis)
Doc
> He was an orthopedic surgeon.

Yankees, Pirates, Athletics, Mariners, Mets, Rangers, Brewers, 1972-1982
Medwick, Joseph (Michael)
Ducky
> For the way he walked.

Ducky-Wucky
> Derogatory name from teammates.

Muscles
> His preferred nickname, self named.

Cardinals, Dodgers, Giants, Braves, 1932-1948
Mee, Tommy [Thomas William]
Judge
Browns, 1910
Meegan, Pete [Peter James]
Steady Pete
Virginians, Alleghenys, 1884-1885
Meek, Frank (James)
Dad
Browns, 1889-1890
Meers, Russ [Russell Harlan]
Babe
Cubs, 1941-1947
Meier, Arthur (Ernst)
Dutch
Pirates, 1906
Meine, Henry (William)
Heinie
> A rhyming name.

The Count of Luxemburg
> Ran a speakeasy in the Luxemburg section of St. Louis.

Speedy
> A minor league name given by the Syracuse Herald.

Speedy Bill
Cousin Heine
> Refers to a pitcher batters love to face.

Browns, Pirates, 1922-1934
Meister, Karl (Daniel)
Dutch
Reds, 1913
Meixell, Merton (Merrill)
Moxie
Naps, 1912
Mejía, Adalberto
{add-al-BARE-toe meh_HEE-ya}
Volador

Twins, Angels, Cardinals, 2016-2019
Melancon, Mark (D){muh-LAN-son}
Stretch
Yankees, Astros, Red Sox, Pirates, Nationals, Giants, Braves, 2009-
Mele, Albert (Ernest){MEE-lee}
Dutch
Reds, 1937
Mele, Sabath (Anthony){MEE-lee}
Sam
    From his initials.
Red Sox, Senators, White Sox, Orioles, Redlegs, Indians, 1947-1956
Melillo, Oscar (Donald)
Spinach
    A doctor told him to eat spinach because of a kidney disease. Probably the inspiration for Popeye.
Ski
    In grammar school, he kicked like a player with that nickname.
Browns, Red Sox, 1926-1937
Meloan, Paul (B)
Molly
    From teammates based on the Irish song *Molly Malone*.
White Sox, Browns, 1910-1911
Melton, Bill [William Edwin]
Beltin' Bill
Beltin' Melton
    A powerful bat.
White Sox, Angels, Indians, 1968-77
Melton, Cliff [Clifford George]
Mickey Mouse
    He had jug ears.
Mountain Music
    A guitar-playing musician in the off-season.
Slim: Cliff the Curver
The Carolina Catapult
    Used only by Grantland Rice.
Giants, 1937-1944
Melville, Tim [Timothy Macgill]
Woody: Smellville
Reds, Twins, Padres, Rockies, 2016-2019
Mendoza, Cristobal (Rigoberto)
Minnie
Twins, 1970
Mench, Kevin (Ford)
Shrek
Rangers, Brewers, Blue Jays, Nationals, 2002-2010
Mendoza, Mario
Manos de Seda
    Spanish for Hands of Silk.
Pirates, Mariners, Rangers, 1974-82
Mendoza, Ramiro
El Brujo
Yankees, Red Sox, 1996-2005
Menefee, John
Jock
    Childhood nickname.
Pirates, Colonels, Giants, Orphans, Cubs, 1892-1903
Menke, Denis (John){MAIN-key}
Tomato Face
Braves, Astros, Reds, 1962-1974
Menosky, Mike [Michael William]
Leaping Mike
    Fearless when crashing into walls chasing fly balls.
Rebels, Senators, Red Sox, 1914-1923
Mensor, Ed [Edward]
The Midget
    He was 5'6", 145 lbs.
Pirates, 1912-1914
Mercer, George (Barclay)
Winner
    From his teenage success pitching for a factory team.
Winnie
Win
    Short forms for Winner.
Senators, Giants, Tigers, 1894-1902
Mercer, Harry (Vernon)
Jack
Pirates, 1910
Mercer, Jordy (Joe)
The Rook
Pirates, Tigers, Yankees, 2012-

Merena, John (Joseph)
   Spike
   Red Sox, 1934
Merewether, Art [Arthur Francis] {MARY-weather}
   Merry
      Short for Merewether.
   Speed
      From his amateur hockey days.
   Pirates, 1922
Merkle, Fred [Carl Frederick Rudolf]
   Bonehead: Leather skull: Ivory Pate
      All based on one play where he failed to touch second base on a penant winning play: a usual custom of the time.
   Giants, Robins, Cubs, Yankees, 1907-1926
Merrifield, Whitley (David)
   Whit Bird
   Royals, 2016-
Merriman, Lloyd (Archer)
   Citation
      Given by minor league fans for his stealing speed.
   Reds, Redlegs, White Sox, Cubs, 1949-1955
Mertes, Sam [Samuel Blair] {MER-Teez}
   Sandow
      Named for a famous strongman of the era.
   Mertes the Spiker
      From high slides in the minors.
   Phillies, Orphans, White Sox, Giants, Cardinals, 1896-1906
Mesa, José (Ramon Nova) {MAY-sa}
   Joe Table
      A literal translation of his name.
   Orioles, Indians, Giants, Mariners, Phillies, Pirates, Rockies, Tigers, 1987-2007
Mesoraco, Devin (Douglas)
   Rocko
   Reds, Mets, 2011-2018
Messenger, Andrew (Warren)
   Bud
   Indians, 1924
Messenger, Charles (Walter)
   Bobby
   White Sox, Browns, 1909-1914
Messersmith, John (Alexander)
   Andy: Bluto
   Channel
      Given by Ted Turner along with no. 17 to promote his TV station.
   Angels, Dodgers, Braves, Yankees, 1968-1979
Metha, Frank (Joseph)
   Scat
      For his baserunning in the minor leagues.
   Tigers, 1940
Metheny, Arthur (Beauregard)
   Bud
   Yankees, 1943-1946
Metkovich, George (Michael)
   Catfish
      From Casey Stengel after an injury getting a hook out of a catfish.
   Cat
      Nickname of his nickname.
   Red Sox, Indians, White Sox, Pirates, Cubs, Braves, 1943-1954
Metzger, Clarence (Edward)
   Butch
      Nicknamed by his sister.
   Giants, Padres, Cardinals, Mets, 1974-1978
Meulens, Hensley (Filemon Acasio)
   Bam-Bam
      Based on the Flintstones character.
   Yankees, Expos, Diamondbacks, 1989-1998
Meusel, Bob [Robert William]
   Long Bob
      6'3".
   Languid Bob
      From some writers.
   Silent Bob
      Quiet demeanor and nonchalant

style of play.
Yankees, Reds, 1920-1930
Meusel, Emil (Frederick) {MEW-zlee}
Irish
Was not Irish but looked Irish. Of German descent.
Senators, Phillies, Giants, Robins, 1914-1927
Meyer, Alex (John)
Bubba
Twins, Angels, 2015-2017
Meyer, Benny [Bernhard]
Earache
Superbas, Terrapins, Blues, Phillies, 1913-1925
Meyer, Lambert (Daniel)
Dutch: Little Dutch
Cubs, Tigers, Indians, 1937-1946
Meyer, Russ [Russell Charles]
Rowdy
Based on his antics on and off the field.
Russ the Red
All his grandparents were natives of Germany.
The Mad Monk
Shaved his head before a high school championship game.
Cubs, Phillies, Dodgers, Redlegs, Red Sox, Athletics, 1946-1959.
Meyerle, Levi (Samuel)
Long Levi
6'1" but only 177 lbs.
Athletics, Whites, White Stockings, Reds, Keystones, 1871-1884.
Meyers, John (Tortes)
Chief
Native American from Cahuilla Mission, California.
Giants, Robins, Braves, 1909-1917
Meyers, Lou [Lewis Henry]
Crazy Horse
Outlaw Reds, 1884
Micelotta, Robert (Peter)
Mickey
Phillies, 1954-1955
Michael, Gene [Eugene Michael]
Stick
Slender frame.
Pirates, Dodgers, Yankees, Tigers, 1966-1975
Michaels, Jason (Drew)
J-Mike
Phillies, Indians, Pirates, Astros, 2001-2011
Middleton, Jim [James Blaine]
Rifle Jim
Giants, Tigers, 1917, 1921
Middleton, John (Wayne)
Lefty
Indians, 1922
Middleton, Keynan (Anthony)
Major Key
Angels, 2017-
Midkiff, Ezra (Millington)
Salt Rock
From his birthplace, Salt Rock, West Virginia.
Reds, Highlanders, Yankees, 1909-13
Mientkiewicz, Doug [Douglas Andrew] {mint-KAY-vich}
Eye Chart
Twins, Red Sox, Mets, Royals, Yankees, Pirates, Dodgers, 1998-2009
Mierkowicz, Ed [Edward Frank]
Autch: Mouse: Butch
Tigers, Cardinals, 1945-1950
Miggins, Larry [Lawrence Edward]
Irish
Born of Irish immigrants.
Cardinals, 1948, 1952
Miklos, John (Joseph)
Hank
Cubs, 1944
Mikolas, Miles (Tice) {MY-ko-lahs}
Lizard King
Padres, Rangers, Cardinals, 2012-
Milan, Clyde [Jesse Clyde] {millin}
Deerfoot
Fast on the bases.
Zeb
Common nickname when from a

small town.
Senators, 1907-1922
Miles, Wilson (Daniel)
Dee
　From his middle name.
Senators, Athletics, Red Sox, 1935-43
Miljus, Johnny [John Kenneth]
Jovo: Big Serb
Rebels, Robins, Pirates, Indians,
1915-1929
Millán, Félix (Bernardo) {mee-YON}
Kitten
　From his skill at running, sliding
　and running some more.
Kit
　Short for Kitten.
El Gatito
　A homeland moniker.
The Cat
　From cartoon, Felix the Cat.
　Cunning and adaptable.
Nacho
　An aunt thought it was a
　nickname for Bernardo (it is not).
Braves, Mets, 1966-1977
Miller, Andrew (Mark)
Miller Time
Tigers, Marlins, Red Sox, Orioles,
Yankees, Indians, Cardinals, 2006-
Miller, Bill F. [William Francis]
Wild Bill
Browns, 1937
Miller, Bill P. [William Paul]
Lefty: Hooks
Yankees, Orioles, 1952-1955
Miller, Brad [Bradley Austin]
Sergio Millar: Rat: Bamboo Brad
Mariners, Rays, Brewers, Indians,
Phillies, Cardinals, 2013-
Miller, Charles (Bradley)
Dusty
Orioles, Browns, Reds, Perfectos,
1889-1899
Miller, Dakin (Evans)
Dusty
Orphans, 1902

Miller, Edmund (John)
Bing
　From the comic strip character,
　George Washington Bings.
Bings
　Before it was shortened to Bing.
Senators, Athletics, Browns, Red Sox,
1921-1936
Miller, Eddie [Edward Robert]
Eppie
Reds, Bees, Braves, Reds, Phillies,
Cardinals, 1936-1950
Miller, Ed [Edwin Collins]
Big Ed
Browns, Indians, 1912-1918
Miller, Elmer (Joseph)
Lefty
Phillies, 1929
Miller, Frank A. (Aloyvisous)
Kohly
Senators, Browns, Phillies, 1892-97
Miller, Frank L. (Lee)
Bullet
　Based on his fastball.
White Sox, Pirates, Braves, 1913-23
Miller, Frederick (Holman)
Speedy
Superbas, 1910
Miller George (Frederick)
Doggie
　He was a dog breeder.
Foghorn
Calliope
　From teammates for his loud
　voice.
Alleghenys, Pirates, Browns,
Colonels, 1884-1896
Miller, Hughie [Hugh Stanley]
Cotton
Phillies, Terriers, 1911-1915
Miller, James (Eldridge)
Hack
Tigers, 1944-1945
Miller, Jim [James McCurdy]
Rabbit
Giants, 1901

Miller, John A (Anthony)
Ox
Gained when he pitched both ends of a doubleheader in the minors.
Senators, Browns, Cubs, 1943-1947
Miller, John B (Barney)
Dots
Childhood nickname.
Hans
He made all the plays at shortstop.
Hans No. 2
Adopted after Hans No. 1 arrived in camp.
Pirates, Cardinals, Phillies, 1909-1921
Miller, Joseph (H)
Cyclone
Chicago/Pittsburgh, Grays, Quakers, Athletics, 1884-1886
Miller, Kenneth (Albert)
Whitey
Giants, 1944
Miller, Laurence (H)
Hack
Resembled strong man, George Hackenschmidt.
Robins, Red Sox, Cubs, 1916-1925
Miller, Leo (Alphonso)
Red
Phillies, 1923
Miller, Lowell (Otto)
Moonie
Superbas, Dodgers, Robins, 1910-22
Miller, Ralph (Henry)
Moose: Lefty
Senators. 1921
Miller, Rick [Richard Alan]
Miller Time
Red Sox, Angels, 1971-1985
Miller, Roland (Arthur)
Ronny
Senators, 1941
Miller, Roscoe (Clyde)
Roxy: Rubberlegs
Tigers, Giants, Pirates, 1901-1904

Miller, Roy (Oscar)
Doc
Became a dermatologist and cancer specialist in the offseason.
Cubs, Doves, Rustlers, Braves, Phillies, Reds, 1910-1914
Miller, Stu [Stuart Leonard]
Little Stu
Cardinals, Phillies, Giants, Orioles, Braves, 1952-1968
Miller, Tom [Thomas P]
Reddy
Athletics, Brown Stockings, 1874-75
Miller, Walter [Jacob Walter]
Jake
Indians, White Sox, 1924-1933
Miller, Ward (Taylor)
Windy: Grump
Pirates, Reds, Cubs, Terriers, Browns, 1909-1917
Miller, Warren (Lemuel)
Gitz
Senators, 1909, 1911
Milligan, John
Jocko
Athletics, Browns, Senators, Orioles, Giants, 1884-1893
Milliken, Bob [Robert Fogle]
Bobo
Dodgers, 1953-1954
Mills, Abbott (Paige)
Jack
Lajoie's Legs
He was pinch runner several times for Nap Lajoie.
Naps, 1911
Mills, Colonel (Buster)
His actual given first name.
Bus
Cardinals, Dodgers, Red Sox, Browns, Yankees, Indians, 1934-1946
Mills, Howard (Robinson)
Lefty
Browns, 1934-1940
Mills, Willie [William Grant]
Wee Willie

Only 5'7", 150 lbs.
Giants, 1901
Milnar, Al [Albert Joseph]
Happy
Indians, Browns, Phillies, 1936-1946
Milne, William (James)
Pete
Giants, 1948-1950
Milner, John (David)
The Hammer
> Named in honor and admiration of Hank Aaron.

Mets, Pirates, Expos, 1971-1982
Milosevich, Mike [Michael]
Mollie
Yankees, 1944-1945
Milstead, George (Earl)
Cowboy
Cubs, 1924-1926
Milton, Larry [Samuel Lawrence]
Tug
Cardinals, 1903
Minahan, Edmund (Joseph)
Cotton
> From his curly blond hair.

Reds, 1907
Minarcin, Rudy [Rudolph Anthony] {min-ARE-sin}
Buster
> Self-described for the Hall of Fame record. Not used.

Potato Head
> From a bad haircut as a seven-year-old.

Redlegs, Red Sox, 1955-1957
Miner, Ray [Raymond Theodore]
Lefty
Athletics, 1921
Minner, Paul [Paul Edison]
Lefty
Babe
> A newspaper-given nickname.

Dodgers, Cubs, 1946-1956
Miñoso, Orestes [Sturnino Orestes Armas] {mi-NO-so}
Minnie
> Short for his last name.

The Cuban Comet: Mr. White Sox
Indians, White Sox, Cardinals, Senators, 1949-1980
Minton, Greg [Gregory Brian]
Moonie
Moon-man
> Based on his escapades in the minor leagues.

Giants, Angels, 1975-1990
Miranda, Guillermo
Willy
> From childhood.

Willie
> When he came to the U.S.

Ringling Brothers
> By Paul Richards from his fielding ability.

Barnum and Bailey
> Also by Paul Richards.

Senators, White Sox, Browns, Yankees, Orioles, 1951-1959
Mitchell, Kevin (Darnell)
World
> Given because he could play infield and outfield.

Mitchell Monster: Talonka
Boogie Bear
> From Giants' teammates.

Mets, Padres, Giants, Mariners, Reds, Red Sox, Indians, Athletics, 1984-98
Mitchell, William (Douglas)
D.J.
Yankees, 2012
Mitterling, Ralph
Sarge
> He was a veteran.

Athletics, 1916
Mitterwald, George (Eugene)
Baron von Mitterwald
Twins, Cubs, 1966-1977
Mize, Johnny [John Robert]
The Big Cat
> From teammate Joe Orengo, when Mize reminded him of a cat playing with a ball. "Why, he's a

big cat!"
Big Jawn
>Refers to his weight gain in the Navy.
Cardinals, Giants, Yankees, 1939-53
Mizell, Wilmer (David)
Vinegar Bend
>He was born near Vinegar Bend, Alabama.
Cardinals, Pirates, Mets, 1952-1962
Mizeur, Bill [William Francis]
Bad Bill
Browns, 1923-1924
Moeller, Ron [Ronald Ralph]
The Kid
>Boyish looks and only 17 at his debut.
Orioles, Angels, Senators, 1956-1963
Mohorcic, Dale (Robert)
Horse
>Short for the major sound of his name.
Rangers, Yankees, Expos, 1986-1990
Mole, Fenton (Leroy)
Muscles
Yankees, 1949
Molina, Bengie [Benjamin Jose]
Big Money
Angels, Blue Jays, Giants, Rangers, 1998-2010
Molitor, Paul (Leo)
The Ignitor
>He generated a spark for his clubs.
Molly
>Used by his friends.
Paulie
>Another name from his friends.
Brewers, Blue Jays, Twins, 1978-1998
Molleken, Dustin (Douglas)
Half Moon
Tigers, 2016
Mollwitz, Frederick (August)
Fritz
>Born in Germany.
Cubs, Reds, Pirates, Cardinals, 1913-1919

Monahan, Edward (Francis)
Rinty
Athletics, 1953
Monday, Robert (James)
Rick
Athletics, Cubs, Dodgers, 1966-1984
Mondesi, Raúl (Ramon) {MON-de-see}
The Buffalo
Dodgers, Blue Jays, Yankees, Diamondbacks, Pirates, Angels, Braves, 1993-2005
Money, Don [Donald Wayne]
Brooks: Easy
Phillies, Brewers, 1968-1983
Monroe, Ed [Edward Oliver]
Peck
Yankees, 1917-1918
Montefusco, John (Joseph, Jr.)
The Count
>After a newspaper declared him the Count of Monty Amarillo.
Giants, Braves, Padres, Yankees, 1974-1986
Montgomery, Jordan (Blackmon)
Gumby
Yankees, 2017-
Moolic, George (Henry)
Prunes
White Stockings, 1886
Moon, Leo
Lefty
Indians, 1932
Moore, Alvin (Earl)
Junior
Braves, White Sox, 1976-1980
Moore, D.C.
>D. C. is his actual given name.
Dee
Reds, Dodgers, Phillies, 1936-1946
Moore, Earl [Alonzo Earl]
Crossfire
>From his sidearm pitch from the end of the rubber.
Big Ebbie
Steam Engine in Boots
>Self-proclaimed after a line drive

tore a foot apart.
Lonzo
> Childhood nickname.

Lon
> Short for Lonzo, which is short for Alonzo.

Lon Mower
> From childhood. Read his name.

Blues, Bronchos, Naps, Highlanders, Phillies, Cubs, Buffeds, 1901-1914

Moore, Euel (Walton)
Chief
> The only major league member of the Chicasaw nation.

Monk
> Given by himself and used by neighbors and friends.

Phillies, Giants, 1934-1936

Moore, Gene Jr. [Eugene]
Rowdy
> Bestowed as one might call a tall person "Shorty."

Reds, Cardinals, Bees, Dodgers, Braves, Senators, Browns, 1931-1945

Moore, Gene Sr. [Eugene]
Blue Goose
Pirates, Reds, 1909-1912

Moore, Jo-Jo [Joe Gregg]
The Gause Ghost
> Born, lived and died in Gause, TX.

The Thin Man
> 5'11", 150 lbs. Skinny and awkward.

Giants, 1930-1941

Moore, Lloyd (Albert)
Whitey
Reds, Cardinals, 1936-1942

Moore, Matt [Matthew Cody]
Matty Moe
Rays, Giants, Rangers, Tigers, 2011-2019

Moore, Maurice
Molly
Atlantics, 1875

Moore, Ray [Raymond Leroy]
Farmer
> Helped on the family farm.

Old Blue
> By his teammates.

Bud
> Childhood family nickname.

Dodgers, Orioles, White Sox, Senators, Twins, 1952-1963

Moore, Tyler (Michael)
T-Mo
Nationals, Marlins, 2012-2017

Moore, Warren (Neal III)
Trey
Expos, Braves, 1998-2001

Moore, Wilcy [William Wilcy]
Cy: Deacon
Yankees, Red Sox, 1927-1933

Moore, William (Allen)
Scrappy
Browns, 1917

Moore William (Austin)
Cy
Robins, Dodgers, Phillies, 1929-1934

Morales, Julio (Ruben)
Jerry
Padres, Cubs, Cardinals, Tigers, Mets, 1969-1983

Morales, Kendrys
{KEHN-dreez more-AH-lez}
Mo Mo
Angels, Mariners, Twins, Royals, Blue Jays, Athletics, Yankees, 2006-2019

Moran, Albert (Thomas)
Hiker
Bees, 1938-1939

Moran, Bill [Carl William]
Bugs
White Sox, 1974

Moran, Charlie [Charles Barthell]
Uncle Charlie
Cardinals, 1903, 1908

Moran, Pat [Patrick Joseph]
Old Whiskey Face
> From his friends.

Beaneaters, Cubs, Phillies, 1901-1914

Moran, Roy (Ellis)
Deedle

Senators, 1912
Morton, William P.
Sparrow
Quakers, 1884
Morandini, Mickey [Michael Robert]
{MORE-in-dee-knee}
Dandy Little Glove Man
Based on his defensive ability.
Mickey Mo: Beaker
Phillies, Cubs, Blue Jays, 1990-2000
Morehead, Dave [David Michael]
Moe
Red Sox, Royals, 1963-1970
Morehead, Seth (Marvin)
Moe
Phillies, Cubs, Braves, 1957-1961
Moreland, Keith [Bobby Keith]
Zonk
Phillies, Cubs, Padres, Tigers, Orioles, 1978-1989
Moreland, Mitch [Mitchell Austin Moreland]
Mitchy Two Bags
Rangers, Red Sox, Padres, 2010-
Moren, Lew [Lewis Howard]
Hicks
Pirates, Phillies, 1903-1910
Moreno, Julio
Jiquí
After a hardwood tree because he threw hard.
The Cuban Bob Feller
From his blazing fastball.
Senators, 1950-1953
Moreno, Omar (Renan)
The Antelope: The Outmaker
Pirates, Astros, Yankees, Royals, Braves, 1975-1986
Morgan, Adam (Christopher)
A-Mo
Phillies, 2015-
Morgan, Chester (Collins)
Chet
Chick
From his association with the Memphis Chickasaws.

Tigers, 1935, 1938
Morgan, Cyril (Arlon)
Cy
Given by sportswriters.
Cid
High school nickname.
Braves, 1921-1922
Morgan, Daniel
Pidgey
Red Stockings, Grays, 1875, 1878
Morgan, Eddie [Edwin Willis]
Pepper
Cardinals, Dodgers, 1936-1937
Morgan, Harry (Richard)
Cy
Browns, Americans, Red Sox, Athletics, Reds, 1903-1913
Morgan, James (Edward)
Red
Americans, 1906
Morgan, Joe [Joseph Leonard]
Little Joe
5'7", 160 lbs.
The Little General
Colt 45s, Astros, Reds, Giants, Phillies, Athletics, 1963-1984
Morgan, Nyjer (Jamid)
Tony Plush
Given to himself as his "gentleman's name."
Pirates, Nationals, Brewers, Indians, 2007-2014
Morgan, Tom (Steven)
Plowboy
He was a farmer.
Yankees, Athletics, Tigers, Senators, Angels, 1951-1963
Morhardt, Meredith (Goodwin)
Moe
Cubs, 1961-1962
Morrill, John (Francis)
Honest John
Red Stockings, Beaneaters, Nationals, Reds, 1876-1890
Morris, Ed [Edward]
Cannonball

Buckeyes, Alleghenys, Burghers, 1884-1890
Morris, W Ed [Walter Edward]
Big Ed
Imposing figure; 6'2", 185 lbs.
Cubs, Red Sox, 1922-1931
Morrison, Johnny [John Dewey]
Jughandle Johnny
Based on his curve ball that jughandled down.
Pirates, Robins, 1920-1930
Morrison, Logan [Justis Logan]
LoMo
Marlins, Mariners, Rays, Twins, Phillies, Brewers, 2010-
Morrissey, Jack [John Albert]
King
Reds, 1902-1903
Morrissey, Michael (Joseph)
Frank: Deacon
Americans, Orphans, 1901-1902
Morrow, Brandon (John)
B Mo
Mariners, Blue Jays, Padres, Dodgers, Cubs, 2007-
Morse, Mike [Michael John]
The Beast
Mariners, Nationals Orioles, Giants, Marlins, Pirates, 2005-2017
Morse, Newell (Obediah Sr.)
Bud
Athletics, 1929
Morse, Pete [Peter Raymond]
Hap
Cardinals, 1911
Morton, Charlie [Charles Alfred]
Ground Chuck: Uncle Charlie
Braves, Pirates, Phillies, Astros, Rays, 2008-
Morton, Guy Jr.
Moose
6'2", 200 lbs.
Hoss: Salty
Red Sox, 1954
Morton, Guy Sr.
The Alabama Blossom

Born and raised in Alabama.
Naps, Indians, 1914-1924
Morton, Wycliffe (Nathaniel)
Bubba
Tigers, Braves, Angels, 1961-1969
Moryn, Walt [Walter Joseph]
Moose
6'2", 205 lbs.
The Blond Adonis
Newspaper nickname for his long, blond hair-never caught on.
Dodgers, Cubs, Cardinals, Pirates, 1954-1961
Moseby, Lloyd (Anthony)
Shaker
From his ability to get away from defenders... in basketball.
Blue Jays, Tigers, 1980-1991
Moses, Wally [Wallace]
Peepsight
Patient and keen eye at the plate.
The Georgia Express
Given by the *Sporting News*.
Athletics, White Sox, Red Sox, 1935-1951
Moskiman, William (Bankhead)
Doc
Went to medical school but never finished.
Red Sox, 1910
Moss, Brandon (Douglas)
Moss Dogg
Red Sox, Pirates, Phillies, Athletics, Indians, Cardinals, Royals, 2007-2017
Mossi, Don [Donald Louis]
Ears
His ears stuck out.
The Sphinx
Very long, slightly crooked nose.
Indians, Tigers, White Sox, Athletics, 1954-1965
Mostil, Johnny [John Anthony]
Bananas
White Sox, 1918-1929
Mott, Elisha (Matthew)

Bitsy
Phillies, 1945
Mottola, Charles (Edward)
Chad
Reds, Blue Jays, Marlins, Orioles, 1996-2006
Mountjoy, Bill [William Henry]
Medicine Bill
Red Stockings, Orioles, 1883-1885
Moustakis, Mike [Michael Christopher] {moo-STOCK-us}
Moose
From Little League coach and fans.
Royals, Brewers, 2011-
Mowrey, Harry (Harlan)
Mike
Mike the Hobo
He was friendly when his sheriff-father let hobos sleep in the jail.
Reds, Cardinals, Pirates, Rebels, Robins, 1905-1917
Moylan, Peter (Michael)
Sledge
Braves, Dodgers, Royals, 2006-2018
Mueller, Bill [William Lawrence]
Hawk
White Sox, 1942, 1945
Mueller, Clarence (Francis)
Heinie
A pre-WWII name for those of German descent.
Cardinals, Giants, Braves, Browns, 1920-1935
Mueller, Don [Donald Frederick] {MYOO-ler}
Mandrake the Magician
He was adept at putting the ball in play and through the infield.
Giants, White Sox, 1948-1959
Mueller, Emmet (Jerome)
Heinie
Phillies, 1938-1941
Mueller, Ray (Coleman)
Iron Man
Caught a National League record 233 consecutive games.
Braves, Bees, Pirates, Reds, Giants, Pirates, 1935-1951
Muich, Ignatius (Andrew)
Joe
Braves, 1924
Mujica, Edward (Jose) {moo-HEE-kah}
The Chief
Indians, Padres, Marlins, Cardinals, Red Sox, Athletics, Tigers, 2006-2017
Mulcahy, Hugh (Noyes)
Losing Pitcher
Never had a full season where he won more than he lost.
Iron Man
Led the league in 1937 with 57 starts.
Phillies, Pirates, 1935-1947
Mullane, Tony [Anthony John]
Count: The Apollo of the Box
Wolverines, Eclipse, Browns, Blue Stockings, Red Stockings, Reds, Orioles, Spiders, 1881-1894.
Mulleavy, Greg [Gregory Thomas]
Moe
White Sox, Red Sox, 1930-1933
Mullen, Ford (Parker)
Moon
From the comic strip *Moon Mullins*.
Phillies, 1944
Mulligan, Joe [Joseph Ignatius]
Big Joe
6'4", 210 lbs.
Red Sox, 1934
Mullin, George (Joseph)
Wabash George
Played semi-pro ball in Wabash, Indiana.
Big George
6'0", 188 lbs.
Tigers, Senators, Hoosiers, Pepper, 1902-1915
Munce, John (Louis)
Big John
Not particularly: 5'8", 160 lbs.

Quicksteps, 1884
Munger, George (David)
Red
    Had thick red hair as a youngster.
Cardinals, Pirates, 1943-1956
Munns, Les [Leslie Ernest]
Nemo: Big Ed
Dodgers, Cardinals, 1934-1936
Munson, Clarence (Hanford)
Red
    Wavy, carrot-top hair.
Phillies, 1905
Munson, Thurman (Lee)
Tugboat: Squatty Body: The Walrus
Yankees, 1969-1979
Murakami, Masanori
Mashi
Giants, 1964-1965
Murchison, Thomas (Malcolm)
Tim
Cardinals, Indians, 1917, 1920
Murff, John (Robert)
Red
Braves, 1956-1957
Murphy, Con [Cornelius B]
Monk: Razzle Dazzle
Quakers, Ward's Wonders, 1884, 90
Murphy, Connie [Cornelius David]
Stone Face
Reds, 1893-1894
Murphy, Dale (Bryan)
The Murph
Mr. Clean
    Clean cut, subdued, quiet manner. As compared to Dr. Dirt (Lenny Dykstra) in a Pinterest photo.
Braves, Phillies, Rockies, 1976-1993
Murphy, Danny [Daniel Joseph]
Handsome Dan
Giants, 1892
Murphy, Dave [David Francis]
Dirty Dave
Beaneaters, 1905
Murphy, Eddie [John Edward]
Honest Eddie
    He was not one of the players involved in the Black Sox Scandal.
Athletics, White Sox, Pirates, 1912-1926
Murphy, Francis (J)
Tony
Metropolitans, 1884
Murphy, Herbert (Courtland)
Dummy
Phillies, 1914
Murphy, John P (Patrick)
Soldier Boy
Cardinals, Tigers, 1902-1903
Murphy, John R (Ryan)
J.R.
Yankees, Twins, Diamondbacks, 2013-
Murphy, Johnny [John Joseph]
Fireman
    One of the top bullpen specialists of the era.
Grandma
    Constantly complained about meals and accommodations.
Fordham Johnny
    Attended Fordham, University.
Yankees, Red Sox, 1932-1947
Murphy, Leo (Joseph)
Red
Pirates, 1915
Murphy, Robert (Sylvester)
Buzz
Braves, Senators, 1918-1919
Murphy, Willie [William H.]
Gentle Willie
    So-named because he was anything but.
Blues, Nationals, 1884
Murphy, William (Henry)
Yale: Tot
Midget
    5'3", 125 lbs.
Giants, 1894-1897
Murray, Arlington (John)
A.J.
Rangers, 2007-2008

Murray, Bill [William Allenwood]
   Dasher
   Senators, 1917
Murray, Eddie (Clarence)
   Steady Eddie
   Orioles, Dodgers, Mets, Indians,
   Angels, 1977-1997
Murray, George (King)
   Smiler
   Tarheel
      He came from North Carolina.
   Yankees, Red Sox, Senators, White
   Sox, 1922-1933
Murray, Jim [James Francis]
   Big Jim
   Robins, 1922
Murray, John (Joseph)
   Red
   Cardinals, Giants, Cubs, 1906-1917
Murray, Ray [Raymond Lee]
   Deacon
      He preached to the umpires.
   Indians, Athletics, Orioles, 1948-54
Musgrove, Joe [Joseph Anthony]
   Moose
      6'5", 235 lbs.
   Astros, Pirates, 2016-
Musial, Stan [Stanley Frank]
   Stan the Man
      From fans who chated, "Here
      comes the man!"
   Stashu {STASH-you}
      Family Polish nickname.
   Stash
      Americanized version of Stashu.
   The Donora Greyhound
      From Donora, as an up-and-
      coming Pennsylvania player.
   Cardinals, 1941-1963
Mussill, Bernard (James)
   Barney
   Phillies, 1944
Mussina, Mike [Michael Cole]
{meu-SEE-na}
   Moose
      The first syllable of his name is
      similar to the animal.
   Orioles, Yankees, 1991-2008
Myatt, George (Edward)
   Mercury
      A threat to steal.
   Stud
      A term he used when he could not
      remember a name.
   Foghorn
      "You could hear him whisper in a
      sawmill."
   Giants, Seantors, 1938-1947
Myer, Charles (Solomon)
   Buddy
   Senators, Red Sox, 1925-1941
Myers, Al [James Albert]
   Cod
   Brewers, Quakers, Cowboys,
   Nationals, Phillies, 1884-1891
Myers, Henry (Harrison)
   Hi: Hy
      The spelling depends upon who is
      writing.
   Superbas, dodgers, Robins, Cardinals,
   Reds, 1909-1925
Myers, Ralph (Edward)
   Hap
   Red Sox, Browns, Braves, Tip-Tops,
   1910-1915
Myers, Randy [Randall Kirk]
   Mr. Mellow
      Facetiously by teammates; a
      ferocious look.
   Mets, Reds, Padres, Cubs, Orioles,
   Blue Jays, 1985-1998
Myers, Wil [William Bradford]
   El Gallo
   Rays, Padres, 2013-
Nagle, Walter (Harold)
   Judge
      He worked in a courthouse.
   Lucky
      At 25, he was given six months to
      live: He died at 91.
   Pirates, Red Sox, 1911
Nahem, Sam [Samuel Ralph]

Subway Sam
: Minor league teammates never met a New Yorker before.
Dodgers, Cardinals, Phillies, 1938-48

Naleway, Frank
Chick
White Sox, 1924

Nance, William (Gideon)
Kid: Doc
Colonels, Tigers, 1897-1901

Napier, Skelton (Leroy)
Buddy
Browns, Cubs, Reds, 1912-1921

Napoli, Mike [Michael Anthony]
Porterhouse
Angels, Rangers, Red Sox, Indians, 2006-2017

Naranjo, Lazaro (Ramón)
{nah-RAHN-ho}
Cholly
: From his grandmother, referring to the shape of his head.
Cholito
: A diminutative form of Choly, which became Cholly.
Gonzalo
: His third given name.
Pirates, 1956

Narleski, Bill [William Edward]
Cap
: Captain of the second team in Spring training with spirited play.
Red Sox, 1929-1930

Narum, Leslie (Ferdinand)
Buster
Orioles, senators, 1963-1967

Nash, Charles (Francis)
Cotton
: Based on his bright blond hair.
Cotton-top
: From an uncle as a child.
The Bayou Bomber
: From his high school basketball ability.
White Sox, Twins, 1967-1970

Nash, Jim [James Edwin]
Jumbo
6'5", 215 lbs.
Athletics, Braves, Phillies, 1966-1972

Nava, Vincent (Irwin)
Sandy
: Played as Sandy Irwin prior to the major leagues.
Grays, Orioles, 1882-1886

Navarro, Julio
Whiplash
: For his sidearm fastball.
El Látigo
: Spanish for Whiplash.
Juju
: Nickname growing up.
Angels, Tigers, Braves, 1962-1970

Navarro, Norberto
Tito
Mets, 1993

Naylor, Josh [Joshua-Douglas James]
Mississauga Masher
: His birthplace in Canada.
Padres, Indians, 2019-

Neal, Theophilus (Fountain)
Offa
Giants, 1905

Neale, Alfred (Earle)
Greasy
: From a name-calling interaction in his youth.
Reds, Phillies, 1916-1924

Needham, Tom [Thomas Joseph]
Deerfoot
Beaneaters, Doves, Giants, Cubs, 1904-1914

Neighbors, Cecil (Fleming)
Cy
Pirates, 1908

Nekola, Francis (Joseph)
Bots
Yankees, Tigers, 1929, 1933

Nelson, Albert (Francis)
Red
Browns, Phillies, Reds, 1910-1913

Nelson, Andy [Andrew Anthony]

Peaches
Battler
> From a newspaper, referring to a popular boxer.
White Sox, 1908
Nelson, Emmett [George Emmett]
Ramrod
Reds, 1935-1936
Nelson, Glenn (Richard)
Rocky
> From a teammate when a ball bounced off his head during a game of pepper. He was unhurt.
Spike
> Childhood nickname.
Cardinals, Pirates, White Sox, Dodgers, Indians, 1949-1961
Nelson, Jimmy [James Jacob]
Big Sweat
Brewers, 2013-
Nelson, John (W)
Candy
> Indicated a quality player at the time.
Haymakers, Eckfords, Mutuals, Blues, Trojans, Ruby Legs, Metropolitans, Giants, Gladiators, 1872-1890
Nelson, Luther (Martin)
Luke
Yankees, 1919
Nelson, Lynn (Bernard)
Line Drive
> From what opposing hitters did to his pitches.
Cubs, Athletics, Tigers, 1930-1940
Nelson, Ray [Raymond]
Kell
Giants, 1901
Nelson, Robert (Sidney)
Tex
> He is from Dallas, Texas.
Babe
> Known in high school as the Babe Ruth of Texas.
Orioles, 1955-1957

Nelson, Roger (Eugene)
Spider
White Sox, Orioles, Royals, Reds, 1967-1976
Neris, Héctor {EK-tor NAIR-iss}
Happy Hector: Compa H
Phillies, 2014-
Nettles, Graig {Greg}
Puff
Twins, Indians, Yankees, Padres, Braves, Expos, 1967-1988
Neuer, John (Stein)
Tacks
> He was either great or terrible.
Bugs
> Had strange behavior on many ocassions.
Highlanders, 1907
Newcombe, Don [Donald]
Tiger
> Duke Snider said, "Roar, Tiger," when Newcombe went to pitch.
Big Newk
Dodgers, Redlegs, Reds, Indians, 1949-1960
Newhouser, Hal [Harold]
Prince Hal
> From the way he carried himself.
Hurricane Hal
> Threw tantrums in the clubhouse when upset.
Tigers, Indians, 1939-1955
Newkirk, Floyd (Elmo)
Three Finger
Yankees, 1934
Newkirk, Joel (Ivan)
Sailor
Cubs, 1919-1920
Newman, Charlie [Charles Frank]
Decker
Giants, Colts, 1892
Newnam, Robert (Albert)
Pat
Browns, 1910-1911
Newsom, Louis (Norman)
Buck

A family nickname.
Bobo
  Never remembered names; everyone was Bobo.
Robins, Cubs, Browns, Senators, Red Sox, Tigers, Dodgers, Athletics, Yankees, Giants, 1929-1953

Newsome, Heber (Hamilton)
Dick
  Since birth, called Dick by his father and everyone.
Red Sox, 1941-1943

Newsome, Lamar (Ashby)
Skeeter
  His friends thought he wasn't much larger than a mosquito.
Athletics, Red Sox, Phillies, 1935-47

Newsome, Ljay (Wyatt)
Quiet Assassin
Mariners, 2020-

Newson, Warren (Dale)
The Deacon
  Bestowed by announcer Ken Harrelson.
White Sox, Mariners, Rangers. 1991-1998

Newton, Eustace (James)
Doc
  He was a dentist.
Reds, Superbas, Highlanders, 1900-1909

Niarhos, Constantine (Gregory) {NYE-uh-hoss}
Gus
  Nickname since birth.
Blood Bank
  From teammates suggesting he needed to put on weight.
Yankees, White Sox, Red Sox, Phillies, 1946-1955

Nicasio, Juan (Ramon)
Arenoso
Rockies, Dodgers, Pirates, Phillies, Cardinals, Mariners, Rangers, 2011-

Nicholas, Don [Donald Leigh]
The Phoenix Flash
  Born in Phoenix.
White Sox, 1952, 1954

Nichols, Charles (Augustus)
Chet
Kid
  Looked more like a batboy than a player.
Nervy Nick
  From the press for daring style of play.
Beaneaters, Cardinals, Phillies, 1890-1906

Nichols, Frederick (C)
Tricky
Elm Cities, Red Stockings, Brown Stockings, Grays, Ruby Legs, Orioles, 1875-1882

Nicholson, Bill [William Beck]
Swish
  From his mighty swing.
Big Bill: Nick
Athletics, Cubs, Phillies, 1936-1953

Nicholson, Fred
Shoemaker
Tigers, Pirates, Braves, 1917-1922

Nicholson, Thomas (Clark)
Parson
  He refused to play baseball on Sunday.
Deacon
Wolverines, Maumees, Senators, 1888-1895

Nicolino, Justin (Brian)
Big Bird
Marlins, 2015-2017

Niebergall, Charlie [Charles Arthur]
Nig
Cardinals, 1921-1924

Niedenfuer, Thomas (Edward)
Buff: Buffalo Head
Dodgers, Orioles, Mariners, Cardinals, 1981-1990

Niekro, Phil [Philip Henry] {NEE-crow}
Knucksie
  From his ability to throw knuckleballs with authority.

Braves, Yankees, Indians, Blue Jays, 1964-1987
Nieman, Elmer (Leroy)
Butch
    Gained as a youngster.
Braves, 1943-1945
Niemes, Jacob (Leland)
Jack
Reds, 1943
Nieve, Fernando (Alexis) {knee-AYVE-ay}
Nightly Nieve
    From TV announcers for his workload.
Astros, Mets, 2006-2010
Niland, Tom [Thomas James]
Honest Tom
Browns, 1896
Niles, Herbert (Clyde)
Harry
Home Run Harry
    Briefly after hitting back-to-back homers.
Hep
    From his semi-pro days.
Browns, Highlanders, Red Sox, Naps, 1906-1910
Nill, George (Charles)
Rabbit
Senators, Naps, 1904-1908
Nitkowski, Christopher (John)
C.J.
Reds, Tigers, Astros, Mets, Rangers, Braves, Yankees, Nationals, 1995-2005
Nixon, Al [Albert Richard]
Humpty Dumpty
Robins, Braves, Phillies, 1915-1928
Noble, Rafael (Miguel) {NO-blay}
Ray
Son
    How his father always referred to him.
Bushman
    Racial epithet by Alvin Dark.
Giants, 1951-1953

Noboa, Miciades (Arturo)
Junior
Indians, Angels, Expos, Mets, Athletics, Pirates, 1984-1994
Nolan, Ed [Edward Sylvester]
The Only Nolan
    Pitched 11 straight games, won them all.
Blues, Alleghenys, Quicksteps, Quakers, 1878-1885
Nolasco, Carlos (Enrique) {nuh-LASS-co}
Ricky
    Father named him after Rick Monday, his favorite player.
Tricky
Marlins, Dodgers, Twins, Angels, 2006-2017
Nomo, Hideo
The Tornado
    Based on his back-to-the-batter wind-up.
Tatsu-maki
    Japanese for The Tornado.
Dodgers, Mets, Brewers, Tigers, Red Sox, Devil Rays, Royals, 1995-2008
Nonnenkamp, Leo (William)
Red: Nonny
Pirates, Red Sox, 1933-1940
Norman, Henry (Willis Patrick)
Bill
White Sox, 1931-1932
Norris, Daniel (David)
D.No
Blue Jays, Tigers, 2014-
Norris, David (Stefan)
Bud: Budsworth
Astros, Orioles, Padres, Braves, Dodgers, Angels, Cardinals, 2009-2018
Norris, Derek (Russell)
Norrisaurusrex
Athletics, Padres, Rays, 2012-2017
Northrop, George (Howard)
Jake: Jerky
Braves, 1918-1919
Norton, Elisha (Strong)
Effie: Leiter

Nova, Iván

Senator, 1896-1897
Nova, Iván (Manuel) {ee-VON NO-vah}
Super Nova
Yankees, Pirates, White Sox, 2010-
Novikoff, Lou [Louis Alexander]
The Mad Russian
Cubs, Phillies, 1941-1946
Novotney, Ralph (Joseph)
Rube
Cubs, 1949
Nutter, Everett (Clarence)
Dizzy
Braves, 1919
Nuxhall, Joe [Joseph Henry]
Ol' Lefthander: Nuxy: Hamilton Joe
Reds, Redlegs, Athletics, Angels, 1944-1966
O'Brien, Frank (Aloysius)
Dink
Phillies, 1923
O'Brien, John F
Cinders
Blues, Spiders, Infants, Reds, 1888-91
O'Brien, John J (Joseph)
Chewing Gum
Grooms, Colts, Colonels, Senators, Orioles, Pirates, 1891-1899
O'Brien, John T (Thomas)
Little John: Johnny O
Pirates, Cardinals, Braves, 1953-1959
O'Brien, Thomas (Joseph)
Buck
  Nickname from an early age.
Red Sox, White Sox, 1911-1913
O'Brien, Tom [Thomas H]
Darby
Ruby Legs, Orioles, Reds, Metropolitans, Brancos, 1882-1890
O'Brien, Tommy [Thomas Edward]
Obie
Pirates, Red Sox, Senators, 1943-1950
O'Connor, Jack J [John Joseph]
Rowdy Jack
  For his role as a "Henchman" for the Spiders.
Peach Pie
  From teammates after he had played for the semi-pro "Peach Pies."
Red Stockings, Solons, Spiders, Perfectos, Cardinals, Pirates, Highlanders, Browns, 1887-1910
O'Connor, Jack W (William)
Oak
Twins, Expos, Orioles, 1981-1987
O'Connor, Johnny [John Charles]
Bucky
Cubs, 1916
O'Day, Darren (Christopher)
Odachowski
Angels, Mets, Rangers, Orioles, Braves, 2008-
O'Day, Hank [Henry Martin Francis]
Tank
  Liked beer.
Peep
The Reverend
  Would not speak a civil word to anyone off the field.
Blue Stockings, Alleghenys, Nationals, Giants, 1884-1890
O'Dea, Paul
Lefty
Indians, 1944-1945
O'Donnell, Harry (Herman)
Butch
Phillies, 1927
O'Doul, Francis (Joseph)
Lefty
The Man in the Green Suit
  An outfit worn daily.
Yankees, Red sox, Giants, Phillies, Robins, Dodgers, 1919-1934
O'Hara James (Francis)
Kid
Beaneaters, 1904
O'Leary, Dan [Daniel]
Hustling Dan

Grays, Red Stockings, Wolverines,
Ruby Legs, Outlaw Reds, 1879-1884
O'Neal, Oran (Herbert)
Skinny
> 5'11" but only 160 lbs.

Phillies,
1925, 1927
O'Neil, Michael
Fancy
> Reportedly from his time as a boxer.

Dark Blues,
1874
O'Neill, Emmett [Robert Emmett]
Pinky
Red Sox, Cubs, White Sox,
1943-1946
O'Neill, Fred [Frederick James]
Tip
Metropolitans
1887
O'Neill, James (Edward)
Tip
The Woodstock Wonder
> The town he grew up in.

Canada's Babe Ruth
> Triple Crown hitter from Canada.

Gothams, Browns, Pirates, Reds,
1883-1892
O'Neill, John [William John]
Tip
Americans, Senators, White Sox,
1904-1906
O'Neill, Paul (Andrew)
The Warrior
> From his passion and love for the game.

Reds, Yankees,
1985-2001
O'Neill, Philip (Bernard)
Peaches
Reds,
1904
O'Rourke, Frank [James Francis]
Blackie
Braves, Robins, Senators, Red Sox,
Tigers, Browns, 1912-1931
O'Rourke, James (Stephen)
Queenie
Highlanders, 1908
O'Rourke, Jim [James Henry]
Orator Jim
> Verbose on field, high intellect and a law degree.

Mansfields, Red Stockings, Grays,
Bisons, Giants, Senators, 1872-1904
O'Rourke, Joseph Sr. (Leo)
Patsy
Cardinals, 1908
O'Rourke, Tim [Timothy Patrick]
Voiceless Tim
Stars, Solons, Orioles, Colonels,
Browns, Senators, 1890-1894
Oakes, Ennis (Telfair)
Rebel
> From Louisiana, given by a sportswriter.

Reds, Cardinals, Rebels, 1909-1915
Oana, Henry (Kawaihoa, Jr.)
Prince
> Used by minor league team owner to promote ticket sales.

Nutsky
> A High school nickname.

Tigers, 1943, 1945
Oberlander, Hartman (Louis)
Doc
> A physician in Montana and elsewhere.

Blues, 1888
Oberlin, Frank (Rufus)
Flossie
> He liked to stay in his hotel room and embroider.

Americans, Senators, 1906-1910
Ock, Harold (David)
Whitey
Dodgers, 1935
Ockey, Walter (Andrew)
Footie
Giants, 1944
Odenwald, Ted [Theodore Joseph]

Lefty
Indians, 1921-1922
Odom, Dave [David Everett]
Blimp
Porky
6'1", 220 lbs.
Braves, 1943
Odom, Johnny (Lee)
Blue Moon
> From grade-school. His face looked like the moon.

Athletics, Indians, Braves, White Sox, 1964-1976
Odor, Rougned (Roberto)
{ROOG-ned oh-DOOR}
Stink: Stinky: El Tipo
Rangers, 2014-
Odwell, Fred [Frederick William]
Fritz
Reds, 1904-1907
Oertel, Chuck [Charles Frank]
Snuffy: Ducky
Orioles, 1958
Ogden, Warren (Harvey)
Curly
> Picked up in childhood for his hair.

Athletics, Senators, 1922-1926
Ogrodowski, Ambrose (Francis)
Bruce: Brusie
Cardinals, 1936-1937
Oh, Seunghwan {Soong-hwan}
Final Boss: Stone Buddha
Cardinals, Blue Jays, Rockies, 2016-2019
Okrie, Frank (Anthony)
Lefty
Tigers, 1920
Oldham, John (Cyrus)
Red
Tigers, Pirates, 1914-1926
Olerud, John (Garrett)
Cheetah
> From college for his lack of speed.

Gabby
> From Blue Jays teammates; he never said much.

Hobbsy
> He had a natural Roy Hobbs-like swing (from *The Natural*).

Johnny O: Big Rude
Blue Jays, Mets, Mariners, Yankees, Red Sox, 1989-2005
Oliver, Al [Albert]
Scoop
Pirates, Rangers, Expos, Giants, Phillies, Dodgers, Blue Jays, 1968-85
Oliver, Nate [Nathaniel]
Pee-Wee
Dodgers, Giants, Yankees, Cubs, 1963-1969
Oliver, Tom [Thomas Noble]
Rebel
> An Alabama native with a southern drawl.

Red Sox, 1930-1933
Olivo, Federico (Emilio)
Chi-Chi {chee-CHEE}
> Meaning: baby; he was the baby of the family.

Braves, 1961-1966
Olson, Gregg [Greggory William]
Otter
Orioles, Braves, Indians, Royals, Tigers, Astros, Twins, Diamondbacks, Dodgers, 1988-2001
Olson, Marv [Marvin Clement]
Sparky
> His nickname primarily as a manager.

Red Sox, 1931-1933
Onis, Manuel (Dominguez)
Ralph: Curly
Dodgers, 1935
Oquendo, José (Manuel) {oh-KEN-dough}
Secret Weapon
> Bestowed by manager Whitey Herzog.

Mets, Cardinals, 1983-1995
Ordenana, Tony [Antonio]
Mosquito
Pirates, 1943

Orrell, Forrest (Gordon)
Joe
Tigers, 1943-1945
Orsino, John (Joseph)
Horse
Giants, Orioles, Senators, 1961-1967
Ortega, Phil [Filomeno Coronada]
Kemo
    Of indian descent.
Dodgers, Senators, Angels, 1960-69
Ortenzio, Frank (Joseph)
Moose
Royals, 1973
Orth, Al [Albert Lewis]
Smiling Al
The Curveless Wonder
    Always relied on speed changes and his control.
Phillies, Senators, Highlanders, 1895-1909
Ortiz, Adalberto
Junior
Pirates, Mets, Twins, Indians, Rangers, 1982-1994
Ortiz, David (Americo)
Cookie Monster: Big O
Big Papi
    Called everyone Papi when he couldn't remember their name.
Señor Octubre
    From his postseason play in 2013.
Cooperstown
    Also from his 2013 postseason.
Twins, Red Sox, 1997-2016
Ortiz, Oliverio
Baby
Senators, 1944
Osborne, Ernest (Preston)
Tiny
    He was 6'4", 215 lbs.
Cubs, Robins, 1922-1925
Osborne, Larry (Sidney)
Bobo
Tigers, Senators, 1957-1963
Osinski, Dan [Daniel]
The Silencer
Athletics, Braves, Red Sox, White Sox, Astros, 1962-1970
Osteen, Claude (Wilson)
Gomer
Reds, Senators, Dodgers, Astros, Cardinals, White Sox, 1957-1975
Ostergard, Roy (Lund)
Red
White Sox, 1921
Ostermueller, Frederick (Raymond)
Fritz: Old Folks: Ostey
Red Sox, Browns, Dodgers, Pirates, 1934-1948
Ostrowski, Joe [Joseph Paul]
Specs
Professor
    He was a teacher before his baseball career.
Browns, Yankees, 1948-1952
Osuna, Antonio (Pedro)
El Cañón
Dodgers, White Sox, Yankees, Padres, Nationals, 1995-2005
Osuna, Roberto
Little Cannon: Osuna Matata
No Panic
Blue Jays, Astros, 2015-
Osuno, José (Gregorio) {oh-SOON-ah}
El Gocho
Pirates, 2017-
Oswalt, Roy (Edward) {OWES-walt}
The Wizard of Os
Astros, Phillies, Rangers, Rockies, 2001-2013
Otey, Bill [William Tilford]
Steamboat Bill
Pirates, Senators, 1907-1911
Otis, Amos (Joseph)
A.O.
    Royals fans chanted "Aaaay Oh! Aaaay Oh!"
Famous Amos
    From an all-star game throw: center field to home.
Mets, Royals, Pirates, 1967-1984
Otis, Harry (George)

Cannonball
Naps, 1909
Otis, Paul (Franklin)
Bill
> Acquired at Williams College. He did not know why.
Highlanders, 1912
Ott, Mel [Melvin Thomas]
Master Melvin: The Shetland Pony
Giants, 1926-1947
Otten, John (G)
Joe
Browns, 1895
Outen, William (Austin)
Chink
Plunging Chink
> Gained in college.
Dodgers, 1933
Overmire, Frank (W)
Stubby
> Based on his size: 5'7", 170 lbs.
Tigers, Browns, Yankees, 1943-1952
Owen, Arnold (Malcolm)
Mickey
> From a manager for his similarity to Mickey Cochrane.
Preacher
> From the minor leagues. He was from the bible-belt.
Cardinals, Dodgers, Cubs, Red Sox, 1937-1954
Owen, Frank (Malcolm)
Yip
> Born in Ypsilanti, Michigan.
Tigers, White Sox, 1901-1909
Owen, Marv [Marvin James]
Freck
> For the freckles on his face.
Tigers, White Sox, Red Sox, 1931-40
Owens, Frank (Walter)
Yip
> Likely from confusion with Frank Owen (no S).
Americans, White Sox, Tip-Tops, Terrapins, 1905-1915
Owens, Furman (Lee)

Jack
Athletics, 1935
Owens, Jim [James Philip]
Bear
Phillies, Reds, Colt .45s, Astros, 1955-1967
Owens, Thomas (Llewellyn)
Red
Phillies, Superbas, 1899, 1905
Owings, Chris [Christopher Scott]
C.O.
Diamondbacks, Royals, Red Sox, Rockies, 2013-
Oyler, Andy [Andrew Paul]
Pepper
Orioles, 1902
Oyler, Ray [Raymond Francis]
Oil Can Harry
Tigers, Pilots, Angels, 1965-1970
Ozmer, Horace (Robert)
Doc
Athletics, 1923
Ozuna, Marcell
The Big Bear
Marlins, Cardinals, Braves, 2013-
Pabor, Charlie [Charles Henry]
The Old Woman in the Red Cap
Forest Citys, Atlantics, Whites, Elm Citys, 1871-1875
Paciorek, Tom [Thomas Marian]
{pa-CHORE-ick}
Wimpy
> Named after he ordered a hamburger rather than steak at a dinner with teammates.
Dodgers, Braves, Mariners, White Sox, Mets, Rangers, 1970-1987
Paddack, Chris [Christopher Joseph]
Sheriff
Padres, 2019-
Padden, Dick [Richard Joseph]
Brains
Pirates, Senators, Cardinals, Browns, 1896-1905
Padgett, Ernie [Ernest Kitchen]
Red

Braves, Indians, 1923-1927
Pafko, Andy [Andrew]
Handy Andy
> From the minors for his versatility.

Pruschka
Cubs, Dodgers, Braves, 1943-1959
Pagán, Ángel (Manuel)
Crazy Horse
El Caballo Loco
> Spanish for Crazy Horse; given by early year teammates.

Cubs, Mets, Giants, 2006-2016
Page, Joe [Joseph Francis]
Fireman
The Gay Reliever
> He was carefree and spent late nights with Joe DiMaggio.

Yankees, Pirates, 1944-1954
Paige, Leroy (Robert)
The Ageless Wonder
> Oldest rookie to enter the majors.

Satchel
> Worked as a train porter at the age of seven.

Indians, Browns, Athletics, 1948-65
Paige, George (Lynn)
Pat: Piggy: Mabel
Naps, 1911
Paine, Phil [Phillips Steere]
Flip
Braves, Cardinals, 1951-1958
Pall, Donn [Donald Steven]
The Pope
White Sox, Phillies, Yankees, Cubs, Marlins, 1988-1998
Palm, Richard (Paul)
Mike
> Given in high school by a coach named Mike... Palm.

Red Sox, 1948
Palmeiro, Rafael
Emerson Lake And
> Chris Bermanism referring to rock group, Emerson, Lake and Palmer.

The Saccharin Slugger
> From fans in his 2015 minor league club.

Cubs, Rangers, Orioles, 1986-2005
Palmer, Eddie [Edwin Henry]
Baldy
Athletics, 1917
Palmer, Jim [James Alvin]
Cakes
> He ate pancakes for breakfast on pitching days.

Orioles, 1965-1984
Papish, Frank (Richard)
Pap
White Sox, Indians, Pirates, 1945-50
Pappas, Milt [Milton Stephen]
Gimpy
Orioles, Reds, Braves, Cubs, 1957-73
Parisse, Louis (Peter)
Tony
Athletics, 1942-1944
Park, Byung Ho
Park Bang
Twins, 2016
Parker, Clarence M. (McKay)
Ace
Athletics, 1937-1938
Parker, Clarence P. (Perkins)
Pat
Browns, 1915
Parker, Dave [David Gene]
The Cobra
> Given by a trainer early in his Pirates career.

Pirates, Reds, Athletics, Brewers, Angels, Blue Jays, 1973-1991
Parker, Douglas (Wooley)
Dixie
> Born and died in Alabama.

Phillies, 1923
Parker, Francis (James)
Salty
Tigers, 1936
Parker, Harley (Park)
Doc
Colts, Reds, 1893-1901

Parker, Wes [Maurice Wesley]
  Mr. Steady
    Won a Gold Glove in seven consecutive years.
  Dodgers, 1964-1972

Parks, Vernon (Henry)
  Slicker
  Tigers, 1921

Parmelee, Roy [Leroy Earl]
  Tarzan
    From a sportswriter for his wildness.
  Bud
    Name in Toledo after a local softball star.
  Doc
    From Casey Stengel because his father was a doctor.
  Big Bess
    Stengel thought he walked like a girl.
  Giants, Cardinals, Cubs, Athletics, 1929-1939

Parnell, Mel [Melvin Lloyd]
  Dusty
    His high school coach said he threw in the dirt a lot.
  Red Sox, 1947-1956

Parnham, James (Arthur)
  Rube
  Athletics, 1916-1917

Parra, Gerardo (Enrique)
  {her-ARR-doe PAR-uh}
  Parra Shark
  Diamondbacks, Brewers, Orioles, Rockies, Giants, Nationals, 2009-2019

Parrish, Lance (Michael)
  Big Wheel
    Kept the Detroit team going on a daily basis.
  Tigers, Phillies, Angels, Mariners, Indians, Pirates, Blue Jays, 1977-1995

Parrott, Tom [Thomas William]
  Tacky Tom
  Tacks
    Possibly from his outrageous and clownish behavior.
  Colts, Reds, Browns, 1893-1896

Parrott, Walter (Edward)
  Jiggs
  Colts, 1892-1895

Parson, William (Edwin)
  Jiggs
  Doves, Rustlers, 1910-1911

Partenheimer, Harold (Philip)
  Steve
  Tigers, 1913

Partridge, James (Bugg)
  Jay
  Robins, 1927-1928

Pascual, Camilo (Alberto)
  Camile
  Little Potato
    His older brother, Carlos, was nicknamed 'Potato.'
  Patato Pequeño
    Spanish for Little Potato, but loosely equal to 'shorty.'
  Senators, Twins, Reds, Dodgers, Indians, 1954-1971

Pascual, Carlos (Alberto)
  Patato
    Spanish for 'short.' He was 5'6".
  Big Potato
    A corruption of the Spanish.
  Senators, 1950

Paskert, George (Henry)
  Dode
    Defined at the time as 'slow witted.'
  Honey Boy
    Because he was a sweet ballplayer.
  Reds, Phillies, Cubs, 1907-1921

Pasquella, Mike [Michael John]
  Toney
  Phillies, Cardinals, 1919

Pastorius, Jim [James Washington]
  Sunny Jim
    From his part in a cereal advertisement.
  Superbas, 1906-1909

Patek, Freddie [Frederick Joseph]
{PAW-tek}
    The Flea: The Cricket
    Pirates, Royals, Angels, 1968-1981

Patterson, Bob [Robert Chandler]
    Glove Doctor
    Padres, Pirates, Rangers, Angles, Cubs, 1982-1998

Patterson, John (William)
    Red
    Dodgers, 2014

Patterson, Roy (Lewis)
    St. Croix
        Lived most of his life in St. Croix Falls, Wisconsin.
    Boy Wonder
    White Sox, 1901-1907

Pattin, Marty [Martin William]
    Bulldog: Duck
    Angels, Pilots, Brewers, Red Sox, Royals, 1968-1980

Pavano, Carl (Anthony)
    American Idle
        From the NY media for his often being disabled.
    Expos, Marlins, Yankees, Indians, Twins, 1998-2012

Pawelek, Ted [Theodore John]
    Porky
    Cubs, 1946

Paxton, James (Alston)
    The Big Maple
    Mariners, Yankees, 2013-

Payne, Harley (Fenwick)
    Lady
    Bridegrooms, Pirates, 1896-1899

Pazos, James (Manuel) {PAH-zohse}
    Papa Paz
    Yankees, Mariners, Rockies, 2015-

Pearce, William (Charles)
    Bunny: Ducky
    Reds, 1908-1909

Pearson, Monte [Montgomery Marcellus]
    Hoot
    Indians, Yankees, Reds, 1932-1941

Pechiney, George (Adolphe)
{PEESH-en-ay}
    Pisch
        Used only after his death by his son-in-law.
    Red Stockings, Blues, 1885-1887

Peden, Les [Leslie Earl]
    Gooch
    Senators, 1953

Pederson, Joc (Russell)
    Dizzy
    Dodgers, 2014-

Pedroes, Charles (P.)
    Chick
    Orphans, 1902

Pedroia, Dustin (Luis)
    The Muddy Chicken: Petey
    The Laser Show
        Blistering line drives.
    Red Sox, 2006-

Peery, George (Allen)
    Red
    Pirates, Braves, 1927, 1929

Peete, Charlie [Charles]
    Mule
        Based on his bulk. 5'9", 195 lbs.
    Cardinals, 1956

Peitz, Henry (Clement)
    Heinie
    Browns, Reds, Pirates, Cardinals, 1892-1913

Pelfrey, Mike [Michael Alan]
    Big Pelf
    Mets, Twins, Tigers, White Sox, 2006-2017

Pelty, Barney
    The Yiddish Curver
        One of the first Jewish players in the American league.
    Browns, Senators, 1903-1912

Peña, Ariel
    Happy Milton
    Brewers, 2015-2016

Peña, Roberto (Cesar)
    Baby
    Cubs, Phillies, Padres, Athletics, Brewers, 1965-1971

Pence, Hunter (Andrew)
    Captain Underpants
        A takeoff of [Team] Captain
        Hunter Pence.
    Wawindaji
    Astros, Phillies, Giants, Rangers,
    2007-

Pennington, George (Louis)
    Kewpie
    Browns, 1917

Pennock, Herb [Herbert Jefferis]
    The Squire of Kennett Square
    The Knight of Kennett Square
        His birthplace, Kennett Square,
        Pennsylvania.
    Athletics, Red Sox, Yankees, 1912-34

Peploski, Joseph (Aloysius)
    Pepper
    Tigers, 1913

Peralta, David [Senger David]
    Freight Train
    Diamondbacks, 2014-

Peralta, Wandy (Luis)
    La Grasa
    Reds, Giants, 2016-

Perdue, Herbert (Rodney)
    Hub: Hurling Hub
    The Tennessee Cyclone
    The Untamed Son of Sumner County
        Born in Bethpage, Sumner
        County, Tenn.
    Rub-Dub-Hub
        From opponents for his 16-4
        record.
    The Gallatin Squash
        Lived and died in Gallatin, TN.
        Shaped like a squash.
    Rustlers, Braves, Cardinals, 1911-15

Pérez, Atanasio
    Tony: Doggie: Big Dog: Big Doggie
    The Mayor of Riverfront
    Flaco
        From family because he was
        skinny.
    Reds, Expos, Red Sox, Phillies,
    1964-1986

Pérez, Chris [Christopher Ralph]
    Pure Rage
    Cardinals, Indians, Dodgers, 2008-14

Pérez, Hernán (Alejandro) {ERR-nahn}
    Pan Blanco
    Tigers, Brewers, Cubs, 2012-

Pérez, Martín [mar-TEEN PAIR-ezz}
    El De Guanare
    Rangers, Twins, Red Sox, 2012-

Pérez, Pascual (Gross)
    I-285
    Perimeter Pascual
        Missed a start when he could not
        find the stadium.
    Wrong-Way Perez
        Got lost on Atlanta's interstate
        285.
    Pirates, Braves, Expos, Yankees,
    1980-1991

Pérez, Salvador (Johan)
    El Nino
    Royals, 2011-

Perkins, Charlie [Charles Sullivan Sebastian]
    Lefty
    Athletics, Dodgers, 1930, 1934

Perkins, Ralph (Foster)
    Cy
        Based on a Broadway character
        named Cy Perkins.
    Athletics, Yankees, Tigers, 1915-34

Pernoll, Henry (Huston)
    Hub: Jud: Piano Legs: Bud: Buddy
    Busher
    Tigers, 1910, 1912

Perrin, Bill [William Joseph]
    Lefty
    Indians, 1934

Perrine, John (Grover)
    Nig
    Senators, 1907

Perritt, William (Dayton)
    Pol
    Cardinals, Giants, Tigers, 1912-1921

Perry, Hank [William Henry]
    Socks

Tigers, 1912
Perry, Melvin (Gray)
Bob
Angels, 1963-1964
Perryman, Emmett (Key)
Parson
Browns, 1915
Pesky, Johnny [John Michael]
The Needle: Mr. Red Sox
Red Sox, Tigers, Senators, 1942-1954
Pestano, Vinnie [Vincent William]
{pez-STON-oh}
VFP
Indians, Angels, 2010-2015
Peters, John (William)
Big Pete: Shotgun
Tigers, Indians, Phillies, 1915-1922
Peters, Otto (Casper)
Rube
First used by minor league press.
White Sox, Tip-Tops, 1912, 1914
Peterson, Carl (Francis)
Buddy
White Sox, Orioles, 1955, 1957
Peterson, Charles (Andrew)
Cap
From his initials.
Giants, Senators, Indians, 1962-1969
Peterson, Fred (Ingles)
Fritz
Yankees, Indians, Rangers, 1966-76
Petoskey, Frederic (Lee)
Ted
Reds, 1934-1935
Petry, Dan [Daniel Joseph]
Peaches
Tigers, Angels, Braves, Red Sox, 1979-1991
Pettibone, Harry (Jonathan)
Jay
Twins, 1983
Pettit, Leon (Arthur)
Lefty
Senators, Phillies, 1935, 1937
Pettit, Paul [GeorgeWilliam Paul]
Lefty

Wizard of Whiff
In high school, pitched 6 no-hitters.
Pirates, 1951, 1953
Petty, Jesse (Lee)
The Silver Fox
Indians, Robins, Pirates, Cubs, 1921-1930
Pezold, Lorenz (Johannes)
Larry
Naps, 1914
Pexxullo, John
Pretzel
From an unusual pitching style.
Phillies, 1935-1936
Pfeffer, Edward (Joseph)
Jeff
Younger brother of Francis "Big Jeff" Pfeffer. Both resembled boxer Jim Jeffries.
Browns, Superbas, Robins, Cardinals, Pirates, 1911-1924
Pfeffer, Francis (Xavier)
Big Jeff
Resembled heavyweight boxer Jim Jeffries.
Cubs, Beaneaters, Doves, Cubs, Rustlers, 1905-1911.
Pfeffer, Fred [Nathaniel Frederick]
Fritz
Unser Fritz
Favorite among German population; meaning Our Fritz.
Dandelion
From his ability to pick ground balls in the infield.
Trojans, White Stockings, Pirates, Colts, Colonels, Giants, 1882-1897
Pfiester, Jack [John Albert]
The Giant Killer
Seven shutouts and a 15-5 record against the Giants.
Pirates, Cubs, 1903-1911
Pfyl, Meinhard (Charles)
Monty
Giants, 1907

Phegley, Josh [Joshua Aaron] {FEG-lee}
PTBNL
White Sox, Athletics, Cubs, 2013-

Phelan, Art [Arthur Thomas]
Dugan
Reds, Cubs, 1910-1915

Phelps, Ed [Edward Jaykill]
Yaller
Pirates, Reds, Cardinals, Dodgers, Superbas, 1902-1913

Phelps, Ernest (Gordon)
Babe
: Build, stance and swing resembled Babe Ruth.

Blimp
: Matured physique; 6'2", 235 lbs.

The Grounded Blimp
: After one trip, he refused to fly with the team.

Senators, Cubs, Dodgers, Pirates, 1931-1942

Phelps, Ken [Kenneth allen]
Digger
Royals, Expos, Mariners, Yankees, Athletics, Indians, 1980-1990

Phillippe, Charles (Louis)
Deacon
: From his reticent demeanor, humility, and way of life.

Colonels, Pirates, 1899-1911

Phillips, Adolfo (Emilio)
Dolpho: Panamanian Flash
Phillies, Cubs, Expos, Indians, 1964-1972

Phillips, Albert (Abernathy)
Buz
Phillies, 1930

Phillips, Bill B [William B]
Silver Bill
Willie
: A family nickname.

Blues, Grays, Cowboys, 1879-1888

Phillips, Bill C [William Corcoran]
Silver Bill: Whoa Bill: Big Bill
Cyclone
: Given by *Sporting Life*.

Blond Bill: Silent Bill: Honest Bill
Allenport Bill
Alleghenys, Reds, 1890-1903

Phillips, Brandon (Emil)
B-Peezy: DatDude
Indians, Reds, Braves, Angels, Red Sox, 2002-2018

Phillips, Charles (Gene)
J.R.
Giants, Phillies, Astros, Rockies, 1993-1999

Phillips, Clarence (Lemuel)
Red
Tigers, 1934, 1936

Phillips, Damon (Roswell)
Dee
Reds, Braves, 1942-1946

Phillips, Jack (Dorn)
Stretch
: Flexible when covering first base. Being 6'4" helped.

Yankees, Pirates, Tigers, 1947-1957

Phillips, John (Melvin)
Bubba
: From his brother in childhood.

The Rebel
: Self given teasing about his Southern heritage.

Tigers, White Sox, Indians, 1955-64

Phillips, William (Taylor)
T-Bone
: To differentiate from a teammate with the same name.

Braves, Cubs, Phillies, White Sox, 1956-1963

Piatt, Wiley (Harold)
Iron Man
: From fans after pitching both ends of a doubleheader. He was the only pitcher in history who lost both games.

Lizzie
: From the newspapers, but it didn't stick.

Phillies, Athletics, White Sox, Beaneaters, 1898-1903

Piazza, Mike [Michael Joseph]
    Pepperoni
        Chris Berman-ism; refers to pizza and his spicy style.
    Monster
        Coach John Stearns said, "The Monster is out of the Cage," after a hit in the 2000 League Championship.
    Dodgers, Marlins, Mets, Padres, Athletics, 1992-2007

Picciolo, Rob [Robert Michael] {PEACH-uh-low}
    Pepperdine Peach
        From his name and his college.
    Athletics, Brewers, Angels, 1977-85

Pickett, Cecil (Lee)
    Ricky
    Diamondbacks, 1998

Pickup, Clarence (William)
    Ty
    Phillies, 1918

Picone, Mario (Peter)
    Babe
    Giants, Redlegs, 1947-1954

Piechota, Al [Aloysius Edward]
    Pie
    Bees, Braves, 1940-1941

Pieh, Edwin (John Otto)
    Cy
        His pitch appeared to come out of a cyclone.
    Yankees, 1913-1915

Pierce, George (Thomas)
    Filbert
    Cubs, Cardinals, 1912-1917

Pierce, Ray [Raymond Lester]
    Lefty
    Cubs, Phillies, 1924-1926

Piercy, Bill [William Benton]
    Wild Bill
    Yankees, Red Sox, Cubs, 1917-1926

Pieretti, Marino (Paul)
    Chick
    Submariner
        Had a sidewinder delivery in the Pacific Coast League.
    Senators, White Sox, Indians, 1945-1950

Pierro, Bill [William Leonard]
    Wild Bill
        Erratic tendencies when pitching.
    Pirates, 1950

Piersall, Jim [James Anthony]
    Waterbury Wizard
        Self-bestowed. He was born in Waterbury, CT.
    Red Sox, Indians, Senators, Mets, Angels, 1950-1967

Pierson, Edmund (Dana)
    Dick
    Metropolitans, 1885

Pierzynski, Anthony (John)
    A.J.
    Twins, Giants, White Sox, Rangers, Red Sox, Cardinals, Braves, 1998-2016

Piez, Charles (William)
    Sandy
    Giants, 1914

Pike, Lipman (Emanuel)
    Lip
    The Iron Batter
        Had 6 home runs in one game, pre-existence of MLB.
    Haymakers, Canaries, Dark Blues, Brown Stockings, Reds, Grays, Ruby Legs, Metropolitans, 1871-1887

Pillar, Kevin (Andrew)
    Superman
    Blue Jays, Giants, Red Sox, Rockies, 2013-

Pillette, Duane (Xavier)
    Dee
    Yankees, Browns, Orioles, Phillies, 1949-1956

Pillette, Herman (Polycarp)
    Old Folks
        Played in the minors until 3 months shy of 50.
    Reds, Tigers, 1917-1924

Pillion, Cecil (Randolph)

Squiz
  Athletics, 1915
Pilney, Antone (James)
  Andy
  Bees, 1936
Pinder, Chad [Chadwick Hudson]
  Swipe Right: Chi
  Athletics, 2016-
Pinelli, Ralph (Arthur)
  Babe
    Playing with older boys on the sandlots.
  White Sox, Tigers, Reds, 1918-1927
Piniella, Lou [Louis Victor]
  Sweet Lou
    From his swing and demeanor.
  Orioles, Indians, Royals, Yankees, 1964-1984
Pinnance, Ed [Elijah Edward]
  Peanuts
  Athletics, 1903
Pinto, Ricardo (Antonio)
  Pinto Bean
  Phillies, Rays, 2017, 2019
Pippen, Henry (Harold)
  Cotton
    Light blonde hair and blue eyes.
  Cardinals, Athletics, Tigers, 1936-40
Piscotty, Stephen (Edward)
  MoMo
  Cardinals, Athletics, 2015-
Pitko, Alex [Alexander]
  Spunk
  Phillies, Senators, 1938-1939
Pitlock, Lee [Lee Patrick Thomas]
  Skip
  Giants, White Sox, 1970-1975
Pittenger, Clarke (Alonzo)
  Pinky
    From a comic-strip character of the day.
  Red Sox, Cubs, Reds, 1921-1929
Pittinger, Charles (Reno)
  Togie
  Beaneaters, Phillies, 1900-1907
Pittman, Joe [Joseph Wayne]
  Shoes
  Astros, Padres, Giants, 1981-1984
Pizarro, Juan (Roman)
  Ter
    Short for Terín.
  Terín
    From neighborhood kids; refers to the Terry and the Pirates character.
  The Ebony Whip
  El Látigo de Ébano
    Spanish for The Ebony Whip.
  Braves, White Sox, Pirates, Red Sox, Indians, Athletics, Cubs, Astros, 1957-1974
Plank, Eddie [Edward Stewart]
  Gettysburg Eddie
  Athletics, Terriers, Cardinals, 1901-1917
Platt, Mizell (George)
  Whitey
  Cubs, White Sox, Browns, 1942-1949
Plouffe, Trevor (Patrick) {PLOOF}
  Special T
  Twins, Athletics, Rays, Phillies, 2010-2018
Podbielan, Clarence (Anthony)
  Bud
  Dodgers, Reds, Redlegs, Indians, 1949-1959
Podgajny, Johnny [John Sigmund] {puh-JONN-ee}
  Specs
  Phillies, Pirates, Indians, 1940-1946
Podsednik, Scott (Eric)
  The Podfather
  Mariners, Brewers, White Sox, Rockies, Royals, Dodgers, Red Sox, 2001-2012
Poetz, Joe [Joseph Frank]
  Bull Montana
    Born, died, and lived in Missouri.
  Giants, 1926
Poffenberger, Cletus (Elwood)
  Boots
  Duke of Duckout

Some days he did not show up for work.
The Baron
Sports writers thought his name sounded royal.
Tigers, Dodgers, 1937-1939
Poindexter, Jennings [Chester Jennings]
Jinx
Red Sox, Phillies, 1936, 1939
Pointer, Aaron (Elton)
Hawk
Colt .45s, Astros, 1963-1967
Polanco, Gregory {poe-LAN-koe}
El Coffee
Pirates, 2014-
Polhemus, Mark (S)
Humpty Dumpty
Hoosiers, 1887
Polivka, Ken [Kenneth Lyle]
Soup
Reds, 1947
Polli, Lou [Louis Americo]
Crip
Short for cripple, after a football injury that put him on crutches.
Browns, Giants, 1932, 1944
Pollock, Allen (Lorenz)
A.J.: Pollo
Diamondbacks, Dodgers, 2012-
Pomeranz, Drew [Thomas Andrew]
Big Smooth
Rockies, Athletics, Padres, Red Sox, Giants, Brewers, 2011-
Pool, Harlin (Welty)
Samson
Reds, 1934-1935
Poole, Jim [James Ralph]
Easy
Athletics, 1925-1927
Porcello, Rick [Frederick Alfred]
Pretty Ricky: Ricky Raindrops
Tigers, Red Sox, Mets, 2009-
Porter, Dick [Richard Twilley]
Wiggles
Twitches
Indians, Red Sox, 1929-1934

Porter, J.W.
No actual given names.
Jay
Firefly
From Satchel Paige for his freckles and red hair.
Browns, Tigers, Indians, Senators, Cardinals, 1952-1959
Porter, Marquis (Donnell)
Bo
Cubs, Athletics, Rangers, 1999-2001
Porterfield, Erwin (Cooledge)
Bob
His father called him Bob from when he was 6.
Yankees, Senators, Red Sox, Pirates, Cubs, 1948-1959
Porto, Al [Alfred]
Lefty
Phillies, 1948
Posada, Jorge (Sado)
{hor-hay poe-SAH-dah}
Sado
Yankees, 1995-2011
Posedel, Bill [William John]
Sailor Bill: Barnacle Bill: Ole Porthole
Nicknames from sportswriters. He served in the Navy.
Chief
From his players because he called everyone Chief.
Dodgers, Bees, Braves, 1938-1946
Poser, John (Falk)
Bob
White Sox, Browns, 1932, 1935
Posey, Gerald (Dempsey)
Buster
Inherited from his father's childhood nickname.
Giants, 2009-
Pott, Nellie [Nelson Adolph]
Lefty
Indians, 1922
Potter, Robert
Squire
Senators, 1923

Potts, Vivian
    Doc
    Senators, 1892
Pounds, Jeared (Wells)
    Bill
    Naps, Superbas, 1903
Powell, Bill [William Burris]
    Big Bill
    Pirates, Cubs, Reds, 1909-1913
Powell, Hershel (Mack)
    Boog
        Named after the more famous
        Boog Powell, by his father to
        avoid confusion. He is Hershel IV.
    Little Mack
        He is Hershel IV.
    Mariners, Athletics, 2017-2018
Powell, Jack [John Joseph]
    Red
    Spiders, Perfectos, Cardinals, Browns,
    Highlanders, 1897-1912
Powell, James (Willard)
    Jay
    Marlins, Astros, Rockies, Rangers,
    Braves, 1995-2005
Powell, John (Wesley)
    Boog
        From his father: kids who got
        into mischief.
    Orioles, Indians, Dodgers, 1961-1977
Powell, Ray [Raymond Raeth]
    Rabbit
    Tigers, Braves, 1913-1924
Powell, Reginald (Bertrand)
    Jack
    Browns, 1913
Powers, Ellis (Foree)
    Mike
    Indians, 1932-1933
Powers, John (Lloyd)
    Ike
    Athletics, 1927-1928
Powers, Michael (Riley)
    Doc
        He was a licensed physician.
    Colonels, Senators, Athletics,
    Highlanders, 1898-1909
Powers, Phil [Philip J.]
    Grandmother
    White Stockings, Red Stockings,
    Blues, Orioles, 1878-1885
Powis, Carl (Edgar)
    Jug
    Orioles, 1957
Pratt, Al [Albert George]
    Uncle Al
        From his interest in the welfare
        of former players.
    Forest Citys, 1871-1872
Pratt, Derrill (Burnham)
    Del
    Browns, Yankees, Red Sox, Tigers,
    1912-1924
Pratt, Frank [Francis Bruce]
    Trackhorse
    White Sox, 1921
Pratt, Lester (John)
    Larry
    Red Sox, Tip-Tops, Pepper, 1914-15
Pratt, Todd (Alan)
    Tank: Tankhead
    Phillies, Cubs, Mets, Braves,
    1992-2006
Preibisch, Mel [Melvin Aloysius]
    Primo
    Bees, Braves, 1940-1941
Prescott, George (Bertrand)
    Bobby
    Athletics, 1961
Presko, Joe [Joseph Edward]
    Baby Joe: Little Joe: Baby Face
    Cardinals, Tigers, 1951-1958
Pressnell, Forest (Charles)
    Tot
        The "tot" who always tagged
        along with his siblings.
    Dodgers, Cubs, 1938-1942
Price, David (Taylor)
    Astro's Dad
    Rays, Tigers, Blue Jays, Red Sox,
    2008-
Price, Jim [Jimmie William]

Smokey
Tigers, 1967-1971
Price, Joe [Joseph Preston]
Lumber
Giants, 1928
Price, John (Thomas Reid)
Jackie
Indians, 1946
Prim, Ray [Raymond Lee]
Pop
> Minor league teammates named him. He was 30 years old.

Pops: Pappy
Squire
> Elegant sophisticated appearance.

Senators, Phillies, Cubs, 1933-1946
Pritchard, Harold (William)
Buddy
Pirates, 1957
Proctor, Noah (Richard)
Red
White Sox, 1923
Proeser, George
Yatz
Blues, 1888
Prothro, James (Thompson)
Doc
> A practicing dentist... before baseball.

Senators, Red Sox, Reds, 1920-1926
Prough, Clint [Herschel Clinton]
Bill
Reds, 1912
Prudhomme, John (Olgus)
Augie
Tigers, 1929
Pruess, Earl (Henry)
Gibby
Browns, 1920
Pruett, Hub [Hubert Shelby]
Shucks
> The strongest word in his vocabulary.

Browns, Phillies, Giants, Braves, 1922-1932
Pruiett, Charles (Leroy)

Tex
> Started his career in Texas.

Americans, Red Sox, 1907-1908
Puccinelli, George (Lawrence)
Pooch: Count
Smoke Ball
> Minor league name after pitching a 4-hitter.

Cardinals, Browns, Athletics, 1930-1936
Puckett, Kirby
The Franchise
Twins, 1984-1995
Puig, Yasiel {YAH-see-el Pweeg}
Wild Horse
> Named by Vin Scully.

Dodgers, Reds, Indians, 2013-
Pujols, Albert [José Alberto] {POO-holes}
Phat Albert: Prince Albert: Machine
Cardinals, Angels, 2001-
Purcell, William (Aloysius)
Blondie
Stars, Reds, Blues, Bisons, Quakers, Athletics, Beaneaters, Orioles, 1879-1890
Purdy, Everett (Virgil)
Pid
White Sox, Reds, 1926-1929
Putz, Joseph (Jason)
J.J.
The Big Guy
> Named by the Mariners' broadcaster.

Mariners, Mets, White Sox, Diamondbacks, 2003-2014
Pyle, Ewald
Lefty
Browns, Senators, Giants, Braves, 1939-1945
Pyle, Harlan (Albert)
Firpo
Reds, 1928
Pyle, Harry (Thomas)
Shadow
Quakers, White Stockings, 1884, 87
Qualters, Tom [Thomas Francis]

Money Bags
A huge signing bonus, then pitched $1/3$ of an inning.
Phillies, White Sox, 1953-1958

Queen, Billy [William Eddleman]
Doc
Braves, 1954

Quick, Hal [James Harold]
Blondie
Senators, 1939

Quilici, Frank [Francis Ralph]
Guido
Twins, 1965-1970

Quinn, Clarence (Carr)
Tad
Athletics, 1902-1903

Quinn, John (Edward)
Pick
Phillies, 1911

Quinn, Wellington (Hunt)
Wimpy
From the hamburger mooch of Popeye cartoon fame.
Cubs, 1941

Quintana, José (Guillermo)
{kin-TAH-nuh}
Q
White Sox, Cubs, 2012-

Quisenberry, Dan [Daniel Raymond]
Q: Quiz
Royals, Cardinals, Giants, 1979-1990

Raburn, Ryan (Neil)
Bobby: Second Half Raburn
Tigers, Indians, Rockies, Nationals, 2004-2017

Rachunok, Steve [Stephen Stepanovich]
The Mad Russian
Dodgers, 1940

Radatz, Dick [Richard Raymond]
Moose
He was 6'6", 230 lbs.
The Monster
Struck out several Yankees in a row. Named by Mickey Mantle.
Red Sox, Indians, Cubs, Tigers, Expos, 1962-1969

Radbourn, Charles (Gardner)
Old Hoss
He was the team's workhorse.
The Great Hercules of Baseball
From a sportswriter after pitching 40 complete games and one relief game out if 51 games in 1884.
The King of Pitchers
A lifetime nickname in respect for his ability.
Grays, Beaneaters, Reds, 1881-1891

Radbourn, George (B)
Dandy: Dordy
Wolverines, 1883

Radcliff, Raymond (Allen)
Rip
Given by his father. We're not sure why.
White Sox, Browns, Tigers, 1934-43

Rader, Dave [David Martin]
Red Rooster
Giants, Cardinals, Cubs, Phillies, Red Sox, 1971-1980

Rader, Doug [Douglas Lee]
Rojo
The Red Rooster
His red hair always stuck out under his cap.
Astros, Padres, Blue Jays, 1967-1977

Rader, Drew (Leon)
Lefty
Pirates, 1921

Radford, Paul (Revere)
Shorty
Only 5'6", 150 lbs.
Little Paul
Beaneaters, Grays, Cowboys, Metropolitans, Bridegrooms, Spiders, Infants, Reds, Senators, 1883-1894

Raether, Hal [Harold Herman]
Bud
Athletics, 1954, 1957

Ragan, Arthur (Garfield)
Rip
Reds, 1903

Raines, Timothy Jr.
   Little Rock
      Son of Tim, Sr. aka Rock.
   Orioles, 2001-2004

Raines, Timothy Sr.
   Rock
      From his physique at an Expo rookie camp.
   Purple
      Chris Bermanism referring to the Prince song "Purple Rain."
   Expos, White Sox, Yankees, Athletics, Orioles, Marlins, 1979-2002

Rajsich, Dave [David Christopher] {RAY-sitch}
   The Blade
   Yankees, Rangers, 1978-1980

Rakow, Ed [Edward Charles] {ROCK-oh}
   Rock
   Dodgers, Athletics, Tigers, Braves, 1960-1967

Ralston, Samuel (Beryl)
   Doc
   Senators, 1910

Rambert, Elmer (Donald)
   Pep
   Pirates, 1939-1940

Rambo, Warren (Dawson)
   Pete
   Phillies, 1926

Ramírez, Alexei (Fernando) {Ah-LECK-say}
   The Cuban Missile
      Speedy and from Cuba.
   White Sox, Padres, Rays, 2008-2016

Ramírez, Hanley
   El Nino: El Trece
   Han-Ram
      Dominican habit of shortening both names.
   Red Sox, Marlins, Dodgers, Indians, 2005-

Ramírez, Juan (Carlos)
   J.C.: Cubanito
   Phillies, Diamondbacks, Mariners, Reds, Angels, 2013-

Ramírez, Manny [Manuel Aristides]
   Manny Being Manny: Man-Ram
   Manny Moments
      From his quirky and fun-loving behavior.
   Mannywood
      After he was named NL Player of the Month.
   Indians, Red Sox, Dodgers, White Sox, Rays, 1993-2011

Ramírez, Mario
   Nato
   Mets, Padres, 1980-1985

Ramos, Alejandro (Hinjos)
   A.J.
   Marlins, Mets, 2012-2018

Ramos, Jesus (Manuel)
   Chucho
   Reds, 1944

Ramos, Pedro
   Pete
      Translation from the Spanish.
   Senators, Twins, Indians, Yankees, Phillies, Pirates, Reds, 1955-1970

Ramon, Wilson (Abraham)
   Buffalo
   Twins, Nationals, Rays, Phillies, Mets, 2010-

Ramsdell, Willie [James Willard]
   Willie the Knuck
      He had a baffling knuckleball.
   Dodgers, Reds, Cubs, 1947-1952

Ramsey, Bill [William Thrace]
   Square Jaw
   Braves, 1945

Ramsey, Thomas (H)
   Toad
   Colonels, Browns, 1885-1890

Randa, Joe [Joseph Gregory]
   The Joker
      He resembled the character in the Batman comics.
   Royals, Pirates, Tigers, Reds, Padres, 1995-2006

Randall, James (Odell)
   Sap

White Sox, 1988
Randolph, Willie (Larry)
Mickey
Pirates, Yankees, Dodgers, Athletics, Brewers, Mets, 1975-1992
Raney, Frank (Robert Donald)
Ribs
Browns, 1949-1950
Rapp, Joseph (Aloysius)
Goldie
Giants, Phillies, 1921-1923
Rariden, Bill [William Angle]
Bedford Bill
> Born and died in Bedford, IN.

Doves, Rustlers, Braves, Hoosiers, Pepper, Giants, Reds, 1909-1920
Raschi, Vic [Victor John Angelo]
Springfield Rifle
> Combined his fastball speed and his birth area.

Yankees, Cardinals, Athletics, 1946-1955
Rasmussen, Henry (Florian)
Hans
Whales, 1915
Raudman, Bob [Robert Joyce]
Shorty
Cubs, 1966-1967
Rautzhan, Clarence (George)
Lance
Dodgers, Brewers, 1977-1979
Rawlings, Johnny [John William]
Red
Reds, Packers, Braves, Phillies, Giants, Pirates, 1914-1926
Ray, Irv [Irving Burton]
Stubby
> He was 5'6," 165 lbs.

Beaneaters, Orioles, 1888-1891
Ray, Jim [James Francis]
Sting
Ray Gun
> From when he struck out 115 in 115 innings.

Astros, Tigers, 1965-1974
Ray, Robert (Henry)

Farmer
Browns, 1910
Rayford, Floyd (Kinnard)
Honey Bear
Rioles, Cardinals, 1980-1987
Raymond, Arthur (Lawrence)
Bugs
> Short for Bughouse; excessive drinking.

Bughouse
> From his zany antics on the mound.

Tigers, Cardinals, Giants, 1904-1911
Raymond, Claude [Jean Claude Marc]
{run-MONE}
Frenchy
> From the province of Quebec.

White Sox, Braves, Colt .45s, Astros, Expos, 1959-1971
Raymond, Harry (H)
Jack
Colonels, Pirates, Senators, 1888-92
Realmuto, Jacob (Tyler)
J.T.
Marlins, Phillies, 2014-
Reardon, Jeff [Jeffrey James]
The Terminator
> An intimidating presence; see the movie.

Mets, Expos, Twins, Red Sox, Braves, Reds, Yankees, 1979-1994
Reberger, Frank (Beall)
Crane
6'5", 200 lbs.
Cubs, Padres, Giants, 1968-1972
Reddick, Josh [William Joshua]
Mr. Irrelevant
> Usually the last person drafted.

Red Dawg
Red Sox, Athletics, Dodgers, Astros, 2009-
Redfern, George (Howard)
Buck
White Sox, 1928-1929
Redman, Julian (Jawonn)
Tike

Pirates, Orioles, 2000-2007
Redmond, Jack [John KcKittrick]
Red
Senators, 1935
Redmond, Mike [Michael Patrick]
Red Dog
Marlins, Twins, Indians, 1998-2010
Reed, Andrew (Joseph)
A.J. : George: Herman: Big Herman
Herm
Astros, White Sox, 2016-2019
Reed, Howie [Howard Dean]
Diz
Athletics, Dodgers, Angels, Astros, Expos, 1958-1971
Reed, Jack [John Burwell]
Mantle's Caddie: Mantle's Legs
Yankees, 1961-1963
Reed Ralph (Edwin)
Ted
Pepper, 1915
Reeder, Julius (Edward)
Icicle
Red Stockings, Senators, 1884
Rees, Stan [Stanley Milton]
Nellie
Senators, 1918
Reese, Calvin
Pokey
  Was a big baby; Grandma mispronounced Porkey.
Reds, Pirates, Red Sox, 1997-2004
Reese, Harold (Henry)
Pee Wee
  From childhood; he was a marbles champion.
The Little Colonel
  Affectionate name while playing for the Colonels.
The Captain
  He was the Dodgers' captain from 1947 on.
Dodgers, 1940-1958
Reeves, Bobby [Robert Edwin]
Gunner
Senators, Red Sox, 1926-1931

Regan, Phil [Philip Raymond]
The Vulture
  From Sandy Koufax for his knack of earning wins in late-inning relief.
Tigers, Dodgers, Cubs, White Sox, 1960-1972
Reiber, Frank (Bernard)
Tubby
Tigers, 1933-1936
Reilley, Alexander (Aloysius)
Duke
Midget
  5'4", 148 lbs.
Naps, 1909
Reilly, Bernard (Eugene)
Barney
White Sox, 1909
Reilly, Charlie [Charles Thomas]
Princeton Charlie
  From Princeton, NJ.
Solons, Pirates, Phillies, Senators, 1889-1897
Reilly, John (Good)
Long John
  6'3" but only 178 lbs.
Reds, Red Stockings, 1880-1891
Reilly, William (Henry)
Josh
Colts, 1896
Reis, Harrie (Crane)
Jack
Cardinals, 1911
Reiser, Harold (Patrick)
Pete
Pistol Pete
  Childhood nickname after Two-Gun Pete, cowboy movie hero.
Dodgers, Braves, Pirates, Indians, 1940-1952
Reisigl, Jacob
Bugs
Naps, 1911
Reising, Charlie [Charles]
Pop
Hoosiers, 1884

Reisling, Frank (Carl)
Doc
Superbas, Senators, 1904-1910

Reitz, Henry (Peter)
Heinie
Orioles, Senators, Pirates, 1893-1899

Reitz, Ken [Kenneth John]
Zamboni
> For his skill at scooping up ground balls.

Cardinals, Giants, Cubs, Pirates, 1972-1982

Rementer, Willis (John)
Butch
Phillies, 1904

Remmerswaal, Wilhelmus (Abraham)
Win: Last Call
Red Sox, 1979-1980

Remy, Jerry [Gerald Peter]
Rem Dawg
Angels, Red Sox, 1975-1984

Rendon, Anthony (Michael)
{ren-DOHN}
Ant: Tone: Tony Two Bags
Nationals, Angels, 2013-

Renfroe, Cohen (Williams)
Laddie
Cubs, 1991

Reniff, Hal [Harold Eugene]
Porky: Whale
Yankees, Mets, 1961-1967

Renna, Bill [William Beneditto]
Big Bill
Yankees, Athletics, Red Sox, 1953-59

Rensa, Tony [George Anthony]
Pug
Tigers, Phillies, Yankees, White Sox, 1930-1939

Renteria, Rick [Richard Avina]
Secret Weapon
Pirates, Mariners, Marlins, 1986-94

Repulski, Eldon (John)
Rip
> From someone in the St. Louis farm system.

Alto
> As in Al the Toe, a college football placekicker.

Cardinals, Phillies, Dodgers, Red Sox, 1953-1961

Rescigno, Xavier (Francis)
Mr. X
Pirates, 1943-1945

Restelli, Dino (Paolo)
Dingo
> A fan in the Pacific Coast league mispronounced Dino.

Pirates, 1949, 1951

Rettig, Adolph (John)
Otto
Athletics, 1922

Reulbach, Ed [Edward Marvin]
{ROYAL-bock}
Big Ed
Cubs, Superbas, Robins, Pepper, Braves, 1905-1917

Reuschel, Rick [Richard Eugene]
{RUSH-el}
Big Daddy
> He had a portly physique.

Cubs, Yankees, Pirates, Giants, 1972-1991

Reyes, José (Bernabe)
La Melaza
Mets, Marlins, Blue Jays, Rockies, 2003-2018

Reyes, Joseph (Albert)
Jo-Jo
Braves, Blue Jays, Orioles, Angels, Marlins, 2007-2016

Reynolds, Allie (Pierce)
Superchief
> A member of the Creek Indian nation and always in command.

Indians, Yankees, 1942-1954

Reynolds, Bob [Robert Allen]
Bullet
Expos, Cardinals, Brewers, Orioles, Tigers, Indians, 1969-1975

Reynolds, Danny [Daniel Vance]
Squirrel
White Sox, 1945

Reynolds, Mark (Andrew)
    Mega-Mark: Sheriff of Swattingham
    Skeletor: Forrest Gump
    Diamondbacks, Orioles, Indians,
    Yankees, Brewers, Cardinals, Rockies,
    Nationals, 2008-2019

Reynolds, Robert (James)
    R.J.
    Dodgers, Pirates, 1983-1990

Reynolds, Ross (Ernest)
    Doc
    Tigers, 1914-1915

Rhawn, Bobby [Robert John]
    Rocky
    Giants, Pirates, White Sox, 1947-49

Rheam, Kenneth (Johnston)
    Cy
    Rebels, 1914-1915

Rhem, Flint [Charles Flint]
    Shad
        He told many fish stories.
    Big Smoky
        College nickname.
    Cardinals, Phillies, Braves, 1924-36

Rhines, Billy [William Pearl]
    Bunker
    Reds, Colonels, Pirates, 1890-1899

Rhoads, Bob [Barton Emory]
    Dusty
    Orphans, Naps, Cardinals, 1902-1909

Rhodes, Charlie [Charles Anderson]
    Dusty
    Cardinals, Reds, 1906-1909

Rhodes, James (Lamar)
    Dusty
        Given by a scout because "all players name Rhodes were called Dusty."
    Giants, 1952-1959

Rhodes, John (Gordon)
    Dusty
    Yankees, Red Sox, Athletics, 1929-36

Rhodes, Karl (Derrick)
    Tuffy
        From childhood for his serious approach to baseball.
    Caburo
        A Japanese nickname.
    Astros, Cubs, Red Sox, 1990-1995

Rice, Edgar (Charles)
    Sam
        Given by a minor league owner.
    Eddie
        A childhood nickname.
    Man o' War
        From his 1920 stolen base total of 63; after the racehorse.
    Senators, Indians, 1915-1934

Rice, Hal [Harold Housten]
    Hoot
    Cardinals, Pirates, Cubs, 1948-1954

Rice, Jim [James Edward]
    Jim Ed: The Boston Strongboy
    Red Sox 1974-1989

Richard, James (Rodney)
    J.R.
    Astros, 1971-1980

Richard, Lee (Edward)
    Bee Bee
    White Sox, Cardinals, 1971-1976

Richards, Fred (Charles)
    Fuzzy
    Cubs, 1951

Richardson, Hardy [Abram Harding]
    Old True Blue
    Bisons, Wolverines, Beaneaters, Reds, Senators, Giants, 1879-1892

Richter, Emil (Henry)
    Reggie
    Cubs, 1911

Rickert, Joe [Joseph Francis]
    Diamond Joe
    Pirates, Beaneaters, 1898, 1901

Rickert, Marv [Marvin August]
    Twitch
    Cubs, Reds, Braves, Pirates, White Sox, 1942-1950

Rickey, Branch [Wesley Branch]
    The Mahatma
        A sportswriter compared him to Gandhi.
    El Cheapo

Reputation prior to breaking the color barrier.
Browns, Highlanders, 1905-1914

Riddle, Johnny [John Ludy]
Mutt
Gained before his college career.
White Sox, Senators, Bees, Reds, Pirates, 1930-1948

Ridgway, Jacob (Augustus)
Jack
Terrapins, 1914

Riebe, Harvey (Donald)
Hank
An early nickname that disappeared over time.
Tigers, 1942-1949

Riefenhauser, Charles (Joseph)
C.J.
Rays, 2014-2015

Righetti, Dave [David Allan]
Rags
Yankees, Giants, Athletics, Blue Jays, White Sox, 1979-1995

Rigney, Bill [William Joseph]
Specs: The Cricket
Giants, 1946-1953

Rigney, Emory (Elmo)
Topper: Trim: Midget
Tigers, Red Sox, Senators, 1922-1927

Riles, Ernest
Easy
An easy-going attitude.
Brewers, Giants, Athletics, Astros, Red Sox, 1985-1993

Riley, Billy [William James]
Pigtail Billy
Westerns, Blues, 1875, 1879

Ripken, Cal Jr. [Calvin Edwin]
Iron Man
Holds the record for most consecutive games played.
The Franchise
Orioles, 1981-2001

Risberg Charles (August)
Swede
White Sox, 1917-1920

Rising, Percival (Sumner)
Pop
He became bald at a young age.
Pop Rising
Popped up at most at-bats in his early career.
Americans, 1905

Ritchey, Claude (Cassius)
Little All Right
Only 5'6" but drove in many runs.
Reds, Colonels, Pirates, Doves, 1897-1909

Ritter, Lew [Lewis Elmo]
Old Dog
Superbas, 1902-1908

Ritter, William (Herbert)
Hank
Phillies, Giants, 1912-1916

Ritterson, Edward (West)
Whitey
Athletics, 1876

Rivera, Ben [Bienvenido]
Big Ben
Braves, Phillies, 1992-1994

Rivera, Jesus (Manuel)
Bombo
Expos, Twins, Royals, 1975-1982

Rivera, Manuel (Joseph)
Jim
Dates from when he was 17.
Big Jim
From 1952, when he started playing for the White Sox.
Jungle Jim
For his unorthodox style and personality.
Browns, White Sox, Athletics, 1952-1961

Rivera, Mariano
Mo: The Ghoul
Super Mariano
A play on Super Mario of Nintendo fame.
The Sandman
Batters facing his cutter were

"put right to bed."
Yankees, 1995-2013
Rivera, Rene
Moncho
Mariners, Twins, Padres, Rays, Mets, Cubs, Angels, Braves, 2004-
Rivera, Thomas (Javier)
T.J.: T-Butta
Mets, 2016-2017
Rivers, John (Milton)
Mickey: Old Gozzlehead
Mick the Quick
A speedy leadoff hitter.
Angels, Yankees, Rangers, 1970-1984
Riviere, Arthur (Bernard)
Tink
Cardinals, White Sox, 1921, 1925
Rixey, Eppa
Jeptha
From his southern drawl.
Phillies, Reds, 1912-1933
Rizzuto, Phil [Philip Francis]
Scooter
From the way he ran the bases.
Yankees, 1941-1956
Roach, Rudolph (Charles)
Born Rudolph Weichbrodt
Skel
From Skeleton.
Skeleton
Minor league teammates couldn't pronouce his name.
Orphans, 1899
Roach, Wilbur (Charles)
Roxey
Highlanders, Senators, Blues, 1910-1915
Robello, Thomas (Vardasco)
Tony
An evolution from Tom.
Tom
An early nickname.
Reds, 1933-1934
Roberge, Joseph (Albert Armand)
Skippy
From childhood.
Braves, 1941-1946
Robert, Luis
La Pantera
White Sox, 2020-
Roberts, Charles (Emory)
Red
Senators, 1943
Roberts, Clarence (Ashley)
Sailor
A gunner's mate in the Navy.
Skipper
A change from Sailor, possibly due to a stutter.
Cardinals, Rebels, Chi-Feds, 1913-14
Roberts, Dale
Mountain Man
Yankees, 1967
Roberts, Dave [David Ray]
Doc
Indians, Dodgers, Red Sox, Padres, Giants, 1999-2008
Roberts, Jim [James Newsom]
Big Jim
6'3", 205 lbs.
Robins, 1924-1925
Roberts, Leon (Joseph)
Bip
Padres, Reds, Royals, Indians, Tigers, Athletics, 1986-1998
Roberts, Ryan (Alan)
TatMan
He has more than 30 tattoos.
Blue Jays, Rangers, Diamondbacks, Rays, Red Sox, 2006-2014
Robertson, Daniel [Daniel Ray]
D-Rob
Rays, Giants, 2017-
Robertson, Daryl (Berdene)
Sonny
Cubs, 1962
Robertson, Dave [David Alan]
Houdini
He walked batters and used strikeouts to escape.
D-Rob
Yankees, White Sox, Phillies, 2008-

Robertson, Preston (James)
    Dick
    Reds, Robins, Senators, 1913-1919
Robinson, Brooks (Calbert)
    Mr. Impossible
    Human Vacuum Cleaner
    Hoover
        Made impossible plays at third.
    Orioles, 1955-1977
Robinson, Don (Allen)
    Caveman
        For his physique and ability to endure injuries.
    Donnie
    Pirates, Giants, Angels, Phillies, 1978-1992
Robinson, Frank
    Robbie: Pencils
    The Judge
        Established the team's kangaroo court.
    Redlegs, Reds, Orioles, Dodgers, Angels, Indians, 1956-1976
Robinson, Jack (Roosevelt)
    Jackie
    Dodgers, 1947-1956
Robinson, John H (Henry)
    Hank: Rube
    Pirates, Cardinals, Yankees, 1911-18
Robinson, John W
    Jack: Bridgeport
    Giants, 1902
Robinson, Wilbert
    Robbie
    Uncle Robbie
        From his managing days showing great player rapport.
    Billy Rob
        Early childhood nickname.
    Butcher Boy
        Partner in a butcher shop.
    Pork Chop
        He was also the son of a butcher.
    Billy Fish
        Drove a fish wagon as a youth.
    Grapefruit
        He tried to catch a grapefruit dropped from a plane.
    Athletics, Orioles, Cardinals, 1886-1902
Robinson, William C (Clyde)
    Rabbit
    Senators, Tigers, Reds, 1903-1910
Robinson, William H
    Yank: Robbie: Willie
    Wolverines, Monumentals, Browns, Burghers, Kelly's Killers, Senators, 1882-1892
Robinson, William Henry
    Bill: Weaser
    Uncle Bill
        From players while a hitting instructor.
    Braves, Yankees, Phillies, Pirates, 1966-1983
Robitaille, Joseph (Anthony)
    Chick
    Pirates, 1904-1905
Robles, Hansel (Manuel)
    {HAND-sol ROBE-lace]
    El Penaco
    Mets, Angels, 2015-
Rocco, Michael (Dominick)
    Mickey
    Indians, 1943-1946
Roche, Jack [John Joseph]
    Red
    Cardinals, 1914-1917
Rodgers, Bill [Wilbur Kinkaid]
    Rawmeat Bill
        From sportswriters after he was seen eating raw meat.
    Indians, Red Sox, Reds, 1915-1916
Rodgers, Robert (Leroy)
    Buck
    Angels, 1961-1969
Rodney, Fernando
    Kimbo: Benjamin
    Tigers, Angels, Rays, Mariners, Cubs, Padres, Marlins, Diamondbacks, Twins, Athletics, Nationals, 2002-
Rodriguez, Alex [Alexander Emmanuel]

A-Rod
The Cooler
    Perception: teams turned cooler when he joined.
A-Fraud
    Teammates and attendants resented his demands.
Mariners, Rangers, Yankees, 1994-2016

Rodríguez, Dereck [Ivan Dereck]
D-Rod
Giants, 2018-

Rodríguez, Eduardo (Jose)
El Gualo
Red Sox, 2015-

Rodríguez, Fernando (Pedro)
Freddy
    Frederick is Fernando in Spanish.
Cubs, Phillies, 1958-1959

Rodríguez, Francisco (José)
K-Rod
    K is the symbol for strikeout.
Frankie
    Short for Francis, Francisco in Spanish.
Angels, Mets, Brewers, Orioles, Tigers, 2002-2017

Rodríguez, Henry (Anderson)
Oh Henry
Dodgers, Expos, Cubs, Marlins, Yankees, 1992-2002

Rodríguez, Iván {ee-VAHN}
Pudge
    Short and stocky from day one.
I-Rod
Rangers, Marlins, Tigers, Yankees, Astros, Nationals, 1991-2011

Rodríguez, José
El Hombre Goma
    Spanish for "The Rubber Man."
Joseíto: Joe
Giants, 1916-1918

Rodríguez, Sean (John)
Serpico
Angels, Rays, Pirates, Braves, Phillies, Marlins, 2008-

Rodríguez, Steven (Francis)
Paco
Dodgers, 2012-2015

Roe, Elwin (Charles)
Preacher
    A minister took him on horse-and-buggy rides.
Ole Preach
Cardinals, Pirates, Dodgers, 1938-54

Roe, James (Clay)
Shad
Senators, 1923

Roebuck, Ed [Edward Jack]
Sears
    From teammates to make the other half of the store.
Dodgers, Senators, Phillies, 1955-66

Roettger, Oscar (Frederick Louis)
Okkie
Yankees, Robins, Athletics, 1923-32

Rogell, Billy [William George]
The Fire Chief
Red Sox, Tigers, Cubs, 1925-1940

Rogers, Kenny [Kenneth Scott]
The Gambler
    Same name as the singer of the song.
Rangers, Yankees, Athletics, Mets, Twins, Tigers, 1989-2008

Rogers, Lee (Otis)
Buck: Lefty
Red Sox, Dodgers, 1938

Rogers, Orlin (Woodrow)
Buck: Lefty
Senators, 1935

Rogers, Stanley (Frank)
Packy
Dodgers, 1938

Rogers, Tom [Thomas Andrew]
Shotgun
Browns, Athletics, Yankees, 1917-21

Rohe, George (Anthony)
Whitey
Orioles, White Sox, 1901-1907

Rojas, Octavio (Victor)
Cuqui

From his mother, meaning charming or adorable.
Cookie
An anglicized version of Cuqui.
Reds, Phillies, Cardinals, Royals, 1962-1977

Rojek, Stan [Stanley Andrew]
Happy Rabbit
Projecting front teeth, good attitude and quick.
Reject
From Pirates' teammates when dumped by the Dodgers.
Dodgers, Pirates, Cardinals, Browns, 1942-1952

Rolfe, Robert (Abial)
Red
First given at Phillips Exeter Academy.
Yankees, 1931-1942

Rollings, William (Russell)
Red
Red Sox, Braves, 1927-1930

Rollins, Jimmy [James Calvin]
J-Roll
Phillies, Dodgers, White Sox, 2000-16

Rollins, Rich [Richard John]
Red
Pie
From teammates after Pie Traynor.
Twins, Pilots, Brewers, Indians, 1961-1970

Romano, John (Anthony)
Honey
Nicknamed by his uncle.
White Sox, Indians, Cardinals, 1958-1967

Romberger, Allen (Isaiah)
Dutch
Athletics, 1954

Romero, Juan (Carlos)
J.C.
Twins, Angels, Red Sox, Phillies, Rockies, Cardinals, Orioles, 1999-2012

Romero, Ricky [Ricardo]
RR Cool Jay
Blue Jays, 2009-2013

Romine, Andrew (James)
Robomb
Angels, Tigers, Mariners, Rangers, 2010-

Romo, Vicente
Huevo
Spanish for "Egg." For the shape of his face.
Dodgers, Indians, Red Sox, White Sox, Padres, 1968-1982

Rondon, Bruce
El Menor
Tigers, White Sox, 2013-

Roof, Philip (Anthony)
Babe
The Duke of Paducah
Born in Paducah, KY.
Braves, Angels, Indians, Athletics, Brewers, Twins, White Sox, Blue Jays, 1961-1977

Root, Charlie [Charles Henry]
Chinski
He pitched near the batter's chin.
Browns, Cubs, 1923-1941

Rosar, Warren (Vincent)
Buddy
From his uncles in his youth.
Yankees, Indians, Athletics, Red Sox, 1939-1951

Rosario, Angel (Ramon)
Jimmy
Giants, Brewers, 1971-1976

Rosario, Eddie (Manuel)
Baudidou
Twins, 2015-

Rosario, Wilin (Arismendy)
Baby Bull
Rockies, 2011-2015

Rose, Pete Sr [Peter Edward]
Charlie Hustle
Gained when he sprinted to first... on a walk.
Reds, Phillies, Expos, 1963-1986

Roseboro, John (Junior)
　Gabby
　　He was extremely quiet.
　Dodgers, Twins, Senators, 1957-1970
Roseman, James (John)
　Chief
　Trojans, Metropolitans, Athletics,
　Grays, Browns, Colonels, 1882-1890
Rosen, Al [Albert Leonard]
　Flip
　　From teenage years, on how he
　　threw a softball and basketball.
　The Hebrew Hammer
　　From minor leagues batting .323.
　Indians, 1947-1956
Rosenberg, Brian (James)
　B.J.
　Phillies, 2012-2014
Rosenthal, Trevor (Jordan)
　Big T
　Cardinals, Nationals, Tigers, Royals,
　Padres, 2012-
Roser, Emerson (Corey)
　Steve
　Yankees, Braves, 1944-1946
Roser, Jack [John William Joseph]
　Bunny
　Braves, 1922
Ross, Chester (Franklin)
　Buster
　Red Sox, 1924-1926
Ross, Cody (Joseph)
　Toy Cannon: Ross the Boss: Smiles
　Tigers, Dodgers, Reds, Marlins,
　Giants, Red Sox, Diamondbacks,
　Athletics, 2003-2015
Ross, Ernie [Ernest Bertram]
　Curly
　Orioles, 1902
Ross, Lee (Ravon)
　Buck
　Athletics, White Sox, 1936-1945
Ross, Robbie [Robert Charles]
　The Lawnmower
　Rangers, Red Sox, 2012-2017
Rossy, Elam (Jose)
　Rico
　Braves, Royals, Mariners, 1991-1998
Rotblatt, Marv [Marvin]
　Rotty
　White Sox, 1948-1951
Roth, Robert (Frank)
　Braggo
　　He was boastful about hitting.
　The Globetrotter
　　He went from team to team.
　White Sox, Indians, Athletics, Red
　Sox, Senators, Yankees, 1914-1921
Rothermel, Edward (Hill)
　Bobby
　Orioles, 1899
Routcliffe, Phil [Philip John]
　Chicken
　Alleghenys, 1890
Rowe, Harland (Stimson)
　Hypie
　Athletics, 1916
Rowe, Lynwood (Thomas)
　Schoolboy
　　Played on an adult team as a 14-
　　year-old.
　Tigers, Dodgers, Phillies, 1933-1949
Rowell, Carvel (William)
　Bama
　　From Citronelle, Alabama.
　Bees, Braves, Phillies, 1939-1948
Rowley, Chris [Christopher Ryan]
　Chipper
　Blue Jays, 2017-
Roy, Normie [Norman Brooks]
　Jumbo
　Braves, 1950
Ruberto, John (Edward)
　Sonny
　Padres, Reds, 1969, 1972
Ruble, Art [William Arthur]
　Speedy
　Tigers, Phillies, 1927, 1934
Rudolph, Dick [Richard]
　Baldy
　　Prematurely thinning hair.
　Giants, Braves, 1910-1927

Rudolph, John (Herman)
    Dutch
    Phillies, Cubs, 1903-1904
Ruel, Herold (Dominic)
    Muddy
        Covered in mud when he entered the house.
    Browns, Yankees, Red Sox, Senators, Tigers, White Sox, 1915-1934
Rueter, Kirk (Wesley) {REE-ter}
    Woody
    Expos, Giants, 1993-2005
Ruether, Walter (Henry)
    Dutch
    The Dutchman
        From his prep school days.
    Cubs, Reds, Robins, Senators, Yankees, 1917-1927
Ruffin, Bruce (Wayne)
    Two Minutes For
        Chris Berman-ism, referring to a hockey penalty.
    Phillies, Brewers, Rockies, 1986-1997
Ruffing, Charles (Herbert)
    Red
    Red Sox, Yankees, White Sox, 1924-1947
Ruiz, Carlos (Joaquin)
    Chooch
        He often muttered "chucha," a Panamanian curse word. Later shortened to Chooch.
    Señor Octubre
        Mr. October in Spanish for his playoff performance.
    Phillies, Dodgers, Mariners, 2006-17
Ruiz, Giraldo
    Chico
    Reds, Angels, 1964-1971
Ruiz, Manuel
    Chico
    Braves, 1978, 1980
Runnels, James (Edward)
    Pete
        From his childhood nickname.
    Little Pete
        Childhood nickname from his father.
    Senators, Red Sox, Colt 45s, 1951-64
Rupp, Cameron (Arthur)
    Pavo
    Phillies, 2013-2017
Rush, Jesse (Howard)
    Andy
    Robins, 1925
Rusie, Amos (Wilson)
    The Hoosier Thunderbolt
        A blazing fastball.
    Hoosiers, Giants, Reds, 1889-1901
Russell, Allen (E)
    Rubberarm
        He could pitch day after day.
    Yankees, Red Sox, Senators, 1915-25
Russell, Bill [William Ellis]
    Ropes
    Dodgers, 1969-1986
Russell, Clarence (Dixon)
    Lefty
    Athletics, 1910-1912
Russell, Ewell (Albert)
    Reb
        From Mississippi.
    Tex
        Moved to Texas as a one-year-old.
    White Sox, 1913-1919
Russell, Glen (David)
    Rip
        Tore his clothes running during a dust storm.
    Cubs, Red Sox, 1939-1947
Russo, Marius (Ugo)
    Lefty
    The Kid From LI
        Born in Brooklyn, went to Long Island Univ.
    Yankees, 1939-1946
Ruth, George (Herman)
    Jidge
        Teammate name for George.
    Babe
        Named as owner Dunn's "Babe."
    The King of Crash

Bambino
   From Italian fans.
The Sultan of Swat: The King of Swing
The Colossus of Clout
   A Boston nickname.
Wizard of Wham: The Bazoo of Bang
Maharajah of Mash: Potentate of Pow
Wali of Wallop: Prince of Pounders
The Southside Phenom
   From the Toronto Daily Star for his first minor league home run.
How-Bouta-Beer Bambino
   From his liking for the suds.
Niggerlips
   Had large facial features when in reform school.
The Big Baboon
   A rookie nickname because he was brash.
Red Sox, Yankees, Braves, 1914-1935
Rutherford, Johnny [John William]
Doc
   Earned his medical degree after his playing days.
Dodgers, 1952
Rutner, Milton
Mickey
Athletics, 1947
Ryan, Cornelius (Joseph)
Connie
Giants, Braves, Reds, Phillies, White Sox, Redlegs, 1942-1954
Ryan, Daniel (R)
Cyclone
Metropolitans, Beaneaters, 1887, 1891
Ryan, Jack
Gulfport
   Began his career in Gulfport, MS.
Coffee Grounds
   How he juiced the ball.
Mud Artist
   His juice concoction resembled dirt.
Naps, Red Sox, Dodgers, 1908-1911
Ryan, Jimmy [James P]
Pony
White Stockings, Pirates, Colts, Orphans, Senators, 1885-1903
Ryan, John (Collins)
Blondy
White Sox, Giants, Phillies, Yankees, 1930-1938
Ryan, Lynn (Nolan)
K-Man
   Has more strikeouts than anyone else in history.
The Ryan Express
   His 100-mph fastball, after the movie, "Von Ryan's Express."
Mets, Angels, Astros, Rangers, 1966-1993
Ryan, Mike [Michael James]
Irish
Red Sox, Phillies, Pirates, 1964-1974
Ryan, Robert, (Victor)
B.J.
Reds, Orioles, Blue Jays, 1999-2009
Ryan, Wilfred (Patrick Dolan)
Rosy
Giants, Braves, Yankees, Dodgers, 1919-1933
Ryba, Dominic (Joseph) {REE-bah}
Mike
Pop
   Made his Boston debut at 35. Lefty Grove nicknamed him.
Cardinals, Red Sox, 1935-1946
Rye, Gene [Eugene Rudolph]
Half Pint
   5'6", 165 lbs.
Red Sox, 1931
Rzepczynski, Marc (Walter) {zep-CHIN-skee}
Scrabble
   For the number of points the letters in his name are worth.
Zep
Blue Jays, Cardinals, Indians, Padres, Athletics, Nationals, Mariners, 2009-2018
Sabathia, Carsten (Charles)

CC: Dub
Indians, Brewers, Yankees, 2001-19
Sabo, Alex [Alexander]
Giz
Senators, 1936-1937
Sabo, Chris [Christopher Andrew]
Spuds
> From Pete Rose for his resemblance to Spuds MacKenzie in Bud Light commercials.
Reds, Orioles, White Sox, Cardinals, 1988-1996
Sadowski, Bob [Robert Frank]
Bo
Cardinals, Phillies, White Sox, Angels, 1960-1963
Sáenz, Olmedo {SIGNS}
Killer Tomato
> From Dodger fans and commentators.
White Sox, Athletics, Dodgers, 1994-2007
Sage, Harry
Doc
Maumees, 1890
Sager, Anthony (Joseph)
A.J.
Padres, Rockies, Tigers, 1994-1998
Sager, Samuel (B)
Pony: Cricket
Forest Citys, 1871
Saito, Takashi
Sammy
The Man from Miyagi
> From Vin Skully. His Japanese team.
Dodgers, Red Sox, Braves, Brewers, Diamondbacks, 2006-2012
Salazar, Argenis (Antonio)
Ángel
Expos, Royals, Cubs, 1983-1988
Sale, Chris [Christopher Allen]
The Condor
> Unorthodox delivery resembles a California Condor.
Stickman: The Conductor
White Sox, Red Sox, 2010-
Salisbury, William (Ansil)
Solly
Phillies, 1902
Sallee, Harry (Franklin)
Slim: Scissors
Slats
> He was 6'3", but only 148 lbs.
Scatter
> He knocked cans and bottles off fence posts with rocks.
Sheriff of Higginsport
> From a sportswriter. He never held the office.
Cardinals, Giants, Reds, 1908-1921
Salmon, Rutherford (Eduardo)
{suh-MONE}
Chico
Indians, Orioles, 1964-1972
Salmon, Tim [Timothy James]
Mr. Angel: Kingfish
Slammin' Salmon
Angels 1992-2006
Saltzgaver, Otto (Hamlin)
Jack
Yankees, Pirates, 1932-1945
Salvo, Manny [Manuel]
Gyp
> Short for Gypsy.
Giants, Bees, Braves, Phillies, 1939-43
Samardzija, Jeff [Jeffrey Allan]
{suh-MAR-jah}
Shark
> From teammates at Notre Dame.
Cubs, Athletics, White Sox, Giants, 2008-
Samuels, Joe [Joseph Jonas]
Shabotch
Tigers, 1930
Samuels, Samuel (Earle)
Ike
Browns, 1895
Sanchez, Aaron (Jacob)
Sanchize
Blue Jays, Astros, 2014-2019
Sanchez, Adrian (Arturo)

El Chamo
Nationals, 2017-
Sánchez, Gary
The Kraken: The Sanchize
Yankees, 2015-
Sánchez, Yolmer (Carlos)
El Del Penonal
White Sox, 2014-
Sand, John (Henry)
Heinie
Phillies, 1923-1928
Sandberg, Ryne (Dee)
The Franchise: Ryno
Kid Natural: Gabby
Berg
> His high school nickname.
Phillies, Cubs, 1981-1997
Sanders, Deion (Luwynn)
Neon Deion
Prime Time
> From a teammate for pickup basketball games during TVs prime time.
Yankees, Braves, Reds, Giants, 1989-2001
Sanders, Ken [Kenneth George]
Daffy
Bulldog
> From Dave Bristol of Milwaukee because he was mean, tough, and stubborn.
Athletics, Red Sox, Brewers, Twins, Indians, Angels, Mets, Royals, 1964-1976
Sanders, Roy G (Garvin)
Butch: Pepe
Reds, Pirates, 1917-1918
Sanders, Roy L (Lee)
Simon
Yankees, Browns, 1918, 1920
Sandoval, Pablo (Emilio)
Fat Ichiro
> Larger version compared to Suzuki.
Round Mound of Pound
Little Money

Kung Fu Panda
> Look and move of the Disney character.
Giants, Red Sox, 2008-
Sanford, Meredith (Leroy)
Mo
Reds, Rockies, Twins, 1991-1995
Sanicki, Ed [Edward Robert]
Butch
Phillies, 1949, 1951
Sanó, Miguel (Angel) {sah-NO}
Bocaton: Boqueton
Twins, 2015-
Santana, Domingo (Alberto)
Showmingo
Astros, Brewers, Mariners, Indians, 2014-
Santana, Ervin (Ramon)
Magic
Angels, Royals, Braves, Twins, White Sox, 2005-2019
Santangelo, Frank-Paul
F.P.
Expos, Giants, Dodgers, Athletics, 1995-2001
Santiago, Benny [Benito]
The Franchise
Padres, Marlins, Reds, Phillies, Blue Jays, Cubs, Giants, Royals, Pirates, 1986-2005
Santiago, Héctor (Felipe)
Bulldoze
White Sox, Angels, Twins, Mets, 2011-
Santiago, José G (Guillermo)
Pantalones
> Translation: Pants. Showed guts when striking out the side with the bases loaded in winter ball.
Indians, Athletics, 1954-1956
Santiago, José R (Rafael)
Palillo
> Spanish for toothpick. He was skinny when young.
Athletics, Red Sox, 1963-1970
Santo, Ron [Ronald Edward]

Pizza
    Cubs, White Sox, 1960-1974
Sargent, Joe [Joseph Alexander]
    Horse Belly
    Tigers, 1921
Sasser, Mackey [Mack Daniel]
    The Hacker
    Giants, Pirates, Mets, Mariners, 1987-1995
Satriano, Tom [Thomas Victor Nicholas]
    Satch: Mr. Everything
    Tommy Trojan
    Angels, Red Sox, 1961-1970
Sauer, Ed [Edward]
    Horn
    Cubs, Cardinals, Braves, 1943-1949
Sauer, Hank [Henry John]
    The Honker
        He had a large nose.
    The Mayor of Wrigley Field
        Power hitter when the Cubs were bad.
    Reds, Cubs, Cardinals, Giants, 1941-1959
Saunders, Joe [Joseph Francis]
    Bazooka Joe
    Safeco Joe
        He pitched well at home for the Mariners.
    Angels, Diamondbacks, Orioles, Mariners, Rangers, 2005-2014
Saunders, Michael (Edward Brett)
    The Condor: Captain Canada
    Mariners, Blue Jays, Phillies, 2009-17
Saupold, Warwick (Anthony)
{sah-POLED}
    Aussie
        Native of Australia.
    Tigers, 2016-2018
Saverine, Bob [Robert Paul]
    Rabbit
    Orioles, Senators, 1959-1967
Savidge, Ralph (Austin)
    Human Ripcord
    The Finger Nail Artist
        Based on a pitch he developed.

    Reds, 1908-1909
Sawatski, Carl (Ernest)
    Swats
        From his name.
    Swisher
    Swish
        From the sound of his bat hitting home runs.
    Butch
        From his stature in the minors.
    Cubs, White Sox, Braves, Phillies, Cardinals, 1948-1963
Sawyer, Carl (Everett)
    Huck
        As in Tom Sawyer and...
    Senators, 1915-1916
Saylor, Phil [Philip Andrew]
    Lefty
        Acquired in college.
    Phillies, 1891
Sborz, John (James)
    Jay
    Tigers, 2010
Scalzi, Frank (John)
    Skeeter
    Giants, 1939
Scanlan, William (Dennis)
    Doc
    Pirates, Superbas, Dodgers, 1903-11
Schaefer, William (Herman)
    Liberty
        Self-adopted after war on Germany declared.
    Germany
    The Prince
        From his on-field flashy showmanship.
    Orphans, Tigers, Senators, Pepper, Yankees, Indians, 1901-1918
Schaeffer, Harry (Edward)
    Lefty
    Yankees, 1952
Schafer, Harry (C)
    Silk Stockings: Dexter
    Red Stockings, 1871-1878
Schalk Ray [Raymond William]

Cracker
White Sox, Giants, 1912-1929
Schaller, Walter
Biff
Tigers, White Sox, 1911, 1913
Scarce, Guerrant (McCurdy)
Mac
Phillies, Mets, Twins, 1972-1978
Schardt, Bill [Wilburt]
Big Bill
6'4", 210 lbs.
Dodgers, 1911-1912
Scharein, Art [Arthur Otto]
Scoop
Browns, 1932-1934
Scharein, George (Albert)
Tom
Phillies, 1937-1940
Scharf, Edward (T)
Nick
Orioles, 1882-1883
Schauer, Alexander (John)
Rube
> Naïve and gullible despite a college education.

Giants, Athletics, 1913-1917
Scheer, Henry (William)
Heinie
> Popular nickname for German ball players.

Yankees, 1922-1923
Scheeren, Fritz [Frederick]
Dutch
Pirates, 1914-1915
Schegg, Gilbert (Eugene)
Lefty
Senators, 1912
Schelle, Gerard (Anthony)
Jim
Athletics, 1939
Schemanske, Fred [Frederick George]
Buck
Senators, 1923
Schemer, Mike [Michael]
Lefty
Giants, 1945-1946

Schepner, Joe [Joseph Maurice]
Gentleman Joe
Browns, 1919
Scherzer, Max [Maxwell M]
Mad Max: Blue Eyes
Diamndbacks, Tigers, Nationals, 2008-
Schesler, Charles
Dutch
Phillies, 1931
Schillings, Elbert (Isaiah)
Red
Athletics, 1922
Schirick, Harry (Ernest)
Dutch
Browns 1914
Schlafly, Harry (Fenton)
Larry
Shoo-fly
> From Chicago bleacherites.

Orphans, Senators, Buffeds, 1902-14
Schlei, George (Henry)
Admiral
Reds, Giants, 1904-1911
Schlesinger, Bill [William Cordes]
Rudy
> From Rudy Redass, derogatory for moody.

Red Sox, 1965
Schliebner, Frederick (Paul)
Dutch
Robins, Browns, 1923
Schlitzer, Victor (Joseph)
Biff
Athletics, Red Sox, Buffeds, 1908-1914
Schlueter, Norm [Norman John]
Duke
White Sox, Indians, 1938-1944
Schmees, George (Edward)
Rocky
Browns, Red Sox, 1952
Schmidt, Charles
Boss
Tigers, 1906-1911
Schmidt, Charles J (John)
Butch

Butcher Boy
> His family was in the meat-packing business.

Highlanders, Braves, 1909-1915

Schmidt, Frederich (Christoph Herman)
Pete
Browns, 1913

Schmit, Frederick (M)
Crazy: Germany
Alleghenys, Orioles, Giants, Spiders, 1890-1901

Schmitz, Johnny [John Albert]
Bear Tracks
> Based on how he shuffled to the mound.

Cubs, Dodgers, Yankees, Reds, Senators, Red Sox, Orioles, 1941-56

Schmutz, Charlie [Charles Otto]
King
Robins, 1914-1915

Schoendienst, Albert (Fred)
Red
Cardinals, Giants, Braves, 1945-1963

Schoeneck, Louis (W)
Jumbo
> 6'2", 223 lbs.

Chicago/Pittsburgh, Monumentals, Hoosiers, 1884-1889

Schofield, Dick [John Richard]
Ducky
> From teammates; his father was "Ducky."

Cardinals, Pirates, Giants, Yankees, Dodgers, Red Sox, Brewers, 1953-71

Schoop, Jonathan (Rufino Jezus) {SCOPE}
Mamba
Orioles, Brewers, Twins, Tigers, 2013-

Schreiber, David (Henry)
Barney
Reds, 1911

Schreiber, Paul (Frederick)
Von
Robins, Yankees, 1922-1945

Schriver, William (Frederick)
Pop
> Advancing age in a 21-year career.

Grays, Quakers, Phillies, Colts, Giants, Reds, Pirates, Cardinals, 1886-1901

Schroeder, Bill [Alfred William]
Rock
Brewers, Angels, 1893-1990

Schroll, Al [Albert Bringhurst]
Bull
> A robust 6'2", 210 lbs.

I.E.
> Family nickname.

Red Sox, Phillies, Cubs, Twins, 1958-1961

Schuble, Henry (George)
Heinie
Kid Boots
> Texas League nickname for his fielding.

Cardinals, Tigers, 1927-1936

Schult, Art [Arthur William]
Dutch
Yankees, Redlegs, Senators, Cubs, 1953-1960

Schulte, Frank (M)
Wildfire
> After a play by the same name.

Cubs, Pirates, Phillies, Senators, 1904-1918

Schulte, Fred (William)
Fritz
Browns, Senators, Pirates, 1927-1937

Schulte, Herman (Joseph)
Ham
Phillies, 1940

Schultz, Charles (Budd)
Buddy
Cubs, Cardinals, 1975-1979

Schultz, George (Warren)
Barney
Cardinals, Tigers, Cubs, 1955-1965

Schultz, Howie [Howard Henry]
Stretch
Steeple
> He was 6'6".

Dodgers, Phillies, Reds, 1943-1948

Schultz, Joe Jr. [Joseph Charles]
Dode
　From childhood.
Pirates, Browns, 1939-1948

Schultz, Joe Sr. [Joseph Charles]
Germany
Braves, Robins, Cubs, Pirates, Cardinals, Phillies, Reds, 1912-1925

Schultz, Wibert (Carl)
Webb
White Sox, 1924

Schumacher, Hal [Harold Henry]
{SHOO-mocker}
Prince Hal
　They already had a King Carl (Hubbell).
Giants, 1931-1946

Schumaker, Jared (Michael)
Skip
Cardinals, Dodgers, Reds, 2005-2015

Schumann, Charles (J)
Hack
Athletics, 1906

Schuster, Bill [William Charles]
Broadway Bill
Pirates, Bees, Cubs, 1937-1945

Schwamb, Ralph (Richard)
Blackie
Browns, 1948

Schwarber, Kyle (Joseph)
Hulk: Warbird
Cubs, 2015-

Schwartz, Bill A [William August]
Scooper Bill: Pop
Buckeyes, Outlaw Reds, 1883-1884

Schwartz, Bill C (William Charles)
Blab
Elmer
　Football nickname from college coaching.
Naps, 1904

Schweitzer, Al [Albert Casper]
Cheese
Browns, 1908-1911

Scoffic, Lou [Louis]
Weaser
Cardinals, 1936

Scoggins, Jim [Lynn James]
Lefty
White Sox, 1913

Scott, Floyd (John)
Pete
Cubs, Pirates, 1926-1928

Scott, George (Charles)
Boomer: Great
Red Sox, Brewers, Royals, Yankees, 1966-1979

Scott, Jim [James]
Death Valley Jim
　Confusion about his birthplace.
Intrepid Nimrod: Wyoming Nimrod
　Both from a reporter.
White Sox, 1909-1917

Scott, Lewis (Everett)
Deacon
Trolley Wire
　From his accurate throws.
Red Sox, Yankees, Senators, White Sox, Reds, 1914-1926

Scott, Marshall
Lefty
Phillies, 1945

Scott, Milt [Milton Parker]
Mikado Milt
　After the Gilbert & Sullivan opera.
White Stockings, Wolverines, Alleghenys, Orioles, 1882-1886

Scott, Ralph (Robert)
Mickey
Orioles, Expos, Angels, 1973-1977

Scott, Rodney (Darrell)
Cool Breeze
Royals, Expos, Athletics, Cubs, Yankees, 1975-1982

Scrivener, Wayne (Allison)
Chuck
Tigers, 1975-1977

Seager, Kyle (Duerr)
Corey's Brother
Mariners, 2011-

Seale, Johnnie [Johnny Ray]

217

Durango Kid
   Played high school and college in Durango, CO.
Tigers, 1964-1965

Seanez, Rudy (Caballero) {see-AHN-yez}
Action Traction
Indians, Padres, Dodgers, Braves, Rangers, Red Sox, Royals, Marlins, Phillies, 1989-2008

Sears, Ken [Kenneth Eugene]
Ziggy
Yankees, Browns, 1943, 1946

Sears, George (Thomas)
Tom Terrific
   Media nickname from a cartoon character.
The Franchise
Mets, Reds, White Sox, Red Sox, 1967-1986

Seaver, Tom [George Thomas]
Tom Terrific: The Franchise
Mets, Reds, White Sox, Red Sox, 1967-1986

Sechrist, Theodore (O'Hara)
Doc
Giants, 1899

Sedgwick, Henry (Kenneth)
Duke
Phillies, Senators, 1921, 1923

See, Charlie [Charles Henry]
Chad
Reds, 1919-1921

Seeds, Bob [Ira Robert]
Suitcase Bob
Indians, White Sox, Red Sox, Yankees, Giants, 1930-1940

Seerey, Pat [James Patrick]
The People's Choice
Fat Pat
   From a writer.
Indians, White Sox, 1943-1949

Segura, Jean (Carlos Enrique)
El Mambo
Angels, Brewers, Diamondbacks, Mariners, Phillies, 2012-

Seibold, Harry
Socks
   Given by his first manager, Connie Mack.
Athletics, Braves, 1916-1933

Selbach, Albert (Karl)
Kip: Baron Selbach
The German Ambassador
   A Washington nickname.
Senators, Reds, Giants, Orioles, Americans, 1894-1906

Selkirk, George (Alexander)
Twinkletoes
   Ran on the balls of his feet.
Yankees, 1934-1942

Sell, Lester (Elwood)
Epp
Cardinals, 1922-1923

Sellers, Oliver
Rube
Doves, 1910

Sellman, Frank [Charles Francis]
Scrubs
Kekiongas, Olympics, Canaries, Nationals, 1871-0875

Selma, Dick [Richard Jay]
Mortimer Snerd
   After the Charlie McCarthy innocent, wisecracking dummy.
Moon Man
   From pitching the day after the first moon landing.
Mets, Padres, Cubs, Phillies, Angels, Brewers, 1965-1974

Selsky, Steve [Steven Garth]
Stone Cold
Reds, Red Sox, 2016-2017

Sembera, Carroll (William)
Pencil
   6' but only 155 lbs.
Astros, Expos, 1965-1970

Semien, Marcus (Andrew)
Mahkus
   New England drawl but raised in California.
White Sox, Athletics, 2013-

Semproch, Roman (Anthony)

Ray: Baby
Phillies, Tigers, Angles, 1958-1961
Senerchia, Emanuel (Robert)
Sonny
Pirates, 1952
Sensenderfer, John (Philips Jenkins)
Count
From his mustache and aristocratic air.
Athletics, 1871-1874
Sentell, Leopold (Theodore)
Paul
Phillies, 1906-1907
Serum, Gary (Wayne)
Truth
As in Truth Serum.
Twins, 1977-1979
Sessi, Walter (Anthony)
Watsie
Cardinals, 1941, 1946
Settlemire, Edgar (Merle)
Lefty
Red Sox, 1928
Sewell, James (Luther)
Luke
From an elementary-school teacher.
Indians, Senators, White Sox, Browns, 1921-1942
Sewell, Truett (Banks)
Rip
Tigers, Pirates, 1932-1949
Seybold, Ralph (Orlando)
Socks
Reds, Athletics, 1899-1908
Seymour, James (Bentley)
Cy
From sportswriters, short for cyclone.
Giants, Orioles, Reds, Braves, 1896-1913
Shafer, Arthur (Joseph)
Tillie
A Momma's boy, named by teammate Cy Seymour.
Giants, 1909-1913

Shafer, George (W)
Orator
From teammates: he talked to himself.
Dark Blues, Mutuals, Whites, Grays, Blues, White Stockings, Bisons, Maroons, Athletics 1875-1890
Shaffer, John (W)
Cannon Ball
Metropolitans, 1886-1887
Shaner, Wally [Walter Dedaker]
Skinny
From a cartoon character of the day.
Nig
A short-lived nickname.
Big Boy
From a Richmond newspaper.
Indians, Red Sox, Reds, 1923-1929
Shanks, Howie [Howard Samuel]
Hawk
Senators, Red Sox, Yankees, 1912-25
Shanley, Harry (Root)
Doc
Browns, 1912
Shannon, Maurice (Joseph)
Red
Braves, Athletics, Red Sox, Senators, Cubs, 1915-1926
Shannon, Mike [Thomas Michael]
Moonman
For the way he dodged a pitch... behind his back.
Cardinals, 1962-1970
Shannon, William (Porter)
Spike
From his teenage years.
Cardinals, Giants, Pirates, 1904-1908
Sharman, Ralph (Edward)
Bally
Athletics, 1917
Sharpe, Bayard (Heston)
Bud
Short for his nickname from his sister-"my little Rosebud."
Beaneaters, Pirates, Doves, 1905, 10

Shaughnessy, Francis (Joseph)
Shag
Senators, Athletics, 1905, 1908
Shaute, Joe [Joseph Benjamin] {SHAY oot}
Lefty
Indians, Robins, Dodgers, Reds, 1922-1934
Shaw, Al [Alfred Louis]
Shoddy
Tigers, Americans, White Sox, Doves, 1901-1909
Shaw, Bryan (Anthony)
Geek
Diamondbacks, Indians, Rockies, Mariners, 2011-
Shaw, Frederick (Lander)
Dupee
He duped batters he struck out by taunting them.
Wizard
Wolverines, Reds, Grays, Nationals, 1883-1888
Shaw, Jim [James Aloysius]
Grunting Jim
He grunted with every pitch.
Senators, 1913-1921
Shaw, Royal (N)
Hunky
Pirates, 1908
Shaw, Travis (R)
Mayor of Ding Dong City
Red Sox, Brewers, Blue Jays, 2015-
Shawkey, Bob [James Robert]
Bob the Gob: Sailor
Athletics, Yankees, 1913-1927
Shay, Arthur (Joseph)
Marty
Cubs, Braves, 1916, 1924
Shea, Francis (Joseph)
Spec
Because of his freckles.
The Naugatuck Nugget
From Naugatuck, Conn.
Yankees, Senators, 1947-1955
Shea, John E (Edward)
Napoleon: Red

Nap
Short for Napoleon.
Shorty
He was 5'5".
Phillies, 1902
Shea, John M (Michael Joseph)
Lefty
Red Sox, 1928
Shea, Patrick (Henry)
Red
Athletics, Giants, 1918-1922
Sheehan, Jim [James Thomas]
Big Jim
Giants, 1936
Sheehan, Timothy (James)
Biff
Browns, 1895-1896
Sheely, Earl (Homer)
Whitey
White Sox, Pirates, Braves, 1921-31
Sheely, Hollis (Kimball)
Bud
White Sox, 1951-1953
Shelton, Andrew (Kemper)
Skeeter: Rabbit: Spider
All based on baserunning speed.
Yankees, 1915
Sherdel, Bill [William Henry]
Wee Willie
5'8", less than 150 lbs.
Cardinals, Braves, 1918-1932
Sherfy, James (Harold)
Wild Thing
Diamondbacks, 2017-2019
Sheridan, Eugene (Anthony)
Red
Robins, 1918, 1920
Sheridan, Neill (Rawlins)
Wild Horse
Based on he way he ran.
Red Sox, 1948
Sherling, Ed [Edward Creech]
Shine
Athletics, 1924
Sherlock, John (Clinton)
Monk

Phillies, 1930
Sherlock, Vince [Vincent Thomas]
    Baldy
    Dodgers, 1935
Sherman, Dan [Lester Daniel]
    Babe: General
    Chi-Feds, 1914
Shields, Ben [Benjamin Cowan]
    Lefty: Big Ben
    Yankees, Red Sox, Phillies, 1924-31
Shields, Francis (Leroy)
    Pete
    Indians, 1915
Shields, Jamie [James Anthony]
    Big Game James: Juego G
    Complete Game James
        After 11 complete games in 2011.
    Devil Rays, Rays, Royals, Padres,
    White Sox, 2006-2018
Shifflett, Garland (Jessie)
    Duck
    Senators, Twins, 1957, 1964
Shinault, Enoch (Erskine)
    Ginger
    Indians, 1921-1922
Shines, Razor [Anthony Razor]
    Ray
    Expos, 1983-1987
Shinnick, Tim [Timothy James]
    Dandy: Good Eye
    Colonels, 1890-1891
Shipke, Bill [William Martin]
    Skipper Bill: Muskrat Bill
    Naps, Senators, 1906-1909
Shipley, Joe [Joseph Clark]
    Moses
    Giants, White Sox, 1958-1963
Shires, Art [Charles Arthur]
    Art the Great
        Self-named.
    Art the Silent
        From writers when he was well-
        behaved.
    White Sox, Senators, Braves, 1928-32
Shirey, Clair (Lee)
    Duke

Senators, 1920
Shirley, Alvis (Newman)
    Tex
    Athletics, Browns, 1941-1946
Shirley, Ernest (Raeford)
    Mule
    Senators, 1924-1925
Shiver, Ivey (Merwin)
    Chick
    Tigers, Reds, 1931, 1934
Shoffner, Milburn (James)
    Milt: Pinky
    Indians, Bees, Reds, 1929-1940
Shorten, Charles (Henry)
    Chick
    Red Sox, Tigers, Browns, Reds,
    1915-1924
Shotton, Burton (Edwin)
    Barney
        Named after Barney Oldfield,
        race car driver.
    Browns, Senators, Cardinals, 1909-23
Shoun, Clyde (Mitchell)
    Hardrock
        Based on his fastball.
    Duster: Lefty
    Cubs, Cardinals, Reds, Braves, White
    Sox, 1935-1949
Shovlin, John (Joseph)
    Brode
    Pirates, Browns, 1911-1920
Shriver, Harry (Graydon)
    Pop
    Robins, 1922-1923
Shriver, William (Frederick)
    Pop
    Grays, Quakers, Phillies, Colts,
    Giants, Reds, Pirates, Cardinals,
    1886-1901
Shuba, George (Thomas)
    Shotgun
        Sprayed line drives with a
        compact swing.
    Dodgers, 1948-1955
Shuck, Jack (Burdett)
    JB

Astros, Angels, Indians, White Sox, Marlins, Pirates, 2011-
Shultz, Wallace (Luther)
Toots
Kaiser
    He supported Germany in 1914.
Phillies, 1911-1912
Siebert, Dick [Richard Walther]
Chief
    From his college coaching days.
Lefty
Dodgers, Cardinals, Athletics, 1932-1945
Siebert, Wilfred (Charles)
Sonny
Indians, Red Sox, Rangers, Cardinals, Padres, Athletics, 1964-1975
Siemer, Oscar (Sylvester)
Cotton
Braves, 1925-1926
Sierra, Rubén (Angel)
The Franchise
El Caballo
    "The Horse" in Spanish.
El Indio
    "The Indian" in Spanish.
Rangers, Athletics, Yankees, Tigers, Reds, Blue Jays, White Sox, Mariners, Twins, 1986-2006
Sierra, Ulises
Candy
Padres, Reds, 1988
Sievers, Roy (Edward)
Squirrel
    From schoolboy basketball.
Browns, Senators, White Sox, Phillies, 1949-1965
Siglin, Wesley (Peter)
Paddy
Pirates, 1914-1916
Silch, Ed [Edward]
Baldy
Bridegrooms, 1888
Silvera, Charlie [Charles Anthony]
Swede
Yankees, Cubs, 1948-1957

Silvestri, Kenneth (Joseph)
Hawk
White Sox, Yankees, Phillies, 1939-51
Simmons, Al [Aloysius Harry Szymanski]
Bucketfoot Al
    Stepped toward third base when hitting.
Athletics, White Sox, Tigers, Senators, Bees, Reds, Red Sox, 1924-1944
Simmons, Andrelton (A)
{ANN-drull-ton}
Simba
Braves, Angels, 2012-
Simmons, George (Washington)
Hack
Tigers, Highlanders, Terrapins, 1910-1915
Simmons, Ted (Lyle)
Simba
    Had collar-length brown hair.
Sleepy
    Laid-back, droopy-eyed appearance.
Cardinals, Brewers, Braves, 1968-88
Simón, Alfredo
Big Pasta
Orioles, Reds, Tigers, 2008-2016
Simon, Syl [Sylvester Adam]
Sammy
Browns, 1923-1924
Simons, Mel [Melbern Ellis]
Butch
White Sox, 1931-1932
Simpson, Harry (Leon)
Suitcase
    From his size 13 shoes.
Goody
    From willingness to run errands for neighbors.
Indians, Athletics, Yankees, White Sox, Pirates, 1951-1959
Simpson, Thomas (Leo)
Duke
Cubs, 1953
Sims, Clarence
Pete

Browns, 1915
Sims, Duane (B)
   Duke
   Indians, Dodgers, Tigers, Yankees, Rangers, 1964-1974
Singer, Bill [William Robert]
   Sing Sing: Billy No-No
   The Singer Throwing Machine
   Dodgers, Angels, Rangers, Twins, Blue Jays, 1964-1977
Singleton, Bert (Elmer)
   Smoky
   Braves, Pirates, Senators, Cubs, 1945-1959
Singleton, John (Edward)
   Sheriff
   Phillies, 1922
Sisler, George (Harold)
   Gorgeous George
      For his good looks.
   Browns, Senators, Braves, 1915-1930
Sisti, Sebastian (Daniel)
   Sibby
   Bees, Braves, 1939-1954
Sitton, Charles (Vedder)
   Carl: CV: Vet
   Naps, 1909
Skaggs, Tyler (Wayne)
   Swaggy
   Diamondbacks, Angels, 2012-2019
Sketchley, Harry (Clement)
   Bud
   White Sox, 1942
Skinner, Elisha (Harrison)
   Camp
   Yankees, Red Sox, 1922-1923
Skizas, Lou [Louis Peter]
   The Nervous Greek
   Yankees, Athletics, Tigers, White Sox, 1956-1959
Skopec, John (S)
   Buckshot
   White Sox, Tigers, 1901, 1903
Showron, Bill [William Joseph]
   Moose
      His haircut looked like Mussolini.

Yankees, Dodgers, Senators, White Sox, Angels, 1954-1967
Slade, Gordon (Leigh)
   Oskie
   Robins, Dodgers, Cardinals, Reds, 1930-1935
Slagle, Jimmy [James Franklin]
   The Mosquito: Rabbit
   Shorty
      5'7"
   Senators, Phillies, Beaneaters, Orphans, Cubs, 1899-1908
Slania, Dan [Daniel Alexander]
   Mr. Incredible
   Giants, 2017
Slaught, Don [Donald Martin]
   Sluggo
      From his slugging ability.
   Royals, Rangers, Yankees, Pirates, Angels, White Sox, Padres, 1982-97
Slaughter, Enos (Bradsher)
   Country
      Florid face, straw-colored hair, tight clothes.
   Warhorse
      From a columnist.
   Cardinals, Yankees, Athletics, Braves, 1938-1959
Slayback, Elbert
   Scottie
   Giants, 1926
Slayton, Foster (Herbert)
   Steve
      Sounded like the sound of him spitting.
   Red Sox, 1928
Sloan, Bruce (Adams)
   Fatso
      Very chubby face.
   Giants, 1944
Sloan, Yale (Yeastman)
   Tod
      After a jockey who crouched.
   Browns, 1913-1919
Sloat, Dwain (Clifford)
   Lefty

Dodgers, Cubs, 1948-1949
Slocumb, Heath [Heathcliff]
   If You Got 'Em
      Chris Berman-ism from the army cliché, "Smoke 'em if you got 'em."
   Cubs, Indians, Phillies, Red Sox, Mariners, Orioles, Cardinals, Padres, 1991-2000
Smalley, Will [William Darwin]
   Deacon
   Farmer Bill
      From newspapers in his youth.
   Spiders, Statesmen, 1890-1891
Smart, Jon (David)
   JD
   Expos, Rangers, 1999, 2001
Smith, Al [Alphonse Eugene]
   Fuzzy
      The first teenager of his friends with a beard.
   Indians, White Sox, Orioles, Red Sox, 1953-1964
Smith, Albert (Edward)
   Edgar
   Beaneaters, 1883
Smith, Aleck [Alexander Benjamin]
   Broadway Aleck
   Bridegrooms, Superbas, Orioles, Giants, Americans, Cubs, 1897-1906
Smith, Armstrong (Frederick)
   Klondike
   Highlanders, 1912
Smith, Bob [Robert Walkup]
   Riverboat
      Coolness and finesse under fire, like a riverboat gambler.
   Red Sox, Cubs, Indians, 1958-1959
Smith, Caleb (Anthony)
   Dr. K
   Yankees, Marlins, Diamondbacks, 2017-
Smith, Charles (Marvin)
   Pop
      Longevity and older appearance.

Reds, Blues, Bisons, Ruby Legs, Athletics, Eclipse, Buckeyes, Alleghenys, Beaneaters, Statesmen, 1880-1891
Smith, Chris M [Christopher Michael]
   Rock N Fire
   Red Sox, Brewers, Athletics, 2008-2017
Smith, Chris W [Christopher William]
   Chip
   Expos, Giants, 1981-1983
Smith, Clarence (Ossie)
   Pop-boy
   White Sox, Indians, 1913-1917
Smith, Dominic (David Rene)
   Sloth Bear
      Teammate said he resembled one in a zoo exhibit.
   Mets, 2017-
Smith, Earl L (Leonard)
   Sheriff
   Cubs, Browns, Senators, 1916-1922
Smith, Earl L (Leonard)
   Sheriff
   Cubs, Browns, Senators, 1916-1922
Smith Earl S (Sutton)
   Oil
      NY fan pronunciation of Earl.
   Giants, Braves, Pirates, Cardinals, 1919-1930
Smith, Elmer (Ellsworth)
   Mike
   Red Stockings, Pirates, Reds, Giants, Beaneaters 1886-1901
Smith, Elwood (Hope)
   Mike
   Giants, 1926
Smith, Ernie [Ernest Henry]
   Kansas City Kid
   White Sox, 1930
Smith, Frank (Elmer)
   Piano Mover
      His offseason job.
   Nig

Minor league nickname, for his dark complexion.
White Sox, Red Sox, Reds, Terrapins, Tip-Tops, 1904-1915

Smith, George A (Allen)
Columbia George
    Played at Columbia University.
Giants, Reds, Robins, Phillies, 1916-1923

Smith, George H (Henry)
Heinie
    German ancestry.
Colonels, Pirates, Giants, Tigers, 1897-1903

Smith, George J
Germany
Mountain City, Blues, Grays, Bridegrooms, Reds, Browns, 1884-1898

Smith, Hal [Harold Raymond]
Cura
Cardinals, Pirates, 1956-1965

Smith, Henry (Joseph)
Happy
Superbas, 1910

Smith James A (Abner)
Stub
    5'6", 145 lbs.
Beaneaters, 1898

Smith, James C (Carlisle)
Red
Dodgers, Superbas, Robins, Braves, 1911-1919

Smith, Jimmy L [James Lawrence]
Greenfield Jimmy
    From a section of Pittsburgh.
Bluejacket
Serpent Tongue
    A bench jockey.
Chi-Feds, Whales, Terrapins, Pirates, Giants, Braves, Reds, Phillies, 1914-1922

Smith, John F (Francis)
Phenomenal
    Gained after pitching a no-hitter.
Athletics, Alleghenys, Grays, Wolverines, Orioles, Phillies, 1884-1891

Smith, John W (William)
Chick
Reds, 1913

Smith, Kevan (Alan)
Szmyoth
White Sox, Angels, Rays, 2016-

Smith, Lewis (Oscar)
Bull
Pirates, Cubs, 1904, 1906

Smith, Lionel (H)
Leo
Broncos, 1890

Smith, Lonnie
Skates
Phillies, Cardinals, Royals, Braves, Pirates, Orioles, 1978-1994

Smith, Marvin (Harold)
Red
Athletics, 1925

Smith, Orlin (Hudson)
Ollie
Colonels, 1894

Smith, Ozzie [Osborne Earl]
The Wizard
    His defensive prowess.
The Wizard of Oz
Padres, Cardinals, 1978-1996

Smith, Ray [Raymond Edward]
Quality: Qualls
Twins, 1981-1983

Smith, Richard (Paul)
Red
Giants, 1927

Smith, Robert (Allan)
Bud
Cardinals, 2001-2002

Smith, Rufus (Frazier)
Shirt
Tigers, 1927

Smith, Samuel (J)
Skyrocket
Colonels, 1888

Smith, Seth [Garry Seth]
Mr. Late Night
Rockies, Athletics, Padres, Mariners,

Orioles, 2007-2017
Smith, Wilbur (Floyd)
Wib
Browns, 1909
Smith, Will (William Dills]
Fresh Prince
Dodgers, 2019-
Smith, Willard (Jehu)
Red
Pirates, 1917-1918.
Smith, Willie
Wonderful Willie
Tigers, Angels, Indians, Cubs, Reds, 1963-1971
Smoak, Justin (Kyle)
Moakey
Rangers, Mariners, Blue Jays, Brewers, Giants, 2010-
Smoker, Josh [Joshua Michael]
Brown Bear
Mets, Pirates, Tigers, 2016-2018
Smoll, Clyde (Hetrick)
Lefty
Phillies, 1940
Smoot, Homer (Vernon)
Doc
Cardinals, Reds, 1902-1906
Smyers, Clarence (Melvin)
Clancy
Dodgers, 1944
Smyth, James (Daniel)
Red
Robins, Cardinals, 1915-1918
Sneed, Cy (R)
Yukon Cornelius
Astros, 2019-
Snell, Blake (Ashton)
Snellzilla
Rays, 2016-
Snell, Wally [Walter Henry]
Doc
A successful mycologist.
Red Sox, 1913
Snider, Edwin (Donald)
Duke
Nickname from age 5.
Duke of Flatbush
Home of the Dodgers.
The Silver Fox
Dodgers, Mets, Giants, 1947-1964
Snider, Travis (James)
Lunchbox
Blue Jays, Pirates, Orioles, 2008-2015
Snipes, Wyatt (Eure)
Roxy: Rock
White Sox, 1923
Snodgrass, Amzie (Beal)
Chappie
Orioles, 1901
Snodgrass, Frederick (Charles)
Snow
Giants, Braves, 1908-1916
Snow, Jack (Thomas)
JT
Yankees, Angels, Giants, Red Sox, 1992-2008
Snover, Colonel (Lester)
Bosco
Giants, 1919
Snyder, Abraham (Conrad)
Coonie
Colonels, 1898
Snyder, Alfred (Joseph)
Chubby
Buffeds, 1914
Snyder, Charles (Nicholas)
Pop
Receding hairline and serious.
Blue Legs, Canaries, Whites, Grays, Red Stockings, Blues, Spiders, Infants, Statesmen, 1873-1891
Snyder, Emanuel (Sebastian)
Redleg
Reds, Quicksteps, 1876, 1884
Snyder, Frank (Elton)
Pancho
Mexican descent.
Cardinals, Giants, 1912-1927
Sockalexis, Louis (Francis)
Chief
Penobscot Indian, impetus for the Indians' team name.

Deerfoot of the Diamond
Spiders, 1897-1899
Sofield, Rick [Richard Michael]
Hollywood
Twins, 1979-1981
Sogard, Eric (Sidney)
Nerd Power
Athletics, Brewers, Blue Jays, Rays, 2010-
Solano, Donovan
Donnie Barrels
Marlins, Yankees, Giants, 2012-
Solano, Jhonatan
Onion
Nationals, Marlins, 2012-2015
Solarte, Yangervis (Alfredo)
{YAWN-hair-vis SO-lahr-tay}
El Ni: Pituki
Yankees, Padres, Blue Jays, Giants, 2014-2019
Solomon, Eddie
Buddy J
Dodgers, Cubs, Cardinals, Braves, Pirates, White Sox, 1973-1982
Solomon, Mose (Hirsch)
The Rabbi of Swat
 Jewish version of the Sultan....
The Jewish Babe Ruth
Hickory
 Childhood nickname.
Giants, 1923
Solters, Julius (Joseph)
Moose
 6', 190 lbs, sollidly built.
Jake: Tarzan: Saltly: Peanuts
Greek: Turk: Zbyszko
Lemons
 Got lemons for the older kids.
Red Sox, Browns, Indians, White Sox, 1934-1943
Somerlott, John (Wesley)
Jock
Senators, 1910-1911
Soria, Joakim (Augustin)
{wah-KEEM SORE-ee-uh}
The Mexicutioner

"The Mexican Executioner."
Jack
Royals, Rangers, Tigers, Pirates, White Sox, Brewers, Athletics, 2007-
Sorrells, Raymond (Edwin)
Chick
Indians, 1922
Sosa, Sammy [Samuel Kelvin Peralta]
Slammin' Sammy
 From announcer Chip Caray.
Say It Ain't
 Chris Berman-ism: "Say it ain't SOsa."
Mikey
 Family, friends nickname.
Rangers, White Sox, Cubs, Orioles, 1989-2007
Soto, Juan (Jose)
La Fiera: Childish Bambino
Nationals, 2018-
Souchock, Stephen
Bud
Yankees, White Sox, Tigers, 1946-55
Southworth, Billy [William Harold]
Billy the Kid
Billy the Heel
 From players for his strict management style.
Naps, Indians, Pirates, Braves, Giants, Cardinals, 1913-1929
Souza, Steven Jr. (Jeffrey)
Souzbot
Nationals, Rays, Diamondbacks, Cubs, 2014-
Sowders, William (Jefferson)
Little Bill
Beaneaters, Alleghenys, 1888-1890
Spalding, Charles (Harry)
Dick: CH
Phillies, Senators, 1927-1928
Span, Keiunta (Denard)
Spanny: D-Span: Spaniard
Twins, Nationals, Giants, Rays, Mariners, 2008-2018
Spangler, Al [Albert Donald]
Spanky

Braves, Colt .45s, Astros, Angels, Cubs, 1959-1971
Sparks, Steve [Steven William]
Phone Book
    Ripped one in half, injuring his shoulder.
Brewers, Angels, Tigers, Athletics, Diamondbacks, 1995-2004
Sparks, Thomas (Frank)
Tully
Sparks the Mysterious
    Telegraphs his pitches and fast ball looks slow.
Phillies, Pirates, Brewers, Giants, Americans, 1897-1910
Speake, Bob [Robert Charles]
Spook
Cubs, Giants, 1955-1959
Speaker, Tris [Tristram Edgar]
Spoke
    Teammate yelled when he got a hit.
The Grey Eagle
    He was prematurely grey.
Americans, Red Sox, Indians, Senators, Athletics, 1907-1928
Speer, George (Nathan)
Kid
Tigers, 1909
Spencer, Daryl (Dean)
Dee: Big Dee
The Monster
    Japanese nickname.
Giants, Cardinals, Dodgers, Reds, 1952-1963
Spencer, Edward (Russell)
Tubby
    5'10" but 215 lbs.
Hippo Spencer
Hackenschmidt
    Big and strong like a famous wrestler.
Browns, Red Sox, Phillies, Tigers, 1905-1918
Spencer, Fred (Calvin)
Hack
    From Hackenschmidt, a famous wrestler.
Kidnapped kid
Browns, 1912
Speraw, Paul (Bachman)
Birdie: Polly
Browns, 1920
Spivey, Ernest (Lee)
Junior
Diamondbacks, Brewers, Nationals, 2001-2005
Sprinz, Joe [Joseph Conrad]
Mule
Indians, Cardinals, 1930-1933
Squires, Mike [Michael Lynn]
Spanky
White Sox, 1975-1985
St. Claire, Edward (Joseph)
Ebba
Braves, Giants, 1951-1954
Stafford, Henry (Alexander)
Heinie
Giants, 1916
Stafford, James (Joseph)
General: Jamsey
Bisons, Giants, Colonels, Beaneaters, Senators, 1890-1899
Stafford John (Henry)
Doc
    Became an optometrist.
Spiders, 1893
Stahl, Charles (Sylvester)
Chick
Beaneaters, Americans, 1897-1906
Stahl, Garland
Jake
    From college fraternity brothers.
Jake the Giant Killer
Americans, Senators, Highlanders, Red Sox, 1903-1913
Stairs, Matt [Matthew Wade]
Wonder Hamster
Expos, Red Sox, Athletics, Cubs, Brewers, Pirates, Royals, Rangers, Tigers, Blue Jays, Phillies, Padres, Nationals, 1992-2011

Stallcup, Thomas (Virgil)
Red
Reds, Cardinals, 1947-1953
Staller, George (Walborn)
Stopper
Athletics, 1943
Stallings, George (Tweedy)
Gentleman George
The Miracle Man
> For managing the Braves from last to first in 1914.

Bridegrooms, Phillies, 1890-1898
Stammen, Craig (Nicholas)
Craigeroo: Trigger
Trig
> Short for Trigger

Nationals, Padres, 2009-
Stanek, Al [Albert Wilfred]
Lefty
Giants, 1963
Stange, Albert (Lee)
Stinger
Twins, Indians, Red Sox, White Sox, 1961-1970
Stanhouse, Don [Donald Joseph]
Stan the Man Unusual
> Parody of Stan 'the man' Musial.

Fullpack
> Manager Weaver smoked many cigarettes when Stanhouse pitched.

Rangers, Expos, Orioles, Dodgers, 1972-1982
Stanky, Eddie [Edward Raymond]
The Brat
> Snarling, clamorous, hot-headed.

Muggsy: Stinky
Cubs, Dodgers, Braves, Giants, Cardinals, 1943-1953
Stanley, Bob [Robert William]
Stanley Steamer: The Steamer
Bigfoot
Red Sox, 1977-1989
Stanley, Fred [Frederick Blair]
Chicken
Pilots, Brewers, Indians, Padres, Yankees, Athletics, 1969-1982
Stanley, John (Leonard)
Buck
Phillies, 1911
Stanley, Mitchell (Jack)
Mickey
Tigers, 1964-1978
Stanton, George (Washington)
Buck
Browns, 1931
Stanton Giancarlo (Cruz-Michael)
Bigfoot
Cruz
> Early nickname from his mother.

Mikey
> From most relatives.

Marlins, Yankees, 2010-
Stargell, Wilver (Dornel)
Willie: Wondrous Willie
Pops
> He was 42 in his last game.

Pirates, 1962-1982
Stark, Monroe (Randolph)
Dolly
Naps, Superbas, Dodgers, 1909-1912
Starr, Ray [Raymond Francis]
Iron Man
> Willing and able to pitch both ends of a doubleheader.

Cardinals, Giants, Braves, Reds, Pirates, Cubs, 1932-1945
Starr, William
Chick
Senators, 1935-1936
Start, Joe [Joseph]
Old Reliable: Rocks
Mutuals, Hartfords of Brooklyn, White Stockings, Grays, Nationals, 1871-1886
Statz, Arnold (John)
Chigger
> Gained when living in Alabama.

Jigger
> Transformation of Chigger.

Giants, Red Sox, Cubs, Robins, 1919-1928

Staub, Daniel (Joseph)
    Rusty
        Named at birth before leaving the hospital.
    Le Grand Orange
        Bright red hair in Montreal.
    Colt .45s, Astros, Expos, Mets, Tigers, Rangers, 1963-1985

Stearns, John (Hardin)
    Bad Dude
        Toughness and confidence.
    Phillies, Mets, 1974-1984

Steele, Bill [William Mitchell]
    Big Bill
    Cardinals, Robins, 1910-1914

Steelman, Morris (James)
    Farmer
    Colonels, Superbas, Athletics, 1899-1902

Stein, Justin (Marion)
    Ott
    Phillies, Reds, 1938

Steiner, James (Harry)
    Red
    Indians, Red Sox, 1945

Stemmyer, Bill [William]
    Cannon Ball
    Beaneaters, Blues, 1885-1888

Stengel, Charles (Dillon)
    Casey
        From Kansas City, MO. Named in a poker game as a rookie.
    The Ol' Perfessor
        As a volunteer coach, he was named an Assistant Professor at the Univ. of Mississippi.
    Dodgers, Pirates, Phillies, Giants, Braves, 1912-1925

Stephen, Louis (Roberts)
    Buzz
    Twins, 1968

Stephens, Jim [James Walter]
    Little Nemo
    Browns, 1907-1912

Stephens, Vern [Vernon Decatur]
    Junior: Buster: Little Slug: Stevie
    Browns, Red Sox, White Sox, Orioles, 1941-1955

Stephenson, Jackson (Riggs)
    Old Hoss
        Reliability as a hitter.
    Warhorse
    Indians, Cubs, 1921-1934

Stephenson, Reuben (Crandol)
    Dummy
        He was deaf.
    Stevey
    Phillies, 1892

Stephenson, Walter (McQueen)
    Tarzan
    Cubs, Phillies, 1935-1937

Sterrett, Charles (Hurlbut)
    Dutch
    Highlanders, Yankees, 1912-1913

Stevens, Ed [Edward Lee]
    Big Ed
        6'1", big for the times.
    Dodgers, Pirates, 1945-1950

Stewart, Charles (Parnell)
    Tuffy
    Cubs, 1913-1914

Stewart, Dave [David Keith]
    Smoke
    Dodgers, Rangers, Phillies, Athletics, Blue Jays, 1978-1995

Stewart, Edward (Perry)
    Bud
    Pirates, Yankees, Senators, White Sox, 1941-1954

Stewart, Glen (Weldon)
    Gabby
    Giants, Phillies, 1940-1944

Stewart, Joe [Joseph Lawrence]
    Ace
    Beaneaters, 1904

Stewart, John D (Davis)
    Stud
    Cardinals, 1922-1925

Stewart, John F (Franklin)
    Stuffy
    Cardinals, Pirates, Robins, Senators, 1916-1929

Stewart, Mark
Big Stick
Reds, 1913

Stewart, Sammy [Samuel Lee]
The Throwin' Swannanoan
Orioles, Red Sox, Indians, 1978-1987

Stewart, Veston (Goff)
Bunky
Senators, 1952-1956

Stewart, Walter C (Cleveland)
Lefty
Tigers, Browns, Senators, Indians, 1921-1935

Stewart, Walter N (Nesbitt)
Neb
Phillies, 1940

Stiely, Fred (Warren)
Lefty
Browns, 1929-1931

Stiles, Rollie [Rolland Mays]
Lena
   Based on an older major leaguer.
Leapin' Lena
Browns, 1930-1933

Stimmel, Archie [Archibald Ray]
Lumbago: Big Stim
Bald Eagle: Baldy
Reds, 1900-1902

Stinson, Bob [Gorrell Robert]
Scrap Iron
Dodgers, Cardinals, Astros, Expos, Royals, Mariners, 1969-1980

Stires, Garret (C)
Gat
Forest Citys, 1871

Stirnweiss, George (Henry)
Snuffy
   He had chewing tobacco and lit a cigar-but no snuff.
Snuffy the Bear
Yankees, Browns, Indians, 1943-1952

Stivetts, Jack [John Elmer]
Happy Jack
   Pleasant demeanor.
Browns, Beaneaters, Spiders, 1889-99

Stocksdale, Otis (Hinkley)
Old Gray Fox
Senators, Beaneaters, Orioles, 1893-1896

Stone, John T (Thomas)
Rocky
Stoney
   Washington fan given.
Tigers, Senators, 1928-1938

Stone, John V (Vernon)
Rocky
Reds, 1943

Stone, William (Arthur)
Tige
Cardinals, 1923

Stoner, Ulysses (Simpson Grant)
Lil
   Infant brother could not pronounce Ulysses.
Bowie Baker
   From an age-16 bakery job.
Tigers, Pirates, Phillies, 1922-1931

Storen, Drew (Patrick)
Homage
Nationals, Blue Jays, Mariners, Reds, 2010-2017

Storie, Howie [Howard Edward]
Sponge
Red Sox, 1931-1932

Story, Trevor (John)
Joe
Rockies, 2016-

Stout, Allyn (McClelland)
Fish Hook
Cardinals, Reds, Giants, Braves, 1931-1943

Stovall, George (Thomas)
Firebrand
   The anarchy of jumping to the Federal League.
Naps, Browns, Packers, 1904-1915

Stovall, Jesse (Cramer)
Scout
Naps, Tigers, 1903-1904

Straily, Dan [Daniel Steven]
Rojo
Athletics, Cubs, Astros, Reds,

Marlins, Orioles, 2012-2019
Strang, Sammy [Samuel Nicklin]
   The Dixie Thrush
   Colonels, Orphans, Giants, White Sox
   Superbas, 1896-1908
Strange, Alan (Cochrane)
   Inky
      A printer in the off-season.
   Browns, Senators, 1934-1942
Strange-Gordon, Dee [Devaris]
   Flash Gordon Jr.
   Dodgers, Marlins, Mariners, 2011-
Stratton, Monty (Franklin Pierce)
   Gander
      From a trick pitch he developed.
   Shorty
      High school, where he was very tall.
   White Sox, 1934-1938
Strauss, Joe [Joseph]
   Dutch: The Socker
   Cowboys, Colonels, Grays, 1884-1886
Strawberry, Darryl (Eugene)
   The Franchise: Master Blaster
   Mets, Dodgers, Giants, Yankees, 1983-1999
Street, Charles (Evard)
   Gabby
      A Southern habitual nickname.
   Old Sarge
   Reds, Beaneaters, Senators, Highlanders, Cardinals, 1904-1931
Street, Huston (Lowell)
   Larry
   Athletics, Rockies, Padres, Angels, 2005-2017
Stricker, John (A)
   Cub
   Athletics, Blues, Spiders, Infants, Reds, Browns, Orioles, Senators, 1882-1893
Strickland, George (Bevan)
   Bo
      Had numerous scrapes and scratches (Booboos).
   Pirates, Indians, 1950-1960

Stricklett, Elmer (Griffin)
   Spitball
   The Little Fox
      He was crafty.
   White Sox, Superbas, 1904-1907
Striker, Wilbur (Scott)
   Jake
   Indians, White Sox, 1959-1960
Strincevich, Nick [Nicholas]
   Jumbo
   Bees, Braves, Pirates, Phillies, 1940-1948
Stripp, Joe [Joseph Valentine]
   Jersey Joe
   Reds, Dodgers, Cardinals, Bees, 1928-1938
Stroman, Marcus (Earl)
   Stro-Show
   Blue Jays, Mets, 2014-
Stromme, Floyd (Marvin)
   Rock
   Indians, 1939
Stroud, Ed [Edwin Marvin]
   Streak
   Creeper
   White Sox, Senators, 1966-1971
Stroud, Ralph (Vivian)
   Sailor
   Tigers, Giants, 1910-1916
Strunk, Amos (Aaron)
   Lightning
   The Flying Foot
      Fast on the basepaths.
   Athletics, Red sox, White Sox, 1908-1924
Struss, Clarence (Herbert)
   Steamboat
   Pirates, 1934
Stryker, Sterling (Alpa)
   Dutch
   Braves, Robins, 1924, 1926
Stuart, Bill [William Alexander]
   Chauncey
   Pirates, Giants, 1895, 1899
Stuart, Dick [Richard Lee]
   Boston Strangler: Stonefingers

Man With the Iron Glove: Iron Glove
The Ancient Mariner
> From the line in the poem: ... "and he stoppeth one of three."

Dr. Strangeglove
> Based on his fielding.

Moby Dick
> While playing in Japan.

Pirates, Red Sox, Phillies, Mets, Dodgers, Angels, 1958-1969

Stuart, Johnny [John Davis]
Stud
Cardinals, 1922-1925

Stuart, Luther (Lane)
Luke
Browns, 1921

Stubbs, Franklin (Lee)
Cadillac
Dodgers, Astros, Brewers, Tigers, 1984-1995

Stubing, Lawrence (George)
Moose
Angels, 1967

Studley, Sy [Seymour L]
Warhorse
Nationals, 1872

Sturdivant, Tom [Thomas Virgil]
Smoke
Snake
> For his great curveball.

Yankees, Athletics, Red Sox, Senators, Pirates, Tigers, Mets, 1955-1964

Stutz, George (Washington)
Kid: Satan
Phillies, 1926

Styles, William (Graves)
Lena
Athletics, Reds, 1919-1931

Suárez, Eugenio (Alejandro)
Nicolle
Tigers, Reds, 2014-

Sudakis, Bill [William Paul]
Suds
Dodgers, Mets, Rangers, Yankees, Angels, Indians, 1968-1975

Suder, Pete [Peter]
Pecky
Athletics, 1941-1955

Sudhoff, Willie [John William]
Wee Willie
Browns, Spiders, Perfectos, Cardinals, Senators, 1897-1906

Sulik, Ernie [Ernest Richard]
Dave
Phillies, 1936

Sullivan, Carl (Mancel)
Jackie
Tigers, 1944

Sullivan, Dan [Daniel C]
Link
Eclipse, Colonels, Browns, Alleghenys, 1882-1886

Sullivan, Florence (P)
Fleury
Alleghenys, 1884

Sullivan, John F (Frank)
Chub
> 6 feet but only 164 lbs.

Reds, Ruby Legs, 1877-1880

Sullivan, John J (Jeremiah)
Lefty
White Sox, 1919

Sullivan, Mike [Michael Joseph]
Big Mike
Nationals, Colts, Athletics, Giants, Reds, Senators, Spiders, Beaneaters, 1889-1899

Sullivan, Paul (Thomas)
Lefty
Indians, 1939

Sullivan, Thomas (Jefferson)
Sleeper
> From his lack of familiarity with Pullman sleeper cars.

Old Iron Hands
Bisons, Brown Stockings, Browns, Eclipse, Maroons, 1881-1884

Sullivan, Timothy (Paul)
Ted
Cowboys, 1884

Summers, Ed [Oren Edgar]
Kickapoo Ed

From the Indiana region where
he was born.
Chief
Tigers, 1908-1912
Summers, John (Junior)
Champ
From his boxing champion
father.
Athletics, Cubs, Reds, Tigers, Giants,
Padres, 1974-1984
Summers, William
Kid
Browns, 1893
Sumner, Carl (Ringdahl)
Lefty
Red Sox, 1928
Sunday, Billy [William Ashley]
Parson: The Baseball Evangelist
The Evangelist
A Christian evangelist.
White Stockings, Alleghenys, Phillies,
1883-1890
Sundra, Steve [Stephen Richard]
Smokey
For his fastball.
Sandy
Yankees, Senators, Browns, 1936-46
Suppan, Jeff [Jeffrey Scot] {SOO-pan}
Soup
Red Sox, Diamondbacks, Royals,
Pirates, Cardinals, Brewers, Padres,
1995-2012
Surhoff, William (James)
BJ
Brewers, Orioles, Braves, 1987-2005
Surkont, Matthew (Constantine)
Max
Childhood nickname.
White Sox, Braves, Pirates, Cardinals,
Giants, 1949-1957
Susce, George (Cyril Methodius)
{SUE-see}
Good Kid
He was eager to help with
mundane tasks.
Sweet Susie

Combative behavior.
Phillies, Tigers, Pirates, Browns,
Indians, 1929-1944
Sutcliffe, Charles (Inigo)
Butch
Bees, 1938
Sutcliffe, Elmer (Ellsworth)
Sy
Old Sy
Looked like a hayseed farmer.
White Stockings, Maroons,
Wolverines, Spiders, Infants,
Statesmen, Orioles, 1884-1892
Sutcliffe, Rick [Richard Lee]
The Red Baron
Dodgers, Indians, Cubs, Orioles,
Cardinals, 1976-1994
Suter, Brent (Michael)
The Raptor
Brewers, 2016-
Suter, Harry (Richard)
Handsome Harry: Rube
White Sox, 1909
Sutherland, Harvey (Scott)
Suds
Went to a bar; ordered not to.
Tigers, 1921
Sutherland, Howard (Alvin)
Dizzy
Senators, 1949
Sutthoff, Jack [John Gerhard]
Sunny Jack
Senators, Perfectos, Reds, Phillies,
1898-1905
Sutton, Don [Donald Howard]
Black & Decker
He had all the tools.
The Secret Spitballer
From a never-aired "secret
identity" interview.
The Mechanic
Dodgers, Astros, Brewers, Athletics,
Angels, 1966-1988
Suzuki, Ichiro
The Wizard: Ichi
Hit Manufacturing Machine

Japanese nickname.
Mariners, Yankees, Marlins, 2001-19
Swacina, Harry (Joseph)
Swats
Pirates, Terrapins, 1907-1915
Swaim, John (Hillary)
Cy
Senators, 1897-1898
Swander, Edward (Otis)
Pinky
Browns, 1903-1904
Swanson, Arthur (Leonard)
Red
Pirates, 1955-1957
Swartz, Sherwin (Merle)
Bud
Browns, 1947
Swartz, Vernon (Monroe)
Monty: Dazzy
Reds, 1920
Sweeney, Charles (Francis)
Buck
Athletics, 1914
Sweeney, Ed [Edward Francis]
Jeff
Highlanders, Yankees, Pirates, 1908-1919
Sweeney, John (J)
Rooney
Orioles, Monumentals, Maroons, 1883-1885
Swett, William (Edward)
Pop
Reds, 1890
Swigler, Ad [Adam William]
Doc
   A dentist.
Giants, 1917
Swindle, Robert (Joseph)
RJ
Phillies, Brewers, 2008-2009
Swoboda, Ron [Ronald Alan]
Rocky
   From his less-than-reliable fielding.
Mets, Expos, Yankees, 1965-1973

Syndergaard, Noah (Seth)
Thor
Mets, 2015-
Taber, Edward (Timothy)
Lefty
Phillies, 1926-1927
Tabler, Pat [Patrick Sean]
Tabby
Mr. Clutch
   Success with bases loaded.
Cubs, Indians, Royals, Mets, Blue Jays, 1981-1992
Tabor, Jim [James Reubin]
Rawhide
   Hustle and toughness.
Red Sox, Phillies, 1938-1947
Taillon, Jameson (Lee) {TIE-own}
Jamo: J-Mo
Pirates, 2016-
Taitt, Doug [Douglas John]
Poco
Red Sox, White Sox, Phillies, 1928-32
Talbot, Frederick (Lealand)
Bubby
White Sox, Athletics, Yankees, Pilots, 1963-1970
Talton, Marion (Lee)
Tim
Athletics, 1966-1967
Tanana, Frank (Daryl)
Daiquiri
   Chris Berman-ism refers to Banana Daiquiri.
Angels, Red Sox, Rangers, Tigers, Mets, Yankees, 1973-1993
Tanaka, Masahiro
{mah-sah-HE-row tuh-na-ka}
Ma-kun
Yankees, 2014-
Tankersley, Lawrence (William)
Leo
White Sox, 1925
Tannehill, Jesse (Niles)
Powder
Reds, Pirates, Highlanders, Americans, Red Sox, Senators, 1894-1911

Tate, Edward (Christopher)
 Pop: Dimples
 Beaneaters, Orioles, 1885-1890
Tate, Lee (Willie)
 Skeeter
 Cardinals, 1958-1959
Tatis, Fernando Jr. (Gabriel)
 El Niño: Bebo
 Padres, 2019-
Tavener, John (Adam)
 Jackie: Rabbit
 Tigers, Indians, 1921-1929
Taveras, Frank (Crisostomo)
 Pittsburgh Stealer
 Pirates, Mets, Expos, 1971-1982
Taylor, Aaron (Wade)
 Big Country
  6'7".
 Mariners, 2002-2004
Taylor, Arlas (Walter)
 Foxy
 Lefty
 Athletics, 1921
Taylor, Ben E [Benjamin Eugene]
 Bleek
 Browns, Tigers, Braves, 1951-1955
Taylor, Billy [William Henry]
 Bollicky Bill
 Ruby Legs, Wolverines, Blues, Alleghenys, Maroons, Athletics, Orioles, 1881-1887
Taylor, C L
 Chink
 Cubs, 1925
Taylor, Chris [Christopher Armand]
 CT3
 Mariners, Dodgers, 2014-
Taylor, Donald (Clyde)
 Dorn
 Pirates, Orioles, 1987-1990
Taylor, Ed [Edgar Ruben]
 Rube
 Cardinals, 1903
Taylor, George (Edward)
 Live Oak
 Hartfords, Trojans, Alleghenys, 1877-1884
Taylor, James (Wren)
 Zack
  He was jokingly and incorrectly called a relative of Zachary Taylor.
 Robins, Braves, Giants, Cubs, Yankees, Dodgers, 1920-1935
Taylor, John B (Besson)
 Jack
 Brewery Jack
  Heavy drinker.
 Giants, Phillies, Browns, Reds, 1891-1899
Taylor, John W (William)
 Jack
 Brakeman
  His offseason occupation.
 Orphans, Cubs, Cardinals, 1898-1907
Taylor, Leo (Thomas)
 Chink
 White Sox, 1923
Taylor, Luther (Haden)
 Dummy
  He was deaf.
 Giants, Bronchos, 1900-1908
Taylor, Robert (Dale)
 Hawk
  His favorite movie serial was "Hawk of the Wilderness."
 Braves, Mets, Angels, Royals, 1957-1970
Taylor, Vernon (Charles)
 Pete
 Browns, 1952
Taylor, Zachary (Hamner)
 ZH
 Canaries, 1874
Teachout, Arthur (John)
 Bud
 Cubs, Cardinals, 1930-1932
Tebbetts, George (Robert)
 Birdie
  Voice sounded like a bird chirping.
 Tigers, Red Sox, Indians, 1936-1952

Tebeau, Charles (Alston)
    Pussy
        Initials are CAT.
    Spiders, 1895

Tebeau, George (E)
    White Wings
        The way he held his hands walking on and off the field.
    Red Stockings, Maumees, Senators, Spiders, 1887-1895

Tebeau, Oliver (Wendell)
    Patsy
    White Stockings, Spiders, Infants, Perfectos, Cardinals, 1887-1900

Teheran, Julio (Alberto) {tey-RON}
    JT
    Braves, Angels, 2011-

Teixeira, Mark (Charles) {Tuh-SHEER-ah}
    Tex
    Rangers, Braves, Angels, Yankees, 2003-2016

Tejada, Miguel (Odalis) {Tay-HAH-duh}
    Miggy
    La Gua Gua
        Spanish for 'the bus.' He drove in many runs.
    Athletics, Orioles, Astros, Padres, Giants, Royals, 1997-2013

Templeton, Garry (Lewis)
    Jumpsteady
    Cardinals, Padres, Mets, 1976-1991

Tenace, Gene [Fury Gene]
    Steamboat
    Athletics, Padres, Cardinals, Pirates, 1969-1983

Terry, Bill [William Harold]
    Memphis Bill: Smiling Bill
    Giants, 1923-1936

Terry, Lancelot
    Yank
    Red Sox, 1940-1945

Terry, William (H)
    Adonis
        Top condition at all times.
    Atlantics, Grays, Bridegrooms, Grooms, Orioles, Pirates, Colts, 1884-1897

Terwilliger, Willard (Wayne)
    Twig
    Cubs, Dodgers, Senators, Giants, Athletics, 1949-1960

Tesch, Al [Albert John]
    Tiny
    Tip-Tops, 1915

Tesreau, Charles (Monroe) {TEZ-row}
    Jeff
        He resembled boxer Jim Jeffries.
    Bullfrog
        Jumped from team to team in the Texas League.
    The Ozark Bear
        Not from the Ozarks and hunted quail, not bear.
    Giants, 1912-1918

Tettelbach, Dick [Richard Morley]
    Tut
    Yankees, Senators, 1955-1957

Tettleton, Mickey (Lee)
    Froot Loops
        Claimed Fruit Loops was the source of his power.
    Athletics, Orioles, Tigers, Rangers, 1984-1997

Thames, Eric (Allyn)
    Sang Namja
    Blue Jays, Mariners, Brewers, Nationals, 2011-

Theodore, George (Basil)
    Stork
    Mets, 1973-1974

Thesenga, Arnold (Joseph)
    Jug
        Shortened form for jughandle.
    Jughandle
        At the time, curveballs were said to resemble jug handles.
    Senators, 1944

Thielman, John (Peter)
    Jake
    Cardinals, Naps, Red Sox, 1905-1908

Thies, Vernon (Arthur) {TEASE}

Jake
Pirates, 1954-1955
Thobe, John (Joseph)
JJ
Expos, 1995
Thomas, Blaine (M)
Baldy
Red Sox, 1911
Thomas, Chester (David)
Pinch
> The nickname that lasted.
Chet: Chess: Chubby: Chatterer Chet
Tom: Thommy: The Baseball Populist
The Golden West Receiver
The Kansan: Goat
Red Sox, Indians, 1912-1921
Thomas, Clarence (Fletcher)
Lefty
Senators, 1925-1926
Thomas, Claude (Alfred)
Lefty
Senators, 1916
Thomas, Dan [Danny Lee]
Sundown Kid
Brewers, 1976-1977
Thomas, Fay (Wesley)
Scow
Giants, Indians, Dodgers, Browns, 1927-1935
Thomas, Forrest
Frosty
Tigers, 1905
Thomas, Frank (Edward)
The Big Hurt
> His power put the big hurt on pitchers.
White Sox, Athletics, Blue Jays, 1990-2008
Thomas, James (Gorman)
Stormin' Gorman
> Pun of 'Stormin' Norman' (Schwarzkoff).
Brewers, Indians, Mariners, 1973-86
Thomas, John (Tillman)
Bud
Browns, 1951

Thomas, Keith (Marshall)
Kite
Athletics, Senators, 1952-1953
Thomas, Lee [James Leroy]
Mad Dog: White Fang
Yankees, Angels, Red Sox, Braves, Cubs, Astros, 1961-1968
Thomas, Luther (Baxter)
Bud
Senators, Athletics, Tigers, 1932-41
Thomas, Myles (Lewis)
Duck Eye
> Coined by Babe Ruth for close-set glasses.
Professor
> Looked like a scholar.
Yankees, Senators, 1926-1930
Thomas, Robert (William)
Red
Cubs, 1921
Thomas, Tom [Thomas Robert]
Savage Tom
> For his pitching wildness.
The Man Killer
> Hit many batters.
Spiders, Perfectos, Carinals, 1894-1900
Thompson, Bobby (LaRue)
Bull
Rangers, 1978
Thompson, Charles (Lemoine)
Tim
Dodgers, Athletics, Tigers, 1954-58
Thompson, Gene [Junior Eugene Earl]
Junior
> Both nickname and given name.
Reds, Giants, 1939-1947
Thompson, Harry [Harold]
Lefty
Senators, Athletics, 1919
Thompson, James (Alfred)
Shag
Athletics, 1914-1916
Thompson, John D (Dudley)
Lee: Lefty
White Sox, 1921

Thompson, John P (Parkinson)
　Tug
　　Red Stockings, Hoosiers, 1882, 1884
Thompson, John S (Samuel)
　Jocko
　　From an early age.
　　Phillies, 1948-1951
Thompson, Milt [Milton Bernard]
　Papa Thompson
　Uncle Milty: Scooter
　　Braves, Phillies, Cardinals, Astros,
　　Dodgers, Rockies, 1984-1996
Thompson, Rich G [Richard Graeme]
　Chopper
　　Angels, Athletics, 2007-2012
Thompson, Rich N [Richard Neil]
　Frankenberry
　　Indians, Expos, 1985-1990
Thompson, Sam [Samuel Luther]
　Big Sam
　　6'2", big for the time.
　　Wolverines, Quakers, Phillies, Tigers,
　　1885-1906
Thomson, Bobby [Robert Brown]
　Flying Scot
　　Born in Glasgow, Scotland.
　The Staten Island Scot
　　Grew up on Staten Island.
　　Giants, Braves, Cubs, Red Sox,
　　Orioles, 1946-1960
Thoney, Jack [John]
　Bullet Jack
　　From the plate to first in 3 $^1/_5$
　　seconds.
　　Bronchos, Orioles, Naps, Senators,
　　Highlanders, Red Sox, 1902-1911
Thormahlen, Herbert (Ehler)
　Hank: Lefty
　　Yankees, Red Sox, Robins, 1917-1925
Thornton, Andre
　Thunder
　　Cubs, Expos, Indians, 1973-1987
Thrasher, Frank (Edward)
　Buck
　　Athletics, 1916-1917
Throneberry, Marvin (Eugene)
　Marvelous Marv
　Acronym
　　Initials matched his team.
　　Yankees, Athletics, Orioles, Mets,
　　1955-1963
Thurston, Hollis (John)
　Sloppy
　　Browns, White Sox, Senators, Robins,
　　Dodgers, 1923-1933
Tiant, Luis (Clemente)
　El Tiante
　Roller 'Rilla
　　Legend: zipped around Yankee
　　Stadium on roller skates.
　　Indians, Twins, Red Sox, Yankees,
　　Pirates, Angels, 1964-1982
Tidrow, Dick [Richard William]
　Dirt
　　Unkempt and dirty before start
　　of game.
　　Indians, Yankees, Cubs, White Sox,
　　Mets, 1972-1984
Tiernan, Mike [Michael Joseph]
　Silent Mike
　　Spoke infrequently. A gentleman.
　　Giants, 1887-1899
Tierney, James (Arthur)
　Cotton
　　Pirates, Phillies, Braves, Robins,
　　1920-1925
Tietje, Les [Leslie William] {TEET-ga}
　Toots
　　Players could not pronounce his
　　name.
　　White Sox, Browns, 1933-1938
Tillman, Johnny [John Lawrence]
　Ducky
　　Browns, 1915
Tillman, Kerry (Jerome)
　Rusty
　　Mets, Athletics, Giants, 1982-1988
Tinning, Lyle (Forest)
　Bud
　　Cubs, Cardinals, 1932-1935
Tipple, Dan [Daniel Slaughter]
　Rusty: Big Dan

Yankees, 1915
Tipton, Eric (Gordon)
   Dukie
      A star at Duke Univ.
   Blue Devil
      The Duke Univ. nickname.
   Eric the Red
      For the explorer after he went through a minor league fence.
   Athletics, Reds, 1939-1945
Titcomb, Ledell (N)
   Cannonball
      Nickname appeared only when he was 82.
   Quakers, Athletics, Giants, Broncos, 1886-1890
Titus, John (Franklin)
   Silent John
      Quiet demeanor.
   Tightpants
      Describes his spending habits.
   Tight Ass
      A play on his last name.
   Phillies, Braves, 1903-1913
Tobin, Jim [James Anthony]
   Abba Dabba
   Shamus
      Referring to Irish descent.
   Pirates, Bees, Braves, Tigers, 1937-45
Tobin, John M (Martin)
   Tip
   Giants, 1932
Tobin, John P (Patrick)
   Jackie
   Red Sox, 1945
Tobin, Marion (Brooks)
   Pat
   Athletics, 1941
Todt, Phil [Philip Julius]
   Hook
   Red Sox, Athletics, 1924-1931
Toenes, William (Harrel)
   Hal
   Senators, 1947
Tolson, Charles (Julius)
   Chick: Toby

Slug
      A power hitter.
   Indians, Cubs, 1925-1930
Tomanek, Dick [Richard Carl]
   Bones
   Indians, Athletics, 1953-1959
Tomás, Yasmany
   {yaz-MA-knee toe-MASS}
   El Tanque
   Diamondbacks, 2015-
Tomlin, Josh [Joshua Aubrey]
   Little Cowboy: Scrubs
   Indians, Braves, 2010-
Tomlin, Randy (Leon)
   Whispers
      Quiet manner and soft voice.
   Pirates, 1990-1994
Tomney, Phil [Philip H]
   Buster
   Colonels, 1888-1890
Tompkins, Ron [Ronald Everett]
   Stretch
   Athletics, Cubs, 1965, 1971
Tonneman, Charles (Richard)
   Tony
   Red Sox, 1911
Tonkin, Harry (Glenville)
   Doc
      Urologist from Baltimore Medical College.
   Senators, 1907
Toporcer, George {ta-PORE-sir}
   Specs
      First major league non-pitcher to wear eyeglasses.
   Baseball's Blind Ambassador
      Motivational speaker after going blind.
   Cardinals, 1921-1928
Torgeson, Clifford (Earl)
   The Earl of Snohomish
      From Snohomish WA.
   Braves, Phillies, Tigers, White Sox, Yankees, 1947-1961
Torkelson, Chester (Leroy)
   Red

Indians, 1917
Torphy, Walter (Anthony)
    Red
    Braves, 1920
Torrens, Luis (Alfonso)
    Churro
    Padres, Mariners, 2017-
Torres, Álex [Alexander Jesus]
    Dark Helmet
    Rays, Padres, Mets, 2011-2015
Torres, Carlos (Ephriam)
    El Carnicero
    White Sox, Rockies, Mets, Brewers, Nationals, Tigers, 2009-
Torres, Rosendo
    Rusty
    Yankees, Indians, Angels, White Sox, Royals, 1971-1980
Tovar, César (Leonardo)
{SAY-zar toe-VAR}
    Pepito
        Spanish for 'Little Seed.'
    Pepi: Mr. Versatility
    Twins, Phillies, Rangers, Athletics, Yankees, 1965-1976
Towles, Justin (Richard) {TOLLS}
    JR
    Astros, 2007-2011
Towne, Jay (King)
    Babe
    White Sox, 1906
Townsend, George (Hodgson)
    Sleepy
    Athletics, Orioles, 1887-1891
Townsend, Ira (Dance)
    Pat
    Braves, 1920-1921
Townsend, John
    Happy
    Phillies, Senators, Naps, 1901-1906
Townsend, Leo (Alphonse)
    Lefty
    Braves, 1920-1921
Tracewski, Dick [Richard Joseph]
{truh-ZOO-ski}
    Trixie

    Dick Tracy
        From fans in his Dodgers years.
    Dodgers, Tigers, 1962-1969
Tramback, Steven (Joseph)
    Red
    Giants, 1940
Trammell, Alan (Stuart)
    The Franchise
    Tigers, 1977-1996
Travers, Joe [Aloysius Joseph]
    Allan
    Tigers, 1912
Travis, Devon (Anthony)
    Mailes
    Blue Jays, 2015-2018
Travis, Sam [Samuel John]
    Doctor Chill: Captain Caveman
    Red Sox, 2017-
Traynor, Harold (Joseph)
    Pie
        Always wanted pie.
    Pie Face
        From his constant request at a grocery store as a child.
    Pirates, 1920-1937
Treadway, Thadford (Leon)
    Red
    Giants, 1944-1945
Treinen, Blake (M) {TRY-nen}
    B-Lockay
    Nationals, Athletics, Dodgers, 2014-
Tremel, Bill [William Leonard]
    Mumbles
    Cubs, 1954-1956
Treviño, Carlos
    Bobby
        Same nickname as his father.
    Angels, 1968
Triandos, Gus
    Tremendous Triandos
        6'3", 215 lbs., impressive minor league stats.
    Golden Greek
    Golden Greek of Chesapeake
    Yankees, Orioles, Tigers, Phillies, Astros, 1953-1965

Triggs, Andrew (Austin)
Triggonometry
Athletics, Giants, Red Sox, 2016-

Trosky, Hal [Harold Arthur]
Hoot
White Sox, 1958

Trout, Mike [Michael Nelson]
Millville Meteor
> The city he grew up in.

Kiiiiid: Prince Fish: God's Gift
King Fish 2.0
> Referring to retired Tim Salmon.

Angels, 2011-

Trout, Paul (Howard)
Dizzy
> Self-named after Dizzy Dean, maybe.

Tigers, Red Sox, Orioles, 1939-1957

Trout, Steve [Steven Russell]
Rainbow
> A species of...

White Sox, Cubs, Yankees, Mariners, 1978-1989

Troy, John (Joseph)
Dasher
Wolverines, Grays, Gothams, Metropolitans, 1881-1885

Troy, Robert (Gustave)
Bun
Tigers, 1912

Truby, Harry (Garvin)
Bird Eye
Colts, Pirates, 1895-1896

Trucks, Virgil (Oliver)
Fire
> First given by a sportswriter.

Tigers, Browns, White Sox, Athletics, Yankees, 1941-1958

Trujillo, John
JJ
Padres, 2002

Tseng, Jen-Ho
Catfish
Cubs, 2017-2018

Tucker, Eddie (Jack)
Scooter
> From grandfather as a child.

Astros, Indians, 1992-1995

Tucker, Preston (M)
Bamm-Bamm
Astros, Braves, Reds, 2015-2018

Tucker, Thomas (John)
TJ
Expos, Nationals, 2000-2005

Tucker, Thurman (Lowell)
Joe E
> Resembled comic Joe E Brown.

White Sox, Indians, 1942-1951

Tucker, Tommy [Thomas Joseph]
Foghorn
> Nickname in Baltimore.

Noisy Tom
> Nickname in Boston.

Tommy Talker
Orioles, Beaneaters, Senators, Bridegrooms, Browns, Spiders, 1887-1899

Tuckey, Tom [Thomas Henry]
Tabasco Tom
Doves, 1908-1909

Turchin, Eddie [Edward Lawrence]
Smiley
Indians, 1943

Turgeon, Eugene (Joseph)
Pete
Cubs, 1923

Turk, Lucas (Newton)
Harlem: Chief
Senators, 1922

Turley, Bob [Robert Lee]
Bullet Bob
> From the velocity of his fastball.

Browns, Orioles, Yankees, Angels, Red Sox, 1951-1963

Turner, George (A)
Tuck
Phillies, Browns, 1893-1898

Turner, Jim [James Riley]
Milkman Jim
> Worked in the family dairy farm.

Colonel
Bees, Reds, Yankees, 1937-1945

Turner, John (Webber)

Jerry
Padres, White Sox, Tigers, 1974-1983
Turner, Justin (Matthew)
RedTurn2
Orioles, Mets, Dodgers, 2009-
Turner, Terry [Terrance Lamont]
Cotton Top
Pirates, Naps, Indians, Athletics, 1901-1919
Turner, Thomas (Lovatt)
Tink
Athletics, 1915
Turner, Trea (Vance)
Triple T
Nationals, 2015-
Tutwiler, Guy (Isbel)
King Tut
Tigers, 1911, 1913
Twineham, Art [Arthur S]
Old Hoss
Browns, 1893-1894
Twining, Howard (Earle)
Twink: Doc
Reds, 1916
Twombly, Clarence (Edward)
Babe
Cubs, 1920-1921
Twombly, Edwin (Parker)
Cy
White Sox, 1921
Twombly, George (Frederick)
Silent George
Reds, Braves, Senators, 1914-1919
Tyler, Fred [Frederick Franklin]
Clancy
Braves, 1914
Tyler, George (Albert)
Lefty
Doves, Rustlers, Braves, Cubs, 1910-1921
Tyler, Johnnie [John Anthony]
Ty Ty
> Owned three dozen neckties.

Katz
Braves, 1934-1935
Tyson, Cecil (Washington)

Turkey: Slim
Phillies, 1944
Uecker, Bob [Robert George] {YOU-kur}
Mr. Baseball
Braves, Cardinals, Phillies, 1962-67
Uhalt, Bernard (Bartholomew)
Frenchy
White Sox, 1934
Uhl, Bob [Robert Elwood]
Lefty
White Sox, Tigers, 1938, 1940
Uhle, George (Ernest) {YOO-lee}
The Bull
Indians, Tigers, Giants, Yankees, 1919-1936
Ullger, Scott (Matthew) {ULL-jer}
Smooth
Twins, 1983
Ulicny, Mike [Michael Edward]
Slugs
Braves, 1945
Ulrich, Frank (W)
Dutch
Phillies, 1925-1927
Upp, George (Henry)
Jerry
Sandusky Singer
> A tenor soloist.

Sweet Singer of Sandusky
Naps, 1909
Upright, Roy (T)
RT: Dixie
Browns, 1953
Upshaw, Willie (Clay)
Chuckie: Wilson
Blue Jays, Indians, 1978-1988
Upton, Justin (Irvin)
J-Up
Diamondbacks, Braves, Padres, Tigers, Angels, 2007-
Upton, Melvin (Emanuel)
BJ
> Stands for 'Bossman Junior,' after his father.

Devil Rays, Rays, Braves, Padres, Blue Jays, 2004-2016

Upton, Tom [Thomas Herbert]
  Muscles
  Browns, Senators, 1950-1952
Urban, Louis (John)
  Luke
  Braves, 1927-1928
Urbina, Ugueth (Urtain)
  {oo-GETT ooor-bee-NAH}
  Oogie
  Expos, Red Sox, Rangers, Marlins,
  Tigers, Phillies, 1995-2005
Ureña, José (Miguel) {oo-RAIN-ya}
  El Nueve
  Marlins, 2015-
Urías, Luis (Fernando) {oo-REE-ahs}
  Wicho
  Padres, Brewers, 2018-
Ury, Louis (Newton)
  Lon: Old Sheep
  Cardinals, 1903
Ussat, William (August)
  Dutch
  Indians, 1925, 1927
Utley, Chase (Cameron)
  The Man: Silver Fox
  Phillies, Dodgers, 2003-2018
Vache, Ernest (Lewis)
  Tex
    Played outfield in the Texas
    League.
  Red Sox, 1925
Vahrenhorst, Harry (Henry)
  Van
  Browns, 1904
Vail, Bob [Robert Garfield]
  Doc
  Pirates, 1908
Valbuena, Luis (Adan) {val-BWAY-nuh}
  Mono
  Mariners, Indians, Cubs, Astros,
  Angels, 2008-2018
Valdés, Rogelio (Lazaro)
  Roy
  Senators, 1944
Valdespino, Hilario
  Sandy
    He looked like Sandy Amoros.
  Twins, Braves, Astros, Pilots, Brewers,
  Royals, 1965-1971
Valentine, Fred (Lee)
  Squeaky
    Made noises as a toddler.
  Orioles, Senators, 1959-1968
Valentine, Harold (Lewis)
  Corky
  Redlegs, 1954-1955
Valenzuela, Benny [Benjamin Beltrán]
  Papelero
    Spanish for 'pretentious' and
    'paper seller.'
  Cardinals, 1958
Valenzuela, Fernando
  El Toro
    Spanish for 'the bull.'
  Dodgers, Angels, Orioles, Phillies,
  Padres, Cardinals, 1980-1997
Valverde, José (Rafael)
  Papa Grande
    Spanish for 'Big Daddy.'
  Diamondbacks, Astros, Tigers, Mets,
  2003-2014
Van Alstyne, Clay [Clayton Emory]
  Spike
  Senators, 1927-1928
Van Atta, Russ [Russell]
  Sheriff
    Served as sheriff of Sussex
    County, NJ.
  Yankees, Browns, 1933-1939
Van Brabant, Camille (Oscar)
  Ozzie
  Athletics, 1954-1955
Van Buren, Edward (Eugene)
  Deacon
  Superbas, Phillies, 1904
Van Haltren, George (Edward Martin)
  Rip
  White Stockings, Ward's Wonders,
  Orioles, Pirates, Giants, 1887-1903
Van Robays, Maurice (Rene)
  Bomber
  Pirates, 1939-1946

Van Slyke, Andy [Andrew James]
  Slick
  Cardinals, Pirates, Orioles, Phillies, 1983-1995
Van Zandt, Charles (Isaac)
  Ike: Izzy
  Giants, Cubs, Browns, 1901-1905
Van Zant, Dick [Richard]
  Foghorn Dick
  Blues, 1888
Vance, Charles (Arthur)
  Dazzy
    Dazzling fastball in semipro.
  The Dazzler
    Dazzled batters.
  Pirates, Yankees, Robins, Dodgers, Cardinals, Reds, 1915-1935
Vance, Gene (Covington)
  Sandy
  Dodgers, 1970-1971
Vance, Joe [Joseph Albert]
  Sandy
  White Sox, Yankees, 1935-1938
Vandenberg, Harold (Harris)
  Hy
  Red Sox, Giants, Cubs, 1935-1945
Vander Meer, Johnny [John Samuel]
  The Dutch Master
  Double No-Hit
    Consecutive no-hitters.
  Reds, Cubs, Indians, 1937-1951
Vander Wal, John (Henry)
  Just Another Brick
    Chris Berman-ism: ... Just Another Brick in The...
  Expos, Rockies, Padres, Pirates, Giants, Yankees, Brewers, Reds, 1991-2004
Vargas, Hediberto
  Eddie
  Pirates, 1982, 1984
Varner, Glen (Gann)
  Buck
  Senators, 1952
Varney, Lawrence (Delano)
  Dike
  Bronchos, 1902
Varney, Richard (Fred)
  Pete
    His father's nickname, inherited.
  White Sox, Braves, 1973-1976
Vaughan, Cecil (Porter)
  Lefty
  Athletics, 1940-1946
Vaughan, Glenn (Edward)
  Sparky
  Colt .45s, 1963
Vaughan, Joseph (Floyd)
  Arky
    Born in Arkansas.
  Pirates, Dodgers, 1932-1949
Vaughn, Fred [Frederick Thomas]
  Muscles
  Senators, 1944-1945
Vaughn, Henry (Francis)
  Harry
  Farmer
    His primary non-baseball work.
  Red Stockings, Colonels, Giants, Kelly's Killers, Brewers, Reds, 1886-1899
Vaughn, Jim [James Leslie]
  Hippo
    6'4", 215 lbs.
  Highlanders, Senators, Cubs, 1908-21
Vaughn, Mo [Maurice Samuel]
  Hit Dog
  Red Sox, Angels, Mets, 1991-2003
Vázquez, Christian (Rafael) {VAZZ-kezz}
  Mini Yadi
  Red Sox, 2014-
Vázquez, Javier (Carlos)
  Silent Assassin
    Quiet demeanor and powerful arm.
  Expos, Yankees, Diamondbacks, White Sox, Braves, Marlins, 1998-2011
Veach, Bill [William Walter]
  Peek-a-boo
    He looked for signals for pickoff attempts.

Cowboys, Colonels, Spiders, Alleghenys, 1884-1890
Veal, Orville (Inman)
Coot
Tigers, Senators, Pirates, 1958-1963
Veil, Frederick (William)
Bucky
High school football fullback runner.
Squire
From days as a magistrate.
Pirates, 1903-1904
Vélez, Otto [Otoniel]
Otto the Swatto
Yankees, Blue Jays, Indians, 1973-83
Venable, William (McKinley)
Max
Giants, Expos, Reds, Angels, 1979-91
Ventura, Yordano
Ace
Royals, 2013-2016
Verban, Emil (Matthew)
Dutch: Antelope
Cardinals, Phillies, Cubs, Braves, 1944-1950
Verble, Gene (Kermit)
Satchel
Senators, 1951, 1953
Verdel, Al [Albert Alfred]
Stumpy
Phillies, 1944
Vereker, John (James)
Tommy
Terrapins, 1915
Vergez, Jean (Louis) {VEER-jess}
Johnny
Giants, Phillies, Cardinals, 1931-1936
Verlander, Justin (Brooks)
JV
Tigers, Astros, 2005-
Vernon, James (Barton)
Mickey
He played the song, "Mickey," as a child.
Senators, Indians, Red Sox, Braves, Pirates, 1939-1960

Versalles, Zoilo (Casanova) {ZOY-low vair-SY-yez}
Zorro
Based on the western TV character.
Senators, Twins, Dodgers, Indians, Braves, 1959-1971
Viciedo, Dayán {die-ON vee-see-AY-dough}
The Tank
White Sox, 2010-2014
Vick, Henry (Arthur)
Ernie
Cardinals, 1922-1926
Vickers, Harry (Porter)
Rube
Reds, Superbas, Athletics, 1902-1909
Vickery, Tom [Thomas Gill]
Vinegar Tom
Phillies, Colts, Orioles, 1890-1893
Vico, George (Steve)
Sam
Tigers, 1948-1949
Victorino, Shane (Patrick)
The Flyin' Hawaiian
Native of Hawaii.
Padres, Phillies, Dodgers, Red Sox, Angels, 2003-2015
Vidal, José
Papito
Indians, Pilots, 1966-1969
Vincent, Nick [Nicholas James]
Hubba Hubba
Padres, Mariners, Giants, Phillies, Marlins, 2012-
Vinson, Ernest (Augustus)
Rube
Naps, White Sox, 1904-1906
Viola, Frank (John)
Sweet Music
From a bedsheet display from a fan.
K-Man
Twins, Mets, Red Sox, Reds, Blue Jays, 1982-1996
Virtue, Jake [Jacob Kitchline]
Guesses

Spiders, 1890-1894
Vizquel, Omar (Enrique) {viz-KELL}
Little O
Mariners, Indians, Giants, Rangers, White Sox, Blue Jays, 1989-2012
Vogt, Stephen (Guy) {VOTE}
I Believe
Rays, Athletics, Brewers, Giants, Diamondbacks, 2012-
Voigt, Ollie [Olen Edward]
Ode
Browns, 1924
Voiselle, Bill [William Symmes]
Ninety-Six
> Attended Ninety-Six HS in Ninety-Six, NC.

Big Bill
> 6'4", 200 lbs.

Giants, Braves, Cubs, 1942-1950
Vólquez, Edinson
Steady Eddie
Rangers, Reds, Padres, Dodgers, Pirates, Royals, Marlins, 2005-
Volz, Jake [Jacob Phillip]
Silent Jake
Base on Balls
> From a sportswriter, for his pitching.

Americans, Beaneaters, Reds, 1901-1908
Von Kolnitz, Alfred (Holmes)
Fritz
Reds, White Sox, 1914-1916
Vorhees, Henry (Bert)
Cy
> Named after Cy Young.

Phillies, Senators, 1902
Votto, Joey [Joseph Daniel] {VAH-toe}
Votto-matic: Tokki 2: JoVo
Reds, 2007-
Vowinkel, John (Henry)
Rip
> Name similar to Rip Van Winkel.

Reds, 1905
Wada, Tsuyoshi {sue-YO-she WAH-duh}
Dr. K
> Given in his college years.

Cubs, 2014-2015
Waddell, Eddie [George Edward] {wa-DELL}
Rube
Colonels, Pirates, Orphans, Athletics, Browns, 1897-1910
Wade, Jake [Jacob Fields]
Whistlin' Jake
> Whistled like a mockingbird.

Tigers, Red Sox, Browns, White Sox, Yankees, Senators, 1936-1946
Wade, Richard (Frank)
Rip
Senators, 1923
Wagner, Albert
Butts
Senators, Bridegrooms, 1898
Wagner, Billy [William Edward]
Billy the Kid
Astros, Phillies, Mets, Red Sox, Braves, 1995-2010
Wagner, Charles F (Francis)
Heinie
Giants, Americans, Red Sox, 1902-18
Wagner, Charlie [Charles Thomas]
Broadway
> He was a snappy dresser.

Red Sox, 1938-1946
Wagner, John [Johannes Peter]
Honus
> Short form of 'Johannes.' {yo-HONN-us}.

Hans
The Flying Dutchman
> Superb speed, German heritage.

Colonels, Pirates, 1897-1917
Wagner, Leon (Lamar)
Daddy Wags
> Distinctive batting style.

Cheeky
> High cheekbones.

Giants, Cardinals, Angels, Indians, White Sox, 1958-1969
Wagner, William (George)
Bull

Superbas, Robins, 1913-1914
Wahl, Bobby [Robert Martin]
  Peanut
  Athletics, Mets, Brewers, 2017-
Walberg, George (Elvin)
  Rube
  Giants, Athletics, Red Sox, 1923-37
Walczak, Ed [Edward Joseph]
  Husky
  Phillies, 1945
Waldbauer, Albert (Charles)
  Doc
  Senators, 1917
Waldrop, Kyle (Michael)
  K-Dub
  Reds, 2015-2016
Walker, Albert (Bluford)
  Rube
    As a batboy, he idolized Rube Robinson.
  Cubs, Dodgers, 1948-1958
Walker, Clarence (William)
  Tillie
  Senators, Browns, Red Sox, Athletics, 1911-1923
Walker, Cleotha
  Chico
  Red Sox, Cubs, Angels, Mets, 1980-93
Walker, Ewart (Gladstone)
  Dixie
  Senators, 1909-1912
Walker, Fred (E)
  Dixie
    His father, Dixie, was Ewart Walker.
  The People's Cherce
    Choice in "Brooklynese."
  Yankees, White Sox, Tigers, Dodgers, Pirates, 1931-1949
Walker, Frederick (Mitchell)
  Mysterious
    Playing as Mitchell, no one knew his last name.
  Reds, Naps, Superbas, Rebels, Tip-Tops, 1910-1915
Walker, Gerald (Holmes)
  Gee
  The Madman from Mississippi
    Based on his antics.
  Tigers, White Sox, Senators, Indians, Reds, 1931-1945
Walker, Harry (William)
  Harry the Hat
    Adjusted his cap between pitches.
  Little Dixie
    Brother and father were called Dixie.
  Cardinals, Phillies, Cubs, Reds, 1940-1955
Walker, Harvey (Willos)
  Hub
  Hubby
    Later shortened to Hub.
  The Mississippi Meteor
    American Association nickname.
  Tigers, Reds, 1931-1945
Walker, James (Roy)
  Dixie
  Jim
    Some newspaper stories.
  Indians, Cubs, Cardinals, 1912-1922
Walker, Joseph (Richard)
  Speed
  Cardinals, 1923
Walker, Larry (Kenneth Robert)
  Booger
    From Montreal fans.
  The Canadian Clubber
  Expos, Rockies, Cardinals, 1989-2005
Walker, Marty [Martin Van Buren]
  Buddy
  Phillies, 1928
Walker, Taijuan (Emmanuel)
  {TIE-wahn}
  Tai-Weezy
  Mariners, Diamondbacks, Blue Jays, 2013-
Wall, Joe [Joseph Francis]
  Gummy
  Giants, Superbas, 1901-1902
Wallace, Clarence (Eugene)
  Jack

Cubs, 1915
Wallace, Frederick (Renshaw)
  Jesse: Doc
  Phillies, 1919
Wallace, Harry (Clinton)
  Huck: Lefty
  Phillies, 1912
Wallace, James (Harold)
  Lefty
  Braves, 1942-1946
Wallace, Roderick (John)
  Bobby: Little Rhody
  Mr. Shortstop
  Spiders, Perfectos, Cardinals, Browns, 1894-1918
Waller, John (Francis)
  Red
  Giants, 1909
Walsh, Ed [Edward Augustin]
  Big Ed
  White Sox, Braves, 1904-1917
Walsh, James (Gerald)
  Junior
  Pirates, 1946-1951
Walsh, Joe F [Joseph Francis]
  Tweet
  Highlanders, 1910-1911
Walsh, Joe P [Joseph Patrick]
  Tweet
  Bees, 1938
Walsh, Joe R [Joseph R]
  Reddy
  Orioles, 1891
Walsh, Leo (Thomas)
  Dee
  Browns, 1913-1915
Walsh, Michael (Timothy)
  Jimmy
  Runt
  Phillies, Terrapins, Terriers, 1910-15
Walters, Alfred (John)
  Roxy
  Yankees, Red Sox, Indians, 1915-25
Walters, Fred (James)
  Whale
    Looked heavier than his 6'1", 210 lbs.
  Red Sox, 1945
Walters, Phillip (DeWayne)
  PJ
  Cardinals, Blue Jays, Twins, 2009-13
Walters, William (Henry)
  Bucky
  Phillies, Reds, Braves, 1934-1950
Walton, Danny [Daniel James]
  Mickey
  Astros, Pilots, Brewers, Yankees, Twins, Dodgers, Rangers, 1968-1980
Wambsganss, Bill [William Adolph]
  {WHAMS-gans}
  Wamby
    Given by headline writers.
  Naps, Indians, Red Sox, Athletics, 1914-1926
Waner, Lloyd (James)
  Little Poison
    Younger brother of 'Big Poison.'
    A Fan's pronunciation of 'Little Person.'
  Scratch
    In high school, he beat out scratch hits.
  Pirates, Braves, Reds, Phillies, Dodgers, 1927-1945
Waner, Paul (Glee)
  Big Poison
    Brooklyn pronunciation of 'big person.'
  Pirates, Dodgers, Braves, Yankees, 1926-1945
Wanner, Clarence (Curtis)
  Jack: Johnny
  Highlanders, 1909
Waniger, Paul (Louis)
  Pee-Wee
    Short stature: 5'7", 150 lbs.
  Yankees, Red Sox, Reds, 1925, 1927
Ward, Frank (Gray)
  Piggy
  Quakers, Pirates, Orioles, Reds, Senators, 1883-1894
Ward, Joe [Joseph Aloysius]

Happy of Manayunk
Phillies, Highlanders, 1906-1910
Ward, John A (Andrew)
Rube
Superbas, 1902
Ward, John F (Francis)
Jay
Twins, Reds, 1963-1970
Ward, Joseph (Nichols)
Hap
Tigers, 1912
Warden, Jon [Jonathan Edgar]
Warbler
   A hitting instructor butchered his last name.
Tigers, 1968
Wares, Clyde (Ellsworth)
Buzzy
   Greeted a girlfriend with a joke buzzer.
Kid
Kiddo
   His first nickname in baseball.
Browns, 1913-1914
Warhop, Jack [John Milton]
Chief
Crab
   Submarine pitcher.
Highlanders, Yankees, 1908-1915
Warmoth, Wallace (Walter)
Cy
Cardinals, Senators, 1916-1923
Warneke, Lon [Lonnie] {WARN-a-key}
The Arkansas Hummingbird
   Sizzling fast pitch delivery.
Country: Dixie: Dixie Dude
   All from Alexandria teammates.
Cubs, Cardinals, 1930-1945
Warner, Hoke (Hayden)
Hooks
Piraes, Cubs, 1916-1921
Warren, Adam (Parrish)
Rocket
Yankees, Cubs, Mariners, Padres, 2012-
Warstler, Harold (Burton)
Rabbit
   In baseball circles.
Rap
   From friends and neighbors.
Red Sox, Athletics, Bees, Cubs, 1930-1940
Warwick, Firman (Newton)
Bill
Pirates, Cardinals, 1921-1926
Wasdin, John (Truman)
Way Back
Athletics, Red Sox, Rockies, Orioles, Blue Jays, Rangers, Pirates, 1995-2007
Washer, William
Buck
   Also his father's nickname.
Phillies, 1905
Washington, Herb [Herbert Lee]
Hurricane Herb
Athletics, 1974-1975
Washington, Sloan (Vernon)
George: Vern
White Sox, 1935-1936
Waszgis, Robert (Michael)
BJ
Rangers, 2000
Wathan, Dustin (James)
Dusty
Royals, 2002
Wathan, John (David)
The Duke
   Great impersonation of John Wayne.
Royals, 1976-1985
Watson, Bob [Robert José]
Bull
Astros, Red Sox, Yankees, Braves, 1966-1984
Watson, Charles (John)
Doc
Cubs, Chi-Feds, Terriers, 1913-1915
Watson, John (Reaves)
Mule
Athletics, Braves, Pirates, Giants, 1918-1624

Watson, Milt [Milton Robert]
Mule
Cardinals, Phillies, 1916-1919
Watson, Walter (L)
Mother
The Zanesville phenomenon
Pre-major league.
Wall
Hometown nickname.
Red Stockings, 1887
Watt, Frank (Marion)
Kilowatt
Phillies, 1931
Watwood, Johnny [John Clifford]
Lefty
Jewel
Given name at birth.
White Sox, Red Sox, Phillies, 1929-39
Weatherly, Cyril (Roy)
Stormy
Indians, Yankees, Giants, 1936-1950
Weaver, Art [Arthur Coggshall]
Six O'Clock
Elongated frame.
Human Hatpin: Scissors: Buck
Stilt
Tall spindly physique.
Cardinals, Pirates, Browns, White Sox, 1902-1908
Weaver, George (Daniel)
Buck
Ginger Kid
After he played with an injured hand.
White Sox, 1912-1920
Weaver, Jered (David)
Three-Six: Dreamweaver
Angels, Padres, 2006-2017
Weaver, Jim B [James Brian]
Fluff
Angels, 1967-1968
Weaver, Jim D [James Dement]
Big Jim: Big James
Senators, Yankees, Browns, Cubs, Pirates, Reds, 1928-1939
Weaver, Monte [Montie Morton]

Prof
College math teacher.
Brain Truster
After FDR's advisors.
Senators, Red Sox, 1931-1939
Weaver, Orville (Forest)
Orlie
Cubs, Rustlers, 1910-1911
Weaver, William (Clinton Bond)
Farmer
Owned and ran a farm.
Buck
Colonels, Pirates, 1888-1894
Webb, Cleon (Earl)
Lefty
Pirates, 1910
Webb, James (Laverne)
Skeeter
Cardinals, Indians, White Sox, Tigers, Athletics, 1932-1948
Webb, Samuel (Henry)
Red
Giants, 1948-1949
Weber, Charlie [Charles P]
Count
Senators, 1898
Wehde, Wilbur
Biggs
White Sox, 1930-1931
Weidman, George (Edward)
Stump
Bisons, Wolverines, Cowboys, Metropolitans, Giants, 1880-1888
Weigel, Ralph (Richard)
Wig
Indians, White Sox, Senators, 1946-1949
Weihe, John (Garibaldi)
Podge
Red Stockings, Hoosiers, 1883-1884
Weik, Dick [Richard Henry]
{rhymes with 'Mike'}
Legs
6'3", only 184 lbs.
Senators, Indians, Tigers, 1948-1954
Weiland, Bob [Robert George]

251

{WHY-lund}
    Lefty
    White Sox, Red Sox, Indians, Browns, Cardinals, 1928-1940

Weilman, Carl (Edward)
    Zeke
    Woolworth
        After the New York building, then tallest in the world.
    The Human Skyscraper
        6'5 ½".
    Browns, 1912-1920

Weimer, Jake [Jacob]
    Tornado Jake
    Cubs, Reds, Giants, 1903-1909

Weinert, Philip (Walter)
    Lefty
    Phillies, Cubs, Yankees, 1919-1931

Weingartner, Elmer (William)
    Dutch
    Indians, 1945

Weintraub, Phil [Philip]
    Mickey
    Giants, Reds, Phillies, 1933-1945

Weis, Arthur (John) {rhymes with 'Rice'}
    Butch
    Cubs, 1922-1925

Weiser, Harry (Budson)
    Bud
        Think beer.
    Phillies, 1915-1916

Welch, Floyd (John)
    Ted
    Terriers, 1914

Welch, Frank (Tiguer)
    Bugger
    Athletics, Red Sox, 1919-1927

Welch, Herb [Herbert M]
    Dutch
    Red Sox, 1925

Welch, James (Thomas)
    Tub
    Maumees, Colonels, 1890, 1895

Welch, Michael (Francis)
    Smiling Mickey
        From a cartoonist for his even temper.
    Trojans, Gothams, Giants, 1880-1892

Welday, Lyndon (Earl)
    Mike
    White Sox, 1907, 1909

Welker, Matt [Matthew Scott]
    Duke
    Pirates, 2013

Wells, Dave [David Lee]
    Boomer
    Blue Jays, Tigers, Reds, Orioles, Yankees, White Sox, Padres, Red Sox, Dodgers, 1987-1998

Wells, Ed [Edwin Lee]
    Satchelfoot
    Slugger
        Given by his church.
    Tigers, Yankees, Browns, 1923-1934

Wells, Greg [Gregory DeWayne]
    Boomer
    Blue Jays, Twins, 1981-1982

Wendell, Steven (John)
    Turk
        A daredevil at the age of 3.
    Cubs, Mets, Phillies, Rockies, 1993-2004

Wensloff, Charles (William)
    Butch: Buster
    Iron Man
        In the minors, he was always ready to pitch.
    Yankees, Indians, 1943-1948

Wenz, Fred [Frederick Charles]
    Fireball
        Struck out more than one per inning in the minors.
    Red Sox, Phillies, 1968-1970

Werden, Perry [Percival Wheritt]
    Moose
        6'2", 220 lbs.
    Maroons, Nationals, Maumees, Orioles, Browns, Colonels, 1884-1897

Werhas, Johnny [John Charles]
    Peaches
    Dodgers, Angels, 1964-1967

Werle, Bill [william George]

Bugs
> Interested in entomology.
Whirling Willie Werle
Pirates, Cardinals, Red Sox, 1949-54
Wert, Don [Donald Ralph]
Coyote
Tigers, Senators, 1963-1971
Werth, Jayson (Richard Gowan)
Werewolf: The Wolf of First Street
Sunshine: Dub: J-Dub
Blue Jays, Dodgers, Phillies,
Nationals, 2002-2017
Werts, Henry (Levi)
Johnny
Braves, 1926-1929
West, David (Lee)
Big Bird
Mets, Twins, Phillies, Red Sox,
1988-1998
West, Milton (Douglas)
Buck
Red Stockings, Spiders, 1884, 1890
West, Weldon (Edison)
Lefty
Browns, 1944-1945
Wetzel, Charles (Edward)
Buzz
Athletics, 1927
Wetzel, Franklin (Burton)
Dutch
Browns, 1920-1921
Weyhing, Gus [August] {WAY-ing}
Cannonball: Rubber Arm Gus
Rubber-Winged Gus
Athletics, Ward's Wonders, Phillies,
Pirates, Colonels, Senators, Cardinals,
Superbas, Blues, Reds, 1887-1901
Wheat, Zack [Zachariah Davis]
Buck
Superbas, Dodgers, Robins, Athletics,
1909-1927
Wheeler, Don [Donald Wesley]
Scott
White Sox, 1949
Wheeler, Floyd (Clark)
Rip
Pirates, Cubs, 1921-1924
Wheeler, George (Harrison)
Heavy
Reds, 1910
Wheeler, Zack [Zachary Harrison]
Wheels
Mets, Phillies, 2013-
Wheelock, Warren (Henry)
Bobby
Beaneaters, Solons, 1887-1891
Whitaker, Lou [Louis Rodman]
Sweet Lou
Tigers, 1977-1995
Whitaker, William (H)
Pat
Orioles, 1888-1889
White, Adel
Abe
Cardinals, 1937
White, Albert (Eugene)
Fuzz
Browns, Giants, 1940, 1947
White, Frank
Smooth: Hoover
Royals, 1973-1990
White, George (Frederick)
Deke
Phillies, 1895
White, Guy (Harris)
Doc
> A dentist.
Phillies, White Sox, 1901-1913
White, James (Laurie)
Deacon
> A silver-tongued orator.
Forest Citys, Red Stockings, White
Stocklings, Reds, Bisons, Wolverines,
Alleghenys, 1871-1890
White, Joyner (Clifford)
Jo-Jo
> From the way he pronounced
> Georgia.
Tigers, Athletics, Reds, 1932-1944
White, Oliver (Kirby)
Red: Buck
Doves, Pirates, 1909-1911

White, Will [William Henry]
Whoop-La
From a newspaper headline and victory shouts.
Red Stockings, Reds, Wolverines, 1877-1886

White, William (Barney)
Bear
Dodgers, 1945

Whitehead, John (Henderson)
Silent John
White Sox, Browns, 1935-1942

Whitehouse, Charlie [Charles Evis]
Lefty
Hoosiers, Pepper, Senators, 1914-19

Whiteman, George
Lucky
Played for pennant-winning teams.
Americans, Yankees, Red Sox, 1907-1918

Whiten, Mark (Anthony)
Hard Hittin'
Blue Jays, Indians, Cardinals, Red Sox, Phillies, Braves, Mariners, Yankees, 1990-2000

Whitman, Frank [Walter Franklin]
Hooker
White Sox, 1946, 1948

Whitney, Arthur (Carter)
Pinky
Phillies, Braves, Bees, 1928-1939

Whitney, Frank (Thomas)
Jumbo
Red Stockings, 1876

Whitney, Jim [James Evans]
Grasshopper Jim
Jumped in his pitching motion.
Red Stockings, Beaneaters, Cowboys, Nationals, Hoosiers, Athletics, 1881-1890

Whitt, Ernie [Leo Ernest]
Mr. Prime Minister
The only one who would talk to Jimy Williams.
Red Sox, Blue Jays, Braves, Orioles, 1976-1991

Whittaker, Walt [Walter Elton]
Doc
A dentist.
Athletics, 1916

Whitted, George (Bostic) {WHITE-ed}
Possum
Either from youth or his hunting tales.
Poffin Belly
Cardinals, Braves, Phillies, Pirates, Robins, 1912-1922

Widner, William (Waterfield)
Wild Bill
From off-field behavior.
Red Stockings, Nationals, Solons, Kelly's Killers, 1887-1891

Wieand, Franklin (Delano Roosevelt)
Ted
Redlegs, Reds, 1958, 1960

Wiedemeyer, Charlie [Charles John]
Chick
Cubs, 1934

Wietelmann, William (Frederick) {WEE-tull-man}
Whitey
Bees, Braves, Pirates, 1939-1947

Wiggs, Jimmy [James Alvin]
Big Jim
6'4", 200 lbs.
Reds, Tigers, 1903-1906

Wight, Bill [William Robert]
Lefty
Yankees, White Sox, Red Sox, Tigers, Indians, Orioles, Redlegs, Cardinals, 1946-1958

Wihtol, Alexander (Ames)
Sandy
Indians, 1979-1982

Wilber, Del [Delbert Quentin]
Babe
From birth.
Skip
As a minor league manager.
Cardinals, Phillies, Red Sox, 1946-54

Wilborn, Thaddeus (Inglehart)

Ted
Blue Jays, Yankees, 1979-1980
Wilhelm, Charles (Ernest)
Spider
From the way he covered shortstop.
Athletics, 1953
Wilhelm, Irvin (Key)
Kaiser
Based on the German emperor.
Little Eva
From minor league newspaper.
Pirates, Beaneaters, Superbas, Terrapins, Phillies, 1903-1921
Wilhelm, James (Hoyt)
Old Sarge
From his military service.
Old Folks
When he was in his late 30s.
Giants, Cardinals, Indians, Orioles, White Sox, Angels, Braves, Cubs, Dodgers, 1952-1972
Wilhelmsen, Thomas (Mark)
{will-HELM-sen}
The Bartender
His other job.
Mariners, Rangers, Diamondbacks, 2011-2017
Wilkie, Aldon (Jay)
Lefty
Pirates, 1941-1946
Wilks, Ted [Theodore]
Cork
He was the team's 'stopper.'
Cardinals, Pirates, Indians, 1944-53
Will, Bob [Robert Lee]
Butch
Cubs, 1957-1963
Williams, Alva (Mitchell)
Rip: Buff
Red Sox, Senators, Indians, 1911-18
Williams, Billy (Leo)
Sweet Billy: Sweet Williams
Sweet-Swinging Billy Williams
Sweet Swingin' Billy From Whistler
Refers to his birthplace in Alabama.
Iron Man
Consecutive game streak of 1,117.
Susie
Grace around first base in semi-pro.
Cubs, Athletics, 1959-1976
Williams, Claude (Preston)
Lefty
The Kid
From fans in Nashville.
Tigers, White Sox, 1913-1920
Williams, David (Carter)
Mutt
Senators, 1913-1914
Williams, Dewey (Edgar)
Dee
Cubs, Reds, 1944-1948
Williams, Don [Donald Reid]
Dino
Twins, 1963
Williams, Earl (Craig)
Big Money
Braves, Orioles, Expos, Athletics, 1970-1977
Williams, Elisha (Alphonso)
Dale
Reds, 1876
Williams, Evon (Daniel)
Denny
Reds, Red Sox, 1921-1928
Williams, Fred
Papa: Pap
Indians, 1945
Williams, Frederick
Cy
From his college years.
Cubs, Phillies, 1912-1930
Williams, Gerald (Floyd)
Ice
Yankees, Brewers, Braves, Devil Rays, Marlins, Mets, 1992-2005
Williams, Gregory (Scott)
Woody
Blue Jays, Padres, Cardinals, Astros,

1993-2007
Williams, Gus [August Joseph]
Gloomy Gus
Browns, 1911-1915
Williams, Johnnie [John Brodie]
Honolulu Johnny
   His birthplace.
Tigers, 1914
Williams, Ken [Kenneth Roy]
Horse Face
Reds, Browns, Red Sox, 1915-1929
Williams, Mark (Westley)
Cadillac
Athletics, 1977
Williams, Marsh [Marshall McDiarmid]
Cap
Athletics, 1916
Williams, Matt [Matthew Derrick]
Carson Crusher
   From high school in Carson City.
Master Blaster: Matt the Bat
The Big Marine
Giants, Indians, Diamondbacks, 1987-2003
Williams, Mitch [Mitchell Steven]
Wild Thing
   Awkward delivery and control problems.
Mitchie-Poo: Dumb Dumb
Rangers, Cubs, Phillies, Astros, Angels, Royals, 1986-1997
Williams, Nick [Billy Nicholas]
Nicky Dubs
Phillies, 2017-
Williams, Rees (Gephart)
Steamboat
   Could eat a 'steaming boatload' of mashed potatoes.
Iron Man
   Pitched 64 games in a minor league season.
Cardinals, 1914, 1916
Williams, Rick [Richard Allen]
Tricky
Astros, 1978-1979
Williams, Robert (Fulton)
Ace
Bees, Braves, 1940, 1946
Williams, Stan [Stanley Wilson]
Big Daddy
6'5", 230 lbs.
The Big Hurt
   Threw at batters for intimidation.
Dodgers, Yankees, Indians, Twins, Cardinals, Red Sox, 1958-1972
Williams, Taylor (Grant)
T-Willy
Brewers, Mariners, Padres, 2017-
Williams, Ted [Theodore Samuel]
The Kid
   The equipment manager said, "The Kid has arrived."
Teddy Ballgame: Thumper
The Splendid Splinter
   Tall, gangly kid.
Ted Threads
   From his clothing habits on the road.
Terrible Ted: Slendid Spitter
Teddy Tantrum
   Supposedly Joe DiMaggio thought of him as a brat.
Red Sox, 1939-1960
Williams, Trevor (Anthony)
Ev
Pirates, 2016-
Williams, Walt [Walter Allen]
No-Neck
   Only 5'6", short neck, muscular.
Colt .45s, White Sox, Indians, Yankees, 1964-1975
Williams, Walter (Merrill)
Pop
Senators, Orphans, Cubs, Phillies, Beaneaters, 1898-1903
Willingham, Josh [Joshua David]
Hammer
Marlins, Nationals, Athletics, Twins, Royals, 2004-2014
Willis, Carl (Blake)
Big Train

Tigers, Reds, White Sox, Twins,
1984-1995
Willis, Charles (William)
Lefty
Athletics, 1925-1927
Willis, Dontrelle (Wayne)
The D-Train
    Speed of his fastball.
Marlins, Tigers, Diamondbacks, Reds,
2003-2011
Willis, Les [Lester Evans]
Wimpy: Lefty
Indians, 1947
Willoughby, Claude (William)
Flunky: Weeping Willie
Phillies, Pirates, 1925-1931
Wills, Elliott (Taylor)
Bump
Rangers, Cubs, 1977-1982
Wilshere, Vernon (Sprague)
Whitey
Athletics, 1934-1936
Willson, Frank (Hoxie)
Kid
White Sox, 1918, 1927
Wilson, Alex [William Alexander]
Dale
Red Sox, Tigers, Brewers, 2013-2019
Wilson, Art [Arthur Earl]
Dutch
Giants, Chi-Feds, Whales, Pirates,
Cubs, Braves, Indians, 1908-1921
Wilson, Brian (Patrick)
The Beard
    Distinctive facial hair.
Giants, Dodgers, 2006-2014
Wilson, Charlie [Charles Woodrow]
Swamp Baby
    Allegedly flooded the diamond to
    avoid practice.
Braves, Cardinals, 1931-1935
Wilson, Christopher (John)
CJ
Rangers, Angels, 2005-2015
Wilson, Frank [Francis Edward]
Squash

Braves, Indians, Browns, 1924-1928
Wilson, Frank E (Ealton)
Zeke
Beaneaters, Spiders, Perfectos,
1895-1899
Wilson, George A (Archer)
Tug
Atlantics, 1884
Wilson, George F (Francis)
Squanto
    Had Native American features.
Tigers, Red Sox, 1911, 1914
Wilson, George P (Peacock)
Icehouse
    Cool under fire...in football.
Tigers, 1934
Wilson, George W (Washington)
Teddy
White Sox, Giants, Yankees, 1952-56
Wilson, Gomer (Russell)
Tex
Robins, 1924
Wilson, Howard (Paul)
Highball
Spiders, Athletics, Senators,
1899-1904
Wilson, Jack [John Francis]
Black Jack
Athletics, Red Sox, Senators, Tigers,
1934-1942
Wilson, Jimmie [James]
Ace
Phillies, Cardinals, Reds, 1923-1940
Wilson, John (Owen)
Chief
    Said to resemble a chief of the
    Texas Rangers.
Pirates, Cardinals, 1908-1916
Wilson, Les [Lester Wilbur]
Tug
Red Sox, 1911
Wilson, Lew [Lewis Robert]
Hack
    Resembled wrestler George
    Hackenschmidt.
Mr. Five-By-Five

Oddball build: 5'6", 195 lbs., size 6 shoe.
Giants, Cubs, Dodgers, Phillies, 1923-1934

Wilson, Michael
Tack
Twins, Angels, 1983, 1987

Wilson, Robert (James)
Red
White Sox, Tigers, Indians, 1951-60

Wilson, Roy (Edward)
Lefty
White Sox, 1928

Wilson, Samuel (Marshall)
Mike
Pirates, 1921

Wilson, Tom [Thomas G]
Slats
Senators, 1914

Wilson, William C (Clarence)
Mutt
Lank
   Tall and lanky.
Tigers, 1920

Wilson, William H (Hayward)
Mookie
   Given as a small child.
Mets, Blue Jays, 1980-1991

Wiltse, George (Leroy) {WILT-sea}
Hooks
   Able to field balls anywhere close.
Giants, Tip-Tops, 1904-1915

Wiltse, Hal [Harold James] {WILT-sea}
Whitey
Red Sox, Browns, Phillies, 1926-1931

Wiltse, Lewis (DeWitt) {WILT-sea}
Snake
   An unusual, twisting delivery.
Pirates, Athletics, Orioles, Highlanders, 1901-1903

Windle, Willis (Brewer)
Bill
Pirates, 1928-1929

Wineapple, Ed [Edward]
Lefty
Senators, 1929

Winfield, Dave [David Mark]
Winny
   Commonly used by other players.
The $23 Million Man
   From sports reporters based on his contract.
Mr. May
   Negative name by George Steinbrenner.
Mr. Jay
   When he led Toronto to a World Series title.
Mullion
   A taunt by opponents.
Big Blood
   Used by pitcher Rudy May.
Padres, Yankees, Angels, Blue Jays, Twins, Indians, 1973-1995

Winford, Jim [James Head]
Cowboy
   Oklahoma upbringing and his physique.
Cardinals, Dodgers, 1932-1938

Wingfield, Frederick (Davis)
Ted
Senators, Red Sox, 1923-1927

Wingo, Absalom (Holbrook)
Al: Red
Athletics, Tigers, 1919-1928

Winham, Lave [Lafayette sharkey]
Lefty
Superbas, Pirates, 1902-1903

Winn, George (Benjamin)
Breezy
   Gained in college.
Lefty
Red Sox, Indians, 1919-1923

Winsett, Tom [John Thomas]
Long Tom
Red Sox, Cardinals, Dodgers, 1930-38

Winter, George (Lovington)
Sassafrass
   Defined a lively player.
Spec
   5'8", 133 lbs., small for a pitcher.
Americans, Red Sox, Tigers, 1901-08

Winters, Jesse (Frank)
  Buck
  T-Bone
    College complaint when served boneless beef after ordering a T-bone steak.
  Giants, Phillies, 1919-1923
Wirts, Elwood (Vernon)
  Kettle
  Cubs, White Sox, 1921-1924
Wise, Kendall (Cole)
  Casey
    From his initials.
  Kick
    Nickname at home.
  Cubs, Braves, Tigers, 1957-1960
Wise, Sam [Samuel Washington]
  Modoc
  Wolverines, Red Stockings, Beaneaters, Nationals, Bisons, Orioles, Senators, 1881-1893
Wistert, Francis (Michael)
  Whitey
  Reds, 1934
Wisterzil, George (John)
  Tex
  Tip-Tops, Whales, Terriers, 1914-15
Witasick, Gerald (Alphonse)
{wi-TASS-ick}
  Jay
  Athletics, Royals, Padres, Yankees, Giants, Rockies, Devil Rays, 1996-2007
Witek, Nicholas (Joseph)
  Mickey
  Giants, Yankees, 1940-1949
Withrow, Frank (Blaine)
  Kid
  Phillies, 1920, 1922
Withrow, Raymond (Wallace)
  Corky
  Cardinals, 1963
Witt, George (Adrian)
  Red
  Pirates, Angels, Colt .45s, 1957-1962
Witt, Lawton (Walter)
  Whitey
  Athletics, Yankees, Robins, 1916-26
Wittgren, Nick [Nicholas James]
  Toothy
  Marlins, Indians, 2016-
Wittig, Johnnie [John Cael]
  Hans
  Giants, Red Sox, 1938-1949
Wolf, Jimmy [William Van Winkle]
  Chicken
    Pre-game eating habits.
  Willie
    As a teenager.
  Eclipse, Colonels, Browns, 1882-1892
Wolf, Ray [Raymond Bernard]
  Grandpa: Bear
  Reds, 1927
Wolf, Walter (Francis)
  Lefty
  Athletics, 1921
Wolfe, Harry [Harold]
  Whitey
  Cubs, Pirates, 1917
Wolfe, Roy (Chamberlain)
  Polly
  White Sox, 1912, 1914
Wolfe, Wilbert (Otto)
  Barney
  Highlanders, Senators, 1903-1906
Wolfgang, Mellie [Meldon John]
  Red
  White Sox, 1914-1918
Wolters, Reinder (Albertus)
  Rynie
  Mutuals, Forest Citys, Resolutes, 1871-1873
Wolverton, Harry (Sterling)
  Fighting Harry
    Heated debates with minor league umpires.
  Sterl
    Nickname growing up.
  Orphans, Phillies, Senators, Beaneaters, Highlanders, 1898-1912
Womack, Horace (Guy)
  Dooley

From a childhood family friend.
Yankees, Astros, Pilots, Athletics, 1966-1970
Womack, Sid [Sidney Kirk]
Tex
Braves, 1926
Wong, Kolten (Kaha)
Wonger
Cardinals, 2013-
Wood, Alex [Robert Alexander]
Woodman
Braves, Dodgers, Reds, 2013-
Wood, Charles A (Asher)
Spades
Pirates, 1930-1931
Wood, Charles S (Spencer)
Doc
Athletics, 1923
Wood, Edward (Robert)
Ted
Wilbur
   In jest after the knuckleballer.
Giants, Expos, 1991-1993
Wood, George (Albert)
Dandy
Ruby Legs, Wolverines, Quakers, Orioles, Athletics, Reds, 1880-1892
Wood, Joe
Smoky Joe
Red Sox, Indians, 1908-1920
Wood, Joe P [Joseph Perry]
JP: Little Joe
Tigers, 1943
Wood, Wilbur (Forrester)
Wilbah
   New England pronunciation.
Red Sox, Pirates, White Sox, 1961-78
Woodend, George (Anthony)
Dandy
Braves, 1944
Woodhead, James
Red
Stars, 1879
Woodling, Gene [Eugene Richard]
Rock
Indians, Pirates, Yankees, Orioles,
Senators, Mets, 1943-1962
Woodman, Dan [Daniel Courtenay]
Cocoa
Buffeds, Blues, 1914-1915
Woodruff, Orville (Francis)
Sam
Reds, 1904, 1910
Woods, George (Rowland)
Pinky
   Childhood confusion with "Pickles."
Pickles
   57 varieties of funny faces at birth.
Red Sox, 1943-1945
Woods, John (Fulton)
Abe
Red Sox, 1924
Woodson, Walter (Browne)
Kerry
Mariners, 1992
Wooten, Earl (Hazwell)
Junior
Senators, 1947-1948
Workman, Harry (Hallworth)
Hoge
   From young days playing in the street.
Red Sox, 1924
Works, Ralph (Talmadge)
Judge
   A scholarly countenance.
Tigers, Reds, 1909-1913
Worley, Vance (Richard)
Vanimal
   'Vance the Animal.'
Phillies, Twins, Pirates, Orioles, Marlins, 2010-2017
Worthington, Al [Allan Fulton]
Red
Giants, Red Sox, White Sox, Reds, Twins, 1953-1969
Worthington, Robert (Lee)
Red
Braves, Cardinals, 1931-1934
Wortman, William (Lewis)

Chuck
Cubs, 1916-1918
Wright, Al [Albert Edgar]
A-1
Braves, 1933
Wright, Albert (Owen)
Ab
Indians, Braves, 1935, 1944
Wright, Ceylon
Cy
White Sox, 1916
Wright, Clyde
Skeeter
    A teammate didn't like 'Clyde'.
Crazy Righto
    Japanes baseball nickname.
Angels, Brewers, Rangers, 1966-1975
Wright, David (Allen)
Captain America
    From the 2013 World Baseball Classic.
Visine: D-Dub
Hollywood
    Clubhouse nicknames.
Mets, 2004-2018
Wright, Forest (Glenn)
Buckshot
    Powerful arm but no accuracy.
Pirates, Robins, Dodgers, White Sox, 1924-1935
Wright, Gene [Clarence Eugene]
Big Gene
Superbas, Bronchos, Naps, Browns, 1901-1904
Wright, Jim [James]
Jiggs
Browns, 1927-1928
Wright, Wayne (Bromley)
Rasty
Browns, 1917-1923
Wright, Willard (James)
Dick
Tip-Tops, 1915
Wright, William Si (Simmons)
Lucky: William the Red: Deacon
The Tontogany Terror
    His hometown.
Naps, 1909
Wright, William Sm (Smith)
Rasty
Stars, Spiders, 1890
Wrigley, George (Watson)
Zeke
Senators, Giants, Superbas, 1896-99
Wuestling, George
Yats
Tigers, Yankees, 1929-1930
Wyatt, Loral (John)
Joe
Indians, 1924
Wynegar, Harold (Delano)
Butch
Twins, Yankees, Angels, 1976-1988
Wynn, Early
Gus
    Someone said he looked like a Gus.
Senators, Indians, White Sox, 1939-1963
Wynn, Jim [James Sherman]
The Toy Cannon
    Bat with 'pop' despite small size.
Colt .45s, Astros, Dodgers, Braves, Yankees, Brewers, 1963-1977
Wyse, Hank [Henry Washington]
Hooks
    Knee-buckling curve ball.
Hankus Pankus
    Clubhouse nickname from Charlie Grimm.
Cubs, Athletics, Senators, 1942-1951
Wysong, Harlan
Biff
Reds, 1930-1932
Yale, William (M)
Ad
Superbas, 1905
Yarnall, Waldo (Ward)
Rusty
Phillies, 1926
Yarrison, Byron (Wardsworth)
Rube

Athletics, Robins, 1922, 1924
Yaryan, Clarence (Everett)
Yam
White Sox, 1921-1922
Yastrzemski, Carl (Michael)
{ya-STREM-ski}
Yaz: Captain Carl
Red Sox, 1961-1983
Yeager, George (J)
Doc
Beaneaters, Blues, Pirates, Giants, Orioles, 1896-1902
Yeager, Joe [Joseph Francis]
Little Joe
Bridegrooms, Superbas, Tigers, Highlanders, Browns, 1898-1908
Yelding, Eric (Girard)
Cool Breeze
Astros, Cubs, 1989-1993
Yellow Horse, Moses (J)
Chief
    Full-blooded American Indian.
Pirates, 1921-1922
Yerkes, Charles (Carroll)
Lefty
Athletics, Cubs, 1927-1933
Yerkes, Stan [Stanley Lewis]
Yank
Orioles, Cardinals, 1901-1903
Yewcic, Tom [Thomas J]
Kibby
Tigers, 1957
Yingling, Earl (Hershey)
Chink
    From minor leagues but never used.
Naps, Dodgers, Superbasd, Reds, Senators, 1911-1918
York, James (Edward)
Lefty
Athletics, Cubs, 1919, 1921
Yost, Edgar (Frederick)
Ned
Brewers, Rangers, Expos, 1980-1985
Yost, Eddie [Edward Frederick Joseph]
The Walking Man
    Propensity for bases on balls.
Senators, Tigers, Angels, 1944-1962
Youkilis, Kevin (Edmund)
{YOU-kih-liss}
Youk
The Greek God of Walks
    Euclis: the fictional God of Walks.
Roly-poly
    By his high school coach.
Pudgy
    By his college coach.
Red Sox, White Sox, Yankees, 2004-2013
Young, Bryan (Owen)
Pete
Expos, 1992-1993
Young, Charlie [Charles]
Cy
Terrapins, 1915
Young, Denton (True)
Cyclone
    Outstanding fastball.
Cy
    Short form of Cyclone.
Farmer
    Worked on the family farm as a child.
Farmboy
Spiders, Perfectos, Cardinals, Americans, Red Sox, Naps, Rustlers, 1890-1911
Young, Dmitri (Dell)
Da Meat Hook: The Big D
Cardinals, Reds, Tigers, Nationals, 1996-2008
Young, Eric Sr. (Orlando)
EY
Dodgers, Rockies, Cubs, Brewers, Giants, Rangers, Padres, 1992-2006
Young, Harley [Harlan Edward]
Cy the Third
Pirates, Doves, 1908
Young, Irv [Irving Melrose]
Young Cy: Cy the Second
Beaneaters, Doves, Pirates, White

Sox, 1905-1911
Young, Joseph (B)
    JB
    Browns, 1892
Young, Kevin (Stacey)
    Little Hurt
    Pirates, Royals, 1992-2003
Young, Lemuel (Floyd)
    Pep
    Pirates, Reds, Cardinals, 1933-1945
Young, Norman (Robert)
    Babe
    Giants, Reds, Cardinals, 1936-1948
Youngblood, Albert (Clyde)
    Chief
    Senators, 1922
Youngs, Royce (Middlebrook)
    Pep
        Based on his hustle and desire.
    Ross
    Giants, 1917-1926
Yount, Herbert (Macon)
    Ducky: Hub
    Terrapins, 1914
Yount, Robin (R)
    The Franchise: Rockin' Robin
    The Kid
        From his first major league at-bat, against Nolan Ryan.
    Brewers, 1974-1993
Yowell, Carl (Columbus)
    Sundown
    Indians, 1924-1925
Zabel, George (Washington)
    Zip
    Cubs, 1913-1915
Zachary, Albert (Myron)
    Chink
    Dodgers, 1944
Zacher, Elmer (Henry)
    Silver
    Giants, Cardinals, 1910
Zackert, George (Carl Harlon)
    Zeke
    Cardinals, 1911-1912
Zambrano, Carlos (Alberto)
    {zam-BRAH-no}
    Big Z
    El Toro
        Spanish for 'the bull.'
    Cubs, Marlins, 2001-2012
Zardón, José (Antonio)
    Guineo
        "Guinea Fowl," common in Cuba.
    Joe
        Americanized nickname.
    Tony
        In Florida and Latin America.
    Senators, 1945
Zarilla, Al [Allen Lee]
    Zeke
        Bowlegs, from California, like a cowboy.
    Browns, Red Sox, White Sox, 1943-53
Zastryzny, Rob [Robert John]
    {za-striz-knee}
    Friday
    Cubs, 2016-2018
Zauchin, Norbert (Henry) {ZOW-chin}
    Norm
    Red Sox, Senators, 1951-1959
Zeider, Rollie (Hubert)
    Bunions
        He was spiked in his 'bunion.'
    Polly
        His hometown nickname.
    White Sox, Yankees, Chi-Feds, Whales, Cubs, 1910-1918
Zeiher, Henry
    Whitey
    Nationals, 1886
Zeile, Todd (Edward)
    The Franchise
    Cardinals, Cubs, Phillies, Orioles, Dodgers, Marlins, Rangers, Mets, Rockies, Yankees, Expos, 1989-2004
Zernial, Gus (Edward)
    Ozark Ike
        After a comic strip character.
    White Sox, Athletics, Tigers, 1949-59
Zettlein, George
    Charmer

White Stockings, Haymakers, Eckfords, Whites, Athletics, 1871-1876
Ziegler, Brad (Gregory)
Unicorn
Athletics, Diamondbacks, Red Sox, Marlins, 2008-2018
Zimmer, Bradley (Clarke)
Machine
Indians, 2017-
Zimmer, Charles (Louis)
Chief
    Captain of Poughkeepsie Indians.
Wolverines, Metropolitans, Blues, Spiders, Colonels, Pirates, Phillies, 1884-1903
Zimmer, Don [Donald William]
Popeye
    Arm resemblance.
Zim: Zip
The Gerbil
    From Bill Lee after losing a playoff game.
Buffalo Head
    Ferguson Jenkins called him the dumbest animal in creation.
El Galleguito
    "The Little Gallician" in Cuba.
El Soldadito
    "Little Soldier" in Mexico and Puerto Rico.
Dodgers, Cubs, Mets, Reds, Senators, 1954-1965
Zimmerman, Henry
Heinie
The Great Zim
    Adapted from 'The Great Houdini.'
Cubs, Giants, 1907-1919
Zimmerman, Ryan (Wallace)
The Z Man: Mr. National: Zim
Mr. Walk-Off
    Has 11 walk-off home runs.
Nationals, 2005-
Zimmermann, Jordan (M)
JZimm: Zim: JZ
Nationals, Tigers, 2009-

Zipfel, Marion (Sylvester)
Bud
Senators, 1961-1962
Zobrist, Ben [Benjamin Thomas] {ZO-brist}
Zobi-Wan Kenobi
    Think Star Wars.
BennyZo: Zoby
Zorilla
    From Rays' manager Joe Maddon.
Devil Rays, Rays, Athletics, Royals, Cubs, 2006-2019
Zoldak, Sam [Samuel Walter]
Sad Sam
Browns, Indians, Athletics, 1944-52
Zuber, Bill [William Henry]
Goober
    Rhymes with Zuber.
Indians, Senators, Yankees, Red Sox, 1936-1947
Zumaya, Joel (Martin) {zoo-MY-ah}
Zoom Zoom
Tigers, 2006-2010
Zupo, Frank (Joseph)
Noodles
Orioles, 1957-1961
Zwilling, Edward (Harrison)
Dutch
White Sox, Chi-Feds, Whales, Cubs, 1910-1916
Zych, Tony [Anthony Aaron] {Zick}
TAZ
Mariners, 2015-2017

Nicknames

$10,000 Beauty
   Kelly, Michael   131
$11,000 Beauty
   Marquard, Richard   153
$11,000 Lemon
   Marquard, Richard   153
$11,000 Peach
   Marquard, Richard   153
$23 Million Man
   Winfield, Dave   258
100 Miles Giles
   Giles, Ken   95
3 AM
   La Stella, Tommy   138
305J
   Jay, Jon   125
3-Dog
   Davis, Willie   66
4th out
   Maldonado, Candido   151
A-1
   Wright, Al   261
A-A-Ron
   Hicks, Aaron   114
Ab
   Wright, Albert   261
Abba Dabba
   Tobin, Jim   240
Abdul Jibber-Jabber
   Bostock, Lyman   34
Abe
   Bowman, Alvah   35
   White, Adel   253
   Woods, John   260

Abie
   Abrams, Cal   13
   Hood, Albie   118
AC
   Cowens, Al   59
Ace
   Aceves, Alfredo   13
   Batch, Emil   24
   Brainard, Asa   36
   Elliott, Allen   77
   Fallenstein, Ed   81
   Hudlin, Willis   121
   Parker, Clarence M   187
   Stewart, Joe   230
   Ventura, Yordano   246
   Williams, Robert   256
   Wilson, Jimmie   257
Ach
   Duliba, Bob   74
Acostica
   Acosta, José   13
Acronym
   Throneberry, Marvin   239
Action Dog
   Cash, Dave   48
Action Traction
   Seanez, Rudy   218
Ad
   Brown, John J   39
   Yale, William   261
Admiral
   Aybar, Erick   20
   Berry, Claude   29

Adonis

Jones, Johnny	127
Schlei, George	215

Adonis
Terry, William	237

A-Fraud
Rodriguez, Alex	207

AG
Garrett, Amir	92

Ageless Wonder
Paige, Leroy	187

Airedale
Drysdale, Don	73

AJ
Burnett, Allan	42
Ellis, Andrew	77
Griffin, Arthur	101
Hinch, Andrew	115
Jones, Adam	126
Murray, Arlington	176
Pierzynski, Anthony	193
Pollock, Allen	195
Ramos, Alejandro	199
Reed, Andrew	201
Sager, Anthony	212

Ajax
Jackson, Austin	123

Al
Bigbee, Lyle	30
Corwin, Elmer	58
Hall, Archibald	104
Wingo, Absalom	258

Alabama Blossom
Morton, Guy Sr	174

Alabama Flash
Byrd, Sammy	43

Alderman
Briody, Frank	38

Alex
Main, Miles	151

Alexander the Great
Alexander, Grover	14

All Rise
Judge, Aaron	128

All-American Out
Durocher, Leo	75

Allan
Travers, Joe	241

Allenport Bill
Phillips, Bill C	192

All-Starlin
Castro, Starlin	49

Altitudinous Twirler
Love, Edward	147

Alto
Repulski, Eldon	202

Amazing
Grace, Mark	99

America's First Baseman
Goldschmidt, Paul	97

American Idle
Pavano, Carl	189

A-Mo
Morgan, Adam	173

Ancient Mariner
Horton, Willie	119
Stuart, Dick	233

Andy
Abad, Fausto	13
González, Angel	97
Messersmith, John	166
Pilney, Antone	194
Rush, Jesse	210

Angel
Gearin, Dennis	93

Ángel
Salazar, Argenis	212

Angel Sleeves
Jones, Ri	127

Animal
Carter, Chris	47

Babe

Grimsley, Ross Jr.	101	Shires, Art	221
Lesley, Brad	144	**Art the Silent**	
Ant		Shires, Art	221
Rendon, Anthony	202	**Ashtabula Midget**	
Antelope		Burns, James	42
Moreno, Omar	173	**Astro Clipper**	
Verban, Emil	246	Eusebio, Tony	79
Antic		**Astro's Dad**	
Anderson, Brian	17	Price, David	196
Antihero		**Athletic Oliver Hardy**	
Decker, Cody	67	Brown, Walter	40
AO		**Augie**	
Otis, Amos	185	Freese, Gene	88
Ape		Prudhomme, John	197
Appier, Kevin	18	**Aussie**	
Apollo of the Box		Saupold, Warwick	214
Mullane, Tony	175	**Autch**	
Apples		Mierkowicz, Ed	167
Lapihuska, Andy	139	**Automatic**	
Archi		Cárdenas, Leo	46
Cianfrocco, Angelo	51	**Available**	
Archie		Jones, Sheldon	127
Lennon, Bob	143	**Ax Man**	
Manning, Rick	152	Axford, John	20
Arenoso		**B Mo**	
Nicasio, Juan	180	Morrow, Brandon	174
Arkansas Assassin		**B Moss**	
Jolley, Smead	126	Anderson, Tim	17
Arkansas Hummingbird		**Babe**	
Warneke, Lon	250	Adams, Charles	13
Arky		Barna, Herbert	22
Vaughan, Joseph	245	Bigbee, Lyle	30
Arm		Bigelow, Elliot	30
Furillo, Carl	89	Birrer, Werner	30
Hafey, Tom	104	Borton, William	34
A-Rod		Butka, Ed	43
Rodriguez, Alex	207	Dahlgren, Ellsworth	63
Arriba		Danzig, Harold	64
Clemente, Roberto	53	Davis, Woody	66
Art the Great		Doty, Elmer	72

Ellison, Bert	77	Machado, Manny	149
Ganzel, Foster	91	**Baby Giraffe**	
Herman, Floyd	113	Belt, Brandon	27
Klee, Ollie	134	Manaea, Sean	151
Klieman, Ed	134	**Baby Goose**	
Linke, Ed	145	McCullers, Lance Sr	159
Marchildon, Phil	152	**Baby Joe**	
Martin, Boris	154	Presko, Joe	196
Meers, Russ	164	**Baby Manny**	
Minner, Paul	170	Díaz, Victor	69
Nelson, Robert	179	**Baby Pedro**	
Phelps, Ernest	192	Martínez, Carlos E	154
Picone, Mario	193	**Baby Prince**	
Pinelli, Ralph	194	Maxwell, Bruce	156
Roof, Philip	208	**Baby Ruth**	
Ruth, George	210	Candelario, Jeimer	45
Sherman, Dan	221	**Baby-Faced Assassin**	
Towne, Jay	241	Graves, Danny	100
Twombly, Clarence	243	**Bad Bill**	
Wilber, Del	254	Dahlen, Bill	63
Young, Norman	263	Eagan, Bill	75
Babe Ruth's Legs		Mizeur, Bill	171
Byrd, Sammy	43	**Bad Dude**	
Baby		Stearns, John	230
Jones, Charley	127	**Bad Henry**	
Martin, Boris	154	Aaron, Henry	13
Ortiz, Oliverio	185	**Bad News**	
Peña, Roberto	189	Galloway, Jim	90
Semproch, Roman	219	Hale, Arvel	104
Baby Bull		**BagPipes**	
Cepeda, Orlando	49	Bagwell, Jeff	21
Rosario, Wilin	208	**Bahnsen Burner**	
Baby Doll		Bahnsen, Stanley	21
Jacobson, William	124	**Bake**	
Baby Face		McBride, Arnold	158
Breuer, Marv	37	**Bak-Pak**	
Presko, Joe	196	Kelly, Shawn	130
Baby Face Assassin		**Bald Billy**	
		Barnie, William	23
		Bald Eagle	

Bartender

Isbell, Frank	123
Stimmel, Archie	231

Bald Eagle of Colorado

McGilvray, Bill	161

Baldy

Jones, Henry	127
Karr, Benn	129
Louden, William	147
Palmer, Eddie	187
Rudolph, Dick	209
Sherlock, Vince	221
Silch, Ed	222
Stimmel, Archie	231
Thomas, Blaine	238

Ball Ball

Didier, Bob	70

Bally

Sharman, Ralph	219

Baltimore Greyhound

Kaline, Al	128

Bam

McCall, Brian	158

Bama

Rowell, Carvel	209

Bam-Bam

Harper, Bryce	107
Meulens, Hensley	166

Bambi

Blanco, Gil	31

Bambino

Ruth, George	211

Bamboo Brad

Miller, Brad	168

Bamm-Bamm

Tucker, Preston	242

Bamtino

Martinez, Tino	155

Bananas

Benes, Joe	28
Mostil, Johnny	174

Banjo Blackie

Mangum, Leo	151

Baquiro

Machi, Jean	149

Barbarian

Conine, Jeffrey	56

Barber

Maglie, Sal	150
McGraw, Frank	161

Barnacle Bill

Posedel, Bill	195

Barney

Gilligan, Andrew	95
Johnson, Walter	126
McFadden, Bernard	160
McLaughlin, Bernard	162
Mussill, Bernard	177
Reilly, Bernard	201
Schreiber, David	216
Schultz, George	216
Shotton, Burton	221
Wolfe, Wilbert	259

Barnicles

Barnes, Matt	23

Barnum and Bailey

Miranda, Guillermo	170

Barnyard

Henderson, Bernie	111

Baron

Knetzer, Elmer	135
Poffenberger, Cletus	195
Selbach, Albert	218

Baron von Mitterwald

Mitterwald, George	170

Barrels

Gosselin, Phil	99

Barry

McCormick, William	159

Bartender

Wilhelmsen, Thomas	255

Base on Balls

Base on Balls
    Volz, Jake   247
Baseball Evangelist
    Sunday, Billy   234
Baseball Populist
    Thomas, Chester   238
Baseball's Blind Ambassador
    Toporcer, George   240
Bash
    Compton, Anna   56
Bash Brother
    Canseco, José   45
Bat Boy
    Davies, Zack   65
Bat Masterson
    Masterson, Justin   155
Batboy
    McGraw, John   161
Battler
    Nelson, Andy   179
Battleship
    Gremminger, Ed   101
Batty
    Abbaticchio, Ed   13
Baudidou
    Rosario, Eddie   208
Bauer Outage
    Bauer, Trevor   24
Bayou Bomber
    Nash, Charles   178
Bazoo of Bang
    Ruth, George   211
Bazooka
    Basinski, Edwin   24
Bazooka Joe
    Charboneau, Joe   50
    Saunders, Joe   214
Be Home
    Blyleven, Bert   32
Beak
    Kravitz, Danny   137
Beaker
    Morandini, Mickey   173
Beanie
    Hall, Bill   104
Beanpole
    Hunt, Ben   122
Beans
    Keener, Harry   130
Bear
    Barraclough, Kyle   23
    Barrett, Aaron   23
    Bryant, Don   40
    Duffy, Danny   73
    Frisella, Danny   88
    Gile, Don   95
    Owens, Jim   186
    White, William   254
    Wolf, Ray   259
Bear Tracks
    Schmitz, Johnny   216
Beard
    Wilson, Brian   257
Beartracks
    Javery, Al   125
Beast
    Acuña, Ron Jr   13
    Foxx, Jimmie   87
    Morse, Mike   174
Beau
    Allred, Dale   15
    Baumann, Frank   24
    Bell, Roy   27
Beauty
    Bancroft, David   22
    McGowan, Fank   161
Bebo
    Tatis, Fernando Jr.   236
Bedford Bill
    Rariden, Bill   200
Bedrock

Bedrosian, Cam 26
Bedrosian, Steve 26
Bee
   Bumbry, Al 41
Bee Bee
   Babe, Loren 20
   Richard, Lee 203
Bee-bo
   Lively, Ben 145
Beef
   Castillo, Welington 48
Beeg Boy
   Carty, Rico 48
Believe
   Kivlehan, Patrick 134
Belleville Basher
   Daubach, Brian 64
Beltin' Bill
   Melton, Bill 165
Beltin' Melton
   Melton, Bill 165
Belve
   Bean, Beveric 25
Ben
   Cardoni, Armand 46
   Conroy, Bernard 57
   Davis, Mark 66
   Egan, Arthur 76
   Koehler, Bernard 135
Benjamin
   Rodney, Fernando 206
Benny Beltner
   Keltner, Ken 131
BennyZo
   Zobrist, Ben 264
Berg
   Sandberg, Ryne 213
Bert
   Cunningham, Elmer 62
   Daniels, Bernard 63

   Gallia, Melvin 90
   Glaiser, John 96
   Kuczynski, Bernard 137
Betty
   Bettis, Chad 29
Betz
   Klopp, Stan 134
Beverly
   Bayne, William 25
Bevo
   LeBourveau, DeWitt 142
BG
   Graham, Bert 99
   Guyer, Brandon 103
B-Ham
   Hamilton, Billy R 105
Bid
   McPhee, John 163
Biddo
   Iott, Frederick 123
Biff
   Maloy, Paul 151
   Schaller, Walter 215
   Schlitzer, Victor 215
   Sheehan, Timothy 220
   Wysong, Harlan 261
Big Baboon
   Ruth, George 211
Big Baby
   Jiménez, Eloy 125
Big Bart
   Colon, Bartolo 55
Big Bear
   García, Edward 91
   Ozuna, Marcell 186
Big Ben
   Cardoni, Armand 46
   Davis, Mark 66
   Rivera, Ben 204
   Shields, Ben 221

Big Bertha

Big Bertha
- Brown, Walter — 40

Big Bess
- Parmelee, Roy — 188

Big Bill
- Abstein, William — 13
- Bagwell, William — 21
- Bolden, William — 33
- Brown, William M — 40
- Chappelle, Bill — 50
- Dinneen, Bill — 70
- Hanlon, Bill — 106
- James, Bill H — 124
- Kelly, Bill — 131
- Lee, Bill C — 142
- Massey, Bill — 155
- McGilvray, Bill — 161
- Nicholson, Bill — 180
- Phillips, Bill C — 192
- Powell, Bill — 196
- Renna, Bill — 202
- Schardt, Bill — 215
- Steele, Bill — 230
- Voiselle, Bill — 247

Big Bird
- Nicolino, Justin — 180
- West, David — 253

Big Blood
- Winfield, Dave — 258

Big Bob
- Lee, Bob — 142

Big Bohemian
- Konetchy, Ed — 136

Big Bopper
- May, Lee — 157

Big Bopper of Birmingham
- May, Lee — 157

Big Bow
- Bowman, Elmer — 35

Big Boy
- Kraft, Clarence — 136
- Lee, Dae-ho — 142
- Shaner, Wally — 219

Big Brownie
- Brown, Walter — 40

Big Cat
- Asher, Alec — 19
- Galarraga, Andrés — 90
- Mize, Johnny — 170

Big Chill
- Mazara, Nomar — 157

Big City
- Adams, Matt — 14

Big Country
- Eldred, Brad — 77
- Taylor, Aaron — 236

Big D
- Drysdale, Don — 73

Big Daddy
- Cain, Matt — 44
- D'Amico, Jeff — 63
- Fielder, Cecil — 83
- Holliday, Matt — 117
- Reuschel, Rick — 202
- Williams, Stan — 256

Big Dan
- Abbott, Dan — 13
- Brouthers, Dennis — 38
- Tipple, Dan — 239

Big Dave
- Davenport, Claude — 65

Big Dee
- Spencer, Daryl — 228

Big Dog
- Pérez, Atanasio — 190

Big Doggie
- Pérez, Atanasio — 190

Big Donkey
- Dunn, Adam — 74

Big Dutch
   Bergman, Alfred   28
Big E
   Cabell, Enos   43
Big Ebbie
   Moore, Earl   171
Big Ed
   Brandt, Ed   36
   Clough, Ed   54
   Crane, Ed   59
   Delahanty, Ed   67
   Donnelly, Ed   71
   Edmondson, George   76
   Hendricks, Ed   112
   Klepfer, Ed   134
   Konetchy, Ed   136
   McCreery, Esley   159
   Miller, Ed   168
   Morris, W Ed   174
   Munns, Les   176
   Reulbach, Ed   202
   Stevens, Ed   230
   Walsh, Ed   249
Big Ern
   Frieri, Ernesto   88
Big Fella
   Hoskins, Rhys   119
Big Finn
   Fiene, Lou   83
Big Fish
   Fisher, Tom G   84
Big Fudge
   Marisnick, Jake   153
Big Game
   García, Freddy   91
Big Game James
   Shields, Jamie   221
Big Gene
   Wright, Gene   261
Big George
   Altman, George   16
   Crowe, George   61
   Mullin, George   175
Big Guy
   Putz, Joseph   197
Big Herman
   Reddick, Josh   201
Big Hosk
   Hoskins, Rhys   119
Big Hurt
   Thomas, Frank   238
   Williams, Stan   256
Big Indian Chief
   Holloman, Alva   118
Big Jack
   Karst, John   129
   Katoll, Jack   129
Big James
   Weaver, Jim D   251
Big Jawn
   Mize, Johnny   171
Big Jeff
   Pfeffer, Francis   191
Big Jim
   Baskette, James   24
   Clinton, Jim   54
   Fridley, Jim   88
   Murray, Jim   177
   Rivera, Manuel   204
   Roberts, Jim   205
   Sheehan, Jim   220
   Weaver, Jim D   251
   Wiggs, Jimmy   254
Big Joe
   Brovia, Joe   39
   Mulligan, Joe   175
Big John
   Anderson, John   17
   Bogart, John   33

Big Kid

Munce, John	175
Big Kid	
Harper, Bryce	107
Big Klu	
Kluszewski, Ted	135
Big Lebowski	
Duda, Lucas	73
Big Mac	
McCovey, Willie	159
McGwire, Mark	162
McReynolds, Kevin	164
Big Maple	
Paxton, James	189
Big Marine	
Williams, Matt	256
Big Masty	
Masterson, Justin	155
Big Mike	
Mahoney, George	150
Sullivan, Mike	233
Big Money	
Molina, Bengie	171
Williams, Earl	255
Big Moose	
Greenberg, Hank	100
Big Mox	
McQuery, William	164
Big Murph	
Johnson, George	126
Big Ned	
Crane, Ed	59
Big Newk	
Newcombe, Don	179
Big O	
Ortiz, David	185
Big Papi	
Ortiz, David	185
Big Pasta	
Simón, Alfredo	222
Big Pelf	
Pelfrey, Mike	189
Big Pete	
McKenry, Frank	162
Peters, John	191
Big Piece	
Howard, Ryan	120
Big Poison	
Waner, Paul	249
Big Potato	
Pascual, Carlos	188
Big Puma	
Berkman, Lance	28
Big Rude	
Olerud, John	184
Big Salad	
Koehler, Tom	135
Big Sam	
Edmonston, Sam	76
Thompson, Sam	239
Big Serb	
Miljus, Johnny	168
Big Sexy	
Colon, Bartolo	55
Big Six	
Auker, Elden	19
Mathewson, Christy	156
Big Smoky	
Rhem, Flint	203
Big Smooth	
Pomeranz, Drew	195
Big Stash	
Lopata, Stan	147
Big Stick	
Stewart, Mark	231
Big Stim	
Stimmel, Archie	231
Big Sugar	
Cain, Matt	44
Big Sweat	
Nelson, Jimmy	179

Big T
    Rosenthal, Trevor   209
Big Time Timmy Jim
    Lincecum, Tim   145
Big Tom
    Gorman, Tom D   98
Big Train
    Asbell, James   19
    Johnson, Walter   126
    Willis, Carl   256
Big Turk
    Farrell, Richard   81
Big U
    Jiménez, Ubaldo   125
Big Unit
    Johnson, Randy   126
Big Vic
    Díaz, Victor   69
Big Wheel
    Parrish, Lance   188
Big Z
    Zambrano, Carlos   263
Bigfoot
    Ladd, Pete   138
    Stanley, Bob   229
    Stanton, Giancarlo   229
Biggs
    Wehde, Wilbur   251
Bigote
    Castro, Ramón   48
Bill
    Bailey, Harry   21
    Bean, Beveric   25
    Bevens, Floyd   29
    Clay, Frederick   53
    Fleming, Leslie   85
    Gilbert, Alfred   95
    Hershberger, Willard   114
    Kay, Walter   130
    Lange, Frank   139
    Norman, Henry   181
    Otis, Paul   186
    Pounds, Jeared   196
    Prough, Clint   197
    Robinson, William Henry   206
    Warwick, Firman   250
    Windle, Willis   258
Billiken
    Howell, Roland   120
Billy
    Arnold, Willis   18
    Baldwin, Robert   22
    Hart, Robert   108
    Martin, Alfred   154
Billy Buck
    Buckner, Bill   41
Billy fish
    Robinson, Wilbert   206
Billy No-No
    Singer, Bill   223
Billy Rob
    Robinson, Wilbert   206
Billy the Heel
    Southworth, Billy   227
Billy the Kid
    Martin, Alfred   154
    Southworth, Billy   227
    Wagner, Billy   247
Bimbo
    Diaz, Carlos   69
Bing
    Miller, Edmund   168
Bingo
    Binks, George   30
Bings
    Miller, Edmund   168
Bip
    Roberts, Leon   205
Bird
    Fidrych, Mark   83

Bird Dog

Friedrich, Christian   88
Bird Dog
  Bird, Greg   30
  Hopper, Bill   119
  Knebel, Corey   135
Bird Eye
  Truby, Harry   242
Birdie
  Burdock, Jack   41
  Lynn, Byrd   149
  Speraw, Paul   228
  Tebbetts, George   236
Biscuit Pants
  Gehrig, Lou   93
Bison
  Kemp, Matt   131
Bitsy
  Mott, Elisha   175
BJ
  Rosenberg, Brian   209
  Ryan, Robert   211
  Surhoff, William   234
  Upton, Melvin   243
  Waszgis, Robert   250
Blab
  Schwartz, Bill C   217
Black & Decker
  Sutton, Don   234
Black Babe Ruth
  Jackson, Reggie   124
Black Cat
  Kiely, Leo   132
Black Jack
  Barry, John J   24
  Burdock, Jack   41
  McDowell, Jack   160
  Wilson, Jack   257
Black Mike
  Cochrane, Gordon   54
Blackie
  Carter, Otis   47
  Clarkson, William   53
  Connolly, Tom   56
  Dark, Alvin   64
  Dente, Sam   68
  Derrington, Jim   68
  Kiely, Leo   132
  Kohlman, Joe   136
  Mancuso, Gus   151
  Mangum, Leo   151
  O'Rourke, Frank   183
  Schwamb, Ralph   217
Blade
  Belanger, Mark   26
  Fossum, Casey   86
  Hall, Tom   105
  Rajsich, Dave   199
Blazer
  Blasingame, Don   32
Bleek
  Taylor, Ben E   236
Blest
  Madson, Ryan   150
Blimp
  Hayes, Frankie   110
  Odom, Dave   184
  Phelps, Ernest   192
Blind Bob
  Emslie, Bob   78
Blitzen
  Benz, Joseph   28
B-Lockay
  Treinen, Blake   241
Blond Adonis
  Moryn, Walt   174
Blond Bill
  Phillips, Bill C   192
Blond Southpaw Hurler
  Johnson, Earl   125

Blondie
    Purcell, William   197
    Quick, Hal   198
Blondy
    Ryan, John   211
Blood Bank
    Niarhos, Constantine   180
Bloody Jake
    Evans, Uriah   80
Blower
    Brown, Lew   39
Blubber
    Malone, Perce   151
Blue Devil
    Tipton, Eric   240
Blue Eyes
    Scherzer, Max   215
Blue Goose
    Moore, Gene Sr.   172
Blue Moon
    Odom, Johnny   184
Blue Sleeve
    Harper, Bill   107
Bluegill
    Hughes, Jim   121
Bluejacket
    Smith, Jimmy L   225
Bluto
    Messersmith, John   166
Bo
    Belinsky, Robert   26
    Boucher, Al   34
    Bowa, Larry   35
    Díaz, Baudilio   69
    Jackson, Vincent   124
    McLaughlin, Michael   163
    Porter, Marquis   195
    Sadowski, Bob   212
    Strickland, George   232
Bo Knows
    Jackson, Vincent   124
Boardwalk
    Brown, Carroll   39
Bob
    Ehmke, Howard   77
    Ewing, George   80
    Glen, Burdette   96
    Koestner, Elmer   136
    Linton, Claud   145
    Perry, Melvin   191
    Porterfield, Erwin   195
    Poser, John   195
Bob the Gob
    Shawkey, Bob   220
Bobby
    Coombs, Raymond   57
    Herrera, Procopio   114
    Locke, Lawrence   146
    Messenger, Charles   166
    Prescott, George   196
    Raburn, Ryan   198
    Rothermel, Edward   209
    Treviño, Carlos   241
    Wallace, Roderick   249
    Wheelock, Warren   253
Bobby-Bo
    Bonilla, Bobby   33
Bobo
    Holloman, Alva   118
    Milliken, Bob   169
    Newsom, Louis   180
    Osborne, Larry   185
Bocaton
    Sanó, Miguel   213
Bocci
    Lombardi, Ernie   146
Bock
    Baker, Charles   21
Body

Boever the Saver

    Kapler, Gabe 129
Boever the Saver
    Boever, Joseph 33
Boileryard
    Clarke, William J 53
Bollicky Bill
    Taylor, Billy 236
Bomber
    Van Robays, Maurice 244
Bombo
    Rivera, Jesus 204
Bonce
    Bahnsen, Stanley 21
Bone
    Buhner, Jay 41
    Hamilton, Billy R 105
Bone Crusher
    Broadway, Mike 38
Bonehead
    Merkle, Fred 166
Bones
    Balboni, Stephen 21
    Blackburn, James 31
    Burton, Ellis 42
    Ely, William 78
    Tomanek, Dick 240
Bonnie
    Hollingsworth, John 117
Boo
    Ferriss, Dave 83
Boo Boo
    Berra, Dale 29
Boob
    Fowler, Joseph 87
    McNair, Eric 163
Boog
    Powell, Hershel 196
    Powell, John 196
Booger
    Walker, Larry 248

Boogie Bear
    Mitchell, Kevin 170
Boom-Boom
    Beck, Walter 25
Boomer
    Blomberg, Ron 32
    Mancici, Trey 151
    Scott, George 217
    Wells, Dave 252
    Wells, Greg 252
Boomstick
    Cruz, Nelson 61
Boon
    Haas, Bruno 103
Boordee
    Boudreau, Lou 34
Booster
    Greason, Bill 100
Booter
    Hill, Marc 115
Bootnose
    Hofmann, Fred 117
Boots
    Day, Charles 66
    Grantham, George 100
    Hollingsworth, Al 117
    Poffenberger, Cletus 194
Bootsie
    Kinsler, Ian 134
Boozy
    Busenitz, Alan 42
Bop
    DeShields, Delino L 69
Boqueton
    Sanó, Miguel 213
Bosco
    Snover, Colonel 226
Boss
    Schmidt, Charles 215
Boston Strangler

Stuart, Dick	232	Kennedy, William	132
Boston Strongboy		**Bridgeport**	
Rice, Jim	203	Robinson, John W	206
Bots		**Bridget**	
Nekola, Francis	178	Donahue, Tim	71
Bourtobello Crushroom		**Brin Diesel**	
Bostock, Lyman	34	Brinson, Lewis	38
Bow Wow		**Bringer of Rain**	
Arft, Hank	18	Donaldson, Josh	71
Bowie baker		**Broadway**	
Stoner, Ulysses	231	Flair, Al	84
Boy Wonder		Jones, Ken	127
Kilroy, Matt	133	Lary, Lyn	140
Patterson, Roy	189	Schuster, Bill	217
Boze		Smith, Aleck	224
Berger, Louis	28	Wagner, Charlie	247
Bozo		**Brock Star**	
Cicotte, Al	52	Holt, Brock	118
B-Peezy		**Brockton Flash**	
Phillips, Brandon	192	Creeden, Pat	60
Braggo		**Brode**	
Roth, Robert	209	Shovlin, John	221
Brain Truster		**Bronco**	
Weaver, Monte	251	Jones, Albert	126
Brains		**Bronk**	
Padden, Dick	186	Brancato, Al	36
Brakeman		**Bronx Thrush**	
Taylor, John W	236	Hassett, John	109
Brat		**Brookfield Bomber**	
Stanky, Eddie	229	Mathews, Eddie	155
Breezy		**Brooks**	
Winn, George	258	Money, Don	171
Brent		**Brotato**	
Billingsley, Brett	30	Hand, Brad	106
Brewery Jack		**Brown**	
Taylor, John B	236	Hockett, Oris	116
Brice		**Brown Bear**	
Hill, Rich	115	Smoker, Josh	226
Brick		**Brown Paper**	
Mansell, Thomas	152	Bagwell, Jeff	21
Brickyard			

Brownie

Brownie
    Foreman, John   86
    Gessler, Henry   94
BroYo
    Arroyo, Bronson   19
Bruce
    Connatser, Broadus   56
    Ogrodowski, Ambrose   184
Bruno
    Block, James   32
Brusie
    Ogrodowski, Ambrose   184
Bruz
    Hamner, Ralph   105
Bryan Boy
    Hudson, Johnny   121
Bryanite
    Hudson, Johnny   121
Bub
    McAtee, Michael   158
    McMillan, Norm   163
Bubba
    Beck, Chris   25
    Carpenter, Charles   46
    Church, Emory   51
    Crosby, Richard   61
    Floyd, Leslie   85
    Frazier, Clint   87
    Harris, Charles   108
    Meyer, Alex   167
    Morton, Wycliffe   174
    Phillips, John   192
Bubbles
    Davis, JD   66
    Hargrave, Eugene   107
Bubby
    Talbot, Frederick   235
Buck
    Becannon, James   25
    Becker, Charles   26
    Brenton, Lynn   37
    Burke, Les   41
    Buxton, Ralph   43
    Carter, Solomon   47
    Collins, Orth   55
    Crouse, Clyde   61
    Danner, Henry   64
    Ebright, Hi   76
    Etchison, Clarence   79
    Ewing, William   80
    Fausett, Robert   81
    Freeman, Alexander   87
    Freeman, Harvey   87
    Freeman, Jerry   87
    Freeman, John   87
    Frierson, Robert   88
    Geggus, Charlie   93
    Gladmon, James   96
    Green, Harvey   100
    Griffith, Bert   101
    Herzog, Charles   114
    Hooker, William   118
    Hopkins, John   118
    Jackson, Grant   123
    Marrow, Charles   153
    Martinez, John   155
    Mays, Willie   157
    McCormick, Frank   159
    Newsom, Louis   179
    O'Brien, Thomas   182
    Redfern, George   200
    Rodgers, Robert   206
    Rogers, Lee   207
    Rogers, Orlin   207
    Ross, Lee   209
    Schemanske, Fred   215
    Stanley, John   229

Bud

Stanton, George	229	Bloomfield, Clyde	32
Sweeney, Charles	235	Bulling, Terry	41
Thrasher, Frank	239	Byerly, Eldred	43
Varner, Glen	245	Clancy, John	52
Washer, William	250	Connolly, Mervin	56
Weaver, Art	251	Daley, Leavitt	63
Weaver, George	251	Davis, John W	66
Weaver, William	251	Freese, George	88
West, Milton	253	Hafey, Daniel	104
Wheat, Zack	253	Hardin, William	107
White, Oliver	253	Harrelson, Derrel	107
Winters, Jesse	259	Haughey, Chris	109

Bucketfoot Al

Simmons, Al	222	Heine, William	111

		Hudson, Hal	121

Buckeye

Grate, Don	100	Hungling, Bernie	122
		Knox, Cliff	135

Bucko

Drake, Oliver	73	Kurtz, Hal	137
		Messenger, Andrew	166

Buckshot

Brown, Thomas	40	Metheny, Arthur	166
May, William	157	Moore, Ray	172
Skopec, John	223	Morse, Newell	174
Wright, Forest	261	Norris, David	181

		Parmelee, Roy	188

Bucky

Brandon, Darrell	36	Pernoll, Henry	190
Dent, Russell	68	Podbielan, Clarence	194
Guth, Charles	103	Raether, Hal	198
Harris, Stanley	108	Sharpe, Bayard	219
O'Connor, Johnny	182	Sheely, Hollis	220
Veil, Frederick	246	Sketchley, Harry	223
Walters, William	249	Smith, Robert	225

Bucky F---ing Dent

Dent, Russell	68	Souchock, Stephen	227
		Stewart, Edward	230

Bud

Anderson, Karl	17	Swartz, Sherwin	235
Bates, Hubert	24	Teachout, Arthur	236
Bicknell, Charles	30	Thomas, John	238
Black, William	31	Thomas, Luther	238
		Tinning, Lyle	239

Buddy

Weiser, Harry	252	
Zipfel, Marion	264	

Buddy
Barker, Raymond	22
Bell, David G	26
Biancalana, Roland	29
Black, Harry	31
Blair, Louis	31
Blattner, Robert	32
Booker, Richard	33
Boshers, Jeffrey	34
Bradford, Charles	35
Brewer, Jack	37
Carlyle, Earl	46
Gilbert, Drew	95
Gremp, Lewis	101
Groom, Wedsel	102
Hancken, Morris	106
Harris, Walter	108
Hassett, John	109
Hicks, Clarence	114
Hunter, Harold	122
Kerr, John Joseph	132
Lewis, Bill	144
Lewis, John	144
Lively, Everett	146
Myer, Charles	177
Napier, Skelton	178
Pernoll, Henry	190
Peterson, Carl	191
Pritchard, Harold	197
Rosar, Warren	208
Schultz, Charles	216
Walker, Marty	248

Buddy J
Solomon, Eddie	227

Budsworth
Norris, David	181

Buff
Niedenfuer, Thomas	180
Williams, Alva	255

Buffalo
Mondesi, Raúl	171
Ramos, Wilson	199

Buffalo Bill
Hogg, William	117

Buffalo Chicken
Kawasaki, Munenori	129

Buffalo Head
Niedenfuer, Thomas	180
Zimmer, Don	264

Bug
Holliday, James	117

Bug-Eater
Hudler, Rex	121

Bugger
Welch, Frank	252

Bughouse
Raymond, Arthur	200

Bugs
Bennett, Joseph	28
Eccles, Harry	76
Grover, Charlie	102
Kommers, Fred	136
Moran, Bill	172
Neuer, John	179
Raymond, Arthur	200
Reisigl, Jacob	201
Werle, Bill	253

Bugsy
Butler, Brett	43

Bull
Durham, Ed	74
Durham, Leon	74
Edwards, Bruce	76
Ferrara, Al	82
Gattis, Evan	92
Godley, Zack	96

Burger

Henry, John	113	Grimes, Austin	101
Hughes, Jared	121	Grimes, Oscar	101
Johnson, Billy	125	**Bump**	
Lawrence, Brooks	141	Akers, William	14
Luzinski, Greg	148	Hadley, Irving	104
Schroll, Al	216	Wills, Elliott	257
Smith, Lewis	225	**Bumps**	
Thompson, Bobby	238	Hadley, Irving	104
Uhle, George	243	**Bumpus**	
Wagner, William	247	Jones, Elijah	127
Watson, Bob	250	**Bun**	
Bull Montana		Troy, Robert	242
Poetz, Joe	194	**Bunch**	
Bulldog		Gillespie, Bob	95
Bouton, Jim	34	**Bunions**	
Fischer, Hank	83	Becker, Heinz	26
Hershiser, Orel	114	Zeider, Rollie	263
Pattin, Marty	189	**Bunk**	
Sanders, Ken	213	Congalton, William	56
Bulldoze		**Bunker**	
		Hill, Carmen	115
Santiago, Héctor	213	Rhines, Billy	203
Bullet		**Bunky**	
Miller, Frank L	168	Stewart, Veston	231
Reynolds, Bob	202	**Bunny**	
Bullet Ben		Brief, Anthony	38
Benson, Allen	28	Corcoran, Art	57
Bullet Bob		Fabrique, Albert	80
Feller, Bob	82	Godwin, John	96
Turley, Bob	242	Hearn, Elmer	110
Bullet Jack		High, Hugh	115
Thoney, Jack	239	Madden, Thomas	150
Bullet Joe		Maranville, Walter	152
Bush, Leslie	42	Pearce, William	189
Bullets		Roser, Jack	209
Bullas, Sim	41	**Bunt**	
Bullfrog		Frisbee, Charlie	88
Dietrich, Bill	70	**Burger**	
Tesreau, Charles	237	King, Ray	133
Bummer			

Burley

Burley
    Bayer, Christopher   25

Burrhead
    Dobson, Joe   71
    Fain, Ferris   80

Bus
    Clarkson, James   53
    McLish, Cal   163
    Mills, Colonel   169

Bush
    Borkowski, Bob   34

Bush Wiz
    Kremer, Remy   137

Busher
    Pernoll, Henry   190

Bushman
    Noble, Rafael   181

Bushy
    Hart, Tom   108

Buster
    Brown, Charles E   39
    Burrell, Frank   42
    Caton, James   49
    Chatham, Charles   50
    Clarence Bray   37
    Freeman, Hersh   87
    Gehrig, Lou   93
    Hoover, William   118
    Keen, Bill   130
    Lucas, Johnny   148
    Maynard, James   157
    McLish, Cal   163
    Minarcin, Rudy   170
    Narum, Leslie   178
    Posey, Gerald   195
    Ross, Chester   209
    Stephens, Vern   230
    Tomney, Phil   240
    Wensloff, Charles   252

Butch
    Alberts, Francis   14
    Benton, Alfred   28
    Davis, Wallace   66
    Edge, Claude   76
    Henline, Walter   112
    Henry, Floyd   112
    Hobson, Clell   116
    Huskey, Robert   122
    Kalloway, Don   136
    Keltner, Ken   131
    Lawing, Garland   141
    McAtee, Michael   158
    Metzger, Clarence   166
    Mierkowicz, Ed   167
    Nieman, Elmer   181
    O'Donnell, Harry   182
    Rementer, Willis   202
    Sanders, Roy G   213
    Sanicki, Ed   213
    Sawatski, Carl   214
    Schmidt, Charles J   215
    Simons, Mel   222
    Sutcliffe, Charles   234
    Weis, Arthur   252
    Wensloff, Charles   252
    Will, Bob   255
    Wynegar, Harold   261

Butcher Boy
    Adkins, Grady   14
    Benz, Joseph   28
    Robinson, Wilbert   206
    Schmidt, Charles J   216

Buttercup
    Dickerson, Lewis   69

Buttermilk Tommy
    Dowd, Tommy   72

Buttons

Candy

Briggs, Herbert	38
Butts	
Wagner, Albert	247
Buz	
Phillips, Albert	192
Buzz	
Arlett, Russell	18
Boyle, Ralph	35
Capra, Lee	46
Clarkson, James	53
Dozier, William J.	73
Eckert, Charlie	76
McWeeny, Doug	164
Murphy, Robert	176
Stephen, Louis	230
Wetzel, Charles	253
Buzzy	
Wares, Clyde	250
Bye-Bye	
Balboni, Stephen	21
Ca Tire	
Flores, Wilmer	85
Cab	
Kalloway, Don	136
Cabbage	
Cabrera, Al	44
Cabbage Patch	
Backman, Walter	20
Cabbie	
Cabrera, Asdrúbal	44
Cabezon	
Guerra, Junior	102
Cabob	
Joseph, Caleb	128
Caburo	
Rhodes, Karl	203
Cactus	
Cravath, Clifford	60
Johnson, Fred	126
Keck, Frank	130
Cadillac	
Stubbs, Franklin	233
Williams, Mark	256
Cadillac Curt	
Blefary, Curt	32
Cafe	
Martínez, Carlos A	154
Martínez, José	155
Cafecito	
Martínez, José	155
Cakes	
Palmer, Jim	187
Cal	
Benge, Ray	28
California	
Brown, William M	40
California Kid	
Knapp, Andrew	135
Callaway Kid	
McBride, Arnold	158
Calliope	
Miller, George	168
Camera Eye	
Bishop, Max	30
Camile	
Pascual, Camilo	188
Camp	
Skinner, Elisha	223
Canada's Babe Ruth	
O'Neill, James	183
Canadian Clubber	
Walker, Larry	248
Candelita	
Iglesias, José	123
Candy	
Candelario, Jeimer	45
Cummings, William	62
Harris, Alonzo	108
LaChance, George	138
Maldonado, Candido	151

Nelson, John 179
Sierra, Ulises 222
Candy Kid
  Konetchy, Ed 136
Candy Man
  Candelaria, John 45
Candyman
  Maldonado, Candido 151
Canena
  Márquez, Luis 153
Cannon Ball
  Shaffer, John 219
  Stemmyer, Bill 230
Cannonball
  Crane, Ed 59
  Morris, Ed 173
  Otis, Harry 186
  Titcomb, Ledell 240
  Weyhing, Gus 253
Cap
  Anson, Adrian 17
  Clark, John 52
  Clarke, Fred 52
  Crowell, Minot 61
  Dillon, Frank 70
  Fahey, Howard 80
  Mattingly, Don 156
  Mays, Willie 157
  McGann, Dan 160
  McGann, Dennis 160
  Narleski, Bill 178
  Peterson, Charles 191
  Williams, Marsh 256
Cap'n Eddie
  Mathews, Eddie 155
Capital Punisher
  Howard, Frank 120
Capt
  Anson, Adrian 17

Captain
  Bando, Sal 22
  Correa, Carlos 58
  Jeter, Derek 125
  Reese, Harold 201
Captain America
  Wright, David 261
Captain Canada
  Saunders, Michael 214
Captain Carl
  Yastrzemski, Carl 262
Captain Caveman
  Travis, Sam 241
Captain Clutch
  Jeter, Derek 125
Captain Hook
  Anderson, George 17
Captain Underpants
  Pence, Hunter 190
Captain Video
  Gwynn, Tony Sr. 103
Cargo
  Gómez, Carlos 97
  González, Carlos 97
Carita
  Devers, Rafael 69
Carl
  Dewald, Charles 69
  Fischer, Charles 83
  Sitton, Charles 223
Carl's Jr
  Edwards, Carl Jr 76
Carlos
  Fisher, Charles 84
Carney
  Flynn, Cornelius 85
Carolina Catapult
  Melton, Cliff 165
Carson Crusher
  Williams, Matt 256
Cascajo

Maldonado, Martín 151
Casey
Collins, Kevin 55
Hageman, Kurt 104
Jones, Charlie 127
Kirsch, Harry 134
Stengel, Charles 230
Wise, Kendall 259
Casper
Asbjornson, Robert 19
Casper the Friendly Ghost
Adair, Jerry 13
Castilian Celt
Gomez, Vernon 97
Cat
Brecheen, Harry 37
Clanton, Uke 52
Clary, Ellis 53
Galarraga, Andrés 90
Metkovich, George 166
Millán, Félix 168
Catfish
Crawford, Jim 60
Hunter, Jim 122
Metkovich, George 166
Tseng, Jen-Ho 242
Catonsville Flash
Maisel, Frederick 151
Caveman
Barnes, Jacob 23
Damon, Johnny 63
Robinson, Don 206
Cayt
Fauver, Clay 81
CB
Burns, Charles 42
CC
Hoffman, Clarence 116
Lee, Chen 142

Sabathia, Carsten 212
Cesita
Hernández, César 113
CH
Spalding, Charles 227
Cha Cha
Cepeda, Orlando 49
Chad
Kimsey, Clyde 133
Mottola, Charles 175
See, Charlie 218
Chairman of the Board
Ford, Edward 86
Champ
Summers, John 234
Chanchi
Martes, Francis 154
Channel
Messersmith, John 166
Chappie
Geygan, James 94
Graff, Louis 99
McFarland, Charles 160
Snodgrass, Amzie 226
Chappy
Charles, Raymond 50
Lane, George 139
Charlie
Blackburn, Foster 31
Cuellar, Jesus 62
Charlie Hustle
Rose. Pete Sr 208
Charmer
Zettlein, George 263
Charron
Desmond, Ian 69
Chattanooga Choo Choo
Layne, Hillis 141
Chatterer Chet
Thomas, Chester 238

Chaucer
    Elliott, Claude   77
Chauncey
    Dubuc, Jean   73
    Stuart, Bill   232
Cheater
    Buxton, Ralph   43
Cheeky
    Wagner, Leon   247
Cheerful Charlie
    Hickman, Charlie   114
Cheerful Hick
    Hickman, Charlie   114
Cheese
    Schweitzer, Al   217
Cheetah
    Olerud, John   184
Chelito
    Hagerman, Zerah   104
Chemist
    Canseco, José   45
Cheo
    Cruz, José   61
Cherokee
    Fisher, William   84
Chess
    Thomas, Chester   238
Chester the Great
    Covington, Chet   59
Chesty
    Covington, Chet   59
Chesty Chet
    Johnson, Chet   125
Chet
    Fowler, Joseph   87
    Nichols, Charles   180
    Thomas, Chester   238
Chewing Gum
    O'Brien, John J   182
Chi
    Pinder, Chad   194
Chi Chi
    González, Alexander   97
Chic
    Ceccarelli, Art   49
Chi-Chi
    Olivo, Federico   184
Chick
    Autry, Martin   20
    Autry, William   20
    Bowen, Emmons   35
    Brandom, Chester   36
    Cuccinello, Tony   62
    Davies, Lloyd   65
    Evans, Charles   79
    Fewster, Wilson   83
    Fraser, Charles   87
    Fullis, Charles   89
    Fulmer, Charles   89
    Gagnon, Harold   90
    Galloway, Clarence   90
    Gandil, Arnold   91
    Hafey, Charles   104
    Hartley, Walter   108
    Hoffer, Bill   116
    Holmes, Elwood   118
    Keating, Walter   130
    King, Charles G   133
    LaPointe, Raoul   140
    Lathers, Charles   140
    Manlove, Charlie   152
    Marshall, Charles   153
    Mattick, Wally   156
    Maynard, Leroy   157
    Morgan, Chester   173
    Naleway, Frank   178
    Pedroes, Charles   189
    Pieretti, Marino   193
    Robitaille, Joseph   206

Shiver, Ivey	221	Cornejo, Mardie	58
Shorten, Charles	221	Eaves, Vallie	76
Smith, John W	225	Ellsbury, Jacoby	78
Sorrells, Raymond	227	García, Freddy	91
Stahl, Charles	228	Geronimo, Cesar	94
Starr, William	229	Gil, Gerónimo	95
Tolson, Charles	240	Hale, Arvel	104
Wiedemeyer, Charlie	254	Harder, Mel	106

Chicken

		Harter, Frank	108
Counsell, Craig	58	Hogsett, Elon	117
Hawks, Nelson	109	Johnson, George	126
Routcliffe, Phil	209	Kahdot, Isaac	128
Stanley, Fred	229	Kelty, John	131
Wolf, Jimmy	259	Koy, Ernie	136

Chicken Man

		LeRoy, Louis	144
Boggs, Wade	33	Meyers, John	167

Chico

		Moore, Euel	172
Cárdenas, Leo	46	Mujica, Edward	175
Carrasquel, Alfonso	47	Posedel, Bill	195
Escarrega, Ernesto	79	Roseman, James	209
Fernández, Humberto	82	Siebert, Dick	222
Fernández, Lorenzo	82	Sockalexis, Louis	226
García, Vinicio	91	Summers, Ed	234
Hernández, Salvador	113	Turk, Lucas	242
Lind, José	145	Warhop, Jack	250
Ruiz, Giraldo	210	Wilson, John	257
Ruiz, Manuel	210	Yellow Horse, Moses	262
Salmon, Rutherford	212	Youngblood, Albert	263
Walker, Cleotha	248	Zimmer, Charles	264

Chief

Aker, Jack	14
Bender, Charles	27
Berroa, Gerónimo	29
Borchers, George	34
Bowles, Emmett	35
Cheeves, Virgil	51
Chouneau, William	51
Cordero, Chad	58

Chigger

Statz, Arnold	229

Childe Harold

Janvrin, Hal	124

Childish Bambino

Soto, Juan	227

Chile

Gómez, José	97

Chili

Chilly

    Buss, Nick   43
    Davis, Charles   65
Chilly
    Chelini, Italo   51
Chin
    Gruber, Kelly   102
Chink
    Heileman, John   111
    Mattick, Wally   156
    Outen, William   186
    Taylor, C L   236
    Taylor, Leo   236
    Yingling, Earl   262
    Zachary, Albert   263
Chinski
    Root, Charlie   208
Chip
    Ambres, Raymond   16
    Bennett, Francis   28
    Coulter, Thomas   58
    Hale, Walter   104
    Lang, Robert   139
    Marshall, Charles   153
    Smith, Chris W   224
Chipper
    Rowley, Chris   209
Chippy
    Gaw, George   93
    McGarr, James B.   160
Chiquitin
    Cabrera, Asdrúbal   44
Chisel
    Kaiser, Bob   128
Chito
    Martinez, Reyenaldo   155
Choke 'em Charley
    Herzog, Charles   114
Cholito
    Naranjo, Lazaro   178

Cholly
    Engle, Charlie   78
    Naranjo, Lazaro   178
Chomo
    Claudio, Álex   53
Chone
    Figgins, Desmond   83
Choo
    Freeman, Raphael   88
Chooch
    Ruiz, Carlos   210
Choo-Choo
    Coleman, Clarence   54
Chopper
    Thompson, Rich G   239
Choppy
    Adair, Jimmy   13
Chops
    Broskie, Sig   38
Chris
    Krug, Everett   137
Christian Gentleman
    Mathewson, Christy   155
Chub
    Aubrey, Harry   19
    Collins, Charles   55
    Sullivan, John F   233
Chubby
    Betts, Harry   29
    Dean, Alfred   67
    Snyder, Alfred   226
    Thomas, Chester   238
Chucho
    Ramos, Jesus   199
Chuck
    Churn, Clarence   51
    Connors, Kevin   57
    Emerson, Chester   78
    Leathers, Hal   142
    Scrivener, Wayne   217

    Wortman, William   261
Chuck Nazty
    Blackmon, Charlie   31
Chuckie
    Upshaw, Willie   243
Chummy
    Gray, George   100
Churro
    Torrens, Luis   241
Cid
    Morgan, Cyril   173
Cigarette
    Leiter, Al   143
Cinco
    Cueto, Johnny   62
Cinders
    O'Brien, John F   182
Circus Solly
    Hofman, Arthur   117
Citation
    Merriman, Lloyd   166
Cito
    Gaston, Clarence   92
CJ
    Fick, Charles   83
    Nitkowski, Christopher   181
    Riefenhauser, Charles   204
    Wilson, Christopher   257
Clancy
    Cutshaw, George   62
    Marshall, Clarence   153
    Smyers, Clarence   226
    Tyler, Fred   243
Clank
    Blefary, Curt   32
Clark
    Kent, Jeff   132
Claw
    Kershaw, Clayton   132
Cliff
    Happenny, John   106
Cliff the Curver
    Melton, Cliff   165
Climax
    Blethen, Clarence   32
Clinkers
    Fagan, Bill   80
Clipper
    Flynn, William   85
Clutch
    Henrich, Tommy   112
CO
    Owings, Chris   186
Coach
    Cozart, Zack   59
Coalyard Mike
    Handiboe, Aloysius   106
Coaster Joe
    Connolly, Joe   56
Cobra
    Driessen, Dan   73
    Lewis, Colby   144
    Parker, Dave   187
Cocky
    Collins, Eddie   55
    Fain, Ferris   80
Coco
    Crisp, Covelli   60
    Laboy, José   138
Cocoa
    Gutiérrez, César   103
    Woodman, Dan   260
Cod
    Myers, Al   177
Cody Love
    Bellinger, Cody   27
Coffee Grounds
    Ryan, Jack   211
Colby Jack
    Coombs, Jack   57

Coldwater Jim
    Hughey, Jim   121
Cole Train
    Cole, Gerrit   54
Collie
    Druhot, Carl   73
Colonel
    Beecher, Roy   26
    Ferson, Alex   83
    Hatfield, Gil   109
    Turner, Jim   242
Colonel Pinch
    Hummel, John   122
Colossus of Clout
    Ruth, George   211
Colt
    Hynes, Joshua   123
Columbia
    Gehrig, Lou   93
Columbia George
    Smith, George A   225
Comando
    Andrus, Elvis   17
Come Hombre
    Castro, Miguel   48
Comet
    Archdeacon, Maurice   18
Commerce Comet
    Mantle, Mickey   152
Commy
    Comiskey, Charles   56
Compa F
    Franco, Maikel   87
Compa H
    Neris, Héctor   179
Complete Game James
    Shields, Jamie   221
Con
    Daily, Cornelius   63
    Dempsey, Cornelius   68
    Lucid, Cornelius   148

Condor
    Guzmán, Ronald   103
    Sale, Chris   212
    Saunders, Michael   214
Conductor
    Sale, Chris   212
Connie
    Creeden, Cornelius   60
    McGeehan, Cornelius   160
    Ryan, Cornelius   211
Connie Mack
    McGillicuddy, Cornelius   161
Conny
    Doyle, Cornelius   72
Control King
    Derringer, Samuel   68
Cooch
    Cuccinello, Tony   62
Cookie
    Carrasco, Carlos   47
    Cuccurullo, Arthur   62
    Lavagetto, Harry   141
    Lupien, Ulysses   148
    Rojas, Octavio   208
Cookie Monster
    Ortiz, David   185
Cookie's Boy
    Lavagetto, Harry   141
Cool
    Hartman, J C   108
Cool Breeze
    Scott, Rodney   217
    Yelding, Eric   262
Cool Papa
    Jordan, Paul   128
Cooler
    Rodriguez, Alex   207
Coonie
    Blank, Frank   31
    Felderman, Marv   82

Snyder, Abraham	226	Nash, Charles	178
Coonskin		**Count**	
Davis, Curt	65	Brainard, Asa	36
Cooperstown		Campau, Charles	45
Ortiz, David	185	Clemens, Clem	53
Coot		Doe, Fred	71
Veal, Orville	246	Garza, Matt	92
Coqui		Gedney, Alfred	93
Fuentes, Rey	89	Lyle, Albert	148
Coral		Montefusco, John	171
Gables, Kenneth	89	Mullane, Tony	175
Corey's Brother		Puccinelli, George	197
Seager, Kyle	217	Sensenderfer, John	219
Cork		Weber, Charlie	251
Wilks, Ted	255	**Count of Luxemburg**	
Corky		Meine, Henry	164
Corcoran, Tommy	57	**Country**	
Valentine, Harold	244	Davis, John W	66
Withrow, Raymond	259	Held, Mel	111
Corns		Littell, Mark	145
Bradley, Hugh	36	Slaughter, Enos	223
Cot		Warneke, Lon	250
Deal, Ellis	67	**Country Breakfast**	
Cotney		Butler, Billy	43
Hopp, Johnny	119	**Cousin Heine**	
Cotton		Meine, Henry	164
Brazle, Al	37	**Cowboy**	
Candiotti, Tom	45	Harrell, Ray	107
Dickson, Brandon	70	Jones, Albert	126
Jones, Howie	127	Lorenzen, Michael	147
Knaupp, Henry	135	Milstead, George	170
Miller, Hughie	168	Winford, Jim	258
Minahan, Edmund	170	**Coyote**	
Nash, Charles	178	Wert, Don	253
Pippen, Henry	194	**Cozy**	
Siemer, Oscar	222	Dolan, Albert	71
Tierney, James	239	Dolan, Patrick	71
Cotton Top		**Crab**	
Turner, Terry	243	Burkett, Jesse	41
Cotton-top			

Evers, Johnny	80	Sager, Samuel	212
Lindsay, Chris	145	**Crime Dog**	
McDonald, Charles	159	McGriff, Fred	161
Warhop, Jack	250	**Crip**	
Cracker		Polli, Lou	195
Hamby, Jim	105	**Crooked Arm**	
Schalk Ray	215	Cremins, Bob	60
Craigeroo		**Crooning Joe**	
Stammen, Craig	229	Cascarella, Joe	48
Crane		**Crossfire**	
Reberger, Frank	200	Moore, Earl	171
Crash		**Crow**	
Allen, Richard	15	Crosetti, Frank	61
Davis, Lawrence	66	**CrunchWrap**	
Crash Davis		Cain, Lorenzo	44
Barnes, William	23	**Crungy**	
Crash Helmet		Cronin, Bill	61
Allen, Richard	15	**Crush**	
Craw Daddy		Davis, Chris	65
Crawford, Jim	60	**Cruz**	
Crazy		Stanton Giancarlo	229
Schmit, Frederick	216	**CT3**	
Crazy Eyes		Taylor, Chris	236
Grimsley, Ross Jr.	101	**Cub**	
Crazy Horse		Stricker, John	232
Meyers, Lou	167	**Cuban Bob Feller**	
Pagán, Ángel	187	Moreno, Julio	173
Crazy Righto		**Cuban Comet**	
Wright, Clyde	261	Miñoso, Orestes	170
Creeper		**Cuban Hero**	
Stroud, Ed	232	Cuppy, George	62
Creepy		**Cuban Missile**	
Crespi, Frank	60	Chapman, Aroldis	50
Crese		Ramírez, Alexei	199
Heismann, Christian	111	**Cuban Warrior**	
C-Rex		Cuppy, George	62
Everett, Carl	80	**Cubanito**	
Cricket		Ramírez, Juan	199
Patek, Freddie	189	**Cuba's Mighty Mite**	
Rigney, Bill	204	Guerra, Fermin	102
		Cuckoo	

Blefary, Curt	32
Christensen, Walter	51
Jamieson, Charlie	124

Cuddles
Marshall, Clarence	153

Cuke
Barrows, Roland	24

Cully
Haworth, Homer	110

Culprit
Keltner, Ken	131

Cuno
Barragan, Facundo	23

Cupid
Childs, Clarence	51

Cuqui
Rojas, Octavio	207

Cura
Smith, Hal	225

Curaçao Kid
Jones, Andruw	126

Curlie
Dorman, Charles	72

Curly
Brown, Charles R	39
Bullard, George	41
Dobson, Joe	71
Jungels, Ken	128
Ogden, Warren	184
Onis, Manuel	184
Ross, Ernie	209

Curry
Foley, Charles	85

Curveless Wonder
Orth, Al	185

Cush
Cooney, Bill	57

Cutch
McCutchen, Andrew	159

Cute Little Lefthander
Lopat, Eddie	146

Cuy
Cuyler, Hazen	62

CV
Matteson, Clifford	156
Sitton, Charles	223

Cy
Alberts, Frederick	14
Barger, Eros	22
Bentley, Clytus	28
Blanton, Darrell	32
Block, Seymour	32
Bowen, Sutherland	35
Cihocki, Ed	52
Falkenberg, Frederick	81
Ferry, Alfred	83
Fried, Arthur	88
Kerlin, Orie	132
Marshall, Roy	153
Moore, Wilcy	172
Moore, William Austin	172
Morgan, Cyril	173
Morgan, Harry	173
Neighbors, Cecil	178
Perkins, Ralph	190
Pieh, Edwin	193
Rheam, Kenneth	203
Seymour, James	219
Swaim, John	235
Twombly, Edwin	243
Vorhees, Henry	247
Warmoth, Wallace	250
Williams, Frederick	255
Wright, Ceylon	261
Young, Charlie	262
Young, Denton	262

Cy the Second
Young, Irv	262

Cy the Third
    Young, Harley   262

Cyclone
    Miller, Joseph   169
    Phillips, Bill C   192
    Ryan, Daniel   211
    Young, Denton   262

Cyclone Jim
    Duryea, James   75

Cyrano of the Iron Mask
    Lombardi, Ernie   146

D Dawg
    Betances, Dellin   29

D.No
    Norris, Daniel   181

DA
    Aardsma, David   13

Da Kid
    Manaea, Sean   151

Da Meat Hook
    Young, Dmitri   262

Dad
    Clark, Fred   52
    Clarke, William H   53
    Clarkson, Arthur   53
    Hale, Ray   104
    Lytle, Edward   149
    Meek, Frank   164

Daddy
    Ethier, Andre   79

Daddy Long-Legs
    Christopher, Russ   51
    Fowler, Dexter   86

Daddy Wags
    Wagner, Leon   247

Daff
    Gammons, John   91

Daffy
    Dean, Paul   67
    Sanders, Ken   213

Dainty
    Gearin, Dennis   93

Daiquiri
    Tanana, Frank   235

Daisy
    Davis, John He   66

Dale
    Williams, Elisha   255
    Wilson, Alex   257

Damo
    García, Dámaso   91

Dan
    Boone, James   34
    Brouthers, Dennis   38
    Ford, Darnell   85
    Griner, Donald   101
    Marion, Donald   153
    McGann, Dennis   160

Dandelion
    Pfeffer, Fred   191

Dandy
    Aylward, Richard   20
    Radbourn, George   198
    Shinnick, Tim   221
    Wood, George   260
    Woodend, George   260

Dandy Little Glove Man
    Morandini, Mickey   173

Dango
    Groth, Ernie   102

Danny
    Bell, Fernando   26
    Boone, Luke   34
    Doyle, Howard   72
    Green, Edward   100

Dapper Dan
    Howley, Dan   120

Darby
    Knowles, Jimmy   135
    O'Brien, Tom   182

Daredevil
    Altizer, David   16
Dark Helmet
    Torres, Álex   241
Dark Knight of Gotham
    Harvey, Matt   109
Darkie
    Clift, Harlond   53
Darling
    Booth, Amos   34
Dasher
    Kearns, Tom   130
    Knox, Andy   135
    Murray, Bill   177
    Troy, John   242
Dashing Dan
    Costello, Dan   58
DatDude
    Phillips, Brandon   192
Dauntless Dave
    Danforth, Dave   63
Dave
    Sulik, Ernie   233
Dave
    Hillman, Darius   115
DaveHuman
    Freese, David   88
Davenport Destroyer
    Brovia, Joe   39
Dazzle
    Gladden, Dan   96
Dazzle Man
    Gladden, Dan   96
Dazzler
    Vance, Charles   245
Dazzy
    Swartz, Vernon   235
    Vance, Charles   245
D-Dub
    Wright, David   261
Deacon
    Brown, Alton   39
    Darby, George   64
    Johnson, Fred   126
    Law, Vern   141
    Leever, Sam   142
    McGuire, James   161
    McKechnie, Bill   162
    Moore, Wilcy   172
    Morrissey, Michael   174
    Murray, Ray   177
    Newson, Warren   180
    Nicholson, Thomas   180
    Phillippe, Charles   192
    Scott, Lewis   217
    Smalley, Will   224
    Van Buren, Edward   244
    White, James   253
    Wright, William Si   261
Deacon Danny
    MacFayden, Danny   149
Deacon Jim
    McGuire, James   161
Dead-Eye
    Gibbs, Jerry   95
Dear Old Roger
    Connor, Roger   57
Death to Flying Things
    Chapman, Jack   50
    Ferguson, Bob   82
    Gutierrez, Franklin   103
Death Valley Jim
    Scott, Jim   217
Decker
    Newman, Charlie   179
Dee
    Brown, Dermal   39
    Cousineau, Edward   58
    Miles, Wilson   168

Deeby

Moore, DC	171	Gearin, Dennis	93
Phillips, Damon	192	Williams, Evon	255
Pillette, Duane	193	**Derby Day Bill**	
Spencer, Daryl	228	Clymer, Bill	54
Walsh, Leo	249	**Desperate**	
Williams, Dewey	255	Beatty, Desmond	25

Deeby
- Foss, George — 86

Destructobeam
- Iannetta, Chris — 123

Deedle
- Moran, Roy — 172

Deuce
- Adduci, Jim — 14
- Duensing, Brian — 73

Deek
- Derrick, Claud — 68

Devil
- Gilliam, Jim — 95

Deerfoot
- Barclay, George — 22
- Bay, Harry — 25
- Kaiser, Al — 128
- Milan, Clyde — 167
- Needham, Tom — 178

Devo the Dragon
- Devenski, Chris — 69

Dewey
- Evans, Dwight — 79
- McDougal, James — 160

Deerfoot of the Diamond
- Sockalexis, Louis — 227

Dexter
- Schafer, Harry — 214

deGroat
- deGrom, Jacob — 67

DH
- Holmberg, David — 118

deGrominator
- deGrom, Jacob — 67

Diamond Jim
- Brady, Jim — 36
- Gentile, Jim — 93

Deke
- White, George — 253

Diamond Joe
- Rickert, Joe — 203

Del
- Howard, Paul — 120
- Pratt, Derrill — 196

Diamond John
- Kelly, John O — 131

Dell
- Darling, Conrad — 64
- Howard, Dave — 120
- Howard, George — 120

Dibby
- Flynn, George — 85

Dice-K
- Matsuzaka, Daisuke — 156

Demon
- Delhi, Lee — 68

Dick
- Barrett, Tracy — 23
- Blaisdell, Howard — 31
- Burrus, Maurice — 42
- Cooley, Duff — 57
- Cox, Elmer — 59
- Gossett, John — 99

Demon Jack
- Dalton, Tolbert — 63

Denny
- Driscoll, John F — 73

Dixie

Harley, Henry	107
Hawke, Bill	109
Hurley, William	122
Newsome, Heber	180
Pierson, Edmund	193
Robertson, Preston	206
Spalding, Charles	227
Wright, Willard	261
Dick Tracy	
Tracewski, Dick	241
Diddy Ball	
Didier, Bob	70
Didi	
Gregorius, Mariekson	100
Diesel	
Lee, David	142
Dig	
King, Lynn	133
Digger	
Graveman, Kendall	100
Hebner, Richie	110
Phelps, Ken	192
Dike	
Varney, Lawrence	245
Dim Dom	
Dallessandro, Dom	63
Dim Dom Dal	
Dallessandro, Dom	63
Dimples	
Dalrymple, Clay	63
Tate, Edward	236
Ding Dong	
Bell, Wilbur	27
Bell, William	27
Ding-a-ling	
Clay, Dain	53
Dingle	
Croucher, Frank	61
Dingo	
Restelli, Dino	202
Dink	
O'Brien, Frank	182
Dinny	
Gearin, Dennis	93
McNamara, John	163
Dino	
Aguilar, Jesus	14
Williams, Don	255
Dinty	
Barbare, Walter	22
Gearin, Dennis	93
Dirt	
Drew, Stephen	73
Tidrow, Dick	239
Dirtbag	
Kipnis, Jason	134
Dirty	
Arroyo, Bronson	19
Dirty Al	
Gallagher, Alan	90
Dirty Craig	
Kimbrel, Craig	133
Dirty Dave	
Murphy, Dave	176
Dirty Jack	
Doyle, Jack	72
Disco	
DeSclafani, Anthony	68
Disco Dan	
Ford, Darnell	85
Dismal Danny	
MacFayden, Danny	149
Divvy	
Davidson, Homer	65
Dixie	
Carroll, Dorsey	47
Davis, Frank	65
Howell, Homer	120
Howell, Millard	120
Leverett, Gorham	144

McArthur, Oland 158
Parker, Douglas 187
Upright, Roy 243
Walker, Ewart 248
Walker, Fred 248
Walker, James 248
Warneke, Lon 250
Dixie Dude
Warneke, Lon 250
Dixie Thrush
Strang, Sammy 232
Diz
Reed, Howie 201
Dizzy
Carlyle, Roy 46
Dean, Jay 67
Nutter, Everett 182
Pederson, Joc 189
Sutherland, Howard 234
Trout, Paul 242
DJ
Carrasco, Daniel 47
Dozier, William H. 73
Houlton, Dennis 119
Jackson, Danny 123
Jennings, Dan 125
Jeter, Derek 125
Mitchell, William 170
D-Lee
Lee, Derrek 142
D-Mac
McGowan, Dustin 161
Doc
Adams, Dan Lu 13
Amole, Morris 16
Ayers, Yancy 20
Bass, William 24
Bowers, Stewart 35

Brown, Robert 40
Bushong, Albert 42
Carney, Pat 46
Carroll, Ralph 47
Casey, James 48
Cook, Luther 57
Cramer, Roger 59
Crandall, James 59
Curley, Walter 62
Daugherty, Harold 64
Doolin, Mickey 71
Edelen, Ed 76
Edwards, Howard 76
Evans, Joe 80
Farrell, Edward 81
Gautreau, Walter 92
Gessler, Henry 94
Gill, Warren 95
Gooden, Dwight 98
Graham, Archibald 99
Hall, Charlie 105
Halladay, Roy 105
Hamann, Elmer 105
Hazleton, Willard 110
Higgins, Eddie 115
Hoblitzell, Dick 116
Irwin, Arthur 123
Kennedy, Michael 132
Kerr, John Jonas 132
Killefer, Wade 133
Knowlson, Tom 135
Lafitte, Ed 138
Land, William 139
Landis, Samuel 139
Lavan, John 141
Legett, Lou 142
Leitner, George A 143

Lowe, George	147	Vail, Bob	244
Mansell, John	152	Waldbauer, Albert	248
Marshall, Eddie	153	Wallace, Frederick	249
Marshall, William	154	Watson, Charles	250
Martell, Marty	154	White, Guy	253
Martin, Harold	154	Whittaker, Walt	254
McJames, James	162	Wood, Charles S	260
McMahon, Henry	163	Yeager, George	262

Doctor Chill

Travis, Sam — 241

Dode

Birmingham, Joseph	30
Brinker, Bill	38
Paskert, George	188
Schultz, Joe Jr.	217

Dodo

Armstrong, Noble	18
Bird, Frank	30
Lane, Hunter	139

Dody

Cicero, Joe — 51

Doe

Boyland, Dorian — 35

Doggie

Miller, George	168
Pérez, Atanasio	190

Dolly

Gray, William	100
Stark, Monroe	229

Dolpho

Phillips, Adolfo — 192

Dominican Comet

Marichal, Juan — 152

Dominican Dandy

Marichal, Juan — 152

Don

Brown, Jim	39
Butera, Drew	43

Donham Bullet

Medich, George	164
Miller, Roy	169
Moskiman, William	174
Nance, William	178
Newton, Eustace	180
Oberlander, Hartman	183
Ozmer, Horace	186
Parker, Harley	187
Parmelee, Roy	188
Potts, Vivian	196
Powers, Michael	196
Prothro, James	197
Queen, Billy	198
Ralston, Samuel	199
Reisling, Frank	202
Reynolds, Ross	203
Roberts, Dave	205
Rutherford, Johnny	211
Sage, Harry	212
Scanlan, William	214
Sechrist, Theodore	218
Shanley, Harry	219
Smoot, Homer	226
Snell, Wally	226
Stafford, John	228
Swigler, Ad	235
Tonkin, Harry	240
Twining, Howard	243

Donie

Darwin, Danny	64		Encarnacion, Edwin	78

Donie
    Bush, Owen   42

Donkey
    Hafner, Travis   104

Donnie
    Lind, Adam   145
    Robinson, Don   206

Donnie Barrels
    Solano, Donovan   227

Donnie Baseball
    Mattingly, Don   156

Donora Greyhound
    Musial, Stan   177

Doof
    Duffey, Tyler   73

Dooley
    Womack, Horace   259

Dooney
    Hardy, Alex   107

Dordy
    Radbourn, George   198

Dorf
    Ainsmith, Ed   14

Dorn
    Taylor, Donald   236

Dory
    Dean, Charles   67

Dot
    Fulghum, James   89

Dots
    Miller, John B.   169

Double
    Dwyer, Joe   75

Double G
    González, Giovany   98

Double No-Hit
    Vander Meer, Johnny   245

Double X
    Foxx, Jimmie   87

Double-E

Doughnut Bill
    Carrick, Bill   47

Dougie Fresh
    Fister, Doug   84

Dowdy
    Hartnett, Charles   109

Downtown
    Brown, Domonic   39
    Brown, Ollie   40

Dr. Death
    Darwin, Danny   64

Dr. Dirt
    Dykstra, Lenny   75

Dr. Funk
    Eichhorn, Mark   77

Dr. Hardball
    Jeter, Derek   125

Dr. K
    Gooden, Dwight   98
    Smith, Caleb   224
    Wada, Tsuyoshi   247

Dr. Smooth
    Brantley, Michael   37

Dr. Sticks
    McKenzie, Triston   162

Dr. Strangeglove
    Stuart, Dick   233

Drago
    Garneau, Dustin   92

Dragon
    Devenski, Chris   69

Dragon Slayer
    Fogg, Josh   85

Dreamweaver
    Weaver, Jered   251

Drew
    Macias, Andres   149

D-Rob
    Robertson, Daniel   205

Robertson, Dave	205

D-Rod

Rodríguez, Dereck	207

D-Span

Span, Keiunta	227

DT

Cromer, David	61

D-Train

Willis, Dontrelle	257

Dub

Sabathia, Carsten	212
Werth, Jayson	253

Duck

Duke, Martin	74
Pattin, Marty	189
Shifflett, Garland	221

Duck Eye

Thomas, Myles	238

Ducky

Detweiler, Robert	69
Hale, George	104
Hemp, William	111
Holmes, Howard	118
Holmes, James	118
Jones, Bob	126
LeJohn, Don	143
Medwick, Joseph	164
Oertel, Chuck	184
Pearce, William	189
Schofield, Dick	216
Tillman, Johnny	239
Yount, Herbert	263

Ducky-Wucky

Medwick, Joseph	164

Dud

Branom, Edgar	36
Lee, Ernest	142

Dude

Derringer, Samuel	68
Duda, Lucas	73
Esterbrook, Thomas	79
Griffin, Doug	101
Latham, Arlie	140
McCormack, Mike	159

Duffman

Duffy, Matt	74

Duffy

Dyer, Don	75
Lewis, George	144

Dugan

Phelan, Art	192

Duke

Brett, Herbert	37
Carmel, Leon	46
Derringer, Samuel	68
Dillinger, Robert	70
Esper, Charles	79
Farrell, Charles	81
Gregerson, Luke	100
Houck, Byron	119
Kelleher, Albert	130
Kenworthy, William	132
Klobedanz, Fred	134
Maas, Duane	149
Massa, Gordon	155
Reilley, Alexander	201
Schlueter, Norm	215
Sedgwick, Henry	218
Shirey, Clair	221
Simpson, Thomas	222
Sims, Duane	223
Snider, Edwin	226
Wathan, John	250
Welker, Matt	252

Duke of Duckout

Poffenberger, Cletus	194

Duke of Flatbush

Duke of Paducah

Snider, Edwin 226
Duke of Paducah
Roof, Philip 208
Duke of Tralee
Bresnahan, Roger 37
Dukie
Tipton, Eric 240
Dumb Dumb
Williams, Mitch 256
Dummy
Deegan, William 67
Dundon, Ed 74
Hoy, William 120
Leitner, George M 143
Lynch, Matthew 149
Murphy, Herbert 176
Stephenson, Reuben 230
Taylor, Luther 236
Dumpling
Childs, Clarence 51
Dupee
Shaw, Frederick 220
Durango Kid
Seale, Johnnie 218
Duster
Mails, John 151
Shoun, Clyde 221
Dusty
Baker, Johnnie 21
Cooke, Allen 57
Kravitz, Danny 137
Miller, Charles 168
Miller, Dakin 168
Parnell, Mel 188
Rhoads, Bob 203
Rhodes, Charlie 203
Rhodes, James 203
Rhodes, John 203
Wathan, Dustin 250

Dut
Chalmers, George 49
Dutch
Bamberger, Harold 22
Beck, Ervin 25
Becker, Heinz 26
Bergman, Alfred 28
Bold, Charles 33
Bolger, James 33
Brenner, Bert 37
Bronkie, Herman 38
Browning, Frank 40
Daulton, Darren 65
Dehlman, Herman 67
Denning, Otto 68
Dietz, Lloyd 70
Distel, George 70
Dotterer, Henry 72
Drescher, Bill 73
Eunick, Ferd 79
Fehring, William 81
Flohr, Mort 85
Gehrman, Paul 93
Hartman, Frederick 108
Henry, Frank 112
Herriage, William 114
Hiller, Frank 115
Hinrichs, William 116
Hoffman, Clarence 116
Holland, Bill 117
Holland, Robert 117
Kemmerer, Russ 131
Kemner, Herman 131
Klaerner, Hugo 134
Klawitter, Al 134
Knabe, Franz 135
Kores, Art 136
Krieger, Kurt 137

Lamlein, Fred	139	Ruether, Walter	210
Legett, Lou	143	**E Jax**	
Leonard, Emil	143	Jackson, Edwin	123
Leonard, Hubert	144	**Eagle Eye**	
Lerchen, Bertram	144	Beckley, Jake	26
Levsen, Emil	144	Hemphill, Charlie	111
Lieber, Charles	145	**Earache**	
McCall, Robert	158	Meyer, Benny	167
Meier, Arthur	164	**Earl of Snohomish**	
Meister, Karl	164	Averill, Earl	20
Mele, Albert	165	Torgeson, Clifford	240
Meyer, Lambert	167	**Ears**	
Romberger, Allen	208	Mossi, Don	174
Rudolph, John	210	**Easy**	
Ruether, Walter	210	Easler, Mike	75
Scheeren, Fritz	215	Money, Don	171
Schesler, Charles	215	Poole, Jim	195
Schirick, Harry	215	Riles, Ernest	204
Schliebner, Frederick	215	**Easy J**	
Schult, Art	216	Jaso, John	124
Sterrett, Charles	230	**Ebba**	
Strauss, Joe	232	St. Claire, Edward	228
Stryker, Sterling	232	**Ebony Whip**	
Ulrich, Frank	243	Pizarro, Juan	194
Ussat, William	244	**Ed**	
Verban, Emil	246	Colgan, William	55
Weingartner, Elmer	252	Manning, Ernie	152
Welch, Herb	252	McCreery, Esley	159
Wetzel, Franklin	253	**Eddie**	
Wilson, Art	257	Rice, Edgar	203
Zwilling, Edward	264	Vargas, Hediberto	245
Dutch Master		**Eddie Mattress**	
Vander Meer, Johnny	245	Mathews, Eddie	155
Dutch Oven		**Edgar**	
Holland, Derek	117	Smith, Albert	224
Dutchman		**Edward the Mighty**	
Blyleven, Bert	32	Konetchy, Ed	136
Fritz, Harry	89	**EE**	
		Encarnacion, Edwin	78
		Effie	

Eggie

Norton, Elisha 181
Eggie
 Lennox, Ed 143
Egyptian
 Healy, John 110
Eiffel Tower
 Love, Edward 147
El Bombi
 García, Adolis 91
El Brujo
 Mendoza, Ramiro 165
El Buitre de Tecamachalco
 López, Aurelio 147
El Caballo
 Lee, Carlos 142
 Sierra, Rubén 222
El Caballo Loco
 Pagán, Ángel 187
El Cabeza
 Fernández, Tony 82
El Cañón
 Osuna, Antonio 185
El Carnicero
 Torres, Carlos 241
El Chamaquito
 Hanson, Alen 106
El Chamo
 Sanchez, Adrian 213
El Cheapo
 Rickey, Branch 203
El Chirizo
 Martínez, Dennis 154
El Coffee
 Polanco, Gregory 195
El Come Dulce
 Abreu, Bobby 13
El Conde
 Heredia, Guillermo 113
El De Guanare
 Pérez, Martín 190
El De La Pica

Escobar, Eduardo 79
El Del Penonal
 Sánchez, Yolmer 213
El Divino Loco
 Hoak, Don 116
El Duque
 Hernández, Orlando 113
El Duquecito
 Hernández, Adrián 113
El Fantasma
 Fernández, Tony 82
El Flaco
 Lamet, Dinelson 139
El fogón Boricua
 Márquez, Luis 153
El Gallo
 Batista, Rafael 24
 Myers, Wil 177
El Gasolino
 Berenguer, Juan 28
El Gatito
 Millán, Félix 168
El Gocho
 Osuna, José 185
El Goofy
 Gomez, Vernon 97
El Grande de Venezuela
 Aparicio, Luis 17
El Grandote Burro
 Brown, Lloyd 39
El Gualo
 Rodríguez, Eduardo 207
El Guapo
 Garcés, Richard 91
El Hombre Diablo
 Cueto, Manuel 62
El Hombre Goma
 Rodríguez, José 207
El Indio
 Sierra, Rubén 222
El Jaliscience

    González, Miguel   98
El Koja
    Beltré, Adrián   27
El Lanzallama
    López, Aurelio   147
El Látigo
    Navarro, Julio   178
El Látigo de Ébano
    Pizarro, Juan   194
El Lindo
    Difo, Wilmer   70
El Mago
    Báez, Javier   20
    González, Erik   98
El Mambo
    Segura, Jean   218
El Menor
    Rondon, Bruce   208
El Meteorico
    Infante, Gregory   123
El Ministro de Defensa
    Machado, Manny   149
El Molleto
    García, Leury   91
El Ni
    Solarte, Yangervis   227
El Nino
    Arcia, Orlando   18
    Pérez, Salvador   190
    Ramírez, Hanley   199
    Tatis, Fernando Jr.   236
El Nueve
    Ureña, José   244
El Oso
    Alfaro, Jorge   15
El Oso Blanco
    Gattis, Evan   92
El Pajaro
    Cabrera, Al   44
El Panqué de Haina

    Alou, Felipe   16
El Papa
    Martinez, Edgar   155
El Penaco
    Robles, Hansel   206
El Pocho
    Alvarado, José   16
El Presidente
    Martínez, Dennis   154
El Pulpo
    Alfonseca, Antonio   15
El Rubio
    Bibens-Dirkx, Austin   30
El Sid
    Fernandez, Sid   82
El Talento
    Céspedes, Yoenis   49
El Tanque
    Tomás, Yasmany   240
El Tiante
    Tiant, Luis   239
El Tipo
    Odor, Rougned   184
El Titan
    González, Adrián   97
El Titere
    Gómez, Carlos   97
El Torito
    Herrera, Odúbel   114
El Toro
    Álvarez, Pedro   16
    Valenzuela, Fernando   244
    Zambrano, Carlos   263
El Trece
    Ramírez, Hanley   199
El Varon
    Almonte, Abraham   15
Eli
    Hodkey, Aloysius   116
Elmer

Elrod

McGuire, Tom 162
Schwartz, Bill C 217
Elrod
McLean, Al 163
Emerson Lake And
Palmeiro, Rafael 187
Entertainer
Alvarez, Henderson 16
Epp
Sell, Lester 218
Eppa
Johnson, Lloyd 126
Eppie
Barnes, Everett 23
Miller, Eddie 168
Eric the Red
Davis, Eric 65
Tipton, Eric 240
Ernie
Vick, Henry 246
Erston
Donalds, Ed 71
Erv
Lange, Erwin 139
ET
May, Rudy 157
McGee, Willie 160
Eude
Curtis, Gene 62
Ev
Williams, Trevor 256
Evangelist
Foster, Eddie 86
Sunday, Billy 234
Eve of Destruction
McGwire, Mark 162
Every Day
Elston, Don 78
Everyday Eddie
Guardado, Eddie 102

EY
Young, Eric Sr. 262
Eye Chart
Mientkiewicz, Doug 167
Eyechart
Gwosdz, Doug 103
Ez
Charles, Ed 50
EZ Mac
McAllister, Zach 158
Famous Amos
Otis, Amos 185
Famous Slow Pitcher
Cuppy, George 62
Fancy
O'Neil, Michael 183
Farmboy
Young, Denton 262
Farmer
Bell, George G 27
Burns, James 42
Moore, Ray 172
Ray, Robert 200
Smalley, Will 224
Steelman, Morris 230
Vaughn, Henry 245
Weaver, William 251
Young, Denton 262
Fast Mail
Mailho, Emil 151
Fat Elvis
Berkman, Lance 28
Fat Freddie
Fitzsimmons, Freddie 84
Fat Ichiro
Sandoval, Pablo 213
Fat Jack
Fisher, Jack 84
Fat Pat
Seerey, Pat 218

Father
    Kelly, John F   131
Fats
    Berger, Joe   28
    Childs, Clarence   51
    Dantonio, John   64
    Fothergill, Bob   86
    Kalin, Frank   128
Fatso
    Sloan, Bruce   223
Fatty
    Briody, Frank   38
    Childs, Clarence   51
    Fothergill, Bob   86
Federalist
    Jay, Jon   125
Fedex
    Federowicz, Tim   81
Felix
    Ayala, Benigno   20
Fibber
    McGhee, Bill   160
Fiddler
    Basinski, Edwin   24
    Corridon, Frank   58
Fiddler Bill
    McGee, Bill   160
Fidgety Phil
    Collins, Philip   55
Fido
    Baldwin, Mark   22
Fien Machine
    Fien, Casey   83
Fighting Harry
    Wolverton, Harry   259
Filbert
    Pierce, George   193
Filipino
    Altizer, David   16
Filthy Fulmer
    Fulmer, Carson   89
Filthy McNasty
    Gallagher, Alan   90
Final Boss
    Oh, Seunghwan   184
Finger Nail Artist
    Savidge, Ralph   214
Finn
    Barry, Hardin   24
Fire
    Cleary, Joe   53
    Trucks, Virgil   242
Fire Chief
    Rogell, Billy   207
Fireball
    Wenz, Fred   252
Firebrand
    Stovall, George   231
Firefly
    Porter, JW   195
Fireman
    Beggs, Joseph   26
    Casey, Hugh   48
    Jackson, Luke   124
    Murphy, Johnny   176
    Page, Joe   187
Firpo
    Marberry, Fred   152
    Pyle, Harlan   197
Fish Hook
    Stout, Allyn   231
Fitz
    French, Walt   88
Five-For-One
    Hayes, Von   110
Flaco
    Chavez, Jesse   51
    Martinez, Julio   155
    Pérez, Atanasio   190
Flaco Fuerte

Flame

Archer, Chris	18
Flame	
Delhi, Lee	68
Flame Thrower	
Fanok, Harry	81
Flash	
Archdeacon, Maurice	18
Fallon, George	81
Flaherty, John	84
Flaherty, Ryan	84
Flaskamper, Ray	85
Gilhooley, Frank	95
Gordon, Joe	98
Gordon, Tom	98
Maisel, Frederick	151
Flash Gordon Jr.	
Strange-Gordon, Dee	232
Flea	
Clifton, Herman	54
Patek, Freddie	189
Fleet Pete	
Bourjos, Peter	34
Fleury	
Sullivan, Florence	233
Flip	
Filipowicz, Steve	83
Lafferty, Frank	138
Paine, Phil	187
Rosen, Al	209
Flip Flap	
Jones, Oscar	127
Flipper	
Fernández, Tony	82
Flit	
Cramer, Roger	59
Floppy	
Hartung, Clint	109
Florida Flamingo	
Causey, Cecil	49
Flossie	
Oberlin, Frank	183
Fluff	
Weaver, Jim B	251
Flunky	
Willoughby, Claude	257
Flushing Flash	
Glynn, Ed	96
Fly	
Jenkins, Fergie	125
Flyin' Hawaiian	
Victorino, Shane	246
Flying Dutchman	
Long, Herman	146
Wagner, John	247
Flying Foot	
Strunk, Amos	232
Flying Scot	
Thomson, Bobby	239
Foghorn	
Bradley, George H.	36
Miller, George	168
Myatt, George	177
Tucker, Tommy	242
Foghorn Dick	
Van Zant, Dick	245
Fonzie	
Alfonzo, Edgardo	15
Footer	
Johnson, Richard	126
Footie	
Ockey, Walter	183
Foots	
Barfoot, Clyde	22
Cress, Walker	60
Footsie	
Blair, Clarence	31
Lenhardt, Don	143
Marcum, Johnny	152
Fordham Flash	
Frisch, Frankie	88

Fordham Johnny
    Murphy, Johnny   176
Forrest Gump
    Reynolds, Mark   203
Fort
    McKenry, Michael   162
Fort McKenry
    McKenry, Michael   162
Four Sack
    Dusak, Erv   75
Fox
    Bridges, Marshall   38
Foxy
    Irwin, Arthur   123
    Taylor, Arlas   236
Foxy Grandpa
    Bannon, James   22
Foxy Ned
    Hanlon, Ed   106
FP
    Santangelo, Frank-Paul   213
Franchise
    Brock, Lou   38
    Clark, Will   52
    Clemens, Roger   53
    Davis, Eric   65
    Dykstra, Lenny   75
    Gooden, Dwight   98
    Griffey, Ken Jr.   101
    Henderson, Rickey   112
    Lincecum, Tim   145
    Mattingly, Don   156
    Puckett, Kirby   197
    Ripken, Cal Jr.   204
    Sandberg, Ryne   213
    Santiago, Benny   213
    Sears, George   218
    Seaver, Tom   218
    Sierra, Rubén   222
    Strawberry, Darryl   232
    Trammell, Alan   241
    Yount, Robin   263
    Zeile, Todd   263
Frank
    Bates, Creed   24
    Freund, Lawrence   88
    Morrissey, Michael   174
Frankenberry
    Thompson, Rich N   239
Frankie
    De La Cruz, Frankie   66
    Rodriguez, Francisco   207
Freak
    Lincecum, Tim   145
Freaky Franchise
    Lincecum, Tim   145
Freck
    Owen, Marv   186
Fred
    House, Willard   120
    Jankowski, Travis   124
    Knouff, Ed   135
Freddy
    Rodriguez, Fernando   207
Free Love
    Arroyo, Bronson   19
Freezy
    Freeman, Sam   88
Freight Train
    Peralta, David   190
Frenchie
    Coulombe, Danny   58
Frenchman
    Kremer, Remy   137
    Lajoie, Nap   138
Frenchy
    Bordagaray, Stanley   34
    Fournier, Henry   86
    Francoeur, Jeff   87

Genins, Frank	93	Tettleton, Mickey	237
LeBlanc, Wade	142	**Frosty**	
LeClair, George	142	Thomas, Forrest	238
Raymond, Claude	200	**Frosty Bill**	
Uhalt, Bernard	243	Duggleby, Bill	74
Fresh Prince		**Frying Dutchman**	
Altherr, Aaron	16	Blyleven, Bert	32
Smith, Will	226	**Fuego**	
Freshest Man on Earth		Feliz, Michael	82
Latham, Arlie	140	Lucchesi, Joey	148
Friday		**Fullpack**	
Zastryzny, Rob	263	Stanhouse, Don	229
Fritz		**Fulm Piece**	
Blanding, Frederick	31	Fulmer, Michael	89
Bratschi, Fred	37	**Fun Police**	
Buelow, Fred	41	McCann, Brian	158
Clausen, Frederick	53	**Fuzz**	
Coumbe, Fred	58	White, Albert	253
Dorish, Harry	72	**Fuzzy**	
Fisher, Frederick	84	Richards, Fred	203
Heimach, Fred	111	Smith, Al	224
Henrich, Frank	112	**Gabby**	
Knothe, Wilfred	135	Cassini, Jack	48
Koster, Fred	136	Glenn, Joe	96
Lucas, Fred	148	Grabarkewitz, Billy	99
Maisel, Frederick	151	Hartnett, Charles	109
Marolewski, Fred	153	Jolly, Dave	126
Mollwitz, Frederick	171	Olerud, John	184
Odwell, Fred	184	Roseboro, John	209
Ostermueller, Frederick	185	Sandberg, Ryne	213
Peterson, Fred	191	Stewart, Glen	230
Pfeffer, Fred	191	Street, Charles	232
Schulte, Fred	216	**Gabe**	
Von Kolnitz, Alfred	247	Gabler, William	89
Froggy		Gebrian, Pete	93
DeMaestri, Joe	68	**Gadget Man**	
Hands, Bill	106	Fernández, Tony	82
Froot Loops		**Gallatin Squash**	
		Perdue, Herbert	190
		Galleguito	

Zimmer, Don 264
Gambler
Rogers, Kenny 207
Gander
Stratton, Monty 232
Gar
Martinez, Edgar 155
Garv Sauce
Garver, Mitch 92
Gary
Gearhart, Lloyd 93
Gas Can
Clark, Bryan 52
Gat
Stires, Garret 231
Gates
Brown, William J 40
Gator
Brown, William J 40
Garr, Ralph 92
Greenwell, Mike 100
Guidry, Ron 102
Gause Ghost
Moore, Jo-Jo 172
Gavvy
Cravath, Clifford 60
Gay Caballero
Gomez, Vernon 97
Gay Reliever
Page, Joe 187
Gazook
Gazella, Mike 93
Gee
Walker, Gerald 248
Gee-Gee
Getz, Gus 94
Gleeson, Jim 96
Geek
Shaw, Bryan 220
Geets

Knudson, Guido 135
General
Crowder, Alvin 61
Sherman, Dan 221
Stafford, James 228
Geno
Espineli, Eugene 79
Gentle Jeems
Galvin, James 90
Gentle Willie
Murphy, Willie 176
Gentleman George
Decker, George A 67
Haddock, George 103
Stallings, George 229
Gentleman Jim
Hickman, Jim 114
Gentleman Joe
Schepner, Joe 215
Gentleman John
Enzmann, Johnny 78
Gentleman's Hurler
Mathewson, Christy 155
Gentlemanly Bob
Clack, Bobby 52
George
De La Rosa, Jorge 67
Reddick, Josh 201
Washington, Sloan 250
Georgia Express
Moses, Wally 174
Georgia Peach
Cobb, Ty 54
Gerbil
Lasorda, Tommy 140
Zimmer, Don 264
German Ambassador
Selbach, Albert 218
Germany
Long, Herman 146

Gettysburg Eddie

Schaefer, William	214	**Gink**	
Schmit, Frederick	216	Fowler, Joseph	87
Schultz, Joe Sr.	217	Hendrick, Harvey	112
Smith, George J	225	**Gint**	
Gettysburg Eddie		Channell, Les	50
Plank, Eddie	194	**Gio**	
Ghost		González, Giovany	98
McNally, Mike	163	**Gitz**	
Ghoul		Miller, Warren	169
Rivera, Mariano	205	**Giz**	
GI Jones		Sabo, Alex	212
Jones, Garrett	127	**Gladiator**	
Giambino		Browning, Louis	40
Giambi, Jason	94	**Glass Arm**	
Giant Killer		Brown, Eddie	39
Coveleski, Harry	59	**Glenn**	
Pfiester, Jack	191	Bolton, Cecil	33
Gibby		**Glider**	
Brack, Gilbert	35	Charles, Ed	50
Gibson, George	95	**Globetrotter**	
Pruess, Earl	197	Roth, Robert	209
Gid		**Gloomy Gus**	
Gardner, Franklin	91	Williams, Gus	256
Gil		**Glove**	
Gallagher, Lawrence	90	Boyer, Clete	35
Gill of the Shamrock		**Glove Doctor**	
Gearin, Dennis	93	Patterson, Bob	189
Gilly		**G-Man**	
Bigelow, Elliot	30	Gaetti, Gary	90
Huber, Clarence	121	Gsellman, Robert	102
Gimpy		Knudson, Guido	135
Brown, Lloyd	39	**G-Money**	
Pappas, Milt	187	Laird, Gerald	138
Ginger		**Gnat**	
Beaumont, Clarence	25	Bowa, Larry	35
Betts, Harry	29	**Go Go**	
Clark, Harvey	52	Goins, Ryan	97
Shinault, Enoch	221	**Goat**	
Ginger Kid		Anderson, Edward	17
Weaver, George	251	Channell, Les	50
		Cochran, Al	54

Thomas, Chester	238	Peden, Les	189
Gob		**Good Eye**	
Buckeye, Garland	41	Shinnick, Tim	221
God's Gift		**Good Kid**	
Trout, Mike	242	Boudreau, Lou	34
Godzilla		Susce, George	234
Matsui, Hideki	156	**Good Time Bill**	
Goggy		Lamar, Bill	139
Meara, Charlie	164	**Goody**	
Go-Go		Simpson, Harry	222
Gómez, Carlos	97	**Goofy**	
Goldbrick		Gomez, Vernon	97
Butler, Frank B	43	**Goofy Joe**	
Golden Boy		Gonzales, Joe	97
Brown, Robert	40	**Gookie**	
Jensen, Jackie	125	Dawkins, Travis	66
Golden Greek		**Gooney Bird**	
Agganis, Harry	14	Larsen, Don	140
Chakales, Bob	49	**Goopy**	
Triandos, Gus	241	Goeddel, Erik	97
Golden Greek of Chesapeake		**Goose**	
Triandos, Gus	241	Easton, John	76
Golden West Receiver		Goslin, Leon	98
Thomas, Chester	238	Gossage, Rich	99
Goldie		Gosselin, Phil	99
Rapp, Joseph	200	Gozzo, Mauro	99
Gomer		**Gor**	
Hodge, Harold	116	Command, Jim	56
Osteen, Claude	185	**Gordo**	
Gonzalo		Blevins, Jerry	32
Naranjo, Lazaro	178	**Gorfax**	
Gonzo		Gorman, Tom P	98
Gonzalez, Luis	98	**Gorgeous**	
Goob		Bourjos, Peter	34
Gruber, Kelly	102	**Gorgeous George**	
Goober		Sisler, George	223
Zuber, Bill	264	**Gorilla**	
Goobers		Gilliford, Paul	95
Bratcher, Joe	37	**Goshen Schoolmaster**	
Gooch		Leever, Sam	142

Governor

Governor
    Brown, William J   40
    Browne, Jerry   40
    Ellerbe, Frank   77
Grand Old Gentleman
    McGillicuddy, Cornelius   161
Grand Old Man of Baseball
    Mack, Connie   149
    McGillicuddy, Cornelius   161
Grande Rojo
    Boyer, Blaine   35
Grandma
    Murphy, Johnny   176
Grandmother
    Powers, Phil   196
Grandpa
    Dickerson, Alex   69
    Wolf, Ray   259
Grandy Man
    Granderson, Curtis   99
Grapefruit
    Robinson, Wilbert   206
Grasshopper
    Lillie, Jim   145
    Mains, Willard   151
    Whitney, Jim   254
Gravedigger
    Hebner, Richie   110
Gray Flamingo
    Brennan, Tom   37
Greased Pole
    Coveleski, Stanley   59
Greasy
    Neale, Alfred   178
Great
    Mails, John   151
    Scott, George   217
Great Gabbo
    Gabler, Frank   89
Great Hambino
    Hamilton, Josh   105
Great Hercules of Baseball
    Radbourn, Charles   198
Great Man
    Dean, Jay   67
Great One
    Clemente, Roberto   53
Great Zim
    Zimmerman, Henry   264
Greek
    George, Charles   94
    Solters, Julius   227
Greek God of Walks
    Youkilis, Kevin   262
Greenfield Jimmy
    Smith, Jimmy L   225
Greenie
    Greenberg, Hank   100
Grey Eagle
    Speaker, Tris   228
Grim Bimbledon
    McLaughlin, Michael   163
Grin
    Bradley, George W.   36
Groove
    Baylor, Don   25
Ground Chuck
    Morton, Charlie   174
Grounded Blimp
    Phelps, Ernest   192
Groves
    Grove, Robert   102
Grump
    Irelan, Hal   123
    Miller, Ward   169
Grumpy
    Clymer, Otis   54
Grunting Jim
    Shaw, Jim   220
Guarenero

Adrianza, Ehire   14
Guesses
   Virtue, Jake   246
Guido
   Quilici, Frank   198
Guinea
   Jolley, Smead   126
Guineo
   Zardón, José   263
Gulfport
   Ryan, Jack   211
Gulliver
   Lehner, Paul   143
Gum
   Charles, Ed   50
Gumby
   Gantner, Jim   91
   Montgomery, Jordan   171
Gummy
   Wall, Joe   248
Gun Boots
   Mathewson, Christy   155
Gunboat
   Gumbert, Harry   102
Gunner
   Cantrell, Guy   46
   McGunnigle, Bill   162
   Reeves, Bobby   201
Gus
   Bell, David R   26
   Bono, Adlai   33
   Keriazakos, Constantine   132
   Niarhos, Constantine   180
   Wynn, Early   261
Gussie
   Gannon, James   91
Guv'nor
   Browne, Jerry   40
Gyp
   Salvo, Manny   212

Hack
   Engle, Clyde   78
   Ennis, Russ   78
   Gibson, George   95
   Hebner, Richie   110
   Miller, James   168
   Miller, Laurence   169
   Schumann, Charles   217
   Simmons, George   222
   Spencer, Fred   228
   Wilson, Lew   257
Hackenschmidt
   Spencer, Edward   228
Hacker
   Hebner, Richie   110
   Sasser, Mackey   214
Hacksaw
   Gomes, Jonny   97
HacMan
   Leonard, Jeffrey   144
Haddie
   Gill, Harold   95
Hakuna Machado
   Machado, Manny   149
Hal
   Luby, Hugh   147
   Mauck, Alfred   156
   Toenes, William   240
Half Moon
   Molleken, Dustin   171
Half Pint
   Rye, Gene   211
Half-Pint
   Leibold, Harry   143
Ham
   Allen, Frank   15
   Connolly, Tom   56
   Schulte, Herman   216
Hamilton Joe
   Nuxhall, Joe   182

Hammer

Hammer
    Aaron, Henry   13
    Hammel, Jason   105
    Milner, John   170
    Willingham, Josh   256
Hammerhead
    Keen, Bill   130
Hammerin' Hank
    Aaron, Henry   13
Hammerin' Cameron
    Maybin, Cameron   157
Hammerin' Hank
    Greenberg, Hank   100
Handsom Ransom
    Jackson, Randy   124
Handsome Dan
    Murphy, Danny   176
Handsome Harry
    McIntire, John   162
    Suter, Harry   234
Handsome Henry
    Boyle, Henry   35
Handsome Hugh
    McQuillan, Alvin   164
Handsome Jack
    Carney, Jack   46
Handsome Lou
    Boudreau, Lou   34
Handy Andy
    High, Andy   115
    Pafko, Andy   187
Haney
    Boney, Henry   33
Hank
    Allen, Harold   15
    Conger, Hyun   56
    DeBerry, John   67
    Garrity, Francis   92
    Griffin, James   101
    Hulvey, James   122
    Karlon, Bill   129
    LaManna, Frank   139
    McCurdy, Harry   159
    Miklos, John   167
    Riebe, Harvey   204
    Ritter, William   204
    Robinson, John H   206
    Thormahlen, Herbert   239
Hank White
    Blanco, Henry   31
Hankus Pankus
    Wyse, Hank   261
Han-Ram
    Ramírez, Hanley   199
Hans
    Ables, Harry   13
    Barthold, John   24
    Grube, Frank   102
    Kluber, Corey   134
    Lobert, John   146
    Miller, John B.   169
    Rasmussen, Henry   200
    Wagner, John   247
    Wittig, Johnnie   259
Hans No. 2
    Miller, John B.   169
Hans Number Two
    Lobert, John   146
Hap
    Collard, Earl   55
    Huhn, Emil   122
    Morse, Pete   174
    Myers, Ralph   177
    Ward, Joseph   250
Happer
    Happ, James   106
Happy
    Bellman, Jack   27
    Buker, Henry   41

Cameron, Jack	45
Chesbro, Jack	51
Feliz, Pedro	82
Felsch, Oscar	82
Finneran, Joseph	83
Foreman, August	86
Hartnett, Pat	109
Hollahan, Bill	117
Hooton, Burt	118
Iott, Frederick	123
Jolley, Smead	126
Kibble, Jack	132
McKain, Archie	162
Milnar, Al	170
Neris, Héctor	179
Peña, Ariel	189
Rojek, Stan	208
Smith, Henry	225
Stivetts, Jack	231
Townsend, John	241
Ward, Joe	250
Hard	
Knox, Cliff	135
Hard Hittin'	
Whiten, Mark	254
Hard Luck	
Horlen, Joe	119
Hardrock	
Johnson, Roy	126
Shoun, Clyde	221
Harlem	
Turk, Lucas	242
Harlem Joe	
Kiefer, Joe	132
Harry	
Baldwin, Howard	22
Fuller, Henry	89
Hannah, James	106
McCormick, Patrick	159
McIntire, John	162
McNeal, John	163
Niles, Herbert	181
Vaughn, Henry	245
Harry the Hat	
Walker, Harry	248
Harry the Horse	
Anderson, Harry	17
Danning, Harry	64
Heilmann, Harry	111
Hartford Jack	
Farrell, Jack	81
Harvard Eddie	
Grant, Eddie	99
Hat	
Lynch, Jerry	148
Hawaiian Hustle	
Kiner-Falefa, Isiah	133
Hawk	
Branca, Ralph	36
Carroll, Clay	47
Dawson, Andre	66
Harrelson, Ken	107
Mueller, Bill	175
Pointer, Aaron	195
Shanks, Howie	219
Silvestri, Kenneth	222
Taylor, Robert	236
Head	
Hollins, Dave	117
Headley	
Hollins, Dave	117
Heap	
McCann, Brian	158
Heater	
Bell, Heath	27
Hembree, Heath	111
Heater from Van Meter	

Heathcliff

Feller, Bob	82	Cruz, Hector	61
Heathcliff		**Hellboy**	
Johnson, Cliff	125	Hellickson, Jeremy	111
Heave-O		**Hendu**	
Hafey, Tom	104	Henderson, Dave	111
Heavy		**Henrietta Hawk**	
Blair, Walter	31	Harrelson, Ken	107
Wheeler, George	253	**Hep**	
Hebrew Hammer		Niles, Herbert	181
Braun, Ryan	37	**Herb**	
Kapler, Gabe	129	Brenton, Lynn	37
Rosen, Al	209	**Herbie**	
Heck		Hrbek, Kent	121
Heifer, Frank	111	**Hercules**	
Heeney		Crane, Ed	59
Majeski, Hank	151	**Herky**	
Heinie		Hinrichs, Paul	116
Batch, Emil	24	**Herky Jerky**	
Beckendorf, Henry	25	Horton, Elmer	119
Berger, Charles	28	**Herm**	
Groh, Henry	101	Doscher, John	72
Heitmuller, William	111	Reddick, Josh	201
Heltzel, William	111	**Herm the Worm**	
Kappel, Henry	129	Herrmann, Chris	114
Manush, Henry	152	**Herman**	
Meine, Henry	164	Reddick, Josh	201
Mueller, Clarence	175	**Hermit**	
Mueller, Emmet	175	Gearin, Dennis	93
Peitz, Henry	189	**Hermosa Hermit**	
Reitz, Henry	202	Killefer, Wade	133
Sand, John	213	**Hi**	
Scheer, Henry	215	Bell, Herman	27
Schuble, Henry	216	Ladd, Arthur	138
Smith, George H	225	Myers, Henry	177
Stafford, Henry	228	**Hibernian-Hildago**	
Wagner, Charles F	247	Gomez, Vernon	97
Zimmerman, Henry	264	**Hick**	
Heity		Cady, Forrest	44
		Carpenter, Warren	46
		Hickey	

Holy

    Hoffman, William   117
Hickory
    Dickson, Walt   70
    Jackson, George   123
    Johnson, Elmer   125
    Solomon, Mose   227
Hickory Bob
    Harmon, Bob   107
Hicks
    Moren, Lew   173
High Pockets
    Hunt, Ben   122
    Kelly, George   131
Highball
    Wilson, Howard   257
Highpockets
    Gregg, Dave   100
Highway to
    Helton, Todd   111
Hiker
    Moran, Albert   172
Hillbilly
    Bildilli, Emil   30
Hinkey
    Haines, Henry   104
Hippity
    Hopp, Johnny   119
Hippo
    Spencer, Edward   228
    Vaughn, Jim   245
Hit 'Em Where They Ain't
    Keeler, Willie   130
Hit Dog
    Vaughn, Mo   245
Hit Man
    Easler, Mike   75
    Mattingly, Don   156
Hit Manufacturing Machine
    Suzuki, Ichiro   234
Hits McGehee
    McGehee, Casey   160
Hitting Machine
    Kim, Hyun Soo   133
Hob
    Hiller, Harvey   115
Hobbsy
    Olerud, John   184
Hobby
    Habenicht, Bob   103
    Hiller, Harvey   115
Hobe
    Ferris, Albert   83
Hoboken Harp
    Carey, Tom   46
Hod
    Eller, Horace   77
    Fenner, Horace   82
    Ford, Horace   86
    Kibbie, Horace   132
    Leverette, Horace   144
    Lisenbee, Horace   145
Hodge
    Berry, Joe Sr.   29
Hoge
    Workman, Harry   260
HoJo
    Johnson, Howard   126
Hoke
    Dillinger, Harley   70
Holley
    Hoelskoetter, Art   116
Hollick
    Cady, Forrest   44
Hollywood
    Bradley, Archie   36
    Hamels, Cole   105
    Snell, Rick   227
    Wright, David   261
Holy
    Good, Ralph   98

Homage

Homage
    Storen, Drew   231
Home Run
    Baker, John   21
    Duffee, Charlie   73
    Johnson, Charlie   125
    Marshall, Joe   153
    Maxwell, Charlie   157
    Niles, Herbert   181
Homer
    Bailey, David   21
Hondo
    Hollmig, Stan   118
    Howard, Frank   120
Hondo Hurricane
    Hartung, Clint   109
Honest
    Anderson, John   17
    Boyle, John   35
    Eubank, John   79
    Godwin, John   96
    Hummel, John   122
    Kelly, John F   131
    Kelly, John O   131
    Morrill, John   173
    Murphy, Eddie   176
    Niland, Tom   181
    Phillips, Bill C   192
Honey
    Barnes, John   23
    Romano, John   208
Honey Bear
    Rayford, Floyd   200
Honey Boy
    Paskert, George   188
Honker
    Branca, Ralph   36
    Sauer, Hank   214
Honolulu Johnny
    Williams, Johnnie   256
Honus
    Lobert, John   146
    Wagner, John   247
Hook
    Carter, Arnold   47
    Henry, Earl   112
    Johnson, Ken   126
    Todt, Phil   240
Hooker
    Whitman, Frank   254
Hooks
    Cotter, Harvey   58
    Dauss, George   65
    Lind, Carl   145
    Miller, Bill P   168
    Warner, Hoke   250
    Wiltse, George   258
    Wyse, Hank   261
Hoosier Hammer
    Klein, Chuck   134
Hoosier Thunderbolt
    Rusie, Amos   210
Hoot
    Evers, Walt   80
    Gibson, Bob   95
    Pearson, Monte   189
    Rice, Hal   203
    Trosky, Hal   242
Hoover
    Robinson, Brooks   206
    White, Frank   253
Hopalong
    Howerton, Bill   120
Horn
    Sauer, Ed   214
Horse
    Brown, Lew   39
    Cain, Matt   44

Colomé, Alex	55	Perdue, Herbert	190
Lee, Bob	142	Pernoll, Henry	190
Mohorcic, Dale	171	Walker, Harvey	248
Orsino, John	185	Yount, Herbert	263

Horse Belly

Hubba Hubba

Sargent, Joe	214	Vincent, Nick	246

Horse Face

Hubby

Williams, Ken	256	Walker, Harvey	248

Hoss

Huck

Bowlin, Weldon	35	Betts, Walter	29
Brown, Lew	39	Conover, Theodore	57
Clarke, Horace	52	Flener, Gregory	85
Hoelskoetter, Art	116	Geary, Eugene	93
Korchek, Steve	136	Sawyer, Carl	214
Morton, Guy Jr.	174	Wallace, Harry	249

Hot Potato

Hamlin, Lewis	105	Romo, Vicente	208

Hot Rod

Huff Daddy

Kanehl, Rod	129	Huff, Aubrey	121
McDonald, Jim	160		

Hotshot

Hug

Mayo, Eddie	157	Huggins, Miller	121

Houdini

Hugo

Robertson, Dave	205	Canavan, Hugh	45

How-Bouta-Beer Bambino

Hulk

Ruth, George	211	Schwarber, Kyle	217

Howdy

Human Crab

Caton, James	49	Evers, Johnny	80
Groskloss, Howard	102		

Human Crash Test Dummy

Howdy-Doody

Evans, Darrell	79	Byrnes, Eric	43

Howie

Human Eyeball

Haworth, Homer	110	Lord, Bris	147

Howling Dan

Human Giraffe

Howley, Dan	120	Love, Edward	147

Hub

Human Hatpin

Harris, Herb	108	Weaver, Art	251
Hart, James	108		

Human Office Building

Knolls, Oscar	135	Love, Edward	147

Human Rain Delay

Báez, Pedro	21	
Hargrove, Mike	107	

Human Ripcord
   Savidge, Ralph   214
Human Skyscraper
   Weilman, Carl   252
Human Vacuum Cleaner
   Robinson, Brooks   206
Hummer
   DeArmond, Charlie   67
   Drott, Dick   73
Humpty
   McElveen, Pryor   160
Humpty Dumpty
   Nixon, Al   181
   Polhemus, Mark   195
Hungarian Hot Shot
   Martin, Boris   154
Hungo
   Hrabosky, Al   120
Hunky
   Hines, Henry   115
   Shaw, Royal   220
Hunnie
   Huhn, Emil   122
Hurling Hub
   Perdue, Herbert   190
Hurricane
   Hazle, Bob   110
Hurricane Hal
   Newhouser, Hal   179
Hurricane Herb
   Washington, Herb   250
Husk
   Chance, Frank   50
   Mathewson, Christy   156
Husky
   Glenn, Harry   96
   Walczak, Ed   248
Hustler from Hustletown
   Latham, Arlie   140
Hustling Dan
   O'Leary, Dan   182

Hy
   Myers, Henry   177
   Vandenberg, Harold   245
Hypie
   Rowe, Harland   209
I Believe
   Vogt, Stephen   247
I-285
   Pérez, Pascual   190
Ice
   Williams, Gerald   255
Ice Box
   Chamberlain, Elton   49
Ice Horse
   Chavis, Michael   51
Ice Man
   Mantei, Matt   152
Icehouse
   Wilson, George P   257
Ichi
   Suzuki, Ichiro   235
Icicle
   Fisler, Wes   84
   Reeder, Julius   201
IE
   Schroll, Al   216
If You Got 'Em
   Slocumb, Heath   224
Ignitor
   Molitor, Paul   171
Igor
   Command, Jim   56
   González, Juan   98
Ike
   Blessitt, Isaiah   32
   Boone, Raymond   34
   Brookens, Edward   38
   Caveney, James   49
   Corey, Ed   58
   Corrales, Pat   58

Danning, Isaac	64	Harrist, Earl	108
Davis, Isaac B	66	Higgins, Eddie	115
Davis, Isaac M	66	McCloskey, Jim	158
Fisher, Isaac	84	McIlveen, Henry	162
Hampton, Isaac	105	Meusel, Emil	167
Kahdot, Isaac	128	Miggins, Larry	167
Kamp, Alphonse	128	Ryan, Mike	211
McAuley, James	158		
Powers, John	196		
Samuels, Samuel	212		
Van Zandt, Charles	245		

I-Rod
    Rodríguez, Iván   207

Immortal Azcue
    Azcue, José   20

Iron Batter
    Pike, Lipman   193

Imp
    Begley, James   26

Iron Duke
    Hall, Herb   105
    Kenworthy, William   132

Impaler
    Guerrero, Vlad   102

Iron Glove
    Stuart, Dick   233

Inch
    Gleich, Frank   96

Iron Horse
    Gehrig, Lou   93

Incredible Hulk
    Downing, Brian   72

Iron Man
    Bader, Lore   20
    Campbell, Archie   45
    Kim, Hyun Soo   133
    McGinnity, Joe   161
    McGlynn, Ulysses   161
    Mueller, Ray   175
    Mulcahy, Hugh   175
    Piatt, Wiley   192
    Ripken, Cal Jr.   204
    Starr, Ray   229
    Wensloff, Charles   252
    Williams, Billy   255
    Williams, Rees   256

Indian Bob
    Johnson, Bob   125

Ing
    Hansen, Roy I   106

Inky
    Strange, Alan   232

Innocent Until Proven
    Gilkey, Bernard   95

Inspector
    Caudill, Bill   49

Intrepid Nimrod
    Scott, Jim   217

Iron Man Pitcher
    Lotz, Joe   147

IPK
    Kennedy, Ian   132

Iron Pony
    Alomar, Santos (Conde)   15

Irish
    Conwell, Ed   57
    Corhan, Roy   58
    Fox, Charlie   87

Ironsides
    Gomes, Jonny   97

Italian Paisano

Itzzy

    Brovia, Joe   39
Itzzy
    Feinberg, Eddie   82
Ivory Pate
    Merkle, Fred   166
Izzy
    Hoffman, Harry   116
    Van Zandt, Charles   245
J Hay
    Harrison, Josh   108
J.C.
    Romero, Juan   208
JA
    Happ, James   106
Jabber
    Lynch, Walt   149
Jabbo
    Jablonski, Ray   123
Jabby
    Appleton, Peter   18
Jack
    Allen, Cyrus   15
    Aragón, Angel   18
    Barrett, John   23
    Cassel, Joseph   48
    Compton, Harry   56
    Dalton, Tolbert   63
    Darragh, James   64
    Dooms, Harry   72
    Enzenroth, Clarence   78
    Farmer, Floyd   81
    Hammond, Walter   105
    Harper, Charles   107
    Horner, William   119
    Jones, Daniel   127
    Kahn, Owen   128
    Knight, Elmer   135
    Kolp, Ray   136
    Leary, John   141
    Little, William   145
    Lively, Henry   146
    McAdams, George   157
    McCandless, Scott   158
    McDonald, Daniel   160
    Mercer, Harry   165
    Mills, Abbott   169
    Niemes, Jacob   181
    Owens, Furman   186
    Powell, Reginald   196
    Raymond, Harry   200
    Reis, Harrie   201
    Ridgway, Jacob   204
    Robinson, John W   206
    Saltzgaver, Otto   212
    Soria, Joakim   227
    Taylor, John B   236
    Taylor, John W   236
    Wallace, Clarence   248
    Wanner, Clarence   249
Jack the Ripper
    Clark, Jack   52
Jackie
    Gallagher, John   90
    Gutiérrez, Joaquin   103
    Hayes, Minter   110
    Hernández, Jacinto   113
    Juelich, John   128
    Price, John   197
    Robinson, Jack   206
    Sullivan, Carl   233
    Tavener, John   236
    Tobin, John P   240
Jackrabbit
    Gilbert, Jack   95
Jake
    Appleton, Peter   18
    Brown, Jerald   39

Jeep

Caulfield, John	49	Heard, Johosie	110
Daubert, Harry	64	Hook, James	118
Dugey, Oscar	74	Kirke, Judson	134
Evans, Uriah	80	Loviglio, John	147
Flowers, D'Arcy	85	Partridge, James	188
Freeze, Carl	88	Pettibone, Harry	191
Gibbs, Jerry	95	Porter, JW	195
Hehl, Herman	111	Powell, James	196
Kruk, John	137	Sborz, John	214
Miller, Walter	169	Ward, John F	250
Northrop, George	181	Witasick, Gerald	259
Solters, Julius	227	**Jazzbow**	
Stahl, Garland	228	Buskey, Joe	43
Striker, Wilbur	232	**JB**	
Thielman, John	237	Bell, Josh	27
Thies, Vernon	238	McHale, Jim	162
Jake the Giant Killer		Shuck, Jack	221
Stahl, Garland	228	Young, Joseph	263
Jakie		**JBJ**	
May, Frank	157	Bradley, Jackie	36
Jamo		**JC**	
Taillon, Jameson	235	Bernard, Joseph	29
Jamsey		Boscan, Jean	34
Stafford, James	228	Camargo, Johan	45
Jap		Gutiérrez, Juan	103
Barbeau, William	22	Martin, Joseph C.	154
Japanese Moe Howard		Ramírez, Juan	199
Matsui, Hideki	156	**JD**	
Jason		Closser, Jeffrey	54
Jackson, Danny	123	DeShaies, James	68
Jasper		Drew, David	73
Davis, Harry H	65	Durbin, Joseph	74
Jay		Martin, John	154
Alou, Jesús	16	Martinez, Julio	155
Avrea, James	20	Smart, Jon	224
Difani, Clarence	70	**J-Dub**	
Franklin, John	87	Werth, Jayson	253
Fry, Johnson	89	**Jeep**	
Gainer, Johnathan	90		

Jeff

Handley, Lee	106	Solomon, Mose	227
Heffner, Don	111	**J-Hey Kid**	
Hughes, Roy	121	Heyward, Jason	114
Jeff		**Jidge**	
Pfeffer, Edward	191	Ruth, George	210
Sweeney, Ed	235	**Jigger**	
Tesreau, Charles	237	Black, Bill	31
Jelly		Lansing, Gene	139
Jelincich, Frank	125	Statz, Arnold	229
Jeptha		**Jiggs**	
Rixey, Eppa	205	Donahue, John A	71
Jerky		Donahue, John F	71
Northrop, George	181	Parrott, Walter	188
Jerry		Parson, William	188
Casale, Gennaro	48	Wright, Jim	261
Morales, Julio	172	**Jim**	
Turner, John	243	Breton, John	37
Upp, George	243	Buckles, Jesse	41
Jersey		Curtiss, Ervin	62
Bakley, Edward	21	Rivera, Manuel	204
Beck, Clyde	25	Schelle, Gerard	215
Jersey Joe		Walker, James	248
Stripp, Joe	232	**Jim Ed**	
Jess		Rice, Jim	203
Cortazzo, John	58	**Jimmy**	
Jesse		Rosario, Angel	208
Duryea, James	75	Walsh, Michael	249
James, Bert	124	**Jimmy Baseball**	
James, Jeff	124	Edmonds, Jim	76
Wallace, Frederick	249	**Jinx**	
Jet		Poindexter, Jennings	195
Jethroe, Sam	125	**Jiquí**	
Johnson, Daniel	125	Moreno, Julio	173
Lemon, Chet	143	**Jittery Joe**	
Jethro		Berry, Jonas	29
Greene, Tommy	100	**JJ**	
Jewel		Cannon, Joe	45
Watwood, Johnny	251	Davis, Jerry	66
Jewish Babe Ruth		Furmaniak, Jason	89

Hardy, James	107	Orrell, Forrest	185
Hoover, James	118	Otten, John	186
Putz, Joseph	197	Rodríguez, José	207
Thobe, John	238	Story, Trevor	231
Trujillo, John	242	Wyatt, Loral	261
		Zardón, José	263

JK
    Kelly, Joe   131

Joe D
    Lewis, John   145
    DiMaggio, Joe   70

J-Mike
    Michaels, Jason   167

Joe E
    Tucker, Thurman   242

J-Mo
    Taillon, Jameson   235

Joe Table
    Mesa, José   166

Joba
    Chamberlain, Justin   49

Joey
    Belle, Albert   27

Jock
    Menefee, John   165
    Somerlott, John   227

Joey Bats
    Bautista, Jose   24

John
    Atz, Jacob   19

Jockey
    Falk, Bibb   80
    Kolp, Ray   136

Johnny
    Guzmán, Dionini   103
    Vergez, Jean   246

Jocko
    Conlan, John   56
    Conlon, Arthur   56
    Flynn, John   85
    Halligan, William   105
    Milligan, John   169
    Thompson, John S   239

    Wanner, Clarence   249
    Werts, Henry   253

Johnny Beisbol
    Cueto, Johnny   62

Johnny O
    O'Brien, John T   182
    Olerud, John   184

Jodie
    Beeler, Joseph   26
    Hunt, Joel   122

Jo-Jo
    Reyes, Joseph   202
    White, Joyner   253

Jody
    Gerut, Joseph   94

Joker
    Randa, Joe   199

Joe
    Boley, John   33
    Dahlke, Jerry   63
    Dawson, Ralph   66
    Decker, George H   67
    Ginsberg, Myron   96
    Muich, Ignatius   175

Jolly Cholly
    Grimm, Charlie   101

Jolly Falstaffian Flinger
    Brown, Walter   40

Jolly Green Giant
    Davis, Bill   65

Jolter

Joltin Joe

Brovia, Joe	39
Joltin Joe	
DiMaggio, Joe	70
Joltin' Joe	
Brovia, Joe	39
Charboneau, Joe	50
Jolting Jabbo	
Jablonski, Ray	123
Jonah	
Derby, George	68
Jonny Lasagna	
Loaisiga, Jonathan	146
Joseíto	
Rodríguez, José	207
Josh	
Billings, John	30
Reilly, William	201
Jot	
Goar, Joshua	96
Jovo	
Miljus, Johnny	168
JoVo	
Votto, Joey	247
JP	
Arencibia, Jonathan	18
Howell, James	120
Wood, Joe P	260
JR	
House, James	119
Murphy, John R	176
Phillips, Charles	192
Richard, James	203
Towles, Justin	241
J-Roll	
Rollins, Jimmy	208
JT	
Bruett, Joseph	40
Realmuto, Jacob	200
Snow, Jack	226
Teheran, Julio	237
Juan Gone	
González, Juan	98
Jud	
Castro, Lou	48
McLaughlin, Justin	163
Pernoll, Henry	190
Judge	
Craghead, Howard	59
Grubbs, Tom	102
Lumley, Harry	148
McCredie, Walter	159
Mee, Tommy	164
Nagle, Walter	177
Robinson, Frank	206
Works, Ralph	260
Juego G	
Shields, Jamie	221
Jug	
Kracher, Joe	136
Powis, Carl	196
Thesenga, Arnold	237
Jughandle	
Morrisson, Johnny	174
Thesenga, Arnold	237
Juice	
Latham, George	140
Juju	
Navarro, Julio	178
Jul	
Kustus, Joe	138
Julio	
Giuliani, Angelo	96
Jumbito	
Díaz, Carlos	69
Jumbo	
Barrett, Robert	23
Barry, Edward	24
Brown, Walter	40
Cartwright, Ed	47
Davis, James	66

Díaz, Jose	69	Spivey, Ernest	228
Dwyer, John	75	Stephens, Vern	230
Harting, Edward	108	Thompson, Gene	238
Latham, George	140	Walsh, James	249
McGinnis, George	161	Wooten, Earl	260
Nash, Jim	178	**Junkman**	
Roy, Normie	209	Lopat, Eddie	146
Schoeneck, Louis	216	**J-Up**	
Strincevich, Nick	232	Upton, Justin	243
Whitney, Frank	254	**Jurassic Carl**	
Jumbo Jim		Everett, Carl	80
Hearn, Jim	110	**Just Another Brick**	
Jumping Jack		Vander Wal, John	245
Jones, Daniel	127	**Just Enough**	
Jumping Joe		Eckstein, David	76
Dugan, Joe	74	**Justin**	
Jumpsteady		Lehr, Charles	143
Templeton, Garry	237	**JV**	
June		Verlander, Justin	246
Calhoun, Willie	44	**JZ**	
Junebug		Zimmermann, Jordan	264
Gilliam, Jim	95	**JZimm**	
Jungle Jim		Zimmermann, Jordan	264
Rivera, Manuel	204	**Kai**	
Junie		Fiers, Mike	83
Andres, Ernest	17	**Kaiser**	
Junior		Shultz, Wallace	222
Boyer, Cloyd	35	Wilhelm, Irvin	255
Cardenal, José	46	**Kangaroo**	
Dagres, Angelo	63	Jones, Davy	127
Frey, Linus	88	**Kansan**	
Gilliam, Jim	95	Thomas, Chester	238
Griffey, Ken Jr.	101	**Kansas City Kid**	
Herndon, Harry	113	Smith, Ernie	224
Holloman, Alva	118	**Kap**	
Kline, Bob	134	Kapler, Gabe	129
Moore, Alvin	171	**Katsy**	
Noboa, Miciades	181	Keifer, Sherman	130
Ortiz, Adalberto	185	**Katz**	
		Tyler, Johnnie	243

Kazmanian Devil
  Kazmir, Scott   130
K-Dub
  Waldrop, Kyle   248
Kell
  Nelson, Ray   179
Kelly
  Holmes, Tommy   118
Kemer
  Brett, Ken   37
Kemo
  Ortega, Phil   185
Kenleyfornia
  Jansen, Kenley   124
Kentucky Colonel
  Combs, Earle   55
Kerry
  Woodson, Walter   260
Kettle
  Wirts, Elwood   259
Kewpie
  Gearin, Dennis   93
  Pennington, George   190
Kewpie Dick
  Barrett, Tracy   23
Khrush
  Davis, Khris   66
Kibby
  Yewcic, Tom   262
Kick
  Kelly, John O   131
  Wise, Kendall   259
Kickapoo
  Kippert, Ed   134
Kickapoo Ed
  Summers, Ed   233
Kid
  Baldwin, Clarence   22
  Bransfield, William   36
  Butler, Frank E   43
  Butler, Willis   43
  Camp, Winfield   45
  Carsey, Wilfred   47
  Carter, Gary   47
  Cochrane, Grodon   54
  DeMars, William   68
  Dugey, Oscar   74
  Eason, Mal   75
  Elberfeld, Norman   77
  Fahey, Howard   80
  Foster, Eddie   86
  Gleason, William   96
  Griffey, Ken Jr.   101
  Heidrick, Emmet   111
  Henriksen, Olaf   112
  Jordan, Charlie   127
  Madden, Michael   150
  McCormack, Mike   159
  McGill, Willie   161
  McLaughlin, James   162
  Moeller, Ron   171
  Nance, William   178
  Nichols, Charles   180
  O'Hara, James   182
  Speer, George   228
  Stutz, George   233
  Summers, William   234
  Wares, Clyde   250
  Williams, Claude   255
  Williams, Ted   256
  Willson, Frank   257
  Withrow, Frank   259
  Yount, Robin   263
Kid Boots
  Schuble, Henry   216
Kid From LI
  Russo, Marius   210
Kid K
  Kershaw, Clayton   132

Kid Natural
    Sandberg, Ryne   213
Kid Twirler
    Jamieson, Charlie   124
Kiddo
    Davis, George W   65
    Wares, Clyde   250
Kidnapped kid
    Spencer, Fred   228
Kif
    Aberson, Clifford   13
Kiiiiid
    Trout, Mike   242
Kiké
    Hernández, Enrique   113
Kiki
    Cuyler, Hazen   63
    Díaz, Edgar   69
    Kiely, Leo   132
Kiko
    Calero, Enrique   44
    Garcia, Alfonso   91
Killa Cam
    Maybin, Cameron   157
Killer
    Contreras, William   57
    Killebrew, Harmon   132
Killer Tomato
    Sáenz, Olmedo   212
Kilowatt
    Watt, Frank   251
Kimbo
    Rodney, Fernando   206
Kimmersak
    Kemmerer, Russ   131
King
    Bailey, Linwood   21
    Brady, Bill   36
    Brady, James W   36
    Brockett, Lewis   38
    Cole, Leonard   54
    Karst, John   129
    Kelly, Michael   131
    Lear, Charles   141
    Lear, Fred   141
    Lehr, Clarence   143
    Lehr, Norm   143
    Leyritz, Jim   145
    Morrissey, Jack   174
    Schmutz, Charlie   216
King Bill
    Kay, Walter   130
King Carl
    Hubbell, Carl   121
King Felix
    Hernández, Félix   113
King Fish 2.0
    Trout, Mike   242
King Kong
    Eldred, Brad   77
    Greenberg, Hank   100
    Keller, Charlie   130
    Kingman, Dave   133
King Krol
    Krol, Ian   137
King Mull
    Malarkey, John   151
King of Crash
    Ruth, George   210
King of Nuts
    Killefer, Wade   133
King of Pitchers
    Radbourn, Charles   198
King of Second Basemen
    Dunlap, Fred   74
King of Swat
    Delahanty, Ed   67
King of Swing
    Ruth, George   211
King Tut

Kingfish

Tutwiler, Guy	243
Kingfish	
Salmon, Tim	212
Kip	
Selbach, Albert	218
Kit	
Carson, Walter	47
McKenna, James	162
Millán, Félix	168
Kite	
Thomas, Keith	238
Kitten	
Haddix, Harvey	103
Millán, Félix	168
Kitten Face	
Gentry, Craig	93
Kitty	
Bransfield, William	36
Brashear, Norman	37
Kaat, Jim	128
KK	
Kim, Kwang Hyun	133
Klondike	
Douglass, William	72
Kane, Harry	129
Smith, Armstrong	224
Klubot	
Kluber, Corey	134
K-Man	
Clemens, Roger	53
Gooden, Dwight	98
Ryan, Lynn	211
Viola, Frank	246
Knapp Time	
Knapp, Andrew	135
Knee	
High, Andy	115
Knight of Kennett Square	
Pennock, Herb	190
Knobby	
Lawing, Garland	141
Knuckles	
Cicotte, Eddie	52
Knucksie	
Niekro, Phil	180
Kohly	
Miller, Frank A	168
Kojak	
Heaverlo, Dave	110
Kong	
Kingman, Dave	133
Koo	
Koufax, Sandy	136
Kraken	
Sánchez, Gary	213
Krane	
Kranepool, Ed	136
K-Rod	
Rodriguez, Francisco	207
Krukker	
Kruk, John	137
Krum	
Kahler, George	128
Kul	
Kustus, Joe	138
Kung Fu Panda	
Sandoval, Pablo	213
LA	
Andersen, Larry	17
La Fiera	
Soto, Juan	227
La Grasa	
Peralta, Wandy	190
La Gua Gua	
Tejada, Miguel	237
La Leche	
Abreu, Bobby	13
La Maquina	
Berríos, José	29
La Maravilla	
García, Adonis	91

La Melaza
    Reyes, José   202
La Mula
    Báez, Pedro   21
La Pantera
    Hechvarría, Adeiny   110
    Robert, Luis   205
La Piedra
    Castillo, Luis   48
La Piña
    Gurriel, Yuli   103
La Potencia
    Céspedes, Yoenis   49
LA Swiftness
    Adams, Lane   14
LaCrosse Lulu
    Konetchy, Ed   136
Laddie
    Link, Fred   145
    Renfroe, Cohen   202
Lady
    Baldwin, Charles   22
    Payne, Harley   189
Lajoie's Legs
    Mills, Abbott   169
Lance
    Rautzhan, Clarence   200
Languid Bob
    Meusel, Bob   166
Lank
    Wilson, William C   258
Lanky
    Greenberg, Hank   100
    Jordan, Raymond   128
Lanky Castilian
    Gomez, Vernon   97
Large
    Bagker, Len   22
Larruper
    Layne, Hillis   141
Larruping Lou
    Gehrig, Lou   93
Larry
    Chapell, LaVerne   50
    Crawford, Charles   60
    Duff, Cecil   73
    Kopf, William   136
    Lajoie, Nap   138
    McLean, John   163
    Pezold, Lorenz   191
    Pratt, Lester   196
    Schlafly, Harry   215
    Street, Huston   232
Laser
    Laureano, Ramón   141
Laser Show
    Pedroia, Dustin   189
Last Call
    Remmerswaal, Wilhelmus   202
Laughing Boy
    Marichal, Juan   152
Laughing Larry
    Doyle, Larry   73
Lave
    Cross, Lafayette   61
Lawnmower
    Ross, Robbie   209
Laz
    Garrett, Clarence   92
Le Grand Orange
    Staub, Daniel   230
Leaky
    Fausett, Robert   81
Leapin' Lena
    Stiles, Rollie   231
Leaping Mike
    Menosky, Mike   165
Leaping Sam
    Crane, Sam   60
Leather Rocket
    Leathersich, Jack   142

Leather Skull

Leather Skull
   Merkle, Fred   166
Leche
   Cabrera, Melky   44
Lee
   Thompson, John D   238
Left Arm of God
   Koufax, Sandy   136
Lefty
   Aber, Al   13
   Alten, Ernie   16
   Anderson, Walter   17
   Anderson, William   17
   Archer, Frederick   18
   Atkinson, Hubert   19
   Baczewski, Fred   20
   Barnes, Frank   23
   Barnes, Junie   23
   Barnes, Robert   23
   Bell, Ralph   27
   Bertrand, Roman   29
   Birkofer, Ralph   30
   Bishop, William   30
   Boggs, Ray   33
   Bonness, William   33
   Boss, Harley   34
   Brown, Charles R   39
   Brunet, George   40
   Burke, Bob   41
   Caldwell, Ralph   44
   Carlton, Steve   46
   Carnett, Eddie   46
   Carter, Arnold   47
   Castner, Paul   48
   Chambers, Cliff   49
   Chase, Ken   50
   Chelini, Italo   51
   Clark, William W   52
   Clarke, Alan   52
   Claset, Gowell   53
   Clauss, Al   53
   Covington, Chet   59
   Craig, George   59
   Cremins, Bob   60
   Cristall, Bill   61
   Crumling, Gene   61
   Dashner, Lee   64
   Davis, Alfonzo   65
   Dillinger, Harley   70
   Dobb, John   70
   Dobens, Ray   71
   Dockins, George   71
   Elliott, Glenn   77
   Fanovich, Frank   81
   Faulkner, Jim   81
   Ferens, Stan   82
   Fieber, Clarence   83
   Fitzgerald, Howard   84
   Gallagher, Ed   90
   Gehrman, Paul   93
   George, Thomas   94
   Gerheauser, Al   94
   Gerner, Ed   94
   Gervais, Lucien   94
   Gessler, Henry   94
   Gilson, Hal   96
   Gomez, Vernon   97
   Good, Wilbur   98
   Goodell, John   98
   Gorman, Howie   98
   Greene, Nelson   100
   Grove, Robert   102
   Guise, Witt   102
   Hallahan, Bill   105
   Harris, Herb   108

Hayden, Eugene	110	Mallonee, Ben	151
Heimach, Fred	111	Mapel, Rolla	152
Heise, Clarence	111	Marr, Charles	153
Herring, Silas	114	Martin, Morrie	154
Herrmann, Marty	114	Masterson, Paul	155
High, Ed	115	Matthews, Joe	156
Hockette, George	116	McBee, Pryor	158
Hoerst, Frank	116	McMullin, John	163
Hopper, Clarence	119	Middleton, John	167
Houtz, Fred	120	Miller, Bill P	168
Hudson, Hal	121	Miller, Elmer	168
Hughes, Vern	121	Miller, Ralph	169
Jackson, Charlie	123	Mills, Howard	169
Jamerson, Charles	124	Miner, Ray	170
James, William	124	Minner, Paul	170
Johns, Augie	125	Moon, Leo	171
Johnson, Art	125	O'Dea, Paul	182
Johnson, Earl	125	O'Doul, Francis	182
Johnson, William	126	Odenwald, Ted	184
Jones, Earl	127	Okrie, Frank	184
Kalfass, Bill	128	Perkins, Charlie	190
Karpel, Herbert	129	Perrin, Bill	190
Kelb, George	130	Pettit, Leon	191
Kennedy, Bill	131	Pettit, Paul	191
Killen, Frank	133	Pierce, Ray	193
Kime, Hal	133	Porto, Al	195
Kraly, Steve	136	Pott, Nellie	195
Lamanske, Frank	139	Pyle, Ewald	197
LaPalme, Paul	139	Rader, Drew	198
Lee, Thornton	142	Rogers, Lee	207
LeFebvre, Bill	142	Rogers, Orlin	207
Leifield, Albert	143	Russell, Clarence	210
Logan, Bob	146	Russo, Marius	210
Lorenzen, Adolph	147	Saylor, Phil	214
Madden, Len	150	Schaeffer, Harry	214
Mahon, Al	150	Schegg, Gilbert	215
Mailho, Emil	151	Schemer, Mike	215

Legend

Scoggins, Jim	217	Williams, Claude	255
Scott, Marshall	217	Willis, Charles	257
Settlemire, Edgar	219	Willis, Les	257
Shaute, Joe	220	Wilson, Roy	258
Shea, John M	220	Wineapple, Ed	258
Shields, Ben	221	Winham, Lave	258
Shoun, Clyde	221	Winn, George	258
Siebert, Dick	222	Wolf, Walter	259
Sloat, Dwain	223	Yerkes, Charles	262
Smoll, Clyde	226	York, James	262
Stanek, Al	229		
Stewart, Walter C	231		
Stiely, Fred	231		
Sullivan, John J	233		
Sullivan, Paul	233		
Sumner, Carl	234		
Taber, Edward	235		
Taylor, Arlas	236		
Thomas, Clarence	238		
Thomas, Claude	238		
Thompson, Harry	238		
Thompson, John D	238		
Thormahlen, Herbert	239		
Townsend, Leo	241		
Tyler, George	243		
Uhl, Bob	243		
Vaughan, Cecil	245		
Wallace, Harry	249		
Wallace, James	249		
Watwood, Johnny	251		
Webb, Cleon	251		
Weiland, Bob	252		
Weinert, Philip	252		
West, Weldon	253		
Whitehouse, Charlie	254		
Wight, Bill	254		
Wilkie, Aldon	255		

Legend
   Alfaro, Jorge   15

Lego
   Gallego, Mike   90

Legs
   Weik, Dick   251

Leiter
   Norton, Elisha   181

Le-Ki
   Kiely, Leo   132

Lem
   Cross, George   61

Lemons
   Solters, Julius   227

Lena
   Blackburne, Russell   31
   Kretlow, Lou   137
   Stiles, Rollie   231
   Styles, William   233

Leo
   Smith, Lionel   225
   Tankersley, Lawrence   235

Lep
   Long, Lester   146

Let's Panic
   Leskanic, Curt   144

LG
   Drake, Logan   73

Li'l Abner

Cathey, Hardin	49	
Erickson, Paul	79	
Liberty		
Bell, George A	26	
Schaefer, William	214	
Lick		
Malloy, Alex	151	
Lief		
Errickson, Dick	79	
Lightning		
Strunk, Amos	232	
Lights Out		
Lidge, Brad	145	
Light-Tower Power		
Ashley, Billy	19	
Lil		
Stoner, Ulysses	231	
Lil D		
d'Arnaud, Travis	63	
Lima Time		
Lima, José	145	
Limb		
McKenry, Frank	162	
Limonar		
Martínez, Rogelio	155	
Line Drive		
Easler, Mike	75	
Nelson, Lynn	179	
Link		
Lowe, Bobby	147	
Sullivan, Dan	233	
Lip		
Durocher, Leo	75	
Pike, Lipman	193	
Lippy		
Durocher, Leo	75	
Little All Right		
Ritchey, Claude	204	
Little Bake		
McBride, Arnold	158	
Little Bill		
Sowders, William	227	
Little Cannon		
Osuna, Roberto	185	
Little Colonel		
Reese, Harold	201	
Little Cowboy		
Tomlin, Josh	240	
Little Dixie		
Walker, Harry	248	
Little Duke		
Hernández, Adrián	113	
Little Dutch		
Meyer, Lambert	167	
Little Eva		
Lange, Bill	139	
Wilhelm, Irvin	255	
Little Forkhander		
Gearin, Dennis	93	
Little Fox		
Stricklett, Elmer	232	
Little General		
Bench, Johnny	27	
Henriksen, Olaf	112	
Morgan, Joe	173	
Little Giant		
Chatham, Charles	50	
Little Globetrotter		
Earle, Billy	75	
Little Hawk		
Long, Tom	146	
Little Henriksen		
Henriksen, Olaf	112	
Little Hug		
Huggins, Miller	121	
Little Hurt		
Grace, Mark	99	
Grebeck, Craig	100	
Young, Kevin	263	
Little Irishman		
Gearin, Dennis	93	

Little Jimmy
    Kaat, Jim   128
Little Joe
    Edwards, James   76
    Ginsberg, Myron   96
    Morgan, Joe   173
    Presko, Joe   196
    Wood, Joe P   260
    Yeager, Joe   262
Little John
    O'Brien, John T   182
Little Louis
    Aparicio, Luis   18
Little Mac
    Macullar, Jimmy   150
    McClellan, Hervey   158
Little Mack
    Powell, Hershel   196
Little Money
    Sandoval, Pablo   213
Little Mr. Chips
    Hudson, Johnny   121
Little Napoleon
    McGraw, John   161
Little Nel
    Fox, Nellie   87
Little Nemo
    Gearin, Dennis   93
    Stephens, Jim   230
Little Ninja
    Amarista, Alexi   16
Little O
    Vizquel, Omar   247
Little Paul
    Radford, Paul   198
Little Pedro
    Martínez, Carlos E   154
Little Pete
    Runnels, James   210
Little Phil
    Geier, Phil   93
Little Poison
    Waner, Lloyd   249
Little Potato
    Pascual, Camilo   188
Little Professor
    DiMaggio, Dom   70
Little Rhody
    Wallace, Roderick   249
Little Rock
    Raines, Timothy Jr   199
Little Sarge
    Matthews, Gary Jr.   156
Little Slug
    Hershberger, Willard   114
    Stephens, Vern   230
Little Steam Engine
    Galvin, James   90
Little Stu
    Miller, Stu   169
Little Unit
    McEwing, Joe   160
Little Willie
    Colgan, William   55
Live Oak
    Taylor, George   236
Liz
    Funk, Elias   89
    Malarkey, John   151
Lizard King
    Luzardo, Jesús   148
    Mikolas, Miles   167
Lizzie
    Piatt, Wiley   192
Lizzy
    Lisenbee, Horace   145
LJ
    Hoes, Jerome   116
Load
    Incaviglia, Pete   123

Loafer
    McAleer, Jimmy   158
Loco
    Herrera, José   113
Logie Bear
    Forsythe, Logan   86
Lollypop
    Killefer, Wade   133
LoMo
    Morrison, Logan   174
Lon
    Goldstein, Leslie   97
    Moore, Earl   172
    Ury, Louis   244
Lon Mower
    Moore, Earl   172
Lone Ranger
    Boris, Paul   34
Long Arm of the Law
    Law, Vance   141
Long Bob
    Ewing, George   80
    Meusel, Bob   166
Long Jim
    Holdsworth, Jim   117
    Korwan, Jim   136
Long John
    Anderson, John   17
    Ewing, John   80
    Healy, John   110
    Reilly, John   201
Long Levi
    Meyerle, Levi   167
Long Tom
    Doran, Tom   72
    Hughes, Tom J   121
    Winsett, Tom   258
Lonnie Baseball
    Chisenhall, Lonnie   51
Lonny
    Frey, Linus   88
Lonzo
    Moore, Earl   172
Loose
    Karger, Ed   129
Lop
    Lopata, Stan   147
Lord
    Jordan, Jimmy   127
Losing Pitcher
    Mulcahy, Hugh   175
Lou
    Brett, George   37
    Brissie, Leland   38
Louie
    Meadows, Mike   164
Louisiana Lightning
    Guidry, Ron   102
Louisville Slugger
    Browning, Louis   40
Low
    Christenbury, Lloyd   51
Loyal
    McCredie, Walter   159
Luck
    Howe, Les   120
Lucky
    Crane, Sam   60
    Glade, Fred   96
    Howe, Les   120
    Kessler, Henry   132
    Lohrke, Jack   146
    Nagle, Walter   177
    Whiteman, George   254
    Wright, William Si   261
Lucky Lucas
    Lucas, Johnny   148
Luis Serge in SR-06
    Cruz, Luis   61
Luisito

Luke

Aparicio, Luis	18	Pujols, Albert	197
Luke		Zimmer, Bradley	264
Appling, Lucius	18	**Mack**	
Etheridge, Bobby	79	Hillis, Malcolm	115
Hamlin, Lewis	105	McCabe, Ralph	158
Lutenberg, Charles	148	McDonnell, Jim	160
Nelson, Luther	179	McGillicuddy, Cornelius	161
Sewell, James	219	McKean, Ed	162
Stuart, Luther	233	**Mack The Knife**	
Urban, Louis	244	Jones, Mack	127
Lumbago		**Mack the Ninth**	
Lombardi, Ernie	146	MacDougal, Robert	149
Stimmel, Archie	231	**Mad Dog**	
Lumbago Bill		Maddux, Greg	150
Doak, Bill	70	Madlock, Bill	150
Lumber		Madson, Ryan	150
Price, Joe	197	Thomas, Lee	238
Lunchbox		**Mad Hungarian**	
Snider, Travis	226	Hrabosky, Al	120
Luscious Luke		**Mad Max**	
Appling, Lucius	18	Scherzer, Max	215
Ma'montro		**Mad Monk**	
Jansen, Kenley	124	Meyer, Russ	167
Mabel		**Mad Russian**	
Paige, George	187	Novikoff, Lou	182
Mac		Rachunok, Steve	198
McClure, Hal	158	**Madman from Mississippi**	
McCovey, Willie	159	Walker, Gerald	248
McFarland, Timothy	160	**Mae**	
McGinnis, George	161	Fleming, Les	85
McHenry, Austin	162	**MaeKen**	
Scarce, Guerrant	215	Maeda, Kenta	150
Mac the Knife		**Magic**	
McAllister, Zach	158	Santana, Ervin	213
Mach One		**Magnet**	
Machemer, Dave	149	Addy, Bob	14
Machine		**Maharajah of Mash**	
Berríos, José	29	Ruth, George	211
LeMahieu, DJ	143	**Mahatma**	
		Rickey, Branch	203

Mahkus
    Semien, Marcus   218
Mail Carrier
    Combs, Earle   55
Mailes
    Travis, Devon   241
Major
    Hach, Irv   103
    Houk, Ralph   119
    Mann, Les   152
Major Key
    Middleton, Keynan   167
Makina
    Chacin, Jhoulys   49
Ma-kun
    Tanaka, Masahiro   235
Mal Tiempo
    Abreu, José   13
Mamba
    Schoop, Jonathan   216
Mambo
    Lima, José   145
Man
    Utley, Chase   244
Man from Miyagi
    Saito, Takashi   212
Man in the Green Suit
    O'Doul, Francis   182
Man Killer
    Thomas, Tom   238
Man Mountain
    Kardow, Paul   129
Man Nobody Knows
    Dickey, Bill   69
Man o' War
    Rice, Edgar   203
Man of Steal
    Henderson, Rickey   112
Man With the Iron Glove
    Stuart, Dick   233
Mandrake
    Layne, Hillis   141
Mandrake the Magician
    Mueller, Don   175
Mandy
    Brooks, Jonathan   38
Manito
    Marichal, Juan   152
Manny
    Kopp, Merlin   136
    Lee, Manuel   142
Manny Being Manny
    Ramírez, Manny   199
Manny Moments
    Ramírez, Manny   199
Mannywood
    Ramírez, Manny   199
Manos de Seda
    Mendoza, Mario   165
Man-Ram
    Ramírez, Manny   199
Mantle's Caddie
    Reed, Jack   201
Mantle's Legs
    Reed, Jack   201
Marion Mule
    Fosse, Ray   86
Mark
    Christman, Marquette   51
    Mauldin, Marshall   156
Marshalltown Infant
    Anson, Adrian   17
Marty
    Hopkins, Meredith   118
    Kutyna, Marion   138
    Shay, Arthur   220
Marvelous Marv
    Throneberry, Marvin   239
Mary
    Calhoun, Bill   44
Mashi

Master Blaster

Murakami, Masanori	176
Master Blaster	
Canseco, José	45
Strawberry, Darryl	232
Williams, Matt	256
Master Melvin	
Ott, Mel	186
Matches	
Kilroy, Matt	133
Matt the Bat	
Williams, Matt	256
Matty Ice	
Bush, Matt	42
Matty Moe	
Moore, Matt	172
Mauer Power	
Maurer, Brandon	156
Max	
Marshall, Milo	153
Surkont, Matthew	234
Venable, William	246
Mayor	
Casey, Sean	48
Mayor of Ding Dong City	
Shaw, Travis	220
Mayor of Riverfront	
Pérez, Atanasio	190
Mayor of Wrigley Field	
Sauer, Hank	214
McCannon	
McCann, James	158
McZilla	
McGwire, Mark	162
Meal Ticket	
Hubbell, Carl	121
Mechanic	
Fossas, Tony	86
Sutton, Don	234
Mechanical Man	
Gehringer, Charlie	93
Medicine Bill	
Mountjoy, Bill	175
Medina Mauler	
Fischer, Charles	83
Mega-Mark	
Reynolds, Mark	203
Melk Man	
Cabrera, Melky	44
Mem	
Lovett, Merritt	147
Memo	
Luna, Guillermo	148
Memphis Bill	
Terry, Bill	237
Meow	
Gilmore, Len	96
Mer	
Duggan, Jim	74
Mercedes	
Benzinger, Todd	28
Mercury	
Myatt, George	177
Merl	
Combs, Merrill	55
Merry	
Merewether, Art	166
Merry Mortician	
Hoyt, Waite	120
Mert	
Hackett, Mortimer	103
Mex	
Hernandez, Keith	113
Mexicutioner	
Soria, Joakim	227
Mick	
Mantle, Mickey	152
Mick the Quick	
Rivers, John	205
Mickey	
Cochrane, Gordon	54
Corcoran, Michael	57

Cross, Frank	61	Jones, Bill	126
Daub, Dan	64	Mensor, Ed	165
Devine, William	69	Murphy, William	176
Finn, Neal	83	Reilley, Alexander	201
Grasso, Newton	100	Rigney, Emory	204
Haefner, Milton	104	**Midget Southpaw**	
Harrington, Charles	108	Gearin, Dennis	93
Harris, Maurice	108	**Miggy**	
Haslin, Michael	109	Tejada, Miguel	237
Hatcher, Michael	109	**Mighty Mite**	
Heath, Minor	110	Fox, Nellie	87
Hughes, Michael	121	Gearin, Dennis	93
Keliher, Maurice	130	Huggins, Miller	121
Klutts, Gene	135	**Mighty Mouse**	
Kreitner, Albert	137	Amarista, Alexi	16
Lopez, Raymond	147	Harrelson, Derrel	107
McDermott, Maury	159	Izturis, Maicer	123
McGowan, Tullis	161	**Mijita**	
Micelotta, Robert	167	Alvarado, Luis	16
Owen, Arnold	186	**Mikado Milt**	
Randolph, Willie	200	Scott, Milt	217
Rivers, John	205	**Mike**	
Rocco, Michael	206	Almeida, Rafael	15
Rutner, Milton	211	Balas, Mitchell	21
Scott, Ralph	217	Bowerman, Frank	35
Stanley, Mitchell	229	Connolly, Mervin	56
Vernon, James	246	Cuellar, Miguel	62
Walton, Danny	249	Cunningham, Mody	62
Weintraub, Phil	252	Dondero, Len	71
Witek, Nicholas	259	Fitzgerald, Justin	84
Mickey Mo		Fornieles, Jose	86
Morandini, Mickey	173	García, Edward	91
Mickey Mouse		Guerra, Fermin	102
Melton, Cliff	165	Handiboe, Aloysius	106
Microwave		Herrera, Ramón	114
Adleman, Tim	14	Knode, Kenneth	135
Midget		Loan, William	146
Gearin, Dennis	93	MacDougal, Robert	149

Mike the Hobo

Mahoney, George 150
Massey, William 155
Mazzera, Mel 157
McCann, Gene 158
McCormick, Myron 159
Mowrey, Harry 175
Palm, Richard 187
Powers, Ellis 196
Ryba, Dominic 211
Smith, Elmer 224
Smith, Elwood 224
Welday, Lyndon 252
Wilson, Samuel 258
Mike the Hobo
   Mowrey, Harry 175
Mikey
   Sosa, Sammy 227
   Stanton Giancarlo 229
Milkman
   Gallen, Zac 90
Milkman Jim
   Turner, Jim 242
Miller Time
   Miller, Andrew 168
   Miller, Rick 169
Millville Meteor
   Trout, Mike 242
Milt
   Shoffner, Milburn 221
Miner
   Brown, Mordecai 40
Mini Miggy
   García, Avisaíl 91
Mini Yadi
   Vázquez, Christian 245
Mini-Hawk
   Harrelson, Derrel 107
Mini-Mart
   Martínez, Michael 155

Minnesota Gopher
   Blyleven, Bert 32
Minnie
   Mendoza, Cristobal 165
   Miñoso, Orestes 170
Minooka Mike
   McNally, Mike 163
Minotaur
   Kershaw, Clayton 132
Miracle Man
   Stallings, George 229
Missile
   Chapman, Aroldis 50
Mississauga Masher
   Naylor, Josh 178
Mississippi Meteor
   Walker, Harvey 248
Mississippi Mudcat
   Bush, Guy 42
   Hebert, Wally 110
Mitchell Monster
   Mitchell, Kevin 170
Mitchie-Poo
   Williams, Mitch 256
Mitchy Two Bags
   Moreland, Mitch 173
Mitty
   Jordan, Mike 127
Mo
   Rivera, Mariano 204
   Sanford, Meredith 213
Mo Mo
   Morales, Kendrys 172
Moakey
   Smith, Justin 226
Moby Dick
   Stuart, Dick 233
Modoc
   Wise, Sam 259
Moe
   Drabowsky, Myron 73

Franklin, Murray 87
Mahoney, Jim 150
Morehead, Dave 173
Morehead, Seth 173
Morhardt, Meredith 173
Mulleavy, Greg 175
Moke
    Kelly, Herb 131
Mollie
    Milosevich, Mike 170
Molly
    Craft, Maurice 59
    Meloan, Paul 165
    Molitor, Paul 171
    Moore, Maurice 172
MoMo
    Piscotty, Stephen 194
Moncho
    Rivera, Rene 205
Mondo
    Harper, Bryce 107
Money Bags
    Qualters, Tom 198
Mongo
    Kusick, Craig 138
Mongoose
    Lukon, Eddie 148
Monk
    Cline, John 54
    Dubiel, Walt 73
    Mattox, Cloy 156
    Moore, Euel 172
    Murphy, Con 176
    Sherlock, John 220
Monkey
    Foreman, Frank 86
    Hotaling, Pete 119
Mono
    Valbuena, Luis 244
Monster
    Piazza, Mike 193
    Radatz, Dick 198
    Spencer, Daryl 228
Monster of the Heisei Era
    Matsuzaka, Daisuke 156
Monte
    Dumont, George 74
Monty
    Basgall, Romanus 24
    Pfyl, Meinhard 191
    Swartz, Vernon 235
Mookie
    Wilson, William H 258
Mookie Batts
    Betts, Mookie 29
Moon
    Gibson, George 95
    Hallahan, Bill 105
    Harris, Joe 108
    Mullen, Ford 175
Moon Man
    Lyons, Steve 149
    Selma, Dick 218
Moonie
    Miller, Lowell 169
    Minton, Greg 170
Moonlight
    Graham, Archibald 99
Moonlight Ace
    Fussell, Fred 89
Moonman
    Shannon, Mike 219
Moon-man
    Minton, Greg 170
Moose
    Alexander, David 14
    Baxter, John 25
    Bowler, Grant 35
    Clabaugh, John 52

Mortimer Snerd

Doll, Art	71	**Mother Maglie**	
Dropo, Walt	73	Maglie, Sal	150
Earnshaw, George	75	**Motormouth**	
Eggert, Elmer	77	Blair, Paul	31
Farrell, Jack A	81	**Mountain Man**	
Grimshaw, Myron	101	Roberts, Dale	205
Haas, Bryan	103	**Mountain Music**	
Korince, George	136	Melton, Cliff	165
Lakeman, Al	138	**Mouse**	
Lee, Bob	142	Brown, Jim	39
Massa, Gordon	155	Eaton, Adam	76
McCormick, Harry	159	Gilligan, Andrew	95
Miller, Ralph	169	Glenn, Ed	96
Morton, Guy Jr.	174	Lyons, Ed	149
Moryn, Walt	174	Mierkowicz, Ed	167
Moustakis, Mike	175	**Mousey**	
Musgrove, Joe	177	Markland, Gene	153
Mussina, Mike	177	**Move Up Joe**	
Ortenzio, Frank	185	Gerhardt, Joe	94
Radatz, Dick	198	**Mowly**	
Showron, Bill	223	Machado, Dixon	149
Solters, Julius	227	**Mox**	
Stubing, Lawrence	233	McQuery, William	164
Werden, Perry	252	**Moxie**	
Mortimer Snerd		Hengel, Emery	112
Selma, Dick	218	Manuel, Mark	152
Mose		Meixell, Merton	164
Eggert, Elmer	77	**Mr. 305**	
Moses		Alonso, Yonder	16
Shipley, Joe	221	**Mr. Angel**	
Mosquito		Salmon, Tim	212
Davis, Ira	66	**Mr. Baseball**	
Ordenana, Tony	184	Bragan, Bobby	36
Slagle, Jimmy	223	Mack, Connie	149
Moss Dogg		McGillicuddy, Cornelius	161
Moss Brandon	174	Uecker, Bob	243
Mother		**Mr. Chips**	
Watson, Walter	251	Chipman, Bob	51
		Hudson, Johnny	121
		Mr. Clean	

Murphy, Dale 176
Mr. Clutch
Tabler, Pat 235
Mr. Cub
Banks, Ernie 22
Mr. Everything
Satriano, Tom 214
Mr. Five-By-Five
Wilson, Lew 257
Mr. Freeze
Belle, Albert 27
Mr. Impossible
Robinson, Brooks 206
Mr. Incredible
Slania, Dan 223
Mr. Irrelevant
Reddick, Josh 200
Mr. Jay
Winfield, Dave 258
Mr. Jello
Andersen, Larry 17
Mr. Late Night
Smith, Seth 225
Mr. Marlin
Conine, Jeffrey 56
Mr. May
Winfield, Dave 258
Mr. Mellow
Myers, Randy 177
Mr. Miami
Machado, Manny 149
Mr. Murder
Irvin, Monte 123
Mr. National
Zimmerman, Ryan 264
Mr. Nice Guy
Garciaparra, Nomar 91
Mr. November
Jeter, Derek 125
Mr. October
Jackson, Reggie 124

Mr. Padre
Gwynn, Tony Sr. 103
Mr. Prime Minister
Whitt, Ernie 254
Mr. Red Sox
Pesky, Johnny 191
Mr. Shortstop
Marion, Marty 153
Wallace, Roderick 249
Mr. Smile
Lindor, Francisco 145
Mr. Steady
Parker, Wes 188
Mr. Sunshine
Banks, Ernie 22
Mr. T
Holland, Al 117
Mr. Team
Elliott, Bob 77
Mr. Tiger
Kaline, Al 128
Mr. Versatility
Tovar, César 241
Mr. Walk-Off
Zimmerman, Ryan 264
Mr. White Sox
Miñoso, Orestes 170
Mr. X
Rescigno, Xavier 202
Muck
McGraner, Howard 161
Mud
Grant, Mark 100
Mud Artist
Ryan, Jack 211
Mudcat
Grant, Jim 99
Muddy
Ruel, Herold 210
Muddy Chicken
Pedroia, Dustin 189

Muggsy

Muggsy
    Stanky, Eddie   229
Mugsy
    McGraw, John   161
Mul
    Holland, Howard   117
Mule
    Dietz, Dick   70
    Fannin, Cliff   81
    Haas, George   103
    Lary, Frank   140
    Peete, Charlie   189
    Shirley, Ernest   221
    Sprinz, Joe   228
    Watson, John   250
    Watson, Milt   251
Mule Ears
    Auker, Elden   20
Mule Trader
    Kimberlin, Harry   133
Mullet
    Brett, George   37
Mullion
    Winfield, Dave   258
Mumbles
    Tremel, Bill   241
Mummy
    Coates, Jim   54
Murph
    Murphy, Dale   176
Murphy
    Johnson, George   126
    Kimberlin, Harry   133
Muscle
    Martin, Russell   154
Muscles
    Gallagher, Joseph   90
    Mantle, Mickey   152
    Mole, Fenton   171
    Upton, Tom   244

    Vaughn, Fred   245
Muskrat Bill
    Shipke, Bill   221
Mutt
    Hodge, Clarence   116
    Riddle, Johnny   204
    Williams, David   255
    Wilson, William C   258
Mutz
    Ens, Anton   78
Mysterious
    Sparks, Thomas   228
    Walker, Frederick   248
Nacho
    Millán, Félix   168
Nails
    Dykstra, Lenny   75
Nanny
    Fernandez, Froilan   82
Nap
    Kloza, John   134
    Shea, John E   220
Napoleon
    Shea, John E   220
Nardi
    Contreras, Arnaldo   57
Nashville Narcissus
    Lucas, Charles   148
Nasty Boy
    Dibble, Rob   69
Nasty Masty
    Masterson, Justin   155
National Det
    Detwiler, Ross   69
Nato
    Ramírez, Mario   199
Natural
    Griffey, Ken Jr.   101
Naugatuck Nugget
    Shea, Francis   220

Navasota Tarantula
    Garvin, Virgil   92
Neb
    Stewart, Walter N   231
Ned
    Connor, Edward   56
    Cuthbert, Edgar   62
    Garvin, Virgil   92
    Yost, Edgar   262
Needle
    Pesky, Johnny   191
Needler
    Bourjos, Peter   34
Nellie
    Rees, Stan   201
Nemo
    Gaines, Willard   90
    Gearin, Dennis   93
    Leibold, Harry   143
    Munns, Les   176
Nene
    Marrero, Chris   153
Neon Deion
    Sanders, Deion   213
Nerd Power
    Sogard, Eric   227
Nervous Greek
    Skizas, Lou   223
Nervy Nick
    Nichols, Charles   180
New Green Monster
    Greenwell, Mike   100
Newt
    Hunter, Frederick   122
    Kimball, Newell   133
Ni
    Castro, Miguel   48
Nick
    Allen, Artemus   15
    Carter, Conrad   47
    Carter, Paul   47
    Handiboe, Jim   106
    Nicholson, Bill   180
    Scharf, Edward   215
Nicky Dubs
    Williams, Nick   256
Nicolle
    Suárez, Eugenio   233
Nig
    Beazley, Johnny   25
    Berry, Joe Jr.   29
    Bragan, Bobby   36
    Clarke, Jay   52
    Cuppy, George   62
    Fuller, Charles   89
    Grabowski, John   99
    Lipscomb, Gerard   145
    Niebergall, Charlie   180
    Perrine, John   190
    Shaner, Wally   219
    Smith, Frank   224
Niggerlips
    Ruth, George   211
Night Hawk
    Mahtook, Mikie   150
Nightly Nieve
    Nieve, Fernando   181
Nin
    Alexander, William   15
Nine
    Conine, Jeffrey   56
Ninety-Six
    Voiselle, Bill   247
Nino
    Bongiovanni, Anthony   33
    Espinosa, Arnulfo   79
    Fernández, José   82
Nixey
    Callahan, Jimmy   45

No Panic
    Osuna, Roberto   185
Noah
    León, Sandy   143
Noisy
    Clarke, Richard   53
    Flick, Lew   85
    Kling, Johnny   134
Noisy Tom
    Tucker, Tommy   242
Nomah
    Garciaparra, Nomar   91
No-Neck
    Williams, Walt   256
Nonny
    Nonnenkamp, Leo   181
Noodle
    Kawasaki, Munenori   129
Noodles
    Hahn, Frank   104
    Zupo, Frank   264
Nook
    Logan, Exavier   146
Noonie
    Marquis, Roger   153
Norm
    Zauchin, Norbert   263
Norrisaurusrex
    Norris, Derek   181
Nub
    Kleinke, Norbert   134
Nubbin
    McLeland, Wayne   163
Nubby
    Barnes, Jesse   23
Nubs
    Jones, Dale   127
Nul
    Hoeft, Billy   116
Nutsky
    Oana, Henry   183
Nuxy
    Nuxhall, Joe   182
Oak
    O'Connor, Jack W   182
Oats
    DeMaestri, Joe   68
OB
    France, Ossie   87
Obbie
    Eckert, Al   76
Obi Yan
    Gomes, Yan   97
Obie
    O'Brien, Tommy   182
OC
    Cabrera, Orlando   44
Ocho
    Braun, Ryan   37
Octopus
    Alfonseca, Antonio   15
    Marion, Marty   153
Odachowski
    O'Day, Darren   182
Ode
    Voigt, Ollie   247
O-Dog
    Cabrera, Orlando   44
    Hudson, Orlando   121
Offa
    Neal, Theophilus   178
Officer
    Dibble, Rob   69
    Karkovice, Ron   129
Oh Henry
    Rodríguez, Henry   207
Oil
    Smith, Earl S   224
Oil Can
    Boyd, Dennis   35
Oil Can Harry
    Oyler, Ray   186

Oisk
    Erskine, Carl   79
Okie
    Fields, Josh   83
Okkie
    Roettger, Oscar   207
Oklahoma Kid
    Mantle, Mickey   152
Ol' Pop
    Haines, Jesse   104
Ol' Stubblebeard
    Grimes, Burleigh   101
Ol' Aches and Pains
    Appling, Lucius   18
Ol' Lefthander
    Nuxhall, Joe   182
Ol' Mate
    Goodman, Ival   98
Ol' Perfessor
    Stengel, Charles   230
Old Authority
    Foley, Charles   85
Old Blue
    Moore, Ray   172
Old Dog
    Ritter, Lew   204
Old Folks
    Arntzen, Orie   19
    Kinder, Ellis   133
    Ostermueller, Frederick   185
    Pillette, Herman   193
    Wilhelm, James   255
Old Fox
    Griffith, Clark   101
Old Gozzlehead
    Rivers, John   205
Old Gray Fox
    Stocksdale, Otis   231
Old Hick
    Carpenter, Warren   46
Old Hickory
    Carpenter, Warren   46
Old Hoss
    Ardner, Joseph   18
    Radbourn, Charles   198
    Stephenson, Jackson   230
    Twineham, Art   243
Old Iron Hands
    Sullivan, Thomas   233
Old Lefthander
    Guise, Witt   102
Old Long Pants
    Hubbell, Carl   121
Old Mose
    Grove, Robert   102
Old Pardee
    Elliott, Claude   77
Old Pete
    Alexander, Grover   14
Old Reliable
    Henrich, Tommy   112
    Start, Joe   229
Old Roman
    Comiskey, Charles   56
Old Sarge
    Street, Charles   232
    Wilhelm, James   255
Old Sheep
    Ury, Louis   244
Old Shufflefoot
    Boudreau, Lou   34
Old Sy
    Sutcliffe, Elmer   234
Old Tomato Face
    Hartnett, Charles   109
Old True Blue
    Richardson, Hardy   203
Old Wax Figger
    Hemming, George   111
Old Whiskey Face
    Moran, Pat   172

Old Woman in the Red Cap
    Pabor, Charlie   186
Ole Porthole
    Posedel, Bill   195
Ole Preach
    Roe, Elwin   207
Ollie
    Bejma, Aloysius   26
    Fuhrman, Alfred   89
    Hanson, Earl   106
    Marquardt, Albert   153
    Smith, Orlin   225
One Arm
    Daily, Hugh   63
One Dog
    Johnson, Lance   126
One Flap Down
    Leonard, Jeffrey   144
One if...
    Baerga, Carlos   20
One-Nut Kruk
    Kruk, John   137
Onion
    Solano, Jhonatan   227
Only Kelly
    Kelly, Michael   131
Only Nolan
    Nolan, Ed   181
Oogie
    Urbina, Ugueth   244
Oom Paul
    Derringer, Samuel   68
    Krueger, Arthur   137
Orator
    Shafer, George   219
Orator Jim
    O'Rourke, Jim   183
Orlandito
    Berríos, José   29
Orlie
    Weaver, Orville   251

Oskie
    Slade, Gordon   223
Oso
    Abreu, José   13
Ostey
    Ostermueller, Frederick   185
Osuna Matata
    Osuna, Roberto   185
Ott
    Stein, Justin   230
Otter
    Olson, Gregg   184
Otto
    Krueger, Arthur   137
    Rettig, Adolph   202
Otto the Swatto
    Vélez, Otto   246
Outlaw
    Kiermaier, Kevin   132
Outmaker
    Moreno, Omar   173
Owl
    Henriksen, Olaf   112
Ownie
    Carroll, Owen   47
Ox
    Brovia, Joe   39
    Eckhardt, Oscar   76
    Goolsby, Ray   98
    Miller, John A.   169
Oyster
    Burns, Thomas   42
Oyster Joe
    Martina, John   154
Ozark Bear
    Tesreau, Charles   237
Ozark Ike
    Zernial, Gus   263
Ozzie
    Van Brabant, Camille   244
Pa

Harkins, John	107
Paca	
Childs, Clarence	51
Packy	
Dillon, Patrick	70
Rogers, Stanley	207
Pac-Man	
Belliard, Rafael	27
Paco	
Rodríguez, Steven	207
Paddy	
Baumann, Charles	24
Creeden, Pat	60
Driscoll, John L	73
Mayes, Adair	157
Siglin, Wesley	222
Paito	
Herrera, Ramón	114
Palillo	
Santiago, José R	213
Palmer Kid	
Karlon, Bill	129
Pan Blanco	
Pérez, Hernán	190
Panama Clipper	
López, Héctor	147
Panamanian Express	
Lewis, Allan	144
Panamanian Flash	
Phillips, Adolfo	192
Pancho	
Comellas, Jorge	55
Herrera, Juan	113
Snyder, Frank	226
Pancho Villa	
Berenguer, Juan	28
Panchón	
Herrera, Juan	113
Pantalones	
Santiago, José G	213
Pap	
Papish, Frank	187
Williams, Fred	255
Papa	
Williams, Fred	255
Papa Grande	
Valverde, José	244
Papa Jack	
Jackson, Ron	124
Papá Montero	
Luque, Dolf	148
Papa Paz	
Pazos, James	189
Papa Thompson	
Thompson, Milt	239
Papa Up	
Jackson, Ron	124
Papelero	
Valenzuela, Benny	244
Papi	
Martinez, Edgar	155
Papicho	
Martinez, Victor	155
Papito	
Bostock, Lyman	34
Vidal, José	246
Papo	
González, Eusebio	98
Hosmer, Eric	119
Pappo	
Jones, Adam	126
Pappy	
Prim, Ray	197
PaquÁn	
Estrada, Frank	79
Parakeet	
Fuentes, Rigiberto	89
Pard	
Epperly, Al	78
Parisian Bob	
Caruthers, Bob	48

Park Bang

Park Bang
    Park, Byung Ho   187
Parkway José
    Canseco, José   45
Parra Shark
    Park, Gerardo   188
Parson
    Lewis, Edward   144
    McGill, Bill   161
    Nicholson, Thomas   180
    Perryman, Emmett   191
    Sunday, Billy   234
Pat
    Ankenman, Frederick   17
    Bohen, Leo   33
    Callahan, Ray   45
    Crawford, Clifford   60
    Deasley, Thomas   67
    Dillard, Robert   70
    Duncan, Louis   74
    French, Frank   88
    Garrett, Henry   92
    Haley, Raymond   104
    Hardgrove, William   106
    Hilly, William   115
    Kilhullen, Joseph   132
    Luby, John   147
    Malone, Perce   151
    McGlothin, Ezra   161
    Newnam, Robert   179
    Paige, George   187
    Parker, Clarence P   187
    Tobin, Marion   240
    Townsend, Ira   241
    Whitaker, William   253
Pat the Bat
    Burrell, Patrick   42
Patato
    Cueto, Manuel   62

    Pascual, Carlos   188
Patato Pequeño
    Pascual, Camilo   188
Patcheye
    Gill, Johnny   95
Patsy
    Cahill, John   44
    McGaffigan, Mark   160
    O'Rourke, Joseph   183
    Tebeau, Oliver   237
Paul
    Sentell, Leopold   219
Paulie
    Molitor, Paul   171
Pavo
    Rupp, Cameron   210
Paw Paw
    Maxwell, Charlie   156
Pea Ridge
    Day, Henry   66
Pea Soup
    Dumont, George   74
Peaceful Valley
    Denzer, Roger   68
Peach
    Fisher, Chauncey   84
Peach Pie
    O'Connor, Jack J   182
Peaches
    Graham, George   99
    Nelson, Andy   179
    O'Neill, Philip   183
    Petry, Dan   191
    Werhas, Johnny   252
Peanut
    Wahl, Bobby   248
Peanuts
    Kantlehner, Erv   129
    Lehner, Paul   143
    Lowrey, Harry   147
    Pinnance, Ed   194

Solters, Julius   227
Pebbly Jack
   Glasscock, Jack   96
Peck
   Lerian, Walt   144
   Monroe, Ed   171
Pecks
   Daly, George   63
Pecky
   Suder, Pete   233
Peco
   Giard, Joe   94
Pedro el Grande
   Martínez, Pedro   155
Pee Wee
   Bowa, Larry   35
   Reese, Harold   201
Peej
   Hughes, Phil   121
Peek-a-boo
   Veach, Bill   245
Peekskill Pete
   Cregan, Pete   60
Peep
   O'Day, Hank   182
Peepsight
   Moses, Wally   174
Peerless Leader
   Chance, Frank   50
   Durocher, Leo   75
Peewee
   Briley, Greg   38
   Hauser, Arnold   109
Pee-Wee
   Oliver, Nate   184
   Waniger, Paul   249
Pegasus
   Chapman, Matt   50
Pelo Buche
   Chirinos, Robinson   51
Pelucita
   Martínez, Michael   155
Pencil
   Sembera, Carroll   218
Pencils
   Robinson, Frank   206
Penguin
   Cey, Ron   49
Penitentiary Face
   Leonard, Jeffrey   144
Pennsylvania Poker
   Brookens, Tom   38
Penny
   Bailey, Frederick   21
People's Cherce
   Walker, Fred   248
People's Choice
   Maxwell, Charlie   157
   Seerey, Pat   218
Pep
   Clark, Harry   52
   Conroy, William F   57
   Deininger, Otto   67
   Florence, Paul   85
   Goodwin, Claire   98
   Harris, Hernando   108
   Johnson, Don   125
   Medeiros, Ray   164
   Rambert, Elmer   199
   Young, Lemuel   263
   Youngs, Royce   263
Pepe
   Frías, Jesus   88
   Sanders, Roy G   213
Pepi
   Tovar, César   241
Pepito
   Tovar, César   241
Pepper
   Austin, James   20

Pepper Kid

Berghammer, Marty	28	Henning, Ernest	112
Clark, Roy	52	Hildebrand, Palmer	115
Clarke, Josh	53	Husting, Bert	122
Griffin, James	101	LaCock, Ralph	138
Martin, Johnny	154	LaForest, Pierre	138
Morgan, Eddie	173	Lamer, Pierre	139
Oyler, Andy	186	LePine, Louis	144
Peploski, Joseph	190	Lister, Morris	145

Pepper Kid

Austin, James	20	Lohman, George	146
		Loos, Ivan	146

Pepperdine Peach

		Manion, Clyde	152
Picciolo, Rob	193	McClanahan, Robert	158

Pepperoni

		McNabb, Edgar	163
Piazza, Mike	193	Milne, William	170

Percy

		Rambo, Warren	199
Coleman, Pierce	55	Ramos, Pedro	199

Perfect Storm

Crawford, Carl	60	Reiser, Harold	201
		Runnels, James	210

Perimeter Pascual

Pérez, Pascual	190	Schmidt, Frederich	216

Perk

		Scott, Floyd	217
Kennedy, William	132	Shields, Francis	221

Perpetual Pedro

		Sims, Clarence	222
Feliciano, Pedro	82	Taylor, Vernon	236

Pete

Alexander, Grover	14	Turgeon, Eugene	242
Allen, Jesse	15	Varney, Richard	245
Aragón, Ángel	18	Young, Bryan	262

Petey

Browning, Louis	40	Martínez, Pedro	155
Center, Marvin	49	Pedroia, Dustin	189
Chapman, Glenn	50		

Petie

Charton, Frank	50	Behan, Charles	26

Phantom

Coachman, Bobby	54	Javier, Julián	125

Phat Albert

Compton, Anna	56		
Daley, Tom	63	Pujols, Albert	197

Phenomenal

Fahrer, Clarence	80		
Flagstead, Ira	84	Smith, John F	225

Phenomenal Kid

Fowler, Jesse	87
Fox, Ervin	87

Kilroy, Matt	133	Traynor, Harold	241
Phil		**Pig**	
Irwin, Bill	123	House, Frank	119
McCullough, Pinson	159	**Pig Pen**	
Philliabuck		Dwyer, Jim	75
Cavarretta, Phil	49	**Pig Tiger**	
Phoenix Flash		Lee, Dae-ho	142
Nicholas, Don	180	**Piggy**	
Phone Book		French, Walt	88
Sparks, Steve	228	Paige, George	187
Piano Legs		Ward, Frank	249
Gore, George	98	**Pigpen**	
Hickman, Charlie	114	Byrnes, Eric	43
Pernoll, Henry	190	Gallagher, Alan	90
Piano Mover		**Pigtail Billy**	
Smith, Frank	224	Riley, Billy	204
Piccolo Pete		**Pimba**	
Elko, Pete	77	Alvarado, Luis	16
Pick		**Pinch**	
Fisher, Ray	84	Thomas, Chester	238
Quinn, John	198	**Pinches**	
Pickle		Kunz, Earl	137
Lockman, Carroll	146	**Ping**	
Pickles		Bodie, Frank	32
Dillhoefer, William	70	**Pink**	
Gerken, George	94	Hawley, Emerson	110
Woods, George	260	**Pinky**	
Pico		Hargrave, William	107
Leclarc, José	142	Higgins, Michael	115
Pid		Lindsay, Chris	145
Purdy, Everett	197	May, Merrill	157
Pidge		O'Neill, Emmett	183
Browne, Prentice	40	Pittenger, Clarke	194
Pidgey		Shoffner, Milburn	221
Morgan, Daniel	173	Swander, Edward	235
Pie		Whitney, Arthur	254
Piechota, Al	193	Woods, George	260
Rollins, Rich	208	**Pinto Bean**	
Traynor, Harold	241	Pinto, Ricardo	194
Pie Face		**Pip**	

Pisch
Koehler, Horace — 136

Pisch
Pechiney, George — 189

Pistol
Mason, Hank — 155

Pistol Pete
Reiser, Harold — 201

Pitching Poet
Kenna, Ed — 131

Pitching Professor
Lewis, Edward — 144

Pittsburgh Stealer
Taveras, Frank — 236

Pituki
Solarte, Yangervis — 227

Pizza
Santo, Ron — 214

Pizza Man
Kazmir, Scott — 130

PJ
Forbes, Patrick — 85
Walters, Phillip — 249

Plowboy
Morgan, Tom — 173

Plunging Chink
Outen, William — 186

Poco
Taitt, Doug — 235

Podfather
Podsednik, Scott — 194

Podge
Weihe, John — 251

Poet
Charles, Ed — 50

Poet Pitcher
Kenna, Ed — 131

Poffin Belly
Whitted, George — 254

Poison
Andrews, Ivy — 17

Pokey

Pol
Reese, Calvin — 201

Pol
Perritt, William — 190

Polar Bear
Alonso, Pete — 15
Datz, Jeff — 64

Poli
Lajoie, Nap — 138

Polish Prince
Krukow, Mike — 137

Polish Wizard
Appleton, Peter — 18

Pollo
Allen, Cody — 15
Pollock, Allen — 195

Polly
McLarry, Howard — 162
Speraw, Paul — 228
Wolfe, Roy — 259
Zeider, Rollie — 263

Polo
Andrews, Stanley — 17

Ponchón
Herrera, Juan — 113

Pongo Joe
Cantillon, Joe — 46

Pony
Ryan, Jimmy — 211
Sager, Samuel — 212

Pooch
Barnhart, Clyde — 23
Puccinelli, George — 197

Poodles
Hutcheson, Joe — 122

Poosh 'Em Up Tony
Lazzeri, Tony — 141

Pop
Anson, Adrian — 17
Corkhill, John — 58
Dillon, Frank — 70

Durham, Joe	74
Fauver, Clay	81
Foster, Clarence	86
Gregory, Paul	101
Haines, Jesse	104
Joiner, Roy	126
Lytle, Edward	149
Prim, Ray	197
Reising, Charlie	201
Rising, Percival	204
Ryba, Dominic	211
Schriver, William	216
Schwartz, Bill A	217
Shriver, Harry	221
Shriver, William	221
Smith, Charles	224
Snyder, Charles	226
Swett, William	235
Tate, Edward	236
Williams, Walter	256

Pop Rising
Rising, Percival	204

Pop-boy
Smith, Clarence	224

Pope
Pall, Donn	187

Popeye
Eichhorn, Mark	77
Erickson, Hank	78
Mahaffey, Roy	150
Mays, Willie	157
Zimmer, Don	264

Poppa
DeShields, Delino D	69

Pops
Fodge, Gene	85
Prim, Ray	197
Stargell, Wilver	229

Pork Chop
Hoffman, John	117
Robinson, Wilbert	206

Pork Chops
Aaron, Henry	13

Porky
Biscan, Frank	30
Howell, Murray	120
Lade, Doyle	138
Odom, Dave	184
Pawelek, Ted	189
Reniff, Hal	202

Porterhouse
Napoli, Mike	178

Poss
Eubanks, Eul	79

Possum
Burright, Larry	42
Whitted, George	254

Pot
LaPorte, Frank	140

Potato
Cueto, Manuel	62

Potentate of Pow
Ruth, George	211

Powder
Tannehill, Jesse	235

Preacher
Blach, Ty	31
Bonnell, Barry	33
Dorsett, Cal	72
Faszholz, Jack	81
Hebert, Wally	110
Law, Vern	141
Owen, Arnold	186
Roe, Elwin	207

Pres
Ermer, Cal	79

Pretty Ricky
Porcello, Rick	195

Pretzel
- Knetzer, Elmer — 135
- Pexxullo, John — 191

Pretzels
- Getzien, Charles — 94

Prexy
- Atherton, Charles — 19

Pride of Havana
- Luque, Dolf — 148

Prime Time
- Coleman, Michael — 54
- Sanders, Deion — 213

Primo
- Preibisch, Mel — 196

Prince
- Oana, Henry — 183
- Schaefer, William — 214

Prince Albert
- Pujols, Albert — 197

Prince Fish
- Trout, Mike — 242

Prince Hal
- Chase, Hal — 50
- Newhouser, Hal — 179
- Schumacher, Hal — 217

Prince of Pounders
- Ruth, George — 211

Princeton Charlie
- Reilly, Charlie — 201

Prof
- Weaver, Monte — 251

Professor
- Craghead, Howard — 59
- Hendricks, Kyle — 112
- Hook, James — 118
- Maddux, Greg — 150
- Ostrowski, Joe — 185
- Thomas, Myles — 238

Project
- Hafner, Travis — 104

Pronk
- Hafner, Travis — 104

Prunes
- Moolic, George — 171

Pruschka
- Pafko, Andy — 187

Psycho
- Lyons, Steve — 149

PTBNL
- Phegley, Josh — 192

Puchy
- Delgado, Luis — 67

Pud
- Galvin, James — 90
- McChesney, Harry — 158

Puddin' Head
- Jones, Willie — 127

Pudge
- Fisk, Carlton — 84
- Gautreaux, Sidney — 92
- Haney, Fred — 106
- Lavelle, Gary — 141
- Rodríguez, Iván — 207

Pudgie
- Delahanty, Frank — 67

Pudgy
- Gould, Al — 99
- Youkilis, Kevin — 262

Puff
- Nettles, Graig — 179

Pug
- Allen, Horace — 15
- Bennett, Justin — 28
- Cavet, Tillar — 49
- Griffin, Francis — 101
- Hallahan, Bill — 105
- Rensa, Tony — 202

Pugger
- Kelb, George — 130

Pumpsie

Green, Elijah	100	Knight, Joe	135
Punch		**Quiet Man**	
Judy, Lyle	128	Alston, Walter	16
Knoll, Charles	135	**Quiz**	
Punjab		Quisenberry, Dan	198
Kardow, Paul	129	**RA**	
Punk		Dickey, Robert	69
Gautreau, Walter	92	**Rabbi of Swat**	
Pup		Solomon, Mose	227
Doherty, John	71	**Rabbit**	
Pupi		Benton, Stan	28
Delgado, Randall	67	Caffie, Joe	44
Pure Rage		Fuller, Frank	89
Pérez, Chris	190	Glaviano, Tommy	96
Purple		Huggins, Miller	121
Raines, Timothy Sr.	199	Lawry, Otis	141
Puss		Maranville, Walter	152
Manning, Walter	152	McHale, Bob	162
Pussy		McNair, Eric	163
Tebeau, Charles	237	Miller, Jim	168
Put-Put		Nill, George	181
Ashburn, Richie	19	Powell, Ray	196
Putsy		Robinson, William C	206
Caballero, Ralph	43	Saverine, Bob	214
Putz		Shelton, Andrew	220
Caballero, Ralph	43	Slagle, Jimmy	223
Q		Tavener, John	236
Quintana, José	198	Warstler, Harold	250
Quisenberry, Dan	198	**Radiant Red**	
Quality		Killefer, Wade	133
Smith, Ray	225	**Radio**	
Qualls		Alberto, Hanser	14
Smith, Ray	225	**Raffy Big Stick**	
Quarterrican		Devers, Rafael	69
Lugo, Seth	148	**Rags**	
Queenie		Faircloth, James	80
O'Rourke, James	183	Righetti, Dave	204
Quiet Assassin		**Rain Man**	
Newsome, Ljay	180	Benes, Andy	27
Quiet Joe			

Rainbow

Rainbow
    Trout, Steve   242
Rajah
    Hornsby, Rogers   119
Rajah of Swat
    Hornsby, Rogers   119
Ralph
    LaPointe, Raoul   139
    Onis, Manuel   184
Ramrod
    Nelson, Emmett   179
Rap
    Warstler, Harold   250
Rapid Robert
    Feller, Bob   82
Raptor
    Suter, Brent   234
Rasty
    Wright, Wayne   261
    Wright, William Sm   261
Rat
    Gaetti, Gary   90
    Miller, Brad   168
Rattlesnake
    Baker, Thomas   21
Rawhide
    Tabor, Jim   235
Rawmeat Bill
    Rodgers, Bill   206
Ray
    Brown, Paul   40
    Knode, Bob   135
    Kremer, Remy   137
    Noble, Rafael   181
    Semproch, Roman   219
    Shines, Razor   221
Ray Gun
    Ray, Jim   200
Razor
    Laureano, Ramón   141
    Ledbetter, Ralph   142
Razzle Dazzle
    Murphy, Con   176
Reading Rifle
    Furillo, Carl   89
Real Deal
    Durbin, Joseph   74
    Harvey, Matt   109
Reb
    Russell, Ewell   210
Rebel
    Adams, Karl   14
    Cooper, Guy   57
    Hundley, Randy   122
    McMillan, Tommy   163
    McTigue, Bill   164
    Oakes, Ennis   183
    Oliver, Tom   184
    Phillips, John   192
red
    McGlothin, Jim   161
Red
    Ames, Leon   16
    Anderson, Arnold   17
    Badgro, Morris   20
    Barbary, Donald   22
    Barnes, Emile   23
    Barrett, Charles   23
    Barrett, Frank   23
    Barron, David   23
    Bennett, James   28
    Bird, James   30
    Bittmann, Henry   30
    Bluhm, Harvey   32
    Booles, Seabron   34
    Borom, Edward   34
    Bowser, James   35
    Branch, Norm   36

Red

Brown, John L	39	Hayworth, Myron	110
Brunet, George	40	Hedlund, Mike	110
Bullock, Malton	41	Herring, Art	114
Busby, Paul	42	Hill, Clifford	115
Calhoun, Jack	44	Hinton, John	116
Callahan, Jim	45	Hittle, Lloyd	116
Camnitz, Howie	45	Hoff, Chester	116
Camp, Howie	45	Holt, James	118
Carroll, Ralph	47	Howell, Murray	120
Cary, Scott	48	Jones, Sam	127
Causey, Cecil	49	Juelich, John	128
Conkwright, Allen	56	Kellett, Donald	130
Connally, John	56	Kelly, Albert	130
Corriden, John Sr	58	Killefer, Wade	133
Cox, Plateau	59	Kinsella, Bob	133
Daughters, Bob	65	Kleinow, John	134
Davis, John Hu	66	Kreitz, Ralph	137
Delhi, Lee	68	Kress, Ralph	137
Desautels, Gene	68	Kuhn, Walt	137
Donahue, Francis	71	Landenberger, Ken	139
Dooin, Charles	71	Lanning, Lester	139
Dorman, Charles	72	Larmore, Bob	140
Downey, Alexander	72	Lively, Everett	146
Downs, Jerome	72	Long, Nelson	146
Durrett, Elmer	75	Lucas, Charles	148
Eaton, Zeb	76	Lutz, Louis	148
Ehret, Philip	77	Lynn, Japhet	149
Embree, Charles	78	Madden, Frank	150
Evans, Russell	80	Mann, Garth	152
Faber, Urban	80	Marion, John	153
Fisher, John	84	Massey, Roy	155
Fisher, Tom C	84	McColl, Alex	159
Friend, Owen	88	McDermott, Frank	159
Gunkel, Woodward	103	McKee, Raymond	162
Gust, Ernie	103	McQuillen, Glenn	164
Hardy, Francis	107	Miller, Leo	169
Harvel, Luther	109	Morgan, James	173

Munger, George	176		Swanson, Arthur	235
Munson, Clarence	176		Thomas, Robert	238
Murff, John	176		Torkelson, Chester	240
Murphy, Leo	176		Torphy, Walter	241
Murray, John	177		Tramback, Steven	241
Nelson, Albert	178		Treadway, Thadford	241
Nonnenkamp, Leo	181		Waller, John	249
Oldham, John	184		Webb, Samuel	251
Ostergard, Roy	185		White, Oliver	253
Owens, Thomas	186		Wilson, Robert	258
Padgett, Ernie	186		Wingo, Absalom	258
Patterson, John	189		Wolfgang, Mellie	259
Peery, George	189		Woodhead, James	260
Phillips, Clarence	192		Worthington, Al	260
Powell, Jack	196		Worthington, Robert	260
Proctor, Noah	197		**Red Baron**	
Rawlings, Johnny	200		Calhoun, Kole	44
Redmond, Jack	201		Greer, Thurman	100
Roberts, Charles	205		Sutcliffe, Rick	234
Roche, Jack	206		**Red Bone**	
Rolfe, Robert	208		Bostock, Lyman	34
Rollings, William	208		**Red Dawg**	
Rollins, Rich	208		Reddick, Josh	200
Ruffing, Charles	210		**Red Dog**	
Schillings, Elbert	215		Killefer, Wade	133
Schoendienst, Albert	216		Redmond, Mike	201
Shannon, Maurice	219		**Red Rooster**	
Shea, John E	220		Rader, Dave	198
Shea, Patrick	220		Rader, Doug	198
Sheridan, Eugene	220		**Red Thunder**	
Smith, James C	225		Frazier, Clint	87
Smith, Marvin	225		**Reddy**	
Smith, Richard	225		Foster, Oscar	86
Smith, Willard	226		Gray, Jim	100
Smyth, James	226		Grey, Romer	101
Stallcup, Thomas	229		Mack, Joseph	150
Steiner, James	230		McMillan, George	163
			Miller, Tom	169

Walsh, Joe R	249
Redleg	
Snyder, Emanuel	226
Reds	
Herrell, Walt	113
McGarr, Jim	160
RedTurn2	
Turner, Justin	243
Reggie	
Richter, Emil	203
Reindeer Bill	
killefer, Bill	132
Reject	
Rojek, Stan	208
Rem Dawg	
Remy, Jerry	202
Rend	
Matz, Steven	156
Reno	
Bertoia, Pierino	29
Rev	
Haseley, Adam	109
Reverend	
O'Day, Hank	182
Rhineland Rocket	
Altherr, Aaron	16
Rhino	
Hitt, Roy	116
Rhys Lightning	
Hoskins, Rhys	119
Ribs	
Raney, Frank	200
Rich Dresser	
Latham, Arlie	140
Rich Homie	
Cunningham, Thomas	62
Rick	
Auerbach, Frederick	19
Honeycutt, Frederick	118
Monday, Robert	171
Ricky	
Jordan, Paul	128
Nolasco, Carlos	181
Pickett, Cecil	193
Ricky F	
Anderson, Tyler	17
Ricky Raindrops	
Porcello, Rick	195
Rico	
Rossy, Elam	209
Rifle Jim	
Middleton, Jim	167
Rifleman	
Connors, Kevin	57
Davis, Eric	65
Griffey, Ken Jr.	101
Rimp	
Lanier, Lorenzo	139
Ringling Brothers	
Miranda, Guillermo	170
Rinty	
Monahan, Edward	171
Rip	
Cannell, Wirt	45
Coleman, Walter	55
Collins, Harry	55
Conway, Richard	57
Egan, Jack	76
Hagerman, Zerah	104
Jordan, Raymond	128
McKay, Reeve	162
Radcliff, Raymond	198
Ragan, Arthur	198
Repulski, Eldon	202
Russell, Glen	210
Sewell, Truett	219
Van Haltren, George	244
Vowinkel, John	247
Wade, Richard	247

Wheeler, Floyd 253
Williams, Alva 255
Rip Zip
  Hagerman, Zerah 104
Ripper
  Collins, James 55
Riverboat
  Smith, Bob 224
RJ
  Reynolds, Robert 203
  Swindle, Robert 235
Road Runner
  Garr, Ralph 92
Roadblock
  Jones, Sherman 127
Roarin' Nick
  Allen, Artemus 15
Roaring Bill
  Hassemaer, Bill 109
  Kennedy, William 132
Rob
  Gardner, Richard 92
Robbie
  Robinson, Frank 206
  Robinson, Wilbert 206
  Robinson, William H 206
Robomb
  Romine, Andrew 208
Rock
  Averill, Earl 20
  García, Freddy 91
  LaRoche, Adam 140
  Raines, Timothy Sr 199
  Rakow, Ed 199
  Schroeder, Bill 216
  Snipes, Wyatt 226
  Stromme, Floyd 232
  Woodling, Gene 260
Rock N Fire
  Smith, Chris M 224
Rocket
  Brock, Lou 38
  Clemens, Roger 53
  Warren, Adam 250
Rockin' Robin
  Yount, Robin 263
Rocko
  Mesoraco, Devin 166
Rocks
  Start, Joe 229
Rocky
  Biddle, Lee 30
  Bridges, Everett 37
  Childress, Rodney 51
  Colavito, Rocco 54
  Coppinger, John 57
  Garrison, Robert 92
  Krsnich, Rocco 137
  Nelson, Glenn 179
  Rhawn, Bobby 203
  Schmees, George 215
  Stone, John T 231
  Stone, John V 231
  Swoboda, Ron 235
Rod
  Correia, Ronald 58
  Dedeaux, Raoul 67
Rojo
  Dyson, Sam 75
  Rader, Doug 198
  Straily, Dan 231
Roller 'Rilla
  Tiant, Luis 239
Rollickig Rollie
  Hemsley, Ralston 111
Rollie
  Hemsley, Ralston 111
Roly-poly

Youkilis, Kevin	262	Moore, Gene Jr.	172
Rome		O'Connor, Jack J	182
Chambers, Richard	50	**Roxey**	
Ronny		Roach, Wilbur	205
Miller, Roland	169	**Roxie**	
Rook		Lawson, Alfred	141
Mercer, Jordy	165	**Roxy**	
Rooney		Crouch, Jack	61
Sweeney, John	235	Miller, Roscoe	169
Rooster		Snipes, Wyatt	226
Burleson, Rick	41	Walters, Alfred	249
Rope		**Roy**	
Boyd, Robert	35	Elsh, Eugene	78
Ropes		Valdés, Rogelio	244
Russell, Bill	210	**Rozycki**	
Roscoe		Kepler, Max	132
Coughlin, William E	58	**RR Cool Jay**	
Rose		Romero, Ricky	208
Barclay, George	22	**RT**	
Rosebud		Upright, Roy	243
Camnitz, Howie	45	**Rubber**	
Ross		Krapp, Gene	137
Barnes, Charles	23	**Rubber Arm**	
Youngs, Royce	263	Krapp, Gene	136
Ross the Boss		**Rubber Arm Gun**	
Ross, Cody	209	Weyhing, Gus	253
Rosy		**Rubberarm**	
Carlisle, Walter	46	Russell, Allen	210
Ryan, Wilfred	211	**Rubberlegs**	
Rotty		Miller, Roscoe	169
Rotblatt, Marv	209	**Rubber-Winged Gus**	
Rough		Weyhing, Gus	253
Carrigan, Bill	47	**Rub-Dub-Hub**	
Round Mound of Pound		Perdue, Herbert	190
Sandoval, Pablo	213	**Rube**	
Rowdy		Adams, Dan Le	13
Bartell, Richard	24	Albosta, Edward	14
Elliott, Harold	77	Benton, John	28
Hummel, John	122	Bressler, Raymond	37
Meyer, Russ	167	Caldwell, Ray	44

Rudy

Dessau, Frank	69	Branyan, Russell	37
Ehrhardt, Welton	77	**Rusty**	
Ellis, George	77	Gerhardt, Allen	94
Foster, George	86	Greer, Thurman	100
Geyer, Jacob	94	Griner, Donald	101
Kinsella, Ed	134	Kemmerer, Russ	131
Kisinger, Charles	134	LaRue, Jason	140
Kroh, Floyd	137	McNealy, Robert	163
Lutzke, Walter	148	Staub, Daniel	230
Manning, Walter	152	Tillman, Kerry	239
Marion, Donald	153	Tipple, Dan	239
Marquard, Richard	153	Torres, Rosendo	241
Marshall, Roy	153	Yarnall, Waldo	261
Novotney, Ralph	182	**Ryan Express**	
Parnham, James	188	Ryan, Lynn	211
Peters, Otto	191	**Rynie**	
Robinson, John H	206	Wolters, Reinder	259
Schauer, Alexander	215	**Ryno**	
Sellers, Oliver	218	Sandberg, Ryne	213
Suter, Harry	234	**Sabbath Smasher**	
Taylor, Ed	236	Maxwell, Charlie	157
Vickers, Harry	246	**Saccharin Slugger**	
Vinson, Ernest	246	Palmeiro, Rafael	187
Waddell, Eddie	247	**Sad Sam**	
Walberg, George	248	Gray, Sam	100
Walker, Albert	248	Jones, Sam	127
Ward, John A	250	Jones, Sam P	127
Yarrison, Byron	261	Zoldak, Sam	264
Rudy		**Sadie**	
Schlesinger, Bill	215	Houck, Sargent	119
Rugger		McMahon, John	163
Ardizoia, Rinaldo	18	**Sado**	
Runt		Posada, Jorge	195
Cox, Frank	59	**Safeco Joe**	
Walsh, Michael	249	Saunders, Joe	214
Russ the Red		**Sage**	
Meyer, Russ	167	Hughes, Roy	121
Russell the Muscle		**Sailor**	
		Newkirk, Joel	179

Sarge

Roberts, Clarence	205
Shawkey, Bob	220
Stroud, Ralph	232

Sailor Bill
Posedel, Bill	195

Sal
Campfield, William	45

Salida Tom
Hughes, Tom L	121

Salt Rock
Midkiff, Ezra	167

Saltly
Solters, Julius	227

Salty
Morton, Guy Jr.	174
Parker, Francis	187

Sam
Barnes, Austin	23
Brenegan, Olaf	37
Covington, Clarence	59
Lanford, Lewis	139
Langford, Elton	139
LaRocque, Simeon	140
Mele, Sabath	165
Rice, Edgar	203
Vico, George	246
Woodruff, Orville	260

Sambo
Leslie, Sam	144

Sammy
Curran, Simon	62
Hale, Arvel	104
Holbrook, James	117
Saito, Takashi	212
Simon, Syl	222

Samson
Pool, Harlin	195

Sanchize
Sanchez, Aaron	212

Sánchez, Gary	213

Sandblaster
Arenado, Nolan	18

Sandman
Rivera, Mariano	204

Sandow
Mertes, Sam	166

Sandusky Singer
Upp, George	243

Sandy
Alomar, Santos Jr.	15
Alomar, Santos, Sr.	15
Amorós, Edmundo	16
Burk, Charles	41
Griffin, Tobias	101
Herring, Art	114
Irwin, Arthur	123
Lajoie, Nap	138
Liebhardt, Glenn	145
McDermott, Thomas	159
McDougal, John	160
Nava, Vincent	178
Piez, Charles	193
Sundra, Steve	234
Valdespino, Hilario	244
Vance, Gene	245
Vance, Joe	245
Wihtol, Alexander	254

Sang Namja
Thames, Eric	237

Santa Barbara Bomber
Mathews, Eddie	155

Sap
Randall, James	199

Sarge
Bagby, James Sr.	21
Connally, George	56
Kuzava, Bob	138
Matthews, Gary Sr.	156

Mitterling, Ralph 170
Sarge Junior
   Matthews, Gary Jr. 156
Sasquatch
   Kuhl, Chad 137
   Ladd, Pete 138
Sassafrass
   Winter, George 258
Satan
   Stutz, George 233
Satch
   Satriano, Tom 214
Satchel
   Paige, Leroy 187
   Verble, Gene 246
Satchelfoot
   Wells, Ed 252
Satsurō
   Kawasaki, Munenori 129
Saturn Nuts
   Arroyo, Bronson 19
Savage Tom
   Thomas, Tom 238
Sawed Off Red Head
   Gearin, Dennis 93
Say Hey Kid
   Mays, Willie 157
Say It Ain't
   Sosa, Sammy 227
Scat
   Cassini, Jack 48
   Davis, Otis 66
   Metha, Frank 166
Scatter
   Sallee, Harry 212
Schnozz
   Lombardi, Ernie 146
Schoolboy
   Cohen, Alta 54
   Hoyt, Waite 120
   Knight, John 135
   Rowe, Lynwood 209
Schoolboy Fritz
   Dorish, Harry 72
Schoolboy Wonder
   Hoyt, Waite 120
Schultz
   Gessler, Henry 94
Scissors
   Foutz, Dave 86
   Sallee, Harry 212
   Weaver, Art 251
Scoop
   Oliver, Al 184
   Scharein, Art 215
Scoop 'em Up
   Carey, George 46
Scooper Bill
   Schwartz, Bill A 217
Scoops
   Carey, George 46
   Carey, Max 46
   Carey, Tom 46
   Cooney, Jimmy 57
Scootch
   Lucey, Joe 148
Scooter
   Conforto, Michael 56
   Gennett, Ryan 93
   Koshorek, Clem 136
   Rizzuto, Phil 205
   Thompson, Milt 239
   Tucker, Eddie 242
Scorpion
   Joseph, Tommy 128
Scott
   Wheeler, Don 253
Scottie
   Slayback, Elbert 223
Scotty

Alcock, John	14	Lange, Frank	139
Barr, Hyder	23	**Seaganbuck**	
Scotty Jetpacks		Lange, Frank	139
Kingery, Scott	133	**Sears**	
Scout		Roebuck, Ed	207
Stovall, Jesse	231	**Seattle Bill**	
Scow		James, Bill L	124
Thomas, Fay	238	**Second Half Raburn**	
Scrabble		Raburn, Ryan	198
Rzepczynski, Marc	211	**Secret Spitballer**	
Scranton Bill		Sutton, Don	234
Coughlin, Bill	58	**Secret Weapon**	
Scrap Iron		Oquendo, José	184
Biecher, Ed	30	Renteria, Rick	202
Courtney, Clint	58	**Secretary of Defense**	
Garner, Phil	92	Maddox, Garry	150
Kenna, Eddie	131	**Senor Octubre**	
Stinson, Bob	231	Ortiz, David	185
Scrappy		**Señor Octubre**	
Carroll, John	47	Ruiz, Carlos	210
Moore, William Allen	172	**Señor Smoke**	
Scrappy Bill		Berenguer, Juan	28
Joyce, Bill	128	López, Aurelio	147
Scratch		**Sensitive John**	
Davis, Ira	66	Clarkson, John	53
Waner, Lloyd	249	**Sep**	
Scroggy		Gantenbein, Joe	91
Durnbaugh, Bobby	74	**Sergio Millar**	
Scrubs		Miller, Brad	168
Sellman, Frank	218	**Serpent Tongue**	
Tomlin, Josh	240	Smith, Jimmy L	225
Scuz		**Shabotch**	
Grimsley, Ross Jr.	101	Samuels, Joe	212
Sea Bass		**Shad**	
González, Álex	97	Barry, John C	24
Sea Lion		Rhem, Flint	203
Hall, Charley	105	Roe, James	207
Seacap		**Shadow**	
Christensen, Walter	51	Carroll, Dick	47
Seagan		Gilmore, Frank	95

Pyle, Harry 197
Shady Bill
    Leith, Bill 143
Shag
    Easterwood, Roy 76
    Shaughnessy, Francis 220
    Thompson, James 238
Shags
    Horan, Joseph 119
Shake 'n Bake
    McBride, Arnold 158
Shaker
    Moseby, Lloyd 174
Shakes
    Huntzinger, Walt 122
Shamus
    Kane, Jim 129
    Tobin, Jim 240
Shaney
    Kissinger, Bill 134
Shang
    Kissinger, Bill 134
Shano
    Collins, John F 55
Shanty
    Daringer, Cliff 64
    Hegan, Jim 111
    Hogan, James 117
Shark
    Bernadina, Roger 29
    Samardzija, Jeff 212
She
    Donahue, Charles 71
Sheriff
    Blake, John 31
    Bridges, Marshall 38
    Chafin, Andrew 49
    Charlton, Norm 50
    Constable, Jim 57
    Ewoldt, Art 80
    Gaddy, John 90
    Gainer, Del 90
    Gassaway, Charlie 92
    Harris, Dave 108
    Jones, Jim 127
    Lee, Hal 142
    Paddack, Chris 186
    Singleton, John 223
    Smith, Earl L 224
    Van Atta, Russ 244
Sheriff of Higginsport
    Sallee, Harry 212
Sheriff of Swattingham
    Reynolds, Mark 203
Shetland Pony
    Ott, Mel 186
Shine
    Cortazzo, John 58
    Sherling, Ed 220
Shirt
    Smith, Rufus 225
Shoddy
    Shaw, Al 220
Shoeless Joe
    Jackson, Joe 123
Shoemaker
    Nicholson, Fred 180
Shoes
    Pittman, Joe 194
Shoo-fly
    Schlafly, Harry 215
Shook
    Brown, Elmer 39
Shooter
    Beck, Rodney 25
Shooty
    Babitt, Mack 20
Shortwave
    Bartell, Richard 24
Shorty

Colgan, William 55
Crawford, Glenn 60
Davenport, Claude 65
Dee, Maurice 67
Des Jardien, Paul 68
Fuller, William 89
Gallagher, Charles 90
Howe, John 120
Radford, Paul 198
Raudman, Bob 200
Shea, John E 220
Slagle, Jimmy 223
Stratton, Monty 232

Shotgun
Chartak, Mike 50
Gardner, Billy 91
Peters, John 191
Rogers, Tom 207
Shuba, George 221

Shovel
Hodge, Clarence 116

Showboat
Fisher, George 84

Showmingo
Santana, Domingo 213

Showrrea
Correa, Carlos 58

Shrek
Mench, Kevin 165

Shucks
Pruett, Hub 197

Shufflin' Phil
Douglas, Phil 72

Si
Blankenship, Homer 32

Sibby
Sisti, Sebastian 223

Sid
Hensiek, Phil 113

Sid
Hickey, Jim 114

Sidee
Caithammer, George 44

Silencer
Osinski, Dan 185

Silent Assassin
Vázquez, Javier 245

Silent Bill
Phillips, Bill C 192

Silent Bob
Meusel, Bob 166

Silent Cal
Benge, Ray 28

Silent George
Hendrick, George 112
Twombly, George 243

Silent Glenn
Elliott, Glenn 77

Silent Jake
Volz, Jake 247

Silent Joe
Boley, John 33
Martin, Joseph S. 154

Silent John
Gillespie, John 95
Hummel, John 122
Titus, John 240
Whitehead, John 254

Silent Mike
Tiernan, Mike 239

Silent Steve
Carlton, Steve 46

Silk
Bryant, Kris 41
Kavanagh, Charlie 129

Silk Stockings
Schafer, Harry 214

Silver
Flint, Frank 85

Silver Bill

Groh, Lewis	101	Weaver, Art	251
King, Charles F	133	**Skates**	
Zacher, Elmer	263	Smith, Lonnie	225
Silver Bill		**Skeeter**	
Phillips, Bill B	192	Barnes, William	23
Phillips, Bill C	192	Bigbee, Carson	30
Silver Fox		Kell, Everett	130
Egan, Jack	76	Newsome, Lamar	180
Petty, Jesse	191	Scalzi, Frank	214
Snider, Edwin	226	Shelton, Andrew	220
Utley, Chase	244	Tate, Lee	236
Simba		Webb, James	251
Simmons, Andrelton	222	Wright, Clyde	261
Simmons, Ted	222	**Skeets**	
Simon		Dickey, George	69
Sanders, Roy L	213	Gregg, Hal	100
Sing Sing		**Skel**	
Singer, Bill	223	Roach, Rudolph	205
Singer Throwing Machine		**Skeleton**	
Singer, Bill	223	Griffin, Doug	101
Singular Senor		Roach, Rudolph	205
Gomez, Vernon	97	**Skeletor**	
Sinker-Slider		Reynolds, Mark	203
Bandy, Jett	22	**Ski**	
Sir Didi		Fiske, Max	84
Gregorius, Mariekson	100	Melillo, Oscar	165
Sir Hugh		**Skids**	
Duffy, Hugh	74	Lipon, Johnny	145
Sir Richard		**Skinner**	
Cooley, Duff	57	Hopkins, Mike	118
Sir Robert		**Skinny**	
Groom, Bob	102	Brown, Hal	39
Sir Timothy		Graham, Arthur	99
Keefe, Tim	130	Graham, Kyle	99
Sis		Kalbfus, Charlie	128
Hopkins, John	118	McNabb, Carl	163
Hopkins, Mike	118	O'Neal, Oran	183
Six		Shaner, Wally	219
Mathis, Jeff	156	**Skins**	
Six O'Clock			

Jones, John 127

Skip
Crouch, Bill 61
Fregosi, Jim 88
Guinn, Drannon 102
Lockwood, Claude 146
Mauch, Gene 156
Pitlock, Lee 194
Schumaker, Jared 217
Wilber, Del 254

Skipper
Donalds, Ed 71
Friday, Grier 88
Roberts, Clarence 205

Skipper Bill
Shipke, Bill 221

Skippy
Byrnes, Milt 43
Knoblauch, Chuck 135
Machado, Dixon 149
Roberge, Joseph 205

Skoonj
Furillo, Carl 89

Skull
Devine, William 69

Sky King
Kingman, Dave 133

Skyrocket
Smith, Samuel 225

Slab
Burns, James 42

Slam
Agnew, Sam 14

Slammin' Salmon
Salmon, Tim 212

Slammin' Sammy
Sosa, Sammy 227

Slats
Blackburne, Russell 31

Davis, Ira 66
Dorman, Charlie 72
Mack, Connie 149
Marion, Marty 153
McConnell, George 159
McGillicuddy, Cornelius 161
Sallee, Harry 212
Wilson, Tom 258

Sled
Allen, Fletcher 15

Sledge
Moylan, Peter 175

Sleeper
Sullivan, Thomas 233

Sleepy
Flanagan, Ed 84
Simmons, Ted 222
Townsend, George 241

Sleepy Bill
Burns, William 42
Johnson, William 126

Slendid Spitter
Williams, Ted 256

Sleuth
Fleming, Tom 85

Slewfoot
Butler, Cecil 43

Slick
Castleman, Clydell 48
Coffman, George 54
Ford, Edward 85
Gardner, Billy 91
Hartley, Grover 108
Host, Gene 119
Johnson, Lou 126
Van Slyke, Andy 245

Slicker
Parks, Vernon 188

Sliding Billy

Slim

Hamilton, Billy	105

Slim

Caldwell, Ray	44
Embry, Charles	78
Emmerich, William	78
Foster, Ed	86
Haislip, Jim	104
Harding, Charlie	107
Harrell, Oscar	107
Harriss, William	108
Kindall, Jerry	133
Kinzy, Harry	134
Love, Edward	147
Lowdermilk, Grover	147
Maybin, Cameron	157
McGrew, Walter	161
Melton, Cliff	165
Sallee, Harry	212
Tyson, Cecil	243

Slim Jim

Earl, Howard	75

Slippery

Eells, Harry	76
Ellam, Roy	77

Sloppy

Thurston, Hollis	239

Sloth Bear

Smith, Dominic	224

Slothful Bill

Lattimore, Bill	141

Slow Joe

Doyle, Judd	72

Slug

Burns, Jack	42
Heilmann, Harry	111
Hutcheson, Joe	122
Tolson, Charles	240

Slugger

Wells, Ed	252

Slugging Cabby

Lajoie, Nap	138

Sluggo

Slaught, Don	223

Slugs

Ulicny, Mike	243

Slydah

Hendriks, Liam	112

Smallest pitcher in captivity

Gearin, Dennis	93

Smellville

Melville, Tim	165

Smiler

Murray, George	177

Smiles

Ross, Cody	209

Smiley

Bischoff, John	30
Keegan, Bob	130
Turchin, Eddie	242

Smiling Al

Maul, Al	156
Orth, Al	185

Smiling Bill

Donovan, Bill	71
Terry, Bill	237

Smiling Bock

Baker, Charles	21

Smiling George

Blackburn, George	31

Smiling Jim

Hughey, Jim	121

Smiling John

Kelly, John O	131

Smiling Mickey

Welch, Michael	252

Smiling Pete

Daniels, Pete	64

Smiling Stan

Hack, Stan	103

Smiling Swedish Southpaw

Johnson, Earl	125	Lyons, George	149
Smiling Tim		Ullger, Scott	243
Keefe, Tim	130	White, Frank	253
Smoke		**Smoothie**	
Herring, Bill	114	Kuiper, Duane	137
Justis, Walt	128	**Smudge**	
Kiefer, Joe	132	Jolley, Smead	126
Stewart, Dave	230	**Snacks**	
Sturdivant, Tom	233	DeShields, Delino D	69
Smoke Ball		**Snags**	
Puccinelli, George	197	Heidrick, Emmet	111
Smoked Herring		**Snake**	
Herring, Bill	114	Arrieta, Jake	19
Smokey		Deal, John	67
Alston, Walter	16	Henry, Frederick	113
Arroyo, Bronson	19	Sturdivant, Tom	233
Fairbank, Jim	80	Wiltse, Lewis	258
Garrett, Henry	92	**Snakeface**	
Gonzales, Joe	97	Downs, Scott	72
Herring, Bill	114	**Snap**	
Hobbs, Bill	116	Dunlap, Grant	74
Lotz, Joe	147	**Snap Dragon 1**	
Maxwell, Charlie	156	McCullers, Lance Jr	159
McIlwain, Stover	162	**Snapper**	
Price, Jim	197	Garrison, Robert	92
Sundra, Steve	234	Kennedy, Sherman	132
Smokey Joe		**Sneak Thief**	
Finneran, Joseph	83	Baylor, Don	25
Lotz, Joe	147	**Snellzilla**	
Martin, Joe	154	Snell, Blake	226
Smoky		**Sniffy**	
Burgess, Forrest	41	Clay, Dain	53
Ishikawa, Travis	123	**Snipe**	
Singleton, Bert	223	Conley, James	56
Smoky Joe		Hansen, Roy E	106
Wood, Joe	260	**Snitz**	
Smoky Rube		Applegate, Frederick	18
Lutzke, Walter	148	Browne, Earl	40
Smooth		**Snooker**	
		Arnovich, Morris	19

Snooks

Snooks
    Dowd, Raymond   72
Snow
    Snodgrass, Frederick   226
Snuffy
    Oertel, Chuck   184
    Stirnweiss, George   231
Snuffy the Bear
    Stirnweiss, George   231
Socker
    Strauss, Joe   232
Socks
    Holden, Joe   117
    Perry, Hank   190
    Seibold, Harry   218
    Seybold, Ralph   219
Soldadito
    Zimmer, Don   264
Soldier
    Carson, Al   47
Soldier Boy
    Curry, George   62
    Murphy, John P   176
Solly
    Salisbury, William   212
Somerville Scot
    MacFayden, Danny   149
Son
    Noble, Rafael   181
Son of Israel
    Arnovich, Morris   19
Sonny
    Dixon, John   70
    Hoffman, William   117
    Hogg, Bert   117
    Horne, Berlyn   119
    Kopacz, George   136
    Robertson, Daryl   205
    Ruberto, John   209
    Senerchia, Emanuel   219
    Siebert, Wilfred   222
Soup
    Campbell, Bill   45
    Campbell, Clarence   45
    Campbell, Dave   45
    Campbell, Eric   45
    Polivka, Ken   195
    Suppan, Jeff   234
Sour Mash Jack
    Daniels, Harold   64
Southern
    Martini, Guido   155
Southside Phenom
    Ruth, George   211
Souzbot
    Souza, Steven Jr   227
Sox
    Husta, Carl   122
Spaceman
    Lee, Bill F   142
Spades
    Wood, Charles A   260
Spaniard
    Span, Keiunta   227
Spanky
    Eaton, Adam   76
    Kirkpatrick, Ed   134
    LaValliere, Mike   141
    Spangler, Al   227
    Squires, Mike   228
Spanny
    Span, Keiunta   227
Sparkles
    Bryant, Kris   41
Sparkplug
    Keenan, Jimmie   130
Sparky
    Adams, Earl   14
    Anderson, George   17
    Lake, Eddie   138

Lyle, Albert	148	Meine, Henry	164
Olson, Marv	184	**Sphinx**	
Vaughan, Glenn	245	Mossi, Don	174
Sparrow		**Spider**	
McCaffrey, Charles	158	Clark, Owen	52
Morton, William	173	James, Art	124
Spartenburg John		Nelson, Roger	179
McMakin, John	163	Shelton, Andrew	220
Spec		Wilhelm, Charles	255
Clough, Ed	54	**Spiderman**	
Harkness, Frederick	107	Hill, Glenallen	115
Hartsfield, Roy	109	Hunter, Torii	122
Shea, Francis	220	**Spike**	
Winter, George	258	Borland, Tom	34
Special T		Brady, Michael	36
Plouffe, Trevor	194	LaRoss, Harry	140
Specs		Merena, John	166
Hill, Carmen	115	Nelson, Glenn	179
Klieman, Ed	134	Shannon, William	219
Meadows, Henry	164	Van Alstyne, Clay	244
Ostrowski, Joe	185	**Spiker**	
Podgajny, Johnny	194	Mertes, Sam	166
Rigney, Bill	204	**Spinach**	
Toporcer, George	240	Melillo, Oscar	165
Speed		**Spitball**	
Geary, Bob	93	Stricklett, Elmer	232
Keeley, Burt	130	**Spittin' Bill**	
Kelly, R.B.	131	Doak, Bill	70
Mahaffey, Roy	150	**Splendid Splinter**	
Martin, Elwood	154	Williams, Ted	256
Merewether, Art	166	**Splinter**	
Walker, Joseph	248	Gerkin, Steve	94
Speedpass		**Spoke**	
Cishek, Steve	52	Emery, Herrick	78
Speedy		Speaker, Tris	228
Meine, Henry	164	**Sponge**	
Miller, Frederick	168	Iannetta, Chris	123
Ruble, Art	209	Storie, Howie	231
Speedy Bill		**Spook**	

Jacobs, Forrest	124	
Speake, Bob	228	
Spooks		
Gerber, Wally	94	
Spork		
Bloomquist, Willie	32	
Sport		
McAllister, Lewis	158	
Spot		
Bethea, Bill	29	
Falk, Chet	81	
Springfield Rifle		
Raschi, Vic	200	
Spud		
Chandler, Spurgeon	50	
Davis, Virgil	66	
Krist, Howie	137	
Spuds		
Sabo, Chris	212	
Spunk		
Pitko, Alex	194	
Squak		
Crist, Ches	60	
Squaky		
Barmes, Bruce	22	
Squanto		
Wilson, George F	257	
Square Jaw		
Ramsey, Bill	199	
Squash		
Wilson, Frank	257	
Squatty Body		
Munson, Thurman	176	
Squeaky		
Bluege, Otto	32	
Valentine, Fred	244	
Squire		
Potter, Robert	195	
Prim, Ray	197	
Veil, Frederick	246	
Squire of Kennett Square		
Pennock, Herb	190	
Squirrel		
McNeal, Jeff	163	
Reynolds, Danny	202	
Sievers, Roy	222	
Squiz		
Pillion, Cecil	194	
St. Croix		
Patterson, Roy	189	
Stan the Man		
Musial, Stan	177	
Stan the Man Unusual		
Stanhouse, Don	229	
Stanley Steamer		
Stanley, Bob	229	
Stanley Struggle		
Bahnsen, Stanley	21	
Starvin' Marvin		
Freeman, Marvin	87	
Stash		
Goletz, Stan	97	
Lopata, Stan	147	
Musial, Stan	177	
Stashu		
Musial, Stan	177	
Staten Island Scot		
Thomson, Bobby	239	
Steady Eddie		
Lopat, Eddie	146	
Mayo, Eddie	157	
Murray, Eddie	177	
Vólquez, Edinson	247	
Steady Pete		
Meegan, Pete	164	
Steam Engine in Boots		
Moore, Earl	171	
Steamboat		
Dreisewerd, Clem	73	
Struss, Clarence	232	

Tenace, Gene	237	Davis, Harry A	65
Williams, Rees	256	Odor, Rougned	184
Steamboat Bill		Stanky, Eddie	229
Otey, Bill	185	**Stone Buddha**	
Steamer		Oh, Seunghwan	184
Flanagan, James	85	**Stone Cold**	
Stanley, Bob	229	Selsky, Steve	218
Steeple		**Stone Face**	
Schultz, Howie	216	Murphy, Connie	176
Sterl		**Stonefingers**	
Wolverton, Harry	259	Stuart, Dick	232
Steve		**Stonewall**	
Brodie, Walter	38	Jackson, Travis	124
Evans, Louis	80	**Stoney**	
Kuczek, Stanislaw	137	Jackson, Travis	124
Partenheimer, Harold	188	McGlynn, Ulysses	161
Roser, Emerson	209	Stone, John T	231
Slayton, Foster	223	**Stooping Jack**	
Stevey		Gorman, John	98
Stephenson, Reuben	230	**Stopper**	
Stevie		Staller, George	229
Stephens, Vern	230	**Stork**	
Stevie Wonder		Theodore, George	237
Henderson, Steve	112	**Storm**	
Stick		Davis, George E	65
Michael, Gene	167	**Stormin' Gorman**	
Stickman		Thomas, James	238
Sale, Chris	212	**Stormin' Norman**	
Still Bill		Cash, Norm	48
Hill, Bill	115	**Stormy**	
Stilt		Weatherly, Cyril	251
Weaver, Art	251	**Strawberry Bill**	
Sting		Bernhard, Bill	29
Ray, Jim	200	**Streak**	
Stinger		Stroud, Ed	232
Clemons, Verne	53	**Stretch**	
Stange, Albert	229	Boyles, Harry	35
Stink		Grunwald, Al	102
Odor, Rougned	184	McCovey, Willie	159
Stinky		Melancon, Mark	165

Strikeout Factory

Phillips, Jack	192	Verdel, Al	246
Schultz, Howie	216	**Sub**	
Tompkins, Ron	240	Mays, Carl	157
Strikeout Factory		**Submarine**	
Lindgren, Jacob	145	Auker, Elden	19
String		**Submariner**	
Gandy, Bob	91	Pieretti, Marino	193
String Bean Slinger		**Subway Sam**	
Edwards, Carl Jr	76	Nahem, Sam	178
Stringer		**Sudden Sam**	
Hunt, Ben	122	McDowell, Sam	160
Stro-Show		**Suds**	
Stroman, Marcus	232	Fodge, Gene	85
Stub		Sudakis, Bill	233
Brown, Richard	40	Sutherland, Harvey	234
Hauser, Arnold	109	**Sugar**	
Smith James A	225	Cain, Merritt	44
Stubby		Cain, Robert	44
Clapp, Richard	52	Díaz, Edwin	69
Erautt, Joe	78	Kane, Frank	128
Mack, Frank	149	Kane, Tom	129
Magner, Edmund	150	**Sugar Bear**	
Mathias, Carl	156	Blanks, Larvell	32
Overmire, Frank	186	**Sugar Boy**	
Ray, Irv	200	Dougherty, Tom	72
Stud		**Suitcase**	
Myatt, George	177	Simpson, Harry	222
Stewart, John D	230	**Suitcase Bob**	
Stuart, Johnny	233	Seeds, Bob	218
Studs		**Sultan of Swat**	
Bancker, John	22	Ruth, George	211
Stuffy		**Sum**	
Butler, Frank B	43	Caldwell, Ray	44
McInnis, Jack	162	**Sun Bear**	
Stewart, John F	230	Davis, JD	66
Stump		**Sunday**	
Weidman, George	251	Hawker, Art	109
Stumpy		**Sunday Charlie**	
Maranville, Walter	152	Maxwell, Charlie	157
		Sunday Punch	

Maxwell, Charlie 157
Sunday Teddy
Lyons, Ted 149
Sundown
Yowell, Carl 263
Sundown Kid
Thomas, Dan 238
Sunny Jack
Sutthoff, Jack 234
Sunny Jim
Bottomly, Jim 34
Dygert, Jimmy 75
Hackett, Jim 103
Mallory, Jim 151
Pastorius, Jim 188
Sunset Jimmy
Burke, Jimmy 41
Sunshine
Clevinger, Mike 53
McLaughlin, James 162
Werth, Jayson 253
Super Joe
Charboneau, Joe 50
McEwing, Joe 160
Super Mariano
Rivera, Mariano 204
Super Nova
Nova, Iván 182
Supercalifragilisticexpialadosius
Brosius, Scott 38
Superchief
Reynolds, Allie 202
SuperJew
Epstein, Mike 78
Superman
Pillar, Kevin 193
Supermanahan
Hannahan, Jack 106
SuperSub
Kennedy, John 132

Sure Shot
Dunlap, Fred 74
Susie
Williams, Billy 255
Swaggy
Skaggs, Tyler 223
Swaggy T
Beckham, Tim 26
Swamp Baby
Wilson, Charlie 257
Swamp Fox
Dark, Alvin 64
Swampy
Donald, Richard 71
Swat
McCabe, James 158
Swats
Sawatski, Carl 214
Swacina, Harry 235
Swede
Burkart, Elmer 41
Carlson, Leon 46
Carlstrom, Albin 46
Delaney, Arthur 67
Hansen, Andy 106
Henriksen, Olaf 112
Hollison, John 118
Johnson, Johnny 126
Larsen, Erling 140
Malmberg, Harry 151
Risberg, Charles 204
Silvera, Charlie 222
Swedish Apollo
Anderson, John 17
Swedish Wonder
Hallstrom, Charlie 105
Sweet Billy
Williams, Billy 255
Sweet Lips
Gilliam, Jim 95

Sweet Lou

Sweet Lou
    Johnson, Lou   126
    Piniella, Lou   194
    Whitaker, Lou   253
Sweet Music
    Viola, Frank   246
Sweet Singer of Sandusky
    Upp, George   243
Sweet Susie
    Susce, George   234
Sweet Swingin' Billy From Whistler
    Williams, Billy   255
Sweet William
    Hallahan, Bill   105
Sweet Williams
    Williams, Billy   255
Sweetbread
    Bailey, Abraham   21
Sweet-Swinging Billy Williams
    Williams, Billy   255
Swipe Right
    Pinder, Chad   194
Swirvin Irvin
    Irvin, Cole   123
Swish
    Nicholson, Bill   180
    Sawatski, Carl   214
Swisher
    Sawatski, Carl   214
Sy
    Sutcliffe, Elmer   234
Symphony Larry
    Ciaffone, Larry   51
Szmyoth
    Smith, Kevan   225
Tabasco Kid
    Elberfeld, Norman   77
Tabasco Tom
    Tuckey, Tom   242
Tabby
    Tabler, Pat   235

Tack
    Wilson, Michael   258
Tacks
    Arroyo, Bronson   19
    Latimer, Clifford   140
    Neuer, John   179
    Parrott, Tom   188
Tacky Tom
    Parrott, Tom   188
Taco
    Bell, George A   26
Tacoby Bellsbury
    Ellsbury, Jacoby   78
Tad
    Quinn, Clarence   198
Tai-Weezy
    Walker, Taijuan   248
Tall Tactician
    Mack, Connie   149
    McGillicuddy, Cornelius   161
Talonka
    Mitchell, Kevin   170
Tami
    Mauriello, Ralph   156
Tank
    O'Day, Hank   182
    Pratt, Todd   196
    Viciedo, Dayán   246
Tankhead
    Pratt, Todd   196
Tarheel
    Murray, George   177
Tarzan
    Parmelee, Roy   188
    Solters, Julius   227
    Stephenson, Walter   230
Taters
    Lary, Frank   140
TatMan
    Roberts, Ryan   205
Tatsu-maki

Nomo, Hideo 181
TAZ
Zych, Tony 264
T-Bone
Giordano, Tommy 96
Koski, Bill 136
Phillips, William 192
Winters, Jesse 259
T-Butta
Rivera, Thomas 205
Teach
Caldwell, Earl 44
Ted
Abernathy, Talmadge 13
Baldwin, Henry 22
Davidson, Thomas 65
Larkin, Henry 140
Lewis, Edward 144
Petoskey, Frederic 191
Reed, Ralph 201
Sullivan, Timothy 233
Welch, Floyd 252
Wieand, Franklin 254
Wilborn, Thaddeaus 255
Wingfield, Frederick 258
Wood, Edward 260
Ted Threads
Williams, Ted 256
Teddy
Kearns, Edward 130
Wilson, George W 257
Teddy Ballgame
Williams, Ted 256
Teddy Tantrum
Williams, Ted 256
Tee the Greene
Greene, Tommy 100
Tennessee Cyclone
Perdue, Herbert 190

Tennis Ball Head
Hovley, Steve 120
Ter
Pizarro, Juan 194
Terín
Pizarro, Juan 194
Terminator
Henke, Tom 112
Reardon, Jeff 200
Terrible Swede
Anderson, John 17
Terrible Ted
Williams, Ted 256
Terry
Larkin, Frank 140
Tex
Aulds, Leycester 20
Carleton, James 46
Clevenger, Truman 53
Covington, Chet 59
Covington, William 59
Creel, Jack 60
Erwin, Ross 79
Garms, Debs 92
Herbert, Ernie 113
Hoffman, Edward 116
Hoyle, Roland 120
Johnson, Rankin 126
Kardow, Paul 129
Kraus, Jack 137
McDonald, Charles 159
Nelson, Robert 179
Pruiett, Charles 197
Russell, Ewell 210
Shirley, Alvis 221
Teixeira, Mark 237
Vache, Ernest 244
Wilson, Gomer 257
Wisterzil, George 259

Texas

Womack, Sid	260
Texas	
Anderson, Chase	17
McNabb, Edgar	163
Texas Con Man	
Clemens, Roger	53
Texas Hill	
Hill, Hunter	115
Texas Jack	
Kraus, Jack	137
McAllister, Lewis	158
Texas Wonder	
Hoffman, Frank	116
The Big D	
Young, Dmitri	262
Thin Man	
Allen, Robert	15
Moore, Jo-Jo	172
Thommy	
Thomas, Chester	238
Thor	
Syndergaard, Noah	235
Three Finger	
Brown, Mordecai	39
Newkirk, Floyd	179
Three Star	
Hennessey, George	112
Three-Six	
Weaver, Jered	251
Thrill	
Clark, Will	52
Throwin' Swannanoan	
Stewart, Sammy	231
Thumper	
DeMerit, John	68
Williams, Ted	256
Thunder	
Thornton, Andre	239
Tice	
Madigan, William	150
Tico	
Almora, Albert	15
Tido	
Daly, Tom	63
Tige	
Stone, William	231
Tiger	
Hoak, Don	116
Kaiser, Don	128
Leppert, Don E	144
Mapes, Cliff	152
Newcombe, Don	179
Tight Ass	
Titus, John	240
Tightpants	
Titus, John	240
Tike	
Redman, Julian	200
Tilden Flash	
Ashburn, Richie	19
Tillie	
Shafer, Arthur	219
Walker, Clarence	248
Tilly	
Bishop, Max	30
Tim	
Burgess, Tom	41
Griesenbeck, Carlos	101
Harkness, Thomas	107
McKeithan, Emmett	162
Murchison, Thomas	176
Talton, Marion	235
Thompson, Charles	238
Tink	
Riviere, Arthur	205
Turner, Thomas	243
Tiny	
Baker, Jesse	21
Bonham, Ernest	33
Chaplin, James	50

Collins, Tim	55
Felder, Mike	82
Graham, Dawson	99
Leonard, Elmer	143
Leverenz, Walt	144
Osborne, Ernest	185
Tesch, Al	237
Tioga George	
Burns, George	42
Tioga Kid	
Burns, George	42
Tip	
O'Neill, Fred	183
O'Neill, James	183
O'Neill, John	183
Tobin, John M	240
Tippy	
Martinez, Felix	155
Titanium Catcher	
Avila, Alex	20
tito	
Bell, Juan	27
Tito	
Francona, John	87
Francona, Terry	87
Fuentes, Rigiberto	89
Herrera, Procopio	114
Landrum, Terry	139
Navarro, Norberto	178
TJ	
Beam, Theodore	25
Mathews, Timothy	155
McFarland, Timothy	160
Rivera, Thomas	205
Tucker, Thomas	242
TK	
Kelly, Tom	131
Kelly, Ty	131
Koehler, Tom	135
T-Mo	
Moore, Tyler	172
Toad	
Ramsey, Thomas	199
Tobacco Chewin' Johnny	
Lanning, Johnny	139
Toby	
Atwell, Maurice	19
Harrah, Colbert	107
Lyons, Thomas	149
Tolson, Charles	240
Toco	
Galvis, Freddy	90
Tod	
Brynan, Charles	41
Dennehey, Thomas	68
Sloan, Yale	223
Todd	
Cunningham, Thomas	62
ToddFather	
Frazier, Todd	87
Todfather	
Helton, Todd	111
Toehead	
Adair, Jerry	13
Togie	
Pittinger, Charles	194
ToJo	
Joseph, Tommy	128
Tokki 1	
Choo, Shin-Soo	51
Tokki 2	
Votto, Joey	247
Tom	
Eaves, Vallie	76
Robello, Thomas	205
Scharein, George	215
Thomas, Chester	238
Tom Terrific	
Sears, George	218

Seaver, Tom	218	Parisse, Louis	187
Tom Thumb		Pérez, Atanasio	190
Force, Davy	85	Robello, Thomas	205
Tomahawk		Tonneman, Charles	240
Collmenter, Josh	55	Zardón, José	263
Tomato Face		**Tony C**	
Cullop, Nick	62	Conigliaro, Tony	56
Lamabe, Jack	139	**Tony Plush**	
Menke, Denis	165	Morgan, Nyjer	173
Tomatoes		**Tony the Tiger**	
Kafora, Jake	128	Clark, Tony	52
Lamabe, Jack	139	**Tony Two Bags**	
Tommy		Rendon, Anthony	202
Atkins, Francis	19	**Tookie**	
Vereker, John	246	Gilbert, Harold	95
Tommy Talker		**Toothpick Sam**	
Tucker, Tommy	242	Jones, Sam	127
Tommy the Cork		**Toothpick Twirler**	
Corcoran, Tommy	58	Groom, Bob	102
Tommy Trojan		**Toothy**	
Satriano, Tom	214	Wittgren, Nick	259
Tommy Two Towel		**Toots**	
Hunter, Tommy	122	Coyne, Martin	59
Tone		Shultz, Wallace	222
Rendon, Anthony	202	Tietje, Les	239
Toney		**Topper**	
Pasquella, Mike	188	Rigney, Emory	204
Tontogany Terror		**Topsy**	
Wright, William Si	261	Hartsel, Tully	109
Tony		Magoon, George	150
Batista, Leocadio	24	**Tornado**	
Boeckel, Norman	33	Nomo, Hideo	181
Daniels, Frederick	64	**Tornado Jake**	
DeFate, Clyde	67	Weimer, Jake	252
Giuliani, Angelo	96	**Tortuga**	
Layne, Hillis	141	Astudillo, Willians	19
Lupien, Ulysses	148	**Tot**	
Madigan, William	150	Murphy, William	176
Murphy, Francis	176	Pressnell, Forest	196
		Total Package	

Toy Bulldog
Brown, Domonic — 39

Toy Cannon
Courtney, Clint — 58

Toys in the Attic
Ross, Cody — 209
Wynn, Jim — 261

Bertaina, Frank — 29
Johnson, Bart — 125

Trackhorse
Pratt, Frank — 196

Trader
Horne, Berlyn — 119

Treads
Johnson, Richard — 126

Tremendous Triandos
Triandos, Gus — 241

Trent
Hubbard, Trenidad — 121

T-Rex
Fuentes, Brian — 89

Trey
Beamon, Clifford — 25
Lunsford, James — 148
Moore, Warren — 172

Trick
McSorley, John — 164

Tricky
Nichols, Frederick — 180
Nolasco, Carlos — 181
Williams, Rick — 256

Trig
Stammen, Craig — 229

Trigger
Stammen, Craig — 229

Triggonometry
Triggs, Andrew — 242

Trim
Rigney, Emory — 204

Triple T
Turner, Trea — 243

Tripp
Cromer, Roy — 61

Trixie
Tracewski, Dick — 241

Trojan
Evers, Johnny — 80

Trolley Line
Butler, John — 43

Trolley Wire
Scott, Lewis — 217

Troy Terrier
Egan, Jim — 76

Truck
Eagan, Charles — 75
Hannah, James — 106
Kearse, Eddie — 130

Truth
Serum, Gary — 219

Tsunami
Martínez, Carlos E — 154

TTT
Markakis, Nick — 153

Tub
Epperly, Al — 78
Welch, James — 252

Tubby
Clemons, Verne — 53
Reiber, Frank — 201
Spencer, Edward — 228

Tuck
Turner, George — 242

Tucker
Ashford, Thomas — 19
Jok, Stan — 126

Tuffy
Stewart, Charles — 230

Tug
Arundel, John — 19
Hulett, Timothy — 122

Malloy, Herm	151	**Twilight Ed**	
McGraw, Frank	161	Killian, Ed	133
Milton, Larry	170	**T-Willy**	
Thompson, John P	239	Williams, Taylor	256
Wilson, George A	257	**Twink**	
Wilson, Les	257	Twining, Howard	243

Tugboat
   Munson, Thurman   176

Twinkles
   Host, Gene   119

Tugger
   McGraw, Frank   161

Twinkletoes
   Selkirk, George   218

Tully
   Sparks, Thomas   228

Twitch
   Rickert, Marv   203

Tun
   Berger, John   28

Twitches
   Porter, Dick   195

Turk
   Curtis, Vern   62
   Delhi, Lee   68
   Farrell, Richard   81
   Lown, Omar   147
   Wendell, Steven   252

Two Gun
   Gettel, Al   94

Two Minutes For
   Ruffin, Bruce   210

Two Pairs
   Bader, Lore   20

Two Silhouettes On
   DeShaies, James   68

Turkey
   Gross, Ewell   102
   Tyson, Cecil   243

Two-story Twirler
   Hunt, Ben   122

Turkey Mike
   Donlin, Mike   71

Ty
   Freigau, Howard   88
   Gainey, Telmanch   90
   Helfrich, Emory   111
   LaForest, Byron   138
   Pickup, Clarence   193

Turkeyfoot
   Brower, Frank   39

Tut
   Jenkins, Tom   125
   Tettelbach, Dick   237

Ty Ty
   Tyler, Johnnie   243

Tweet
   Walsh, Joe F   249
   Walsh, Joe P   249

U
   Jiménez, Ubaldo   125

U.S.
   Bonds, Barry   33

Twig
   Little, Bryan   145
   Terwilliger, Willard   237

Ubbo Ubbo
   Hornung, Joe   119

Twiggy
   Harrelson, Derrel   107
   Hartenstein, Chuck   108

UFO
   Evans, Darrell   79

Ug

Wally

Balboni, Stephen	21	Coleman, Vince	55
Caster, George	48	**Vinegar Bend**	
Ugly		Mizell, Wilmer	171
Dickshot, Johnny	70	**Vinegar Bill**	
Uncle		Essick, Bill	79
Alvord, William	16	**Vinegar Tom**	
Anson, Adrian	17	Vickery, Tom	246
Bannon, Thomas	22	**Virgil Van Mijk**	
McCurdy, Harry	159	Massey, William	155
Moran, Charlie	172	**Visine**	
Morton, Charlie	174	Wright, David	261
Pratt, Al	196	**Vito**	
Robinson, Wilbert	206	Butera, Drew	43
Robinson, William Henry	206	**Voiceless Tim**	
Thompson, Milt	239	O'Rourke, Tim	183
Unicorn		**Volador**	
Ziegler, Brad	264	Mejía, Adalberto	164
Union Man		**Von**	
Holke, Walter	117	Schreiber, Paul	216
Unser Choe		**Votto-matic**	
Hauser, Joe	109	Votto, Joey	247
Unser Fritz		**Vulture**	
Pfeffer, Fred	191	Regan, Phil	201
Untamed Son of Sumner County		**Wabash George**	
Perdue, Herbert	190	Mullin, George	175
Van		**Waddy**	
Vahrenhorst, Harry	244	MacPhee, Walter	150
Vanimal		**Wagon Tongue**	
Worley, Vance	260	Adams, Joe	14
Vern		Keister, Bill	130
Washington, Sloan	250	**Wahoo Sam**	
Vet		Crawford, Sam	60
Sitton, Charles	223	**Waiter**	
VFP		Combs, Earle	55
Pestano, Vinnie	191	**Wali of Wallop**	
Victory		Ruth, George	211
Faust, Charlie	81	**Walking Man**	
Vince		Yost, Eddie	262
Gonzales, Wenceslao	97	**Wall**	
Vincent Van Go		Watson, Walter	251
		Wally	

Wally World
    Goldsmith, Warren   97

Wally World
    Joyner, Wally   128

Walrus
    Munson, Thurman   176

Walter the Whale
    Brown, Walter   40

Wamby
    Wambsganss, Bill   249

Wampum Walloper
    Allen, Richard   15

Warbird
    Schwarber, Kyle   217

Warbler
    Warden, Jon   250

Ward Six
    Bannon, Thomas   22

Warhorse
    Slaughter, Enos   223
    Stephenson, Jackson   230
    Studley, Sy   233

Warrior
    Friend, Bob   88
    O'Neill, Paul   183

Washington Monument
    Howard, Frank   120

Waterbury Wizard
    Piersall, Jim   193

Watsie
    Sessi, Walter   219

Wattie
    Holm, Roscoe   118

Watty
    Clark, William   52
    Lee, Wyatt   142

Wawindaji
    Pence, Hunter   190

Way Back
    Wasdin, John   250

Wayward Son
    Carreon, Mark   47

Weasel
    Bessent, Fred   29

Weaser
    Robinson, William Henry   206
    Scoffic, Lou   217

Webb
    Schultz, Wibert   217

Webbo
    Clarke, Vibert   53

Wedo
    Martini, Guido   155

Wee Carolinian
    May, Frank   157

Wee Davy
    Force, Davy   85

Wee Dinny
    Gearin, Dennis   93

Wee Sprig of the Shamrock
    Gearin, Dennis   93

Wee Willie
    Clark, Willie   52
    Dammann, Bill   63
    Keeler, Willie   130
    Ludolph, Willie   148
    McGill, Willie   161
    Mills, Willie   169
    Sherdel, Bill   220
    Sudhoff, Willie   233

Weeping Willie
    Willoughby, Claude   257

Weiser Wonder
    Johnson, Walter   126

Welcome Back
    Kapler, Gabe   129

Werewolf
    Werth, Jayson   253

Whale
    Reniff, Hal   202
    Walters, Fred   249

Whammy
    Douglas, Charles   72
What a Pair of Hands
    López, Héctor   147
What is That
    Manwaring, Kirt   152
What's the Use
    Chiles, Pearce   51
Wheels
    Wheeler, Zack   253
Wheezer
    Dell, William   68
Whip
    Blackwell, Ewell   31
Whiplash
    Navarro, Julio   178
Whirling Willie Werle
    Werle, Bill   253
Whispering Bill
    Barrett, William   23
Whispers
    Tomlin, Randy   240
Whistlin' Jake
    Wade, Jake   247
Whit Bird
    Merrifield, Whitley   166
White Bear
    Gattis, Evan   92
White Fang
    Thomas, Lee   238
White Rat
    Herzog, Dorrel   114
    Kuzava, Bob   138
White Shark
    Blanco, Grégor   31
White Wings
    Tebeau, George   237
Whitey
    Alpermann, Charles   16
    Appleton, Edward   18
    Ashburn, Richie   19
    Baker, Kirtley   21
    Blanco, Andrés   31
    Ellam, Roy   77
    Federoff, Al   81
    Ford, Edward   85
    Gardner, Billy   91
    Gibson, Leighton   95
    Glazner, Charles   96
    Graves, Sid   100
    Guese, Theodore   102
    Hayes, Jim   110
    Herzog, Dorrel   114
    Hilcher, Walter   115
    Hilley, Ed   115
    Hurd, Tom   122
    Konikowski, Alex   136
    Kurowski, George   137
    Lockman, Carroll   146
    Miller, Kenneth   169
    Moore, Lloyd   172
    Ock, Harold   183
    Platt, Mizell   194
    Ritterson, Edward   204
    Rohe, George   207
    Sheely, Earl   220
    Wietelmann, William   254
    Wilshere, Vernon   257
    Wiltse, Hal   258
    Wistert, Francis   259
    Witt, Lawton   259
    Wolfe, Harry   259
    Zeiher, Henry   263
Whiteyball
    Herzog, Dorrel   114
Whiz
    Gee, Johnny   93
Whoa Bill
    Fisher, Chauncey   84

Whoop-La

Phillips, Bill C   192
Whoop-La
    White, Will   254
Whoops
    Creeden, Pat   60
Wib
    Smith, Wilbur   226
Wicho
    Figueroa, Luis   83
    Urías, Luis   244
Wick
    Bell, Chad   26
Wickey
    McAvoy, James   158
Wid
    Conroy, William E   57
Wig
    Emslie, Bob   78
    Weigel, Ralph   251
Wiggles
    Porter, Dick   195
Wilbah
    Wood, Wilbur   260
Wilbur
    Wood, Edward   260
Wild Bear
    Fielder, Cecil   83
Wild Bill
    Connelly, William   56
    Donovan, Bill   71
    Everitt, Bill   80
    Hallahan, Bill   105
    Hunnefield, Bill   122
    Hutchison, Bill   122
    Leard, Bill   141
    Luhrsen, William   148
    Miller, Bill F   168
    Piercy, Bill   193
    Pierro, Bill   193

Widner, William   254
Wild Elk of the Wasatch
    Heusser, Ed   114
Wild Horse
    Puig, Yasiel   197
    Sheridan, Neill   220
Wild Horse of the Osage
    Martin, Johnny   154
Wild Man
    Byrne, Tommy   43
Wild Thing
    Magnifico, Damien   150
    Sherfy, James   220
    Williams, Mitch   256
Wildcat
    McCormick, Frank   159
Wildfire
    Craft, Harry   59
    Schulte, Frank   216
Wiley
    Dunham, Henry   74
Willi
    Casilla, Santiago   48
William the Red
    Wright, William Si   261
Willie
    Miranda, Guillermo   170
    Phillips, Bill B   192
    Robinson, William H   206
    Stargell, Wilver   229
    Wolf, Jimmy   259
Willie Mac
    McCovey, Willie   159
Willie the Knuck
    Ramsdell, Willie   199
Willie the Wonder
    Horton, Willie   119
Willy
    Miranda, Guillermo   170
Wilson

Upshaw, Willie 243
Wimpy
Harder, Mel 106
Paciorek, Tom 186
Quinn, Wellington 198
Willis, Les 257
Win
Batchelder, Joe 24
Mercer, George 165
Remmerswaal, Wilhelmus 202
Windy
Bradshaw, Dallas 36
McCall, John 158
Miller, Ward 169
Winner
Mercer, George 165
Winnie
Mercer, George 165
Winny
Winfield, Dave 258
Wish
Egan, Aloysius 76
Wito
Cone, Ramón 56
Witto
Alomá, Luis 15
Wiz
Kremer, Remy 137
Wizard
Hoffer, Bill 116
Shaw, Frederick 220
Smith, Ozzie 225
Suzuki, Ichiro 234
Wizard of Os
Oswalt, Roy 185
Wizard of Oz
Smith, Ozzie 225
Wizard of Wham
Ruth, George 211
Wizard of Whiff

Pettit, Paul 191
Wobby
Hammond, Walter 105
Wolf of First Street
Werth, Jayson 253
Wonder Dog
Hudler, Rex 121
Wonder Hamster
Stairs, Matt 228
Wonderful Willie
Mays, Willie 157
Smith, Willie 226
Wonderful Wop
Bodie, Frank 33
Wondrous Willie
Stargell, Wilver 229
Wonger
Wong, Kolten 260
Woodman
Wood, Alex 260
Woodstock Wonder
O'Neill, James 183
Woody
Holtgrave, Vern 118
Main, Forrest 151
Melville, Tim 165
Rueter, Kirk 210
Williams, Gregory 255
Woolworth
Weilman, Carl 252
Woonsocket Rocket
Baldelli, Rocco 21
Workhorse
Black, Joe 31
Crompton, Herb 61
Mahaffey, Roy 150
World
Mitchell, Kevin 170
Wrench
Craig, Allen 59

Gladden, Dan	96	Wuestling, George	261
Wrong-Way Perez		**Yatz**	
Pérez, Pascual	190	Proeser, George	197
Wyoming Nimrod		**Yaz**	
Scott, Jim	217	Yastrzemski, Carl	262
X Factor		**Yiddish Curver**	
Eckstein, David	76	Pelty, Barney	189
Xanthos		**Yip**	
Gruber, Kelly	102	Owen, Frank	186
X-Man		Owens, Frank	186
Hernancez, Xavier	113	**Yoandry**	
Yahtzee		Margot, Manuel	152
Foster, George A	86	**Yogi**	
Yale		Abreu, José	13
Murphy, William	176	Berry, Lawrence	29
Yaller		**You Sunk My**	
Phelps, Ed	192	Blankenship, Lance	32
Yaller Bill		**Youk**	
Harbridge, Bill	106	Youkilis, Kevin	262
Yam		**Young Collegian**	
Yaryan, Clarence	262	Jamerson, Charles	124
Yanimal		**Young Cy**	
Gomes, Yan	97	Young, Irv	262
Yank		**Young Skinny**	
Brown, Charles E	39	Graham, Arthur	99
Robinson, William H	206	**Yo-Yo**	
Terry, Lancelot	237	Epps, Aubrey	78
Yerkes, Stan	262	**YRG Jr**	
Yankee Clippard		Grandal, Yasmani	99
Clippard, Tyler	54	**Yucca**	
Yankee Clipper		Kelliher, Frank	130
DiMaggio, Joe	70	**Yukon Cornelius**	
Yankee Killer		Sneed, Cy	226
Beazley, Johnny	25	**Z Mac**	
Lary, Frank	140	McAllister, Zach	158
Yatch		**Z Man**	
Logan, Johnny	146	Zimmerman, Ryan	264
Yatcha		**Zack**	
Logan, Johnny	146	Taylor, James	236
Yats		**Zamboni**	

Reitz, Ken 202
Zanesville phenomenon
Watson, Walter 251
Zaza
Harvey, Ervin 109
Zbyszko
Solters, Julius 227
Zeb
Milan, Clyde 167
ZeeZee
Hagerman, Zerah 104
Zeke
Allen, Myron 15
Barnes, Virgil 23
Bella, John 27
Bonura, Henry 33
Weilman, Carl 252
Wilson, Frank E 257
Wrigley, George 261
Zackert, George 263
Zarilla, Al 263
Zen Master
Lorenzen, Michael 147
Zep
Rzepczynski, Marc 211
ZH
Taylor, Zachary 236

Ziggy
Hasbrook, Robert 109
Sears, Ken 218
Zim
Zimmer, Don 264
Zimmerman, Ryan 264
Zimmermann, Jordan 264
Zip
Collins, John E 55
Jaeger, Joe 124
Zabel, George 263
Zimmer, Don 264
Zobi-Wan Kenobi
Zobrist, Ben 264
Zoby
Zobrist, Ben 264
Zonk
Moreland, Keith 173
Zoom Zoom
Zumaya, Joel 264
Zoombiya
Dyson, Jarrod 75
Zorilla
Zobrist, Ben 264
Zorn
Gaetti, Gary 90
Zorro
Versalles, Zoilo 246
ZZ
Hagerman, Zerah 104

Acknowledgements

Many sources were consulted during the compilation of this book. The authors are indebted to the following:

ArcaMax.com, Arizona Diamondbacks, Baltimore Sun, Baseball-Almanac.com, Baseball Hall of Fame, Baseball History Daily, Baseball in Wartime (baseballinwartime.com), BaseballLibrary.com, Baseball-Reference.com, *Baseball State by State* by Chris Jensen, TheBaseballPage.com, The Baton Rouge Advocate, The Big Book of Jewish Baseball, Biography.com, Cincinnati Reds Hall of Fame & Museum, Classic Minnesota Twins!, Marna L. Clemons on Ancestry.com, Colby Curry (KC Royals' Communications coordinator), Corpus Christi (TX) Caller-Times, Diamondsinthedusk.com, David Eskenazi on SportspressNW.com, ESPN.com, Charles Faber in "New Century, New Team: The 1901 Boston Americans," Findagrave.com, Dan Fulghum on Ancestry.com, Funtrivia.com.

Also, Johnny Goodtimes in Philly Sports History, Tim Gannon (Times-review), The Great Encyclopedia of Nineteenth-Century Major League Baseball, Walter Johns in the (Florida) Daily Independent, Brent Kelley in Baseball's Bonus Babies, Stephen M Lombardi in The Baseball Same Game, Los Angeles Angels of Anaheim, Bruce Markusen (The Hardball Times), Chance Michaels in Borchertfield.com, MLB.com, Houston Mitchell in the Los Angeles Times, Eric Nadel, TheNationalPastimeMuseum.com, New York Times, Thomas Nelshoppen on the APBA blog, David Nemek in the Great Encyclopedia of Nineteeth Century Baseball, North Carolina Sports Hall of Fame, Oregon Sports Hall of Fame, Our Game (https://ourgame.mlblogs.com), People.com, PSA Card Facts, Rockland County Journal News.

The work of many members of SARB are referenced. They include Marc Z. Aaron, Stephen Able, Niall Adler, Arthur R. Ahrens, William Akin, David W. Anderson, Ron Anderson, Will Anderson, Sheldon Appleton, Mark Armour, Eric Aron, Rich Arpi, Tyler Ash, Bob Bailey, Lawrence Baldassaro, Ed Bartholemy, Jeff Barto, Anthony Basich, John Bennett, Ralph Berger, Jay Berman, Michael Betzold, Sam Bernstein, Charley Bevis, Robert W. Bigelow, Dennis Bingham, Bill Bishop, Peter C. Bjarkman, Gil Bogen, Rich Bogovich, Terry Bohn, Maurice Bouchard, Jeff Bower, Bob Brady, Ryan Brecker, Ryan Brodeur, Thomas J. Brown Jr., Bob Buege, Tony Bunting.

Also, Brian Campf, Zita Carno, Tommy Carella, Charles Carey, Dave Cicotello, Alan Cohen, Phil Cola, Tim Connaughton, Stephen Constantelos, John Contois, Mike Cooney, Warren Corbett, Rory Costello, Edwin Fernandez Cruz,

Dan D'Addona, Jon Daly, Aaron Davis, Sidney Davis, Dominick Denaro, Paul E. Doutrich, William Dowell, Jonathan Dunkle, Steve Dunn, Don Duren, Alexander Edelman, Rob Edelman, James Elfers, Eric Enders, Greg Erion, Brian Erts, Amy Essington, Charles F. Faber, Scott Ferkovich, Scott Fiesthumel, Dan Fields, Jan Finkel, David Finoli, Brian Flaspohler, David Fleitz, David Fletcher, James Forr, Dave Forrester, Eddie Frierson, Eric Frost, John Fuqua, John Gabcik, Cappy Gagnon, Dave Gagnon, Paul Geisler Jr., Gary Gillette, Austin Gisriel, Peter M. Gordon, Mike Grabek, John F. Green, Nelson 'Chip' Greene, Rebecca Gildewell-Hall, Nancy Snell Griffith.

And Donna L. Halper, Rex Hamann, Eric Hanauer, Craig Hardee, Don Harrison, Chip Hart, Steve Hatcher, Charles Hausberg, John Heiselman, Tim Herlich, Lou Hernandez, Mark Hodermarsky, Paul Hofmann, Dan Holmes, Donald J. Hubbard, Mike Huber, Rick Huhn, Joanne Hulbert, Bob Hurte, John R Husman, Dwayne Isgrig, Don Jensen, Bill Johnson, Janice Johnson, Rodney Johnson, David Jones, Chris Kabout, Maxwell Kates, Jimmy Keenan, Thomas Kern, Norm King, Bill Kirwin, Wendy Knickerbocker, David Krell, Jim Kreuz, Tara Krieger, Mike Lackey, Bryan Lake, Bill Lamb, Bill Lamberty, Craig Lammers, Tom Larwin, David Laurila, Ted Leavengood, Jim Leeke, Bob LeMoine, R.J. Lesch, Patrick Lethert, Peter Levine, Daniel R. Levitt.

Also Dick Leyden, James Lindberg, Dan Lindner, Angelo Louisa, Mitch Lutzke, Mike Lynch, Jim Mackay, Peter Mancuso, Jeffrey Marlett, Mel Marmer, Kevin McCann, Mike McClary, Andy McCue, Brian McKenna, John McMurray, Steven McPherson, Roger Melin, Mark Miller, Paul Mittermeyer, Frank Morris, Jack Morris, Peter Morris, Ralph Moses, Art Mugalian, David Nemec, Todd Newville, Jim Nitz, Bill Nowlin, Dan O'Shea, Clifton Parker, Royse, Parr, Len Pasculli, Scott Pero, Catherine Petroski, Mike Piazzi, Hugh Poland, Neal Poloncarz, David Porter, J.G. Preston, Bill Pruden, Rich Puerzer, Christine Putnam, Jane Allen Quevedo, Al Quimby, Chris Rainey, Jose Ramirez, James Lincoln Ray, George Rekela, Ron Rembert, Stephen V. Rice, Mike Richard, Bob Rives, C. Paul Rogers III, Dick Rosen, Bruce Roth, Frank Russo, Paul-Michael Russo, John Saccoman, Ruth Sadler, Eric Sallee, Paul Sallee, Jim Sandoval, Jim Sargent, Gary Sarnoff, Gabriel Schechter.

Others also include Andrew Schiff, Stuart Schimler, Steven Schmitt, Dan Schoenholz, Fred Schuld, Ron Schuler, Joe Schuster, Michael See, Andrew Sharp, Scott Schul, David Shiner, Matthew Silverman, Tom Simon, Terry Simpkins, John Simpson, Matt Sisson, David Skelton, Doug Skipper, Larry Slagle, Jack Smiles, Richard Smiley, Steve Smith, Mike Sowell, Glen Sparks, Lyle Spatz, John Stahl, Bill Staples Jr., Fred Stein, Steve Steinberg, Brian Stevens, Mark Stewart, Trey Strecker, John Struth, Andy Sturgill, Josh Sullivan, Rick Swaine, Bill

Swank, Jim Sweetman, Judith Testa, Bob Tholkes, Joan M. Thomas, Dick Thompson, Stew Thornley, Rich Thurston, Clayton J. Trutor, Alfonso L. Tusa, Adam Ulrey, Al Ulrey, Fred Veil, Edward Veit, Cort Vitty, Dale Voiss, John Vorperian, Nick Waddell, Joe Wancho, Guy Waterman, Jeremy Watterson, Charlie Weatherby, John Wickline, Robert Wiggins, Ken Willey, Dave Williams, Joe Williams, Phil Williams, Saul Wisnia, Gregory H. Wolf, Allan Wood, Steve Wulf, Jack Zerby, and Don Zminda.

Thanks also to: Sarasota Herald-Tribune, Betsy Schwartz (Chicago Cubs), Bill Selnes in the Melfort Journal (Canada), SB Nation, Bill Shenley, The Sporting News, SportsPool.com, St. Louis Post Dispatch, Strangest names in American Political History, David Sturm in the Baltimore Sun, Gypsi Tompkins, Toledo Blade, Texas State Historical Assn, TribLive.com (Pittsburgh Tribune), and Wikipedia.org.

Any errors or omissions belong to the authors.

About the Authors
Joseph Ross

Joseph Ross is the owner of Rosstrum Publishing and its chief editor. He has been involved in sports for many years, serving as an official in basketball and soccer and has served in baseball as an official scorer, scoreboard operator and color commentator for game broadcasts. Joe also prepares and distributes a daily email feature, "Today in Baseball History," which is distributed every day of the year to subscribers across the continent.

He is also a member of SABR (Society for American Baseball Research). He never anticipated that this book would be as long and as involved as it became. Joe is already planning his next book which promises to be at least as cumbersome and involved as this one.

Richard M. Renneboog

Richard M. "Boog" Renneboog resides in southwestern Ontario, Canada, about midway between the home of the Detroit Tigers and Canada's back-to-back World Series champions, the Toronto Blue Jays, and not far from Beachville, home of the first documented game of 'base ball' in North America (1837). He has been a lifelong fan and player of the great sport of baseball in its many forms since being introduced to the sport in the 1950s. Now in his late 60's, he continues to be a powerful force with a bat from both sides of the plate and an adept player in any position on the field, although the speed of his game has decreased somewhat. The game has kept him young and win or lose, a day playing baseball is better than any other day... unless the championship game suddenly gets rained out and can't be played.

"Boog" also serves as an editor for many environmental and scientific books as well as fiction works of other authors.

www.ingramcontent.com/pod-product-compliance
Lightning Source LLC
Chambersburg PA
CBHW070044080526
44586CB00013B/909